LEE BAILEY'S
THE
WAY I
COOK

Lee Bailey

ALSO BY LEE BAILEY

COUNTRY WEEKENDS

CITY FOOD

COUNTRY FLOWERS

GOOD PARTIES

COUNTRY DESSERTS

SOUP MEAL

SOUTHERN FOOD & PLANTATION HOUSES

CALIFORNIA WINE COUNTRY COOKING

COOKING FOR FRIENDS

LEE BAILEY'S TOMATOES

NEW ORLEANS

LEE BAILEY'S CORN

LONG WEEKENDS

LEE BAILEY'S BERRIES

LEE BAILEY'S ONIONS

DINNERS AT HOME

PORTABLE FOOD

CLARKSON POTTER/PUBLISHERS
NEW YORK

LEE BAILEY'S
THE WAY I COOK

BY LEE BAILEY

PHOTOGRAPHS BY TOM ECKERLE

Copyright © 1996 by Lee Bailey

Photographs copyright © 1996 by Tom Eckerle

All rights reserved. No part of this book may be reproduced or
transmitted in any form or by any means, electronic or
mechanical, including photocopying, recording, or by
any information storage and retrieval system, without permission
in writing from the publisher.

Published by Clarkson Potter/Publishers,
201 East 50th Street, New York, New York 10022.
Member of the Crown Publishing Group.

RandomHouse, Inc. New York, Toronto, London, Sydney, Auckland

http://www. randomhouse.com/

CLARKSON N. POTTER, POTTER, and colophon
are trademarks of Clarkson N. Potter, Inc.

Most of the recipes in this work were originally published in
previous Lee Bailey cookbooks.

Printed in the United States of America

Design by DONNA AGAJANIAN

Library of Congress Cataloging-in-Publication Data
is available upon request

ISBN 0-517-59751-9

10 9 8 7 6 5 4 3 2 1
First Edition

This book is
lovingly dedicated to
Carol Southern.

I would like to thank Francine
Maroukian for her time and toil on
this project. Ditto to James Lartin.

And, of course, Tom Eckerle.

Finally to all my friends,
both in and out of the food game,
and to my readers, heartfelt
thanks for your help and
encouragement over the years.

CONTENTS

INTRODUCTION xii

MY NEW MENUS xv

EGGS 1

SOUPS AND CHOWDERS 8

SALADS 43

PASTA 77

VEGETABLES AND SIDES 99

GRAINS, RICE, POTATOES, AND BEANS 165

POULTRY AND GAME BIRDS 196

MEATS 225

SEAFOOD AND FISH 255

BREAD, ROLLS, BISCUITS, AND MUFFINS 293

PIZZAS, FRITTERS, CRISPBREADS, AND SANDWICHES 322

SAUCES, SALSAS, CHUTNEY, AND MORE 345

PIES, TARTS, COBBLERS, AND CRISPS 373

CAKES AND COOKIES 409

OTHER DESSERTS 456

ICE CREAM AND SORBETS 488

INDEX 505

INTRODUCTION

THE WAY I COOK IS ROOTED IN THE FIRM belief that sharing food together is one of the great simple joys available to us all—and that the occasions, small and large, when we gather for a meal ought to be a blessing to both body and spirit.

Which is what all my books have been about—along with my own takes on the rich, creative imagination and just plain good cooking I have encountered in the near and sometimes far places I have been over the last fifteen years.

In my first book, *Country Weekends*, I detailed how I planned and prepared meals at my Long Island country house. In my second, *City Food*, I went on to explore another aspect of cooking that had intrigued me—which is how much we had absorbed the foods of all the many different cuisines that are reflected in our country's great ethnic diversity—and almost without noticing it. I said at the time, "Without even being aware of what was going on we have gotten to know pita bread as well we do corn-bread, quiche and pizza pie as well as apple pie, tomato sorbet as well as lemon ice—sometimes liking the new even better than the familiar. On top of that, the perva-siveness of this 'mix' has helped raise us to the enviable position of having our choice of most of these ethnic ingredients." Today we find once-exotic ingredients everywhere, even in our large supermarkets.

Then there was *Good Parties* in which I continued to explore what I call home cooking. After that came single-subject books, one called *Country Desserts*, the title of which is self-explanatory (and a book that is dear to my heart) and *Soup Meals*, which came about when I noticed something I had been doing more and more over the years, namely serving soup as a main course.

Next I returned to my roots and wrote *Southern Food &
Plantation Houses,* which combined the sort of food and
antebellum settings I grew up with. Then it was out West
to do *California Wine Country Cooking.* And the following year took me to Europe and the Caribbean to produce
Cooking for Friends. After that it was back to Louisiana,
where it all began for me, to work with my old friend Ella
Brennan and her legendary restaurant clan for *New
Orleans.* Which led me to hanker to see more of my own
country than just airports. The result of my travels was
Long Weekends.

Dinners at Home was another shot at trying to encour-
age entertaining on home ground, which I still think is
the best place to do it. That was followed by *Portable Food,*
an idea that had been kicking around in the back of my
head and wanted to come out, which it did last spring.

Along with the full-scale cookbooks, I have turned out
a quartet of small-sized books devoted to particular culi-
nary favorites of mine: tomatoes, corn, onions, and
berries. And in deference to my fellow gardeners, I ought
to mention *Country Flowers,* my book on gardening that
somehow sprouted between cookbooks.

All in all I have kept pretty busy, and I've had the time
of my life. So far so good .

MY NEW MENUS

THE IDEA OF COOKING AS ART WITH A capital A has always made me uneasy. I consider it craft at best—and in some very gifted hands a sublime one. But Art, I don't think so. Certainly not the way I cook.

However, I suspect I flex the art and design muscles I developed in college and at the Parsons School of Design when I make menus. Somehow I visualize tastes and textures working together in a meal the same way I visualize shapes and colors working together in a room.

As a sort of demonstration of this process I have made a group of new menus with new recipes. There are 24 menus in all—a dozen for warm weather and a dozen for cold—with more than 90 new recipes.

I believe these menus accurately reflect my current feelings about cooking, which has evolved for me into something more lighthearted and playful. I still like to try stuff I've never cooked before and to utilize ingredients I have not used until recently, such as tortillas.

Also I'm still a sucker for quick and easy and quirky— witness the Winter menu that starts with onion rings and then moves on to a friend's version of Philadelphia cheese steak accompanied by creamy stuffed potatoes. Finishing with a dessert pie of green tomatoes and apples.

Read on—and remember that having a good time in the kitchen is what cooking is all about.

S U M M E R

1

Avocado Salad with Cilantro Vinaigrette
(page 59)

Chicken and White Bean Chili *(page 209)* with
Roasted Corn Salsa
(page 355)

Cornsticks
(page 308)

Grilled Pineapple with Rum Cream Sauce
(page 460)

2

Savoy Mushroom Salad
(page 128)

Roasted Chicken Breasts with Pan Gravy
(page 206)

Asparagus with Shallots
(page 101)

Boiled Rice
(page 170)

Individual Crustless Lemon Meringue Pies
(page 380)

M E N U S

3

Ham Fajitas with Fresh Salsa Ranchera
and Scrambled Eggs
(page 331)

Chicken Fajitas with Avocado Dressing
(page 333)

Jicama Slaw
(page 56)

Sour Cream Pound Cake with Poached Fruit
(page 428)

4

Roasted Vidalia Onion Salad
(page 133)

Individual Grilled Pizzas
(page 324)

Peach Cobbler
(page 403)

SUMMER

5

Baked Thin-Sliced Salmon
(page 279)

Bulgur Salad
(page 167)

Fresh Fruit with Yogurt and
Warm Sun Honey
(page 461)

6

Grilled Pita Chips *(page 328)*
with Sun-Dried Tomato Dip
(page 353)

Mediterranean Patties
(page 249)

Grilled Potato Pockets
(page 184)

Grilled Asparagus Pockets
(page 101)

Layered Fresh Fruit with Raspberry Sauce
(page 462)

M E N U S

7

Roasted Red Pepper and Butter Sandwiches
(page 339)

Red Bean and Rice Salad
(page 178)

Carrot Slaw
(page 62)

Cinnamon Walnut Twists
(page 450)

8

Sweet Pea Soup
(page 17)

Fried Soft-Shell Crabs
(page 256)

New Potato, Red Pepper, and Corn Salad
(page 191)

Mango with Blackberries
(page 458)

XIX

SUMMER

9

The Tuscan Sandwich
(page 340)

Grilled Shrimp with
Cole Slaw on Pepper Bread
(page 340)

Grilled Portobello Burger
(page 339)

Pickled Okra
(page 162)

Melon Slices with Raspberry Puree
(page 459)

Spices Sables
(page 449)

10

Artichokes with Black Olive Butter
(page 100)

Swordfish Steak Salad with
Tomato Vinaigrette
(page 284)

Poached Oranges
(page 463)

M E N U S

11

Cold Sesame Noodles with Carrots
and Cucumbers
(page 78)

Garlic Smoked Tenderloin of Beef
(page 226)

Grilled Green Bean Pockets
(page 104)

Lemon Rice
(page 171)

Lemon Squares
(page 453)

12

Green Olive, Walnut, and Parsley
Sauce/Crostini Topping
(page 95)

Uncooked Tomato Sauce/Crostini Topping
(page 92)

Ricotta, Basil, and Prosciutto Sauce/
Crostini Topping
(page 96)

Cappuccino Brownies
(page 453)

W I N T E R

1

Southwestern Caesar Salad with
Cornbread Croutons
(page 51)

Spaghetti with Garlic and Rosemary Oil
(page 81)

Banana Pudding Cake
(page 430)

2

Onion Rings
(page 133)

Cheese Steak Sandwiches
(page 342)

Stuffed Baked Potatoes
(page 183)

Apple and Green Tomato Pie
(page 374)

M E N U S

3

Stuffed Portobello Mushrooms
(page 127)

Lamb Shanks with Black Olives
and Orange Zest
(page 236)

Orzo and Rice Pilaf
(page 174)

Date Tart
(page 388)

4

Roasted Onions with Balsamic Vinegar
(page 130)

Venison with Grainy Mustard Sauce
(page 252)

Sautéed Spinach
(page 139)

Oven-Roasted Cottage Fries
(page 182)

Flourless Chocolate and Walnut Cake
(page 427)

W I N T E R

5

Warm Potato Salad with Sherry Vinaigrette
(page 190)

Roast Loin of Pork with Natural Gravy
(page 240)

Butternut Squash Puree
(page 140)

Blackberry Jam Tart
(page 388)

6

Warm Curried Fruit
(page 461)

Carrot Cake Waffles
(page 320)

Baked Ham
(page 247)

Café au Lait
(page 372)

M E N U S

7

Wilted Salad with Pancetta
(page 55)

Boiled Smoked Pork Butt with Vegetables
(page 248)

Pumpkin Pudding
(page 477)

8

Pan-Grilled Eggplant on
Sun-Dried Tomato Toasts
(page 118)

Beefsteak Florentine
(page 231)

Linguine with Greens and Pine Nuts
(page 81)

Poached Dried Fruit
(page 466)

XXV

WINTER

9

Haricots Verts with Anchovy Vinaigrette
(page 104)

Duck Sausage and New Potatoes
(page 224)

Milk Chocolate Macaroons
(page 438)

10

Fennel, Celery, and Parsley Salad
with Shaved Parmesan
(page 65)

Roasted Herb Turkey Breast *(page 217)*
with Pan-Roasted Sweet Potatoes
(page 188)

Sautéed Broccoli
(page 106)

Ambrosia Crumble
(page 404)

M E N U S

──── 11 ────

Warm Green Bean Salad
(page 62)

Whole Red Snapper
(page 283)

Basmati and Wild Rice with Swiss Chard
(page 175)

Fresh Fig Baked Custard
(page 473)

──── 12 ────

Smoked Salmon Salad
(page 292)

Spaghetti Squash with Roasted Vegetables
(page 140)

New World Spice Cookies
(page 443)

EGGS

BEING A TRADITIONALIST AT HEART, I REGARD BREAKFAST as sacred—every day, including Sunday. Lots of people apparently share my Sunday-morning feelings—even those who don't ordinarily care for breakfast during the week. I'm sure that for me this attitude has to do with my natural self-indulgent weekend ways, but who cares. ✦ Whatever, even though I start my Sunday morning with such standard fare as orange juice, dry cereal with skimmed milk, and a pot of tea, I still like eggs at noon on Sunday. (I know many people would call this "brunch," but I have always hated that word.) This light lunch, which includes bacon and/or sausage and café au lait (a childhood holdover), is one I look forward to all week. ✦ A few dishes here are versions of the imaginative, traditional vegetable/egg combinations native to other countries—the omelet in France, tortilla de huevos in Mexico, and in Italy, the frittata. Whatever the origins, they are an extremely flexible group, utiliz-  ing combinations of seasonal vegetables and herbs that can be varied even further with the addition of meats.

EGGS POACHED IN CHILI-TOMATO SAUCE

For this, it's best to serve the plates in the kitchen, because even if the eggs are fairly firm the dish is still tricky to handle. Put half a Cold-Water Corn Cake (page 310) on each plate, overlap it with a slice of ham, and top with two eggs and sauce. Salad had better be on separate plates, because this dish can be runny. Break up the remaining cornbread and serve warm, wrapped in a towel.

> 1 large garlic clove, peeled
> 1/4 cup safflower oil
> 1 large onion, coarsely chopped
> 1 can (4 ounces) mild to medium-hot green
>   chilies, drained and chopped
> 1 1/2 pounds tomatoes, roasted (see page 20)
>   and peeled, with stem end cut out
> 3/4 teaspoon salt
> 2 teaspoons tomato paste (optional)
> 1 1/2 cups Chicken Stock (page 41), hot
> 8 large eggs

Sauté garlic in hot oil in a large skillet and discard the garlic. Turn off heat and add onion, tossing to coat with oil. Wilt over low heat. Add chilies, tomatoes, salt, and tomato paste, if using. Stir and simmer for about 10 minutes to blend flavors and reduce liquid a bit.

When ready to cook the eggs, add hot stock and bring to a simmer. Add eggs, one at a time, by cracking each into a flat saucer and sliding it into the stock. Cover and continue to simmer for 6 to 8 minutes, or until eggs are at the desired degree of firmness.

SERVES 4

CHILI-TOMATO EGGS IN BREAD CRUMB CUPS

These make a very pretty presentation. Any left over are good to take to the beach or on a picnic. They take a little doing, but give them a try. The recipe is in two parts, and the cups can be done ahead of time.

BREAD CRUMB CUPS
> 9 slices white bread, cut into quarters
> 12 tablespoons (1 1/2 sticks) unsalted butter
> 1 teaspoon salt
> 1/2 teaspoon freshly ground black pepper
> 2 egg whites

FILLING
> 6 large eggs
> 1/2 teaspoon salt
> 1/4 cup safflower oil
> 1 cup seeded, peeled, and chopped tomatoes
> 3 tablespoons chopped white onion
> 3 tablespoons chopped red bell pepper
> 1 small hot Mexican pepper, finely chopped
> 1 chili pepper, finely chopped

Preheat oven to 375 degrees. Grease six 3 1/2-inch muffin-tin cups. Cut a circle of wax paper the size of the bottom of each cup. Put in cups and grease them.

To make cups: Coarsely chop bread in a food processor, then bake on a cookie sheet for 10 minutes. Let cool. Put crumbs, butter, salt, and pepper into processor with a metal blade. Process briefly until mixture is crumbly but not pasty.

Beat egg whites until foamy and stir into crumb mixture. Divide among the cups and press against sides and bottom to form a shell. Bake for about 15 minutes. Butter will foam up but will subside after it cools. (This preparation may be done a day before and kept covered in the refrigerator, in the muffin tin. Heat in the oven for 3 minutes before using.)

To make filling: Mix eggs lightly with salt and set aside. Put oil in a skillet over high heat, add tomatoes, onion, and peppers, and fry for about 2 minutes, stirring all the while (a bit longer if tomatoes are giving off a lot of juice). Reduce heat and stir in eggs. Cook quickly until whites just begin to turn. Remove from heat and spoon into crumb cups. Bake 15 to 20 minutes. Timing will depend on how well done you want your eggs. They are practically cooked when you put them in the oven. Allow to cool just a few minutes before serving. Carefully loosen sides and lift out. Carefully peel off the wax paper.

SERVES 6

BAKED BROWNED BUTTER EGGS

These baked eggs would obviously make a very good nucleus around which to build a party breakfast. Just add the usual bacon, sausages, and a salad.

6 tablespoons thinly sliced green onions
6 tablespoons (³/₄ stick) unsalted butter, melted and browned
6 teaspoons balsamic vinegar
6 large eggs
¹/₂ teaspoon salt, or to taste
Freshly ground black pepper, to taste
6 round or square pieces toast

Preheat oven to 400 degrees.

Divide green onions, butter, and vinegar among 6 small ramekins. Drop an egg into each. Add salt and pepper.

Place on a baking sheet and bake for 9 to 10 minutes, depending on how firm you like the yolk.

To serve, turn eggs out onto toast, letting the juices be absorbed.

SERVES 6

EGGS IN BROWN BUTTER

My friend Diane Judge taught me how to make these eggs. She says the recipe came to her from her Dutch grandmother. It is truly a treat, and one of my favorite ways of eating eggs.

This recipe allows one egg per guest. If this is not enough, you might want to double it. If so, cook the eggs in two large batches (or even three) and keep them on a warm plate in a warm oven until all are done. Have everyone ready at the table as you finish frying.

6 tablespoons (³/₄ stick) butter
4¹/₂ teaspoons cider vinegar
6 large eggs
Snipped fresh chives
Salt and freshly ground black pepper, to taste

Brown half the butter in a small pan and add vinegar, which will slightly boil away. Set aside to keep warm.

In a skillet large enough to fry 3 eggs comfortably, melt half of the remaining butter. Cook eggs to the desired degree of doneness and put one on each warm plate. Repeat with the remaining butter and eggs. Pour the browned butter over each egg and top with chopped chives. Season with salt and pepper.

SERVES 6

VARIATION

You may also bake eggs in individual ramekins. In that case, pour the browned butter with vinegar over them and add the chives after they are cooked.

CORN OMELET

You should use tender white corn just cut from the cob when you make this. Be sure to scrape the cobs.

Making an omelet is simple and quick after you get the technique down—as those who've made them know. If omelet making is new to you, give it a try with your breakfast eggs mixed with a little water, salt, and pepper. Some people also add about a tablespoon of chopped chilled butter to the mixture just before adding it to the pan. You'll get the hang of it quickly.

> 2 or 3 large eggs
> 1 1/2 teaspoons water
> 1/2 cup fresh white corn kernels
> 2 teaspoons snipped fresh chives
> Salt and freshly ground black pepper, to
>   taste
> 1 1/2 teaspoons unsalted butter

Beat eggs and water together lightly. Stir in corn, chives, salt, and pepper. Heat an omelet pan or a small skillet with curved sides. Melt butter in the pan over medium heat, tilting it as you do so the entire surface is coated.

When butter stops bubbling and is just beginning to turn brown, pour in egg mixture. Stir a few seconds with the tines of a fork, without scraping the bottom. Lifting the pan slightly off the heat and shaking, lift the edges of the congealing egg to allow as much egg as possible to run under. At the same time start tilting the pan slightly and begin inching one side of the cooked omelet to fold it over. When it is almost folded, tilt the pan enough to make the omelet roll onto the far side of the pan. Allow to cook a few seconds more before inverting onto a warmed plate.

MAKES 1 OMELET

"LIGHT" TOMATO SOUFFLÉ

This isn't exactly a diet dish, but it doesn't have egg yolks in it, and there's only a little butter and milk per serving. Whatever, it's great for lunch.

Sometimes the base isn't reduced properly, so the bottom of the soufflé ends up a little watery. This doesn't matter—it's just as good.

> 4 tablespoons (1/2 stick) unsalted butter
> 3 pounds tomatoes, coarsely chopped
> 1 tablespoon minced tarragon
> 1 tablespoon tomato paste
> 3 tablespoons flour
> 1 cup milk
> 1/4 cup freshly grated parmesan cheese
> 1/4 teaspoon freshly ground black pepper
> Salt, to taste
> 5 egg whites
> 1/2 teaspoon cream of tartar

Preheat oven to 350 degrees and prepare a 2-quart soufflé dish, or 6 to 8 individual soufflé dishes, by buttering lightly and dusting inside with flour. Set aside.

Melt 1 tablespoon of the butter in a large skillet over medium heat. Add tomatoes and tarragon and cook over medium-low heat for 40 minutes to reduce well. Stir occasionally to prevent sticking and scorching. Put through a food mill to strain out the seeds and skins. Be sure to press as much pulp as possible before discarding the waste. Stir in tomato paste. Set aside until slightly cooled, about 15 minutes.

Melt remaining butter in the top of a double boiler. Add flour, mixing well, and cook for another 4 minutes, stirring. Whisk in milk, making sure all lumps are dissolved. Cook until sauce thickens. Add tomato mixture and cheese and stir until it melts. Stir in pepper and salt.

Beat egg whites until foamy, add cream of tartar, and beat until stiff but not dry. Stir a quarter of the beaten whites into the tomato mixture. Pour this over remaining egg whites and fold in gently. Do not overmix; a few lumps are okay.

Pour into the soufflé dish and bake in the center of the oven for 30 minutes, until puffy and lightly browned on top.

SERVES 6 TO 8

SCRAMBLED EGGS AND ONIONS

Onions add zip to traditional scrambled eggs.

2 tablespoons unsalted butter
½ cup finely chopped onion
4 large eggs or 2 eggs plus 2 portions egg substitute
1 tablespoon water
¼ teaspoon salt
⅛ teaspoon freshly ground black pepper

Melt butter in a cast-iron or nonstick skillet over medium-high heat. Add onion and sauté, stirring occasionally, until golden brown, 8 to 10 minutes.

Meanwhile, beat eggs with a whisk until light and fluffy. Add water and whisk to combine.

When onions are golden, pour eggs in over them through a strainer. Reduce heat to medium and scramble until cooked to your liking, usually 2 to 3 minutes. Sprinkle with salt and pepper. Serve immediately.

SERVES 2

MEXICAN EGGS

What this actually amounts to is scrambled eggs with salsa—so just scramble your eggs the way you like them and top with Basic Tomato Salsa (page 356).

A variation of this is to thin out the salsa with a bit of chicken stock and add a little more Tabasco Sauce to make it hotter. Heat this in a saucepan and poach the eggs in the liquid. *Then* top it with fresh salsa.

EGGS IN PIQUANT MAYONNAISE

The recipe for this piquant mayonnaise came from Silvestro Baraldo, who is the chef and owner of the popular Bar Centrale on the square in San Casciano dei Bagni.

When I make this, I usually double the piquant mayonnaise recipe to have extra to use on sandwiches.

¾ cup Homemade Mayonnaise (page 348)
2 tablespoons hot pepper oil (see Note)
½ teaspoon Worcestershire Sauce
2 teaspoons fresh lemon juice
3 large hard-cooked eggs, finely chopped

Whisk together mayonnaise, hot pepper oil, Worcestershire, and lemon juice. Fold in eggs.

Note: Silvestro makes hot pepper oil by heating fiery small dried peperoncini (peppers) in olive oil and then allowing them to steep. Chinese hot pepper oil could be substituted here.

MAKES 1¼ CUPS

SCRAMBLED EGG SALAD

This salad is a good alternative to the more typical egg salad and may be served either slightly warm or slightly chilled. I'm beginning to lean more in the direction of slightly chilled. Either way, it doesn't take too much time to put together.

I have been meaning to include pine nuts in this because I like them in plain chopped egg salad. I keep forgetting to, but you might give it a try.

½ pound thickly sliced Canadian bacon
1 large red bell pepper, roasted, peeled,
*   and seeded (see Note, page 74), cut into*
*   large dice*
1 bunch green onions, with some of the
*   green, cut into rings*
1 tablespoon capers, drained and dried
½ teaspoon salt
¼ teaspoon freshly ground black pepper
2 tablespoons cider vinegar
2 tablespoons olive oil
2 tablespoons safflower oil
4 drops Tabasco Sauce
2 tablespoons mayonnaise
12 large eggs, lightly beaten

Starting in a cold skillet, fry bacon to the degree of doneness you like. Drain it on paper towels, cut into strips or dice, and put in a salad bowl. Add the diced red pepper, green onions, and capers.

Make dressing in a small bowl. Mix together salt, pepper, and vinegar. Whisk in the oils and add Tabasco. If you are not going to serve the salad right away, stop here. If you are ready to go, add the mayonnaise and mix. Set aside while you scramble the eggs.

I use a nonstick pan coated with vegetable cooking spray to do the eggs in, and I scramble them in two batches. The trick is to have the pan fairly hot, then put in half the eggs and stir them around briefly until they set. Do the same with the other half. What you don't want to do is put them in a skillet that is not hot enough; that way they take too long to set and must be stirred too much, resulting in a mealy texture. You should have to chop the eggs after you scramble them.

So chop the eggs and add to the other ingredients in the salad bowl. Toss thoroughly but carefully. Add dressing and toss again. Correct seasoning if necessary.

SERVES 6

GORGONZOLA SOUFFLÉ WITH CUCUMBER SAUCE

Gorgonzola cheese has a pleasingly tangy flavor. It makes a perfect soufflé topped with cucumber sauce.

Freshly grated parmesan cheese
4 tablespoons (½ stick) unsalted butter
3 tablespoons all-purpose flour
1 cup milk
1 teaspoon green peppercorn mustard
1 teaspoon salt
¼ teaspoon cayenne
2 cups mild gorgonzola cheese, cubed
6 large eggs, separated
2 large egg whites
¼ teaspoon cream of tartar
Cucumber Sauce (recipe follows)

Generously butter a 6-cup or a 2-quart soufflé dish and dust with grated parmesan cheese, or use 6 similarly prepared individual soufflé dishes. Set aside.

Put a kettle of water on to heat over low heat.

Melt the butter in a medium saucepan over medium heat. Add the flour and mix well. Slowly whisk in the milk and cook until thickened, whisking constantly. Stir in mustard, salt, cayenne, and cheese. Blend well. Beat egg yolks in a small bowl and warm them with a little of the cheese mixture before whisking them in, in a slow steady stream. Cook just a few minutes. Transfer to a large bowl and let cool.

Beat egg whites until foamy, sprinkle with cream of tartar, and beat until stiff but not dry.

Fold egg whites into the cheese mixture, mixing just until all white streaks disappear. Pour into soufflé dish. Sprinkle the top with grated parmesan cheese, if you like.

Put soufflé dish in a larger pan and surround with boiling water. Place in a cold oven and turn on to 325 degrees. Bake until puffy and brown, about 50 minutes.

Serve immediately with sauce.

SERVES 6

CUCUMBER SAUCE
    1 English cucumber, peeled, seeded, and
        coarsely chopped
    2 tablespoons tarragon vinegar
    1 tablespoon safflower oil
    ¹/₂ cup Chicken Stock (page 41)
    2 tablespoons very finely chopped red onion
    1 tablespoon chopped fresh lemon thyme or
        parsley
    1 teaspoon salt
    ¹/₄ teaspoon white pepper

Purée cucumber, vinegar, oil, and stock. Whisk in the other ingredients. Do not refrigerate.

MAKES ABOUT 1¹/₂ CUPS

SPECIAL EGG SALAD ON WATER BISCUITS

I call this egg salad "special" because it has the flavor of cumin (which is what makes chili taste like chili and Indian food taste like Indian food). It alters the color of the salad slightly, but the unexpected flavor is worth losing a bit of the yellow intensity. I am very partial to thin English water biscuits to serve this salad on, my favorite brand being Carr's.

    6 large eggs, hard-cooked, peeled,
        and grated
    3 tablespoons mayonnaise, commercial or
        homemade (page 348)
    ¹/₄ teaspoon salt, or to taste
    1 teaspoon ground cumin, or to taste
    Grind of black pepper
    2 teaspoons snipped fresh chives (optional)
    2 or 3 drops Tabasco Sauce (optional)

Mix all ingredients thoroughly and refrigerate for at least 30 minutes before serving. Taste and adjust seasonings if necessary.

Note: To make eggs easier to peel after cooking, they should be plunged immediately into cold water.

SERVES 6

7

SOUPS AND CHOWDERS

FOR THE LONGEST TIME I THOUGHT OF SOUP BASICALLY AS something you had for a quick lunch, or occasionally for Sunday supper. However, several years back I began to consider soups to

be appropriate as the center-piece of a regular meal rather than simply as a lead-in to the main event—which in turn led me to experiment with numerous types of soups that I had never thought of trying before. The result of all this noodling around was my book *Soup Meals*. Of course, I still think soup makes a fine first course—I've just expanded my horizons. ✦ Soups that I make in warm weather are often lighter in texture and more pronounced in flavor than my winter favorites. That means I leave dried beans and meats to the cold months when the longer preparations and simmering times are both satisfying and necessary, and sturdy soups a boon and a blessing.

VEGETABLE SOUPS

ASPARAGUS SOUP

I think you will find this soup's texture creamy enough with simple chicken stock enhanced by the merest amount of half-and-half, but you certainly could replace part of the stock with skim or regular milk or light cream. This might cause the finished soup to require a bit more seasoning, so be sure to check it before serving if you decide to do this.

You also could serve this soup at room temperature or only slightly chilled, if you think that would suit you more than the more traditional iced soup.

1 1/2 pounds fresh asparagus, tough ends
   removed, washed
4 tablespoons (1/2 stick) unsalted butter
1/2 cup chopped onion
1 cup carefully washed and chopped leeks,
   white parts only
1/2 cup chopped celery
1 small baking potato, peeled and cubed
3 1/2 cups Chicken Stock (page 41)
1 teaspoon fresh lemon juice
Salt and white pepper, to taste
Paprika, to taste (optional)
1/2 cup half-and-half

Crème fraîche or whipped cream

Snap off asparagus tips. Cut the stalks into large pieces and set aside. Melt butter in a deep skillet with a lid. Add asparagus tips, onion, leeks, celery, and potato. Cover tightly and cook over the very lowest heat until vegetables are soft, 20 minutes or more.

Meanwhile, place stock in a large saucepan with the reserved asparagus stalks. Bring to a boil and simmer, tightly covered, for about 30 minutes. Discard stalks and set stock aside.

Purée softened vegetables in a food processor and add to the asparagus stock. Season with lemon juice, salt, white pepper, and paprika, if desired.

Let cool and then refrigerate for at least 4 hours.

Just before serving, stir in half-and-half and garnish with a dollop of crème fraîche or whipped cream and a sprinkling of paprika, if desired.

SERVES 6

BEET, CARROT, AND SWEET POTATO SOUP

1/2 pound beets, scrubbed
1/2 pound sweet potatoes, scrubbed
1 large yellow onion
4 shallots
4 garlic cloves
1 pound carrots, scraped and roughly
   chopped
4 cups Chicken Stock (page 41)
1/4 cup buttermilk
1 teaspoon fresh lemon juice
1/2 teaspoon salt
1/4 teaspoon freshly ground black pepper
1 cup frozen petit pois, rinsed well under hot
   water

Preheat oven to 400 degrees.

Wrap beets in foil and place them in the oven with sweet potatoes. Roast until tender, about 1 1/2 hours for the beets and 1 hour for the sweet potatoes, depending on size. Remove from oven and let cool.

Peel and quarter onion, shallots, and garlic. Combine them with carrots and stock in a medium saucepan and cook, covered, over medium heat until carrots are tender, about 20 minutes. Set the soup aside to cool slightly.

Peel beets and sweet potatoes and combine them with the cooled soup. Purée mixture in batches in a food processor and strain back into the saucepan. Stir in buttermilk, lemon juice, salt, pepper, and petit pois. Warm through and serve.

SERVES 6 TO 8

BROCCOLI RABE SOUP

You have to know your guests' tastes to serve this soup. Broccoli rabe—which I love—can be very bitter (too bitter for some), so if you think your guests won't much like its flavor, substitute spinach.

1 pound fresh broccoli rabe, stems trimmed
3 cups Chicken Stock (page 41)
2 tablespoons unsalted butter
1 medium onion, coarsely diced
1 large potato, peeled and diced
Salt and freshly ground black pepper, to taste
6 lemon slices (optional)
Sour cream or crème fraîche (optional)

Wash broccoli rabe and place in a covered saucepan with just the water clinging to it. Add about ½ cup of stock and cook slowly until tender, about 20 minutes.

Melt butter in a skillet and sauté the onion until tender, about 5 minutes. Add potato and remaining chicken stock. Cover and simmer until potato is tender, about 12 minutes. Strain out potato and onion, saving liquid, and combine with cooked broccoli rabe and its liquid. Purée. Return to saucepan and add reserved liquid. Heat and correct seasoning with salt and pepper. Add more stock if soup is too thick.

Serve in warm bowls garnished with a slice of lemon and/or a dollop of sour cream or crème fraîche, if desired.

SERVES 6

PURÉED BROCCOLI RABE SOUP

¼ cup olive oil
1 pound broccoli rabe, stems trimmed, coarsely chopped
7¼ cups Chicken Stock (page 41)
1 large onion, diced
2 large carrots, scraped and diced
2 celery ribs, diced
1 cup water
2 small baking potatoes, peeled and diced
2 garlic cloves, minced
½ teaspoon salt
¼ teaspoon freshly ground black pepper

Put 2 tablespoons of olive oil in a deep pot over high heat. Wash the chopped broccoli rabe and add it to the oil with any water clinging to it. Toss and add ¼ cup of stock. Reduce heat to medium, cover, and cook until tender, about 15 minutes.

Put remaining 2 tablespoons of olive oil in another pot over medium heat and add onion, carrots, and celery. Cook until wilted, about 5 minutes. Add remaining 7 cups stock, the water, potatoes, and garlic. Bring to a boil over high heat. Turn back to a slow boil and cook until potatoes are soft, about 15 minutes. Add broccoli rabe and mix. Cook for 5 minutes to blend flavors.

Let cool slightly, then purée in a food processor or through a food mill. Season with the salt and pepper. Serve warm.

SERVES 6

CARROT AND TOMATO SOUP

I love the flavor of this soup. As it is made below, it will be fairly thick. If you like a slightly thinner consistency, add extra chicken stock after you have made it. If you see fresh coriander at the market, it looks very pretty on top of each serving.

5 tablespoons unsalted butter
1 pound carrots, scraped and coarsely
    shredded
1 pound potatoes, peeled and coarsely
    shredded
2 large shallots, chopped
1 small onion, coarsely chopped
3 cups Chicken Stock, or more to taste
    (page 41)
1½ pounds ripe tomatoes, peeled, seeded,
    and coarsely chopped
1 teaspoon salt, or to taste
1 teaspoon sugar
1 tablespoon tomato paste
½ teaspoon ground coriander, or to taste

Chopped fresh coriander leaves (optional)

Melt butter in a medium-size saucepan over very low heat. Add carrots, potatoes, shallots, and onion. Mix to coat with butter and cover. Cook for 10 minutes, shaking pan occasionally to prevent scorching. Add ¼ cup of the stock and continue cooking, covered, for 10 minutes. Add tomatoes. Mix and simmer, uncovered, for 10 minutes more. Add remaining stock, salt, sugar, tomato paste, and ground coriander. Simmer for 10 minutes more. Correct seasoning if necessary.

Pour soup in a food processor and pulse for just a few seconds. The texture should remain coarse. Garnish individual servings with chopped coriander leaves, if desired.

Note: The soup can be reheated in a double boiler.

SERVES 6

CARROT AND DILL SOUP

The combination of carrots and dill is a match made in heaven. Add as much dill as you like.

¾ pound sweet potato
½ pound baking potato
2 tablespoons unsalted butter
1 large onion, coarsely chopped
5 cups Chicken Stock (page 41)
1¾ pounds carrots, scrubbed and cut into
    rings
1½ teaspoons salt
½ teaspoon white pepper
1 tablespoon fresh lemon juice
2 to 3 tablespoons finely chopped fresh dill
Milk or heavy cream (optional)
Sour cream, plain yogurt, or crème fraîche

Preheat oven to 400 degrees.

Place sweet and baking potatoes in oven and bake until soft, about 1 hour. Meanwhile, melt butter in a medium skillet and sauté onion until light golden and just beginning to brown.

Scrape sautéed onion into a food processor, deglaze pan with a little of the stock, and add to the onion. Add carrots and purée. Scoop out pulp from potatoes and add to processor along with salt, white pepper, and lemon juice. Purée until thoroughly mixed and very fine. Pour mixture into a saucepan. Add dill and remaining stock and simmer over very low heat for about 15 minutes.

Soup may be thinned with additional stock, milk, or cream. Correct seasoning and serve warm with a dollop of sour cream, yogurt, or crème fraîche on top.

SERVES 6 TO 8

CARROT AND RED BELL PEPPER SOUP

For a slightly heartier soup, add cooked shrimp and serve the soup warm.

> 6 cups grated carrots
> 3 cups milk
> 2 fresh savory sprigs
> 6 cups Chicken Stock (page 41)
> 4 large red bell peppers, roasted and peeled (see Note, page 74), coarsely chopped
> 1/2 cup coarsely chopped red onion
> 2 teaspoons fresh lemon juice
> 1/4 teaspoon salt, or to taste
> Freshly ground black pepper, to taste
> Sour cream, plain yogurt, or crème fraîche (optional)

Combine carrots, milk, one of the savory sprigs, and half the stock in a saucepan. Simmer for 15 minutes over medium heat.

Strain the carrots from milk and set aside, reserving liquid. Place the peppers and onion in remaining stock with remaining savory sprig. Simmer rapidly over high heat for about 10 minutes. Lower heat to medium and add reserved carrots and cooking liquid, lemon juice, and salt and pepper. Heat for 5 minutes. Do not boil. Allow to cool, then purée in batches.

Reheat to serve warm or refrigerate for at least 4 hours and serve chilled. Serve garnished with a dollop of sour cream, yogurt, or crème fraîche, if desired.

SERVES 8 TO 10

CAULIFLOWER AND CRESS SOUP

There are often a number of types of peppery cress available in specialty markets in summer. Upland cress, for example, is cultivated in garden soil instead of water and is a relative of watercress. Some cresses are stronger than others, and almost any one of them will work here. However, I do think the stronger the flavor the better, since cauliflower has a pretty potent taste and the cress should be able to stand up to it.

> 1 1/2 cups small cauliflower florets
> Low-fat milk
> 6 tablespoons (3/4 stick) unsalted butter
> 3/4 cup finely chopped green onions, with some of the green
> 3/4 teaspoon salt
> 1 1/2 cups peeled and finely diced potatoes
> 2 1/2 cups Chicken Stock (page 41)
> 8 ounces cress, trimmed and heavy stems removed
> 1/4 teaspoon white pepper, or to taste

> Crème fraîche
> Sprigs of cress

In a small saucepan, cover cauliflower with milk and bring to a simmer. Continue to cook until fork-tender, approximately 10 minutes. When done, set aside (in the milk).

Meanwhile, melt butter in a large skillet and add green onions. Sauté over medium-low heat until limp, approximately 5 minutes. Add salt, potatoes, and stock. Bring to a simmer and cover tightly. Cook for 10 minutes.

Add the cress to the potatoes, cover again, and cook an additional 10 minutes, shaking pan occasionally. Test potatoes for doneness. They should pierce easily with the tines of a fork. Add white pepper. Drain the cauliflower (reserve milk), and add to skillet. Put vegetables in a food processor and purée thoroughly. Return to skillet and add 1 cup of the reserved cauliflower milk. If you do not have enough milk, add plain milk to make up the difference. Heat, and correct seasoning if necessary.

Serve warm but not piping hot. Garnish with crème fraîche and a sprig of cress.

SERVES 6

CREAMED CORN AND RED BELL PEPPER SOUP

This delightful soup freezes quite well. For that reason, I always make a double batch and freeze individual portions.

2 tablespoons unsalted butter
2 cups thinly sliced leeks, white parts only
1 cup thinly sliced shallots
6 cups Chicken Stock (page 41) or low-sodium canned broth
1 baking potato, peeled and diced
1/2 cup diced red bell pepper
3 cups fresh or frozen yellow corn kernels
Salt, to taste
1/2 teaspoon white pepper

Crème fraîche or plain yogurt (optional)
Snipped fresh chives (optional)

Melt butter over medium heat in a heavy medium saucepan with a tight-fitting lid. Add leeks and shallots and toss in butter; cover with the lid. Reduce heat to very low and sweat vegetables, stirring several times, until wilted but not browned, about 15 minutes.

Stir in stock and bring quickly to a boil over high heat. Then turn back to a simmer. Add potato and bell pepper. Cover and simmer for 15 minutes. Add corn and bring to a simmer. Cover and cook for 5 minutes.

Purée soup mixture in a food processor or blender. Push through a sieve and discard solids. Season strained purée with salt and pepper. Serve warm or refrigerate for at least 4 hours and serve chilled. Garnish with dollops of crème fraîche or yogurt and chives, if you like.

SERVES 8

VARIATION

Omit potato and bell pepper for a tasty, easy-to-prepare, plain "creamy" corn soup that's made without cream or milk.

CORN CHOWDER

Corn is a terrific main ingredient in soups and it holds very well.

3 thick slices bacon, cut into 1/4-inch strips
1 cup coarsely chopped onion
4 cups peeled and cubed potatoes
2 cups water
1 cup crushed oyster crackers
1/2 cup milk
2 cups fresh corn kernels, cut and scraped from the cobs
1 1/2 teaspoons salt, or to taste
3 dashes Tabasco Sauce
1/2 teaspoon freshly ground black pepper, or to taste
1 cup Chicken Stock (page 41)

Fry bacon in a large saucepan. Remove and drain on paper towels. Pour out all but 2 tablespoons of fat. Add onion and sauté until lightly browned, about 5 minutes. Add potatoes and water. Cook over low heat until potatoes are tender, about 10 minutes.

Combine oyster crackers and milk in a small bowl and let sit for a few minutes. Stir into chowder along with corn, reserved bacon, salt, Tabasco, pepper, and stock. Simmer over very low heat for 10 minutes more. Serve warm.

SERVES 4 TO 6

CORN AND GREEN CHILI CHOWDER

This recipe comes from John Schmitt, chef-owner of the Boonville Hotel, in Boonville, north of San Francisco.

*1/4 cup olive oil or 4 tablespoons (1/2 stick)
    unsalted butter*
1 large onion, chopped
2 to 3 garlic cloves, chopped
1 yellow bell pepper, seeded and chopped
2 to 3 new potatoes, scrubbed and sliced
4 cups Chicken Stock (page 41), boiling
1/2 teaspoon ground cumin
Salt, to taste
*3 cups fresh corn kernels, cut and scraped
    from cobs*
1 can (8 ounces) green chilies, drained
1 jalapeño, seeded and chopped
1/2 cup coarsely chopped fresh cilantro
Freshly ground black pepper, to taste
Sour cream

Place 2 tablespoons olive oil in a heavy pot over medium heat and sauté onion, garlic, yellow pepper, and potatoes until onion is wilted, about 5 minutes. Add boiling stock, cumin, and salt. Continue to cook until potatoes are soft.

Meanwhile, heat 2 tablespoons olive oil in a large sauté pan and sauté corn, chilies, jalapeño, and cilantro until just heated through. Add salt and mix with the stock.

Purée mixture in a food processor in batches. Pour through a sieve to remove corn kernel skins. Adjust seasoning with pepper and more salt if necessary.

Serve hot or refrigerate for at least 4 hours and serve chilled. Garnish with a dollop of sour cream.

SERVES 6

GREEN SOUP

This soup has the texture of vichyssoise and also has potatoes as one of its principal ingredients. But, unlike vichyssoise, it has marvelous green-leaf vegetables in it. Best of all, it is made with no cream or milk. Guests are always surprised when I tell them this, because it has such a creamy texture. I serve it hot in the fall and winter and at room temperature during the warmer months.

1/4 cup sliced green onions
5 tablespoons unsalted butter
2 cups diced potatoes
1 teaspoon salt
2 cups Chicken Stock (page 41)
1 cup torn arugula leaves
1 cup torn spinach leaves, stems removed
2 cups torn lettuce leaves
Salt and white pepper, to taste
Sour cream or crème fraîche
Snipped fresh chives

Sauté green onions in butter for 5 minutes, until wilted. Add potatoes and salt and 1 cup of stock. Simmer, covered, for 10 minutes. Add the arugula, spinach, and lettuce. Simmer for 10 minutes more and test the potatoes for doneness. Purée vegetables in a food processor. Taste for seasoning, add the rest of the stock, and simmer for 1 or 2 minutes.

Serve either hot or at room temperature, with a dollop of sour cream or crème fraîche and a sprinkling of chopped chives on top.

SERVES 6

GREENS, TURNIP, AND CORN SOUP

If you don't see mustard greens around, and you are near a market that sells really fresh produce, have them ask their supplier about turnip greens. Kale and collard greens are the other choices, but neither compares with mustard or turnip greens.

2 strips of thick-sliced bacon
2 tablespoons olive oil
2 tablespoons unsalted butter
2 large shallots, coarsely chopped
1 pound onions, coarsely chopped
1 celery rib, coarsely chopped
1 large garlic clove, minced
2½ pounds mustard greens
2 packages instant chicken stock
2 teaspoons salt
1 teaspoon freshly ground black pepper
½ teaspoon dried thyme
6 cups Chicken Stock (page 41)
2 teaspoons fresh lemon juice
¼ teaspoon Tabasco Sauce
1¼ pounds small white turnips, peeled and cubed
6 large ears of corn, kernels cut from the cob and cobs scraped for milk

Snipped fresh chives (optional)
6 thin lemon slices (optional)

In a deep pot, fry bacon until crisp. Set aside. Reserve 1 tablespoon fat. Add olive oil and butter. Sauté shallots, onions, and celery until lightly browned, about 5 minutes. Add garlic.

Carefully wash greens and remove tough stems. Tear into large pieces and place in pot with only the water clinging to them. Sprinkle with instant chicken stock, salt, pepper, and thyme. Cover tightly and cook over medium heat until greens are wilted and tender, about 10 minutes.

Transfer to a food processor and purée. Return to soup pot and add chicken stock, lemon juice, and Tabasco. Bring to a slow boil and add turnips. Simmer until they start to become tender, about 10 minutes.

Add corn kernels and milk. Continue cooking for 5 minutes more. Correct seasoning, turn off heat, and let sit, uncovered, for 15 to 20 minutes before serving. Garnish with snipped chives or a slice of lemon.

SERVES 6

MUSHROOM CONSOMMÉ

This has a very gentle flavor.

6 cups Chicken Stock (page 41), clarified
1 cup dry white wine
1 teaspoon dried tarragon
½ teaspoon salt
2 tablespoons unsalted butter
3 cups thinly sliced mushrooms

In a large saucepan, combine stock, wine, tarragon, and salt. Simmer for about 30 minutes to reduce and intensify the flavor.

Melt butter in a medium skillet over medium heat. Add mushrooms and sauté 2 to 3 minutes, until they begin releasing their liquid.

To serve, combine mushrooms with stock and reheat.

SERVES 8

15

OKRA CHOWDER

If you can't find pancetta (Italian unsmoked bacon), substitute a good smoked bacon, preferably not sugar cured. Be sure to blanch it before using.

Should you want to have this chowder in winter, both okra and corn freeze tolerably well.

*¼ pound pancetta in 1 piece, cut into
    medium dice*
2 tablespoons unsalted butter
¼ cup safflower oil
1 large onion, coarsely chopped
2 medium shallots, finely chopped
*1 pound fresh okra, tops and tips removed,
    cut into ½-inch slices*
*1 can (14½ ounces) peeled tomatoes,
    drained and coarsely chopped*
7 cups Chicken Stock (page 41)
1 teaspoon salt
½ teaspoon dried thyme
*2 medium baking potatoes, peeled and
    coarsely diced*
*2 large ears of yellow corn, kernels cut off
    and milk scraped out*

Bring a saucepan of water to a boil and blanch the pancetta for 2 minutes. Drain and set aside.

Place butter and safflower oil in a deep pot and when hot, add the pancetta. Brown the pieces and reserve. Add onion, shallots, and okra. Cook over medium heat until onion begins to brown. Add tomatoes and cook another 5 minutes, stirring. Add stock, salt, and thyme. Simmer, skimming any foam, for 10 minutes.

Add potatoes and slowly boil for 10 minutes, skimming the oil that has started to rise to the surface. Add corn kernels, corn milk, and pancetta. Simmer for 2 minutes more, then turn off the heat. Let rest for 15 minutes before serving.

SERVES 6 TO 8

GREEN PEA SOUP WITH HAM

Like most of my other soups, this one is pretty thick. If you like a thinner soup, add more chicken stock and check the seasoning.

If you decide to make this in the winter with frozen peas—which are surprisingly good in a soup—put them into the soup unthawed and cook them just long enough to warm them through, a couple of minutes at most.

1 tablespoon olive oil
2 tablespoons unsalted butter
*¼ pound ham steak, trimmed and finely
    diced*
⅓ cup finely chopped celery
⅓ cup finely chopped carrots
1 cup finely chopped onion
½ pound buttom mushrooms, sliced
1 small garlic clove, minced
4 cups Chicken Stock (page 41), hot
1 teaspoon salt
½ teaspoon paprika
¼ teaspoon freshly ground black pepper
*½ head Boston lettuce, washed and
    shredded*
2 cups shelled green peas

Heat olive oil and butter in a deep saucepan and add diced ham. Fry over medium heat until ham begins to crisp. Remove, drain, and reserve.

Add celery, carrots, and onion, and sauté until vegetables wilt and begin to turn golden, about 3 minutes. Add mushrooms and continue cooking for another 2 minutes, tossing all the while. Stir in garlic, then add stock, salt, paprika, and pepper.

Add lettuce and peas to the soup. Bring to a boil and then reduce heat to a simmer. Cook for 10 minutes and turn off the heat. Stir in reserved ham and let sit for 15 minutes before serving.

SERVES 6

COLD PIMIENTO SOUP

A friend told me about a pimiento soup he had in the South of France, which sounded so good that I was moved to try to re-create it. After experimenting, I came up with this version. It is indeed delicious and, incidentally, is a perfect way to utilize some of those inexpensive tomatoes and red bell peppers that come on the market at the end of the summer. It also freezes well. The tomatoes should be vine-ripened for the right flavor.

2¼ pounds ripe tomatoes
2 large red bell peppers
1 tablespoon unsalted butter
½ pound onions, coarsely chopped
¼ celery rib, coarsely chopped
1 small carrot, coarsely grated
4 cups Chicken Stock (page 41)
Sour cream or crème fraîche

Put tomatoes on a low-sided baking sheet and set under the broiler. Roast them as you would peppers, turning with tongs until the skin blackens, about 10 minutes. Put them on a plate and set aside. They will give up quite a bit of liquid by the time you are ready to use them; drain it off and discard.

Roast red bell peppers as you did the tomatoes. When they are blackened, put them in a paper bag and fold the top shut. Set aside.

Put butter, onions, celery, and carrot in a saucepan with 1 or 2 tablespoons of the stock. Simmer, covered, over low heat for 10 minutes. Shake or stir to prevent sticking; do not allow to brown. When vegetables are soft, set aside.

Peel tomatoes and cut out stem ends. Add tomatoes to wilted onion mixture and simmer, covered, for 15 minutes. Stir occasionally to prevent scorching. Mash the solids through a strainer to get rid of the seeds. (Putting the strained pulp through a food processor or food mill first makes this a bit easier.) Return strained vegetables to saucepan and add remaining stock. Simmer 30 minutes, uncovered. Skim as necessary.

Peel, seed, and purée the peppers. Add to the tomato mixture and let simmer for just a few minutes. Let cool and then correct seasoning. Refrigerate for 1 hour and serve slightly chilled with a large spoonful of sour cream or crème fraîche on top.

SERVES 4 TO 6

SWEET PEA SOUP

2 tablespoons unsalted butter
¾ cup finely chopped white onion
1½ cups frozen sweet peas, thawed
1 cup water
½ cup sour cream
½ cup yogurt
3 tablespoons (loosely packed) cilantro leaves, torn
1 teaspoon salt
2 teaspoons freshly ground black pepper

Melt butter in a medium saucepan over medium-high heat. Add ½ cup of the chopped onion and 1¼ cups of the peas, cooking until peas begin to sweat and onions look translucent, about 10 to 12 minutes.

Pour the peas, onions, and water into a food processor, add the remaining peas and onions, and purée for 1 or 2 minutes. Leave the mixture slightly chunky.

Add sour cream, yogurt, cilantro, salt, and pepper and purée until almost smooth. Serve warm or refrigerate for at least 4 hours and serve chilled.

SERVES 6

POTATO AND RED BELL PEPPER SOUP

1 tablespoon unsalted butter
1 small onion, coarsely chopped
2 garlic cloves, minced
4 cups Chicken Stock (page 41)
2 large baking potatoes, peeled and each cut
into 8 pieces
1 large red bell pepper, roasted, peeled, and
seeded (see Note, page 74), chopped
1 teaspoon salt
1/4 teaspoon freshly ground black pepper

Melt butter in a saucepan over medium-high heat. Add onion and cook, covered, until just starting to brown, about 7 minutes. Add garlic and cook, stirring constantly, for 1 minute. Add stock and potatoes. Bring to a boil. Cover, reduce the heat, and simmer until the potatoes are tender, about 20 minutes. Stir in the bell pepper.

Allow the soup to cool slightly, then purée it in batches in a food processor. Strain the purée and season with salt and pepper. Serve warm.
SERVES 6

SWEET POTATO VICHYSSOISE

Quick, easy, and tasty!

3 cups peeled and sliced sweet potatoes
1 3/4 cups sliced green onions, mostly white
parts
5 cups Chicken Stock (page 41)
Salt and white pepper, to taste
1/2 cup half-and-half
Snipped fresh chives (optional)

Put sweet potatoes and green onions in a medium saucepan. Add enough stock to cover the potatoes and bring to a boil over high heat. Reduce the heat to low and simmer until tender, about 15 minutes. Allow to cool for several minutes, then strain, reserving the liquid. Purée the solids in a food processor or put through a food mill and return to the saucepan with the reserved liquid. Season with salt and pepper. Simmer a few minutes, then set aside off the heat until cool. Refrigerate, covered, for at least 4 hours.

To serve, stir in half-and-half. Place in chilled soup bowls. Garnish each serving with some snipped chives, if you like.
SERVES 6 TO 8

COLD RADISH SOUP

Make this as thick or as thin as you choose. You may use additional chicken stock (which I do), low-fat milk, or light cream. I always make enough of this soup to have leftovers for another meal or an afternoon snack.

1 tablespoon unsalted butter
1 cup thinly sliced green onions, mostly
white parts
2 cups small-cubed white potatoes
2 cups thinly sliced radishes
2 2/3 cups Chicken Stock (page 41)
1/2 teaspoon white pepper
Salt, to taste
Chopped radish
Snipped fresh chives

Melt butter in a medium saucepan and stir in green onions. Cover tightly and sweat over very low heat about 15 to 20 minutes, until wilted. Do not allow to brown. Add potatoes and radishes and enough stock to cover.

Bring to a boil, turn heat to low, and simmer, covered, until potatoes are very tender, about 20 minutes.

Transfer to a food processor and purée until smooth. Return to the saucepan and add the remaining stock. Add pepper and salt.

Refrigerate for at least 4 hours and serve chilled with chopped radish and snipped chives on top of each serving.
SERVES 8

SORREL SOUP

Here it is—sorrel soup my way.

 3 tablespoons unsalted butter
 1 pound onions, coarsely chopped
 1 small garlic clove, minced
 6 cups Chicken Stock (page 41)
 $^1/_2$ pound red potatoes, peeled and coarsely
   diced
 $^3/_4$ pound sorrel, trimmed and torn into
   large pieces
 Salt and freshly ground black pepper, to
   taste
 Sour cream

Heat butter in a deep pot and sauté onions until wilted and turning golden, about 5 minutes. Add garlic and cook for another minute. Add stock and heat, then add potatoes. Simmer until potatoes are done, about 10 minutes. Stir in sorrel and heat thoroughly.

   Transfer to a food processor and purée. Return to the heat and cook for another few minutes, correcting seasoning with salt and pepper if necessary.

   Serve with a dollop of sour cream on top of each serving.

SERVES 6

SPINACH SOUP

The recipe for this marvelously strong-flavored soup came to me from a friend, Mary Allen of Roxbury, Connecticut. The only time-consuming thing about it is stemming the spinach; the rest is a breeze. Just make sure the spinach is well washed, as it tends to be sandy and the merest hint of sand ruins it for me.

 3 pounds fresh spinach, large stems removed
   and leaves carefully washed
 4 tablespoons ($^1/_2$ stick) unsalted butter
 $1^1/_2$ cups finely chopped onion
 2 cups Chicken Stock (page 41)
 2 cups low-fat milk
 Salt and freshly ground black pepper, to
   taste
 Dash of freshly grated nutmeg (optional)
 6 thin lemon slices
 Snipped fresh chives

Place spinach in a large pot with just the water clinging to the leaves. Cover and cook over high heat until wilted and tender.

   Meanwhile, melt butter in a large skillet and sauté onion until golden.

   Drain spinach, reserving the liquid, and place spinach in a food processor along with the onion. Purée until smooth. Combine puréed spinach-onion mixture with stock, spinach pan juice, and milk. Slowly bring to a simmer. Add salt and pepper, and a dash of nutmeg, if using.

   Float a slice of lemon on top of each serving and sprinkle with snipped chives.

SERVES 6

19

ACORN SQUASH AND TURNIP SOUP

As you might imagine, this has a pronounced turnip flavor. If turnips are not one of your favorite vegetables, maybe this soup is not for you. But you can cut down on the turnip flavor by reducing their number or by adding a cubed small potato to the combination. This is the sort of soup that invites innovation.

1 large acorn squash, split and seeded, cut
   surface rubbed with a little butter
4 tablespoons (¹/₂ stick) unsalted butter or
   half butter, half margarine
1 medium leek, white part only, carefully
   washed and coarsely chopped
1 cup coarsely chopped onion
³/₄ cup coarsely grated carrot
1 small garlic clove, cut into several pieces
1 teaspoon sugar
3 to 4 white turnips, peeled
5 cups Chicken Stock (page 41)
¹/₄ teaspoon white pepper
1 teaspoon salt
¹/₄ teaspoon ground coriander
Crème fraîche or sour cream

Preheat oven to 375 degrees.

Place squash in a foil-lined pan and bake until fork-tender, about 30 minutes.

Melt butter in a stockpot and toss with leek, onion, carrot, and garlic. Sprinkle sugar over all and cover tightly. Sweat over lowest possible heat for 20 minutes. Do not allow to burn. Add turnips, 2 cups of the stock, white pepper, salt, and coriander. Simmer until turnips are tender, about 20 minutes.

Transfer vegetables and liquid to a food processor. Scoop out pulp of acorn squash and add to vegetables. Purée all and return to pot. Stir in remaining stock and heat. Correct seasoning if necessary. Serve with a dollop of crème fraîche or sour cream.

SERVES 6 TO 8

COLD ROASTED TOMATO SOUP WITH CHERVIL

Roasting tomatoes seems to enhance their flavor. Of course, this soup should be made only when vine-ripened tomatoes are available. Happily, at the same time they come on the market, you can usually get fresh chervil, one of my favorite herbs.

1 tablespoon unsalted butter
¹/₂ pound onions, coarsely chopped
¹/₄ celery rib, coarsely shredded
1 small carrot, coarsely shredded
4 cups Chicken Stock (page 41)
2¹/₄ pounds fresh tomatoes, roasted
   (see Note)
1 tablespoon chopped fresh Italian flat-leaf
   parsley
2 tablespoons chopped fresh chervil
Salt, to taste
Freshly ground black pepper (optional)

Put butter, onions, celery, and carrot in a saucepan with about 1 cup of stock and simmer, covered, over low heat for about 10 minutes. Stir to prevent sticking. Do not let brown.

Add tomatoes and the rest of the stock. Continue to simmer, covered, over low heat for 15 minutes more. Stir to prevent scorching. When tomatoes become pulpy, purée in a food processor, then strain out the tomato seeds and skin, pushing the solids through.

Return purée to saucepan and add parsley, chervil, salt, and pepper, if using. Simmer, uncovered, for another 10 minutes. Cool, then refrigerate for at least 4 hours. Serve chilled.

Note: To roast tomatoes, put them in a rimmed pan under the broiler and roast them, turning with tongs until the skin begins to blacken, 5 to 10 minutes. Transfer to a plate and set aside. Peel the tomatoes and cut out the stem ends.

SERVES 4

VARIATION

This soup is also delicious served hot, with rice added. Add 2 tablespoons raw rice to the soup for the last 10 minutes of the cooking time and test for doneness.

COLD ROASTED TOMATO AND RED BELL PEPPER SOUP

I always keep a batch of this in my refrigerator during the summer. One taste is all you need to be converted.

1 tablespoon unsalted butter
1/2 pound onions, coarsely chopped
1/2 celery rib, coarsely chopped
1 small carrot, grated
4 cups Chicken Stock (page 41)
2 1/2 pounds ripe tomatoes, roasted
    (see page 20)
2 large red bell peppers, roasted
    (see Note, page 74)
Salt and white pepper, to taste
Sour cream or crème fraîche

Put butter, onions, celery, and carrot in a saucepan with 1 or 2 tablespoons of the stock. Shaking the pan to prevent sticking, simmer, covered, over low heat for 10 minutes, until vegetables are soft but not browned. Add tomatoes and simmer, covered, for 15 minutes. Stir occasionally to prevent scorching.

Purée the mixture briefly in a food processor and then put it through a strainer or food mill to get rid of the seeds. Return the purée to the saucepan and add the remaining stock. Simmer, uncovered, for 30 minutes, skimming.

Peel, seed, and purée the peppers. Add to the saucepan and simmer for just a few more minutes. Let cool. Correct the seasoning with salt and pepper, if necessary. Serve chilled with a large spoonful of sour cream or crème fraîche on top.

SERVES 4 TO 6

HOT TOMATO AND RICE SOUP WITH SAUSAGE BALLS

If you would like to freeze this, leave out the rice and sausage. Add them when you serve it.

1 tablespoon unsalted butter
1/2 pound onions, coarsely chopped
1/4 celery rib, coarsely chopped
1 small carrot, grated
4 cups Chicken Stock (page 41)
2 1/4 pounds ripe tomatoes, roasted
    (see page 20)
1 tablespoon minced fresh Italian flat-leaf
    parsley
2 tablespoons minced fresh chervil
Salt and freshly ground black pepper, to
    taste
2 tablespoons raw long-grain rice
1/2 to 3/4 pound sausage meat

In a saucepan, combine butter, onions, celery, and carrot with 1 cup of stock and simmer, covered, over low heat for 10 minutes. Add the rest of the stock.

Drain off any juice from the tomatoes. Add the tomatoes to the saucepan, cover, and simmer over low heat for another 15 minutes, stirring occasionally.

Purée the mixture briefly in a food processor and then put it through a strainer or food mill. Discard the seeds and return the purée to the saucepan. Add parsley, chervil, and salt and pepper. Bring to a simmer and add rice. Simmer for 10 minutes, or until rice is tender.

Meanwhile, roll sausage meat into walnut-size balls. Brown them and add them to individual servings of the soup.

SERVES 6

SUMMER TOMATO SOUP

Make sure to string the celery before you chop it.

>*2 tablespoons olive oil*
>*2 cups finely diced onions*
>*1/2 cup finely diced green bell pepper*
>*1/3 cup roughly chopped celery*
>*1 1/2 pounds tomatoes, peeled, seeded, and*
>*   roughly chopped*
>*2 cups Chicken Stock (page 41)*
>*1/2 teaspoon salt*
>*1/4 teaspoon freshly ground black pepper*
>*1 tablespoon tarragon vinegar*

Pour the oil in a large cast-iron skillet. Heat over medium-high heat until hot. Add the onions and sauté for 5 minutes, stirring occasionally. Add the bell pepper and celery. Stir to combine, cover, and cook for 5 minutes, stirring occasionally. Add the tomatoes and stir. Increase the heat to high and cook for 5 minutes, until the tomatoes give up their juice and become tender. Add the stock, salt, and pepper and stir. Heat the soup thoroughly; there's no need to boil it. Add the vinegar just before serving.

SERVES 4

SPRING SOUP

This soup is eminently portable, but don't keep it too long, as the lettuce should look fresh.

>*2 tablespoons unsalted butter*
>*1 1/2 cups carefully washed and coarsely*
>*   chopped leeks, white parts only*
>*1/3 cup sliced shallots*
>*1/3 cup sliced green onions*
>*3/4 cup grated carrots*
>*4 cups roughly chopped romaine lettuce*
>*3/4 cup small peas, fresh or frozen*
>*5 cups Chicken Stock (page 41)*
>*1 cup cooked rice*
>*3/4 teaspoon salt*
>*1/4 teaspoon freshly ground black pepper*

Melt butter in a large saucepan over medium-high heat. Add leeks and cook, stirring occasionally, until just beginning to brown, approximately 10 minutes. Add shallots and stir. Cover and cook for 2 minutes. Add green onions, carrots, lettuce, and peas. Stir to combine and cook, covered, for 3 minutes. Add stock and cook, covered, for 5 minutes. Add rice and stir to combine. Add salt and pepper and adjust seasoning if necessary.

SERVES 6

UNCOOKED TOMATO SOUP

You could stir a bit of crabmeat or boiled small shrimp into this soup and make a meal of it.

>*3 pounds ripe tomatoes, peeled and seeded*
>*1 medium green bell pepper, seeded and*
>*   coarsely chopped*
>*1 small cucumber, peeled, seeded, and*
>*   coarsely chopped*
>*3 large celery ribs, peeled*
>*10 small basil leaves, coarsely chopped*
>*1 tablespoon chopped fresh tarragon*
>*2 tablespoons olive oil*
>*1/4 cup tarragon vinegar*
>*Salt and freshly ground black pepper, to taste*
>*1 cup Vegetable Stock (page 40)*
>*3 tablespoons minced roasted red bell pepper*
>*   (see Note, page 74) (optional)*
>*Yogurt or crème fraîche (optional)*
>*Sprigs of herb*

Put all the vegetables, herbs, oil, and vinegar in a food processor and pulse until roughly chopped. Pour into a large bowl and stir in salt and pepper and stock. If the soup is too thick, thin with a little extra stock.

Serve at room temperature or refrigerate for 1 hour and serve chilled. Garnish with roasted red pepper, a dollop of yogurt or crème fraîche, and a sprig of herb, if you like.

SERVES 8

ZUCCHINI AND BUTTERNUT SQUASH SOUP

Many combinations of summer vegetables work well when puréed together. For my money, one of the best flavor combinations is the slight sweetness of butternut squash when added to zucchini.

1 small butternut squash, split and seeded, the cut surface rubbed with a little butter
4 tablespoons (1/2 stick) unsalted butter or half butter and half margarine
1 medium leek, white part only, carefully washed and coarsely chopped
1 cup coarsely chopped onion
1 cup grated carrots
1 small garlic clove, cut into several pieces
1 teaspoon sugar
1 pound zucchini, trimmed and cut into large rounds
5 cups Chicken Stock (page 41)
1/4 teaspoon white pepper
1 teaspoon salt
1/4 teaspoon ground coriander
Yogurt (optional)

Preheat oven to 375 degrees.

Place butternut squash in a foil-lined pie pan and bake until fork-tender, about 30 to 40 minutes.

Melt butter in a stockpot and add leek, onion, carrots, and garlic. Toss well, then sprinkle sugar over all and cover tightly. Sweat over the lowest possible heat for 20 minutes. Do not allow to burn. Add zucchini, 2 cups of the stock, white pepper, salt, and coriander. Cook, uncovered, over medium heat until zucchini is very soft, about 10 minutes.

Transfer vegetables and liquid to a food processor. Scoop out the pulp of the squash, making sure you get it all, and add to vegetables in food processor. Purée everything together and return to pot.

Stir in the remaining stock and heat. Correct seasoning if necessary. Serve with a dollop of yogurt on top of each serving, if desired.

SERVES 6 TO 8

CHILLED BUTTERMILK VEGETABLE SOUP

I think you will love this tangy soup. You could experiment by adding a few other kinds of vegetables after you have made this the first time.

2 tablespoons unsalted butter
1 large onion, chopped
3 medium apples, peeled, cored, and coarsely chopped
3 cups water
1 tablespoon instant chicken broth granules
2 1/2 cups buttermilk
1 cup peeled, seeded, and finely diced cucumber
1 cup peeled, seeded, and finely diced tomato
1 cup corn cut from the cob, steamed
1 1/2 teaspoons salt
1/4 cup finely chopped fresh dill
2 tablespoons chopped red bell pepper

Melt butter in a skillet and sauté onion over medium heat until wilted but not browned, about 5 minutes. Add apples, water, and chicken broth granules. Simmer until apples are soft, about 5 to 10 minutes. Purée in a blender or food processor. (Soup may be frozen at this point.)

Add buttermilk, vegetables, and salt. Refrigerate, covered, until well chilled. Serve garnished with dill and red pepper.

SERVES 6 TO 8

FIVE BEAN SOUP

This meal is for those of you who like to have a real Tex-Mex fix. There are plenty of spices in the soup.

½ cup dried black beans
½ cup dried red kidney beans
½ cup dried navy beans
½ cup dried black-eyed peas
½ cup dried baby lima beans
¾ pound andouille sausage
1 medium smoked ham hock
4 cups water
1 large carrot, scrubbed and broken into
*   several pieces*
3 large celery ribs, broken into several large
*   pieces*
3 large Italian flat-leaf parsley sprigs
1 very large onion, coarsely chopped
¼ cup olive oil
2 large garlic cloves, finely chopped
1 large bay leaf
2½ teaspoons salt
2 teaspoons paprika
2 teaspoons ground cumin
2 teaspoons chili powder
1 teaspoon freshly ground black pepper
¼ teaspoon ground cinnamon
2 cups chopped canned whole tomatoes in
*   paste*
2 cups Beef Stock (page 42)
1 teaspoon red wine vinegar

Put all beans except the baby limas and peas in a bowl and cover with water. Soak overnight or use the quick-soak method (see Note, page 25). Soak limas separately.

Cover sausage and ham hock with the water and bring to a boil. Add carrot, celery, and parsley. Turn back to just simmering and simmer for 1 hour, removing sausage after about 15 minutes. Set aside.

Sauté chopped onion in olive oil until wilted and brown, about 5 minutes. Add garlic and set aside.

Drain and degrease liquid in which sausage and hock were cooked. Discard vegetables and remove any meat from hock. Chop coarsely. Discard skin and bones.

Drain mixed beans and place in a large pot. Measure degreased liquid and add enough water to make 4 cups. Pour over beans and bring to a boil. Add onion-garlic mixture and turn heat back to a simmer. Add bay leaf, salt, spices. Simmer until almost tender, about 1½ to 2 hours.

Add chopped tomatoes and beef stock to the pot. When simmering, add drained baby limas. Simmer until they are just cooked, about 30 minutes.

Cut sausage into ¼-inch rings. Add to soup along with ham and vinegar. Simmer another few minutes.

SERVES 6 TO 8

BLACK BEAN AND MACARONI SOUP

I am especially fond of the combination of beans and macaroni. And with red bell peppers—oh boy!

1 cup dried black beans, soaked overnight or
*   by the quick-soak method (see Note)*
About 8 cups Chicken Stock (page 41)
2 small bay leaves
¼ cup olive oil
1 large onion, coarsely chopped
1 small garlic clove, finely chopped
1 cup drained and chopped canned
*   tomatoes*
2 tablespoons red wine
1 teaspoon sugar
¼ teaspoon freshly ground black pepper
1½ cups elbow macaroni
2 very large red bell peppers, roasted and
*   peeled (see Note, page 74), cut into*
*   medium dice*
Finely chopped fresh Italian flat-leaf parsley
Finely chopped green onions

Drain beans and cover with 3 cups of the stock. Bring to a boil and turn heat down to a simmer. Add bay leaves. Simmer until the beans start to get tender, about 1 hour and 30 minutes.

Meanwhile, heat olive oil and sauté onion until wilted and starting to brown, about 5 minutes. Stir in garlic and continue to cook for another minute or so. Scrape onion-garlic mixture into beans and add tomatoes. Continue cooking, adding more stock as necessary, until beans are done. This can take up to 1 hour. Add wine, sugar, pepper, and the remaining stock.

To serve, boil macaroni in very well salted water for 6 minutes. Drain and add to the bean mixture along with the diced red pepper. Simmer just long enough to completely cook the macaroni. Allow to sit for about 5 minutes before serving. This probably will not need salt, but correct seasoning if necessary.

If you have cooked the soup too rapidly you may have evaporated too much of the liquid. In that case, add a bit more stock. However, this should be a very thick soup.

Sprinkle with chopped flat-leaf parsley and green onions, if desired.

Note: To use the quick-soak method, cover beans with 1 inch water and bring to a rapid boil. Boil for 2 minutes and turn off heat. Allow to sit, covered, for 1 hour.

SERVES 6

BEAN, BACON, POTATO, AND RED PEPPER SOUP

I have soup at least three times a week and I make it out of anything handy. Here is one of my favorites. You may make this soup with sweet potatoes and other types of dried beans. Use whatever you've got.

1/4 pound hickory-cured slab bacon, with rind, cut into 3/8-inch dice
1 tablespoon unsalted butter
1/2 small onion, diced small
1/2 large carrot, scraped and diced small
1 small celery rib, diced small
6 cups Chicken Stock (page 41)
3/4 teaspoon salt
1/4 teaspoon white pepper
2 medium leeks, white parts only, carefully washed and cut into 1/2-inch rounds
2 medium baking potatoes, peeled and cut into 1-inch cubes
3/4 large red bell pepper, diced
1 can (10 1/2 ounces) white kidney beans, rinsed and drained

Cover bacon with water in a large pot and simmer for 5 minutes. Drain and press dry in paper towels. Wipe out pot and return bacon. Fry until golden and crisp over medium-low heat, about 4 minutes. Remove to a paper towel and reserve. Discard all rendered fat except 2 teaspoons; add butter and return to heat. When foamy, add onion, carrot, and celery. Sauté until brown, about 5 minutes. Add the stock, reserved bacon, salt, and pepper. Simmer, skimming foam, for 5 minutes. Add leeks and potatoes. Simmer 5 minutes then add red bell pepper. Continue cooking, skimming as needed, until potatoes are just tender when pierced with the point of a knife, about 5 more minutes. Add beans and simmer for another minute or so. Correct seasoning, turn off the heat, and allow the soup to sit 30 minutes before serving.

SERVES 6

WHITE BEAN AND SAUSAGE SOUP

You can use any sausage that appeals to you for this. And incidentally, this method of cooking sausage is a good one to know about—it's foolproof, and always improves the flavor of whatever sausage you are preparing.

2 cups dried navy beans
8 cups Chicken Stock (page 41)
1 large bay leaf
¹/₄ teaspoon dried thyme
¹/₄ cup olive oil
1¹/₂ cups coarsely chopped onion
¹/₂ cup coarsely chopped celery
2 large carrots, peeled and cut into rounds
¹/₄ large green bell pepper, coarsely chopped
12 links pork sausage (1 to 1¹/₄ pounds)
2 large garlic cloves, minced
¹/₄ cup dry red wine

Pick over beans and soak overnight, or use the quick-soak method (see Note, page 25).

Drain and put beans, 3 cups stock, bay leaf, and thyme in a large pot. Bring to a simmer and continue to cook, simmering as necessary, until beans begin to get tender and fall apart, 1¹/₂ to 2 hours. Add another 2 cups of stock, or to taste, if soup has reduced too much at the end of the cooking time.

Meanwhile, place olive oil in a large skillet and sauté onion, celery, carrots, and bell pepper until they start to brown. Scrape into a food processor and purée. Reserve this purée and add to the beans for the last 30 minutes of their cooking time.

Place sausages in a cold skillet and cook over high heat for 6 minutes, turning often. Pour off the fat. Add garlic and red wine. Simmer, covered, for another 15 minutes. Cut sausages into rounds and add to the soup. Deglaze the pan with a few tablespoons of water or stock, then add to soup. Add more stock if necessary. Serve warm.

Note: To cut down on the cooking time, substitute dried baby lima beans for the navy beans. Limas require only about 45 minutes to cook.
SERVES 6 TO 8

TWO BEAN SOUP WITH BROCCOLI RABE AND SAUSAGE

As recently as five years ago, broccoli rabe was available only in specialty shops. Happily, now it is cropping up everyplace. This soup is a small celebration of the emergence of this vegetable, which the Italians have enjoyed for ages.

1 cup dried black-eyed peas, rinsed and
  picked over
1 cup dried navy beans, rinsed and picked
  over
8 cups Chicken Stock (page 41)
4 medium onions, chopped
2 large garlic cloves, crushed
2 bay leaves
¹/₂ teaspoon dried thyme
¹/₂ teaspoon freshly ground black pepper
1¹/₂ tablespoons olive oil
1 pound bulk breakfast sausage, formed into
  1-inch balls
¹/₂ pound broccoli rabe, stems trimmed,
  coarsely chopped
Salt, to taste

Soak peas and beans in water using the quick-soak method (see Note, page 25).

Drain peas and beans and return to the pot. Add stock and bring to a boil over moderate heat. Add onions, garlic, bay leaves, thyme, and pepper. Simmer until beans are tender, skimming as necessary; this will take about 30 to 60 minutes or more, depending on age of beans.

Meanwhile, heat ¹/₂ tablespoon of olive oil in a large skillet over moderate heat. Add sausage balls and cook, turning, until browned

26

all over and cooked through, about 10 minutes. Drain on paper towels.

When beans are tender, add broccoli rabe and return to a simmer. Continue to simmer until broccoli rabe is tender, skimming if necessary. Stir in remaining olive oil and sausage balls. Season with salt if necessary. Heat through, then let stand for 15 minutes before serving.

SERVES 6 TO 8

PASTA AND BEAN SOUP

There is a very simple way to alter the flavor of this soup. The recipe calls for crushed tomatoes, which are available with and without tomato paste added. If you use the one without paste, the tomato flavor is a bit more subtle; with the paste the flavor is more pronounced. It's good both ways.

1/4 pound thick-sliced bacon
5 tablespoons olive oil
1/2 cup minced onion
1/2 cup minced celery
1/2 cup minced carrot
1 1/2 cups canned crushed tomatoes
2 cans (19 ounces) cannellini beans, rinsed and drained
8 cups Chicken Stock (page 41)
1 teaspoon salt
1/2 teaspoon freshly ground black pepper
1 cup small elbow macaroni

Bring a small saucepan of water to a simmer. Cut bacon strips into 4 equal pieces each, add to water, and blanch for 5 minutes. Drain, dry bacon well, and fry until crisp. Set bacon aside and reserve 2 tablespoons of bacon fat.

Heat bacon fat and olive oil in a stockpot over medium heat. Add onion, celery, and carrot. Cover and cook, stirring occasionally, until vegetables begin to brown, about 10 minutes. Add tomatoes and increase the heat to high. Cook, stirring, until reduced and slightly darkened, about 8 minutes. Add beans, stock, salt, and pepper. Bring to a boil, then turn back to a simmer. Cook 5 minutes. Use the back of a spoon to mash some of the beans (this will thicken the soup slightly). You can prepare the recipe up to this point in advance. Set it aside, covered.

Add reserved bacon and the macaroni. Bring back to a boil and cook for 5 minutes. Cover the pot and remove it from the heat. Allow to rest 5 minutes before serving. Serve immediately.

SERVES 6

LENTIL, FENNEL, AND CRESS SOUP

This soup freezes fairly well because it does not depend as much on texture as it does on overall flavor.

3 tablespoons olive oil
1 cup coarsely chopped fennel, tender parts only and no tops
3/4 cup coarsely chopped onion
1/2 cup coarsely chopped celery
1/4 cup finely chopped carrot
1/4 cup finely chopped red bell pepper
About 1/2 pound watercress, large stems removed
1 medium garlic clove, minced
1 1/2 cups brown lentils, picked over, rinsed, soaked for several hours, and drained
5 to 6 cups Chicken Stock (page 41), hot
1/8 teaspoon dried thyme
1/4 teaspoon salt, or to taste
1/4 teaspoon freshly ground black pepper, or to taste
1 medium bay leaf
4 dashes of Tabasco Sauce
2 tablespoons unsalted butter (optional)

Sprigs of watercress

Place olive oil in a deep pot and add fennel, onion, celery, carrot, and red pepper. Sauté until vegetables start to brown and turn soft, a few minutes. Add watercress and cook until just wilted, a few more minutes. Add garlic, lentils, and about 4 cups of the stock. Bring to a simmer and add thyme, salt, pepper, bay leaf, and Tabasco. Cook over very low heat for about 20 minutes, until lentils are tender and falling apart, adding a bit more stock if necessary.

Place soup in a food processor and purée. Return to pot and add remaining stock and heat thoroughly. I prefer this soup rather thick, but it can be diluted with additional stock if you like. Stir in butter, if desired.

Serve with a sprig of watercress on top.

SERVES 6 TO 8

CHICKEN, MEAT, AND SEAFOOD SOUPS

LEMON CHICKEN SOUP

This soup has a light hint of Mexico.

6 chicken thighs, skin removed
7 cups Chicken Stock (page 41) or low-
 sodium canned broth
Juice and grated zest of 1 large lemon
2 tablespoons unsalted butter
1 large onion, coarsely chopped
2 medium garlic cloves, crushed
5 medium ears of corn, kernels cut off and
 scraped out, or 2 cups frozen corn kernels
2 large tomatoes, coarsely chopped
6 green onions, coarsely chopped
1/2 cup coarsely chopped fresh cilantro, or to
 taste
Salt and freshly ground black pepper, to
 taste

5 corn tortillas, cut into bite-size pieces
6 thin slices of lemon
Sprigs of cilantro

Put chicken thighs in a saucepan and cover with a generous amount of cold water. Bring to a boil and simmer until meat is very tender, about 45 minutes. Remove chicken and let cool. Reserve the cooking liquid and shred the chicken.

Measure 4 cups of cooking liquid (add more water if you don't have enough to make that amount) and combine it with the stock in a large saucepan. Bring to a simmer and add chicken meat, lemon juice, and lemon zest.

Meanwhile, melt butter in a medium skillet over medium heat and sauté onion and garlic until lightly golden, about 5 minutes. Add this and the corn kernels and pulp to the simmering stock. Simmer a few more minutes. Add tomatoes, green onions, chopped cilantro, and salt and pepper. Simmer 15 minutes longer. Skim fat.

To serve, place some tortilla pieces in each of 6 soup bowls, ladle in the soup, garnish with lemon slices and cilantro, and serve.

SERVES 6

CHICKEN AND DILL SOUP

The amount of dill called for in this recipe gives this soup a fairly mild dill flavor. Frankly, when I make it for myself I use almost double the amount. If you really like the flavor of dill, as I obviously do, you might want to increase the amount, too.

Salt and freshly ground black pepper, to taste
2½ pounds chicken breast, with bones and skin, split in half
2 very large onions, very coarsely chopped
6 cups Chicken Stock (page 41)
6 ounces carrots, cut into rounds
¾ pound baking potato, peeled and diced
¼ teaspoon dried thyme
¼ teaspoon ground mace or freshly grated nutmeg
3 tablespoons chopped fresh dill leaves

Preheat oven to 375 degrees.

Salt and pepper the chicken breasts generously. Spread half the chopped onions on the bottom of a baking dish large enough to hold the chicken breasts in a single layer. Put the remaining onions on top of the chicken. Bake, uncovered, for 20 minutes. Heat 1 cup of the stock and pour into pan. Bake another 20 minutes, or until chicken is cooked through.

Remove bones and skin from chicken and discard. Set chicken aside.

Strain the baked onions from the pan juices. Place onions in a large pot with the remaining stock. Heat. Meanwhile, degrease pan juices and add to pot along with carrots, potato, thyme, mace, dill, and salt and pepper. Simmer for 8 minutes, skimming if necessary. When carrots and potato are almost fork-tender, cut chicken into large cubes and add. Turn off heat and let sit for about 15 minutes before serving.

SERVES 6 TO 8

TURKEY VEGETABLE SOUP

This soup has a few surprising elements in it. Just be sure to brown the turkey meat and bones properly and make certain that the chicken stock is nice and flavorful.

2 tablespoons safflower oil
1 raw turkey breast carcass with some meat on it, chopped roughly into 4 to 5 pieces
7 cups Chicken Stock (page 41) or low-sodium canned broth
4 cups water
½ very large red onion, thinly sliced
2 cups green beans, tipped and puréed to the consistency of relish
1½ pounds white potatoes, peeled and cubed
4 large Italian flat-leaf parsley sprigs without stems, chopped
½ teaspoon freshly ground black pepper
1 package (10 ounces) frozen peas

Heat the safflower oil and carefully and thoroughly brown turkey carcass parts and any bits of leftover raw meat. This may take about 5 minutes or more. Add stock and water. Bring to a simmer and continue to cook for about 40 minutes, skimming occasionally. Remove the bones and meat and let them cool. Remove the meat from the bones and chop it coarsely. Discard the bones.

Add onion and green beans to the liquid and simmer over very low heat. Add potatoes, parsley, and pepper. (The black pepper is very important here, so don't be shy about the amount.) Add the reserved turkey meat and simmer just long enough to finish cooking potatoes. Add peas and continue cooking for just 1 or 2 minutes to heat them through. Serve warm.

Note: This soup can be frozen with no loss in flavor, although the potatoes and peas get a little mushy. Should you want to prepare this soup well in advance, do it up to the time you put in the potatoes and peas and complete this last step just before serving.

SERVES 8

DUCK, TURNIP, AND SQUASH SOUP

The important thing to remember when preparing this soup—or any soup that includes assorted vegetables—is not to overcook them. This mistake is best avoided by allowing the vegetables to complete their cooking by retained heat. When they are almost tender let the soup sit off the heat for up to thirty minutes before it is served.

Finishing the soup by this method will guarantee not only that the vegetables retain their individual flavors and texture but that the soup is at the proper temperature, not too hot.

MARINADE

1 teaspoon dried thyme
2 large bay leaves
12 juniper berries
1 tablespoon salt
2 teaspoons freshly ground black pepper
Large garlic clove
1 tablespoon balsamic vinegar

1 5-pound duck
1 large bay leaf
1 large onion, cut in half
1 large carrot, scrubbed and broken in half
3 large celery ribs, with leaves, broken into large pieces
1 teaspoon dried thyme
2 teaspoons salt, or to taste
1 teaspoon freshly ground black pepper
2 teaspoons balsamic vinegar
1 tablespoon tomato paste
2 leeks, white parts only, carefully washed and cut into 1/4-inch rounds
1 cup peeled and cubed turnips
2 cups peeled and cubed butternut squash
2 cups peeled and cubed potatoes

Put the ingredients for the marinade in a food processor and purée to a paste. Rub duck inside and out with it and cover tightly. Marinate duck overnight.

Preheat oven to 325 degrees.

Drain and pat duck dry. Split down the back and cut each half in two. Place in a roasting pan with a rack. Roast for 1 hour. Turn pieces and roast for another hour.

Place roasted duck in a deep pot and cover with about 2 quarts of cold water. Add bay leaf, onion, carrot, and celery. Bring to a simmer and allow to cook very slowly for 1 hour or more until the meat is coming off the bone. Pour the fat out of the roasting pan and ladle a cup or so of the liquid from the pot into the pan. Place over low heat and scrape browned bits from the bottom of the pan, dissolving them where you can. Pour this back into the soup pot. Remove duck, and when cool, remove meat, dice, and reserve. Strain stock and discard vegetables, along with the bones and skin. Either degrease the stock or refrigerate overnight and lift congealed fat off the top before going on with the soup.

Measure out 8 cups of degreased stock. Refrigerate any leftover for another soup. Add thyme, salt, pepper, and vinegar. Dissolve tomato paste in a cup of the heated pot liquid and add. Bring to a simmer. Add leeks and bring to a boil. Simmer for 10 minutes, then add all the other vegetables. Simmer 5 minutes more, and add duck meat, skimming if necessary. Simmer another 3 minutes before testing vegetables for doneness. They should be almost fork-tender. Turn off heat and allow to rest for up to 30 minutes before serving. Correct seasoning if necessary.
SERVES 6 TO 8

HAM, MUSTARD GREEN, RED BEAN, AND SWEET POTATO SOUP

This soup calls for an unusual green, mustard greens, arguably my favorite of them all. It combines perfectly with the taste of sweet potato.

4 pounds smoked ham hocks
3 quarts water
1½ cups dried red kidney beans, soaked overnight or by the quick-soak method (see Note, page 25)
4 very large garlic cloves, crushed
1½ teaspoons freshly ground black pepper
1 teaspoon salt
4 large sprigs of fresh curly parsley
2 bay leaves
1½ teaspoons dried thyme
3 medium to large leeks, white parts only, carefully washed and cut into rounds
2 medium onions, cut into large rings
1 pound sweet potatoes, peeled and cubed
1½ pounds mustard greens, washed, stemmed, and torn into large pieces
½ cup or more cubed cooked ham (optional)

Pat ham hocks in a large stockpot and cover with water. Bring to a boil and turn down to a simmer. Cook, partly covered, for about 2 hours. Skim as necessary. Remove hocks and allow to cool.

Degrease liquid in the stockpot. Drain beans and add to the pot. Bring to a simmer and add garlic, pepper, salt, parsley, bay leaves, and thyme. Simmer until beans are just tender, 1 to 1½ hours.

While beans are cooking, remove meat from hocks and discard skin and bones. Coarsely chop and add to beans when they are done.

Bring soup back to a simmer and add leeks, onions, and sweet potatoes. Cook, barely simmering, for another 15 minutes. Correct seasoning if necessary. Add mustard greens and cook just until tender, about 10 minutes. Do not overcook.

Add cubed ham, if using, and let sit in the pot for 15 minutes before serving. Add more hot water if mixture is too thick. It should, however, be almost like a vegetable stew.
SERVES 8

OSSO BUCO SOUP

Obviously, this is a very hearty soup and should be served with a knife and fork as well as the soup spoon. If you think it would be easier to eat, you could cut each veal slice into bite-size pieces, but I prefer to serve it unsliced.

8 small meaty slices veal shank, cut 1 to 1½ inches thick, with bone in (2½ to 3 pounds)
Salt
Freshly ground black pepper
Flour for dusting
¼ cup olive oil
4 tablespoons (½ stick) unsalted butter
1 medium onion, finely chopped
1 medium carrot, finely chopped
1 large celery rib, finely chopped
1½ cups dry light red wine
1 strip (½ inch wide) lemon zest
12 large pitted green olives
6 small fresh sage leaves
2 teaspoons fresh rosemary leaves
1 small garlic clove
2 tablespoons capers, drained
5¾ cups Chicken Stock (page 41) or veal stock
¾ cup basmati or long-grain rice

Dry veal shank slices, salt lightly, and dust generously with pepper. Flour both sides, shaking off excess. Heat half of the oil and half of the butter in a deep heavy pot and brown the floured veal, being careful not to burn the butter. Do this in batches. Set meat aside.

Meanwhile, heat the remaining oil and butter in a large skillet and sauté onion, carrot, and celery until wilted, about 5 minutes. Add ¾ cup of the red wine and boil over medium heat until reduced to a few tablespoons, 6 to 8 minutes. Set aside.

Mince together lemon zest, olives, sage leaves, rosemary leaves, garlic, and capers. Pour oil and butter from the pot in which veal was browned. Return veal to the pot and add the sautéed vegetables with the reduced wine and minced ingredients. Pour in the remaining red wine plus ¾ cup of the stock. Bring to a boil and turn back to a simmer. Cover tightly and cook for 40 minutes.

Add the remaining stock and continue to simmer, uncovered, until veal is fork-tender, about another hour. Skim off oil and fat as it rises.

To serve, cook rice in well-salted water, then drain. Place several generous spoonfuls of rice in a flat-bottom soup bowl and top with a veal slice. Pour soup over all.

SERVES 6 TO 8

LAMB AND BEET SOUP

4 thick shoulder lamb chops (at least 2 pounds)

MARINADE

5 tablespoons bourbon
¼ cup soy sauce
¼ cup (tightly packed) light brown sugar
2 tablespoons olive oil
3 tablespoons Dijon mustard
1 teaspoon Worcestershire Sauce
1 teaspoon freshly ground black pepper
½ teaspoon salt
⅛ teaspoon cayenne
½ medium onion, coarsely sliced

1 pound fresh beets, trimmed with 1 inch of tops
4 cups water
2 cups Beef Stock (page 42)
1 large onion, coarsely chopped
1 medium carrot, cut into large rounds
3 large fresh Italian flat-leaf parsley sprigs
½ teaspoon dried thyme
1 large bay leaf
3 medium carrots, coarsely grated
½ pound green cabbage, cored and thinly shredded
1 can (16 ounces) peeled tomatoes, thoroughly drained
2 tablespoons red wine vinegar
½ teaspoon salt
½ teaspoon freshly ground black pepper
2 large baking potatoes, peeled and cubed
3 tablespoons chopped fresh dill
Sour cream
Snipped fresh chives

Place chops in a shallow glass or ceramic dish in a single layer. Mix marinade ingredients thoroughly and pour over all, allowing onion slices to remain on top. This liquid should cover the chops. Cover with foil wrap and refrigerate overnight. Turn once.

Lift chops out of the marinade, leaving onion on top, and place in a shallow baking pan in a cold oven. Turn the oven on to 350 degrees and bake for 1½ hours, turning chops once.

Place beets in a foil-lined pan and cover with foil. Put in the oven with the chops. When chops are done, remove. Test beets for doneness. If not tender, turn oven up to 400 degrees and continue to cook until they can be pierced easily with the point of a knife. When beets are tender, peel and chop into small dice. Set aside.

Meanwhile, place chops in a large pot along with any pan juice, degreased. Add water, stock, onion, carrot rounds, parsley, thyme, and bay leaf. Simmer, uncovered, over very low heat for 1 hour.

Remove lamb and cut into strips or cubes, discarding any fat, gristle, and bone. Set aside.

Strain pot liquid. Discard vegetables and return liquid to the pot. Add beets, grated carrots, cabbage, tomatoes, vinegar, salt, and pepper. Simmer for 30 minutes, adding lamb after about 15 minutes.

While this is simmering, boil the potatoes in salted water until fork-tender, about 10 to 12 minutes. Drain and set aside.

To serve, ladle soup into bowls and place a few cooked potatoes in the middle. Sprinkle generously with chopped dill, then add a dollop of sour cream topped with chives. Serve additional dill and sour cream on the side.

SERVES 6

LAMB, PUMPKIN, AND LIMA BEAN SOUP

When I make lamb soups, I always use lamb from the leg. It tends not to have so much fat, which I don't like at all.

If pumpkins are not in season, use a hard winter squash instead.

> ¼ cup safflower oil
> 1½ pounds lamb cut from the leg, trimmed and cut into 1-inch cubes
> 3 tablespoons unsalted butter
> 2 cups coarsely chopped onion
> 2 tablespoons sugar
> 8 cups Beef Stock (page 42), heated
> 1 cup dried baby lima beans, soaked overnight or by the quick-soak method (see Note, page 25)
> 1 teaspoon dried thyme
> 1 bay leaf
> 1½ teaspoons salt
> ½ teaspoon black pepper
> 2 cups pumpkin, cut into ½-inch dice
> Strips of green onion

Heat oil in a deep pot and quickly sear meat until it is completely brown. Remove with a slotted spoon and set aside. Pour out oil and add butter. Sauté onion until wilted, about 5 minutes, then sprinkle with sugar and stir. Continue to cook until sugar begins to turn golden and caramelize. Add stock and stir to melt the sugar.

Add lima beans, thyme, bay leaf, salt, pepper, and lamb. Bring to a boil and then turn back to a simmer. Cook for about 20 to 25 minutes, skimming very often, until beans and meat are almost tender.

Stir in pumpkin and cook until just tender, about 8 to 10 minutes. Do not overcook the pumpkin or it will lose its flavor and texture. Correct seasoning if necessary.

Serve garnished with strips of green onion.

SERVES 6 TO 8

CRAB GAZPACHO

When made with Dungeness crab, this gazpacho has a definite California twist.

¼ cup olive oil
¼ cup dry white wine
1 tablespoon red wine vinegar
1 tablespoon fresh lime juice
3 medium tomatoes, peeled and seeded
1 medium red bell pepper, seeded and
  coarsely chopped
1 medium green bell pepper, seeded and
  coarsely chopped
1 medium cucumber, peeled, seeded, and
  coarsely chopped
2 cups tomato juice
½ medium sweet onion, diced
2 tablespoons snipped fresh chives or
  chopped green onions
2 tablespoons chopped fresh cilantro
¼ to ½ medium jalapeño, minced
1 teaspoon salt, or to taste
1 to 2 teaspoons Tabasco Sauce, or to taste
Freshly ground black pepper, to taste
1 cooked Dungeness crab
Plain yogurt (optional)
Sprigs of cilantro (optional)

Whisk together oil, wine, vinegar, and lime juice and set aside. In a food processor, combine tomatoes, bell peppers, and cucumber. Add tomato juice and pulse several times until mixture is fine but not puréed. Pour into a large bowl and stir in onion, chives or green onions, cilantro, and jalapeño. Mix and add salt, Tabasco, and pepper.

Crack and clean the crab. Remove the meat and reserve the whole claws for garnish. Flake the balance of the meat and stir into the soup. Chill in a covered bowl for at least 4 hours.

Serve in chilled bowls each garnished with a dab of yogurt and a sprig of cilantro, if desired.
SERVES 6

CRAB CORN BISQUE

Since you must go to the bother of making a stock base, this recipe is for a large quantity. But that's fine, because the soup freezes well.

STOCK
2 tablespoons unsalted butter
1 pound onions, coarsely chopped
2 large celery ribs, coarsely chopped
8 large garlic cloves, peeled
2½ pounds smashed blue crab shells, from
  5 to 6 pounds fresh whole crabs
1 cup dry white wine
8 cups water
1 tablespoon minced fresh thyme
½ cup whole peppercorns
3 large bay leaves

ROUX
8 tablespoons unsalted butter
½ cup all-purpose flour

BISQUE
4 tablespoons (½ stick) unsalted butter
Kernels from 3 ears of corn or 1 package
  (10 ounces) thawed frozen corn
6 green onions, with a lot of green,
  julienned
1 pound crabmeat, picked over
⅓ cup brandy
3 tablespoons Louisiana Hot Sauce
Salt and freshly ground black pepper, to
  taste

To make stock: Melt butter in a 10-quart stockpot over high heat. Sauté onions, celery, garlic, and crab shells for about 5 minutes, until the vegetables are translucent. Add wine, water, and seasonings. Bring back to a boil, then reduce heat to a simmer. Cook for 30 minutes, skimming occasionally. Strain, discarding solids. Reserve stock.

To make roux: Heat butter in a large skillet over medium heat. Add flour a few tablespoons at a time, whisking all the while.

34

Continue to cook and whisk until mixture turns dark golden. Set aside.

To complete bisque: Melt butter in a 10-quart stockpot over medium heat. Add corn and green onions and sauté until corn is tender, about 2 minutes. Add crabmeat and stir; add brandy and stir. Cook another couple of minutes. Add the reserved stock and bring to a simmer. Stir in roux, whisking to avoid lumps. Simmer for another 30 minutes. Off the heat, stir in the hot sauce, salt, and pepper.

SERVES 12

CRAWFISH BISQUE

This is another soup that freezes well.

STOCK

  5 pounds live crawfish
  1 large head garlic, cloves peeled and
    coarsely chopped
  3 large celery ribs, coarsely chopped
  1 pound onions, coarsely chopped
  3 large bay leaves, crumbled
  1/4 cup black peppercorns
  6 quarts water

ROUX

  2 medium green bell peppers, finely
    chopped
  3/4 pound celery ribs, finely chopped
  2 pounds onions, finely chopped
  16 medium garlic cloves, about 1 1/2 heads,
    peeled and minced
  2 1/2 cups peanut oil
  3 cups all-purpose flour
  2 tablespoons Creole Seasoning
  2 tablespoons Worcestershire Sauce
  1 cup peeled, seeded, and chopped tomatoes

  Stuffed Crawfish Heads (recipe follows)

To make stock: Plunge crawfish into boiling water. Cook for 1 1/2 minutes. Drain and reserve 3 dozen heads. Peel enough tails, reserving shells, to get 1 pound of meat. Set aside.

Put shells and the remaining whole boiled crawfish in a large stockpot with garlic, celery, onions, bay leaves, and peppercorns. Sauté, mashing and chopping with a large spoon, over high heat for 1 to 2 minutes. Add the water, bring to a boil, and simmer for 30 minutes. Strain and keep warm.

To make roux: Toss all the chopped vegetables together in a large bowl. Heat oil in a large heavy pot to the smoking point. Add flour gradually, about 1/2 cup at a time, stirring constantly with a wooden spoon. Turn heat down to medium and continue to cook, stirring, until roux is a dark color. Add the reserved vegetables, stir, and remove from heat. Stir in warm stock. Return to stove and continue to simmer over medium heat until thickened, about 4 minutes. Stir in seasonings and the chopped tomato.

Serve garnished with Stuffed Crawfish Heads.

SERVES 12

STUFFED CRAWFISH HEADS

  8 tablespoons (1 stick) unsalted butter
  2 tablespoons minced garlic
  1 medium celery rib, diced
  1/2 medium onion, diced
  1/2 medium green bell pepper, diced
  1 pound crawfish tails (reserved from
    bisque), coarsely chopped
  1 tablespoon Creole Seasoning
  1/2 teaspoon salt
  1/2 teaspoon cayenne
  1 1/2 cups dry bread crumbs
  1/2 egg white
  3 dozen crawfish heads (reserved from
    bisque)

Preheat oven to 350 degrees.

Heat butter in a large heavy skillet over medium heat and stir in vegetables. Sauté until translucent, about 4 minutes. Stir in crawfish tails, seasonings, and 1 cup of the bread crumbs. Remove from heat and mix lightly. Mix in egg white. Stuff heads with mixture and roll in the remaining bread crumbs. Place on a baking sheet and bake for 4 to 5 minutes, until heated through and browned.

MAKES 36

LOBSTER SOUP

This looks like a long, involved recipe, but in truth lots of it has to do with making the base for the soup. It's not as difficult as it seems on first sight.

5 pounds live lobsters
3 tablespoons olive oil
2 cups coarsely chopped onion
1 large carrot, coarsely chopped
2 celery ribs, coarsely chopped
1 large leek, white part only, carefully washed and coarsely chopped
2 teaspoons minced fresh ginger
2 large garlic cloves, minced
1/4 cup brandy
Pinch of cayenne
2 bay leaves
2 tablespoons minced fresh parsley
5 pounds ripe tomatoes, peeled, seeded, and coarsely chopped
3 cups Fish Stock (page 42) or bottled clam juice
2 cups Chicken Stock (page 41)
1 tablespoon tomato paste
Salt and freshly ground black pepper, to taste
2 cups cooked white rice
1 tablespoon sheery (optional)
1 tablespoon unsalted butter
1 large potato, peeled, cut into 1/2-inch cubes, and boiled

1 large red bell pepper, roasted, peeled, and seeded (see Note, page 74), cut into 1/2-inch pieces

Put on a large stockpot of water. When boiling, plunge lobsters in just long enough to kill them. Remove and pour out water. While lobsters are cooling, wipe out pot and add olive oil. Sauté onion, carrot, celery, leek, ginger, and garlic over medium heat for about 5 minutes. Meanwhile, remove meat from tails and claws of the lobsters. Set aside. Remove the green mass (tomalley) and any roe (coral) from the body of the lobsters. Crush all the shells.

Pour the brandy over the sautéed vegetables. Ignite and allow to burn off. Add crushed shells and any liquid. Sauté for another 10 minutes, until vegetables are completely wilted. Add cayenne, bay leaves, parsley, and tomatoes. Cover and cook about 10 minutes, shaking pan occasionally. Add the stocks and tomato paste. Bring to a boil, turn heat down, and simmer for about 15 minutes, skimming. Scoop out as many large shell pieces as you can with a slotted spoon and discard. Place a colander over a large bowl and pour stock through, pressing as many solids and as much liquid through as possible. Discard shells and pulp. Measure stock and if you have more than 6 cups, reduce to that amount over high heat. Strain through cheesecloth and season with salt and pepper.

To serve, heat stock and keep warm. Place 1 cup of the stock and the 2 cups of cooked rice in a food processor and process to a smooth purée. Whisk the purée into the hot stock. Stir in sherry, if using. Melt butter in a small skillet and sauté lobster meat over medium heat until cooked through, about 3 minutes. Slice meat and divide among 6 heated bowls. Divide the potato and red pepper as well. Ladle stock over each portion.

SERVES 6

SMOKED SALMON AND CORN CHOWDER

Obviously this may be made without corn, but I like corn with salmon. You could add small oysters, too.

3 tablespoons unsalted butter
1/2 to 2/3 cup finely chopped onion
1/2 to 2/3 cup finely chopped celery
1/2 to 2/3 cup finely chopped red bell pepper
2 tablespoons all-purpose flour
3 cups Chicken Stock (page 41), hot
2 cups low-fat milk
1/2 teaspoon salt
Freshly ground black pepper, to taste
2 cups canned or frozen whole kernel corn, drained
4 ounces smoked salmon, chopped into pea-size pieces
Chopped fresh Italian flat-leaf parsley, dill, or chervil, to taste

Melt butter in a large saucepan. Sauté onion, celery, and red bell pepper over medium heat until wilted and onion is just beginning to brown, about 8 to 10 minutes. Stir in flour and cook, stirring constantly, for another minute or so. Add stock and cook for 2 to 3 minutes, stirring. Add milk and turn heat down to a simmer. Cook for 3 to 4 minutes, stirring occasionally. Add salt, pepper, and corn. Bring back to a simmer and turn off heat. Stir in salmon. Serve with a sprinkling of chopped herbs.

If you prefer a thinner soup, use more stock or milk.

SERVES 6

ROASTED TOMATO, RICE, AND SCALLOP SOUP

1 1/2 tablespoons unsalted butter
3/4 pound onions, coarsely chopped
1 small celery rib, coarsely chopped
2 very small carrots, coarsely shredded
6 cups Chicken Stock (page 41)
3 1/2 pounds ripe tomatoes, roasted (see page 20)
1 1/2 tablespoons chopped fresh Italian flat-leaf parsley
3 tablespoons chopped fresh chervil
3 tablespoons raw long-grain white rice
Salt and freshly ground black pepper, to taste
1 pound shucked bay scallops
1/2 cup dry white wine
1 small bay leaf
2 fresh Italian flat-leaf parsley sprigs

Put butter, onions, celery, and carrots in a saucepan with about 1 cup of the stock. Simmer, covered, over low heat for about 10 minutes. Stir to prevent sticking and do not allow to brown. Add tomatoes and 4 1/2 cups of the remaining stock. Continue to simmer over low heat for another 15 minutes. Stir to prevent scorching.

When tomatoes become pulpy, purée in a food processor, in batches if necessary, then strain out seeds and skin, pushing through the solids. Return to saucepan and add parsley, chervil, rice, salt, and pepper. Simmer, uncovered, for 10 minutes. Test rice for doneness and cook another few minutes if not done.

Meanwhile, place scallops, wine, remaining 1/2 cup stock, bay leaf, and parsley sprigs in a small saucepan. Bring rapidly to a simmer and cook until just tender, about 3 minutes if scallops are small. Remove bay leaf and parsley, and stir scallops and pan juice into the tomato soup.

SERVES 6 TO 8

CURRIED SHRIMP AND POTATO SOUP

I bet fresh corn off the cob would be good in this soup, and sometime you probably should try substituting rice for the potatoes used here. The shrimp dish that inspired this curried soup was always served over rice.

4 tablespoons (½ stick) unsalted butter
1 cup finely chopped tart apple
1 cup finely chopped celery
3 cups finely chopped onion
3 cups water
2 cups light cream or half-and-half
5 tablespoons curry powder
2 teaspoons salt
½ teaspoon finely ground black pepper
2 cups Fish Stock (page 42), hot
2 cups Chicken Stock (page 41), hot
1 pound cooked and peeled medium shrimp, each cut in half
1 pound white potatoes, peeled and cut into ½-inch dice
Snipped fresh chives

Melt butter in a deep skillet and sauté apple, celery, and onion until wilted and the onion is turning golden, about 5 minutes. Add the water and bring to a simmer. Continue simmering until almost all the water has evaporated, about 10 minutes. Purée the mixture in a food processor until smooth.

Return mixture to the skillet and whisk in cream, curry powder, salt, and pepper. Simmer over very low heat, whisking regularly, until reduced and thickened, about 10 minutes. Stir in the fish and chicken stocks. Mix thoroughly, add shrimp, and simmer for a few minutes.

Meanwhile, cover diced potatoes with well-salted water and bring to a boil. Boil slowly for 5 minutes, then drain and add to the soup. Simmer the soup for another 2 or 3 minutes.

Garnish each serving with chives.
SERVES 6

CORN AND OYSTER CHOWDER

Some people add a little diced red bell pepper to this, but I like it best as is.

8 tablespoons (1 stick) unsalted butter
1 cup finely chopped onion
1 cup finely chopped celery
2 cups cubed potatoes (½-inch cubes)
2 cups Chicken Stock (page 41)
2 cups water
½ teaspoon dried basil
¼ teaspoon salt
3 tablespoons all-purpose flour
2 cups milk
1 can (20 ounces) whole kernel corn, drained, or about 2 cups fresh or frozen corn
20 medium oysters, shucked, with 2 table-spoons oyster liquor

In a large pot, melt butter over medium heat and add onion and celery. Sauté about 10 minutes, until slightly browned. Add potatoes, stock, water, basil, and salt. Simmer over low heat for 30 to 45 minutes, until potatoes are tender and falling apart.

In a small saucepan, whisk together flour and ½ cup of the milk. Bring this to boiling over low heat and whisk into the simmering stock. Add the remainder of the milk and the corn. Heat, but do not boil, the soup over low heat for another few minutes.

Just before serving, add oysters and liquor. Heat about 5 to 6 minutes, until oysters puff up and edges are curly.
SERVES 8 TO 10

38

WHITE CORN AND OYSTER CHOWDER WITH ANCHO CHILI CREAM

With its croutons and chili cream, this silky soup is almost a meal in itself.

1 1/2 cups dry white wine
18 oysters, shucked, with liquor reserved
2 tablespoons unsalted butter
1/2 cup coarsely chopped onion
1/2 cup coarsely chopped celery
6 medium ears white corn, kernels cut from cobs and milk scraped out, cobs reserved
2 quarts Fish Stock (page 42)
1 cup heavy cream
1 medium garlic head, roasted (see page 185)
1 tablespoon coarsely chopped fresh sage
6 tablespoons dry sherry
Salt and freshly ground black pepper, to taste
6 to 8 toasted rounds of French or Italian bread
Ancho Chili Cream (recipe follows)

Bring wine to a boil in a medium pot and add oysters. Remove from the heat and let oysters cool in the wine. When cool, remove oysters and set aside, covered. Reduce wine by half over high heat, 5 minutes or more. Set aside.

In a soup pot, melt butter over medium heat. Add the onion and celery and sauté until wilted, about 5 minutes. Add the reserved corn cobs, fish stock, oyster liquor, and reduced wine to the vegetables. Bring to a low boil and simmer for 30 minutes.

Add three-fourths of the corn kernels (saving the balance for garnish), the cream, garlic pulp squeezed from the roasted head, and sage. Continue to simmer for 20 minutes more.

Remove cobs and discard. Purée soup in a food processor or blender and strain through a medium strainer. Stir in sherry and add salt and pepper.

To serve, ladle the soup into heated soup bowls. Float a crouton in each and top with oysters. Drizzle Ancho Chili Cream over each portion.

SERVES 6 TO 8

ANCHO CHILI CREAM

1/4 cup ancho chilies (2 ounces)
4 sun-dried tomatoes
1 cup dry white wine or water, warm
1 cup heavy cream, reduced to 1/2 cup
2 tablespoons dry sherry
Pinch of chili powder
Pinch of ground cumin
Pinch of dried oregano
Salt and freshly ground black pepper, to taste
Cayenne, to taste

Place chilies and tomatoes in separate bowls and pour 1/2 cup warm wine or water over each. Let soak for 10 minutes. When reconstituted, drain and discard the liquid from both. Carefully remove and discard the stems and seeds from chilies. Scrape the chilies and tomatoes to remove the pulp and reserve. Discard skins. Place all ingredients in a blender and purée until smooth.

MAKES ABOUT 1 1/2 CUPS

FISH SOUP

I really don't like this as well when made with
an oily fish, so I keep to fish with white flesh.

2 tablespoons unsalted butter
2 tablespoons olive oil
*³/₄ pound fennel bulb, trimmed and sliced
    into ³/₄-inch pieces*
1 pound onions, coarsely sliced
2 carrots, scraped and cut into coarse rings
2 large celery ribs, cut into thick slices
1 very large garlic clove, minced
8 cups Fish Stock (page 42), heated
1 tablespoon fresh lemon juice
1 teaspoon dried thyme
1 large bay leaf
2 cups peeled and diced potatoes
*1 pound tomatoes, peeled, seeded, and
    coarsely chopped*
3 fresh marjoram sprigs, tied together
*1 pound firm-fleshed white fish fillets, such
    as tilefish, cut into 1-inch cubes*
Salt and freshly ground black pepper, to taste

Heat butter and oil in a soup pot and sauté fennel, onions, carrots, and celery until wilted,
about 5 minutes. Stir in garlic, fish stock,
lemon juice, thyme, bay leaf, and potatoes.
Simmer for 10 minutes, skimming foam as
necessary.

Add tomatoes, marjoram, and fish.
Simmer until fish is done, another 8 to 10 minutes. Do not overcook. Remove marjoram
sprigs, add salt and pepper, and serve.
SERVES 6 TO 8

VEGETABLE STOCK

1 tablespoon safflower oil
1 small onion, coarsely chopped
*1 large leek, with some green part, carefully
    washed and cut into large rings*
*1 medium carrot, scrubbed and cut into
    large rings*
*¹/₄ large fennel bulb, including tough outer
    layers, coarsely chopped*
*1 large celery rib, with some leaves, coarsely
    chopped*
1 small tomato, coarsely chopped
*¹/₈ very small head cabbage, coarsely
    chopped*
10 cups water
1 bay leaf

Place oil in a deep pot and add onion, leek, carrot, and fennel. Toss and cover tightly; cook
over very low heat for about 5 minutes, shaking pan occasionally to keep vegetables from
scorching. Add celery, tomato, and cabbage.
Toss again and cover tightly. Continue to cook
over very low heat for an additional 10 minutes, shaking pan occasionally. Add water and
bay leaf. Bring to a simmer and cook, barely
simmering, for 30 minutes, skimming as necessary. Put ingredients through a strainer
which has been lined with a double thickness
of damp cheesecloth. Allow to cool and refrigerate, sealed, or freeze.

*Note: You may make a heartier-flavored stock
by roasting the onion, leek, carrot, fennel, and
celery, as for Beef Stock (page 42). When they
have browned, add them with the dissolved pan
juices to the tomato and cabbage after you have
sweated them. Then follow the rest of the recipe.*
MAKES ABOUT 4 CUPS

CHICKEN STOCK

*3 pounds chicken wings, backs, or other
    bones (see Note)*
1 medium veal knuckle, cracked
4 quarts water
3 large onions, peeled and cut in half
*2 large carrots, scrubbed and cut into large
    rings*
*2 medium leeks, carefully washed and cut
    into large rings*
Several large shallots, peeled but left whole
1 large bay leaf
8 fresh Italian flat-leaf parsley sprigs
*8 large celery ribs, with leaves, broken into
    large pieces*
1 teaspoon dried thyme
1 tablespoon salt
2 teaspoons freshly ground black pepper
1 whole clove

Select a stockpot large enough to comfortably
hold all the above ingredients. Place chicken,
veal knuckle, and water in pot and bring to a
boil. Skim foam, and add all the other ingredients. Bring back to a boil and reduce to the lowest possible heat; you want this to be barely
simmering. Continue cooking for about 2½
hours, skimming occasionally as necessary.

    Strain the cooked stock through a damp
cheesecloth-lined colander. Discard all solids.
Cool and refrigerate the stock. When fat has
congealed on top, remove and discard it. The
stock may be used as is or frozen.

    *Note: Whenever I cook chicken or fry chicken
wings, I cut off the tip joint and freeze it. There is
a lot of gelatin in this (also in veal knuckle). And
when I buy a cut-up chicken, I usually freeze the
back uncooked as well–unless I know a guest likes
chicken backs. (My Aunt Freddie does.) You will
wind up with 3 pounds of uncooked chicken bones
before you know it.*

MAKES 3½ TO 4 QUARTS

TURKEY STOCK

Since the flavor of both turkey gravy and
turkey stuffing depends to some degree on the
flavor of the stock, make sure it is not bland,
but has a rich taste. Add more seasoning and
more bouillon cubes if required.

Turkey neck and giblets, except the liver
1 medium onion, cut in half
*1 large celery rib, with leaves, broken into
    several pieces*
1 large carrot, scrubbed and broken in half
Few sprigs of fresh Italian flat-leaf parsley
2 chicken bouillon cubes
6 cups water
*Salt and freshly ground black pepper, to
    taste*

Put turkey neck and giblets and the vegetables
in a stockpot. Add bouillon cubes and water
and cook for 1 hour, skimming as necessary.
Strain, discarding vegetables and reserving
meat. Correct seasoning if necessary and set
aside.

    Remove meat from the neck, discarding
skin, and chop along with giblets. These may
be added to turkey stuffing or gravy or divided
between the two.

MAKES ABOUT 4 CUPS

BEEF STOCK

5 pounds mixed beef and veal bones
2 large carrots, scrubbed and broken into
  several pieces
2 large celery ribs, broken into several pieces
2 large onions, cut in half
Water
2 tablespoons tomato paste
6 fresh Italian flat-leaf parsley sprigs
1 teaspoon dried thyme
18 peppercorns
2 medium garlic cloves, crushed

Preheat oven to 500 degrees.

Place bones in a single layer in a roasting pan and scatter carrots, celery, and onions among the bones. Roast for 30 to 45 minutes until meat, bones, and vegetables begin to brown, even burn a little. Put all into a deep stockpot. Pour about a half inch of water into the roasting pan and dissolve any bits that have stuck to the bottom of the pan. Pour over bones. Add more water to several inches above bones. Bring to a boil and stir in tomato paste. Add parsley, thyme, peppercorns, and garlic. Cook, barely simmering, for several hours, adding more hot water as necessary. Strain and boil slowly until reduced and flavor is intensified. Allow to cool and skim any fat from the top. Refrigerate, tightly covered, or freeze.

MAKES ABOUT 8 CUPS

FISH STOCK

4 pounds fish bones, heads, and tails from
  any nonoily white fish, gills removed,
2 medium onions, coarsely chopped
4 large shallots, coarsely chopped
4 celery ribs, with leaves, broken into sev-
  eral pieces
3 large carrots, scrubbed and, broken into
  several pieces
3 cloves
2 large bay leaves
6 sprigs of fresh Italian flat-leaf parsley
1 1/2 teaspoons dried thyme or a large sprig of
  fresh thyme
18 peppercorns
2 strips lemon zest
4 cups water
2 cups dry white wine

Wash fish bones, heads, and tails in cold water and place in a large stockpot. Add all other ingredients. Bring quickly to a boil, then reduce heat until liquid is just barely simmering. Cook at this heat level for 20 to 30 minutes, skimming foam as necessary.

Place a double thickness of damp cheesecloth in a colander and pour the stock through it. Allow to drain thoroughly, but do not press down. Discard solids. Allow stock to cool and then refrigerate.

Note: Do not use oily fish like mackerel or salmon. If you have any shrimp, lobster, or crab shells, however, do include them.

MAKES 6 TO 8 CUPS

SALADS

THERE ARE TIMES WHEN NOTHING IS QUITE SO PLEASING OR right as plain green salad dressed with the simplest vinaigrette—I like mine after the main course, thank you. Then there are also occasions when salads need a more complicated combination of flavors and textures and have to be more substantial all around— usually when they're served as a first course. Both extremes suit

me, but basically I see them as two different things. ✦ What I don't like is greens that have not been prop- erly washed and dried. Gritty salad is inedible as far as I'm concerned. Period. Anyway, these cleaning tasks are the first and most critical steps in good salad making. In addi- tion, salads should be well-dressed so that the leaves are coated but not drenched. You may be surprised at how little dressing this will actually take. ✦ Finally, of course, the addition of meats, cheeses, and cooked vegetables can turn a salad into something substantial enough to be the whole meal. And it's a great way to make use of any bits and pieces that are in the refrigerator.

GREEN SALADS

GREEN SALAD WITH WHITE WINE VINAIGRETTE

Whatever combination of greens you favor would be fine for this. Serve with melba toast or a round of toasted French bread.

6 to 8 cups mixed salad greens, washed, dried, and torn into pieces if large
3 thin slices red onion, separated into rings and cut in half

WHITE WINE VINAIGRETTE
3 tablespoons olive oil
1 tablespoon vegetable oil
1 tablespoon white wine vinegar
Salt and freshly ground black pepper, to taste

Toss greens in a bowl with the onion.
Whisk together the remaining ingredients. Spoon enough vinaigrette over greens, tossing, to coat leaves.
SERVES 6

MIXED GREEN SALAD WITH RED WINE VINAIGRETTE

Accompany the salad with a wedge of cheese, such as asiago, at room temperature.

RED WINE VINAIGRETTE
6 tablespoons olive oil
2 tablespoons red wine vinegar
2 teaspoons Dijon mustard
Salt and freshly ground black pepper, to taste

8 cups mixed salad greens, washed, dried, and torn into pieces if large

Whisk together ingredients for the vinaigrette. Arrange greens on 6 individual plates and drizzle with the vinaigrette. (Store leftover vinaigrette in the refrigerator.)
SERVES 6

GARDEN SALAD WITH BALSAMIC VINAIGRETTE AND FONTINA

Any combination of garden greens, such as Boston, Bibb, or leaf lettuce, is fine here.

8 cups (loosely packed) mixed garden greens, washed, dried, and torn into bite-size bits

BALSAMIC VINAIGRETTE
3/4 teaspoon salt
Freshly ground black pepper, to taste
1 heaping teaspoon Dijon mustard
3 tablespoons balsamic vinegar
6 tablespoons olive oil

6 small wedges fontina

Place greens in a bowl, cover with a kitchen towel, and refrigerate.
Combine salt, pepper, mustard, and vinegar. Whisk. Add oil, continuing to whisk until well combined.
Spoon 2 tablespoons of the vinaigrette over the greens and toss to coat leaves. Add more vinaigrette as desired. (Store leftover vinaigrette in the refrigerator.)
Serve with a wedge of fontina.
SERVES 6

VARIATION
Red wine vinegar may be substituted for the balsamic.

SIMPLE SALAD

Use this dressing on an assortment of your favorite greens. Serve the salad with a wedge of cheese if you like.

SIMPLE VINAIGRETTE

3 tablespoons canola oil
6 tablespoons olive oil
3 tablespoons red wine vinegar
1 teaspoon grainy Dijon mustard
1/2 teaspoon salt
1/2 teaspoon freshly ground black pepper
2 tablespoons minced shallots

8 to 10 cups mixed salad greens, washed, dried, and torn into pieces if large

Whisk together all vinaigrette ingredients except the shallots. Stir in shallots after vinaigrette is combined.

Put greens in a bowl, add enough dressing to coat leaves, toss, and serve. (Store leftover dressing in the refrigerator.)
SERVES 8

GREEN SALAD WITH SHERRY–RED WINE VINAIGRETTE

Use only as much vinaigrette as you need to coat the greens. Do not overdress them. Store leftover vinaigrette in the fridge.

3 to 4 medium to small heads lettuce, washed, dried, and torn into pieces

SHERRY–RED WINE VINAIGRETTE

2 tablespoons red wine
1/4 cup sherry vinegar
1/3 cup olive oil
2 tablespoons peanut oil
1 teaspoon fresh lemon juice
Pinch of sugar
Salt and freshly ground black pepper, to taste
1 large garlic clove

Mix lettuces in a large bowl and refrigerate until ready to serve.

Meanwhile, whisk together the wine, vinegar, oils, lemon juice, sugar, salt, and pepper. Mash the garlic slightly and float on top. Remove and discard the garlic before using the vinaigrette. Toss vinaigrette with the greens and serve.
SERVES 6

GREEN SALAD WITH RASPBERRIES AND RASPBERRY VINAIGRETTE

6 to 8 cups mixed salad greens, washed, dried, and torn into pieces if large

RASPBERRY VINAIGRETTE

3/4 teaspoon salt, or to taste
1 teaspoon Dijon mustard
2 tablespoons raspberry vinegar
3 tablespoons vegetable oil
2 tablespoons olive oil
1/4 cup fresh raspberries

About 20 fresh raspberries

Put the greens in a salad bowl and place in the refrigerator.

Whisk together the salt, mustard, vinegar, and oils. Mash raspberries and stir in. Toss with the greens and arrange on individual salad plates. Garnish with a few whole raspberries.
SERVES 6

MIXED GREENS WITH CHAMPAGNE VINAIGRETTE

With the fillip of sliced cucumber, you can use any combination of greens you find fresh in your market.

CHAMPAGNE VINAIGRETTE
3 tablespoons Champagne vinegar
½ cup olive oil
½ teaspoon salt
Pinch of freshly ground black pepper
2 teaspoons minced red onion

5 cups mixed salad greens, washed, dried, and torn into pieces if large
1 small cucumber, peeled, seeded, and cut into medium-thick half rings

Whisk together the vinegar, oil, salt, and pepper. Stir in the onion.

Toss greens and cucumber together. Spoon enough vinaigrette over all to coat greens when they are tossed. (Store leftover vinaigrette in a jar with a lid in the refrigerator.)
SERVES 6

MIXED GREEN SALAD WITH SHERRY–RICE WINE VINAIGRETTE

I like some sort of melba toast or water biscuits with salad, especially when it is served with cheese. Try a creamy Saint-André.

SHERRY–RICE WINE VINAIGRETTE
1 tablespoon sherry vinegar
1 tablespoon rice wine vinegar
1 tablespoon fresh lemon juice
¼ cup olive oil
2 tablespoons canola oil
¼ teaspoon salt
¼ teaspoon freshly ground black pepper
¼ teaspoon dry mustard

9 cups mixed salad greens, washed, dried, and torn into pieces if large

Whisk together vinaigrette ingredients and correct the seasoning.

Toss the greens with enough vinaigrette to coat the leaves. Divide salad among 6 individual serving plates. (Store any leftover vinaigrette in the refrigerator.)
SERVES 6

MIXED BABY LETTUCES WITH HONEY-LEMON DRESSING

Many wine connoisseurs will tell you that wine cannot be served with the salad course because it reacts with the vinegar in the dressing. This simple dressing makes it possible to have wine with this course if you like.

HONEY-LEMON DRESSING
2 medium shallots, minced, or 2 tablespoons minced onion
3 tablespoons honey
3 tablespoons fresh lemon juice
1 tablespoon olive oil
Salt and freshly ground black pepper, to taste

6 cups mixed baby lettuces and greens or mesclun, washed and dried

Place dressing ingredients in a small bowl and whisk. Toss greens with dressing and serve.
SERVES 6

MESCLUN SALAD WITH PEARS, BLUE CHEESE, AND PORT DRESSING

A port wine–based dressing works well with any sort of fruit-and-cheese combination salad.

PORT DRESSING

1/2 cup mayonnaise
1/2 cup plain yogurt
1 teaspoon minced fresh tarragon
1 tablespoon minced fresh chives
1 tablespoon minced red onion
2 tablespoons tawny port
1 tablespoon fresh lemon juice
Salt and freshly ground black pepper,
*   to taste*

3/4 pound mesclun, washed and dried (see
*   Note)*
3 ripe pears, peeled, cored, sliced thick, and
*   rubbed with lemon juice*
6 ounces blue cheese

Whisk together mayonnaise and yogurt and stir in tarragon, chives, onion, port, and lemon juice. Mix well. Add salt and pepper and set aside.

Toss the greens with just enough vinaigrette to coat them well. Serve on individual plates garnished with pear slices and crumbled blue cheese.

Note: Mesclun is the name given to a combination of baby salad greens, made up of different textures and flavor.

SERVES 6 TO 8

MESCLUN SALAD WITH CHÈVRE VINAIGRETTE

If you can't find mesclun, use any combination of greens you like, just as long as you have a good mixture of textures and flavors. For the chèvre, any creamy goat cheese will do.

8 cups mesclun, washed and dried

CHÈVRE VINAIGRETTE

2 tablespoons cider vinegar
6 tablespoons vegetable oil
2 ounces creamy chèvre cheese
Salt and freshly ground black pepper, to
*   taste*

Place mesclun in a large salad bowl and refrigerate, covered.

Whisk together the vinegar and oil. Whisk in chèvre until well combined. Add salt and pepper. Pour over greens and toss.

SERVES 6

ARUGULA, BOSTON LETTUCE, AND JULIENNE RED PEPPER SALAD

Strips of red pepper make the salad look appealing and add a bit of extra flavor. Serve this with pipo crem' cheese, which has a mild Roquefort-like flavor and creamy texture.

1 bunch arugula
2 heads Boston lettuce
1 red bell pepper, cut into julienne strips
Red Wine Vinaigrette (page 44)

Wash and dry greens. Cut stems off arugula. Tear lettuce into bite-size pieces. Toss together with red pepper and keep, covered, in refrigerator until ready to serve. Just before serving, add enough vinaigrette to lightly coat the greens and toss.

SERVES 6

ARUGULA AND LETTUCE SALAD WITH RICE WINE VINAIGRETTE

I like to combine a mild lettuce with arugula. It can be Boston or Bibb—or red-leaf lettuce, if the color appeals to you.

*2 bunches arugula, stemmed, washed,
    dried, and torn into pieces*
*1 small head Boston lettuce, washed, dried,
    and torn into pieces*

RICE WINE VINAIGRETTE
1/3 cup rice wine vinegar
3/4 cup vegetable oil
1/4 cup olive oil
1/2 teaspoon salt
1/4 teaspoon freshly ground black pepper
3 tablespoons minced red onion

Put greens in a serving bowl and toss to mix.

Whisk together all vinaigrette ingredients except onion, or put them in a jar and shake. Mix in onion. Use just enough to lightly coat greens. (Store leftover dressing in the refrigerator.)
SERVES 6 TO 8

ARUGULA AND SWISS CHEESE SALAD

You should not substitute any other green in this delightful salad, as the bite of arugula is very important.

*1 1/2 pounds imported Swiss cheese, shredded
    on a grater*
*3 tablespoons grainy mustard, preferably
    Moutarde de Meaux*
1 1/2 tablespoons red wine vinegar
3/4 teaspoon freshly ground black pepper
1/4 teaspoon salt
1/2 cup olive oil
*1 bunch (6 to 8 ounces) arugula, washed
    and dried*

Put the cheese in a bowl. In another bowl make the vinaigrette by combining the mustard, vinegar, pepper, and salt, and then whisking in the oil.

When ready to serve, add the dressing to the cheese and toss very lightly and carefully with two forks. Arrange several sprigs of arugula on each plate and mound the cheese in the middle.
SERVES 8

BIBB LETTUCE AND CHEESE SALAD

I don't know about your location, but for some reason, the Bibb lettuce we get around here is loaded with sand. If you have the same problem, be sure to wash it carefully. Nothing ruins a salad quicker than grit.

My method of washing is to separate the leaves in running water and then put them in a large bowl of water to soak. I then lift out the lettuce and change the water.

LEMON-OIL DRESSING
3/4 teaspoon salt
1/4 teaspoon freshly ground black pepper
1 teaspoon grainy mustard
2 tablespoons fresh lemon juice
2 tablespoons mild olive oil
4 tablespoons safflower oil

*3 medium to large heads Bibb lettuce, leaves
    separated, washed, and dried*
6 slices Saint Albry or other soft cheese

Put the salt, pepper, and mustard in a small bowl and mix in the lemon juice. Whisk in the oils. If you do this in advance, do not refrigerate.

To serve, arrange lettuce leaves on individual plates with a slice of cheese in the middle. Spoon some of the dressing over all.
SERVES 6

48

BIBB LETTUCE SALAD WITH PEPPERCORN VINAIGRETTE

2 small heads Bibb lettuce

PEPPERCORN VINAIGRETTE
  1 tablespoon balsamic vinegar
  ½ teaspoon salt
  ½ teaspoon green peppercorn mustard
  Freshly ground black pepper, to taste
  3 tablespoons safflower oil
  2 tablespoons olive oil

Wash and dry lettuce leaves. Refrigerate in a bowl, covered with paper towels.

Make the vinaigrette by combining the vinegar, salt, mustard, and pepper. Whisk in the oils.

To serve, dress the leaves with enough vinaigrette to coat them. (Refrigerate any leftover vinaigrette.)

SERVES 4

BOSTON LETTUCE SALAD WITH SHERRY VINAIGRETTE

If you don't have sherry vinegar, don't buy it just for this vinaigrette—unless you are unfamiliar with its flavor and want to taste it. A good red wine vinegar is a perfectly acceptable substitute.

SHERRY VINAIGRETTE
  ½ teaspoon salt
  ¼ teaspoon freshly ground black pepper
  1 teaspoon Dijon mustard
  2 tablespoons sherry vinegar
  3 tablespoons safflower oil
  2 tablespoons olive oil

3 small or 2 large heads Boston lettuce, leaves separated, washed, and dried

Put the salt, pepper, and mustard in a small bowl and add the vinegar. Mix. Whisk in the oils. (If you are not using this right away, do not refrigerate.)

To serve, arrange the lettuce on individual salad plates and spoon a little of the vinaigrette over each. (Store rest in the refrigerator.)

SERVES 6

BOSTON LETTUCE SALAD WITH TOASTED GOAT CHEESE

I like the salad greens for this to be as simple as possible—Boston lettuce is my preference, but any mild lettuce would do.

  8 cups lettuce, washed, dried, and torn into bite-size pieces
  12 thick slices mild goat cheese
  12 slices (½ inch thick) French bread
  Red Wine Vinaigrette (page 44)

Put the lettuce in a bowl and refrigerate, covered.

Put slices of cheese on the French bread slices and toast under the broiler. While this is toasting, toss the lettuce with enough vinaigrette to coat and divide among 6 individual plates. Serves with cheese toasts on the plate. (Store leftover vinaigrette in the refrigerator.)

SERVES 6

BOSTON LETTUCE SALAD WITH WALNUT VINAIGRETTE AND CAMBAZOLA

Cambazola cheese, a mild, creamy blue, is complemented by the walnuts in the salad.

8 cups (loosely packed) Boston lettuce, washed, dried, and torn into bite-size pieces
1/3 cup walnut pieces, broken into bits

WALNUT VINAIGRETTE

1 teaspoon Champagne mustard
2 tablespoons white wine vinegar
1/2 teaspoon salt
1/4 teaspoon white pepper
1/4 cup walnut oil

6 wedges Cambazola
Freshly ground black pepper

Place lettuce in a bowl and toss with nuts. Cover and refrigerate.

Combine vinaigrette ingredients in a jar and shake to blend. Add to lettuce and toss to coat leaves.

To serve, arrange salad on 6 plates and garnish each with a wedge of Cambazola topped with a grind of pepper.
SERVES 6

BOSTON LETTUCE SALAD WITH PEAS AND ANCHOVY VINAIGRETTE

Anchovy vinaigrette is also very good on fresh tomatoes.

6 cups Boston lettuce or other salad greens, washed, dried, and torn into large pieces
48 sugar snap peas, blanched for 1 minute in boiling water

ANCHOVY VINAIGRETTE

2 tablespoons red wine vinegar
1 teaspoon grainy Dijon mustard
2 tablespoons olive oil
3 tablespoons safflower oil
Freshly ground black pepper, to taste
4 flat anchovy fillets, drained and mashed

Place the lettuce and peas in a large salad bowl and refrigerate, covered, until ready to use. Whisk together the vinegar, mustard, oils, and pepper. Stir in the anchovies and mix until they "dissolve." Toss with the greens and peas.
SERVES 6

BOSTON AND BIBB LETTUCE SALAD WITH FRUIT VINAIGRETTE

Use a mixture of several light lettuces in this salad, which marries well with a dressing utilizing a fruit vinegar. Although the flavor of this vinegar is interesting, I use it sparingly because it can become a bit cloying.

1 small head Boston lettuce
1 small head Bibb lettuce
1/2 small head loose-leaf garden lettuce

FRUIT VINAIGRETTE

1/2 teaspoon salt
1/2 teaspoon dry mustard
Freshly ground black pepper
1 tablespoon fruit vinegar, raspberry or other
1 1/2 tablespoons safflower oil
1 tablespoon mild olive oil

Wash lettuces thoroughly and pat dry. Tear into bite-size pieces. Whisk together the vinaigrette ingredients and dress the lettuce lightly.
SERVES 6

50

SOUTHWESTERN CAESAR SALAD

If salmonella is a problem in your area (it isn't in mine), make a different salad, one that does not have raw egg in the dressing.

2 small heads romaine lettuce

CAESAR DRESSING
6 anchovy fillets, drained
6 roasted garlic cloves (see page 185), peeled and smashed
3 tablespoons fresh lemon juice
2 teaspoons Worcestershire Sauce
1 teaspoon Tabasco Sauce
6 tablespoons olive oil
1 large egg

Cornbread Croutons (recipe follows)
1 red bell pepper, cored, seeded, and julienned
1 green bell pepper, cored, seeded, and julienned
1/3 to 1/2 cup shaved parmesan
Freshly ground black pepper

Twist and pull off root base from romaine. Discard. Separate and wash greens, removing the tough outer leaves. Dry thoroughly. This is most important because the Caesar dressing will not cling to wet leaves. Tear greens into small pieces. You should have about 8 cups. Wrap lettuce in a kitchen towel and refrigerate to store. Remove and unwrap to bring to room temperature when you are ready to make the dressing.

To make the dressing: In a large salad bowl (the same bowl you will use to toss the salad), combine anchovies with garlic and smash together using the tines of a fork until they form a paste. Add lemon juice, Worcestershire, and Tabasco, stirring to combine. Slowly add oil, whisking constantly to emulsify. Add egg, whisking to combine.

Add the greens to the dressing and toss until the leaves are well coated.

Add croutons, peppers, and parmesan, reserving some of each for garnish. Grind some black pepper over all. Toss the salad again. Taste the salad for seasoning, adding salt only if necessary. The anchovy and parmesan are naturally salty.

Arrange salad on individual plates and garnish with reserved croutons, peppers, and parmesan.

SERVES 8

CORNBREAD CROUTONS
2 tablespoons unsalted butter, melted
2 cups white cornmeal
1/2 cup all-purpose flour
3 1/2 teaspoons baking powder
1/2 teaspoon baking soda
1/2 teaspoon salt
1 1/2 cups buttermilk
2 eggs, lightly beaten

Preheat corn stick molds in 450-degree oven.

Melt butter in a small saucepan over low heat.

In a large mixing bowl, sift together cornmeal, flour, baking powder, baking soda, and salt. Make a well in the center of the dry ingredients and lightly stir in buttermilk and then eggs. Do not overmix.

Carefully remove molds from oven and coat with melted butter. Fill molds one-third full and bake 8 minutes or until the sticks are crispy outside. Reduce oven temperature to 350 degrees.

Allow corn sticks to cool and break into bite-size pieces. Place these pieces on an ungreased baking sheet and return to the oven for 6 to 8 minutes, tossing at least twice. Cool and reserve for use as croutons.

MAKES 4 CUPS

ENDIVE AND RADICCHIO SALAD WITH RED WINE VINAIGRETTE

*6 Belgian endive leaves, washed, dried,
 and coarsely chopped*
*6 radicchio leaves, washed, dried, and torn
 into bite-size pieces*
*12 small leaves curly leaf lettuce, washed,
 dried, and torn into bite-size pieces*
*1 cup peeled, seeded, and coarsely chopped
 ripe tomatoes*
1/2 cup sliced mushrooms
*1 teaspoon minced fresh Italian flat-
 leaf parsley*
Red Wine Vinaigrette (page 44)

Combine salad ingredients in a large bowl. Sprinkle with parsley and mix well; toss with enough vinaigrette to coat the salad well.
SERVES 6

VARIATION
ENDIVE AND RADICCHIO WITH WHITE CHEDDAR
Toss together torn leaves of radicchio and cut or broken pieces of Belgian endive. Toss with Balsamic Vinaigrette (page 44) and serve with a piece of good white cheddar.

ENDIVE, RADICCHIO, APPLE, AND PEPPER WITH ROQUEFORT VINAIGRETTE

This is a delicious combination.

*2 heads Belgian endive, leaves separated,
 washed and dried*
*1 small head radicchio, leaves separated,
 washed and dried*
*1 medium tart apple, peeled, cored, and
 diced*
*1/2 medium yellow bell pepper, seeded and
 cut into thin julienne*

ROQUEFORT VINAIGRETTE
3 tablespoons vegetable oil
1 tablespoon rice wine vinegar
1/4 teaspoon freshly ground black pepper
4 ounces Roquefort cheese, crumbled

Toss endive, radicchio, apple, and yellow pepper together in a large salad bowl.
   Whisk together oil, vinegar, and pepper. Stir in cheese. Toss salad again with vinaigrette.
SERVES 6

ENDIVE AND CARROT SALAD WITH BERRY VINAIGRETTE

*6 large heads Belgian endive, leaves sepa-
 rated, washed, and dried*
*2 carrots, scraped and cut into very thin
 strips with a vegetable peeler or coarsely
 grated*

BERRY VINAIGRETTE
3/4 teaspoon salt
1/2 teaspoon freshly ground black pepper
2 tablespoons berry vinegar
6 tablespoons canola oil
3 tablespoons olive oil
1/4 cup fresh berries

Freshly ground black pepper (optional)

Arrange endive leaves on individual salad plates and sprinkle carrot strips over the center of each. Whisk together the remaining ingredients for the vinaigrette except the berries. Just before spooning over the endive, mash in the berries. Grind more pepper over each salad, if you like.
SERVES 6

VARIATION
Cut the endive crosswise into 1/2-inch pieces and toss with carrots instead of arranging them on individual plates.

ENDIVE SALAD WITH BLACKBERRY VINAIGRETTE

Fruit vinegars are a very good foil for the slightly sweet-bitter taste of endive.

BLACKBERRY VINAIGRETTE
6 tablespoons olive oil
3 tablespoons blackberry vinegar
1/2 teaspoon salt
1/4 teaspoon freshly ground black pepper
1/2 teaspoon Dijon mustard
1 1/2 teaspoons minced shallot
6 to 8 large blackberries

5 heads Belgian endive, separated into
    spears
Additional blackberries, for garnish
    (optional)
Freshly ground black pepper (optional)

Whisk together the oil, vinegar, salt, pepper, and mustard. Stir in the shallot and mash in the blackberries.

Place endive spears on individual plates and spoon some of the vinaigrette over each. Garnish with another blackberry on each plate and a grind of black pepper, if you like.
SERVES 6

ENDIVE SALAD WITH OIL AND LEMON DRESSING

6 large heads Belgian endive, washed
Juice of 1/2 lemon

OIL AND LEMON DRESSING
2 tablespoons fresh lemon juice
1 teaspoon salt
Dash of freshly ground black pepper
2 tablespoons safflower oil
4 tablespoons mildly flavored olive oil

Toss endive rings with lemon juice in a large bowl and set aside.

Put the dressing ingredients in a small bowl and whisk to combine. Toss endive rings with enough of the dressing to coat well.
SERVES 6

VARIATION
Add one 5-ounce can water chestnuts, drained and thinly sliced, to the salad. Sprinkle with 1 tablespoon minced fresh Italian flat-leaf parsley.

MÂCHE AND RADICCHIO SALAD WITH SPARKLING WINE VINAIGRETTE

You might want to serve Monterey Jack cheese with this salad.

6 cups (lightly packed) mixed mâche and
    torn radicchio, washed and dried

SPARKLING WINE VINAIGRETTE
6 medium shallots, minced
1 tablespoon Dijon mustard
1/2 cup sparkling white wine
1/2 cup Champagne vinegar
1/2 cup virgin olive oil
Salt and freshly ground black pepper, to taste

Wedges of Monterey Jack cheese (optional)

Place the greens in a bowl and refrigerate, covered.

Combine shallots, mustard, wine, and vinegar in a bowl and whisk together. Whisk in oil, then salt and pepper. Check for seasoning and add more oil if desired. Do not refrigerate. (This makes about 1¾ cups of vinaigrette.)

Toss greens with a few tablespoons of vinaigrette, adding more to taste as well as more salt and pepper if desired. Serve with a wedge of cheese, if desired. (Store leftover dressing in the refrigerator.)
SERVES 6 TO 8

MÂCHE SALAD

Mâche is one of my favorite salad greens. I like it on its own.

6 cups mâche, roots cut off, washed and
  dried
2 tablespoons plus 1½ teaspoons white wine
  vinegar
1 teaspoon grainy mustard
½ teaspoon soy sauce
Freshly ground black pepper, to taste
4 tablespoons olive oil

Tear mâche leaves into several pieces and place in a salad bowl.

Whisk together remaining ingredients and dress salad. Top each serving with a grind of black pepper.

SERVES 6

WATERCRESS SALAD
WITH EGG DRESSING

The egg dressing used with the watercress is a variation of one I've known for years, dating back to the time I lived in New Orleans. It is still one of my favorite ways of dressing salad greens.

3 bunches (6 to 8 ounces each) watercress,
  washed and dried, tough stems broken off

EGG DRESSING
  1½ tablespoons balsamic vinegar
  ¾ teaspoon salt
  1 teaspoon green peppercorn mustard
  Freshly ground black pepper, to taste
  5 tablespoons safflower oil
  3 tablespoons olive oil
  2 tablespoons mayonnaise (optional)

  6 hard-cooked eggs, finely chopped or
    shredded

Put the watercress in a large bowl.

Whisk together the dressing ingredients until well blended. Pour enough dressing over the watercress so that when it is tossed all the greens will be generously coated. Just before serving, toss in the eggs, reserving a little to sprinkle over the top.

SERVES 8

HARD-COOKED EGG
AND GARDEN GREEN
SALAD

Versions of this simple salad have been a Gulf Coast favorite for generations. This makes more vinaigrette than you'll need, but you'll use it later.

FLAVORED VINAIGRETTE
  ¼ cup red wine vinegar
  ¼ teaspoon salt
  ½ teaspoon freshly ground black pepper
  ½ teaspoon Tabasco Sauce
  1 teaspoon Worcestershire Sauce
  ½ teaspoon dried marjoram
  1 tablespoon honey
  1 cup oil

  6 cups mixed garden greens, washed, dried,
    and torn into bite-size pieces
  6 hard-cooked eggs, sliced
  Salt and freshly ground black pepper, to
    taste

Whisk or shake vinaigrette ingredients together until well blended.

Divide the greens among 6 salad plates. Top each with slices of egg and some of the vinaigrette. Sprinkle with salt and a good grind of black pepper.

SERVES 6

CHOPPED LETTUCE AND EGG SALAD

This is essentially an iceberg lettuce salad with an egg garnish. Gourmets may grimace, but iceberg lettuce is traditional for this salad in New Orleans.

> *6 cups (loosely placed) chopped or shredded*
> *   iceberg lettuce*
> *Simple Vinaigrette (page 45)*
> *Homemade Mayonnaise (page 348)*
> *   (optional)*
> *4 hard-cooked eggs, finely chopped or put*
> *   through a ricer*
> *Salt and freshly ground black pepper, to*
> *   taste*

Before serving, toss the lettuce with enough vinaigrette to just coat it. Toss in a tablespoon of homemade mayonnaise, if you like. Dilute with a teaspoon of vinaigrette if it is stiff. Sprinkle the eggs over all and toss again lightly. Season with salt and pepper.
SERVES 6

RUSTIC SALAD

This salad is always a great hit with guests.

> *12 thick bacon slices, cut into $1/2$-inch pieces*
> *2 tablespoons safflower oil*
> *2 tablespoons finely minced onion*
> *2 tablespoons red wine vinegar*
> *$1/4$ teaspoon salt*
> *$1/2$ teaspoon freshly ground black pepper*
> *$1 1/2$ cups large cubes of French bread*
> *3 tablespoons olive oil*
> *3 heads romaine lettuce, washed, dried, and*
> *   torn into bite-size pieces*
> *6 large eggs*

Preheat oven to 350 degrees.

Fry bacon until crisp. Set aside to drain on paper towels. Reserve 3 tablespoons of the bacon fat, add the safflower oil to it, and heat.

Sauté onion until golden. Add vinegar, salt, and pepper. Set aside on the stove.

Put the bread cubes on a baking sheet and toast in the oven. When golden, heat the olive oil and fry them. Set aside.

To serve, toss together the croutons, bacon, and lettuce. Add just enough dressing to lightly coat the lettuce leaves. Put on large individual plates and set aside.

Poach eggs in a large shallow pan of simmering water by breaking individual eggs into a saucer and sliding each into the water. Carefully remove eggs with a slotted spoon, blot to dry, and place on top of the salads. Spoon a little of the dressing over eggs and pass the rest.
SERVES 6

WILTED SALAD WITH PANCETTA

> *1 pound mixed greens, such as arugula,*
> *   mâche, and red leaf lettuce, washed and*
> *   dried*
> *$1/2$ pound pancetta, thickly sliced*
> *$1/3$ cup red wine vinegar*
> *Salt and freshly ground black pepper, to*
> *   taste*

Place greens in a large mixing bowl and set aside.

Stack pancetta slices and cut into strips. In a heavy frying pan over medium-high heat, cook pancetta until it is crisp, stirring occasionally. This takes about 5 minutes.

Pour pancetta and rendered cooking fat over the greens and toss until the greens are wilted. Pour vinegar into the frying pan, bring to a boil, stirring to dissolve any pan juices, and reduce by one third.

Pour over the wilted greens and toss well to coat evenly. Season with salt and pepper; serve warm.
SERVES 4

COLESLAW I

I like my coleslaw simple: just cabbage and red pepper with a basic mayonnaise dressing.

MAYONNAISE DRESSING
*1 cup mayonnaise, preferably homemade
    (page 348)*
4 teaspoons olive oil
2 tablespoons safflower oil
2 teaspoons sugar
1 teaspoon salt
1 teaspoon green peppercorn mustard
2 tablespoons balsamic vinegar
7 drops Tabasco Sauce
1/2 teaspoon freshly ground black pepper

5 cups finely shredded cabbage
1 medium red bell pepper, finely chopped

Whisk together all ingredients for the dressing until well blended. Mix cabbage and bell pepper together with a generous amount of dressing. (You will probably have more dressing than you need. Refrigerate if not using right away.)
SERVES 6

COLESLAW II

*1/2 cup mayonnaise, preferably homemade
    (page 348)*
1 tablespoon wine vinegar
2 teaspoons sugar
1/4 teaspoon salt
1/4 cup sweet pickle juice
2 cups shredded green cabbage
2 cups shredded red cabbage
1/2 cup shredded carrot
1/4 cup finely chopped green bell pepper
2 tablespoons minced onion

Whisk together the mayonnaise, vinegar, sugar, salt, and pickle juice. Chill.
  Toss remaining ingredients together in a large bowl and combine with the dressing.
SERVES 6 TO 8

NEW ORLEANS COLESLAW

This is a typically pungent mix.

4 cups shredded green cabbage
1/2 cup shredded carrot
6 tablespoons mayonnaise
2 1/2 tablespoons Creole mustard
1 1/4 tablespoons white wine vinegar
1/2 teaspoon salt
1/2 teaspoon white pepper
1/2 teaspoon sugar
*1 1/2 teaspoons minced fresh Italian flat-leaf
    parsley*
1 tablespoon fresh lemon juice

Toss cabbage and carrot together in a large bowl. Beat together all other ingredients and pour onto vegetables. Toss to coat well.
SERVES 6

JICAMA SLAW

1 1/2 cups grated, peeled jicama
1 cup grated carrots
*1 head Belgian endive, halved, quartered,
    and julienned*
1/2 cup roughly chopped watercress
1 tablespoon finely chopped garlic
1/2 teaspoon grated fresh ginger
1 teaspoon grated orange zest
1/4 cup fresh orange juice
1/2 teaspoon salt
1/4 teaspoon freshly ground black pepper

Combine jicama, carrots, endive, and watercress in a medium mixing bowl. Combine remaining ingredients in a small jar with a tight-fitting lid and shake vigorously to combine. Pour over vegetable mixture and toss well to combine.
SERVES 6

56

VEGETABLE SALADS

WARM ARTICHOKE SALAD

6 or 8 large artichokes
Lemon juice
1/3 cup olive oil
2 large garlic cloves, finely chopped
1/4 cup finely chopped shallots
1 tablespoon minced fresh Italian flat-leaf
  parsley
2 tablespoons chopped fresh mint
1/2 cup water
1 teaspoon salt
Freshly ground black pepper
2 tablespoons red wine vinegar

Trim artichokes by snapping off and discarding the coarse outer leaves. Using a small sharp knife, trim off the green fibrous parts, rubbing all cut surfaces with lemon as you work. Cut each artichoke heart in half and scoop out fibrous choke with a spoon.

In a shallow pan heat olive oil over medium heat. Add garlic and shallots; turn heat to low and cook just long enough to soften the garlic and shallots, 2 or 3 minutes. Add remaining ingredients except vinegar and artichokes, and bring to a slow boil. Add artichokes and cover. Cook over medium heat until tender, about 10 minutes. Remove artichokes with a slotted spoon. If any water is remaining in the pan, increase heat and boil until evaporated. Deglaze the pan with the vinegar, scraping any brown bits and herbs from the bottom of the pan. Pour over artichokes and toss.

SERVES 6 TO 8

RAW ASPARAGUS AND LETTUCE SALAD WITH MUSTARD VINAIGRETTE

I am particularly fond of the tiny asparagus that you can get in the early spring. Their tender crunchiness is perfect in a salad.

1/2 pound thin asparagus
1 large head Boston lettuce

MUSTARD VINAIGRETTE
1/4 cup red wine vinegar
1 tablespoon Dijon mustard
1/4 cup olive oil
1/4 cup safflower oil
1 large egg yolk
1 tablespoon chopped fresh chives
1 tablespoon chopped fresh Italian flat-leaf
  parsley
1 teaspoon chopped shallots

Wash and dry asparagus. Cut into 1-inch pieces, discarding the bottom third of each stalk if it is the least bit tough. Wash and dry lettuce and tear into bite-size pieces. Combine with asparagus and refrigerate, covered, until you need it.

Combine the vinegar and mustard in a small bowl; whisk in the oils, then the egg yolk. Add the chives, parsley, and shallots and mix. Let stand at room temperature.

When you are ready to serve, toss the greens with a bit of the dressing. (Store leftover dressing in the refrigerator.)

SERVES 6

57

ASPARAGUS VINAIGRETTE

2 to 3 pounds medium asparagus, stems
*   peeled*
Balsamic Vinaigrette (page 44)
2 hard-cooked eggs, finely diced
Freshly ground black pepper, to taste

Bring a large pan of well-salted water to the boil. Put asparagus in and bring back to a boil. Cook until just tender, about 5 minutes. Drain and refresh under cold water.

Arrange the cooled asparagus on a platter or individual plates, and spoon vinaigrette over all. Sprinkle with egg and top with a grind of pepper.
SERVES 6

VARIATION
Make the vinaigrette with half vegetable oil, half olive oil.

SLICED AVOCADO SALAD WITH LEMON VINAIGRETTE

You may vary this vinaigrette by using salt instead of the soy sauce and mashing in a couple of anchovy fillets.

3 ripe avocados, peeled, pitted, and sliced
*   thick*
Fresh lemon juice

LEMON VINAIGRETTE
1/4 teaspoon freshly ground black pepper
1 teaspoon soy sauce, or to taste
2 tablespoons fresh lemon juice
1 teaspoon grainy mustard
5 tablespoons olive oil

1/2 small red onion, cut into thin rings or
*   chopped*

Rub each avocado slice with a little extra lemon juice to prevent from turning dark. Place in a salad bowl.

Meanwhile, combine pepper, soy sauce, lemon juice, and mustard in a small bowl and whisk together. Whisk in oil. Spoon sauce over avocados or serve on the side. Garnish with red onion.
SERVES 6

VARIATION
Substitute Red Wine Vinaigrette (page 44) for the Lemon Vinaigrette.

AVOCADOS WITH LIME VINAIGRETTE

If you are rushed, a simple oil and vinegar dressing is fine on avocados. Or if you are really a minimalist, just add a squeeze of lemon or lime juice. Whatever you do, rub the cut surfaces of avocado with citrus juice to keep them from discoloring before being served.

LIME VINAIGRETTE
1/4 cup olive oil
2 tablespoons fresh lime juice
1/2 teaspoon salt, or to taste
1/2 teaspoon freshly ground black pepper
1 tablespoon mayonnaise
3 to 4 dashes Tabasco Sauce (optional)
1 teaspoon Dijon mustard
2 tablespoons minced shallots
3 tablespoons finely chopped red bell pepper

3 ripe avocados, peeled, pitted, and
*   quartered*

In a small glass bowl, whisk together the olive oil, lime juice, salt, and pepper. Whisk in mayonnaise, Tabasco, if using, and mustard, then fold in shallots and red pepper.

To serve, drizzle vinaigrette over prepared avocado quarters.
SERVES 6

AVOCADO SALAD WITH CILANTRO VINAIGRETTE

CILANTRO VINAIGRETTE
1 teaspoon grainy mustard
3 tablespoons white wine vinegar
Juice of 1 lime
3 tablespoons vegetable oil
6 tablespoons olive oil
2 tablespoons (loosely packed) torn cilantro
*   leaves*

3 avocados, halved, pitted, skinned, and
*   cut lengthwise into thin slices*
2 small red onions, sliced into thin rings
1 medium cucumber, peeled, halved,
*   seeded, and thinly sliced (approximately*
*   1½ cups)*

Combine mustard, vinegar, and lime juice. Gradually add oils, whisking constantly to emulsify. Gently stir in cilantro leaves.

Place avocados, onions, and cucumber in a mixing bowl and combine gently with vinaigrette.
SERVES 6

CHOPPED AVOCADO, ONION, TOMATO, AND HOT PEPPER SALAD

Use a Hass avocado for this if possible. Hass is the one with the dark, rough skin.

3 tablespoons fresh lemon juice
6 tablespoons olive oil
Salt and freshly ground black pepper
1 tablespoon minced fresh cilantro
1 cup medium red onion, chopped
2 cups peeled, seeded, and coarsely chopped
*   fresh tomatoes*
1 large avocado, peeled, seeded, and
*   coarsely chopped*
1 teaspoon minced jalapeño, or to taste

Whisk together lemon juice, olive oil, salt, pepper, and cilantro. Set aside.

Combine onion, tomatoes, avocado, and jalapeño and toss with the vinaigrette. This can sometimes be rather liquid, so serve it with a slotted spoon.
SERVES 6

COLD BEETS

These beets contain no seasoning, just a squeeze of lemon over them.

2 to 3 pounds beets
2 lemons, cut into wedges

Cut tops from the beets, scrub, and cover with water in a saucepan. Bring to a boil. Simmer until tender, about 30 minutes, depending on the size. Let cool in their juice. Slip off the skin and root. Slice and serve with lemon wedges.
SERVES 6

FRESH BEET SALAD

2 to 3 pounds beets
1 tablespoon minced shallots
2 tablespoons olive oil
2 tablespoons balsamic or red wine vinegar

Preheat oven to 400 degrees.

Scrub beets and cut off stems about 2 inches from the bulb. Leave root on. Place beets in a small foil-lined pan. Bake until tender to the touch, about 1 hour. When cool, peel and stem, cutting off and discarding the tops. Cut beets into ½-inch dice. Toss with shallots.

Whisk together the oil and vinegar. Pour over beets and toss.
SERVES 6

CHOPPED BEET, ENDIVE, AND RED ONION SALAD

This can be made with canned beets, but they don't compare with the earthy flavor of fresh ones.

>   2 to 3 pounds beets, boiled or baked (see
>   pages 105 to 106)
>   6 medium heads Belgian endive, leaves sep-
>   arated, washed, dried, and cut into 1/2-
>   inch rings
>   1 medium red onion, cut into thin rings
>   Simple Vinaigrette (page 45)

Slip off beet skins. Chop into medium-size chunks. Toss beets, endives, and onion together. Dress sparingly with vinaigrette.

SERVES 6

VARIATION

Substitute Balsamic Vinaigrette (page 44) for the Strong Vinaigrette.

BEET SALAD WITH ONION

>   3 small onions
>   1 tablespoon olive oil
>   1 tablespoon balsamic vinegar
>   Salt and freshly ground black pepper, to
>   taste
>   2 pounds beets
>   1 tablespoon raspberry vinegar
>   1 tablespoon balsamic vinegar
>   2 tablespoons olive oil

Preheat oven to 400 degrees.

Peel onions and cut into quarters. Drizzle 1 teaspoon each of the oil and balsamic vinegar on each onion. Sprinkle with salt and pepper. Wrap each onion in aluminum foil and twist at the top to seal. Bake until tender, about 1 hour. Reserve any liquid for the dressing.

Place the beets on a foil-lined baking sheet. Bake until tender, 1 to 1 1/2 hours. Set aside to cool.

Peel the beets and cut into 1/4-inch slices, then into thick sticks. Place in a large mixing bowl. Break up the quartered onions and add them to the beets.

Whisk together vinegars, oil, salt, and pepper. Stir in any reserved liquid from the onions. Pour the dressing over the salad and toss.

SERVES 6

WILTED RED ONIONS AND PICKLED BEET SALAD

These onions make delicious sandwiches or a topping for tomatoes. Like the beets, they keep well in the refrigerator.

WILTED ONIONS

>   1 1/2 pounds red onions, peeled and sliced
>   thin
>   1/2 cup safflower oil
>   1/2 cup white vinegar
>   1/2 cup water
>   1/2 teaspoon freshly ground black pepper
>   2 teaspoons salt
>   1 tablespoon sugar
>   3 or 4 drops Tabasco Sauce

PICKLED BEETS

>   1 1/2 cups white vinegar
>   1/2 cup sugar
>   1/2 teaspoon salt
>   1 teaspoon whole allspice
>   1 1/2 cups water
>   9 unpeeled medium beets, roots and tops
>   removed, cut into 4 wedges
>   6 green onions, including some of the green,
>   cut into 1/2-inch lengths
>   2 sprigs fresh tarragon or 1 teaspoon dried
>   tarragon

To make wilted onions: Put onions in a crockery bowl. Mix all other ingredients together in a saucepan and bring to a boil. Pour over the onions. When cool, cover and refrigerate overnight.

To make pickled beets: Combine vinegar, sugar, salt, allspice, and water in a medium saucepan. Simmer over moderate heat (if using dry tarragon, add it now). Reduce heat and simmer 10 minutes. Add beets, cover, and cook over moderate heat 10 to 15 minutes, or until beets are tender. Cool beets in cooking liquid for about 30 minutes and skin them.

Transfer beets and liquid to a jar or bowl. Add green onions and fresh tarragon. Cover with cheesecloth and let stand overnight. Next day, remove cheesecloth and refrigerate, covered.

To serve, put a portion of beets and onions on each individual salad plate.

SERVES 6, WITH LEFTOVERS

LIMA BEAN AND CHEESE SALAD

*2 packages (10 ounces each) frozen lima
  beans
Balsamic Vinaigrette (page 44)
Salt and freshly ground black pepper, to
  taste
2 tablespoons snipped fresh chives
6 ounces sharp cheddar, cubed*

Cook beans according to package directions and drain. Pour vinaigrette over beans while still warm. Marinate, refrigerated, until ready to serve. Remove from the refrigerator, season with salt and pepper, and toss in the chives and cheese.

SERVES 8

TWO-BEAN SALAD

*2 pounds green beans, stem ends snapped off
1 can (16 ounces) kidney beans, drained
1 large red onion, thinly sliced
2 tablespoons sugar
1/4 cup vegetable oil
3 tablespoons distilled white vinegar
1/4 teaspoon salt
1/4 teaspoon freshly ground black pepper*

Cook green beans in lightly salted boiling water until tender, about 12 minutes. Drain and run under cold water until cool. Drain again and pat dry.

In a large mixing bowl, combine green beans with kidney beans and red onion. In a small bowl, combine sugar, oil, vinegar, salt, and pepper. Stir to mix well and dissolve the sugar. Add the dressing to the beans and toss to mix.

SERVES 6

BABY GREEN BEAN, ONION, AND TOASTED PINE NUT SALAD

You may substitute asparagus here for the green beans.

*1 pound baby green beans (haricots verts),
  stemmed and tipped
1 medium Vidalia, or red onion, or 4 green
  onions, coarsely chopped
Red Wine Vinaigrette (page 44)
2 tablespoons pine nuts, toasted
Freshly ground black pepper*

Steam beans until crisp-tender and allow to cool. Toss with onion and enough vinaigrette to coat lightly. Arrange on a plate and sprinkle pine nuts over all. Top with a grinding of black pepper.

SERVES 6

WARM GREEN BEAN SALAD

I'm very fond of this salad because it's so flexible. You may serve the beans tossed with hot vinaigrette at the last minute, but you may also add any number of ingredients, either tossed in with them or as a garnish. Consider minced red onion, celery, red bell pepper, shallots, parsley, or dill. Or what about a topping of toasted slivered almonds, pimiento, crumbled crisp bacon, or chopped hard-cooked egg?

Anyway, here is the basic "recipe."

Balsamic Vinaigrette (page 44)
1¼ pounds baby green beans (haricots verts), tipped, stemmed, and steamed to crisp-tender
Freshly ground black pepper

Heat vinaigrette in a small saucepan and toss with the freshly steamed beans. Combine or garnish with any of the ingredients suggested above. Top with a grind of fresh pepper.
SERVES 6

BABY GREEN BEAN SALAD

1 pound baby green beans (haricots verts), stems snapped off
2 tablespoons salt
1 tablespoon red wine vinegar
6 tablespoons olive oil
2 medium garlic cloves, minced

Bring a medium saucepan of water to a boil. Add beans and salt. Cook until beans are just beginning to get tender, about 3 minutes. Drain and rinse in cold water to preserve color and stop their cooking.

Whisk together vinegar, oil, and garlic. Pour over beans and toss.
SERVES 6

GREEN BEAN AND CHEESE SALAD

¾ pound green beans, cut into 1-inch pieces
1 cup grated gruyère
8 large shallots, minced
2 tablespoons olive oil
2 tablespoons red wine vinegar
1 tablespoon grainy Dijon mustard
¼ teaspoon salt
⅛ teaspoon freshly ground black pepper

Blanch green beans in boiling salted water for 5 minutes. Drain and run under cold water to stop the cooking. Drain well, then combine with cheese in a large mixing bowl.

Whisk together all remaining ingredients for dressing. Combine with the green beans and cheese. Mix well.
SERVES 6

CARROT SLAW

½ cup chopped fresh Italian flat-leaf parsley
¼ cup red wine vinegar
1 teaspoon grainy mustard
2 garlic cloves, chopped
1 heaping tablespoon brown sugar
½ cup olive oil
¼ cup vegetable oil
6 cups chopped carrots

Combine parsley, vinegar, mustard, garlic, brown sugar, and oils in a small jar with a tight-fitting lid and shake vigorously. Toss with carrots to coat. Let stand at room temperature for at least 1 hour.
SERVES 6

THAI SALAD WITH CARROT AND CUCUMBER

*3 medium cucumbers, peeled, seeded, and
    sliced*
2 medium carrots, peeled and grated
4 large shallots, sliced
1/2 red onion, sliced
1 small red chili, minced
3/4 cup rice wine vinegar
1/4 cup plus 2 tablespoons sugar
3 tablespoons finely chopped fresh cilantro
1/2 cup peanuts, roughly chopped

Combine cucumbers, carrots, shallots, onion,
and chili in a bowl.

Place vinegar and sugar in a small saucepan.
Bring to a boil and then reduce heat to a simmer. Simmer uncovered for 5 minutes, until
the mixture is syrupy. Allow to cool.

Pour the sweetened vinegar over the vegetables and toss. Add cilantro and peanuts and
toss again.

SERVES 6

SWEET CARROT AND CUCUMBER SALAD

I especially like this combination of flavors.

*2 medium cucumbers, peeled, seeded, and
    cut into 1/4-inch-thick half-moons*
*1 medium carrot, scraped and sliced into 1/4-
    inch-thick rounds*
1/4 medium red onion, coarsely chopped
*1 medium pickled jalapeño, seeds removed,
    minced*
1 cup water
1/4 cup granulated sugar
1/4 cup (packed) light brown sugar
1/3 cup distilled white vinegar
2 tablespoons nuoc mam *(see Note)*

Toss vegetables together in a medium bowl.
Heat water, sugars, vinegar, and *nuoc mam*
over medium heat, stirring, until sugar dissolves. Remove from heat and pour over vegetables. Refrigerate until ready to serve.

This will keep for up to 3 days in the
refrigerator.

Note: Nuoc mam *is a fermented fish sauce
used in Vietnamese and other Asian cuisines. It is
available in specialty stores and in the Oriental
section of many supermarkets.*

SERVES 6

CHOPPED CELERY, APPLE, AND PEAR SALAD

3 cups thinly sliced celery
*2 large Granny Smith apples, peeled, cored,
    and thinly sliced*
*2 large Bosc pears, peeled, cored, and thinly
    sliced*
1 medium garlic clove, cut in half
1/2 teaspoon salt
1/4 cup olive oil
1/4 cup fresh raspberries
1/4 cup fresh orange juice
2 tablespoons raspberry vinegar

Toss celery, apples, and pears together in a
bowl. Combine all other ingredients in a food
processor and process until smooth. Toss with
the celery and fruit. Chill, covered, for 1 hour
before serving.

SERVES 8

CORN SALAD

In this recipe the corn is just barely cooked. Sugar is added to enhance the flavor, because most of the corn sold in city groceries is at least several days old. This recipe is based on using large-kernel yellow corn; less cooking time is required for the more delicate white variety.

4 ears of corn, kernels cut off and scraped
from cob
1¹/₂ tablespoons milk or water
¹/₂ teaspoon salt
1 red bell pepper, roasted, peeled, and
seeded (see Note, page 74), coarsely
chopped
2 teaspoons fresh lemon juice
1¹/₂ teaspoons sugar
Freshly ground black pepper, to taste

Put corn kernels and scraped pulp in the top of a double boiler and add milk and salt. Cook covered, over simmering water, for about 10 minutes. Stir occasionally to prevent sticking. Pour corn into a bowl and let cool. (If corn has stuck to the bottom of the pan, immediately fill it with cold water and let soak.)

Combine corn and red pepper in a bowl and add lemon juice, sugar, and black pepper. Mix.

SERVES 4

CUCUMBER, WALNUT, AND ENDIVE SALAD WITH WALNUT VINAIGRETTE

The combination of cucumbers, walnuts, and endive is a surprisingly satisfying mix of flavors that you might not think would work together. It also makes a very appealing presentation.

1 small cucumber, peeled, seeded, and diced
³/₄ cup walnuts, coarsely chopped
6 medium heads Belgian endive, leaves sep-
arated, washed, and dried

Walnut Vinaigrette (page 50)

Combine cucumbers and walnuts. Arrange endive leaves on individual plates and heap the cucumber mixture over them. Spoon the vinaigrette over all.

SERVES 6

CUCUMBER AND MINT SALAD

Yogurt marries well to cucumber. Sometimes I peel and seed cucumbers in advance, salt them, and put them in the refrigerator to draw out a good bit of their water. Of course, this changes their texture, making them less crunchy, but I like them that way.

3 cucumbers, peeled, seeded, and cut into
half-moons
1 tablespoons very finely chopped fresh mint
leaves
¹/₂ cup plain yogurt
4 tablespoons rice wine vinegar
1 teaspoon brown sugar
¹/₈ teaspoon white pepper
Salt, to taste

Put cucumbers in a bowl and mix with mint. In another bowl, combine all the remaining ingredients. Put the cucumbers on small individual plates and spoon some of the yogurt dressing over them.

SERVES 6

CUCUMBER SALAD WITH SESAME DRESSING

Whenever you use sesame oil, be sure it is the dark Asian variety. Some brands sold in health food stores have absolutely no taste or odor.

I always seed cucumbers before I use them, but this is not really necessary if you don't mind seeds.

3 small cucumbers, peeled, seeded, and cut
   into 1/2-inch strips

SESAME DRESSING
   2 tablespoons rice wine vinegar
   1 tablespoon dark brown sugar
   1 tablespoon soy sauce
   1 tablespoon dark sesame oil

Put cucumbers in a bowl. Mix the remaining
ingredients and pour over them. Refrigerate
until ready to use.
SERVES 6

FENNEL AND ORANGE SALAD WITH SHAVED PARMESAN AND BLACK OLIVES

You may substitute peaches for the oranges in
this salad.

   6 medium to small seedless oranges, peeled
      with pith scraped
   6 small or 3 medium fennel bulbs, trimmed
      and cored
   36 black olives in oil
   Balsamic Vinaigrette (page 44)
   Shaved parmesan, to taste
   Freshly ground black pepper, to taste

Cut oranges crosswise into 8 slices each. Place
in a salad bowl. Halve fennel bulbs lengthwise
and cut into medium to thin slices. Place on
oranges. Drain olives and add. Toss lightly.

   Add 3 tablespoons vinaigrette to the salad
and toss, using more if necessary. Arrange on
individual plates and top with shaved parmesan. Grind black pepper over all.
SERVES 6

FENNEL AND BOSTON LETTUCE SALAD

This salad can be served in very small portions.

   1 large head Boston lettuce, washed, dried,
      and torn into rather large pieces
   1 large bulb fennel, trimmed, washed, and
      very thinly sliced
   Simple Vinaigrette (page 45)
   Salt and freshly ground black pepper, to
      taste

Divide the lettuce among 6 plates. Heap fennel
on top of each serving of lettuce. Drizzle a
modest amount of vinaigrette over each serving, and sprinkle with salt and pepper.
SERVES 6

FENNEL, CELERY, AND PARSLEY SALAD WITH SHAVED PARMESAN

   2 1/4 cups thinly sliced fennel bulb
   2 1/4 cups thinly sliced celery
   1 1/4 cups minced fresh Italian flat-leaf
      parsley
   Balsamic Vinaigrette (page 44)
   Shaved parmesan, to taste
   Freshly ground black pepper, to taste

Toss fennel, celery, and parsley together. Add
3 tablespoons vinaigrette and toss. Add more
as necessary. Place on individual serving plates
and top with shaved parmesan and a good
grind of black pepper.
SERVES 6

VIDALIA ONIONS AND LEEKS WITH TARRAGON VINAIGRETTE

This combination is almost a meal in itself.

*2 large Vidalia or other sweet onions,
    trimmed and peeled*
*3 leeks, trimmed to include 1½ inches of the
    light green, halved lengthwise and care-
    fully washed*

TARRAGON VINAIGRETTE
1 cup extra virgin olive oil
½ cup tarragon vinegar
1½ tablespoons grated onion
1½ tablespoons Dijon mustard
1 teaspoon sugar
*Salt and freshly ground black pepper, to
    taste*
Lettuce leaves
*1 cup peeled, seeded, and chopped ripe
    tomatoes*
*2 hard-cooked eggs, pushed through a sieve
    or finely chopped*
*½ cup finely chopped mixed fresh herbs,
    such as chervil, tarragon, and Italian
    flat-leaf parsley*

Steam onions, covered, over boiling water until tender, about 20 minutes. Remove and set aside.

Steam leeks over boiling water until tender, about 15 minutes. Remove and set aside.

In a large jar with a tight-fitting lid, combine oil, vinegar, grated onion, mustard, sugar, and salt and pepper. Cover and shake well to emulsify.

Line two salad plates with lettuce. Quarter each onion. Split each leek half lengthwise. Divide the onions and leeks between the plates. Garnish with tomatoes and eggs. Shake the dressing again and spoon some over each salad. Sprinkle with fresh herbs and serve.
SERVES 2

GREEN PEA SALAD

You might add other ingredients to this, such as finely chopped celery, but I really prefer it as it is. If you are especially fond of dill, the amount in the dressing might not be enough for you.

*2 packages (10 ounces each) frozen green
    peas, steamed until barely tender*
3 tablespoons chopped fresh dill
2 tablespoons sour cream
2 tablespoons mayonnaise
2½ teaspoons fresh lemon juice
4 teaspoons olive oil
1 teaspoon Dijon mustard
½ teaspoon salt
¼ teaspoon freshly ground black pepper
Few drops of Tabasco Sauce
Sprigs of dill

Mix the peas and chopped dill and set aside. Whisk together sour cream, mayonnaise, lemon juice, olive oil, mustard, salt, pepper, and Tabasco. Add about three quarters of the dressing to peas and toss lightly. Cover and refrigerate.

To serve, correct the seasoning and mix in the rest of the dressing. (This may be done several hours in advance.) Garnish each portion with a sprig of fresh dill.
SERVES 6

VARIATION
Omit the sour cream and mayonnaise. Substitute red wine vinegar for the lemon juice.

RICE, GREEN PEA, AND OLIVE SALAD WITH ORANGE-CILANTRO VINAIGRETTE

I use frozen tiny green peas in this salad, uncooked but thawed at the last minute, and I cook the rice in chicken stock.

3 cups cooked rice
2/3 cup sliced pitted green olives
1 cup frozen tiny green peas

ORANGE-CILANTRO VINAIGRETTE
3 tablespoons olive oil
6 tablespoons fresh orange juice
1 tablespoon grated orange zest
1 tablespoon lemon zest
1 teaspoon salt, or to taste
1/2 teaspoon paprika
1/4 cup finely chopped cilantro

Toss rice and olives together. Place peas in a strainer and run very hot tap water over them for 1 minute, shaking, to thaw. Shake dry and add to the rice and olives. Toss

Whisk together vinaigrette ingredients and dress the salad just before serving, tossing well.
SERVES 6 TO 8

MUSHROOM AND WALNUT SALAD

This interesting combination of flavors is a nice change from the traditional green salad.

1/2 pound button mushrooms, washed, trimmed, and thinly sliced
1 tablespoon fresh lemon juice
1 cup walnuts
2 tablespoons red wine vinegar
1/2 teaspoon salt, or to taste
Freshly ground black pepper, to taste
3 tablespoons walnut oil
2 tablespoons safflower oil
3 small heads Boston lettuce, washed, dried, and torn into bite-size pieces

Wash and slice mushrooms, toss with lemon juice, and refrigerate. Do not do this more than an hour before you are ready to serve. Chop walnuts coarsely.

Make dressing by whisking together vinegar, salt, and pepper and then adding the oils. Do not refrigerate.

When ready to serve, toss mushrooms, walnuts, and lettuce together, and drizzle with the dressing. Taste and correct seasoning if necessary.
SERVES 6 TO 8

GREENS AND MUSHROOM SALAD

Use any kind or combination of fresh mushrooms you like in this salad. If you wish, you can substitute red bell pepper for the other bell peppers.

1/3 cup white wine vinegar
1 cup olive oil
1 teaspoon salt, or to taste
1/4 teaspoon white pepper, or to taste
1 tablespoon minced shallots
1 tablespoon minced garlic
1 tablespoon diced roasted red bell pepper (see Note, page 74)
1 tablespoon diced roasted yellow bell pepper
1 tablespoon diced roasted green bell pepper
3 cups mixed greens, washed, dried, and torn into bite-size pieces
1 cup sliced mushrooms

Whisk together vinegar, oil, salt, and pepper. Stir in shallots, garlic, and bell peppers.

Toss greens and mushrooms together. Spoon enough vinaigrette over all to coat. Toss.
SERVES 6

SAUTÉED RED AND YELLOW PEPPER SALAD

1 tablespoon olive oil
1¹/₂ cups sliced red bell peppers, 2 × ¹/₄ inch
1¹/₂ cups sliced yellow bell peppers, 2 × ¹/₄ inch
1 tablespoon capers, drained
2 ounces niçoise olives, pitted and roughly chopped
2 tablespoons balsamic vinegar

Place olive oil into a very large skillet and heat over high heat. Add peppers and sauté until just tender, about 3 or 4 minutes, shaking or stirring constantly.

Remove sautéed peppers to a bowl. Add capers, olives, and balsamic vinegar. Toss to mix.

SERVES 6

ROASTED PEPPER SALAD

I use several colors of peppers for this, but you could use all of one variety.

1 red bell pepper
1 yellow bell pepper
1 orange bell pepper
1 purple bell pepper
2 tablespoons minced shallots
¹/₂ cup olive oil
¹/₃ cup dry white wine
¹/₂ cup white wine vinegar
1 teaspoon dried oregano
1 tablespoon sugar
¹/₂ teaspoon cayenne

Roast, peel, and seed peppers as described on page 74. Cut each pepper into strips and place in a shallow dish. Combine all other ingredients in a small saucepan and bring to a simmer. Pour over peppers. Allow to cool and refrigerate. Bring back to room temperature before serving.

SERVES 8

GREEN PEPPER AND CUCUMBER SALAD

This salad is quite easy to prepare. Just be sure to give the cucumbers enough time to give up their water, or the whole thing can get too liquid.

2 large cucumbers, peeled, seeded, and cut into thick slices
1 teaspoon salt
6 tablespoons plain yogurt
3 tablespoons wine vinegar
¹/₄ teaspoon freshly ground black pepper
¹/₂ teaspoon sugar
1 medium garlic clove, cut in half
2 very large green bell peppers, roasted, peeled, and seeded (see Note, page 74), cut into large dice
¹/₂ small red onion, thinly sliced

Put cucumber slices in a bowl and salt them generously. Refrigerate for at least 1 hour. When you are ready to use them, drain and squeeze between paper towels to dry.

Make a dressing by combining yogurt, vinegar, pepper, sugar, and garlic. Combine the cucumbers and bell pepper and pour the dressing over all. Just before serving, remove the garlic and stir. Top with thin rings of red onion.

SERVES 6

NEW POTATO SALAD WITH GREENS AND LEMON-DILL CHARDONNAY VINAIGRETTE

This salad has potatoes in it, but they taste so unusual you would think they were a different vegetable.

2 pounds red new potatoes, scrubbed
Salt

LEMON-DILL CHARDONNAY VINAIGRETTE

1/4 cup fresh lemon juice
2 tablespoons chardonnay
3 tablespoons chopped fresh dill
1 teaspoon Dijon mustard
Freshly ground black pepper, to taste
1/2 cup olive oil

Assorted mixed greens, such as red leaf, Bibb, and butter lettuce, washed, dried, and torn into pieces
2 to 3 heads of Belgian endive, leaves separated, washed, and dried
Freshly ground black pepper

Boil potatoes in a large pot of lightly salted water until tender enough to pierce through with a fork. Drain and cool. Set aside.

Combine lemon juice, wine, dill, and mustard in a small bowl and whisk. Add salt and pepper. Whisking, pour in oil in a steady stream.

Halve the potatoes and toss with some of the vinaigrette. Make a bed of the assorted greens and endive on individual salad plates. Arrange 3 or 4 leaves on top and divide potato halves among the plates.

Drizzle remainder of the vinaigrette over all and top with a grinding of fresh pepper.

SERVES 6

WARM GREEN BEAN AND NEW POTATO SALAD

Some people cook these vegetables separately when serving them this way, but I just dump them all in a pot together. I like the flavor the cooking juice adds to the potatoes.

2 pounds green beans, snapped into several pieces, ends removed
2 pounds small red new potatoes, scrubbed
2 large onions, coarsely chopped
1 piece (1 inch) salt pork
Salt and freshly ground black pepper, to taste

Lemon-Oil Dressing (page 48)
Chopped fresh Italian flat-leaf parsley (optional)

Put beans and potatoes in a saucepan. Cover with water and add onions, salt pork, and salt and pepper. Simmer for 30 to 40 minutes. The beans should be very tender. They can cool a bit in the liquid. When ready to serve, if they have gotten completely cold, bring the liquid back to a boil and then turn off the heat. Allow vegetables to sit in it while you whisk together all the ingredients for the dressing.

Drain the vegetables, discarding the cooking liquid or keeping it for soup. Peel and cut the potatoes into chunks. Put potatoes and beans in a serving bowl and toss with the dressing. Garnish with chopped parsley, if desired. Correct seasoning if necessary.

SERVES 6 TO 8

TOMATO AND BREAD SALAD

When I make this salad, I make a double batch of the crunchy croutons and freeze them.

1/2 small baguette (about 12 inches long)
1 large garlic clove, mashed
Olive oil
6 medium to large ripe tomatoes, cut into
  large chunks
1/2 medium onion, chopped
3 tablespoons coarsely chopped fresh basil
1/4 cup balsamic vinegar
1/2 cup olive oil

Preheat oven to 300 degrees.

Split baguette in half lengthwise. Rub the cut sides very well with mashed garlic. Brush liberally with olive oil. Cut each half in half again lengthwise and then cut these strips into 3/4-inch pieces. Place croutons on a cookie sheet, crust side down. Bake until dark golden, about 30 minutes or more.

If croutons are made in advance, place tomatoes in a large mixing bowl a bit before you intend to mix salad, then drain and discard any juice that may have accumulated in the bottom of the bowl.

To serve, add the croutons, onion, and basil to the tomatoes. Whisk together vinegar and oil, pour over salad, and toss.
SERVES 6

TOMATO AND RED ONION WITH OLIVES AND ROMANO

You don't need a recipe for this salad. All you do is peel and slice tomatoes and top them with slices of red onion. Spoon a little Simple Vinaigrette (page 45) over, and sprinkle with salt and a grind of black pepper. Add curls of romano cheese, made with a vegetable peeler. Garnish the salad with black olives.

TOMATOES WITH CITRUS DRESSING

The slightly sweet taste of this dressing is a very nice complement to the tomatoes.

3 large ripe tomatoes, peeled and thickly
  sliced
3 tablespoons minced shallots
2 teaspoons grated orange zest
1/2 cup fresh orange juice
1/4 cup olive oil
1 teaspoon grated lime zest
3 tablespoons fresh lime juice
1 teaspoon grated lemon zest
1 tablespoon fresh lemon juice
Salt and freshly ground black pepper, to
  taste

Divide tomatoes among 6 plates. Whisk all other ingredients together. Spoon a little of the dressing over each serving of tomatoes.
SERVES 6

TOMATOES WITH LEMON SLICES

These tomatoes are served without any dressing. I chop up the end pieces of the tomato and heap them on top of the slices.

4 medium to large ripe tomatoes, peeled and
  cut into thick slices (see Note)
2 lemons, sliced and seeded
Snipped fresh chives

Arrange tomatoes in rows with the slices alternating with lemon rounds. Let marinate in the refrigerator for 30 minutes before serving. Garnish with chives.

Note: I dip the tomatoes in boiling water a few hours before they are to be used and refrigerate them unpeeled until they are going to be served. Then I peel them at the last minute. If you peel them and let them sit in the refrigerator, they lose some of their texture and flavor.
SERVES 6

CREOLE TOMATOES WITH AVOCADO MAYONNAISE

Everyone in Louisiana looks forward to the arrival of the first Creole tomatoes of the season. Naturally, locals think they're the best, and I'm inclined to agree. But I was born in these parts. Must be in the genes.

6 medium ripe tomatoes, preferably Creole, peeled and sliced
Salt and freshly ground black pepper, to taste
1 ripe Hass avocado, peeled and pitted
2 tablespoons fresh lime juice
¼ cup mayonnaise
2 dashes of Worcestershire Sauce
2 dashes of Tabasco Sauce

Arrange tomatoes on 6 individual plates and sprinkle with salt and pepper.

Mash the other ingredients together. The amounts are at best mere guidelines. Add more of anything you like. Serve avocado mayonnaise on the side.

SERVES 6

CHOPPED LETTUCE AND TOMATO SALAD WITH PEPPER MAYONNAISE

Iceberg lettuce is what's used for this salad all over the South. Of course, you could substitute any crisp lettuce you fancy.

PEPPER MAYONNAISE
2 egg yolks
½ teaspoon salt
1 teaspoon red wine vinegar
½ teaspoon fresh lemon juice
¾ cup vegetable oil
¼ cup olive oil
1 tablespoon freshly ground black pepper

1 head iceberg lettuce, washed and coarsely chopped
2 very large tomatoes, peeled, seeded, and coarsely chopped
Salt, to taste

Process egg yolks, salt, and half the vinegar in a food processor for a few seconds to mix. With the machine running, add the remaining vinegar, the lemon juice, and the oils in a thin stream, continuing until all is incorporated. Mix in pepper.

Toss lettuce and tomatoes with a little of the pepper mayonnaise and arrange on individual serving plates. Add salt and serve remaining mayonnaise on the side.

SERVES 8

FETA AND TOMATO SALAD

This is another salad almost everyone has had.

4 large ripe tomatoes, peeled and thickly sliced
1 sweet yellow onion, such as Vidalia, or red onion, cut into medium rings, wilted (see page 60) or raw
¼ cup feta cheese, crumbled
1 tablespoon minced fresh Italian flat-leaf parsley
Mustard Vinaigrette (page 57)
Freshly ground black pepper

Arrange tomato slices on 4 individual plates. Top each with onions. Toss crumbled cheese and parsley together and sprinkle over all. Spoon a little mustard vinaigrette over the top and serve some on the side. Top with freshly ground black pepper.

SERVES 4

TOMATO ASPIC WITH MAYONNAISE

When this was made at home, our cook prepared extra to serve with sandwiches and the like. This recipe also will give you extras.

1/2 cup boiling water
2 envelopes unflavored gelatin
3 cups thick tomato juice, warmed
1 small onion, very finely minced
2 celery ribs, very finely minced
1 tablespoon fresh lemon juice
2 teaspoons Worcestershire Sauce
1 teaspoon salt
1/2 teaspoon freshly ground black pepper
1/2 teaspoon Tabasco Sauce
8 ounces cream cheese, softened
Homemade Mayonnaise (page 348)
Sprigs fresh Italian flat-leaf parsley or
*   watercress*

Pour the hot water into a shallow bowl and sprinkle gelatin over it. When gelatin is completely dissolved, stir in warmed tomato juice, making sure all lumps are gone; if they persist, reheat the mixture briefly. Stir in all other ingredients except cream cheese and cool slightly. Meanwhile, divide the cream cheese by spoonfuls among twelve 1/2-cup molds. Pour tomato mixture in each and refrigerate until set, several hours.

To serve, run a knife around the top of each mold and set in a bowl of hot water just long enough to loosen gelatin. Place a serving plate on top and invert to unmold. If water has melted the aspic too much, rerefrigerate long enough to set again. Put a dab of mayonnaise on each and garnish with a sprig of green, if you like.

SERVES 12

FRESH TOMATO AND FETA CHEESE ASPIC

5 tablespoons water
2 tablespoons unflavored gelatin
4 cups tomato pulp (see Note)
1 1/2 teaspoons salt
1 medium green bell pepper
1 small onion
2 tablespoons lemon juice
1 tablespoon Worcestershire Sauce
1/2 teaspoon Tabasco Sauce
1 cup feta cheese, in 1/4-inch cubes
Homemade Mayonnaise (page 348)

Put water in a deep saucer and sprinkle gelatin over it. Set aside.

Place tomato pulp in a small saucepan and stir in salt. Grate the green pepper and onion over the tomato pulp, allowing the juice and pulp of the pepper and onion to drop into the pan. Stir in lemon juice, Worcestershire, and Tabasco.

Heat mixture over medium heat and stir in softened gelatin. Continue to heat and stir until gelatin is dissolved, about 1 minute.

Pour half the mixture into a 4- to 6-cup ring mold. Place in the refrigerator. Allow the remaining tomato mixture to cool in the saucepan for about 30 minutes, then put it in the refrigerator. When the mixture in the mold is beginning to set—in about an hour or so—sprinkle the cheese over it and carefully pour the second batch of tomato mixture over the cheese. Some cheese may float to the top; if so, press it below the surface gently with your fingers or the back of a spoon. Return to the refrigerator and allow to jell completely, another hour at least.

An hour before serving, unmold by placing the mold in a pan of hot water just long enough to loosen the aspic, about 30 seconds. Place the serving plate over the mold and quickly invert. If the aspic does not come out, hold the inverted mold tightly against the plate and give it a good downward shake or two to loosen it. Return unmolded aspic to the refrigerator for an hour to allow any melted aspic to set again.

Serve with mayonnaise.

Note: There are several ways of "making" the tomato pulp, and my favorite is to roast the tomatoes (see page 20). Cut out the stem end and discard the skin. Put tomatoes through a strainer to remove seeds. Twelve tomatoes should give you about 4 cups of pulp. If you are a little short, add tomato juice.

SERVES 6 TO 8

SLICED TOMATOES WITH LEMON JUICE

If I had to choose just one way to eat tomatoes, I think my choice would be to simply top them with freshly squeezed lemon juice about 30 minutes prior to serving, with maybe a grind of black pepper (and salt if you like).

COMPOSED SALAD

Feel free to delete from or add to the list of vegetables below.

1 large onion
1 teaspoon olive oil
1 teaspoon balsamic vinegar
Salt and freshly ground black pepper, to taste
18 medium to large asparagus, woody ends snapped off
12 small red potatoes
Lettuce leaves for garnish (optional)
1 large red bell pepper, roasted, peeled, and seeded (see Note, page 74), cut into strips
6 hard-cooked eggs, peeled and halved
Roughly grated parmesan cheese
Peppercorn Vinaigrette (page 49)

Preheat oven to 350 degrees.

Peel onion and cut it through, top to root end, into 6 wedges. Tear off a square of foil and stand the cut onion in the center. Spoon the olive oil and balsamic vinegar over it and sprinkle with salt and pepper. Bring the corners of the foil up and twist to close, pressing the foil against the onion. Place on a small pan and bake for 1 hour and 20 minutes, until tender. Open the foil pack to let the onion cool.

Bring a skillet of salted water to a boil. Add asparagus and cook over medium-low heat for 4 or 5 minutes, until just barely tender. Drain and immediately run under cool water to stop the cooking. Pat dry and set aside. If not using right away, wrap the cooled asparagus in damp paper towels.

Scrub potatoes and cut each in quarters. Place in a saucepan and cover with cold water. Add salt to taste. Bring to a boil over high heat. Turn the heat down and cook at a slow boil for about 10 minutes, until tender. Drain the potatoes, rinse them in cold water, pat them dry, and set aside.

Have all ingredients at room temperature. Place a small, crisp lettuce leaf, if using, on a luncheon or dinner plate. Top this with 3 asparagus spears. Place a wide strip of roasted pepper over the asparagus. Surround the asparagus with a wedge of onion, some potatoes, and 2 egg halves. Sprinkle the whole plate with the roughly grated parmesan. Spoon a little vinaigrette over each serving.

SERVES 6

VARIATION

Prepare the recipe as above. Bring a medium pan of salted water to a boil. Add 18 large shrimp (in their shells) to the water and boil until pink and cooked through. Drain the shrimp, peel them, and add them to the plate.

VEGETABLE SALAD

Free feel to add any other vegetable you like, but blanch any fibrous ones.

1 cup julienned carrots
1 cup green beans, stems and strings removed
1 cup wax beans, stems and strings removed
1/4 cup green onions, with some of the green, cut into small rings
1/2 cup small yellow squash, cut into small rings
1 medium red bell pepper, roasted and cut into 1/4-inch strips (see Note)
3 tablespoons olive oil
1 tablespoon white wine vinegar
1/2 teaspoon salt
1/4 teaspoon freshly ground black pepper
1/4 cup chopped fresh dill (no stems)

Bring a medium saucepan of water to a boil over medium-high heat.

Add carrots and cook for 6 minutes, until just barely tender. Take carrots out with a skimmer and place in a bowl of ice water to stop the cooking. Add green and wax beans to the water and cook for 10 minutes, until just barely tender. Drain and place beans in the ice water with carrots. When vegetables are cool, drain them well and dry them with paper towels.

Place blanched vegetables in a large bowl with green onions, squash, and roasted pepper. Toss.

In a small bowl, whisk together olive oil, vinegar, salt, and pepper. Stir in dill and pour over vegetables. Toss.

Note: Here's my simple method for roasting peppers. Place 1 or 2 bell peppers on a foil-lined baking sheet and place under a preheated broiler. Turn them carefully with tongs from time to time until the skin is black and charred all over. Take them off the baking sheet and place in a small paper bag. Fold the bag shut and let sit for 15 to 20 minutes. Remove and discard the skin, core, and seeds.

SERVES 6

COOKED VEGETABLE SALAD

Vegetables may be lightly steamed or blanched. Dry well before using. I feel a starchy vegetable, such as potato, provides a nice balance to this combination.

1 carrot, julienned
1 cup broccoli spears
1 cup asparagus tips
1/4 pound green beans, tipped and stemmed
1 red bell pepper, roasted, peeled, and seeded (see Note, left), cut into strips
4 small new potatoes, boiled in their skins and cut in half
Red Wine Vinaigrette (page 44)
Homemade Mayonnaise (page 348)

Either toss all the ingredients together with a little vinaigrette (mayonnaise on the side), or arrange on individual plates and serve with vinaigrette and mayonnaise on the side. I like both dressings on my salad.

SERVES 6

SUMMER GARDEN SALAD

You can substitute any other combination of greens that you like.

HONEY-MUSTARD DRESSING
1 teaspoon Dijon mustard
1/2 teaspoon honey
1 tablespoon lemon juice
1 1/2 tablespoons olive oil

1/4 cup slivered almonds
1/2 cup peeled, seeded, and coarsely chopped cucumbers
1/2 cup coarsely chopped yellow summer squash
1/2 cup coarsely chopped zucchini
1/2 cup chopped radishes
1/2 cup chopped green bell peppers
1 cup torn red leaf lettuce
1 cup torn romaine

To make the dressing, place mustard, honey, lemon juice, and olive oil in the bottom of a large salad bowl and whisk together. Toss lightly with all salad ingredients.

SERVES 6 TO 8

MARINATED SUMMER MÉLANGE

During the middle of the warm months, when all sorts of young fresh vegetables are available, this is one of my favorite salads. You may use virtually any vegetable you like as long as it has a decent texture.

1/2 pound green beans, stemmed, tipped, and broken in half
2 carrots, scraped and cut into 1/2-inch rounds
1 zucchini, cut into 1/2-inch rounds
1 red bell pepper, cut into thick strips
1 cup cauliflower florets
1 celery rib, sliced thin
Red Wine Vinaigrette (page 44)
Lettuce leaves
4 small new potatoes, boiled in their jackets and quartered
6 green onions, with some of the green, coarsely chopped
4 tomatoes, cut into wedges

Toss together green beans, carrots, zucchini, pepper, cauliflower, and celery. Cover with vinaigrette and marinate overnight, covered. A glass jar with a seal top is a good container.

To serve, place lettuce on 6 individual salad plates, with a few potato quarters on top. Spoon the drained mixed vegetables over and top with chopped green onions. Garnish with tomato wedges.

SERVES 6

CHOPPED SPRING SALAD

I like this chopped fairly fine except maybe for the tomatoes, which should be a little coarser. If all you can find is big asparagus, blanch it.

1 cup diced red bell pepper
1 cup seeded and coarsely chopped tomato
1 cup shredded zucchini
1 cup thinly sliced, on the diagonal, tender thin asparagus
2 tablespoons olive oil
2 teaspoons balsamic vinegar
8 dashes Tabasco Sauce
Salt and freshly ground black pepper, to taste

Toss together pepper, tomato, zucchini, and asparagus. Whisk together the remaining ingredients. Dress just before serving (pour out any liquid that may have accumulated in the bottom of the bowl of vegetables before adding the dressing).

SERVES 8

WINTER VEGETABLE MÉLANGE

This is when I use dried beans. I often combine several kinds along with fresh vegetables.

1 cup cooked and drained navy beans
1 cup cooked and drained red kidney beans
1 cup frozen corn kernels, steamed and cooled
1 small onion, minced
1 small green bell pepper, coarsely chopped
Red Wine Vinaigrette (page 44)
Arugula leaves
Freshly ground black pepper

Toss the beans, corn, onion, and bell pepper with a bit of red wine vinaigrette. Arrange arugula leaves on a plate and top with vegetables and a grind of black pepper.

SERVES 6

CHOPPED WINTER SALAD

Let these vegetable quantities be a rough guide. You can add more of any one you might like. I use all of the dressing, but some people like their salad less dressed.

4 cups shredded and chopped green cabbage
1 large red bell pepper, diced
2 small carrots, scraped and shredded
1 large bunch watercress (8 ounces), stems included, coarsely chopped

BALLPARK MUSTARD DRESSING
5 tablespoons olive oil
2 tablespoons balsamic vinegar
1 teaspoon salt
1/2 teaspoon freshly ground black pepper
8 dashes Tabasco Sauce
2 generous teaspoons ballpark (yellow) mustard
2/3 cup prepared mayonnaise
1/3 cup low-fat sour cream
2 tablespoons minced shallots

In a large bowl, combine cabbage, red pepper, carrots, and watercress. Toss.

Combine oil, vinegar, salt, pepper, Tabasco, and mustard in a small bowl, and whisk until smooth. Add mayonnaise and sour cream. Stir until smooth. Stir in shallots.

Add about three quarters of the dressing to the vegetables and toss. Add the remainder, if desired.
SERVES 6

MELON AND GRAPE SALAD

Of course, almost any combination of melon will work, but in this case, watermelon and cantaloupe are awfully good.

1 cup cubed cantaloupe
1 cup cubed and seeded watermelon
2 cups green seedless grapes
5 tablespoons lime juice
1/2 cup honey
2 tablespoons Dijon mustard

Toss fruit with 1 tablespoon lime juice and refrigerate, covered. When ready to serve, pour out any liquid, drying out the serving bowl. Whisk together the remaining lime juice, honey, and mustard. Toss with the fruit.
SERVES 6

WATERMELON AND RED ONION SALAD

This is my take on Jeremiah Tower's inventive creation.

2 cups cubed seeded watermelon
1/2 red onion, thinly sliced
Raspberry Vinaigrette (page 44)
Boston lettuce leaves

Toss watermelon with red onion in a large bowl.

Pour on the dressing and toss with the watermelon and red onion. Cover and refrigerate until very cold. Serve on chilled plates, garnished with the lettuce.
SERVES 4

PASTA

I AM ASTONISHED WHEN I THINK HOW OUR UNDERSTANDING
and attitudes have changed toward pasta in the last ten years.
Time was when Italian cooking, in most folks' minds, meant
some version of spaghetti and meatballs. This, of course, was
before spaghetti became pasta—and pasta became multishaped
and multigrained. Slowly but surely, it began to dawn on us that

pasta could be sauced with anything from basic tomato to spicy
meat and/or vegetable combinations, to subtle cream and cheese
mixtures. ✦ Besides being versa-
tile, pasta is easy to prepare for a
large group. It can even be cooked
hours in advance, washed in cold
running water, dried, tossed with

little vegetable oil, and then set aside. To serve, plunge the pasta
into boiling water briefly and drain. ✦ Smaller portions of these
pasta dishes make fast first courses, side dishes for roasted meats,
and, with the addition of a green salad, good bread, and a glass of
wine, they can become quick lunches in themselves.

RIGATONI WITH WHITE BEANS, GREEN BEANS, AND PINE NUTS

1 cup dried cannellini beans, soaked
overnight or by the quick-soak method
(see Note, page 25)
6 cups Chicken Stock (page 41)
1 teaspoon dried oregano
Pinch of cayenne
2 large garlic cloves, crushed
1½ cups tipped, stemmed, and snapped
green beans
¾ pound dried rigatoni
Salt
¼ cup olive oil
4 tablespoons (½ stick) unsalted butter
Freshly ground black pepper, to taste
¾ cup pine nuts, toasted
Freshly grated parmesans, to taste

Drain the soaked cannellini beans and cover with 4 cups of stock. Add oregano, cayenne, and garlic. Bring to a medium boil, then reduce heat to low. Simmer until very tender, about 1 hour and 10 minutes. Cool in the liquid.

Cover green beans with remaining stock and bring to a simmer over medium heat. Cook until beans are just beginning to get tender, about 9 minutes. Set beans aside to cool in the liquid.

Cook rigatoni in a large pot of boiling salted water until tender. Meanwhile, in a skillet heat 2 tablespoons each of oil and butter. Drain cannellini and green beans, add to the skillet, and heat in the oil and butter. Place remaining oil and butter in a large bowl and heat it in the oven. Drain pasta and put into the heated bowl, then toss to coat. Add cannellini and green beans and toss. Season with salt and pepper. Place in individual heated bowls and sprinkle with pine nuts. Serve with grated parmesan.
SERVES 8

COLD SESAME NOODLES WITH CARROTS AND CUCUMBERS

The talented food writer Michael McLaughlin keeps a container of these spicy noodles in the refrigerator, handy for snacking.

⅔ cup peanut butter
⅔ cup plus 1 teaspoon dark sesame oil
½ cup soy sauce
½ cup freshly brewed strong black tea, hot
3 tablespoons (packed) dark brown sugar
2½ tablespoons Asian chili oil
2 tablespoons red wine vinegar
4 garlic cloves, peeled and chopped
1 slice of fresh ginger ¾ inch thick and
about 1 inch in diameter, peeled and
chopped
1 pound fresh linguine
1 tablespoon salt
3 green onions, with some of the green,
thinly sliced
1 cup peeled and coarsely shredded carrots
1 cup seeded and coarsely shredded English
or hothouse cucumber

In the bowl of a food processor fitted with a metal blade, combine peanut butter, ⅔ cup sesame oil, soy sauce, ¼ cup of the hot tea, sugar, chili oil, vinegar, garlic, and ginger and process until smooth. Add more tea by tablespoons and process briefly to thin the dressing as needed. It should be the consistency of melted ice cream.

Cook noodles in a large pot of boiling salted water until al dente. Drain and toss with remaining teaspoon of sesame oil to keep from sticking. Cool and toss with the sauce. Top with green onions, carrots, and cucumber.
SERVES 6

78

WAGON WHEELS WITH GREEN BEAN PURÉE

If you can't find ruoti—wagon-wheel–shaped pasta—substitute small shells or other pasta that will trap the sauce in its crevices.

1 pound green beans, trimmed
³⁄₄ cup Chicken Stock (page 41)
Salt, to taste
White pepper, to taste
¹⁄₂ cup crème fraîche
1¹⁄₂ pounds dried ruoti
3 tablespoons unsalted butter

Steam green beans until soft. Reduce stock to ¹⁄₂ cup over high heat Purée beans with stock in a food processor. Correct seasoning with salt and pepper. Remove to a double boiler and stir in the crème fraîche. Cook gently over barely simmering water; do not allow to boil.

Meanwhile, bring a large pot of salted water to a boil. Cook pasta until tender. Drain and toss with butter in a large bowl. Top with the warm purée just before serving.

SERVES 8

PASTA WITH BROCCOLI

1¹⁄₂ pounds broccoli, washed
4 tablespoons olive oil
3 garlic cloves, smashed
¹⁄₂ teaspoon crushed red pepper
¹⁄₄ cup Chicken Stock (page 41)
1 pound dried penne rigate or other medium pasta
4 tablespoons (¹⁄₂ stick) unsalted butter, melted
1 cup shaved parmesan
Salt, to taste
Freshly ground black pepper, to taste

Divide broccoli into florets and stems. Peel stems. Blanch florets and stems in a large pot of boiling salted water for 2 minutes, or until broccoli is bright green and still firm. Drain and run under cold water to stop the cooking. Chop florets and stems into 1¹⁄₂-inch pieces. Dry and set aside.

Heat olive oil in a large heavy pan and sauté garlic until it is tinged with brown, 2 to 3 minutes. Discard the garlic. Add broccoli, red pepper, and chicken stock and heat.

Meanwhile, cook pasta in a large pot of boiling salted water until tender. Drain pasta and toss with the broccoli, melted butter, parmesan, salt, and pepper. Serve immediately.

SERVES 6

PENNE WITH FENNEL AND ONIONS

The subtle flavor of fennel is a perfect complement to the sweet flavor of onions.

2 tablespoons unsalted butter
¹⁄₄ cup olive oil
1 pound yellow onions, roughly chopped
1¹⁄₂ pounds fennel bulb, trimmed and cut into strips the size of the penne
¹⁄₂ cup Chicken Stock (page 41)
¹⁄₄ teaspoon salt
¹⁄₄ teaspoon freshly ground black pepper
1 pound dried penne
Shaved parmesan

Melt butter with olive oil in a large skillet over medium-high heat. Add onions and sauté until lightly browned, 10 to 12 minutes.

Add fennel to the onions and stir to combine. Stir in chicken stock, salt, and pepper, and bring to a boil. Reduce the heat to medium-low, cover, and cook until fennel is crisp-tender.

Meanwhile, cook pasta in a large pot of boiling salted water until tender. Drain and toss with the sauce. Serve immediately with the parmesan.

SERVES 6

FETTUCCINE WITH ASPARAGUS AND ONION SAUCE

Other fresh vegetable combinations can be used instead of the asparagus and bell pepper, such as green onions and summer squash—both blanched as you would the asparagus.

4 tablespoons (1/2 stick) unsalted butter
1/3 cup plus 1 tablespoon olive oil
5 cups coarsely chopped onions
1/3 cup fine fresh bread crumbs, toasted (see Note)
3 ounces creamy mild goat cheese
Salt
3/4 pound asparagus, trimmed
1 pound dried fettuccine
1 large yellow bell pepper, seeded and cut into thin slices

Heat butter and 1/3 cup of olive oil in a heavy skillet over medium heat. Add onions and cook, stirring occasionally, until golden and slightly browned, 10 to 15 minutes. Set aside.

In a small bowl, combine bread crumbs and chèvre with a fork until crumbly. Set aside.

Bring a medium pot of water to a boil. Salt the water and blanch the asparagus for 3 minutes. Drain and plunge into cold water. Pat dry and cut diagonally into 1/2-inch pieces. Set aside.

Meanwhile, bring a large pot of water to a boil. Salt the water and cook the fettuccine until al dente.

Heat remaining 1 tablespoon olive oil in a medium skillet over medium heat. Add yellow bell pepper and cook, stirring, until pepper starts to get tender, about 3 minutes. Add asparagus and cook, tossing, for 1 or 2 minutes, until heated through.

Drain the pasta and return it to the cooking pot. Toss with the onions and divide among 6 warm plates. Top each serving with the asparagus and bell pepper mixture, using it all. Sprinkle with the chèvre–bread crumb mixture.
SERVES 6

Note: Fresh bread crumbs are best for this dish. To make them, remove the crusts from a slice of good white bread and run the bread through a food processor to make fine crumbs. Toast them in a dry skillet over medium heat, stirring, until they're golden brown, 5 to 7 minutes.

FETTUCCINE WITH GORGONZOLA AND WHITE CORN SAUCE

The thing to remember here is not to allow this sauce to boil after the cheese is stirred in or when it is reheated—it will become bitter.

6 tablespoons minced red onion
1/4 cup olive oil
1/4 teaspoon salt, or to taste
1 1/2 cups evaporated skimmed milk
6 ounces gorgonzola, crumbled
Tabasco Sauce, to taste
1 pound dried fettuccine
1 1/2 teaspoons grated fresh lemon zest
12 large basil leaves, cut into thin strips
6 large mint leaves, cut into thin strips
3 ears of white corn, kernels cut from cob and scraped (about 1 1/2 to 1 3/4 cups)
8 thick slices of bacon, fried crisp and chopped

Wilt onion in olive oil in a medium skillet over medium heat without browning, stirring, about 5 minutes. Add salt and evaporated milk, and heat. Add cheese and Tabasco, and continue to cook over medium-low heat, stirring, until melted and thickened. Remove from heat.

Put fettuccine on to cook in boiling salted water. When the pasta is almost done, reheat the sauce. Add lemon zest, basil, mint, and corn, stirring. Toss the drained pasta with about 1/2 cup of the sauce and divide among 8 warmed bowls. Top each serving with more sauce (use it all) and sprinkle with bacon.
SERVES 8

SPAGHETTI WITH GARLIC AND ROSEMARY OIL

This flavored oil was inspired by something I read by the great Marcella Hazan. If you have time, make this sauce the day before and leave it out in a cool spot, unrefrigerated and unstrained.

The oil is also delicious brushed on bread and grilled.

1 cup beef broth
2 tablespoons olive oil
6 tablespoons unsalted butter
4 fresh rosemary (3 inches) sprigs
4 large garlic cloves, coarsely chopped
3/4 pound dried spaghetti
Freshly grated parmesan, to taste

Reduce broth in a small saucepan over high heat to 1 tablespoon, about 20 minutes.

Heat olive oil and butter over medium heat in a small pot. Add rosemary and garlic. Cook until garlic begins to soften and browns lightly, about 5 minutes. Stir in reduced broth and set aside.

Cook spaghetti until al dente in boiling salted water. Drain and strain the infused oil over it. Toss. Serve with parmesan on the side.
SERVES 4

LINGUINE WITH GREENS AND PINE NUTS

Almost all greens are delicious as far as I'm concerned, and broccoli rabe is one of the best. Its flavor is strong, and here it is enhanced by garlic oil.

1 1/2 pounds broccoli rabe
1 tablespoon instant chicken bouillon
1/8 teaspoon crushed red pepper
Salt, to taste
1/2 pound dried linguine
1/4 cup olive oil
2 large garlic cloves, finely minced
4 ounces pine nuts, darkly toasted

Cut large stems from broccoli rabe and discard. Place in a very large container of water and let soak. Carefully lift rabe from the water, giving it a few shakes, and place in a large, deep pot with just the water clinging to the leaves. Sprinkle instant bouillon over all. Cover and cook until tender, about 8 minutes, depending on the age of the rabe. Stir and turn over several times during the cooking and shake the pan back and forth. When cooked, quickly boil off the liquid (uncovered). If this takes too long, pour out liquid. Add crushed red pepper and toss; add salt. Using 2 knives, chop the broccoli rabe into coarse bits.

Cook linguine in a large pot of boiling salted water until al dente. Meanwhile, warm olive oil and add garlic. Warm for 10 minutes, covered, to flavor the oil. Do not cook. Turn up heat and sauté, uncovered, for a few minutes until garlic is just starting to turn color. Stir and pour over the broccoli rabe. Drain fettuccine and toss with broccoli rabe, using 2 forks to disperse it evenly in the pasta. Top each serving with pine nuts.
SERVES 4

TORTELLINI AND WILD MUSHROOMS WITH BUTTERMILK DRESSING

White mushrooms, or a combination of mushrooms, may be substituted.

> 2 tablespoons light vegetable oil
> 2 medium garlic cloves, minced
> 2 shallots, minced
> 1/2 pound fresh shiitake or chanterelle mushrooms, sliced
> 1 cup dry white wine
> 1/4 cup chopped fresh Italian flat-leaf parsley
> 1 pound cheese-filled tortellini, cooked according to package instructions
> Buttermilk Dressing (recipe follows)
> Chopped nasturtiums (optional)

Heat oil in a large skillet. Add half the garlic and shallots and sauté over medium heat until wilted, about 5 minutes. Add mushrooms and sauté 8 to 10 minutes over low heat, until mushrooms give up liquid and begin to get tender. Add wine and remaining garlic and shallots along with half the parsley. Toss and sauté an additional 2 to 3 minutes, until mushrooms are tender.

Toss cooked tortellini with dressing. Sprinkle with remaining parsley and surround with mushrooms. Garnish with nasturtiums, if using.

SERVES 6 TO 8

BUTTERMILK DRESSING

> 2 cups buttermilk
> 8 ounces low-fat cream cheese
> 2 medium garlic cloves, minced
> 1/2 teaspoon Tabasco Sauce
> Freshly ground black pepper, to taste

Place all ingredients except pepper in a food processor. Process until smooth. Add pepper and refrigerate until ready to use. May be made a day in advance.

MAKES ABOUT 3 CUPS

ORZO WITH ONIONS AND BLACK OLIVES

Orzo with onions and olives is always a winner. I serve it very often in both summer and winter.

> 4 tablespoons (1/2 stick) unsalted butter
> 2 cups coarsely chopped onions
> 1 cup pitted oil-cured black olives
> 2 cups orzo
> Salt and freshly ground black pepper, to taste

Melt butter over medium to low heat and add onions. Sauté until soft but not browned, about 5 minutes. Toss in olives and set aside.

Boil orzo in well-salted water until tender and drain well. Place onion-olive mixture over low heat to warm it, then toss orzo in with it. Season with salt and pepper.

SERVES 6

FETTUCCINE WITH RED BELL PEPPER SAUCE

This is the same sauce I serve with stuffed crepes (see page 321). It may be used in many other ways—on fish or roast veal.

> 2 tablespoons unsalted butter
> 2 tablespoons olive oil
> 2 1/4 cups chopped red onions
> 2 large garlic cloves, minced
> 3 large red bell peppers, roasted, peeled, and seeded (see Note, page 74), chopped
> 2 cups Chicken Stock (page 41)
> 1/4 teaspoon freshly ground black pepper
> Salt, to taste
> 3/4 pound dried fettuccine
> Freshly grated parmesan, to taste

Heat butter and oil in a large skillet over medium heat and sauté onions until they start to turn slightly brown in spots, about 4 minutes. Add garlic and sauté another minute.

Add peppers and cook another 2 minutes. Add stock and black pepper. Cook for 10 minutes. Transfer to a food processor and purée; add salt.

Cook fettuccine in a large pot of boiling salted water until al dente. Drain and toss with sauce and place in heated individual bowls. Serve with grated parmesan.

SERVES 4

ANGEL HAIR WITH SPINACH, TOMATOES, AND THREE CHEESES

Pasta is always a delightful main dish for a simple supper. Here is another great one for your files. If the tomatoes are not really fresh and ripe, it is better to use canned.

6 tablespoons olive oil
3 medium garlic cloves, chopped
3 pounds fresh spinach, washed, stemmed, drained, and coarsely chopped
³/₄ cup freshly grated asiago or parmesan
³/₄ pound ricotta cheese
³/₄ pound mascarpone cheese
1¹/₂ cups coarsely chopped walnuts
¹/₄ teaspoon grated nutmeg
³/₄ teaspoon salt
¹/₄ teaspoon freshly ground black pepper
3 cups fresh tomato sauce (see Note)
¹/₄ cup coarsely chopped fresh basil
1¹/₂ pounds dried angel hair pasta

Place olive oil in a large frying pan. Sauté garlic over medium-high heat for about 2 minutes, until golden brown. Add spinach and cook until limp, tossing, about 5 minutes. Remove from heat and place in a large bowl. Toss with asiago cheese and set aside.

In another bowl, combine ricotta, mascarpone, walnuts, nutmeg, salt, and pepper. Bring a large pot of water to a boil.

Meanwhile, in a medium saucepan, heat tomato sauce, adding basil. Cook about 5 minutes, to completely incorporate basil flavor.

Place pasta in boiling salted water and cook only 1 minute if fresh, according to package instructions if dried. Drain pasta and immediately toss with the tomato sauce.

Place pasta in 8 warmed serving bowls. Top each with a scoop of the spinach mixture and one of the ricotta mixture. Toss lightly.

Note: To make fresh tomato sauce, peel and seed 3 pounds of plum tomatoes and add salt to taste. Simmer over low heat to reduce liquid by half, 45 minutes to 1 hour.

SERVES 8

FUSILLI WITH RED ONION, TOMATO, BASIL, AND GOAT CHEESE

This is one of my all-time favorite summer pasta dishes.

1 pound dried fusilli
¹/₄ cup olive oil
2 tablespoons butter
1¹/₂ cups roughly chopped red onions
1¹/₂ pounds ripe tomatoes, peeled, seeded, and roughly chopped
¹/₂ cup tightly packed shredded basil leaves
4 ounces fresh goat cheese, crumbled
¹/₂ teaspoon salt
¹/₄ teaspoon freshly ground black pepper

Cook the pasta in plenty of boiling salted water until tender.

Meanwhile, heat oil and butter in a large skillet.

Drain the pasta. Add it to the skillet and toss with the hot butter and oil mixture. Turn off the heat. Add onions, tomatoes, and basil and toss to mix well. Add cheese and toss to combine. Season with salt and pepper. Serve at once.

SERVES 4

RIGATONI WITH YELLOW TOMATOES, PEPPERS, AND CORN

Tomato sauce in almost any form freezes very well, so I make several batches to enjoy later in the year. If you want to freeze this sauce, make it up to the point of adding the corn and prosciutto. Then toss the prosciutto in the butter as directed, but do not cook the corn. Put it in the mixture raw; it will cook when the sauce is rewarmed later.

4 medium to large onions, unpeeled
2 large garlic cloves, unpeeled
4 large yellow bell peppers, roasted, peeled, and seeded (see Note, page 74)
2 tablespoons olive oil
3 pounds yellow tomatoes, peeled and seeded
1 teaspoon salt
1/4 teaspoon freshly ground black pepper
1 1/2 tablespoons finely chopped fresh tarragon leaves
2 tablespoons finely chopped fresh Italian flat-leaf parsley
1 pound dried rigatoni
3 tablespoons unsalted butter
4 ounces prosciutto, diced
4 ears of corn, kernels cut from cob (about 2 1/4 to 2 1/2 cups)
Freshly grated parmesan

Preheat oven to 425 degrees.

Roast the onions and garlic until soft to the touch. Onions will take from 1 to 1 1/4 hours, garlic cloves about 25 minutes. Cut up peppers and purée them in a food processor. Set aside.

Peel onions and garlic and purée them together. Heat olive oil in a large skillet and add onion-garlic purée. Stir to mix and add tomatoes. Simmer for about 25 minutes, or until they fall apart. When this is simmering briskly, add salt, black pepper, and tarragon. Add parsley in the last 10 minutes and stir in the puréed peppers.

Put a large pot of salted water on to boil.

When it is boiling rapidly, put in the rigatoni and cook until tender. Rigatoni should be cooked more than al dente.

While the pasta is cooking, melt 2 tablespoons of the butter in a medium skillet and add diced prosciutto. Sauté a minute or two to heat through and then add corn. Cook corn until just done. This will be only a few minutes. Add prosciutto and corn to the heated tomato mixture. Mix well.

Drain the pasta and toss with the remaining 1 tablespoon of butter. Put in 8 individual warmed bowls and top with the sauce. Sprinkle with grated parmesan and serve immediately.
SERVES 8

PENNE WITH MIXED GRILLED VEGETABLES

6 thick slices of peeled eggplant
Salt
3 medium leeks, well washed and blanched
6 large diagonal slices of zucchini
3 medium red bell peppers, cut into quarters, lengthwise, and seeded
Olive oil
Salt and freshly ground black pepper, to taste
1 1/2 pounds dried penne
2 tablespoons unsalted butter
2 cups Basic Tomato Sauce (page 352), heated
Balsamic or red wine vinegar, to taste

Sprinkle eggplant slices generously with salt and allow to drain for 30 minutes. Wash off salt and pat dry.

Cut blanched leeks in half lengthwise. Rub eggplant, leeks, zucchini, and bell peppers generously with olive oil. Place zucchini and peppers on the grill. Sprinkle with salt and pepper. Cook about 1 minute, then add eggplant slices and leeks. Sprinkle with salt and pepper. Cook all about 4 minutes longer, turning and sprinkling other sides with salt and pepper.

Meanwhile, cook the penne in a large pot of boiling salted water until tender. Drain and add butter to pot. Dump pasta back in and toss. Add tomato sauce and toss.

Cut vegetables into large chunks. Put pasta on individual plates and top each serving with vegetables. Sprinkle vegetables with a little vinegar.

SERVES 8

ORECCHIETTE WITH TOMATOES, CILANTRO, AND GOAT CHEESE

This "little ear" pasta is also very good served with roasted meats.

1 cup dry white wine
4 large tomatoes, peeled and seeded,
  chopped, with juice reserved
1 cup green onions, with some of the green,
  roughly chopped
2 heaping tablespoons finely chopped
  cilantro
1/2 pound dried orecchiette
6 ounces mild goat cheese
Salt and freshly ground black pepper, to
  taste
Cilantro leaves

In a large nonreactive skillet, combine wine and tomato juice and bring to a boil. Cook over medium heat until reduced by half, about 5 minutes. Add tomatoes, green onions, and cilantro and simmer for about 2 minutes. Set aside.

Meanwhile, cook pasta in lightly salted water until tender. Drain and add to the sauce. Reheat quickly if necessary. Crumble cheese and add; toss and season with salt and pepper. Garnish with cilantro leaves.

SERVES 4

FETTUCCINE WITH SPICY TOMATO AND BACON SAUCE

I've made this pasta almost everywhere we have gone for a vacation. The necessary ingredients are almost always available in one form or another. If there are no fresh tomatoes, substitute a large can of tomatoes, drained and chopped.

1/2 pound thick bacon slices
3 tablespoons olive oil
2 1/2 large onions, chopped
3 garlic cloves, crushed
5 large tomatoes (about 3 pounds), peeled,
  seeded, and chopped
1 tablespoon salt
1 tablespoon dried tarragon
1/4 teaspoon crushed red pepper or cayenne
1 teaspoon freshly ground black pepper
4 tablespoons finely chopped fresh Italian
  flat-leaf parsley
1 pound dried fettuccine
Unsalted butter
Grated parmesan

Fry bacon until crisp, drain on paper towels, and set aside. Pour out all the fat except for 1 tablespoon. Add olive oil to this, and when hot, add onions. Wilt (about 5 minutes) and add garlic and tomatoes. Simmer for a few minutes, then add salt, tarragon, and red and black peppers. Simmer for 30 minutes, stirring occasionally. Add parsley. Simmer for 5 minutes. Crumble the bacon and stir it in. The sauce may be used now or reheated later.

To serve, cook the pasta in a large quantity of boiling salted water until al dente. Drain. Put it back in the pot and toss with a little butter. Mix with some of the sauce and pass the rest. top each serving with freshly grated parmesan.

SERVES 6

PASTA SAUSAGE

One of the best things about this dish, aside from the way it tastes and looks on the plate, is that it does not have to be served piping hot—so long as it is not refrigerator-cold, it is fine.

The taste of lemon zest is a very pleasant addition of flavor. So far as I am concerned, edible garnishes that enhance the taste of the dish are a must whenever possible.

One 12 × 15-inch sheet of fresh pasta,
  homemade or store-bought (see Note)
2 tablespoons unsalted butter
1/2 cup diced boiled ham
4 large green onions, finely chopped
1 ounce dried mushrooms, soaked, patted
  dry, and coarsely chopped
5 ounces stemmed fresh or frozen spinach,
  steamed and squeezed dry
8 ounces cream cheese, at room temperature
1/4 cup parmesan
1/2 cup ricotta
1 egg
1/8 teaspoon white pepper
3 tablespoons finely chopped fresh Italian
  flat-leaf parsley
3 ounces prosciutto, sliced
Melted butter for sealing edges
Chicken Stock (page 41)
Zest of 1 lemon, cut into thin strips
Uncooked Green Sauce (page 93)

Lay out the pasta on a sheet of wax paper. Cover with another sheet of wax paper and set aside.

Melt butter and add ham, green onions, and mushrooms. Sauté for 3 minutes. Mix in spinach. Set aside. In another bowl, beat together cream cheese, parmesan, and ricotta. Add egg, pepper, parsley, and ham mixture. Mix well.

Spread the mixture on the pasta sheet, leaving a 2-inch border at one of the short ends. Arrange the prosciutto on top of that. Brush the edge with melted butter. Roll up the pasta like a jelly roll. Wrap it in a doubled piece of cheesecloth. Tie the ends very securely.

Fill a large kettle (or a fish poacher) with chicken stock and bring to a boil. Place the pasta roll in the stock and simmer gently for 25 minutes. Remove and drain. Let it rest for a few minutes before carefully removing the cheesecloth. Garnish with strips of lemon zest. Slice into 1/2-inch pieces after the roll has cooled slightly, making sure each portion has a few lemon strips on top. Serve with Uncooked Green Sauce.

Note: You can buy sheets of pasta fresh at some Italian markets and specialty shops. They are also available frozen, in which case let them thaw out before using them. If you cannot find a 12 × 15-inch sheet, join two sheets by overlapping them slightly, dampening the seam where they join, and then pressing them together.
SERVES 8

ORZO WITH BUTTER AND PARSLEY

Orzo is one of the many kinds of 100-percent semolina pasta now available. Cooked, it looks a lot like long-grain rice. After it is buttered, it will hold in a warm spot on the stove.

1/2 pound orzo
3 tablespoons unsalted butter, melted
3 tablespoons finely chopped fresh Italian
  flat-leaf parsley
Salt and freshly ground black pepper, to
  taste
Paprika (optional)

Cook the orzo in a medium pot of boiling salted water until tender, testing frequently for doneness. Drain and put back into the pot. Mix in the butter and parsley. Correct seasoning if necessary. Add a dash of paprika, if you like.
SERVES 4

PENNE WITH CABBAGE AND LAMB

The lamb sauce has to cook for three hours, but it's the sort of sauce that can be made a few days in advance—as a matter of fact, it's better if it is.

LAMB SAUCE

1 ounce dried porcini mushrooms
2 cups hot water
10 tablespoons olive oil
8 cups sliced onions
3½ tablespoons minced garlic
½ pound fresh white mushrooms, sliced
Salt and freshly ground black pepper
1½ pounds very well trimmed boneless lamb
  shoulder or leg, cut into 1-inch pieces
Flour, for dredging
1½ cups dry white wine, warmed
2 cups beef stock, warmed
1 large bay leaf
5 fresh rosemary sprigs (4 inches)

HOT OIL

1 tablespoon crushed red pepper
½ cup olive oil

CABBAGE

1 large head green cabbage, about 2
  pounds, cored and coarsely shredded
3 tablespoons rice wine vinegar
1 teaspoon salt
1 teaspoon freshly ground black pepper

1 pound dried penne

To make the lamb sauce: Place porcini in a bowl and cover with the hot water. Allow to sit for at least 1 hour. Drain, reserving liquid. Pour liquid through a fine cloth to remove any grit. Set aside.

Heat 4 tablespoons of the oil in a large skillet and sauté onions until brown, about 12 minutes. Add garlic and sauté another minute. Remove onions and garlic with a slotted spoon and set aside.

Add 2 more tablespoons of the oil to the pan and sauté white mushrooms until golden, about 2 minutes. Remove and add to the onions and garlic. Set aside.

Salt and pepper the lamb pieces liberally and dredge them in flour. Using the same pan and the remaining oil, sauté the meat in batches until very brown.

When all the meat is browned, return it to the pan along with the onion mixture and the porcini mushrooms. Add the wine, stock, mushroom liquid, bay leaf, and rosemary. Bring to a boil, reduce to a simmer, cover, and cook very slowly for 2 hours, stirring occasionally. Remove the lid and simmer for another hour or until the meat is falling apart and the sauce is thick. If necessary, thin the sauce with just a little water or stock. Correct seasoning.

To make the hot oil: Combine crushed red pepper and oil in a small saucepan. Heat over medium heat. When oil is hot but not boiling, remove from heat and set aside to cool.

Strain before using, discarding crushed red pepper.

To make the cabbage: Place cabbage in a glass bowl and toss in remaining ingredients. Cover tightly with plastic wrap. Make a steam hole in the top and cook in the microwave on highest setting until crisp-tender, about 5 minutes in a full-power oven. Allow to rest, still covered, for another several minutes. If it's not cooked to your taste, you can cook it slightly longer, but it should not be too limp.

To do this without a microwave, combine the cabbage and other ingredients in a stainless-steel skillet. Cook over medium heat, stirring frequently, until it's crisp-tender, about 5 minutes.

To assemble the dish: Cook pasta according to package directions. Toss with 2 tablespoons of the strained hot oil (reserve any leftover oil for another time) and all the cooked cabbage. Divide among 8 warmed serving bowls and top each with lamb sauce. (Do not serve with cheese.)

SERVES 6

SPAGHETTI WITH BACON AND BAKED TOMATO SAUCE

The tomatoes in this recipe are cooked in an unusual—and easy—way. Put them in to bake while you fry the bacon and onions and bring the pasta water to a boil. Dinner will be on the table in less than half an hour.

2 pounds fresh tomatoes, peeled
Salt and freshly ground black pepper, to taste
Pinch of crushed red pepper
3/4 cup good olive oil
6 strips of thick bacon
2 cups coarsely chopped onions
1 1/2 pounds dried spaghetti
2 tablespoons chopped fresh Italian flat-leaf parsley
Freshly grated parmesan

Preheat oven to 400 degrees and put a large pot of salted water on to boil.

Slice each tomato into 3 thick rounds. Place a layer of tomato slices on the bottom of an ovenproof baking dish. Sprinkle with salt and pepper. Place another layer on top of this and sprinkle with salt and pepper as well as the pinch of red pepper. (Crushed red pepper is very necessary to the taste of this dish, but as it is also very potent, use less than 1/4 teaspoon.) Finish off with the final layer of tomatoes and sprinkle with salt and pepper. Pour 1/2 cup of the olive oil over the tomatoes and bake, uncovered, for 20 minutes.

While tomatoes are baking, fry bacon until crisp. Set aside to drain on paper towels.

Pour off all the rendered bacon fat and wipe out the skillet. Return 1 tablespoon of fat and the remaining 1/4 cup olive oil to the skillet. Bring to high heat and add onions; reduce the heat to medium and cook the onions until they become wilted and softened. Set aside. Crumble the bacon and set aside.

About 5 minutes before the tomatoes are to come out, put the spaghetti in to boil. Cook until al dente and drain. While it is draining, pour the tomatoes into a large warmed bowl, then sprinkle the onions over them. Place cooked spaghetti on top of the sauce and sprinkle with bacon and parsley. Toss gently to mix well. Serve with grated cheese on the side.
SERVES 6

FETTUCCINE WITH FOUR CHEESES

If you like, add some chopped prosciutto. As a matter of fact, by adding ham and steamed fresh green peas to this dish you have the makings of a quick and easy Sunday supper. All you need then is a salad and a bit of fruit for dessert.

1/2 cup minced onion
1 tablespoon minced garlic
1/4 cup (1/2 stick) unsalted butter
1 cup ricotta cheese
4 ounces mild goat cheese
1/2 teaspoon salt
Pinch of cayenne
1 1/2 ounces freshly grated parmesan
1 pound dried fettuccine, cooked al dente and drained
1/2 cup mild olive oil, heated
1/2 pound mozzarella, cut into small cubes
2 tablespoons chopped fresh chives

Sauté onion and garlic in butter until just wilted, 4 to 5 minutes. Stir in ricotta and goat cheese. Let cheese melt over low heat, stirring. Mix in salt, cayenne, and parmesan.

Toss pasta and oil together, then add the ricotta mixture and toss again. Add mozzarella and chives and toss quickly. Serve before the mozzarella has a chance to melt completely.

Serve on individual warmed plates, with additional parmesan on the side, if desired.
SERVES 6

PASTA WITH CRAWFISH SAUCE

This recipe is typical of the way crawfish are cooked throughout Louisiana, only there, more cayenne is used. So add as much as you like, but if you are not familiar with it use a light touch, because a little cayenne can be mighty powerful.

When choosing pasta for this dish, use something with a shape that will capture some of the sauce in it, like spirals or shells.

3 tablespoons unsalted butter
2 tablespoons safflower oil
4 tablespoons all-purpose flour
1/2 cup finely chopped shallots
1 cup finely chopped onion
3/4 cup finely chopped green bell pepper
3/4 cup finely chopped celery
2 tablespoons finely chopped celery leaves
   (optional)
3 cups Fish Stock (page 42)
2 large garlic cloves, crushed
2 cups cooked crawfish tails, with fat if possible (see Note)
1 tablespoon tomato paste
1 tablespoon Worcestershire Sauce
2 teaspoons fresh lemon juice
1 teaspoon salt
1 teaspoon freshly ground black pepper
1/8 teaspoon cayenne
1 tablespoon capers, rinsed and drained
1 tablespoon chopped fresh Italian flat-leaf parsley
1 pound dried medium shape pasta
Chopped green onion tops

Put 2 tablespoons of the butter and the oil in a skillet with flour and cook slowly, moving it around with the back of a pancake turner, until it turns golden brown. Immediately add vegetables and continue to cook, stirring and scraping the bottom, for 5 minutes or so, until they are wilted. In the meantime, put on the fish stock to heat. When vegetables have wilted,

add about 2 cups of stock and stir as it thickens. Add garlic and crawfish. Stir and then add tomato paste, Worcestershire, lemon juice, salt, black pepper, and cayenne. Add the rest of the stock and simmer for about 5 minutes more. Add capers and parsley. Set aside.

Cook pasta in a large quantity of salted water until tender. Drain it, then dump it back in the hot pot and mix with remaining tablespoon of butter. Divide it among individual warmed bowls and top with the crawfish sauce. Sprinkle with chopped green onion tops. Do not add cheese.

Note: If you are using frozen crawfish tails, cook them just as you would shrimp.
SERVES 6

BUCATINI WITH BLACK PEPPER, BREAD CRUMBS, AND PECORINO

The bread crumbs give this a little extra crunch, but leave them out if you're in a hurry. Parmesan could be substituted for the pecorino.

1/4 cup olive oil
4 tablespoons (1/2 stick) unsalted butter
1 cup grated hard pecorino
1 tablespoon freshly ground black pepper, or to taste
3/4 pound dried bucatini, also called perciatelli
1 cup fresh bread crumbs, toasted

Heat oil and butter together. Combine cheese and pepper.

Cook the pasta in boiling salted water until tender. Drain and put into a heated bowl. Pour the oil and butter over and toss quickly. Add the cheese and pepper and toss again. Place in individual serving bowls and top each serving with a sprinkling of bread crumbs.
SERVES 6

ROTINI WITH SMOKED SALMON, GOAT CHEESE, AND CORN

I used to make creamy cheese-based sauces with reduced heavy cream, but now I use evaporated skimmed milk instead.

6 tablespoons minced red onion
1/4 cup olive oil
1/2 teaspoon salt, or to taste
1 1/2 cups evaporated skimmed milk
8 ounces mild goat cheese, crumbled
1 1/2 teaspoons Tabasco Sauce
1 pound dried rotini
1 tablespoon grated lemon zest
1/2 teaspoon lemon pepper
12 large basil leaves, cut into strips
6 large mint leaves, cut into strips
3 ears white corn kernels, cut from the cob
  (1 1/2 to 1 3/4 cups)
10 ounces smoked salmon, cut into large
  pea-size pieces or flaked, all bones out
6 basil leaves, cut into strips
3 mint leaves, cut into strips

Wilt onion in olive oil in a medium skillet over medium heat without browning, stirring, about 5 minutes. Add salt and milk and heat. Add cheese and Tabasco and continue to cook over medium heat, stirring, until thick and smooth. Remove from heat.

Put pasta on to cook in boiling salted water and when it's almost done, reheat the sauce. Stir in lemon zest, lemon pepper, basil, mint, and corn.

When pasta is done, drain and place in a warm bowl. Mix salmon into the sauce and pour half over the pasta, tossing. Divide among 6 to 8 individual warmed plates. Place a large spoonful of the sauce on each and sprinkle with strips of basil and mint.

SERVES 6 TO 8

SPAGHETTI WITH TUNA, OLIVES, CAPERS, AND CAYENNE

3 cups Basic Tomato Sauce (page 352),
  heated
1 cup sliced pimiento-stuffed green olives
6 tablespoons capers, drained
1 can (6 1/2 ounces) tuna in oil, drained
Cayenne, to taste
1 1/2 pounds dried spaghetti
2 tablespoons unsalted butter
Freshly grated parmesan

Heat tomato sauce and stir in olives, capers, and tuna, breaking tuna chunks with a fork. Add cayenne and set aside.

Cook spaghetti in plenty of well-salted water. When it's cooked al dente, drain it. Add butter to the pot and dump hot, drained pasta in, tossing. Add 1 1/2 cups of sauce to the pasta and toss. Top each serving with 1/4 cup of the remaining sauce and a sprinkling of parmesan.

SERVES 8

CONCHIGLIE WITH GRILLED CHICKEN BREASTS AND GOAT CHEESE

3 large boned chicken breasts, cut in half
6 tablespoons fresh lime juice
6 tablespoons olive oil
3 large garlic cloves, sliced thin
1½ pounds dried conchiglie (medium shells)
2 tablespoons unsalted butter
2 cups Basic Tomato Sauce (page 352), heated
1½ cups cubed goat cheese
Freshly ground black pepper

Place chicken in a shallow dish. Whisk together lime juice, oil, and garlic; pour over chicken. Cover and marinate for at least 2 hours, in the refrigerator, turning once. Grill until done over coals or under the broiler, about 5 to 7 minutes per side. (It depends on how hot the coals are and how close the chicken is to them.) Do not overcook.

Meanwhile, cook pasta in plenty of boiling salted water until tender. Drain and add butter to pot. Dump pasta back in and toss. Add sauce and toss, then add cheese and toss again. Place on individual warm plates. Skin the chicken breast halves, discarding skin, and slice. Place on top of each plate of pasta. Top with a grind or two of black pepper.

SERVES 6

PASTA SHELLS WITH UNCOOKED TUNA AND TOMATO SAUCE

If you are not too keen on anchovies, reduce the amount called for by half or even more. But don't leave them out altogether, as they are an important element.

1 can (6½ ounces) Italian tuna in olive oil, drained
1 can flat anchovies, drained and chopped
½ cup black oil-cured olives, pitted and chopped
5 tablespoons basil olive oil (see Note)
2 tablespoons safflower oil
1 tablespoon fresh lemon juice
¼ cup finely chopped fresh Italian flat-leaf parsley
3 medium garlic cloves, mashed and finely chopped
6 green onions, with some of the green, finely chopped
1 pound dried medium shells
2 medium tomatoes, coarsely chopped

Break up tuna into small pieces and add all remaining ingredients except pasta and tomatoes. Mix thoroughly and cover. Refrigerate overnight.

To serve, let the sauce come to room temperature and cook the shells in a large quantity of boiling salted water until tender. Drain and toss with the sauce. Sprinkle with chopped tomatoes or pass the tomatoes separately.

Note: Put 2 teaspoons dried basil in 5 tablespoons olive oil and let it marinate for several days. Strain the oil, discarding the solids.

SERVES 6

PASTA SAUCES

FRESH TOMATO SAUCE

*2 cups peeled, seeded, and coarsely chopped
    tomatoes*
2 tablespoons balsamic vinegar
1 teaspoon salt
1/2 teaspoon white pepper
1 tablespoon minced fresh dill

Place all ingredients in a blender or food
processor and process just long enough to
blend.
MAKES ENOUGH FOR 1 POUND OF
PASTA

UNCOOKED TOMATO SAUCE

You have to let your taste buds be your guide
here. When you toss this together, add the
smaller amounts of vinegar and oil, a little salt
and pepper, and a dash of Tabasco if you like.
Taste and go on from there.

*6 medium to large tomatoes, cut into large
    chunks*
1 small garlic clove, minced
1 tablespoon minced shallot
1/2 medium onion, chopped
3 tablespoons coarsely chopped fresh basil
3 to 4 tablespoons balsamic vinegar
6 to 8 tablespoons olive oil
Salt and freshly ground black pepper, to taste
Tabasco Sauce, to taste (optional)

Drain off and discard any liquid from the
tomatoes. Mix tomatoes with all of the remaining ingredients. Let the mixture stand at room
temperature for about 20 minutes.
MAKES ENOUGH FOR 1 1/2 POUNDS OF
PASTA

SMOKED TOMATO SAUCE

This sauce is especially good on angel hair
pasta. Shaved curls of Romano cheese complement it nicely.

*3 pounds Smoked Tomatoes, peeled and
    seeded (page 143)*
1 1/2 teaspoons chopped fresh thyme
2 small bay leaves
1/4 teaspoon dried oregano
1/4 teaspoon dried marjoram
1 tablespoon paprika
1 teaspoon minced garlic
Pinch of crushed red pepper
1/4 cup Chicken Stock (page 41)
2 tablespoons rice wine vinegar
1/4 cup heavy cream
*4 tablespoons (1/2 stick) unsalted butter,
    softened*

Put tomatoes in a saucepan over medium heat.
Add thyme, bay leaves, oregano, marjoram,
paprika, garlic, and crushed red pepper.
Simmer for 6 to 8 minutes, stirring occasionally. Remove from the heat. Discard bay leaves.
Purée mixture in a food processor. Return it to
the heat and stir in stock and vinegar. Bring to
a boil, turn the heat down, and simmer for
another 6 to 8 minutes to thicken the sauce.

To finish the sauce, add cream and reheat.
Off the heat, beat in butter. Correct the season-
ing if necessary.
MAKES ENOUGH FOR 1 POUND OF
PASTA

TOMATO AND RED BELL PEPPER SAUCE

The flavor of this sauce is dependent on the freshness of the tomatoes. If they are not vine ripened you should boost the sauce's flavor with a little tomato paste before continuing. Do this sparingly, however, tasting as you go along.

1/4 cup olive oil

3 medium garlic cloves, cut in half

3 large onions, coarsely chopped

3 1/2 pounds ripe tomatoes, peeled, seeded, and chopped

16 fresh tarragon leaves

15 Italian flat-leaf parsley sprigs, without stems, finely chopped

1 very large red bell pepper, roasted, peeled and seeded (see Note, page 74)

1 teaspoon salt

1/4 teaspoon freshly ground black pepper

2 tablespoons tomato paste (optional)

Heat oil in a large skillet and add garlic. Mashing down on the pieces, sauté it until it starts to brown, then remove and discard it. Sauté onions in the oil until they are translucent and then add tomatoes and tarragon leaves. Simmer for 30 minutes. Add parsley and simmer for another 10 minutes.

Purée in a food processor (this may be either smooth or coarse) and return it to the pan. Purée bell pepper, add it and the salt, black pepper, and tomato paste to the sauce, and simmer for 5 minutes.

MAKES ENOUGH FOR 2 POUNDS OF PASTA

UNCOOKED GREEN SAUCE

Correct the flavor of this sauce after puréeing all the ingredients together. Often it will need a bit more salt and pepper or oil and vinegar.

This sauce should always be served at room temperature, but refrigerate any that is left over. Let it come back to room temperature before using it again.

Toss the pasta with a bit of butter first, then sauce, then grated parmesan cheese and peeled, seeded, and diced tomatoes. The tomatoes may need a bit more salt. This is also useful as a sauce for poached fish.

1 slice dense white bread (such as Tuscan bread)

3 tablespoons wine vinegar

1 large shallot, peeled

4 large green onions, with some of the green

1 small garlic clove, peeled

1 medium tomato, peeled and seeded

1 small cucumber, peeled and seeded

3 tablespoons chopped fresh Italian flat-leaf parsley, without stems

4 flat anchovy fillets

2 tablespoons capers, drained, rinsed, and dried

2 tablespoons olive oil

2 tablespoons safflower oil

1 tablespoon green peppercorn mustard

Tabasco Sauce, to taste

3/4 teaspoon salt

1/2 teaspoon freshly ground black pepper

Put bread in a deep saucer and pour vinegar over it. Coarsely chop all vegetables and put them in a food processor, along with the remaining ingredients. Add the soaked bread and vinegar that was not absorbed. Process to a fine purée, stopping to scrape down the sides several times.

MAKES ENOUGH FOR 1 POUND OF PASTA

TWO SAUCES FOR PASTA

This brown sauce is one of the many versions of the classic Bolognese sauce. It can be served as suggested here or over rice or any other kind of baked pasta dish. The tomato sauce is cooked very briefly to preserve its strong tomatoey freshness. Toss al dente pasta with the Brown Sauce, and serve the Tomato Sauce on the side. This way the Tomato Sauce, which has a light, fresh flavor, won't be absorbed by the more pungent Brown Sauce. A bit of freshly chopped parsley can be sprinkled over the top of the dressed pasta, if you like.

BROWN SAUCE
1 ounce dried mushrooms, preferably porcini
¼ cup olive oil
1 medium onion, finely chopped
1 carrot, finely chopped
1 stalk of celery, finely chopped
5 Italian flat-leaf parsley sprigs, finely chopped
1 large garlic clove, peeled and finely chopped
1 small strip of lemon zest, chopped
½ pound ground chuck
½ cup dry red wine
1 1-pound can Italian plum tomatoes (without basil or paste)
1 tablespoon tomato paste
Salt and freshly ground black pepper, to taste
2 cups Chicken Stock (page 41), hot

TOMATO SAUCE
4 tablespoons olive oil
1 very large red Bermuda onion, sliced medium thin
3 pounds ripe plum tomatoes, peeled and seeded
6 large garlic cloves, peeled and finely chopped
Salt, to taste

2 pounds dried fusilli
¼ cup finely chopped Italian flat-leaf parsley (optional)

To make Brown Sauce: Cover mushrooms with lukewarm water and set aside for 30 minutes.

Put olive oil in large skillet and sauté onion, carrot, celery, parsley, garlic, and lemon zest until golden brown, about 20 minutes. Add ground chuck and sauté for an additional 15 minutes. Add wine and cook until it evaporates, about 20 minutes. Add tomatoes and tomato paste, mixing thoroughly, and salt and pepper. Simmer very slowly for 25 minutes.

Drain the soaked mushrooms. (The soaking liquid can be refrigerated and used later in soup.) Add mushrooms to sauce and continue to simmer very slowly for another 1½ hours, adding hot chicken stock as more liquid is needed. If you do not have enough liquid to complete the cooking time, add the mushroom water. The finished sauce should not be too liquid but of medium density. Set aside until ready to serve; be careful not to scorch when it is reheated.

To make Tomato Sauce: Put the olive oil in a large skillet and sauté onion until wilted but not brown. Add tomatoes, garlic, and salt. Simmer gently for 30 minutes, until flavor develops and some water evaporates. Do not overcook.

To assemble: When the tomato sauce is nearly finished, cook fusilli in a large pot of boiling salted water until tender. Gently reheat the brown sauce. Drain the pasta, place in a large bowl, and toss with the brown sauce. Sprinkle with chopped parsley, if using. Serve in warmed individual bowls with the tomato sauce on the side.

Note: The tomato sauce freezes very well, so if you find yourself swamped with an abundance of tomatoes, you might make a few containers to use in the winter.

SERVES 12

94

GREEN OLIVE, WALNUT, AND PARSLEY SAUCE

Use a pasta with ridges, like penne or ziti rigate, so the sauce will cling to it. This sauce is also good as a topping for crostini.

5 tablespoons walnut oil
1/3 cup walnut pieces
3 garlic cloves, minced
3/4 cup green olives, pitted and finely chopped
1/3 cup fresh Italian flat-leaf parsley, finely chopped
Pinch of crushed red pepper
2 teaspoons freshly ground black pepper
1/4 cup freshly grated parmesan

Heat 2 tablespoons of the walnut oil in a large sauté pan over medium-high heat. Add walnuts and sauté for 3 minutes, tossing to coat with oil. Add garlic and sauté only until golden brown, about 1 minute. Allow this mixture to cool completely and then process as fine as possible in the bowl of a food processor fitted with a metal blade.

Combine olives, parsley, crushed red pepper, black pepper, parmesan, and remaining 3 tablespoons of walnut oil. Add the ground walnut and garlic mixture and let sit for at least 1 hour before serving.

MAKES ENOUGH FOR 1 POUND OF PASTA

CHILI SAUCE WITH SAUSAGE

1/2 pound ground sirloin
1/2 pound sweet Italian sausage, removed from casing
1/2 pound hot Italian sausage, removed from casing
1 tablespoon olive oil
1 large onion, roughly chopped
3 tablespoons chili powder
2 tablespoons ground cumin
1 can (35 ounces) whole Italian tomatoes, including liquid
1 1/2 cups tomato juice
1 can (15 1/2 ounces) black beans, rinsed and drained

Preheat oven to 350 degrees.

Combine meats, place in a large roasting pan, and bake for approximately 25 minutes. Remove pan from oven, drain grease, and set aside to cool. When meat is cool, break into small pieces for the sauce, but do not crumble.

In a large skillet, heat olive oil over medium-high heat until almost smoking. Add onion and sauté until tender and beginning to color, about 8 to 10 minutes. Lower heat, add chili powder and cumin, and stir constantly to coat onion with the spices. Continue cooking the spices and the onion until the mixture takes on a rich dark color, about 3 to 5 minutes. (Keep stirring so the mixture does not burn.) Add cooked meats, stirring just to combine.

Break up the canned tomatoes with a spoon and add, with their juice and the additional tomato juice, to the meat mixture. Stir well and bring to a boil. Reduce heat and simmer uncovered for about 45 minutes, stirring occasionally. Add rinsed drained beans just before serving.

MAKES ENOUGH FOR 2 POUNDS OF PASTA

RICOTTA, BASIL, AND PROSCIUTTO SAUCE

A large tube-shape pasta like cavatelli or riga-toni is what you want with this sauce. Try it also on top of crostini.

2 cups ricotta, drained
1/2 cup finely shredded basil
1 tablespoon freshly ground black pepper
8 garlic cloves, minced
16 slices prosciutto, cut into thin strips
1 tablespoon olive oil

Combine ricotta, basil, and pepper in a large mixing bowl. Set aside.

In a large skillet over medium heat, sauté garlic and prosciutto in oil, turning frequently. This will take only about 2 minutes; the garlic will be fragrant and the prosciutto will begin to brown on the edges. Add the cooked garlic and prosciutto to the ricotta cheese mixture and stir well to combine. Use immediately.

MAKES ENOUGH FOR 1 POUND OF PASTA

BAKED PASTA

SAUSAGE PASTA CAKE

This may be served right out of the oven or it can wait for an hour. It is quite good just warm. Any leftovers should be rewarmed slightly.

PASTA SHELL
4 1/2 tablespoons unsalted butter
4 tablespoons bread crumbs
3/4 pound dried spaghettini
1 small onion, finely chopped
3 tablespoons all-purpose flour
1 1/2 cups Chicken Stock (page 41), hot
1/4 teaspoon white pepper
1 teaspoon fresh lemon juice

6 tablespoons freshly grated parmesan
1 cup grated mild cheddar
3 large eggs
1/2 teaspoon salt

SAUSAGE FILLING
3/4 pound Italian sausage, removed from casings
1 tablespoon unsalted butter
1 tablespoon safflower oil
3/4 cup coarsely chopped green bell pepper
1 3/4 cups coarsely chopped onion
1/3 cup grated mild cheddar
3 tablespoons chopped fresh Italian flat-leaf parsley
1/2 teaspoon freshly ground black pepper

Tomato and Red Bell Pepper Sauce (page 93)

Preheat oven to 375 degrees. Butter a spring-form pan with 1 tablespoon of the butter and sprinkle with 3 tablespoons of the bread crumbs. Set aside.

Drop pasta into a large pot of boiling salted water. Cook at a rolling boil for 7 minutes. Drain and run cold water over it. Set aside.

Starting in a cold skillet, brown sausage meat slowly, crumbling it as it cooks.

While sausage is cooking, make a white sauce for the pasta by melting 3 tablespoons of the butter in a skillet and browning the chopped onion. Then add flour and mix well. Slowly pour in heated stock, and continue to simmer for a few minutes until the mixture thickens. Add white pepper and lemon juice.

In a large bowl combine pasta, sauce, parmesan, cheddar, eggs, and salt. Mix well. Set aside for a few minutes.

Remove the browned sausage meat from the skillet and pour out any fat. Wipe out the skillet and add butter and safflower oil. Sauté green pepper and onion until they are limp and add this to the meat, along with cheddar, parsley, and black pepper. Mix well.

To assemble the dish, put half the pasta mixture in the pan. Make a deep depression in the middle, leaving a ½-inch space around the edges. Heap the meat mixture into the depression, mounding it in the middle. Pat it down solidly. Place the rest of the pasta on top and smooth it over. Top with the remaining bread crumbs and dot with the remaining butter.

Bake for 35 or 40 minutes, until the top is brown. Let stand for a few minutes before removing the outside ring of the pan. Do not bother to remove the bottom. Serve with tomato and red bell pepper sauce.

SERVES 8

PASTA SALADS

SUMMER PASTA SALAD

½ pound dried fusilli or rotelle
¾ cup chopped dill pickle
½ cup chopped red onion
¼ cup chopped fresh dill
¼ cup mayonnaise
¼ cup sour cream
¼ teaspoon salt
⅛ teaspoon freshly ground black pepper

Cook pasta according to package directions. Drain, run under cold water, and drain again thoroughly. Put in a large bowl.

Combine the remaining ingredients and stir well. Add to the pasta and toss.

SERVES 6

ORZO AND VEGETABLE SALAD

1 pound orzo
⅓ cup plus 2 tablespoons olive oil
1 large red bell pepper, cut into fine julienne
1 large red onion, diced
1 pound asparagus
½ cup chopped green onions, with some of the green
2 tablespoons raspberry vinegar
¼ teaspoon salt
¼ teaspoon freshly ground black pepper
1 tablespoon minced shallot
¼ cup freshly grated parmesan

Cook orzo according to package directions. Drain, run under cold water, and drain again thoroughly. Put in a large bowl.

Heat 1 tablespoon olive oil in a large skillet over medium heat. Add bell pepper and sauté until just tender, 3 or 4 minutes. Add to the orzo.

Heat 1 tablespoon olive oil in the same pan and add onion. Sauté until translucent, 4 or 5 minutes. Add to the orzo.

Break off and discard the woody ends of the asparagus. Blanch asparagus in boiling water until tender, about 4 minutes. Drain, run under cold water, and drain again. Dry asparagus on paper towels, then cut on the diagonal into 1-inch pieces. Add them, along with the green onions, to the orzo and vegetables.

Make a vinaigrette by whisking the remaining ⅓ cup oil with the vinegar, salt, pepper, and shallot. Pour over the salad and toss. Add parmesan and toss again.

SERVES 6

ORZO WITH MUSTARD BALSAMIC VINAIGRETTE

This can be made in advance, but I like it better if it hasn't been refrigerated.

1/2 pound orzo
2 1/2 tablespoons balsamic vinegar
1 teaspoon salt
Freshly ground black pepper, to taste
1 tablespoon Dijon mustard
1/4 cup minced shallots
1/2 cup olive oil

Drop the orzo into a large saucepan of lightly salted boiling water. Return to a boil and cook until just tender, about 8 minutes. Drain, but do not rinse.

Whisk together the other ingredients. Pour the vinaigrette over the drained, still-warm orzo. Allow to cool, stirring several times.

SERVES 6 TO 8

MACARONI AND CHEESE SALAD

1/2 pound dried elbow macaroni
1/2 cup diced canned pimiento
1 cup grated Monterey Jack cheese
1 cup grated cheddar cheese
1 large red onion, finely chopped
4 tablespoons olive oil
2 tablespoons red wine vinegar
1 teaspoon salt
1/2 teaspoon freshly ground black pepper

Cook macaroni according to package directions. Drain, run under cold water, and drain again thoroughly. Put in a large bowl.

Add pimiento and Jack and cheddar cheeses. Add onion and toss.

Whisk together oil, vinegar, salt, and pepper. Add to the salad and mix well.

SERVES 6

98

VEGETABLES AND SIDES

THIS IS A CATEGORY I AM VERY WELL acquainted with because, during my early years, every main meal included three or four. We also had all-vegetable dinners once a week—what we now call vegetarian although no one knew them by that name at the time. ✦ When vegetables like corn or asparagus are in season I usually cook them the pure and simple way only once or twice at the beginning of the season. After that, to prevent monotony, I prepare them in slightly different ways and in different combinations. There are combinations of vegetables that are traditional, repeated in every country where they thrive together. Think of eggplant and tomato or okra and tomato. Or how about snap beans and potatoes, corn and lima beans. There are dozens more. ✦ And don't forget that a vegetable pureed with a bit of butter or cream may be prepared ahead then reheated in a double boiler—much easier than trying to steam them at the last minute.

ARTICHOKES

STEAMED ARTICHOKES

Use any kind of dipping sauce you like with these. Garlic Mayonnaise (page 348) would be nice.

*8 medium artichokes, ¼ inch cut off bottoms
    and ¾ inch cut off tops
3 quarts water
2 tablespoons salt
½ lemon, squeezed, with shell reserved
2 tablespoons vinegar*

Remove tough outer leaves from artichokes and trim pointed tips off all remaining leaves. Put in a large pot and add other ingredients, including lemon shell. Bring to a boil over high heat, turn down to a slow boil, and cook until artichoke bottoms are tender, 30 to 45 minutes. Drain and cool, inverted, on a towel.
SERVES 8

ARTICHOKES WITH
BLACK OLIVE BUTTER

*6 large artichokes, rinsed and trimmed
1 teaspoon salt
2 bay leaves
1 lemon, halved
2 tablespoons unsalted butter
1 teaspoon black olive paste*

In a large pot with a tight-fitting lid, bring 1½ inches of water to a boil.

Place artichokes, stem end up, in water and sprinkle with salt. Add the bay leaves and lemon halves. Cover and steam over medium-high heat for approximately 40 minutes.

In a small saucepan over medium heat, melt butter and olive paste, stirring to combine. This mixture will not be smooth.

Remove artichokes with tongs and drain in a colander, stem side up. Invert and spoon warm olive butter over them to serve.
SERVES 6

STUFFED ARTICHOKE
BOTTOMS

It's important to rub the artichokes with lemon juice as you trim them so they don't turn dark.

*2 medium lemons
8 medium artichokes, leaves snapped off
    and edges trimmed, chokes removed
3 cups pitted and chopped oil-cured black
    olives
12 anchovy fillets, drained and coarsely
    chopped
¾ cup capers, rinsed and drained
¾ cup coarsely chopped fresh Italian flat-
    leaf parsley
3 medium garlic cloves
3 hard-cooked eggs, finely chopped
¼ cup olive oil
Freshly ground black pepper, to taste*

Use one of the lemons to rub artichokes as you trim them, dropping each artichoke into a large saucepan of water into which you have squeezed the other lemon. When all artichokes are trimmed, bring the water to a boil and cook over medium heat until artichoke bottoms are tender, 30 to 45 minutes. Remove with a slotted spoon and let cool.

Meanwhile, combine all the other ingredients except the eggs, olive oil, and pepper. Chop and toss lightly to combine the flavors. Do not chop too fine. Mix with the eggs and oil, adding pepper and more oil if desired. Top artichoke bottoms with equal amounts of the mixture, using it all.
SERVES 8

ASPARAGUS

SIMPLE SAUTÉED ASPARAGUS

36 small to medium asparagus, trimmed
Salt
1 tablespoon peanut oil
1 tablespoon rice wine vinegar

Place asparagus in a pot of well-salted boiling water. Blanch for 3 minutes. Drain and pat dry. Cut on the diagonal into 1-inch pieces.

Heat oil in a large skillet over high heat. Sauté asparagus, tossing, for 1½ minutes, until just crisp-tender. Off the heat, toss in the vinegar and salt to taste.

SERVES 4

GLAZED ASPARAGUS

What a feast for the eyes these are.

2 quarts Chicken Stock (page 41)
½ cup olive oil
5 pounds fresh asparagus, trimmed and
*   peeled*
1 large red bell pepper, cut into thin strips
Zest of 1 large lemon

Place chicken stock and olive oil in a large pot and bring to a hard boil. Add asparagus, and when the liquid returns to a boil, cook for 2 or 3 minutes, or until barely cooked and crisp.

Remove with a wire strainer and let cool. Save this stock-oil mixture to use in soup.

To serve, arrange neatly on a platter interspersed with strips of bell pepper and sprinkled with the lemon zest.

SERVES 12 TO 15

ASPARAGUS WITH SHALLOTS

2 pounds thin asparagus, trimmed and
*   peeled*
2 tablespoons unsalted butter
1 tablespoon olive oil
2 shallots, minced
1 teaspoon salt
½ teaspoon freshly ground black pepper

Blanch asparagus in boiling water, allowing them to cook for 2 to 3 minutes, but do not overcook. Immediately remove from heat and shock in cold water. Drain, dry, and set aside.

Melt butter and oil in a large heavy pan over medium heat. Sauté shallots, stirring frequently, until browned. Add asparagus and turn with tongs to coat and heat through, 3 to 5 minutes. Season with salt and pepper.

SERVES 6

GRILLED ASPARAGUS POCKETS

36 medium asparagus (about 3 pounds),
*   trimmed and peeled*
¼ cup olive oil
2 teaspoons salt
1 teaspoon freshly ground black pepper
2 shallots, minced

Prepare an outdoor grill. Place the asparagus in a large bowl and toss with olive oil, salt, and pepper. Divide asparagus among 6 aluminum foil squares, distribute the shallots evenly, and wrap tightly. Grill with the cover down until tender, about 8 to 10 minutes, turning occasionally. Do not unwrap but place one pocket on each individual plate to serve.

SERVES 6

ASPARAGUS WITH WARM TOMATO VINAIGRETTE

This warm vinaigrette is also very good on little boiled new red potatoes or steamed fresh cauliflower, or a combination of the two tossed with a little crumbled crisp bacon.

1/4 cup finely chopped shallots
1/4 cup olive oil
1 cup peeled, seeded, and chopped vine-ripened tomatoes
1/4 cup red wine vinegar
1 large garlic clove, finely minced
2/3 cup dry white wine
1/4 teaspoon salt
Freshly ground black pepper, to taste
18 to 24 medium to large asparagus, steamed until crisp-tender

Sauté shallots in oil over medium heat until wilted but not browned, about 5 minutes. Add tomatoes and bring to a simmer. Cook for another 5 minutes, stirring to prevent sticking, then add vinegar, garlic, wine, salt, and pepper. Simmer for 15 to 20 minutes to reduce and thicken the vinaigrette.

Serve warm over just-warm or room-temperature asparagus spears.

SERVES 6

TINY FRESH ASPARAGUS

When the very thin asparagus first become available I always have at least one "pig out" meal of them. Nothing but lots of asparagus. Multiply the amounts to serve more than just yourself.

1 handful of pencil-thin asparagus
1 tablespoon unsalted butter
Salt and freshly ground black pepper, to taste
Lemon slices or wedges

Bend the asparagus stalks to break off tough ends and discard ends. Place butter in a skillet. Wash asparagus tops, then put them on the butter with just the water that clings to them. Cover tightly and cook over high heat, shaking pan often, for 5 minutes. If not quite done, give them another minute. Do not overcook.

Remove asparagus to a plate and pour the pan juices over all. Add salt and pepper. Serve with lemon slices or wedges.

SERVES 1

VARIATIONS

Garnish with chopped or sliced tomatoes, red bell pepper strips, sliced hard-cooked eggs, or chopped hard-cooked egg yolk.

BEANS

GREEN BEANS IN MUSTARD MARINADE

1 tablespoon dried rosemary
2 pounds fresh green beans, trimmed and washed

MUSTARD MARINADE
1 teaspoon grainy mustard
1 1/2 teaspoons red wine vinegar
4 1/2 tablespoons extra virgin olive oil
Salt and freshly ground black pepper, to taste

Fill a 1 1/2-quart saucepan with water and bring to a boil. Add rosemary and boil rapidly for about 2 minutes. Toss in beans and continue to boil for about 10 minutes, or until beans are crisp without being tough. As soon as beans are done, drain them and rinse with cold water to stop the cooking process. Drain and set the beans aside.

To make marinade: Combine mustard, vinegar, and oil in a small bowl. Whisk together and add salt and pepper.

Dry the beans and toss them in the marinade. Refrigerate until ready to serve.

SERVES 8

VARIATIONS

Omit the rosemary.

Omit the mustard marinade and serve with butter and salt and pepper to taste.

GREEN BEANS WITH JICAMA

Green beans are old dependables. Unfortunately, in many restaurants today they seem to be served barely cooked. I suppose some chefs prefer crunch to flavor. This way of preparing green beans seems to be a good compromise—the beans are steamed until tender (which I think improves their flavor) and the crunch is supplied by the jicama.

Jicama is a vegetable from Mexico that became popular in the West and has moved east in the last few years. It has a marvelous texture and a very pleasant taste. It is often served raw, cut into strips, as a crudité with dip in California—which is how and where I first encountered it.

1¹/₂ pounds green beans, washed and trimmed
1 cup peeled and finely diced jicama
1 tablespoon unsalted butter
Fresh lemon juice, to taste
Salt, to taste

Put green beans in a steamer and cook them to the degree of tenderness you like. Test beans with the tines of a fork, and when they start getting soft, add jicama to warm it through.

To serve, toss beans and jicama with butter, a squeeze of lemon, and salt.

SERVES 6

GREEN BEANS AND MUSHROOMS

This is a simple Syrian method of preparing green beans. You can use either butter or oil (oil is traditional), and cook the beans to the degree of doneness that you prefer.

4 tablespoons (¹/₂ stick) unsalted butter
2 medium onions, coarsely chopped
1¹/₂ pounds green beans, washed and trimmed
1 pound mushrooms, sliced
1 teaspoon salt
Juice of ¹/₂ lemon

Heat butter in a large heavy skillet with a lid. Add onions and sauté until they start turning brown. Add beans and on top of them the mushrooms, sprinkling with a little salt as you go along. Cover and cook over low heat. Shake occasionally to prevent scorching. Test for doneness after 15 minutes. If they have to wait (covered), they will continue cooking slightly—so keep that in mind. Finish by tossing in the lemon juice.

SERVES 6

GRILLED GREEN BEAN POCKETS

1 1/2 pounds green beans, trimmed and
washed
3 tablespoons unsalted butter
1 teaspoon salt
1/2 teaspoon freshly ground black pepper

Prepare an outdoor grill. Divide green beans and place on 6 large squares of aluminum foil. Top each portion with 1/2 tablespoon of butter and season with salt and pepper. Wrap to seal tightly.

Grill over high heat for several minutes, turning once or twice to coat with melted butter. Transfer to cooler side of grill and cover. Cook for about 10 to 15 minutes, turning occasionally. Do not unwrap but place one pocket on each individual plate to serve.

SERVES 6

HARICOTS VERTS WITH ANCHOVY VINAIGRETTE

The haricots verts will be quite spicy from the seasoned cooking water and salty from the anchovies, so additional salt or pepper should be left to the individual.

ANCHOVY VINAIGRETTE
 6 anchovy fillets, drained
 1/2 teaspoon grainy mustard
 2 tablespoons red wine vinegar
 6 tablespoons olive oil

 2 tablespoons Tabasco Sauce
 2 tablespoons freshly ground black pepper
 1 1/2 pounds haricots verts (baby green
  beans), trimmed and washed
 2 lemons, each cut into 6 wedges

To make the vinaigrette: In a small bowl, mash anchovy fillets with mustard until a paste is formed. Stir in vinegar to combine, then slowly whisk in oil. Set aside.

In a heavy saucepan over high heat, bring 4 quarts of water to a rolling boil. Add Tabasco and black pepper, and boil for several minutes. (Although this may make your eyes sting, it does season the water for more flavorful beans.)

Plunge haricots verts into boiling water and cook until tender but still firm, about 4 to 6 minutes. Shock immediately in cold water, drain, and dry. Toss with vinaigrette, place on individual plates, add lemon wedges, and serve.

SERVES 6

BAKED LIMA BEANS AND PEARS

Presoaked and cooked dried limas can also be used in this recipe, but I find it much easier to use frozen ones.

6 cups frozen lima beans (three 10-ounce
 packages)
6 large ripe pears, peeled, cored, and sliced
1/4 cup light molasses
1/4 cup brown sugar
1/4 cup finely chopped onion
1 cup Chicken Stock (page 41)
1 teaspoon salt
Freshly ground black pepper, to taste

Preheat oven to 200 degrees.

Combine all ingredients in a heavy casserole with a tight-fitting lid and bake, covered, for 8 hours or longer. If there is excess moisture in the casserole at the end of the cooking time, continue to bake with the top ajar to evaporate part of it. Personally, it doesn't matter to me if they are a bit liquid. The beans can wait for hours in the turned-off oven after they are done.

SERVES 8

STEAMED LIMA BEANS WITH BROWN BUTTER

Lima beans are the one vegetable that I use frozen: They taste almost as good as fresh and save a lot of time. Steam two 10-ounce packages according to the directions. Carefully brown butter to nut color in a skillet and pour over all just before serving.

SERVES 6 TO 8

BUTTER BEANS WITH BACON

These are smaller than their cousin, lima beans, and have a different texture.

> 2 pounds fresh butter beans, shelled
> 4 slices bacon
> 5 cups water
> 1 teaspoon sugar
> 1 teaspoon salt
> 1 teaspoon freshly ground black pepper
> 3 tablespoons unsalted butter

Wash beans and set aside. Cut bacon into several pieces and sauté over low heat in a deep saucepan for 10 minutes. Drain off all but 2 tablespoons of fat. Add beans, water, sugar, salt, and pepper. Cook, uncovered, over medium heat for 30 minutes or longer, until very tender. Stir in bacon and butter just before serving.

SERVES 6

VARIATION

Omit the bacon and use 1 tablespoon bacon fat or oil.

Fry 1 small minced onion until golden in the fat before adding the beans.

BEETS

GRATED BAKED BEETS

These beets reheat very well. For a change, pique their flavor with a tablespoon of fresh orange juice added with the butter.

> 6 medium beets
> 3 tablespoons unsalted butter, cut into small
>   pieces
> 1 teaspoon salt
> 1/2 teaspoon freshly ground black pepper

Preheat oven to 400 degrees.

Wash beets and trim off their tops, leaving the roots on. Place them in a foil-lined baking pan. Cover snugly with another sheet of foil and bake for 1 1/2 hours, or until beets can be easily pierced with a fork. When cool enough to handle, skin them (the skins will slip right off) and grate them coarsely. Toss with the butter, salt, and pepper.

MAKES 6 SERVINGS

BUTTERED BEETS

You could also cook these in a hot oven if you like (see above).

> 16 small to medium beets
> 1 teaspoon sugar
> 1 teaspoon salt
> 2 tablespoons unsalted butter, cut into small
>   pieces

Wash and cut tops from beets. Place them in a saucepan and cover with water. Add sugar and salt. Cook over medium heat for about 45 minutes, or until tender when pierced with the point of a knife.

Drain, peel, and cut in half. Toss with butter, and serve hot.

SERVES 6

BABY BEETS AND GREENS

Many people think beet greens are too bitter, but if they are served with a bit of fresh lemon juice or a sprinkling of vinegar they can be very tasty. Besides, you will have bought them anyway, so you might as well give them a try.

2 dozen baby red beets with tops
2 dozen baby yellow beets with tops
1½ teaspoons balsamic vinegar
1 tablespoon Dijon mustard
Salt and freshly ground black pepper, to
    taste
¾ cup olive oil
2 medium shallots, minced
1 large garlic clove, minced
Beet Greens (recipe follows)

Wash beets well and cut off tops, leaving about 1 inch of stem. Reserve tops. Trim roots. In separate saucepans cover red and yellow beets with water and boil, uncovered, over medium heat until tender, 20 to 25 minutes. Drain. When cool enough to handle, slip off skins. Cut each beet in halves or quarters, depending on size, and place in a large bowl.

While beets are cooking, whisk together vinegar, mustard, salt, and pepper. Whisk in oil until well combined, then stir in shallots and garlic. Pour the sauce over beets. Cover and marinate overnight in the refrigerator.

Drain beets and serve with greens.

SERVES 6 TO 8

BEET GREENS

Beet tops from 4 dozen baby beets
2 tablespoons olive oil
1 small garlic clove, minced
Salt and freshly ground black pepper, to
    taste
1 tablespoon balsamic vinegar, or to taste

Wash and stem the beet greens. Dry carefully. Heat oil over medium heat in a large pot and sauté garlic until wilted, 2 to 3 minutes. Add greens and continue to cook, tossing until wilted and tender, 6 to 8 minutes. Season with salt and pepper. Sprinkle with balsamic vinegar just before serving.

SERVES 6 TO 8

BROCCOLI

BASIC BROCCOLI

You could steam the broccoli instead of blanching it—it holds well either way.

2 pounds broccoli, florets only
1 tablespoon unsalted butter
½ teaspoon salt
½ teaspoon white pepper

Blanch florets in salted boiling water for 1½ minutes. Immediately immerse in ice water. Drain and set aside.

To serve, toss in butter over medium heat to warm through. Season with salt and pepper.

SERVES 6

SAUTÉED BROCCOLI

2 pounds broccoli, washed and trimmed
3 tablespoons unsalted butter
2 tablespoons olive oil
1 teaspoon salt
½ teaspoon freshly ground black pepper

Blanch broccoli in plenty of boiling water, 3 to 5 minutes. Drain, chop into pieces, and reserve. This can be done in advance.

Melt butter and oil together in a heavy skillet over medium-high heat. When the mixture begins to sizzle, add broccoli pieces and toss until entirely coated and heated through. Season with salt and pepper.

SERVES 6

STEAMED BROCCOLI AND CAULIFLOWER

I made this dish in a microwave, which cooked the vegetables perfectly and quickly. But you could also cook these quickly in a steamer, then toss them with the lemon juice, butter, salt, and pepper.

2 pounds broccoli, florets and tender
stems only
1 medium head cauliflower, florets only
3 tablespoons fresh lemon juice
1 tablespoon unsalted butter, or more to
taste
1/2 teaspoon salt
1/2 teaspoon freshly ground black pepper

Combine ingredients in a large glass bowl and cover tightly with plastic wrap. Make a steam vent in the plastic wrap using a fork or knife. Microwave on HIGH for 5 minutes. Toss and then cook 5 minutes more. Remove from oven and allow to stand, covered, for another few minutes. Correct seasoning and add more butter if you like.
SERVES 8 TO 10

BRUSSELS SPROUTS

BRUSSELS SPROUTS WITH MUSTARD

Mustard is a perfect balance for the flavor of brussels sprouts.

4 cups brussels sprouts
5 cups salted water
2 tablespoons unsalted butter
2 tablespoons grainy mustard
1/2 teaspoon freshly ground black pepper

Carefully wash sprouts, trim stems, and cut an × into bottom of each with a sharp knife. Bring salted water to a boil and drop in sprouts. Boil about 15 minutes, until fork-tender. Drain well.

Melt butter in a large skillet and stir in mustard and pepper. Add sprouts and toss to coat well. Add more salt and pepper, if desired.
SERVES 8

BRUSSELS SPROUTS, ROASTED SHALLOTS, AND ROASTED YELLOW BELL PEPPERS

3/4 pound shallots
1 1/2 pounds brussels sprouts
2 medium yellow bell peppers, roasted,
peeled, and seeded (see Note, page 74),
coarsely chopped
1/2 teaspoon salt
4 teaspoons fresh lemon juice
1 tablespoon plus 2 teaspoons unsalted
butter
1 tablespoon crème fraîche
Dash of white pepper
Dash of freshly grated nutmeg

Preheat oven to 400 degrees.

Line a small pie pan with foil and place the unpeeled shallots in it. Bake until soft when squeezed, about 25 minutes. Set aside to cool slightly.

While shallots are cooling, trim brussels sprouts and cut an × into the root end. Steam until fork-tender. Place brussels sprouts in a food processor with the roasted peppers.

Peel shallots by snipping off tops and bottoms with kitchen shears and squeezing out the soft center into the food processor. Add salt, lemon juice, butter, crème fraîche, pepper, and nutmeg. Purée. Correct the seasoning if necessary.
SERVES 6

CABBAGE

STEAMED CABBAGE

I think this vegetable is not used often enough. Many people think it is too homely. Give it a chance.

4 cups finely shredded cabbage, tightly packed
1 tablespoon fresh lemon juice
4 tablespoons (1/2 stick) unsalted butter, melted
3/4 teaspoon salt
Dash of freshly ground black pepper

Put cabbage in the top of a steamer and steam for 7 minutes, or until tender. Do not overcook.

Remove to a serving dish. Stir lemon juice into butter and pour over cabbage. Add salt and pepper and toss to coat well.

SERVES 6

STEAMED GREEN CABBAGE

These instructions are for the microwave, but you can cook the cabbage, covered, on top of the stove over medium heat for about 10 minutes.

1/2 head of green cabbage, cored and coarsely shredded (about 8 cups)
1 1/2 tablespoons rice wine vinegar or fresh lemon juice
1/2 teaspoon salt
1/4 teaspoon freshly ground black pepper
1/4 teaspoon sugar (optional)
2 tablespoons unsalted butter, cut into small pieces

Place cabbage in a glass bowl and toss with vinegar, salt, pepper, and sugar, if using. Cover tightly with plastic wrap. Make a steam hole in the top and microwave on HIGH until crisp-tender, 6 to 8 minutes. Let rest, still covered, for several minutes. Toss with butter.

SERVES 6

CABBAGE STUFFED WITH GRAINS, NUTS, AND VEGETABLES

This whole stuffed cabbage makes a very pretty presentation. You could also just bake the stuffing in a casserole and serve it with a simple tomato sauce.

1 large head of green cabbage
3 tablespoons olive oil
1 cup chopped onion
2 cups thickly sliced white mushrooms
1/2 cup minced celery
3/4 cup minced red bell pepper
1 large garlic clove, finely chopped
1/2 cup shredded carrot
1/2 green onion finely sliced lengthwise, with some of the green
2 tablespoons minced fresh Italian flat-leaf parsley
1/2 cup coarsely chopped toasted pecans or hazelnuts
Salt and freshly ground black pepper
1/4 teaspoon dried thyme
Pinch of cayenne
6 1/2 cups Chicken Stock (page 41)
1/2 cup medium bulgur
1/2 cup acini di pepe or other very small soup pasta
1/2 cup long-grain white rice
2 tablespoons butter
4 1/2 teaspoons rice wine vinegar

Peel several outer leaves from cabbage head and set aside. (These will be used to decorate the dish when it is served.) Cut off core end of cabbage. Remove core without disturbing outer walls and discard. Using a small pointed paring knife and making short, slashing, crosshatch motions, hollow out the entire cabbage head, leaving about a ¾-inch outer wall intact. Reserve both the cabbage shell and the chopped cabbage.

Heat 1 tablespoon of oil in a heavy skillet over medium-high heat. Add onion and cook until golden, about 10 minutes. Set aside in a large bowl. Add another tablespoon of the oil to the skillet and sauté mushrooms over high heat until browned, about 4 minutes. Add to the bowl with the onion. Add the last tablespoon of oil to the skillet and sauté celery and bell pepper over medium-high heat for a minute. Add the garlic and cook another minute. Set aside in the bowl with the other vegetables.

Toss the carrot, green onion, parsley, and pecans with the cooked vegetables. Sprinkle with ¾ teaspoon salt, ¼ teaspoon pepper, thyme, and cayenne. Toss to mix. Stir in ½ cup of the chicken stock. Set aside.

Heat the remaining stock in a deep saucepan over high heat. When boiling, add bulgur, pasta, and rice. Bring back to a boil. When boiling, turn the heat down to medium and cook until almost tender, about 10 minutes. Drain and discard any remaining stock. Add the pasta and grains to the other ingredients. Toss to mix well.

Spread a 4-foot length of doubled cheesecloth on the counter. Place the cabbage, open side up, in the center. Spoon the stuffing mixture into the cavity, pressing down lightly. When the cabbage is full, pile the rest on top, pressing down gently to make a mound. Gather the ends of the cheesecloth together and tie it shut around the stuffed cabbage.

Put 2 inches of water in a large pot and bring to a boil over high heat. Insert a steamer (I use a pasta pot with a perforated insert for this). Add the cabbage, cover, and steam until the cabbage is tender, about 1 hour. Be sure to check the water from time to time so it doesn't boil away.

Bring an inch of water to a boil in a saucepan. Insert a steamer, add the reserved chopped cabbage, and steam for about 4 minutes, until tender. Season with butter, vinegar, salt, and pepper.

To serve, make a bed of steamed chopped cabbage on a platter. Top with the stuffed cabbage and the reserved outer leaves. Cut into wedges and mound each serving with the stuffing.
SERVES 8

SAUTÉED CABBAGE AND CARROTS WITH GINGER

A quick and easy way to prepare this savory combination.

¼ cup vegetable oil
1 cup sliced green onions
1 large garlic clove, minced
3 tablespoons peeled and finely chopped
  fresh ginger
½ teaspoon crushed red pepper
1½ tablespoons sesame oil
1 large head green cabbage, shredded
  (about 10 to 12 cups)
2 large carrots, peeled and shredded

Heat oil in a large skillet or wok over medium heat and add green onions, garlic, ginger, and crushed red pepper. Sauté for 3 minutes, until green onions have started to wilt. Add sesame oil, cabbage, and carrots. Stir-fry for 5 minutes, tossing. Cover and cook over low heat until tender, about 3 to 4 minutes.
SERVES 6

WARM SLAW

3 tablespoons olive oil
1/2 pound cremini mushrooms, thinly sliced
2 cups shredded carrots
1 cup finely diced red onion
6 cups shredded green cabbage
3 tablespoons red wine vinegar
1 tablespoon sugar
2 teaspoons salt
1 tablespoon freshly ground black pepper

In a heavy sauté pan over medium heat, heat oil and cook vegetables separately in the order they are listed, until just beginning to brown, about 3 to 5 minutes. Remove vegetables and deglaze pan with vinegar and sugar. Add salt and pepper, stirring to combine. Return vegetables to pan and toss to coat.

SERVES 6

CABBAGE, POTATO, BELL PEPPER, AND ONION MÉLANGE

This dish is something my housekeeper Grace Monroe taught me to cook.

1 strip thick bacon, cut into 6 pieces
1 tablespoon unsalted butter
1 large potato, sliced
3/4 pound green cabbage, shredded
1/2 red bell pepper, seeded and cut into strips
1/2 yellow bell pepper, seeded and cut into strips
1 large onion, sliced thick
2 tablespoons water
1/2 teaspoon salt
1/2 teaspoon freshly ground black pepper

Fry bacon pieces in a medium to large saucepan over medium heat until half-crisp. Pour out fat. Continue frying until crisp. Add butter and melt. Add potato. Rinse cabbage

with cold water and add to saucepan with whatever water is clinging to it. Add peppers and onion. Sprinkle the water over all. Season with salt and pepper.

Cover tightly and simmer or steam for 10 minutes. Toss and continue cooking, tossing once more to mix until potato is cooked, about 30 minutes in all. Do not overcook.

SERVES 6 TO 8

CARROTS

CANDIED CARROTS AND TURNIPS

Carrots and turnips are a nice duo. Their flavors complement each other well, especially when they are lightly glazed. But if the prospect of glazing doesn't strike your fancy, you can always just squeeze a lemon over them and add a dab of butter instead.

1 pound carrots, scraped and cut into rounds
1 pound white turnips, peeled and cut into rounds
Salt
4 tablespoons (1/2 stick) unsalted butter
4 tablespoons granulated brown sugar

Steam carrots and turnips separately for about 6 minutes each, until tender. Salt very lightly.

Melt butter in a large skillet and add brown sugar. Mix well and add vegetables. Continue to cook gently for 4 minutes, turning until well glazed.

Note: You may steam the carrots and turnips a little in advance and use the glazing to heat them through.
SERVES 6

GLAZED CARROTS, TURNIPS, AND ONIONS

You can add rutabagas to this combination if you like.

1½ cups scraped and sliced carrots
1½ cups peeled and cubed white turnips
  (½-inch cubes)
1½ cups very small peeled white onions
  (see Note)
2 cups water
½ teaspoon salt
3 tablespoons unsalted butter
¼ cup honey
2 tablespoons fresh lemon juice

Place vegetables in a saucepan with water and salt. Simmer about 20 minutes, just until fork-tender. Meanwhile, simmer butter, honey, and lemon juice in a small saucepan for 10 or 15 minutes, until slightly reduced. Drain vegetables well. Toss with glaze before serving.

Note: Drop onions into a pot of boiling water for about 1 minute. The skins will slip right off.

SERVES 6 TO 8

WHITE PEPPER CARROTS

You could also use baby carrots for this recipe.

2 tablespoons unsalted butter
2 tablespoons sugar
1 to 2 teaspoons salt, to taste
1 teaspoon white pepper
2½ to 3 cups carrot rounds, steamed tender,
  about 5 minutes
1 tablespoon minced fresh Italian flat-leaf
  parsley

Melt butter in a large skillet over medium heat. Stir in sugar, salt, and pepper. Add carrots, tossing lightly. Heat through. Toss with parsley.

SERVES 6

LEMON CARROTS

Sprinkle a little nutmeg on these if you like.

1½ pounds small carrots, scraped and cut
  into julienne strips
Salt
Juice of ½ large lemon
1 tablespoon unsalted butter

Put carrots in a saucepan and cover with well-salted water. Boil, uncovered, for about 10 minutes, or until crisp-tender.

Drain and toss with lemon juice and butter. If desired, add more of each to taste.

SERVES 6

BUTTERED CARROTS AND YELLOW BELL PEPPERS WITH PARSLEY

This is a nice contrast of textures and colors.

4 large carrots, scraped and cut into ½-inch
  slices
1 tablespoon unsalted butter
1 medium yellow bell pepper, seeded and cut
  into medium dice
¼ cup coarsely chopped fresh Italian flat-
  leaf parsley
¼ teaspoon salt
¼ teaspoon white pepper

Cover carrots with well-salted water and bring to a boil. Reduce heat to medium and cook until tender, about 10 minutes. Plunge into cold water and drain.

To serve, melt butter in a skillet and toss carrots and yellow pepper together long enough to heat them through, 2 or 3 minutes. Off the heat, stir in parsley, salt, and pepper.

SERVES 6

111

HONEY CARROTS

Carrots prepared this way can sit for ten minutes or so after they are done. Don't wait too much longer, as they begin to lose their flavor.

4 cups scraped and sliced carrots
4 tablespoons honey
3 tablespoons unsalted butter
1/4 teaspoon salt
1/2 teaspoon freshly grated nutmeg
3 tablespoons fresh lemon juice

Mix all ingredients in a skillet with a tightly fitting lid. Cook, covered, over medium-high heat until the liquid evaporates and the carrots begin to just brown. If they are tender and there is still liquid in the pan, remove the cover and boil it down rapidly. The timing on this can vary greatly, depending on the thickness of the slices and the age of the carrots—10 minutes more or less.

SERVES 6

STEAMED CARROTS WITH APRICOTS

You won't believe how successful this combination is until you try it.

1 cup dried apricots
3 cups peeled and thinly sliced carrots
3 tablespoons water
2 tablespoons unsalted butter, or more to taste
1/4 teaspoon salt

Soak apricots in hot water for 1½ hours. Pat dry and julienne.

Put carrots in a skillet with a tight-fitting lid and add water, butter, and salt. Cover and cook over medium heat for 10 minutes, or until they are fork-tender. Shake occasionally to prevent sticking. Stir in apricots and cover until ready to serve. Check for seasoning, and add more butter if you like.

SERVES 6 TO 8

CARROT CUSTARD

This has a surprisingly sweet taste that is very nice with meat. It also reheats remarkably well. To do so, place in a pan over just simmering water for 30 minutes before serving.

1 pound carrots, scraped and cut into
1-inch pieces
2 tablespoons unsalted butter, at room
temperature
2 eggs
1/2 cup milk
3 tablespoons evaporated skimmed milk
1/2 teaspoon freshly grated nutmeg
1/2 teaspoon salt
Dash of freshly ground black pepper

Preheat oven to 375 degrees and put rack in the middle position. Butter a 9-inch round cake pan and set aside. Put a kettle of water on to boil.

Boil carrots until very tender, about 30 minutes, and drain. In a food processor with a metal blade, process carrots with butter for 10 seconds. Add remaining ingredients and process for 30 seconds more, until well puréed. Adjust seasoning if necessary.

Pour mixture into the cake pan and put the pan in a large ovenproof pan. Pour enough boiling water around it to come halfway up the side of the cake pan. Put in the oven and bake for 30 to 35 minutes. Mixture will be firm and set. If using immediately, allow enough time to let it rest for 10 minutes after it has been taken out of the water. Do not remove from the pan if you intend to reheat it later. When ready to serve, loosen edges gently with a knife and invert it onto the serving platter.

SERVES 6

CELERY ROOT

CORN

CELERY ROOT RÉMOULADE

Although I always envision this as part of a first course, it could be served as a side dish.

> *2 tablespoons Creole or brown mustard*
> *1 tablespoon paprika*
> *1/2 teaspoon salt*
> *1/4 cup cider vinegar*
> *2 medium garlic cloves, coarsely chopped*
> *1/4 cup finely chopped celery*
> *1/4 cup minced fresh Italian flat-leaf parsley*
> *1/4 cup minced green onions*
> *2 tablespoons mayonnaise*
> *2 large celery roots*
> *Juice of 1 lemon*

Place mustard, paprika, salt, vinegar, and garlic in a processor and process until smooth. Pour into a bowl and stir in celery, parsley, green onions, and mayonnaise.

Peel celery roots and cut into 1/4-inch julienne strips. Cover with water in a small saucepan and add lemon juice. Simmer until tender, 1 to 2 minutes. Drain and dry. Combine with enough sauce to coat well and refrigerate.

SERVES 6

STEAMED CORN ON THE COB

This method of cooking corn is the best I've ever encountered. It eliminates that problem of keeping corn warm once it's been cooked, without overcooking. Here's how you do it.

Use a steamer and arrange the ears standing on the stalk ends. Cover tightly and bring the water to a boil over high heat. When the water begins to steam and the lid starts to jump around, time it for 1 minute and then turn off the heat. (If you're using an electric stove, remove the steamer from the coil.) Allow corn to continue to cook by retained heat for 10 minutes more, covered (or a little longer if the corn is not young and fresh), before serving. It can stay like this for up to 1 hour.

CORN OFF THE COB

While fresh corn on the cob quickly steamed or boiled and slathered with butter certainly must be one of our national favorites, I must confess I prefer it cut from the cob and cooked very briefly in a skillet.

Allow two ears or more per person and slice the kernels off with a sharp knife (you do not have to cut too deep). Then, using the back side of the knife, scrape out the juice and pulp. Place corn, juice, and pulp in a large skillet and add 2 or 3 tablespoons of butter, salt and pepper to taste, plus 1 or 2 tablespoons milk. (If the corn is old you might want also to add a pinch of sugar.) Bring rapidly to a simmer, stirring all the while to prevent sticking. This will need only a few minutes of cooking time, depending on the age and type of corn.

BARBECUED CORN ON THE COB

This barbecued corn on the cob is a specialty of Trey Wilson, chef-owner of Grandville Cafe in Charleston, South Carolina.

1 cup cider vinegar
2 garlic cloves, minced
1/2 cup Jack Daniels bourbon
2 tablespoons chili powder
2 tablespoons ground cumin
Pinch of cayenne pepper
1 medium red onion, diced
2 14-ounce bottles ketchup
1 1/2 teaspoons ballpark mustard

Fresh corn on the cob

Combine vinegar, garlic, bourbon, chili powder, cumin, cayenne, and onion in a medium saucepan. Bring to a boil, stirring, then reduce heat to a simmer and cook for 10 minutes. Stir in ketchup and mustard off the heat. Let cool, then refrigerate.

Husk the corn, clean it, and roast it over coals. While it's still hot, brush it all around with the sauce. Store any leftover sauce, tightly covered, in the refrigerator.

MAKES ABOUT 4 CUPS SAUCE

FRIED CORN

The taste of corn prepared this way sends me right back to my childhood. It's important to cook the corn long enough for it to start turning slightly golden and develop a nutty flavor. If I remember correctly, sometimes it was combined with chopped red bell pepper, but I like it better plain.

2 tablespoons canola oil
1 tablespoon unsalted butter
1 tablespoon bacon fat
12 ears of corn, kernels cut and scraped from cobs
Salt

Heat oil, butter, and bacon fat in a large skillet over medium-high heat until very hot. Add corn quickly, stirring to coat. Continue to stir as the corn cooks, later scraping up any that sticks to the bottom. Sample after a few minutes for doneness. The cooking time will depend on the age and kind of corn. Add salt if desired.

SERVES 6

VARIATIONS

Substitute 3 tablespoons additional butter for the oil and bacon fat.

Sprinkle the corn with 2 teaspoons sugar and cook for 10 to 15 minutes.

CREAMED CORN

This is a good way to use older large-kernel corn.

4 cups fresh corn kernels, cut from the cob and scraped (about 6 medium ears)
2 cups milk or light cream
1 1/4 cups warm water
1 teaspoon sugar
1/4 teaspoon salt
2 teaspoons unsalted butter (optional)

Put corn and milk in a small saucepan and bring to a boil. Reduce heat and simmer, stirring with a fork every once in a while, until milk is almost completely reduced, about 15 minutes. Add water and cook another 10 minutes, until liquid has reduced to just below the surface of the corn. Remove from the heat and stir in sugar and salt. Process 3/4 cup of the kernels in a food processor, then stir the purée back in with the kernels. Add butter, if using.

SERVES 6

SKILLET CREAMED CORN

Evaporated skimmed milk can be substituted for the half-and-half. And if the corn is past its prime, a dash of sugar will help.

2 tablespoons unsalted butter
3 cups fresh corn kernels, cut from the cob
*   and scraped (about 4 large ears)*
1/2 cup half-and-half
1 teaspoon salt
1/2 teaspoon freshly ground black pepper

Melt butter in a large skillet. When it begins to bubble, add corn and mix. Stir in half-and-half, salt, and pepper. Sauté over medium heat, for 6 minutes, just long enough to heat thoroughly and cook corn.

VARIATIONS

Use only 2 tablespoons half-and-half or milk and stir in 3 ounces thinly sliced prosciutto, cut into thin strips, at the end.

Thaw 1 cup frozen peas in a strainer under running hot tap water. Stir in when the corn is done. Let stand for 1 or 2 minutes to warm through.

SERVES 8

SKILLET BAKED CORN

Everyone loves this easy-to-prepare concoction. The trick is to have the iron skillet in which it is cooked super-hot when the corn mixture goes in.

2 tablespoons vegetable oil
8 medium ears of white corn, kernels cut
*   and scraped from the cobs*
1/2 teaspoon salt
1/2 cup all-purpose flour

Preheat oven to 425 degrees. Place an 8-inch cast-iron skillet in oven. After about 20 minutes, pour vegetable oil into the skillet.

Meanwhile, combine corn, salt, and flour to make a thick batter.

Remove the skillet from the oven and pour and scrape the batter in. Do not stir; press the batter into place. Be careful not to burn yourself.

Bake until a nice crust forms on the bottom and the top starts to brown. Remove and invert onto a serving plate. Cut into 4 wedges. This will be rather crumbly, so use a spatula and a fork to serve.

SERVES 4

CORN TIMBALES

An old Southern favorite—tasty and simple. You might want to garnish these with roasted red bell peppers, chopped or cut into strips.

1/4 cup heavy cream
1/2 cup Chicken Stock (page 41)
1/4 teaspoon freshly ground black pepper
2 cups fresh corn kernels, cut from the cob
*   and scraped (about 3 medium ears)*

Preheat oven to 350 degrees. Grease eight 1/2-cup ramekins.

Combine cream, stock, pepper, and 1 cup of the corn kernels. Place mixture in a food processor and process until smooth. Stir in the reserved kernels and divide among the ramekins. Bake in a hot water bath for 25 minutes, or until set. Allow to rest a few minutes before loosening edges and unmolding.

SERVES 8

CORN AND RICE

Here's a dish I grew up with. I'm not going to give you a recipe, just a method, and the proportions are completely subjective. I suspect this was a way to use leftover rice in our kitchen.

Cook rice in good rich chicken stock. Meanwhile, cut kernels from the cob and cook them in a skillet with just a little milk, cream, or half-and-half until tender. If the corn is fresh and young this won't take but a few minutes. Season with salt and pepper to taste (and a little sugar, if you like). Toss with the rice, pour browned butter over it all, and toss it again. Delicious!

CREAMED CORN PUDDING

The important element in this recipe is the fresh corn base. Because fresh corn varies in water content, it is almost impossible to say exactly the number of ears you will require. It may be anywhere from six to eight, or even more if they are small or dry. I would rather have a bit more. (You can always eat any leftover corn, as is, with a dab of butter.)

2½ cups fresh corn kernels, cut from the cob
and scraped (about 4 medium ears)
1 cup light cream or evaporated skimmed
milk
1 tablespoon sugar
1½ teaspoons salt
¼ teaspoon white pepper
3 tablespoons butter, melted
5 eggs, well beaten
3 cups milk
1 tablespoon cornstarch
1 tablespoon cold water

Preheat oven to 350 degrees. Generously butter a shallow 2-quart baking dish.

Place corn in the top of a double boiler along with the light cream or evaporated skimmed milk. Slowly cook for 10 to 20 minutes to reduce it slightly. Stir often to prevent sticking. This should produce a thickened creamy mixture. If it starts to dry out, add more cream, or if it is too liquid, cook a little longer.

Measure out 2½ cups of this corn mixture to use in the custard. If you don't have quite enough to make the measure, stir in a few more tablespoons of cream. Cool slightly. (The mixture may be set aside for up to 30 minutes.)

Combine corn mixture with sugar, salt, pepper, butter, eggs, and milk. Dissolve cornstarch in the water and add. Pour into the prepared baking dish and bake for about 1 hour or until custard is firm.

SERVES 6 TO 8

MAQUE CHOUX

This is a very popular way of serving corn in my native Louisiana—and, because it was a favorite of my father's, it's a dish I have had many times. Make it when tomatoes and corn are at their best.

1 tablespoon bacon fat
3 tablespoons unsalted butter
1 medium onion, finely chopped
4 cups fresh corn kernels, cut from the cob
and scraped (about 6 medium ears)
2 medium tomatoes, peeled, seeded, and
diced
Salt and freshly ground black pepper, to
taste

Put bacon fat and butter in a large skillet and sauté onion until wilted, about 5 minutes. Do not let it brown. Add corn and tomatoes. Simmer for about 10 minutes and season with salt and pepper. If it begins to dry out, add a few tablespoons of milk or chicken stock. Serve warm.

SERVES 6 TO 8

CUCUMBERS

STEAMED CARAWAY CUCUMBERS

Cucumbers are too often thought of as something just to have in a salad. Here's a change of pace.

6 large cucumbers, peeled, cut in half
   lengthwise, and seeded
2 teaspoons caraway seeds
1 tablespoon unsalted butter
1 tablespoon plain yogurt
Salt, to taste

Cut cucumbers into ½-inch-thick half circles. Sprinkle with caraway seeds, then place in a large steamer. Steam about 20 minutes, until tender. Remove to a warm bowl and toss with butter, yogurt, and salt. Serve warm or hot.
SERVES 12

MARINATED CUCUMBERS AND YELLOW PEPPERS WITH DILL AND MINT

Serve this as an accompaniment to grilled fish —it's a perfect combination.

8 cups thinly sliced peeled cucumbers
4 cups thinly sliced yellow bell peppers
½ teaspoon minced fresh jalapeño
¼ cup snipped fresh dill
2 tablespoons fresh mint, cut into strips
4 teaspoons salt
¼ cup finely chopped red onion
¼ cup olive oil
4 teaspoons red wine vinegar
½ teaspoon freshly ground black pepper
½ cup coarsely snipped radish sprouts
   (optional)

Toss cucumbers, peppers, jalapeño, dill, and mint together with salt in a shallow bowl. Cover with a plate that fits inside and weight down with a couple of heavy cans. Refrigerate for at least 1 hour. Remove from the refrigerator and drain well, squeezing the vegetables out with your hands. Toss the mixture with onion, olive oil, vinegar, and pepper. Add sprouts and toss lightly. Add more salt if necessary.
SERVES 8

EGGPLANT

FRIED EGGPLANT STICKS

Eggplant cooked this way has a crunchy texture.

2 large eggplants cut into finger-size sticks
Salt
2 eggs
½ cup milk
Cornmeal as necessary
Safflower oil for deep-frying

Sprinkle cut eggplant generously with salt and let stand for an hour. When ready to use, drain and pat dry with absorbent towels.

Beat eggs and milk in a bowl large enough to hold a number of sticks at one time. Pour a quantity of yellow cornmeal onto a sheet of wax paper.

Put about 1 inch of oil in a large pan and start it heating. When oil is very hot, dip eggplant in the egg-milk mixture and then roll in cornmeal to coat. Prepare in batches of 6 or 7 sticks and fry in the hot oil until golden brown. (Since these sticks are comparatively thin, be very careful not to burn them.)
SERVES 6

117

PAN-GRILLED EGGPLANT ON SUN-DRIED TOMATO TOASTS

If you have a grill pan with small ridges, this is the perfect time to use it.

2 small eggplants, about ³/4 pound each, uniform in shape
3 tablespoons olive oil
Salt and freshly ground black pepper
6 slices country-style bread, cut about ³/4 inch thick
2 teaspoons sun-dried tomato paste

Split each eggplant in half lengthwise, discard ends, and cut each half into 6 slices (half-circles). You will have 24 slices. Brush with 1 tablespoon of the olive oil and sprinkle with salt and pepper.

In a heavy skillet or grill pan over medium-high heat, heat the remaining olive oil until almost smoking. Grill eggplant until golden brown on both sides, turning only once. This will take 3 to 5 minutes per side. Remove to a sheet pan, season with pepper, and keep warm.

Grill or toast the bread on both sides. While the bread is still warm, spread each slice with sun-dried tomato paste on one side only. Place the bread, sun-dried tomato paste side up, on a plate, and arrange 2 eggplant slices on each. If desired, drizzle each with additional olive oil and season with black pepper.

Note: Sun-dried tomato paste varies widely in saltiness so this recipe goes easy on the added salt. You may want to place a small bowl of kosher salt on the table for individual adjustments.
SERVES 6

GRILLED EGGPLANT WITH RICOTTA AND TWO TOMATOES

This is very good served warm if you can manage it. If not, it works fine at room temperature.

12 to 18 slices (¹/4 inch) unpeeled eggplant
1 teaspoon salt
6 to 7 tablespoons olive oil
¹/4 cup dehydrated sun-dried tomatoes, cut into thin strips
2 medium fresh tomatoes, peeled
Freshly ground black pepper, to taste
1 tablespoon minced fresh oregano
6 tablespoons fresh ricotta
6 medium green onions, with some of the green, cut into thin rings

Preheat the grill or oven broiler. Place eggplant slices on a flat pan and sprinkle with ¹/2 teaspoon salt. Drizzle 2 or 3 tablespoons olive oil over them and turn to coat slices with oil. Set aside for at least 5 minutes.

Cover sun-dried tomatoes with hot water and set aside.

Quarter the fresh tomatoes, and remove and discard the seeds and watery pulp. Cut the flesh into a medium julienne. Put in a bowl. Drain and dry the sun-dried tomatoes, add to the fresh tomato with the remaining olive oil and ¹/2 teaspoon of salt. Stir in oregano. Set aside.

Grill eggplant slices until golden on both sides, 4 to 5 minutes, turning several times. Keep warm.

To assemble, place a tablespoon of ricotta in the center of 6 small plates. Divide grilled eggplant among the plates, arranging the slices over the cheese. Spoon tomato topping over each and sprinkle with green onions.
SERVES 6

WHOLE BABY EGGPLANT IN OIL

These baby eggplants are usually available year round in specialty food markets.

12 small finger eggplants (each about
  4½ inches long)
Salt
¼ cup olive oil
3 large garlic cloves, cut in half
¼ cup Chicken Stock (page 41)
2 teaspoons soy sauce
Lemon juice
Freshly ground black pepper, to taste

Cut each eggplant in half, leaving it attached at the stem on top. Sprinkle the flesh with salt and set aside in the refrigerator for 30 minutes.

Heat oil in a large skillet and add garlic. Fry garlic until it is almost golden. Wipe eggplants dry and add them, flesh side down, to the pan with the garlic. Cook eggplants over medium heat for several minutes. Add stock and soy sauce. Cover and simmer for 6 or 7 minutes. Test for doneness on the flesh side.

Place eggplants on a platter and make an incision down the length of each half. Squeeze lemon juice over all and pour the pan oil on top of this. Add salt and pepper.

Serve either hot or at room temperature.

SERVES 6

FENNEL

BROILED FENNEL WITH PANCETTA

Cooked fennel is a fairly new enthusiasm for me. I had always just assumed that I wouldn't like its taste. I've mended my ways.

3 large fennel bulbs, trimmed and cut
  lengthwise into ¼-inch slices
6 or more tablespoons olive oil
1 large lime
Salt and freshly ground black pepper, to taste
¼ pound pancetta, thinly sliced (see Note)
6 or more tablespoons coarsely grated
  parmesan
Lime slices
1 large red bell pepper, roasted, peeled, and
  seeded (see Note, page 74), cut into strips
Oil-cured black olives

Preheat broiler.

Place slices of fennel in a single layer in a shallow pan. Smear generously with olive oil, then sprinkle with juice of ½ lime. Salt and generously pepper.

Broil for 5 minutes. Some edges will blacken slightly. Carefully cover fennel completely with pancetta and return to the broiler. Broil until pancetta is crisp, about 1½ minutes. Using flat-end tongs, turn individual slices of fennel with the pancetta so that the pancetta is on the bottom. Place under broiler for 3 more minutes. Remove and sprinkle with parmesan, making sure all surfaces are coated. Return to broiler until cheese starts to brown, about 1½ to 2 minutes.

Let cool in the pan until ready to serve. Do not refrigerate, but serve at room temperature.

To serve, arrange slices of fennel and pancetta on individual plates and squeeze the remaining ½ lime half over all. Pour oil from the pan over each serving. (Add more oil if there is not enough.) Additional pepper may be added also.

Garnish each with a small slice of lime, a few strips of roasted red pepper, and black olives.

Note: When you purchase the pancetta, have the very thin slices placed on a sheet of wax paper, not touching or overlapping. If one slice is put on top of the other without paper in between, they will stick together.

SERVES 6 TO 8

FENNEL NIÇOISE

This dish can be prepared early in the day and reheated. It doesn't have to be very hot—I like it best just warm.

8 fennel bulbs
2 tablespoons unsalted butter
4 tablespoons olive oil
2 medium onions, thinly sliced
2 large garlic cloves, thoroughly crushed
2 pounds tomatoes, peeled, seeded, and cut
    into chunks
2 tablespoons fresh lemon juice
2 tablespoons wine vinegar
1 heaping tablespoon tomato paste
1/4 teaspoon dried thyme or 1 fresh thyme
    sprig
1/4 teaspoon salt
1/4 teaspoon coarsely ground black pepper
2 green onions, with some of the green,
    chopped
1 tablespoon minced fresh Italian flat-leaf
    parsley
1 cup small niçoise olives

Trim fennel, removing any tough outer layers as well as the piece of root at the end. Cut into 1/2-inch slices. Melt butter in a large skillet and sauté fennel, covered, for 15 minutes or less, just until tender. Remove from the pan and set aside.

Add olive oil to the pan, and when it is hot add onions and garlic. Sauté, uncovered, until they have wilted. Add tomatoes and simmer until most of their liquid has evaporated. Mix in lemon juice, vinegar, tomato paste, thyme, salt, pepper, green onions, and parsley. Cover and simmer until the liquid is reduced. Add fennel and cook for a few more minutes before adding olives. Correct the seasoning if necessary.
SERVES 6

GARLIC

ROASTED GARLIC WITH HERBS

You'll find countless uses for roasted garlic. Try it first spread on a piece of bread with a salad. Save the oil to use in vinaigrettes.

3 garlic heads
1 cup olive oil
1 1/2 teaspoons minced fresh thyme
1 tablespoon minced fresh rosemary
Salt and freshly ground black pepper

Preheat oven to 350 degrees.

Cut off tops of garlic heads to expose cloves. Brush generously with olive oil, then place in a small, ovenproof pan with the remaining oil. Sprinkle with thyme and rosemary and season with salt and pepper. Roast for about 1 hour, or until the garlic is tender and spreadable.
MAKES 3 HEADS

VARIATION
Omit the herbs and pepper.

GREENS

OLD-FASHIONED TURNIP GREENS

Turnip greens have a strong flavor, which I love. You can also combine them with other greens.

3 pounds turnip greens
4 slices of bacon
2 tablespoons sugar
1/2 teaspoon salt
1/2 teaspoon freshly ground black pepper
1/2 cup water

Strip leaves from stems, discarding stems. Place leaves in a sinkful of water and swish them around.

Meanwhile, in a very large, heavy pot, cook bacon over low heat for about 7 minutes, until translucent. Carefully lift greens from the water, shaking off excess, and add to the pot. Turn several times with a wooden spoon. Add sugar, seasonings, and water. Simmer over very low heat for 3 hours. Remove from liquid with a slotted spoon and serve hot.

SERVES 6

MUSTARD GREENS

In some areas it is hard to find mustard greens. But if you like them and have a little piece of sunny garden plot, they are remarkably easy to grow, being ready to harvest in as little as six weeks.

The Hot Pepper Vinegar gets more potent with time. After using it once, you may wish to increase the number of peppers. It is also good on scrambled eggs.

3 pounds mustard greens
2 large onions, coarsely chopped
6 ounces salt pork
4 green onions, chopped (optional)
Hot Pepper Vinegar (recipe follows)

Soak the greens in a large pan of water to get rid of any sand. Change the water, washing out any sand that may have settled to the bottom of the pan. Strip the leaves from the stems and discard the stems.

Put onions and salt pork in a large pot and put in the greens with just the water clinging to them. Cover and simmer for about 45 minutes. May be served with chopped green onions on top, if desired, and a sprinkling of the vinegar.

SERVES 6

HOT PEPPER VINEGAR
1 pint bottle red wine vinegar
3 or 4 hot peppers, cut

Pour out a bit of the vinegar and force hot peppers, including the seeds, into the bottle. Pour vinegar back into the bottle to fill. Allow to marinate for several days before using.

MAKES 1 PINT

WILTED MIXED SUMMER GREENS

You may use any combination of greens you find in the market.

4 pounds mixed greens (see Note)
5 tablespoons olive oil
1/2 cup Chicken Stock (page 41)
Salt and freshly ground black pepper

Wash and stem the greens and tear into bite-size pieces. Heat oil in a very large skillet (these will reduce considerably, but you will need a large skillet or pot to start) and add the washed greens. Stir as the greens wilt. When wilted, add stock, cover tightly, and cook over low heat until tender, about 15 minutes. Toss in some salt and a good dose of pepper

Note: It is rather difficult to give a precise quantity here, but if you cook too much, the leftovers freeze. After you strip greens of their stems, the weight is usually reduced by half. The weight measure here is with stems.

SERVES 6

WILTED MUSTARD GREENS WITH OLIVE OIL AND LEMON

Mustard greens, like their relatives collards and kale, are very sturdy vegetables and may be reheated without destroying their texture. Broccoli rabe or spinach could be substituted for mustard greens.

2 tablespoons mild olive oil
1 medium onion
2 small shallots
2 tablespoons Chicken Stock (page 41)
2 small garlic cloves, finely mined
2 pounds mustard greens, washed, with
*   large stems removed*
2 teaspoons fresh lemon juice
1/2 teaspoon salt
1/4 teaspoon freshly ground black pepper
Lemon wedges
Green onions
Hard-cooked egg, grated

In a deep pot with a lid, heat olive oil and sauté onion and shallots until golden, about 10 minutes. Mix in chicken stock and garlic. Place washed greens on top. Cover and cook over medium heat for about 20 minutes. This will reduce considerably in volume, and greens should be turned several times during the cooking period. Sprinkle with lemon juice, salt, and pepper. Toss

Serve warm with extra olive oil on the side. Garnish with lemon wedges, green onions, and grated hard-cooked egg.
SERVES 6

BRAISED WINTER GREENS

6 green onions, with some of the green,
*   chopped*
2 tablespoons olive oil
2 1/2 pounds winter greens, such as mustard,
*   beet, and turnip greens and broccoli*
*   rabe, cleaned and trimmed*
1 1/2 cups Chicken Stock (page 41)
Dash of Tabasco Sauce

In a large, heavy pot with a tight-fitting lid, brown the green onions in the olive oil over medium heat. Add greens and toss to coat. Add stock and Tabasco, cover, lower heat, and cook for 10 to 15 minutes, until tender and just wilted.

Note: A larger bunch of mustard greens should be used to balance the bitterness of the other greens.
SERVES 6

KOHLRABI

SAUTÉED KOHLRABI

Kohlrabi has a distinctive flavor that I especially like. When you see it in your market, buy some and prepare it in this uncomplicated way.

2 cups peeled and diced kohlrabi (1/2-inch
*   dice)*
Salt, to taste
1 tablespoon unsalted butter
1/4 teaspoon white pepper
1 tablespoon minced fresh Italian flat-leaf
*   parsley*

Cover kohlrabi with salted water and bring quickly to a boil. Turn the heat to medium and cook until tender, about 8 minutes. Drain and keep warm, covered with a damp tea towel.

To serve, melt butter in a medium skillet and sauté kohlrabi, tossing, until heated. Sprinkle with salt and pepper and toss with parsley.

SERVES 6

LEEKS

STEAMED LEEKS WITH RED ONION

Steamed leeks are one of my favorite vegetables. Topped with finely chopped red onion, they are delicious.

16 medium leeks, root end and most of the green top removed
1 medium red onion, chopped fine

To clean leeks, let stand in a large quantity of cold water for 30 minutes or so. Before putting leeks in soaking water, stand on root end and, using downward motion, with a sharp knife cut halfway down the length of the stem so that the water can get in between the leaves. Pour out water, replacing it with new, pulling the leaves back slightly to make sure all the sand is out.

Steam for 45 minutes. Serve the leeks whole or cut in two, with chopped onion sprinkled over the top.

Note: The leeks may also be covered with Chicken Stock (page 41) and simmered until very tender, about 15 to 20 minutes. Let cool in the stock.

SERVES 8

LEEKS NIÇOISE

This is a pretty glamorous first-course salad by any measure.

¼ cup safflower oil
¼ cup olive oil
2 tablespoons minced garlic
1 tablespoon dried thyme
1 teaspoon freshly ground black pepper
6 medium to large leeks, trimmed to include 2 to 3 inches of the light green, halved lengthwise, and washed well
½ cup Chicken Stock (page 41), heated
½ pint cherry tomatoes, stemmed, washed, and dried
½ cup drained niçoise olives
1 teaspoon salt

Combine oils in a large skillet set over very low heat. Stir in garlic, thyme, and pepper and heat for about 5 minutes to flavor and warm the oils and herbs without cooking them.

Add leeks to oil, tightly cover the pan, and simmer over low heat for 10 minutes. Turn leeks with tongs and add hot chicken stock. Cover again, increase the heat to medium, and simmer until leeks are tender, 5 to 8 minutes. Remove leeks to a serving dish.

Add tomatoes, olives, and salt to the skillet and sauté over medium heat, shaking the pan gently to heat through without mashing the tomatoes, about 3 minutes.

Pour the mixture over the leeks. Serve at room temperature.

SERVES 6

BRAISED LEEK AND HERB CUSTARD

This is like a crustless quiche.

> 2 tablespoons unsalted butter, plus additional for molds
> 1 cup finely diced (well-washed) leek, mostly white part
> ½ cup finely diced onion
> 4 eggs
> 1 cup half-and-half
> 2 tablespoons grated parmesan
> 1 teaspoon minced mixed fresh Italian flat-leaf parsley and fresh rosemary
> Salt and freshly ground black pepper, to taste

Preheat oven to 325 degrees and butter six 4-ounce molds. Set aside.

Place butter in a small skillet and sauté leek and onion over medium heat until wilted, 3 to 5 minutes. In another bowl, combine eggs, half-and-half, cheese, herbs, and seasonings. Stir in leek and onion mixture. Pour into molds. Place molds in a larger pan and surround with boiling water. Bake until firm, 15 or 20 minutes, or until a knife inserted in the center comes out clean.

SERVES 6

MUSHROOMS

MUSHROOM, FENNEL, AND ARTICHOKE RAGOUT

> 3 tablespoons olive oil
> 3 large shallots, thinly sliced
> 3 medium garlic cloves, thinly sliced
> 1 medium carrot, scraped and chopped fine
> 3 tablespoons unsalted butter
> ½ pound fresh porcini mushrooms, cut into 1-inch cubes
> ½ pound matsutake mushrooms, thinly sliced
> ½ pound chanterelle mushrooms, thickly sliced
> ½ pound shiitake mushrooms, thickly sliced
> 1 small fennel bulb, trimmed, sliced, and blanched for 5 minutes in salted water
> 3 large cooked and trimmed artichoke hearts, cut into quarters
> ½ teaspoon fennel seeds, toasted
> ½ teaspoon minced fresh thyme
> Salt and freshly ground black pepper, to taste

Put oil in a 12-inch skillet and, over low heat, cook shallots, garlic, and carrot until tender but not browned, about 7 minutes. Add butter and turn heat to high. When butter is melted, add mushrooms, fennel, and artichokes. Toss and cook until mushrooms give up their liquid and liquid has evaporated and mushrooms are tender. This will take only a few minutes over high heat. Be sure to keep tossing lightly and shaking pan. When almost done, sprinkle fennel seeds and thyme over all, tossing. Correct seasoning.

SERVES 6 TO 8 AS A FIRST COURSE

SMOKED BACON AND WILD MUSHROOMS IN PUFF PASTRY

Vol au vent is a flaky pastry shell with a top. You can make them yourself (which I never do) or buy packages of individual ones frozen. (Pepperidge Farm is the brand available most places.)

This is often served as a first course in a restaurant, but it makes a fine luncheon dish with just a salad and a fruit dessert.

6 individual frozen pastry shells
1 egg, beaten
1 tablespoon unsalted butter
6 ounces smoked bacon strips (about 6 strips), cut into 1/2-inch pieces
3/4 pound mixed fresh wild mushrooms, such as chanterelle, shiitake, and oyster, carefully cleaned and chopped into large pieces
1/2 teaspoon chopped fresh thyme
1/2 teaspoon chopped garlic
Salt and freshly ground black pepper, to taste
3 cups heavy cream
1 cup Chicken Stock (page 41) or veal stock, reduced to 1/3 cup
6 fresh thyme sprigs

Preheat oven to 400 degrees. Place frozen pastries on a baking sheet. Mix beaten egg with 1 tablespoon of water and brush on pastries. Bake according to package directions. When golden, remove to a warm spot. Keep oven at 400 degrees.

Melt butter in a large skillet and add bacon. Sauté over medium to low heat until just transparent, several minutes. Add mushrooms, thyme, garlic, salt, and pepper. Turn heat up slightly and continue to sauté until mushrooms begin to brown slightly, 3 or more minutes. Add cream and stock. Reduce by half, 10 or more minutes.

Taste and adjust the seasoning if necessary. Cut the tops from the pastry shells and reheat the bottoms in the oven for a few minutes. Place bottoms on individual plates and fill with the mushroom mixture. Return tops to filled shells and garnish each with a sprig of thyme.
SERVES 6

FRIED OYSTER MUSHROOMS

These mushrooms would also be awfully good with salsa instead of the mayonnaise.

1 1/2 cups all-purpose flour
1/4 cup cornstarch
1/2 teaspoon paprika
3/4 teaspoon salt
1/2 teaspoon freshly ground black pepper
2 tablespoons minced fresh Italian flat-leaf parsley
2 eggs
1 1/3 cups milk
18 unbroken well-shaped oyster mushrooms
Vegetable oil for frying
Watercress Mayonnaise (page 349)

Toss together in a bowl the flour, cornstarch, paprika, salt, pepper, and parsley. Set aside. In another bowl beat together eggs and milk.

Toss mushrooms in flour, then egg wash, and then back in flour.

Heat oil in a deep-fryer to 365 degrees. Fry mushrooms for about 4 minutes, or until golden. Drain and serve immediately with the mayonnaise.
SERVES 6

GRILLED PORTOBELLO MUSHROOMS WITH BLACK OLIVES AND TOMATOES

If you don't have an outdoor grill handy, do the mushrooms under the broiler. You might also want to try this with sliced domestic white or brown mushrooms sautéed in a little hot oil. However, the texture of portobellos is especially well suited to this dish.

18 small whole shallots, peeled
¼ cup plus 3 tablespoons olive oil
1 head of garlic
Salt and freshly ground black pepper, to taste
3 large portobello mushrooms (about 12 ounces total weight)
2 tablespoons capers, rinsed and drained
24 oil-cured black olives
2 tablespoons red wine vinegar
2 large tomatoes, cut into wedges

Preheat oven to 350 degrees.

Rub shallots with 1 tablespoon of the oil. Wrap them all in foil in a single package. Slice the top off the head of garlic to expose the cloves, rub with 1 tablespoon of the oil, and lightly sprinkle with salt and pepper. Wrap in foil. Place the shallots and garlic in the oven and roast for an hour or more, until tender. Set aside.

Meanwhile, prepare an outdoor grill or preheat the broiler.

Remove the stems from the mushrooms and discard. Brush mushrooms with 1 tablespoon of the oil and grill until tender, 4 to 5 minutes per side. Remove to a cutting board and cut into medium dice.

Place mushrooms in a bowl and toss with capers, olives, and roasted shallots. Squeeze the roasted garlic out of the skins and into the bowl with the mushroom mixture. In a small bowl, whisk the remaining ¼ cup oil and the vinegar together. Pour over the other ingredients in the bowl and toss.

Mound in the center of a serving plate and surround with tomato wedges.

SERVES 6

SAUTÉED MUSHROOMS

Wild mushrooms don't require much attention. Milder mushrooms might be more flavorful with a dash of Tabasco and a small quantity of Worcestershire Sauce.

3 tablespoons olive oil
1 tablespoon unsalted butter
3 cups very coarsely chopped mushrooms, caps and stems
1½ teaspoons fresh lemon juice
Salt and freshly ground black pepper, to taste
1 tablespoon minced fresh Italian flat-leaf parsley (optional)

Heat oil and butter in a large skillet. Add mushrooms and sauté over medium heat until they give up most of their liquid and are tender, about 10 to 15 minutes. Add lemon juice and season with salt and pepper. Sprinkle with parsley, if using.

SERVES 4

STUFFED PORTOBELLO MUSHROOMS

1/2 cup grated parmesan
1/2 cup chopped fresh Italian flat-leaf parsley
6 large (about 1/4 pound each) portobello mushrooms, wiped clean, stems reserved
5 tablespoons unsalted butter
3 tablespoons olive oil
4 large shallots, minced
4 small zucchini, shredded and drained of extra liquid (about 3 cups)
1/2 pound goat cheese
1/2 cup fresh bread crumbs
2 teaspoons curry powder
2 teaspoons paprika
1/2 teaspoon freshly ground black pepper

Preheat oven to 350 degrees. Lightly butter a rimmed baking sheet and set aside. Reserve 1 tablespoon each of parmesan and chopped parsley for garnish. Coarsely chop mushroom stems and set aside.

Melt butter and oil to combine in heavy skillet over low heat. Sauté mushrooms, cap side down, until golden brown. Remove and drain any liquid that may have collected inside the cap. Place mushrooms, cap side down, on prepared baking sheet.

In the same skillet over medium heat, sauté mushroom stems and shallots until mushrooms are golden in color, about 2 to 5 minutes. If the mixture begins to stick to the cooking surface of the skillet, use additional butter and oil, being careful the mixture does not become too wet.

Add shredded zucchini, stirring to combine, and remove the vegetable mixture from heat. Transfer to a large bowl. Immediately toss with both cheeses, parsley, bread crumbs, and dry seasonings. Do not overwork this mixture or it will become too sticky.

Fill each mushroom cap with stuffing mixture and bake until heated through, about 8 to 10 minutes.

Arrange on serving dishes and sprinkle with reserved parmesan and parsley.
SERVES 6

WARM GRILLED MUSHROOM SALAD

Try this also with fresh porcini mushrooms if they're available, or put together several different kinds.

18 medium shiitake mushrooms, brushed and wiped clean with stems trimmed to 1/4 inch
1/4 teaspoon salt
1/4 teaspoon white pepper
2 tablespoons olive oil
2 small heads red oak leaf lettuce, washed and dried
2 small heads frisée lettuce, washed and dried

RICE VINAIGRETTE
1/4 cup olive oil
2 teaspoons rice wine vinegar
Pinch of salt
Pinch of white pepper

Preheat grill or broiler.

Place mushrooms in a bowl and sprinkle with half the salt and pepper. Drizzle 1 tablespoon of the oil over all and toss to coat. Grill or broil until just tender, 3 to 4 minutes. Do not overcook. Place in a small warmed metal bowl as they cook and toss with the remaining salt, pepper, and olive oil. Keep warm.

Tear greens into bite-size pieces. Whisk together ingredients for the vinaigrette and toss with the greens.

To serve, arrange greens on individual plates and place 3 mushrooms on each, pouring any oil and juice which may have accumulated in the mushroom bowl over each plate.
SERVES 6

SAVOY MUSHROOM SALAD

This delectable salad is served at the intimate Savoy Restaurant in New York City. Owner Peter Hoffman and chef David Wurth were generous enough to give it to me to use here. You'll love it. Incidentally, the olive combination may be made in advance and keeps quite well. The spiced olives are great for picnics.

2 cups Kalamata olives
1 cup Picholine olives
¹/₂ cup white wine
¹/₂ cup olive oil
4 garlic cloves
2 teaspoons crushed red pepper
¹/₂ cup fresh oregano leaves
1 cup fresh Italian flat-leaf parsley leaves
¹/₂ cup red wine vinegar
¹/₄ cup olive oil
¹/₂ pound small cremini mushrooms
1 pound shiitake mushroom caps
2 tablespoons olive oil
Salt and freshly ground black pepper
2 cups arugula
1 pound fresh mozzarella, thinly sliced

Combine both types of olives and cover with cool water. Allow to soak for about 30 minutes, changing water twice. Drain well.

Preheat oven to 350 degrees. Place drained olives on a baking sheet large enough to hold them in a single layer. Pour white wine and olive oil over them. Stir well to combine.

Cover the pan with aluminum foil, sealing well. Bake for 1 hour, shaking pan occasionally.

While the olives are baking, make the spice paste. In a food processor, combine garlic, crushed red pepper, and herbs. Process until fairly smooth. Add vinegar and process just to combine. While the machine is running, slowly add oil to form a smooth paste.

When olives are done, remove from the oven and uncover. Increase oven temperature to 400 degrees. Prick each olive several times with the tines of a fork. Cover olives with the paste and stir well to combine. Let olives cool.

Toss mushrooms lightly with oil but do not coat. Sprinkle with salt and pepper. Place on a baking sheet in a single layer (do not allow mushrooms to touch or they will steam rather than roast) and roast for about 15 minutes. Remove from pan and cool.

To assemble individual salads, evenly distribute arugula on 6 plates, arrange mushrooms and olives on top, and place two thin slices of mozzarella next to each portion of salad.

SERVES 6

FRESH PORCINI MUSHROOMS BAKED WITH BACON

Fresh porcini mushrooms are so delicious they don't require much doing. Here they are combined with bacon to create a first course as tasty as it is easy to prepare.

4 very large, fresh porcini mushrooms
(about ³/₄ pound each), brushed,
trimmed, and split in half
Olive oil
16 slices thick-cut lean bacon (about ¹/₂
pound or more), each cut in half
lengthwise
Freshly ground black pepper

Preheat oven to 450 degrees.

Generously brush mushroom halves on all sides with olive oil. Wrap each in bacon and place on a baking sheet. Bake until bacon crisps, about 8 to 10 minutes. Remove to warmed serving plates and top with a generous grind of black pepper.

SERVES 8

128

OKRA

SAUTÉED OKRA, TOMATOES, AND CORN

Okra for some is an acquired taste. If you are among them, you might start by trying this recipe. I've found most people's objection has to do with its viscous texture, and most of that is cooked away here. What is left combines wonderfully with onions and tomatoes. This dish can be served hot or just warm. Personally, I prefer the latter, because the flavors seem at their most distinct.

2 pounds okra, stems and tips discarded
3 pounds tomatoes, peeled and seeded
2 tablespoons unsalted butter
2 tablespoons safflower oil
1 pound onions, coarsely chopped (about 4 cups)
3 teaspoons salt
4 cups fresh corn kernels, cut from the cob and scraped (about 8 large ears; optional)
Freshly ground black pepper, to taste

Cut okra into ¼-inch rounds. Set aside. There should be approximately 6 cups.

Put tomatoes in a stainless or enameled pan and cook slowly for about 30 minutes to get rid of some excess liquid. Do not scorch. There should be approximately 2 cups of reduced pulp when finished. Pour off any excess liquid before measuring.

Heat butter and safflower oil in a large deep skillet. When medium hot, add okra and onions together. Cook until onions are completely wilted and okra has begun to brown on the edges. Turn and scrape the bottom of the pan often with a spatula. This can take from 10 to 15 minutes. Add reduced tomatoes and salt. Simmer for 5 minutes. There should not be too much liquid from the tomatoes in the pan. Pour out any excess.

Add corn, if using, cooking just long enough to heat thoroughly, about 3 or 4 minutes. Add pepper, and more salt if desired. Serve hot or warm.

Note: You will have enough leftovers for a delicious vegetable lunch. A little Hot Pepper Vinegar (page 121) sprinkled over the top is very good.

SERVES 6, WITH LEFTOVERS

STEAMED OKRA WITH WARM TOMATO VINAIGRETTE

The wonderful warm vinaigrette is good on any steamed vegetable, not just okra.

1 pound okra, stems and tips trimmed
Warm Tomato Vinaigrette (page 354)

Steam okra for 5 minutes, or until just fork-tender. Allow to cool. Do not refrigerate. Serve the sauce warm over the okra.

SERVES 6

ONIONS

BARBECUED ONIONS

This little trick will work with any barbecue sauce.

2 pounds yellow onions, quartered
¹/₂ cup store-bought barbecue sauce

Preheat oven to 400 degrees.

Break up the quartered onions into a mixing bowl. Add barbecue sauce and mix to coat thoroughly. Scatter the coated onions over the bottom of a small roasting pan; cover with foil.

Roast for 10 minutes.

Remove the foil and roast until the onions are tender, 10 to 15 minutes longer.

SERVES 6

ROASTED ONIONS WITH BALSAMIC VINEGAR

Guests love these very simple-to-do onions. And they don't take much doing.

6 small Vidalia or other sweet onions, peeled
*   and left whole*
2 tablespoons olive oil
2 tablespoons balsamic vinegar
¹/₂ teaspoon salt
¹/₄ teaspoon freshly ground black pepper

Preheat oven to 350 degrees.

Quarter onions lengthwise but leave them attached at the root ends. Place each onion on a small square of aluminum foil.

Gently open each onion slightly and drizzle with some of the oil and then some of the balsamic vinegar, salt, and pepper. Wrap each onion in its foil and twist closed at the top.

Bake the onions until tender, 45 to 60 minutes.

SERVES 6

SAUTÉED ONIONS

Serve this with your favorite meat dish.

3 Spanish onions, thickly sliced
¹/₄ cup olive oil
2 tablespoons unsalted butter
¹/₂ teaspoon salt
¹/₄ teaspoon freshly ground black pepper
¹/₄ cup balsamic vinegar

In a large skillet set over medium-high heat, sauté onions in oil and butter, stirring occasionally, until golden brown, 10 to 12 minutes.

Season with salt and pepper. Pour in vinegar and stir to coat onions. Cook for 1 minute. Serve hot or cool.

SERVES 6

CARAMELIZED ONIONS

4 tablespoons olive oil or unsalted butter
3 medium onions, halved and sliced or
*   coarsely chopped*
1 teaspoon salt
Pinch of white pepper
1 teaspoon red wine or balsamic vinegar
*   (optional)*

Heat oil in a large skillet over medium-high heat until very hot. Add onions and stir to coat. Add salt and pepper and continue to cook, stirring occasionally, until they color and start to caramelize, 10 to 12 minutes for sliced onions, 30 minutes for chopped. Stir in vinegar, if using.

SERVES 4

SAUTÉED VIDALIA ONIONS

Vidalia onions are available in most grocery stores in spring.

4 tablespoons (1/2 stick) unsalted
4 large Vidalia onions, sliced or coarsely
chopped

Melt butter over low heat and add onions, coating well. Cook about 8 minutes, until translucent and soft. Increase heat to caramelize sugar in onions, about 5 minutes. Stir constantly.
SERVES 6 TO 8

ONIONS IN SEASONED OLIVE OIL

Try this combination with your summertime sandwiches.

1 pound small white onions, peeled
1/3 cup olive oil
1 tablespoon honey
2 tablespoons white wine vinegar
3/4 cup water
1/2 teaspoon coriander seeds
1/4 teaspoon fennel seeds
1/4 teaspoon celery seeds
6 shallots, sliced
1/4 teaspoon salt
10 black peppercorns, crushed
2 tablespoons chopped fresh Italian flat-leaf
parsley

Place onions in a nonreactive heavy saucepan and cover with all the remaining ingredients except the parsley. Cover and cook over medium-high heat for 10 minutes.

Uncover the pan and cook for another 2 minutes or so, letting onions brown slightly. Turn out into a serving dish and sprinkle with the parsley. Serve warm or at room temperature.
MAKES 1 1/2 CUPS

ONION POTATOES ANNA

This is a variation of a classic I think you will find very pleasing. Use a sharp, not sweet, onion here.

2 pounds onions, thinly sliced
4 tablespoons unsalted butter
2 pounds new potatoes, peeled and thinly
sliced
1 teaspoon salt
1/4 teaspoon freshly ground black pepper

In a large skillet set over medium-high heat, sauté onions in 3 tablespoons of the butter, stirring occasionally, until golden brown, 10 to 12 minutes.

Preheat oven to 350 degrees.

Melt the remaining 1 tablespoon butter in a medium cast-iron skillet set over medium-high heat. Arrange a single layer of the potato slices in concentric circles, overlapping them slightly, over the bottom of the skillet. Sprinkle the potatoes with some of the salt and pepper. Spread one third of the cooked onions on top of the potatoes. Repeat, layering the potatoes, salt and pepper, and onions until you have 3 layers of onions and 4 of potatoes.

Increase the heat to high and cook until the bottom layer of potatoes is golden brown, about 5 minutes. Check by picking up the edge of the potatoes with a metal spatula. When the bottom layer is browned, remove the skillet from the heat and tightly cover the pan with aluminum foil.

Bake until the potatoes are tender when stabbed with the tip of a sharp knife, about 45 minutes.

Remove the skillet to a wire rack, uncover, and let cool and set up slightly, 10 to 15 minutes.

Loosen the bottom of the potatoes with a spatula and by shaking the pan back and forth. Invert a serving dish over the skillet and flip the two together to unmold. Slice the potatoes and onions into 6 wedges and serve.
SERVES 6

STUFFED ONIONS, CUBAN STYLE

These spicy stuffed onions make a delicious centerpiece for a luncheon or can be served as a first course.

6 medium white onions
2 tablespoons olive oil
½ pound ground beef
½ pound ground pork
1 can (16 ounces) Italian plum tomatoes,
  drained and chopped
1 can (4 ounces) mild green chilies, drained
  and chopped
¼ cup raisins
2 tablespoons tomato paste
2 garlic cloves, minced
1 tablespoon cider vinegar
¼ teaspoon ground cinnamon
⅛ teaspoon ground cloves
1 teaspoon salt
½ teaspoon freshly ground black pepper
½ cup coarsely chopped pimiento-stuffed
  olives
¼ cup coarsely chopped pimiento
2 cups Beef Stock (page 42), boiling
Minced fresh Italian flat-leaf parsley

Peel onions and remove ¼ inch of the stem end. Using a melon baller, scoop out the center of each onion, leaving a ¼-inch shell. Finely chop the onion you removed and reserve 1 cup for the filling.

Blanch the onion shells in boiling salted water for 5 minutes. Remove from the water, rinse under cool water, and drain upside down on a wire rack until cooled to room temperature.

Preheat oven to 350 degrees.

In a large, heavy skillet set over medium heat, sauté reserved chopped onion in olive oil until onion is translucent, 3 to 4 minutes. Add ground meats and cook, stirring occasionally, until they are no longer pink, 3 to 5 minutes. Stir in tomatoes, green chilies, raisins, tomato paste, garlic, vinegar, cinnamon, cloves, salt, and pepper. Cook stirring, until the excess liquid evaporates but the mixture is still moist, about 10 minutes. Stir in olives and pimiento.

Sprinkle drained onion shells with salt and pepper. Divide stuffing equally among them, mounding the tops. Arrange stuffed onions in a casserole or baking dish. Pour hot stock around the onions into the bottom of the dish. Cover the dish with foil.

Bake for 45 minutes.

Serve hot, sprinkled with parsley.

SERVES 6

FRIED THIN ONION RINGS

You'll be pleased with how simple these are to make. The only problem is that you never seem to have quite enough of them.

3 medium onions
Vegetable oil, for frying
¾ cup all-purpose flour
Salt

Cut off the stem end of each onion and peel. Slice very thin—you might have to use a mandoline-type slicer to ensure even, thin slices. Separate the onions into rings.

Pour about 2 inches of oil into a deep-fryer or large sauté pan and heat to 365 degrees.

Meanwhile, combine flour and pepper in a plastic bag. Add onion rings and shake to coat; remove and shake off any excess flour.

Working in batches, drop some of the coated onions into the hot oil and fry very quickly until golden all over, about 2 minutes. Adjust the heat as necessary. Remove with a slotted spoon or tongs; drain on paper towels. Sprinkle with salt and serve hot.

SERVES 4

VARIATION

Add 1 tablespoon freshly ground black pepper to the flour.

ROASTED VIDALIA ONION SALAD

2 cups shredded radicchio
6 leaves Boston lettuce
6 roasted small Vidalia Onions with
   Balsamic Vinegar (see page 130)

DRESSING
2 tablespoons olive oil
1 teaspoon red wine vinegar
1/4 teaspoon salt
1/2 teaspoon freshly ground black pepper

Arrange radicchio on individual plates and top each with a leaf of Boston lettuce.

Unwrap roasted onions and place one on each plate. Pour any remaining liquid into a container and reserve.

To make the dressing: Combine the reserved onion juice with the remaining ingredients in a small container with a tight-fitting lid. Shake until well combined. Pour over onion salad.
SERVES 6

ROASTED ONION AND POTATO SALAD

1 tablespoon olive oil
2 teaspoons balsamic vinegar
1 teaspoon Dijon mustard
1 tablespoon chopped fresh Italian flat-leaf
   parsley
1/4 teaspoon salt
1/4 teaspoon freshly ground black pepper
3 medium onions
2 pounds small red new potatoes

Preheat oven to 400 degrees.

Place oil, vinegar, mustard, parsley, salt, and pepper in a jar with a tight-fitting lid. Shake well.

Peel and quarter onions. Place each onion on a large square of aluminum foil. Drizzle about a third of the dressing over the onions and twist the foil to seal the packets. Bake until tender, approximately 1 hour.

Scrub potatoes and cut them into quarters. Place in a large saucepan and barely cover with cold salted water. Bring to a boil and then reduce heat to a simmer. Cook until fork-tender, approximately 20 minutes. Drain and toss potatoes with the remaining vinaigrette while they are still warm. Break up onions and add to potatoes, along with any liquid in the packets. Toss. Serve warm or at room temperature.
SERVES 8

ONION RINGS

You must use enough oil so the onion rings are floating freely and can brown from all sides. This will depend on the size and depth of the pot.

1 cup all-purpose flour
3 eggs, lightly beaten with 3 tablespoons milk
2 cups fresh bread crumbs
Vegetable oil for deep-frying
6 large yellow onions, cut into 1/2-inch slices
2 teaspoons salt
1/2 teaspoon freshly ground black pepper

Preheat oven to 200 degrees.

Place flour, egg wash, and bread crumbs in 3 separate dishes. Pour about 2 inches of oil into a deep-fryer or large sauté pan and heat to 365 degrees.

Lightly coat each onion ring with flour, shaking off excess. Dip floured ring into egg wash, being careful to coat all surfaces, and dredge through bread crumbs. Shake off excess.

Carefully place the breaded onion rings into the hot oil, using long tongs. Do not overcrowd because the onion rings will not brown properly. Cook in small batches until golden brown. Drain on paper towels and keep in warm oven.

Season with salt and pepper. Stack to serve.
SERVES 6

REFRIGERATOR WILTED ONIONS

Try these on sandwiches.

½ cup white vinegar
½ cup water
1 cup oil
⅛ teaspoon freshly ground black pepper
½ teaspoon sugar
1 large onion, thinly sliced

Whisk together vinegar, water, oil, pepper, and sugar.

Place onion slices in a deep, narrow dish or measuring cup. Pour the liquid over the onions, cover, and refrigerate overnight.

Drain the onions and serve.

MAKES 2½ CUPS

PEAS

TINY GREEN PEAS WITH DILL BUTTER

3 packages (10 ounces) frozen tiny green
*   peas*
3 tablespoons minced fresh dill
4 to 6 tablespoons (½ to ¾ stick) unsalted
*   butter, softened*
¼ teaspoon sugar
½ to ¾ teaspoon salt, or to taste

Place frozen peas in a strainer and let them stand in a bowl, covered with boiling water, until they are heated through, about 1 minute. Shake them dry.

Meanwhile, mash dill into the softened butter. Combine hot peas with the dill butter, sugar, and salt.

SERVES 8

SPRING PEAS AND GREEN ONIONS

1 tablespoon unsalted butter, or to taste
6 green onions, coarsely chopped, including
*   some of the green*
3 cups fresh or frozen green peas
½ teaspoon salt, or to taste
½ cup water

Melt butter in a medium saucepan and add green onions. Sauté about 5 minutes, until just wilted, being careful not to let them brown. Add peas and sprinkle with salt. Add water and cover tightly. Simmer for about 10 minutes, until peas are tender. Timing will depend on age and size of the peas and if they are fresh or frozen. Frozen peas take only a few minutes. If, when the peas are almost tender, there is too much liquid, uncover, turn the heat up to high, and quickly boil some out. Serve immediately.

SERVES 6

GARDEN PEAS IN SHALLOT BUTTER

2 cups water
Salt
6 cups fresh green peas, about 8 pounds in
*   the pod*
½ cup minced shallots
5 tablespoons unsalted butter, softened
Freshly ground black pepper (optional)

Bring the water to a boil, salt it well, and add peas. Cook over medium-high heat until tender, about 5 minutes. Cover and let rest for 5 minutes. Drain.

While peas are cooking, sauté shallots in 1 tablespoon of the butter until wilted, about 5 minutes. Season to taste with salt and a little pepper, if desired. Mash the shallots into the remaining 4 tablespoons of butter.

To serve, toss the hot peas with most of the butter, reserving about 2 tablespoons so you may place a dab on top of each serving.
SERVES 8

STEAMED GREEN PEAS

This might be more peas than you need, but if any are left over, I put them in a salad the next day.

4 pounds green peas in the pod
4 tablespoons (1/2 stick) unsalted butter
Salt and freshly ground black pepper, to taste

Shell peas, and steam in steamer basket until tender. The time will vary according to how old and how large the peas are. Toss with butter, season with salt and pepper, and serve.
SERVES 6

PEPPERS

CHEESE-AND-HERB– STUFFED PASILLA CHILES

The basic work on these may be done in advance so I think they would make a terrific lunch dish—all you need is sliced avocados and salsa.

6 to 8 large pasilla chiles (see Note)

FILLING
4 medium garlic cloves, minced
3 tablespoons minced green onions or shallots
3 medium pieces oil-packed sun-dried tomatoes, minced
1/2 cup (loosely packed) fresh cilantro leaves, finely chopped

1/4 cup (tightly packed) fresh basil leaves, minced
1/2 cup mild dry goat cheese, crumbled
1 cup grated soft Monterey Jack cheese
1/2 teaspoon dried thyme
1/2 teaspoon dried dill
Salt and freshly ground black pepper, to taste

1 egg
2 to 3 tablespoons heavy cream
1 cup blue cornmeal (yellow can be substituted)
2 or 3 tablespoons peanut oil

Roast and peel chiles as you would bell peppers (see Note, page 74). Leave stem on and after they are peeled, carefully slit the chiles starting at the stem to about halfway down their length. Lift out seeds and discard. Set aside.

Combine all the filling ingredients, mixing well. Gently place enough cheese mixture into each chile to fill the cavity without overstuffing. Close by overlapping the seams. Put stuffed chiles on a tray and refrigerate, covered, until needed.

Remove chiles from refrigerator at least 30 minutes before continuing with the recipe.

Lightly beat together egg and cream. Spread cornmeal on a sheet of wax paper. Dip each chile in the cream mixture, letting excess run off; dredge in cornmeal, lightly shaking off excess. Place coated chiles on a plate or a sheet of wax paper next to the stove as you finish them.

Heat peanut oil in a large skillet and gently sauté chiles until golden brown on all sides and cheese mixture has softened and warmed. This will take several minutes, depending on how hot the oil is. Don't cook these too fast or they will burn before the stuffing is heated through. Serve at once.

Note: Pasilla chiles can be found in specialty markets or Latin markets.
SERVES 6 TO 8

MIXED PEPPERS IN OIL AND VINEGAR

Obviously this looks best if you can find several colors of peppers, but if the mixed colors are not available, use three red and one small green bell pepper.

1 each red, yellow, orange, and purple bell
  pepper
2 tablespoons olive oil
2 teaspoons balsamic vinegar
Salt and freshly ground black pepper

Seed the peppers and cut into strips. Heat oil over medium-high heat and add peppers. Cook until just crisp-tender, tossing all the while, about 10 to 12 minutes. Sprinkle with vinegar and then salt and pepper. Toss to mix.
   Serve hot or warm.
SERVES 6

BELL PEPPERS AND ONION

I use more than one color of peppers for this, but that is mostly because I like the way it looks. Red bell peppers alone would do fine.

2 tablespoons olive oil
2 tablespoons unsalted butter
1 medium onion, coarsely chopped
2 medium garlic cloves, minced
1 large yellow bell pepper, seeded and diced
1 large red bell pepper, seeded and diced
1/4 cup water or stock

Heat oil and butter in a large skillet over medium heat and sauté onion until slightly wilted, about 5 minutes. Add garlic and sauté another minute or so. Add peppers and water. Cover and cook over low heat until peppers are soft, about 30 minutes, stirring occasionally.
MAKES ABOUT 1½ CUPS

BAKED CHILES RELLEÑOS

In most kitchens stuffed mild green chiles are filled and fried. I like this version, which does away with the frying.

24 fresh mild green chiles
Vegetable oil
1 cup diced onion
1/2 cup golden raisins
1 cup fresh yellow corn kernels, cut and
  scraped from the cob (about 2 ears)
1/2 cup pine nuts
1 1/4 cups shredded mozzarella
1 1/4 cups shredded cheddar
4 large eggs, lightly beaten
1/2 teaspoon salt
Few dashes of Maggi seasoning
4 tablespoons unsalted butter, melted
1 cup evaporated skimmed milk
1/4 teaspoon freshly ground black pepper
1 teaspoon minced fresh oregano or 1/2 tea-
  spoon dried oregano

Preheat oven to 450 degrees. Rub chiles with vegetable oil and place on a baking sheet. Bake until skin begins to blister, about 10 to 15 minutes. Place in a brown paper bag and fold shut. Let cool. Reduce oven temperature to 350 degrees.

   Meanwhile, place a heavy skillet over high heat and when it is very hot add the onion (no oil). Do not stir. When the onion begins to caramelize, start shaking the pan from time to time. When well caramelized, remove to a bowl.

   Lightly grease a 2-quart casserole. Rub skins off the peppers and split each in half, removing seeds. Place one third of the halves in a layer on the bottom of the casserole. Sprinkle with a third of the onion, raisins, corn, and pine nuts. Combine cheeses and sprinkle a third of it over the onion. Repeat to make 3 layers, finishing with the cheese.

Mix the remaining ingredients and pour over the layered peppers. Stir slightly to make sure it gets under the bottom layer.

Bake, covered, for 30 minutes. Remove cover and bake another 30 minutes or until set and cheese is bubbly.

SERVES 6

RED BELL PEPPER ASPIC

Many of you know how I am about aspics. Here's a favorite.

5 tablespoons water
2 envelopes unflavored gelatin
2 tablespoons unsalted butter
2 tablespoons olive oil
2¼ cups coarsely chopped red onion
2 medium garlic cloves, minced
3 very large red bell peppers, roasted, peeled, and seeded (see Note, page 74), chopped
2 cups Chicken Stock (page 41)
Salt and freshly ground black pepper
Mayonnaise, preferably homemade (see page 348)

Put water in a small saucer and sprinkle the gelatin over it; let the gelatin dissolve.

Heat butter and oil in a skillet over medium-high heat and sauté onion until lightly browned, about 5 minutes. Add garlic and cook another minute. Add peppers, stock, salt, and pepper. Pour into a processor and process until smooth. Transfer to a bowl and stir in the gelatin, stirring until dissolved. Pour into a ring mold and refrigerate until set, about 3 hours.

To serve, place the mold in a bowl of hot water for a few seconds, just long enough to loosen it. Place the serving plate over it and invert. Refrigerate until melted gelatin sets again. Serve with a dab of mayonnaise.

SERVES 8

PEPPERS STUFFED WITH CORN

You can use green peppers for this, but I like the way red or yellow ones look. And they *are* slightly sweeter in taste. Either way, choose peppers that will stand easily.

6 medium red or yellow bell peppers
2 tablespoons unsalted butter
6 tablespoons minced celery
6 tablespoons minced onion
2 cups fresh corn kernels, cut from the cob and scraped (about 4 large ears)
1½ cups peeled, seeded, and chopped tomatoes
1½ teaspoons salt, or to taste
Pinch of freshly ground black pepper
1 cup soft bread crumbs
2 eggs, lightly beaten, or egg substitute
1 cup shredded emmentaler

Preheat oven to 350 degrees.

Slice off the stem ends of the peppers and remove the seeds and membranes. Place in a pot of boiling water and cook for about 5 minutes to soften. Drain and set aside.

Meanwhile, melt butter in a medium skillet over medium heat and cook celery and onion until wilted, about 5 minutes. Place in a bowl and add corn, tomatoes, salt, and pepper and toss. Toss in bread crumbs and then stir in the eggs. Stuff the peppers, mounding with the stuffing. Place in a pan with about ½ inch of hot water, top with cheese, and cover with oiled aluminum foil. Bake for 50 minutes, uncover, and bake for another 10 minutes to brown.

SERVES 6

RADICCHIO

GRILLED RADICCHIO

This delicious first course is a bit time-consuming but at least part of it, such as the sauce reduction and mixing the poaching liquid, can done ahead of time.

2 cups red zinfandel wine
6 medium to large shallots, minced
3 cups Chicken Stock (page 41)
3 cups veal stock
2 bay leaves
2 fresh thyme sprigs
4 cups water
1 cup Champagne vinegar
1 cup dry white wine
¼ cup lemon juice
2 medium heads radicchio, quartered
Olive oil
Salt and freshly ground black pepper, to taste
2 tablespoons black olive paste
10 medium basil leaves
3 tablespoons chilled unsalted butter, cut into bits
Coarsely chopped fresh Italian flat-leaf parsley

Place red wine and shallots in a large saucepan and reduce over medium-high heat to about 1⅓ cups, 10 to 15 minutes. Add stocks, bay leaves, and thyme and reduce to about 3½ cups, 20 minutes or more. Strain and set aside.

Combine water, vinegar, white wine, and lemon juice and bring to a boil. Turn back to a simmer and drop radicchio quarters in to poach for 1 minute, being sure they are submerged all the while. Carefully remove radicchio and place in a bowl of ice water to stop cooking. Drain. Brush radicchio lightly with olive oil, sprinkle with salt and pepper, and grill (or broil) lightly until hot and marked by the grill. Set aside covered lightly.

Bring red wine sauce to a boil and add olive paste and basil. When slightly viscous, about 5 minutes, stir in butter.

Serve radicchio on top of a pool of sauce and sprinkled with parsley.

SERVES 8

SHALLOTS

PAN-ROASTED SHALLOTS

1 tablespoon olive oil
16 medium shallots, peeled
¼ teaspoon salt
¼ teaspoon white pepper

Preheat oven to 275 degrees.

Heat oil in an ovenproof skillet over medium-high heat. Add shallots, salt, and pepper, and toss. Cook, stirring, until shallots begin to brown slightly and caramelize. Bake until very tender, about 10 to 15 minutes.

SERVES 4

SPINACH

SAUTÉED SPINACH

3 garlic cloves, smashed
2 tablespoons olive oil
3 tablespoons unsalted butter
2 pounds spinach, washed well and drained
   (but not dried)
1 tablespoon salt
2 tablespoons freshly ground black pepper

In a large skillet over medium-high heat, sauté garlic in oil and butter until it has a tinge of brown, about 2 to 3 minutes. Remove garlic and discard.

   Add spinach and sauté, stirring frequently, until the greens absorb the butter and oil, 3 to 5 minutes. Season with salt and pepper and serve.
SERVES 4

CREAMY SPINACH
Poached pears are also quite good puréed with spinach.

4 pounds fresh spinach, carefully washed
   and stemmed
1½ cups sliced bananas
2 teaspoons fresh lemon juice
Salt and freshly ground black pepper

Place the undrained spinach in a deep pot. Cook over high heat, shaking pan. Stir and fold spinach once, mashing down as it wilts, and cook about 4 minutes, until tender. Remove to a colander and press with the back of a wooden spoon to get rid of excess moisture. Place spinach and other ingredients in a food processor and purée until mixture is creamy.
SERVES 8

SQUASH

BAKED ACORN SQUASH
Of course these may be cooked in a regular oven, but they are done much quicker in a microwave. Take your pick.

3 medium acorn squash, split and seeded
3 tablespoons unsalted butter
Lemon pepper, to taste
Salt, to taste

Place split squash halves in a covered dish and dot with butter. Season with lemon pepper and salt.

   To bake in a microwave oven, cover and place in microwave set at HIGH. Cook for about 18 minutes in a full-wattage oven or longer in a smaller oven, checking every 6 minutes for doneness.
SERVES 6

VARIATION
To bake squash in a conventional oven, preheat oven to 350 degrees. Place squash cut side down on a baking dish and bake for 30 minutes. Turn the squash over and dot with butter, pepper, and salt. Bake for about 30 minutes more, or until fork-tender.

SWEET SQUASH CASSEROLE

I use acorn squash for this, but any winter squash will do.

4 medium acorn squash
6 to 8 tablespoons (³/4 to 1 stick) unsalted
*   butter*
6 tablespoons granulated brown sugar
¹/4 teaspoon salt
¹/2 teaspoon freshly grated nutmeg

Preheat oven to 350 degrees.

Halve and seed the squash. Rub them lightly with a little of the butter and sprinkle each half with about ¹/2 teaspoon of the sugar. Place in a shallow baking pan and bake until tender, about 1 hour.

Let cool slightly, then scoop out the flesh. Mash, then beat until smooth with 4 tablespoons butter, 4 tablespoons sugar, salt, and nutmeg. Lightly butter an 8-cup soufflé dish and scrape the squash in. Dot with remaining butter and sprinkle remaining sugar over it all.

Bake for about 30 minutes, until top is bubbly.
SERVES 8

BUTTERNUT SQUASH PURÉE

2 pounds butternut squash
4 tablespoons buttermilk
2 tablespoons maple syrup
¹/2 teaspoon ground allspice

Preheat oven to 350 degrees.

Cut squash lengthwise in half and remove seeds. Place, cut side down, on lightly oiled baking sheet and bake for 35 to 40 minutes. Remove and cool cut side up to avoid condensation. While squash is still warm, scoop from skin and place in food processor. Add remaining ingredients and purée until smooth.
SERVES 6

SPAGHETTI SQUASH WITH ROASTED VEGETABLES

Lightly grilled or toasted country bread is a good accompaniment.

SPAGHETTI SQUASH
2 small spaghetti squash (1¹/2 to 2 pounds
*   each)*
2 tablespoons unsalted butter
2 tablespoons olive oil
3 garlic cloves, finely minced with 1 tea-
*   spoon salt to make a paste*
¹/2 cup chopped fresh Italian flat-leaf parsley
1 teaspoon salt
1 tablespoon freshly ground black pepper

ROASTED VEGETABLES
3 large red or yellow bell peppers, cored,
*   seeded, and julienned*
3 small zucchini, cut lengthwise into
*   quarters*
3 small red onions, peeled, halved, and cut
*   through the roots into quarters*
1 pound asparagus (at least 12 stalks of
*   medium asparagus), rough ends*
*   trimmed and peeled*
3 medium portobello mushroom caps, wiped
*   clean and quartered*
4 stems of fresh rosemary, broken into small
*   pieces*
6 fresh thyme sprigs, torn into small pieces
1 tablespoon salt
2 tablespoons freshly ground black pepper
2 to 4 tablespoons olive oil

Freshly grated parmesan (optional)

To make squash: Preheat oven to 350 degrees.

Pierce squash carefully, but deeply, with a long knife and place on a baking sheet. Bake until the squash can be pierced easily by the same knife, about 45 minutes. Remove squash and increase oven temperature to 475 degrees.

Let the squash cool until it is easier to handle but still warm. Cut lengthwise in half, scoop out seeds, and, using a fork, scrape the flesh into strands and place in a large mixing bowl.

In a small heavy saucepan, melt together butter, olive oil, and garlic paste, stirring constantly. Add parsley, salt, and pepper. Toss with the spaghetti squash.

To roast vegetables: Divide vegetables between 2 large roasting pans. If you have 2 heavy-gauge sheet pans (10 × 15-inch), these would be ideal. Do not overcrowd because the vegetables will steam rather than roast. You may even need to hold some back for a third batch.

Scatter herbs, salt, and pepper over the vegetables and drizzle, but do not soak, with olive oil.

Roast the vegetables, turning occasionally to cook them evenly and to prevent sticking, until tender. This should take approximately 30 minutes, but you may begin checking for doneness earlier. Do not overcook.

Remove and arrange over spaghetti squash to serve. Pass grated parmesan, if using.

SERVES 6

BUTTERED ACORN SQUASH

The touch of nutmeg in this recipe piques the flavor of the squash very nicely. You can add more butter if you like.

1 acorn squash
¼ teaspoon grated nutmeg, or to taste
½ teaspoon salt
2 tablespoons unsalted butter

Cut squash into medium-thick slices, about ¼ inch or more. Discard seeds and stem. Peel with a very sharp paring knife. Place slices in a steamer, cover, and cook about 20 minutes, until fork-tender. While still hot, sprinkle with nutmeg and salt. Toss with butter.

SERVES 4

TOMATOES

SAUTÉED CHERRY TOMATOES

Mix whatever cherry tomatoes you find in your market. If you see nothing but red, they will be fine alone.

2 tablespoons unsalted butter
1 pint yellow pear tomatoes, washed, dried, and cut in half
1 pint red or orange cherry tomatoes, washed, dried, and cut in half
¼ cup minced fresh Italian flat-leaf parsley
½ teaspoon salt, or to taste
¼ teaspoon freshly ground black pepper

Melt butter over medium heat in a large skillet. Add tomatoes and toss. Sprinkle parsley, salt, and pepper over all and continue to cook, tossing lightly, until warmed through and skins are beginning to brown, several minutes.

SERVES 6

STEWED TOMATOES

Tomatoes are popular any way they are prepared in the South.

2 tablespoons unsalted butter
2 coarsely chopped onions
2 teaspoons red wine vinegar
5 cups peeled and seeded tomatoes
1 teaspoon dried basil

Melt butter over low heat in a deep saucepan. Add onions and sauté for 15 minutes. Add vinegar and sauté for another 2 minutes. Add tomatoes and basil. Cook for 2 hours over very low heat. Serve warm.

SERVES 6

SLOW-BAKED TOMATOES

These may also be chopped coarsely with fresh basil or tarragon and tossed with pasta.

5 tablespoons peanut oil
8 medium tomatoes
2 teaspoons sugar
¹/₂ teaspoon salt
¹/₄ teaspoon freshly ground black pepper
3 medium garlic cloves, minced
1 tablespoon olive oil
¹/₂ cup minced fresh Italian flat-leaf parsley

Preheat oven to 300 degrees.

Spread oil in a jelly-roll pan. Cut off one third of the stem end of the tomatoes and discard. Place tomatoes in the pan, cut side down, and bake for 30 minutes. Turn and bake for another 30 minutes, basting with the pan juices occasionally. Sprinkle with sugar, salt, and pepper. Bake for another 1½ hours until tomatoes are flattened.

Sauté garlic in olive oil over medium heat until soft, about 4 minutes. Do not brown. Stir in parsley and sprinkle over cooked tomatoes.
SERVES 8

OVEN-DRIED TOMATOES

This is how you can "sun-dry" tomatoes in the privacy of your own kitchen. Maybe they aren't Tuscan, but then how many of us are? And besides tossing 'em in with your pasta, you can use them to make Tomato Spoon Bread (page 311) or Tomato Gougère (page 299).

Set your oven to its lowest, below 200 degrees. Slice plum tomatoes in half, top to bottom. Scoop out the seeds with your fingers. Place, cut side down, directly on the oven racks and let them dry out for 12 to 15 hours. I usually put them in when I go to bed and let them go all night.

OVEN-CURED TOMATOES

This method comes from Larkin Selman, formerly of Gautreau's Restaurant in New Orleans. Use these tomatoes in everything from composed salads to vinaigrettes.

6 medium tomatoes, peeled and cut in half
  crosswise
1 tablespoon minced garlic
1 tablespoon chopped fresh thyme
2 tablespoons olive oil
¹/₄ teaspoon salt
¹/₄ teaspoon freshly ground black pepper

Line a baking sheet with foil and lightly oil it. Place tomatoes on the foil, cut side down. Combine remaining ingredients and rub each tomato half with the mixture.

Place in the oven and turn it to 225 degrees. Bake for 5 hours, until the tomatoes are soft but retain their shape. To store, cover with olive oil and refrigerate them.
MAKES 1 DOZEN

BAKED HONEY TOMATOES

A lot of people don't realize how well the flavors of tomato and honey go together. This is an old Southern dish.

8 ripe medium tomatoes
¹/₂ cup fresh coarse bread crumbs
2 teaspoons salt
2 teaspoons freshly ground black pepper
1 tablespoon dried tarragon
Tabasco Sauce (optional)
4 teaspoons honey
4 teaspoons unsalted butter

Preheat oven to 350 degrees. Slice off the stem ends of the tomatoes and carefully scoop out the seeds. Place open side up in a buttered baking dish.

Mix bread crumbs with the salt, pepper,

and tarragon. Mix a few drops of Tabasco into the honey, if you like. Drizzle the honey over tomatoes, rubbing it down into the cavities. Sprinkle tomatoes with crumb mixture and dot with butter. Bake, uncovered, for 30 minutes, until tomato skins begin to wrinkle. Place under the broiler for another 5 minutes, or until crumbs begin to brown.

Serve hot or at room temperature.

SERVES 8

WARM COUSCOUS-STUFFED TOMATOES

6 medium tomatoes, about $\frac{1}{2}$ pound each
2 tablespoons olive oil
6 tablespoons minced onion
$\frac{3}{4}$ cup minced red bell pepper
2 tablespoons coarsely chopped fresh Italian
    flat-leaf parsley
$2\frac{1}{2}$ cups couscous cooked in chicken stock
Salt and freshly ground black pepper

Preheat oven to 350 degrees.

Cut off a slice from the top of each tomato and use a grapefruit knife to clean out all pulp. Be careful to leave the wall of the tomato intact. Reserve the pulp and invert the tomato shells onto a paper towel.

Place oil in a large skillet and sauté onion and red pepper until wilted, about 5 minutes. Add 1 cup plus 2 tablespoons of the reserved tomato pulp. Cook over medium-high heat to reduce for about 10 minutes. Stir in parsley and couscous. Season well with salt and pepper.

Rub the inside of each tomato with salt and pepper and heap the couscous mixture into each, mounding the tops. Coat a pan just large enough to hold the 6 tomatoes tightly with vegetable spray and place them in. Bake until heated through, about 15 minutes. If you overcook them they will split and collapse, so keep an eye on them.

SERVES 6

SMOKED TOMATOES

This method comes from chef Gerard Maras at Mr. B's Restaurant in New Orleans. Use the smoked pulp to make any sort of sauce.

If you have a smoker, follow the directions to prepare it for smoking. You can also use a charcoal grill with a cover—such as a Weber—and get a medium-size charcoal fire going.

Prepare about 3 pounds of tomatoes for smoking. With a melon baller, core out the stem end of each tomato. With a sharp knife, make an × incision in the other end.

When the coals are covered with white ash, sprinkle moistened chips (hickory, mesquite, pecan, grape cuttings) over them to produce a heavy smoke. Place the tomatoes on an oiled grill, × side down. Replace the cover and adjust the vents to an almost-closed position; the coals should smoke but not flame up.

The smoking process should take anywhere from 45 minutes to 1 hour. Check the tomatoes shortly after putting them on to make sure your fire is not too hot. If they seem to be cooking, add more moistened wood chips to cool the fire down. The tomatoes are ready when they are very soft but retain their basic shape. The skins will be splitting and the tomatoes a bit wrinkled; the cored end will be full of liquid. To save all the juices, keep the tomatoes upright as you transfer them to a colander placed over a bowl. When they are cool enough to handle, slip off the skins and separate the seeds from the pulp. Reserve the pulp and juice and discard the skins and seeds. If not using right away, store the pulp and juice in an airtight container in the refrigerator.

BAKED TOMATOES STUFFED WITH ANDOUILLE SAUSAGE AND RICE

These stuffed tomatoes are sometimes dry, so bake them with a little broth in the pan. The juices can be spooned over the tomatoes when they're served. These are good hot or at room temperature.

TOMATO SHELLS
4 large tomatoes
Salt and freshly ground black pepper, to taste
2 teaspoons olive oil
1/4 teaspoon Tabasco Sauce
1 teaspoon minced garlic (optional)

FILLING
2 tablespoons olive oil
1/2 cup finely diced onion
1/2 cup finely diced yellow bell pepper
1/2 pound andouille sausage, finely chopped
1 cup cooked rice
2 tablespoons chopped fresh Italian flat-leaf parsley
1/4 teaspoon freshly ground black pepper
3 tablespoons fresh bread crumbs
1 tablespoon unsalted butter
1/4 cup Chicken Stock (page 41)

To prepare tomato shells: Hollow out tomatoes from the stem end. Discard seeds and chop pulp. Set pulp aside for the filling.

Invert shells on a rack and drain for 10 to 15 minutes. Sprinkle insides with salt and pepper, then rub them with a mixture of the oil, Tabasco, and garlic, if using. Place hollowed side up in a greased gratin dish.

Preheat oven to 375 degrees.

To make filling: Heat oil over medium-high heat and sauté onion, stirring, for 2 minutes. Add bell pepper and sausage. Cook for 3 minutes longer. Stir in the reserved tomato pulp and cook for another minute or so. Off the heat, stir in rice, parsley, and black pepper (the sausage adds enough salt). Correct the seasoning. Spoon the filling into the tomato shells. Top each with bread crumbs and a bit of butter. Pour the stock into the dish. Bake for 25 to 30 minutes, until the tops are light golden and the skins start to shrivel. Spoon juices over all when serving.

SERVES 4

VARIATION
Substitute another spicy smoked sausage for the andouille.

TOMATO SLICES WITH FETA AND CHOPPED HERBS

2 ripe tomatoes, cut in half crosswise and seeded
2 ounces feta cheese
1 tablespoon minced fresh chives
1 tablespoon minced fresh Italian flat-leaf parsley
4 basil leaves, shredded
Salt and freshly ground black pepper

STRONG VINAIGRETTE
1 teaspoon salt, or to taste
1 heaping teaspoon green-peppercorn mustard
Scant 1/2 teaspoon freshly ground black pepper
2 tablespoons balsamic vinegar
3 tablespoons vegetable oil
2 to 3 tablespoons olive oil

Place tomatoes on a platter and top with crumbled cheese. Sprinkle with chives, parsley, basil, salt, and pepper.

Whisk all vinaigrette ingredients together and spoon over salad.

SERVES 2

TOMATO SOUFFLÉ

I think it is best to make the tomato base for this in advance, so you can be relaxed about the soufflé. If the base doesn't taste tomatoey enough, stir in a little extra good quality tomato paste to give it a lift.

Freshly grated parmesan to dust inside of
soufflé dish
3 tablespoons chopped shallots
5 tablespoons unsalted butter
1½ tablespoons minced garlic
2 tablespoons chopped fresh tarragon
¼ cup all-purpose flour
1 teaspoon salt
½ teaspoon freshly ground black pepper
2 cups peeled, seeded, and coarsely chopped
vine-ripened tomatoes
2 tablespoons tomato paste
4 egg yolks, lightly beaten
5 egg whites
¼ teaspoon salt
¼ teaspoon cream of tartar

Preheat oven to 350 degrees. Generously butter a 6- to 8-cup medium to shallow soufflé dish. Dust with finely grated parmesan and set aside.

Sauté shallots in butter over medium heat until wilted, about 5 minutes. Add garlic and tarragon, then cook, few minutes more. Sprinkle with flour and cook for a few minutes, until well blended. Add salt, pepper, and tomatoes. The mixture will lump up, but keep stirring and mashing until the tomatoes begin to give up their water and a thick paste is formed. Stir in tomato paste, then add egg yolks and cook a few more minutes. Set aside.

Beat egg whites until foamy, then add salt and cream of tartar. Beat until stiff. Pile whites on top of the tomato mixture and fold in with an over-and-under motion until lightly mixed. Do not overmix; there can be a few streaks or lumps of white in the mixture when you pour it into the prepared dish. Place soufflé dish in a larger pan and surround with hot water. Bake until set, about 35 to 40 minutes. Serve immediately.
SERVES 6

FRESH TOMATO ASPIC

I'd wager there's not a soul from the Deep South who didn't grow up with tomato aspic. Whether you loved it or could leave it alone, it was always there. I love it.

3 pounds tomatoes, peeled and seeded,
juices saved
1 medium green bell pepper, seeded and
grated
1 medium onion, grated
1½ teaspoons salt
½ teaspoon freshly ground black pepper
3 tablespoons Worcestershire Sauce
2 teaspoons Tabasco Sauce
3 tablespoons fresh lemon juice
3 envelopes unflavored gelatin soaked in ¾
cup water

Chop enough of the tomatoes into small dice to make 1 cup. Purée the rest, and add enough of the reserved juice to make 3½ cups. (If short, add a little canned tomato juice.)

Combine diced tomato, bell pepper, onion, salt, black pepper, Worcestershire, Tabasco, and lemon juice. Set aside.

In a small saucepan, warm the purée over low heat. Stir in the softened gelatin and stir to dissolve. Add the reserved diced-tomato mixture and taste for seasoning. Pour into a 6-cup mold and refrigerate for several hours, until set.

To unmold, place the mold in a pan of hot water long enough to loosen the edges, cover with a serving plate, and invert. Return to the refrigerator for 15 to 20 minutes, then serve.
SERVES 8

CORNMEAL PAN-FRIED GREEN TOMATOES

These are great as a Sunday-morning treat with sausage. Some folks sprinkle them with sugar instead of salt and pepper.

Flour
1 egg beaten with a little milk
Yellow cornmeal
8 ¼-inch slices green tomato
Oil for frying
Salt and freshly ground black pepper, to taste

Spread flour on a sheet of wax paper. Put egg wash in a shallow dish. Spread cornmeal on a sheet of wax paper.

Dredge tomato slices in flour and shake off the excess. Dip each slice in egg and drain off the excess. Coat with cornmeal, shaking off the excess lightly.

Heat oil in a large heavy skillet over a medium flame. When hot, add tomatoes. Cook several minutes, until golden, then turn. Sprinkle with salt and pepper.

SERVES 2

TOMATOES WITH HONEY AND BLACK PEPPER

Honey is a great complement to the flavor of tomatoes (tomatoes, you may remember, are technically fruits). Peel a large tomato, cut it into thick slices, and spread each slice thinly with honey. Sprinkle the honeyed slices with salt and freshly ground black pepper, then reassemble the tomato. Brush it lightly with more honey, and give it a sprinkle of salt and pepper. Refrigerate for about 20 minutes, and serve cool.

GREEN TOMATO RATATOUILLE

I like this served just warm or at room temperature.

6 tablespoons olive oil
1 pound green tomatoes, very coarsely chopped
1 large green bell pepper, seeded and coarsely chopped
3 very large garlic cloves, minced
1 pound white onions, coarsely chopped
1¾ pounds ripe tomatoes, coarsely chopped
1 pound zucchini, cut into medium-thin rounds
1 tablespoon salt
1 teaspoon freshly ground black pepper
Pinch of crushed red pepper
1 tablespoon minced fresh basil or ½ teaspoon dried basil

Heat oil in a large skillet and add green tomatoes, bell pepper, garlic, and onions. Sauté, stirring lightly, until vegetables are wilted, 7 to 8 minutes. Add ripe tomatoes and zucchini. Cook until zucchini is tender and tomatoes have given up a lot of liquid. Add seasonings and mix carefully. Continue to simmer at higher heat, stirring lightly, until most of the liquid has evaporated and what is left has thickened. Keep scraping from the bottom to keep it from scorching and sticking.

To serve hot, reheat in a double boiler.

SERVES 6 TO 8

TOMATOES AND LEMONS

The trick here is to slice the lemon *very* thin and to put the whole thing together about 30 minutes before you eat it, to give the salad time to marinate in the refrigerator. Arrange lemon slices alternating with tomato slices. I take all the end slices of tomato, chop them, and heap them in a line along the middle of the dish. Just before serving, sprinkle with salt and freshly ground black pepper.

TURNIPS

TURNIPS AND BEETS

The method of cooking and preparation for both of these vegetables is the same, but they should be cooked separately to keep the turnips from being colored by the beets.

6 medium turnips, peeled and quartered
Salt
6 medium beets, peeled and quartered
2 tablespoons unsalted butter
White pepper, to taste
4 tablespoons minced fresh Italian flat-leaf
*   parsley*

Place turnips in a saucepan and cover with well-salted water. Bring to a boil over high heat, then turn heat down to a light boil and cook until just fork-tender, about 15 minutes. If not using right away, plunge in cold water and drain.

Prepare beets the same way as the turnips. They may take longer to be tender, up to 30 minutes.

To serve, melt 1 tablespoon butter in a large skillet and sauté turnips until warmed through, about 2 minutes. Toss with salt, pepper, and 2 tablespoons of the parsley. Repeat with the beets. Combine and serve.

SERVES 8

TURNIP CUSTARD

Turnips prepared this way are mild and have a subtle flavor that is perfect with fish.

³/₄ pound peeled white turnips
1 small white potato
3 tablespoons butter
2 large eggs
¹/₂ cup milk
3 tablespoons evaporated skimmed milk
¹/₂ teaspoon freshly grated nutmeg
¹/₂ teaspoon salt, or to taste
Chopped fresh Italian flat-leaf parsley

Put kettle of water on to boil. Butter a 9-inch cake pan and set the oven rack in the middle position. Preheat to 375 degrees.

Boil turnips until very tender, about 30 minutes. If they are large, cut into several pieces. Cut potato into pieces and, in a separate pan, boil until tender. In a food processor with a metal blade, process turnips and butter until puréed, about 10 seconds. Scrape down the sides of the bowl. Add eggs, milk, evaporated milk, nutmeg, and salt and process for 30 seconds. Rice the potato and add to the mixture. Adjust seasoning if necessary.

Pour the mixture into the cake pan and set it into a larger pan. Pour in boiling water to come up ¹/₂ inch. Bake for 30 minutes, or until the custard sets. Remove from water bath and let rest. When ready to serve, run a knife around the edge and invert onto a platter. Decorate with parsley.

Note: This custard can be prepared ahead and set aside, unmolded. Reheat by putting in water bath and simmering for 30 minutes on top of stove. When unmolding it, if parts should stick, carefully remove them with a spatula and mold the parts together with your hands. You will hardly be able to see the seams, and the parsley garnish will also help hide any imperfections.

SERVES 6

GRATED TURNIPS

On several occasions when I have served this, my guests were not quite sure what it was at first. I think you will like this unusual way of serving this sharp-tasting little vegetable.

2 tablespoons unsalted butter
2 tablespoons finely chopped onion
1 tablespoon sugar
2 pounds white turnips, peeled and coarsely shredded
About 1 cup Chicken Stock (page 41), reduced, hot
3/4 teaspoon salt

Melt butter in a large heavy saucepan and add onion and sugar. Cook over low heat until mixture begins to caramelize. Add turnips and mix. Add 1 cup of hot stock and the salt. Simmer, covered, for about 30 minutes. Add more stock if necessary and correct seasoning.
SERVES 6

WATERCRESS

STIR-FRIED WATERCRESS

This is really a delicious way of doing watercress, and it requires almost no cooking time.

2 pounds watercress
1 tablespoon rice wine vinegar
1 teaspoon salt
1 tablespoon peanut oil
2 large garlic cloves, finely minced

Wash and thoroughly dry watercress. Remove the large tough stems.

Combine vinegar and salt in a small bowl. Put oil in a large wok or skillet and heat to very hot. Add garlic and stir-fry for 10 seconds. Continuing at high heat, add watercress and stir-fry until it is wilted, about 15 seconds. Add the vinegar-salt mixture and continue to toss for another 5 or 6 seconds. Serve at once.
SERVES 6

YELLOW SQUASH AND ZUCCHINI

GRILLED YELLOW SQUASH AND TOMATO

Yellow tomatoes are best for this dish, but use red ones if the yellow are not available.

4 medium garlic cloves, minced
1/2 cup olive oil
1/4 cup balsamic vinegar
Salt and freshly ground black pepper
1 1/2 pounds yellow summer squash, cut into 1/4-inch slices
2 green onions, with some of the green, finely sliced
1/4 cup minced shallots
1 large yellow tomato, coarsely chopped

Preheat a grill or broiler. Combine garlic, oil, vinegar, salt, pepper, and squash. Marinate for 10 to 15 minutes. Drain the squash, reserving the marinade, and grill until golden. (The timing will depend on how hot the grill is and how far the grate is from the heat.)

Chop the squash into large chunks and place in a bowl. Add the remaining ingredients as well as the marinade. Toss lightly.
SERVES 6

SUMMER SQUASH AND PEPPERS WITH BALSAMIC VINEGAR BUTTER

Balsamic vinegar butter is good on almost any vegetable, so remember it.

3 cups sliced or cubed summer squash
2 large green bell peppers, seeded and cut into thin strips

BALSAMIC VINEGAR BUTTER
2 tablespoons unsalted butter, softened
1½ teaspoons balsamic vinegar

Salt, to taste
Dash of white pepper (optional)

Put squash and peppers in a steamer. Steam for 6 minutes, or until the degree of doneness desired. Do not overcook.

Meanwhile, blend butter and vinegar.

Drain vegetables and toss with vinegar, butter, salt, and a dash of white pepper, if you like.

SERVES 6

BROILED ZUCCHINI

The cooking time will vary slightly according to the size of the zucchini and how mature it is. Test it with the tines of a fork. You may also sprinkle almost any herb you particularly like on the zucchini before broiling it.

6 small zucchini, cut in half lengthwise
2 tablespoons unsalted butter, melted
Salt and freshly ground black pepper, to taste

Preheat broiler.

Place zucchini halves on a lightly greased pan, skin side down. Score the flesh with the point of a knife. Drizzle butter over all and sprinkle with salt and pepper.

Put under the broiler and cook for 5 minutes, until tender.

SERVES 6

SHREDDED ZUCCHINI

Not only is this fast, it's also my favorite way of preparing zucchini.

2 cups shredded zucchini
1 teaspoon salt
2 tablespoons unsalted butter
½ cup coarsely chopped onion

Place shredded zucchini in a colander, sprinkle with salt, and toss. Put in the sink or over a plate and cover with a tea towel. Allow to drain for at least 1 hour. Squeeze as much additional liquid from the zucchini as possible. Set zucchini aside.

Melt butter in a large skillet over medium heat and add onion. Sauté until wilted and lightly browned, about 5 minutes. Add zucchini and toss. Continue to cook over medium heat until zucchini is turning tender, about 6 to 8 minutes. Do not overcook.

SERVES 6

YELLOW SQUASH AND ONIONS

You can cook zucchini this way, too.

4 tablespoons (½ stick) unsalted butter
4 cups coarsely chopped onions
2 pounds yellow summer squash, sliced
1 teaspoon sugar
1 teaspoon salt
½ teaspoon freshly ground black pepper
¼ cup water

Melt butter in a medium saucepan over low heat. Add onions, cover, and cook for 15 minutes, stirring occasionally to prevent sticking, until translucent but not browned. Add squash, sugar, salt, pepper, and water. Cook for 1 hour, stirring occasionally until squash and onions are very tender. Remove from liquid with a slotted spoon and serve hot.

SERVES 6

EGGPLANT, ZUCCHINI, AND PARMESAN TORTINO

The recipe for this tortino comes courtesy of Michael Romano, chef at Danny Meyer's marvelous Union Square Cafe in New York City.

3/4 cup plus 2 tablespoons olive oil
1 pound sweet onions, peeled and cut into 1/4-inch slices
Salt and freshly ground black pepper
1 pound eggplant, peeled and quartered lengthwise, cut into 1/4-inch slices
1/2 pound zucchini, washed and sliced into 1/4-inch rounds
1/2 pound yellow summer squash, washed and sliced into 1/4-inch rounds
5 large eggs
2 tablespoons balsamic vinegar
1 cup heavy cream
1/2 cup freshly grated parmesan

Preheat oven to 325 degrees.

Heat 1/4 cup of the olive oil in a large skillet and cook onions over medium-high heat until very tender, 5 to 6 minutes. Season with salt and pepper and put into a large mixing bowl.

Using another 1/4 cup of the olive oil, sauté eggplant, zucchini, and yellow squash over high heat until tender, 6 to 8 minutes. Add to the onions.

In a medium bowl, whisk together eggs, 1/4 cup of olive oil, the vinegar, cream, and half the parmesan. Pour this over the vegetables and mix gently.

Use the remaining 2 tablespoons olive oil to oil a 2-inch-deep 2-quart baking dish. Pour in the vegetable mixture. Cover with foil and bake for 45 minutes. Remove foil and sprinkle with the remaining parmesan. Bake for an additional 15 minutes. Run under the broiler briefly to brown lightly. Let rest for 30 minutes. Cut into squares or wedges to serve.

Note: A lighter version can be made using slightly less oil, egg substitute for 3 of the 5 eggs, and evaporated skimmed milk for the cream.
SERVES 6

YELLOW SQUASH SOUFFLÉ WITH TOMATO AND RED BELL PEPPER SAUCE

Zucchini squash can be substituted for the yellow squash.

2 cups sliced yellow summer squash (1-inch rounds)
1 cup coarsely chopped onion
9 tablespoons unsalted butter
1 tablespoon sugar
Salt and freshly ground black pepper, to taste
6 tablespoons all-purpose flour
2 cups milk, scalded
Dash of nutmeg
1 tablespoon cornstarch
1 tablespoon water
1/4 teaspoon cayenne
2 teaspoons Worcestershire Sauce
8 eggs, separated
Tomato and Red Bell Pepper Sauce (page 93)

In a saucepan, combine squash, onion, 4 tablespoons of the butter, sugar, and salt and pepper. Cover with water and bring quickly to a boil. Simmer about 45 minutes, until vegetables are very tender. Drain, mash, and set aside. You should have about 1 1/2 cups of pulp.

Preheat oven to 400 degrees and butter a 2-quart soufflé dish. Set aside.

Melt remaining 5 tablespoons butter in a saucepan over moderate heat until small bubbles form. Whisk in flour well. Add milk in a steady stream, whisking rapidly, until sauce is thick and smooth. Add salt, pepper, and nutmeg. Cook for one or two minutes more.

Combine cornstarch and water to make a paste, add to sauce, and stir. Cook for another minute before adding cayenne and Worcestershire.

Beat yolks lightly. Add a few tablespoons of white sauce to the yolks to warm them. Put sauce over low heat and pour in yolks in a thin stream, whisking. Add squash mixture and blend. Remove from heat. Set aside.

Beat whites until stiff. Fold into squash mixture with an over-and-under movement. Do not overmix. Pour mixture into soufflé dish and place in oven. Immediately lower heat to 375 degrees and bake for about 30 minutes, until puffy and golden.

Serve on a slick of sauce, and pass the remaining sauce.

SERVES 6 TO 8

VEGETABLE PURÉES

PURÉED CARROTS AND CAULIFLOWER

1 pound carrots, peeled and cut into thin
*   rounds*
1/2 pound cauliflower florets
3 tablespoons unsalted butter
1 teaspoon sherry vinegar
3 tablespoons milk
1/2 teaspoon salt
Freshly grated nutmeg

Put vegetables in the top of a steamer and steam for 6 minutes, until tender. Put them in a food processor, along with the rest of the ingredients. Purée until smooth, scraping down the sides of the bowl as needed. Correct the seasoning, if necessary.

SERVES 6

PURÉE OF BEETS AND CARROTS

The thing to remember about this and most other purées is to season them to your personal taste. They can be puréed to a completely smooth texture or be left rather coarse, as you wish.

You can use crème fraîche, butter, yogurt, or a little stock to achieve the consistency and taste you like. A squeeze of lemon or a few drops of vinegar will also pique the flavor of most vegetables.

3 cups grated carrots
3 cups coarsely chopped, peeled baked beets
*   (see page 105)*
1 1/2 tablespoons fresh lemon juice
1/8 teaspoon freshly grated nutmeg
4 tablespoons (1/2 stick) unsalted butter
2 tablespoons plain yogurt or sour cream
Salt

Place carrots in a small pot and just barely cover with water. Bring to a boil and cook slowly for about 15 minutes, until tender. Drain and place in a food processor along with all other ingredients except salt. Purée to desired consistency. Add salt to taste and more of any of the other ingredients you desire.

Reheat in the top of a double boiler, stirring as it heats.

SERVES 12

PURÉE OF CARROTS AND BAKED ONIONS

*3 pounds carrots, scraped and cut into
   rounds*
*3 pounds large onions, preferably Vidalia,
   roasted (see page 130)*
3 tablespoons unsalted butter
1 tablespoon sherry vinegar
2 tablespoons sugar
Salt, to taste

Cover carrots with lightly salted water in a
large saucepan and simmer for about 15 minutes, until fork-tender. Drain carrots and keep
warm.

   Let roasted onions cool until you can just
handle them and peel off the first couple of
layers. Cut the onions in half and put them in a
food processor, along with the carrots, butter,
vinegar, and sugar. Process until puréed. Add
salt and correct the seasoning.
SERVES 8

CARROT AND BROCCOLI PURÉE

*1 1/4 pounds carrots, scraped and cut into 1/2-
   inch rounds*
1/2 pound broccoli florets
2 large garlic cloves
1 1/4 pounds roasted onions (see page 130)
1 teaspoon balsamic vinegar
1 teaspoon salt
2 tablespoons unsalted butter
1 tablespoon crème fraîche
Few grinds of black pepper

Simmer carrots in lightly salted water for 10
minutes, until fork-tender. Drain. Do the same
with the broccoli. Put the vegetables in a food
processor, add remaining ingredients, and
purée. Correct the seasoning if necessary.
SERVES 6

PURÉE OF LEEKS AND WAX BEANS

*1 1/4 pounds leeks (white part only), carefully
   washed and chopped into 1/2-inch slices*
*1 1/4 pounds wax beans, ends and stems
   removed*
1 teaspoon raspberry vinegar
1 tablespoon plus 1 teaspoon unsalted butter
1 teaspoon salt, or to taste
3 tablespoons crème fraîche
1/2 teaspoon white pepper

Simmer leeks in lightly salted water for 15 minutes, or until fork-tender. Drain. Simmer wax
beans for 12 minutes, or until fork-tender.
Drain. Put leeks, beans, and remaining ingredients in a food processor and purée. Correct
the seasoning if necessary.
SERVES 6

ROASTED ONION, CAULIFLOWER, AND LEEK PURÉE

*1/2 pound leeks (white part only), cleaned
   and cut into 1/2-inch rings*
3/4 pound cauliflower florets
Milk
1 pound roasted onions (see page 130)
1 tablespoon plus 1 teaspoon unsalted butter
1 tablespoon plus 1 teaspoon crème fraîche
1 teaspoon salt
1 teaspoon lemon juice
Few grinds of black pepper

Cover leeks with lightly salted water and simmer for 15 minutes, until fork-tender. Drain.
Cover cauliflower with milk and simmer for 10
minutes, until fork-tender. Drain.

   Put everything in a food processor and
purée. Correct the seasoning if necessary.
SERVES 6

152

GREEN BEAN AND POTATO PURÉE

This dish is a winner. It can even hold for a few minutes while you get everything else ready to serve.

1 pound white potatoes, peeled and cut into
*   cubes*
2 teaspoons salt
1 pound green beans, stemmed and broken
*   into several pieces*
5 tablespoons unsalted butter
Freshly grated nutmeg, to taste

Preheat oven to 450 degrees.

Put potato cubes in a saucepan and cover with water; add salt. Bring to a boil and add green beans. Cook for about 10 minutes. The beans should be just getting tender.

Drain and put into a food processor fitted with a metal blade. Purée, scraping down a few times. Add 4 tablespoons of the butter, cut into bits, and mix. Add nutmeg, and correct seasoning.

Pour into a baking dish and top with the remaining butter, cut into small pieces. Bake for 20 minutes. Serve from the baking dish.
SERVES 6

PURÉE OF ROASTED ONION, PEAR, AND CAULIFLOWER

1¼ pounds cauliflower, separated into
*   florets*
Milk
1¼ pounds roasted onions (see page 130)
6 ounces peeled and cored pear
1 tablespoon plus 1 teaspoon fresh lemon
*   juice*
1 teaspoon salt
3 tablespoons crème fraîche
Few grinds of black pepper

Cover cauliflower with milk and simmer gently for 10 minutes, until fork-tender. Drain. Put everything in a food processor and purée. Correct the seasoning if necessary.
SERVES 6

GREEN PEA AND WATERCRESS PURÉE

Aside from its soothing texture and flavor, this dish is useful because it can be made several hours in advance and reheated in a double boiler. If you plan to do this, do not refrigerate.

3 10-ounce packages frozen green peas
2 bunches watercress, large stems removed
Chicken Stock (page 41), hot
3 tablespoons unsalted butter
Salt

Put peas and watercress in a pot and add just enough hot stock to cover. Bring to a simmer and cook for 4 minutes. Drain and reserve stock. Put peas and watercress in a food processor and purée along with the butter and ¼ cup of the reserved stock. Correct seasoning by adding salt if necessary.

To reheat, put in the top of a double boiler over hot but not boiling water. Stir occasionally; otherwise, keep covered. Continue until hot.
SERVES 8

153

GREEN PEA AND FENNEL PURÉE WITH MINT

1 pound green peas, shelled
6 medium fresh mint leaves
³/₄ pound fennel, tender parts only (no
*   leaves or core)*
¹/₂ teaspoon salt
1 tablespoon plus 2 teaspoons crème fraîche

Simmer peas and mint leaves in lightly salted water to just cover for 5 minutes, or until tender. Do not overcook. Drain and place in a food processor.

Coarsely chop fennel and simmer for 4 minutes, or until tender. The length of time will depend on how fresh the fennel is. Drain and add to the peas and mint. Add salt and crème fraîche. Purée. Correct the seasoning if necessary.

SERVES 6

PEAR AND KOHLRABI PURÉE

1 pound peeled and cubed kohlrabi
¹/₂ pound ripe pears, peeled, quartered, and
*   cored*
1 tablespoon unsalted butter
¹/₄ teaspoon white pepper
¹/₂ teaspoon fresh lemon juice
1 teaspoon salt, or to taste
Few grinds of nutmeg

Simmer kohlrabi in lightly salted water for 18 minutes, until fork-tender. Drain. Steam the pears for 3 minutes. Put everything in a food processor and purée. Correct the seasoning if necessary.

SERVES 6

PURÉED PEARS AND TURNIPS

The flavor of turnips can be especially strong, so I like to add something to the purée to reduce their bitterness. This combination was suggested to me by Christopher Idone a few years back. I think it is unusually successful.

2¹/₂ pounds turnips
4 firm pears
¹/₂ lemon, cut in half
4 to 6 tablespoons unsalted butter (to taste)
1 tablespoon sugar
Salt and freshly ground black pepper, to
*   taste*

Peel and cut turnips into 1-inch cubes and steam until fork-tender.

While the turnips are cooking, peel and core the pears. Cut in half and put in a saucepan, just covered with water. Add lemon pieces. Bring to a simmer. Cook just a few minutes, until tender; do not overcook. Let stand in the water.

When turnips are done, purée them with the butter and sugar. Remove pears carefully to a strainer and drain for a few minutes, pressing slightly against the strainer to remove more of the liquid. Discard water and lemon. Add pears to puréed turnips and purée briefly. Add salt and pepper. If not serving immediately, reheat later in top of double boiler.

SERVES 8

VARIATION

Substitute 1 pound boiled potatoes for the pears. Omit the sugar.

BUTTERNUT SQUASH AND LEEK PURÉE

1¼ pounds butternut squash, split lengthwise and seeded
Butter
½ pound leeks (white part only), cleaned
   and cut into rounds
1 tablespoon plus 1 teaspoon crème fraîche
¾ teaspoon salt
¼ teaspoon freshly ground black pepper
Few grinds of nutmeg

Preheat oven to 400 degrees.

Put a dab of butter in the cavity of each squash half. Line a pan with foil and bake the squash in their skins, for approximately 1 hour, until fork-tender. Cover leeks with lightly salted water and simmer for 15 minutes, until tender. Drain.

Scoop out the squash pulp and put everything in a food processor and purée. Correct the seasoning if necessary.
SERVES 6

PURÉE OF YELLOW AND GREEN SUMMER SQUASH AND ROASTED ONION

1¼ pounds mixed yellow and green summer
   squash, cut into ½-inch rounds
¾ pound roasted onions (see page 130)
1 tablespoon plus 1 teaspoon unsalted butter
¾ teaspoon salt
¼ teaspoon white pepper
¼ teaspoon ground cumin

Cover squash with lightly salted water and cook for 6 to 8 minutes, until fork-tender (or steam them). Put everything in a food processor and purée. Correct the seasoning if necessary.
SERVES 6

PURÉED ACORN SQUASH AND GREEN BEANS

1 pound acorn squash, halved
¾ pound green beans, ends and stems
   snapped off
3 tablespoons unsalted butter
1 teaspoon salt
2 teaspoons sugar
Sprinkling of ground cinnamon
¼ teaspoon freshly ground black pepper

Preheat oven to 400 degrees.

Line a pan with aluminum foil and place squash in it. Bake for 1 hour, until fork-tender. Scoop cooked squash from skins and put in food processor.

Cover beans with lightly salted water and simmer for 12 minutes, until fork-tender.

Add beans and remaining ingredients to food processor and purée. Correct the seasoning if necessary.
SERVES 6

VEGETABLE CONFITS, TERRINES, AND LASAGNA

CONFIT OF GARDEN VEGETABLES

This recipe was originated by Randi Middleton.

1 pound eggplant, cut into 1-inch cubes
1½ pounds tomatoes, peeled, seeded, and
*   cut into 1-inch dice*
1 teaspoon table salt
1 pound red bell peppers, quartered length-
*   wise, roasted, and peeled (see Note, page*
*   74), cut into 1-inch dice*
1 pound red onions, cut into 1-inch dice
1 pound zucchini, cut into quarters length-
*   wise, then into 1-inch sections*
About 1 cup olive oil
About 2 tablespoons kosher salt
1 large garlic head
¼ cup Chicken Stock (page 41)
½ cup chopped mixed fresh Italian flat-leaf
*   parsley, basil, marjoram, and thyme*

Preheat oven to 375 degrees.

Sprinkle eggplant and tomatoes with table salt, then let drain about 30 minutes. Rinse eggplant and pat it dry.

Place one vegetable at a time in individual mixing bowls and toss with just enough olive oil to coat. As you finish, spread the vegetables in single layers on separate baking sheets lined with baking parchment. Sprinkle with kosher salt.

Bake until the vegetables caramelize. They should still be tender and a bit chewy but should retain their shape. The eggplant, zucchini, and onions will take about 40 minutes, the peppers about 30. As each vegetable is finished, remove to a large bowl for a communal toss while still warm.

Meanwhile, break apart the head of garlic, removing the paper but leaving skins on the whole cloves. In a small saucepan, toss the garlic with olive oil to just coat. Sprinkle with table salt. Add chicken stock, cover, and simmer over low heat until tender, 30 to 45 minutes. Push through a sieve to remove the skins. Add garlic purée to the vegetables. Toss.

When confit has cooled somewhat, add herbs and toss again. Serve at room temperature and garnish (recipe follows).
MAKES 4 CUPS

SAUTÉED VEGETABLE GARNISH

1 to 2 tablespoons oil
1 to 2 tablespoons unsalted butter
2 large red onions, peeled and cut into ¼-
*   inch rings*
2 pounds eggplant, sliced ½ inch thick,
*   salted, and drained for 30 minutes,*
*   washed and dried*
1 pound medium zucchini, split lengthwise

Combine oil and butter in a large skillet and fry vegetables, turning as necessary, over medium heat until brown, about 10 minutes.
SERVES 6

VEGETABLE TERRINE WITH WATERCRESS MAYONNAISE

2 pounds ham hocks or meaty smoked pork
   neck bones
3 quarts water
1 large carrot, broken into several pieces
1 large onion, quartered
Several ribs celery, broken into large pieces
2 bay leaves
2 carrots, peeled and cut into julienne strips
4 medium leeks, well washed with tough
   outer layers removed
2 medium potatoes, peeled and cut into thick
   sticks
1/4 pound green beans, tips and stems
   removed
1 large yellow or red bell pepper, roasted (see
   Note, page 74), peeled, and seeded
4 envelopes unflavored gelatin
Salt, to taste
1/4 teaspoon freshly ground black pepper
2 egg whites, lightly beaten
2 egg shells
Several dashes Tabasco Sauce
1 tablespoon cognac
Strips of 1/4-inch-thick cooked ham
   (optional)
Watercress Mayonnaise (page 349)

Cover ham hocks or neck bones with the water and bring to a boil. Turn down to simmer and add carrot pieces, onion, celery, and bay leaves. Allow to slowly boil, uncovered, for several hours. Strain out the bones and either discard the meat or reserve it to make a sandwich spread. Discard vegetables and bay leaves. Refrigerate liquid if you have time, then remove congealed fat from the top; otherwise, carefully skim fat off.

To assemble the terrine, select a 4- to 6-cup loaf pan and refrigerate. Meanwhile, separately cook carrot strips, leeks, potato sticks, and green beans in the skimmed liquid until tender, being careful not to cook the potatoes so much that they fall apart. Cut leeks in lengthwise strips after cooking. Refresh all vegetables in cold water, dry them, and refrigerate. Strain the liquid once more and measure out 4 cups. If you don't have enough liquid, make up the difference with a little chicken stock or water.

Cut the bell pepper into thin strips. Set aside.

Place liquid in a saucepan and sprinkle the gelatin over it. When gelatin has softened, add salt, pepper, egg whites, and egg shells. Place saucepan over medium heat and bring to a boil, stirring all the while. Off the heat, add Tabasco and cognac. Line a strainer with a double layer of dampened cheesecloth and place over a medium bowl. Pour liquid through, then discard cloth and particles. Allow gelatin to cool slightly.

Pour a thin layer of gelatin in the bottom of the cold loaf pan. Allow to set for a few minutes, then arrange a layer of one of the vegetables neatly over it. Cover this vegetable layer with more gelatin mixture and allow gelatin to set for a few minutes in the refrigerator before proceeding. Continue with layers of each vegetable and the ham, if you are using it, repeating the thin gelatin layer over each. When complete, cover all with gelatin up to the top of the pan. Refrigerate, covered, until set.

To serve, set in a pan of hot water just long enough to loosen the sides. Invert onto a serving platter, then chill to reset gelatin before slicing, 30 to 45 minutes.

Serve with Watercress Mayonnaise.

SERVES 6

VEGETABLE LASAGNA

Here is a delicious concoction. All the vegetables should be thinly sliced, but they don't have to be peeled. A mandoline is handy for slicing.

> 1 medium eggplant, trimmed and thinly
>   sliced lengthwise
> 4 medium onions, peeled and thinly sliced
> ³/₄ teaspoon salt
> ³/₄ teaspoon white pepper
> 1 tablespoon minced garlic
> 6 medium green zucchini, trimmed and
>   thinly sliced lengthwise
> 8 ripe tomatoes, thinly sliced
> 1 cup freshly grated parmesan
> 1 to 1¹/₂ tablespoons minced fresh Italian
>   flat-leaf parsley

Preheat oven to 325 degrees.

Generously oil the bottom and sides of an 8 × 10-inch gratin dish. Cover the bottom of the dish with slightly overlapping eggplant slices. Top this with a layer of slightly overlapping onion slices. Sprinkle with ¹/₄ teaspoon each of salt and pepper and some of the garlic. Layer the zucchini, then tomatoes, and then again zucchini. Season again as above. Press down with your hand to compact the layers. Put on another layer of slightly overlapping tomatoes and finish with a layer of eggplant and the final seasoning. Sprinkle cheese and parsley over all. Cover with foil and bake for 15 minutes. Remove foil and bake until lightly brown, about another 10 to 15 minutes. Remove from oven and pour off excess liquid. Serve either warm or at room temperature.

SERVES 6 TO 8

CRUDITÉS AND VEGETABLE PLATTERS

ASSORTED VEGETABLES

These do not have to be done in any particular order. Just plunge in when you have a free moment. Arrange the vegetables nicely on a platter shortly before serving.

> New potatoes
> Broccoli
> Asparagus
> Artichokes
> Green beans
> Red bell peppers
> Tomatoes

Scrub potatoes, cover with water, and bring to a boil. Cook for about 15 minutes, or until tender. Leave in skins.

Clean broccoli and cut off the tough stem and leaves. Divide into sections, leaving florets intact. Stand on their ends in a steamer and steam until just fork-tender. This can be as little as 5 minutes depending on the age and freshness of vegetable. It is better to undercook than overcook in this case.

Trim off hard end of the asparagus and peel away the skin about an inch up from the bottom. A potato peeler can be used for this. Steam for only 3 or 4 minutes, tied in a bunch and standing upright. Do not overcook.

Cut off artichoke stems even with the bottom and trim the sticky end of each leaf straight across, cutting away about ¹/₂ inch. Soak covered with cool water for about 30 minutes. Drain and cover with fresh water and simmer 10 to 15 minutes. Test for doneness by poking the cut-off bottom with a fork to see if it is tender. Drain and set aside.

Snip off stem ends of green beans and plunge into boiling salted water. Cook only until crisp-tender.

Grill whole red peppers under the broiler until they are completely blackened. Store in a paper bag with the top folded over until ready to peel, seed, and quarter.

Dip tomatoes in hot water for 4 or 5 seconds. Refrigerate, unpeeled, until ready to slice.

COLD VEGETABLES WITH MUSTARD SAUCE

This is a very easy and eye-catching combination.

4 medium carrots, scraped and cut into thin julienne
4 medium zucchini, cut into thin julienne
4 medium yellow summer squash, cut into thin julienne
1½ pounds small green beans, tipped and stemmed
1½ pounds very small new red potatoes
Salt
1 tablespoon minced shallot
2 tablespoons Dijon mustard
3 tablespoons boiling water
½ cup olive oil
Freshly ground black pepper, to taste
Fresh lemon juice, to taste
2 tablespoons minced Italian flat-leaf parsley or other herb of your choice

Steam carrots, zucchini, and yellow squash separately until just crisp-tender, 2 to 3 minutes or less. Refresh with cold water. Drain well and dry in paper towels. Place in plastic bags and store in refrigerator.

Steam the beans for 4 to 8 minutes, refresh, dry thoroughly, and place in a plastic bag and refrigerate.

Drop the unpeeled potatoes in lightly salted boiling water and cook until just tender, 5 to 8 minutes depending on size. Refresh in cold water and store, whole, in the refrigerator.

Rinse a mixing bowl in hot water, then dry. Place shallot and mustard in bowl and whisk in boiling water a few drops at a time. Whisk in olive oil in a steady stream. Add salt, pepper, and lemon juice, mixing well. Mix in herbs.

To serve, toss carrots, zucchini, and yellow squash lightly with 3 tablespoons of the sauce. Thinly slice the potatoes and arrange vegetables on a cold serving platter. Drizzle remaining sauce over potatoes and green beans.

SERVES 8

CRUDITÉS WITH WATERCRESS MAYONNAISE

Include any selection of fresh vegetables you like—jicama, green onions, red and white radishes, cucumbers, carrots, cauliflower, broccoli, small mushrooms, small turnips, or red, yellow, and green bell peppers. Simply wash and clean them carefully and cut them neatly into strips and slices.

For mushrooms, peel and stalk them (save stalks for another use) and marinate overnight in olive oil and lime juice, mixed in a proportion of 1 cup mild olive oil to the juice and zest of 1 large lime. Add salt and pepper to taste.

To serve, dry all vegetables well, drain mushrooms, and arrange neatly on individual plates. Serve with Watercress Mayonnaise (page 349).

RAW VEGETABLES ON ICE

Cut celery, carrots, and green peppers into strips of even length. Cut the roots and tops off green onions, leaving a little of the green. Wash and cut into even lengths. Wash radishes, and cut top and root off. Remove stems from pear tomatoes and wash.

Serve all vegetables on a bed of crushed ice.

PICKLED AND MARINATED VEGETABLES

PICKLED ONIONS

I make these and just store them in the refrigerator because I am too lazy to go through the hassle of processing them; they keep for a good while in the refrigerator.

8 cups small white pickling onions or pearl
*   onions, peeled*
1/2 cup salt
4 cups distilled white vinegar
1 cup sugar
2 tablespoons yellow mustard seeds
1 tablespoon drained prepared horseradish
20 white peppercorns
4 bay leaves
1/2 cup drained pimiento strips

Sprinkle onions with the salt. Cover with cold water and let stand for 6 to 8 hours or overnight. Rinse thoroughly with cold water, and drain well.

Combine vinegar, sugar, mustard seeds, and horseradish in a nonreactive large saucepan and bring to a boil over high heat. Reduce the heat and simmer for 10 minutes.

Meanwhile, divide onions among 4 clean pint-size jars. Add a few peppercorns, a bay leaf, and some of the pimiento to each jar. Pour the boiling hot vinegar mixture over the onions, leaving abut 1/2 inch of head space at the top. Put the lids on, let cool, then refrigerate the jars for up to 2 weeks.

MAKES 4 PINTS

REFRIGERATOR PICKLED BROCCOLI

These pickles are simple to make and will keep for weeks in a covered container in the refrigerator.

2/3 cup cider vinegar
1/3 cup olive oil
1/4 cup Pommery mustard
2 tablespoons honey
1/2 teaspoon curry powder
Salt, to taste
4 cups broccoli florets
1/2 medium green bell pepper, cut into 1/4-
*   inch strips 1 inch long*

Whisk together vinegar, oil, mustard, honey, and curry. Add salt and set aside.

Blanch broccoli in boiling water for 2 to 3 minutes. Drain and transfer to a glass container. Pour in marinade and lay green pepper strips on top. Cover container and let cool. Refrigerate for 48 hours before using.

SERVES 6

MARINATED MUSHROOMS WITH OREGANO

1 pound button mushrooms, cleaned,
*   trimmed, and quartered*
2 teaspoons minced fresh oregano
1 teaspoon minced garlic
1/4 cup plus 2 tablespoons red wine vinegar
1 cup olive oil
1/2 teaspoon salt
1/4 teaspoon freshly ground black pepper

Put mushrooms in a medium mixing bowl. Whisk together oregano, garlic, vinegar, oil, salt, and pepper in a small bowl. Pour over mushrooms and mix well. Let sit for at least 1 hour before serving.

MAKES ABOUT 4 CUPS

MARINATED MUSHROOMS WITH ROSEMARY AND CHIVES

These mushrooms are a good addition to any quick meal.

1 pound button mushrooms, washed and trimmed
2 tablespoons wine vinegar
2 tablespoons safflower oil
3 tablespoons olive oil
1 teaspoon Dijon mustard
1 teaspoon salt, or to taste
Few grinds of black pepper
1 teaspoon chopped fresh chives
1/4 teaspoon chopped fresh rosemary

Put mushrooms in a crockery bowl. Whisk together all the ingredients for the marinade. Sprinkle chives and rosemary over mushrooms and toss with the marinade. Marinate for at least 1 hour before using. Refrigerate if not using that day.

SERVES 6

MARINATED MUSHROOMS WITH CARROTS AND GREEN ONIONS

These are a good accompaniment to almost any kind of sandwich. Serve with fancy toothpicks.

1 pound small mushrooms, cleaned and thinly sliced
1 large carrot, coarsely shredded
2 bunches green onions (with some of the green), cut into rings
1 cup good-quality olive oil
3/4 cup raspberry vinegar
1 teaspoon dry mustard
Pinch of salt
1/4 teaspoon freshly ground black pepper

Combine mushrooms, carrot, and green onions in a bowl. Whisk together the rest of the ingredients and pour over all. Toss and refrigerate.

SERVES 6 TO 8

TERRELL'S PICKLES IN A HURRY

5 Kirby cucumbers
5 fresh dill sprigs, or 1 teaspoon dried dill
3 garlic cloves, minced
3/4 cup cider vinegar
1/3 cup kosher salt
Pinch of dill seed
2 whole cloves
1 teaspoon pickling spices
1 teaspoon Tabasco Sauce
2 bay leaves
12 black peppercorns
3 cups water

Wash cucumbers and place them in a crock or glass bowl. Add dill and garlic.

Place remaining ingredients in a medium saucepan and bring to a boil. Reduce the heat, cover, and simmer for 5 minutes. Remove from heat and let cool.

Pour pickling liquid over cucumbers. Submerge cucumbers by weighting them with a plate and a heavy can. Cover the crock and refrigerate for 3 days.

Skim off any foam, slice cucumbers, and store in a clean jar.

MAKES 4 CUPS

SPICED MARINATED MUSHROOMS

These should be served at room temperature.

1 pound white mushrooms, brushed clean
¼ cup plus 2 tablespoons olive oil
½ cup finely chopped shallots
2 tablespoons minced garlic
3 tablespoons fresh lemon juice
½ cup dry white wine
1¾ cups Chicken Stock (page 41), hot
1 large bay leaf
½ teaspoon crushed coriander seeds
½ teaspoon crushed black peppercorns
¼ teaspoon paprika
1 tablespoon chopped fresh thyme

Separate mushroom caps from stems and set caps aside. Coarsely chop stems.

In a nonreactive skillet, heat ¼ cup of the olive oil and sauté shallots over medium-high heat, tossing, until they begin to brown very lightly, about 5 minutes. Add mushroom stems and continue to cook, stirring occasionally, until they give off their liquid and start to turn golden, about 15 to 20 minutes.

Add garlic to the mushrooms and cook another minute or so, stirring. Add lemon juice, wine, and 1½ cups stock. Bring to a boil and add remaining ingredients. Stir to deglaze pan. Turn heat back to a simmer and add mushroom caps. Poach 2 to 3 minutes, until tender. Remove with a slotted spoon and set aside.

Reduce poaching liquid over medium-high heat until almost all has evaporated, about 20 to 25 minutes. Whisk in the remaining olive oil and the remaining ¼ cup of heated chicken stock. Pour over caps and toss. Refrigerate, covered, overnight. Bring to room temperature before serving.
SERVES 6

PICKLED OKRA

This recipe comes from Laura Godfrey. It's essential to use small okra; large simply will not do.

2 pounds fresh, small okra
4 cups 5-percent distilled white vinegar
2 tablespoons salt
1 tablespoon Tabasco Sauce
1 tablespoon Worcestershire Sauce
5 garlic cloves, peeled
1 tablespoon dried dillweed
1 tablespoon mustard seeds
5 small whole hot or mild peppers

Wash okra and soak for 1 hour in cold water. Meanwhile, sterilize and keep hot 5 pint jars and lids. Put the vinegar, salt, Tabasco, Worcestershire, garlic, dried dill, and mustard seeds in a pot. Bring to a boil and boil for 5 minutes. Pack okra, 1 pod up and 1 down, in the hot jars and add 1 pepper and 1 clove of garlic to each jar. Carefully cover with the boiling liquid and seal. Store in a cool, dry place.
MAKES 5 PINTS

WATERMELON RIND PICKLES

These are wonderful with hot or cold ham or pork. This recipe also comes from Laura Godfrey.

Rind of 1 large watermelon
Pickling lime
3½ pounds sugar
2 cups distilled white vinegar
1 ounce stick cinnamon
1 ounce whole cloves

Cut off the green skin and most of the pink meat (leave a tiny bit for color) from the watermelon rind. Cut rind into 1-inch cubes, cover with water, and mix in ½ ounce of lime for

162

every gallon of water. Soak overnight, then drain the rind but do not rinse.

In a large pot, cover rind with water again and cook over medium heat for about 1½ hours, or until rind can be pierced with a fork. Drain again. Mix sugar, vinegar, cinnamon, and cloves, then cover the rind with this mixture and cook for 1 hour. While this is cooking, sterilize 6 pint jars and keep them hot. Place fruit in hot jars with a slotted spoon and then fill each jar with liquid. Leave spices in the liquid. Seal and process in a hot-water bath.

MAKES ABOUT 6 PINTS

OLIVE SALAD

Add cheese, French bread, and tomatoes to this and you would have a fine little lunch— and an easy one to pack up and take along. This is the sort of thing that can rest for weeks in the refrigerator, getting better as the flavors meld together.

If you can't find jicama, you could substitute water chestnuts or celery for a little crunch.

¾ cup halved pitted small green olives
¾ cup coarsely chopped pitted Greek olives in oil
1 red bell pepper, roasted (see Note, page 74), peeled, and seeded, cut into strips
1 tablespoon capers, rinsed and drained
½ cup jicama, peeled and cut into small dice
¼ cup wine vinegar
¼ cup olive oil
Salt and freshly ground black pepper, to taste
1 small red onion, cut into thin rings and separated

Put olives, red pepper, capers, and jicama in a bowl and toss. Whisk together vinegar and oil. Pour over other ingredients. Add salt and pepper. Refrigerate. Garnish with onion rings.

MAKES 4 CUPS

MARINATED MIXED VEGETABLES

This combination of vegetables is one I like personally, but any firm vegetable can be used. You can even add button mushrooms.

1 very small head cauliflower, separated into florets
1 package frozen lima beans, cooked 4 minutes
3 carrots, cut into rounds
1 large green bell pepper, cored, seeded, and cut into strips
½ pound green beans, ends snapped off and cut into pieces
1 large zucchini, cut into strips

MARINADE
3 garlic cloves, crushed
1 cup safflower oil
1¾ cups wine vinegar
⅓ cup sugar
2 teaspoons salt, or to taste
2 teaspoons dry mustard
Freshly ground black pepper, to taste

Put vegetables into a refrigerator container with a cover. Mix all ingredients of the marinade and pour into the container with the vegetables. This will probably not cover all the vegetables but don't worry, they will settle. Marinate in the refrigerator for at least 48 hours, stirring once or twice.

SERVES 8

FRUIT SIDE DISHES

BRAISED APPLES AND RED ONIONS

This would be perfect served with ham or some other kind of pork.

3 tablespoons olive oil
3 large red onions, peeled and chopped into 1-inch pieces
3 large Granny Smith or Newtown Pippin apples, peeled, cored, and cut into 1-inch slices
3 cups dry red wine, preferably pinot noir
Salt and freshly ground black pepper, to taste

Place oil in a large, nonreactive sauté pan, add onions, and sauté over medium-low heat until wilted and translucent, about 7 minutes. Add apples and continue cooking over medium-low heat until softened, about 5 minutes. Add wine and raise heat to medium-high, cover, and cook approximately 5 minutes or until wine is completely reduced and apples and onions are completely soft. Add salt and pepper.
SERVES 6

SAUTÉED APPLES

Sautéed apples are good served with sausages and cornbread for an easy cold-weather meal.

1 tablespoon unsalted butter
1 tablespoon vegetable oil
3 firm apples, cored, peeled, and cut into 6 lengthwise slices
3 tablespoons granulated brown sugar

Heat butter and oil in a large skillet over high heat and add apple slices, tossing to coat. Brown lightly, turning, until tender, about 5 minutes. Pour off any liquid or fat and sprinkle brown sugar over all. Stir and toss lightly until well coated.
SERVES 6

PEPPERED PEACHES

This dish is East Indian in origin and has a nice tang that goes well with poultry and meat dishes. After you have made this once, you can increase the amounts of pepper to suit your taste.

6 large peaches
3 tablespoons fresh lemon juice
2 tablespoons sugar
1 teaspoon salt
Freshly ground black pepper
Cayenne pepper

To peel peaches, dip in boiling water for 6 seconds. Skins should then slip off easily. Cut each peach in half and remove the pit. Put peach halves in a single layer on a plate and coat with lemon juice. Sprinkle sugar and salt over all. Add black pepper and cayenne pepper sparingly.

(This dish can be prepared up to 3 hours in advance. Don't refrigerate. The lemon juice keeps the peaches from discoloring.)
SERVES 6

GRAINS, RICE, POTATOES, AND BEANS

WHILE GRAINS, RICE, AND beans have always played an important part in my menus, I tended to think of them as balance and connectors to a main course. But lately that's changed. Whether it is part of an ongoing search for healthy cuisine or the vastly improved availability of new varieties that dramatically broadened my tastes (or both), I've started to think of these in terms of main courses. In any capacity, grains, rice, and beans practically invite innovation, as you'll see in this section. And as with pastas, when it comes to topping almost anything goes. Also don't overlook any of them as the principal ingredient of a main course salad.
✦ We didn't have a lot of potatoes when I was growing up, except for mashed and picnic-staple salad. And of course there were plenty of sweet potatoes. The potato dishes here came later—let's refer to them as my grown-up potato favorites.

GRAINS

GRITS WITH BUTTER

Grits are simply hulled corn kernels ground coarsely. Their appeal, aside from their flavor, is their creamy texture. Grits are packaged in three forms. The first is the old-fashioned variety, which must be cooked about thirty minutes. The flavor is excellent, but the grits have to be watched to keep from sticking and getting lumpy. The second, which I often use, can be prepared in about five minutes and is referred to as "quick grits." The last is the instant type, which I would avoid because the flavor is too bland.

1½ cups quick grits
1½ teaspoons salt
6 cups boiling water
Melted unsalted butter

Stir grits slowly into salted boiling water. Return to a slow boil and reduce heat. Cook 5 minutes, stirring constantly. Top with melted butter when served.

Note: After grits are poured from the cooking pan, immediately fill the pan with cold water. This will keep any grits left in the pot from sticking to it.
SERVES 6

BAKED BOUILLON GRITS

This is sort of a mock grits soufflé.

4 cups Chicken Stock (page 41)
1 cup quick grits (not instant)
½ teaspoon salt
4 eggs, separated

Preheat oven to 350 degrees. Generously grease 2-quart soufflé or Pyrex baking dish. Bring the stock to a boil in large saucepan and stir grits in slowly. Add salt and after it has returned to a boil, simmer for 5 minutes. Remove from heat and cover. Let stand for 5 minutes.

Meanwhile, beat the yolks until light yellow; whisk the whites until they stand in peaks. Combine yolks with grits, then fold in whites. Pour into baking dish and bake for 20 to 25 minutes, until puffy and light golden. Serve immediately.
SERVES 6

BAKED CREAMY GRITS

Cooking grits in milk instead of water gives them a very creamy texture and flavor. When you take this out of the oven, drape a dish towel over it. It can sit for ten to fifteen minutes this way.

4½ cups milk
1 cup quick grits (not instant)
4 tablespoons (½ stick) unsalted butter
1 teaspoon salt
2 eggs

Preheat oven to 350 degrees.

Generously butter 1½- or 2-quart casserole and set aside. Bring 4 cups milk carefully to a boil. Do not scorch. Add 1 cup quick grits in a steady stream, stirring all the while. Cook 4 minutes, continuing to stir. Remove from heat and add the butter, salt, and remaining ½ cup milk. Mix well. Beat the eggs well and add to the mixture. Mix and pour into prepared casserole. Bake for 1 hour.
SERVES 6

BULGUR SALAD

1½ cups carrot juice
4 tablespoons fresh lemon juice
2 tablespoons soy sauce
¼ teaspoon cumin
⅛ teaspoon ground cloves
1 cup coarse bulgur
½ cup chopped fresh Italian flat-leaf parsley
2 teaspoons salt
Freshly ground black pepper, to taste
1 large cucumber, peeled, seeded, and
*   chopped*
2 tomatoes, seeded and chopped
½ cup crumbled feta

Combine carrot juice, lemon juice, soy sauce, cumin, ground cloves, and bulgur in large bowl, allowing room for the bulgur to expand. Cover tightly and refrigerate overnight.

Unwrap, bring to room temperature, and toss with the chopped parsley. Add more carrot and lemon juice if dry. Season with salt and pepper.

Place on large serving dish or individual plates. Garnish with chopped cucumber, chopped tomato, and feta.
SERVES 6

BUTTERED BULGUR WITH BLACK OLIVES

Many people think of bulgur only as something to use to make tabbouleh. That's too bad —it has a marvelous nutty flavor when served hot. Try this.

2 cups Chicken Stock (page 41)
1 cup bulgur
1 tablespoon unsalted butter
¼ cup pitted and coarsely chopped oil-cured
*   black olives*

Place stock in small saucepan and stir in the bulgur. Cover and bring quickly to a boil. Turn back to simmer and cook, covered, until wheat is soft and liquid has been absorbed. Stir in butter.

To serve, make a mound of bulgur on each plate and sprinkle with chopped black olives.
SERVES 4

PASTA AND GRAIN PILAF

The bulgur wheat gives this pilaf a distinctive nutty flavor I know you'll like.

3 tablespoons unsalted butter
½ cup minced onion
¼ cup minced red bell pepper
¼ cup minced celery
1 tablespoon minced shallots
½ cup long-grain white rice
½ cup bulgur
½ cup spaghetti, broken into small pieces
3 cups Chicken Stock (page 41), hot
½ teaspoon salt
¼ teaspoon freshly ground black pepper

Preheat oven to 350 degrees.

Melt butter in skillet over medium heat. Add onion and cook until wilted, about 3 minutes. Add bell pepper, celery, and shallots and sauté for 2 minutes, to coat well with butter. Add rice, bulgur, and spaghetti pieces; cook, stirring, for 2 minutes. Add stock, salt, and pepper and bring to a boil. Pour into 1½- to 2-quart casserole with a tight lid. Bake, covered, until all the liquid is absorbed, about 30 minutes.
SERVES 6

TABBOULEH

Bulgur is very popular throughout the Middle East. It can be used as a substitute for rice. Here it is soaked in water to make it expand, instead of being cooked.

1³/4 cups fine bulgur
7 cups boiling water
1 medium cucumber, peeled, seeded, and
*   cut into small chunks*
¹/2 cup minced green onions
2 tablespoons chopped fresh mint leaves

LEMON DRESSING
2 teaspoons salt, or to taste
3 tablespoons safflower oil
7 tablespoons olive oil
5 tablespoons fresh lemon juice
¹/4 teaspoon freshly ground black pepper

2 large tomatoes, peeled, seeded, and
*   coarsely chopped*
1 head romaine lettuce

Put bulgur in large bowl and pour boiling water over it. Cover and let stand for 2 to 3 hours. Drain off excess water and put into a sieve and shake dry. Return to a serving bowl and add the cucumber, green onions, and mint.

Make a dressing by whisking together the salt, oils, lemon juice, and pepper. Pour this into the salad and mix. Chill, covered, until ready to serve. Before serving, mix in the tomatoes, draining off any liquid that may have accumulated in the container in which they were stored. Garnish with individual leaves of romaine.

SERVES 6

ADRIANA'S GNOCCHI

Adriana is the maid in the house we visit in Tuscany, and she often makes this dish for us for supper. I'd never made gnocchi in my life, but I liked hers so much I got her to teach me.

2 cups milk
2 cups water
¹/2 teaspoon salt
6 tablespoons unsalted butter
1 cup semolina
¹/2 cup freshly grated parmesan

Tear off a sheet of foil about 2 feet long, lay it on the counter, and butter it well. Butter a 12 × 9-inch baking dish and set it aside.

Combine the milk, water, salt, and 4 tablespoons butter in saucepan and heat, without boiling. When butter is melted, start stirring in the semolina. When all the semolina is in the pot, turn up the heat and bring to a slow boil, stirring. Cook, stirring, until smooth and thick, about 30 minutes. Pour out onto buttered foil and smooth to a thickness of slightly less than ½ inch. Allow to cool and set, about 1 hour.

Cut semolina into 2-inch squares and place in buttered dish, touching. Dot with the remaining 2 tablespoons of butter and sprinkle with the parmesan. This may be put aside for a few hours at this point, covered with a tea towel but not refrigerated.

Preheat oven to 350 degrees and bake the gnocchi until golden and bubbly, about 50 to 60 minutes.

SERVES 6

168

OVEN POLENTA, TOMATO FONDUE, AND SONOMA JACK CHEESE

Golden Pheasant is the brand of prepared polenta I used here.

OVEN POLENTA

4 tablespoons (½ stick) unsalted butter
½ medium onion, minced fine
1 cup coarse polenta
1 tablespoon kosher salt
1 teaspoon cracked black peppercorns
4 cups boiling water

TOMATO FONDUE

1 tablespoon unsalted butter
¼ cup extra-virgin olive oil
1 medium garlic clove, minced
2 medium shallots, minced
3 to 4 medium tomatoes, peeled, seeded, and finely chopped
1 tablespoon tomato paste
¼ bay leaf
1 tablespoon sugar
Salt and freshly ground black pepper, to taste

ASSEMBLY

6 ounces dry Sonoma Jack cheese, shaved
1½ cups heavy cream

Preheat oven to 350 degrees.

To make polenta: In an ovenproof pan, melt the butter. Sauté onion over low heat until translucent, about 5 minutes, then remove from heat and add polenta, stirring. Add salt and pepper to boiling water and pour over polenta. Mix lightly. Bake for about 30 minutes. Polenta should be firm, but still liquid enough to spread with a spatula. Spread polenta on an oiled 10 × 15-inch jelly roll pan; smooth the top. This will give you a layer approximately ½ inch thick. Cool and refrigerate, covered, until ready to assemble. This may be done 2 days in advance.

To make tomato fondue: Place butter and olive oil in a medium skillet over medium heat. Sauté garlic and shallots until translucent, about 5 minutes. Add remaining ingredients and simmer 20 minutes. Adjust the seasoning and remove bay leaf.

To assemble: Preheat oven to 350 degrees. Butter an 8-inch-square gratin dish and smear the bottom with some of the tomato fondue. Cut the cold polenta into 8 strips (see Note) approximately 7½ by 2½ inches. Place the first strip up against one side of the dish. Spoon tomato fondue along the length of the strip leaving about ½ inch uncovered (by the fondue) along the side that touches the edge of the dish. Sprinkle cheese on top of the line of fondue you have just put on the strip of polenta. Overlap the next polenta strip to cover just the line of fondue and cheese. Proceed as with the first strip, overlapping as you go, until you use all the strips. You may have to push the strips more tightly together to make them all fit. Drizzle the cream over all and bake until the top is golden and bubbly, about 35 to 40 minutes.

If you have any cheese left over after assembling the dish, sprinkle it over the top before baking. Any extra leftover fondue may be passed when the dish is served.

Note: You may cut the cold polenta into any shape you choose as long as the shape is one that will overlap the piece underneath easily when the dish is assembled. Triangles of polenta look very nice.

SERVES 6

GREEN CHILI POLENTA

8 tablespoons (1 stick) unsalted butter
5 cups Chicken Stock (page 41)
2 cups coarse polenta (Golden Pheasant, if available)
1 can (8 ounces) roasted and diced green chilies, drained

Butter large baking sheet with a short lip with 2 to 3 tablespoons of the butter. Set aside.

Combine another 4 tablespoons butter with the chicken stock and bring to a boil in large pot. Over medium heat, pour in the polenta in a steady stream, stirring constantly to prevent lumps from forming. Add the chilies, stirring, and continue to cook for 5 minutes, until thick and sticky. Quickly spoon mixture out onto baking sheet, spreading to a thickness of about ½ inch, using a buttered spatula. Rub more butter all over the top. As the polenta cools, it will become firm. Cut into triangles.
SERVES 8 TO 10

SPAETZLE

These little dumplings are terrific with stew.

1¾ cups all-purpose flour
Salt
2 eggs
¼ cup milk
½ cup club soda
4 tablespoons unsalted butter
Freshly ground black pepper

Combine flour and ½ teaspoon salt in large mixing bowl.

In another bowl, combine eggs, milk, and club soda, stirring well. Add to the flour mixture. Using a wooden spoon, beat for several minutes until a smooth dough forms. Allow the batter to rest for 30 minutes.

While the batter is resting, bring large pot of salted water to a boil. Using a spaetzle maker, pour the batter into the maker and shape the dough into the boiling water. Alternately, push the dough through a colander with holes the size of peas into the boiling water. Bring each batch of batter to a boil, then remove with a slotted spoon. Drain in colander and cool under cold running water. Spread on paper towels to allow to dry.

To serve, heat butter in large skillet. Add spaetzle and toss to coat; warm thoroughly. Season with salt and pepper.
SERVES 6

RICE

BOILED RICE

To add a little extra flavor to the rice you could cook it in chicken stock.

1 cup long-grain white rice
5 cups cold water
1 tablespoon salt

Combine all the ingredients in deep saucepan. Bring to a boil, uncovered, over medium-high heat. Turn the heat down so the rice cooks at a slow, rolling boil. Test for doneness after 10 minutes. Drain in colander and wash briefly with hot water. Fluff with a fork.
SERVES 6

VARIATION

When you fluff the rice, stir in 1 tablespoon softened butter and 2 tablespoons minced fresh Italian flat-leaf parsley.

170

STEAMED YELLOW RICE

2 tablespoons butter or margarine
1 teaspoon saffron threads, or more to taste
2 cups long-grain rice
3 cups water
1/2 teaspoon salt, or to taste

Melt butter in saucepan over medium heat, add saffron, and stir. Add rice, stir well, then add water and salt. Bring to a boil. Cover and cook over low heat for about 18 minutes, or until rice is tender and all the liquid has been absorbed.
SERVES 8

VARIATION
For plain steamed rice, omit the saffron.

RICE WITH FRESH DILL

I thought dill would be a tasty addition here. Adjust the amount to suit your own preference. This quantity will give the rice a medium-strong flavor of the herb.

1 cup converted rice
2 tablespoons unsalted butter
2 tablespoons chopped fresh dill

Boil or steam the rice as directed above. Stir in the butter and toss. Add the dill just before serving. Rice may rest in the pot for 5 to 10 minutes before serving.
SERVES 4

GINGER SESAME RICE

2 tablespoons minced fresh ginger
1 tablespoon toasted sesame oil
1 cup basmati rice
1 1/2 cups water
4 tablespoons teriyaki marinade

In heavy saucepan over low heat, brown minced ginger in sesame oil and add rice, stirring to coat. Add water and marinade. Bring to a boil and cover. Reduce heat and simmer until water is absorbed, about 20 minutes. Let rest for 10 minutes and fluff with fork.
SERVES 6

LEMON RICE

I almost cook rice this way in chicken stock, but you can substitute salted water if you like.

1 1/4 cups long-grain rice
Chicken Stock (page 41)
3 to 4 tablespoons melted unsalted butter
Grated zest of 1 large lemon
Salt and freshly ground black pepper, to taste

Boil or steam the rice as directed above. Mix in butter and grated lemon zest. Season with salt and pepper. The rice will hold for about 10 minutes. Fluff with a fork before serving.
SERVES 6

BUTTERED RICE AND MUSHROOMS

2 tablespoons unsalted butter, or more to taste
2 cups sliced fresh mushrooms
4 cups cooked long-grain rice
Salt and freshly ground black pepper, to taste

Melt 2 tablespoons butter in medium skillet and sauté mushrooms over medium heat for a few minutes until they give up liquid. Sauté another 2 minutes and toss with rice. Add more butter, if desired, and season with salt and pepper.
SERVES 6 TO 8

SMOKED SALMON AND SPINACH RISOTTO

A mouthwatering blend of ingredients!

2 tablespoons unsalted butter
1/4 medium onion, chopped
1 pound Arborio or Carnaroli rice
1 cup dry white wine
2 3/4 cups Chicken Stock (page 41), hot
1 bunch of spinach, large stems removed
     and julienned to 1/8-inch wide
1/4 cup minced fresh chives
6 ounces smoked salmon
3/4 cup (6 ounces) mascarpone cheese
Salt and freshly ground black pepper, to
     taste
2 ounces tobiko (Japanese flying fish roe) or
     golden caviar

Heat half the butter over medium heat in heavy-bottomed 6-quart pot. Add onion and cook until wilted but not brown, about 3 minutes. Add rice and stir well for 30 seconds to coat. Add wine and stir. Add 1/2 cup of the stock, turn up heat, and bring to a boil. Turn heat immediately back to a simmer, stirring with a wooden spoon every minute or so. When rice becomes dry, add another 1/2 cup of stock. Rice should be covered with a "veil" of stock during cooking. Repeat until all stock is added, about 13 minutes. Add spinach, half the chives, and the salmon. Mix and cook for another 3 to 4 minutes, stirring constantly so that the rice doesn't stick. Remove from heat and stir in cheese and remaining butter. Season with salt and pepper.

Transfer risotto to individual warmed plates and sprinkle with tobiko or caviar and remaining chives. Serve immediately.

SERVES 4 AS AN ENTRÉE OR 8 AS AN APPETIZER

BAKED ITALIAN RICE

This is really a very simple dish, but it requires that you make a portion of risotto first. To do that properly, you should use only Arborio or another medium-grain Italian rice. These varieties of rice are available in many Italian markets and specialty stores.

4 tablespoons (1/2 stick) unsalted butter
1 medium onion, finely chopped
2 cups Arborio rice
1/2 cup dry white wine
6 cups Chicken Stock (page 41), hot
3 large eggs, lightly beaten
Salt, to taste
1 cup coarsely grated gruyère

Preheat oven to 400 degrees. Lightly grease a 1 1/2-quart casserole or flat pan.

Heat half the butter in heavy saucepan and sauté the onion until it is translucent. Add rice and coat well with butter. Stir for a few seconds, then add wine. When it evaporates, start adding stock to the rice, 1/2 cup at a time. Stir it well after each addition of stock and once or twice as it is begin absorbed. You want this to be just barely simmering, not boiling. Repeat until all the stock has been absorbed and the mixture is al dente and creamy. Add the rest of the butter and let the rice rest.

Add the eggs to the rice and mix well, leaving no lumps. Add salt. Pour half of the rice into the casserole and cover it with the grated cheese. Top with the remaining rice. Smooth this over and bake for 40 minutes, or until the top begins to turn golden.

If you would like to serve this unmolded instead of spooned out, let it cool for about 5 minutes and then run a knife around the edges and invert onto a serving plate.

SERVES 8

172

LETTUCE-PROSCIUTTO RISOTTO

This is based on Barbara Kafka's wonderful recipe. I use her basic recipe and add to it whatever I have on hand—from lettuce or mustard greens to beans.

2 tablespoons unsalted butter
2 tablespoons olive oil
1/2 cup minced onion
1 cup Arborio rice
3 1/4 cups Chicken Stock (page 41), hot
1 cup shredded lettuce
1 cup shredded prosciutto (about 4 ounces)
Freshly ground black pepper, to taste
Freshly grated parmesan (optional)

Place butter and oil in a 14 × 11 × 2-inch dish and cook 2 minutes on high, uncovered, in a microwave oven. Stir in onion and cook 2 minutes. Stir in rice and cook another 2 minutes. Pour in hot stock and cook 9 minutes. Stir in lettuce and prosciutto and cook 9 minutes more. Allow to rest for several minutes before serving, topped with a grind of fresh pepper. Serve with a sprinkling of parmesan, if desired.
SERVES 6

VARIATION

You may omit the lettuce and/or the prosciutto.

PECAN RICE

No matter how I use pecans, I almost always toast them first—except when I'm making a pecan pie. Toasting vastly improves their favor.

1 cup pecans
1 tablespoon unsalted butter
3 cups hot cooked long-grain rice, rinsed
*   well*
Salt and freshly ground black pepper
*   (optional)*

Preheat oven to 250 degrees. Place pecans in a single layer on a baking sheet and toast about 15 minutes, until golden but not burned. Chop coarse and set aside.

When ready to serve, melt butter in a skillet and add pecans, stirring to coat with butter. Add rice and toss with pecans. Season with salt and pepper, if you like.
SERVES 6

VARIATION

Substitute 1/2 cup toasted slivered almonds.

RICE AND PASTA

Cooking rice and pasta together is a special treat.

3 tablespoons unsalted butter
1/4 cup finely chopped onion
1 1/2 cups rice
1 1/2 cups spaghettini, broken into 1/2-inch
*   pieces*
4 cups Chicken Stock or Fish Stock (pages
*   41 and 42), hot*

Melt butter in a large skillet. Add onion and sauté for several minutes, until slightly wilted. Add rice and spaghettini. Sauté, stirring, over moderate heat until rice is turning white and pasta begins to darken. Do not let burn.

Add about 2 cups of hot stock. Stir and simmer until this is absorbed. Add more as needed. Do not boil. Test for doneness after about 15 minutes. If not done, simmer for another 5 minutes.
SERVES 6

173

RICE AND PEANUT PILAF

I've got to confess—I like peanuts in almost anything.

4 tablespoons (1/2 stick) unsalted butter
3/4 cup minced onion
1 cup long-grain rice, washed
2 cups Chicken Stock (page 41), hot
3/4 cup toasted lightly salted peanuts

Preheat oven to 375 degrees.

Melt butter in an ovenproof pot over medium heat and add onion. Sauté until wilted, about 5 minutes. Mix in rice and stir in hot stock and peanuts. Bring quickly back to a boil.

Cover, reduce heat to low, and bake until rice is tender, 20 to 25 minutes. Fluff rice before serving.

SERVES 6

BASMATI AND WILD RICE WITH SWISS CHARD

3/4 cup basmati rice
1/4 cup wild rice
2 tablespoons unsalted butter
1 shallot, finely minced
2 1/2 cups water
1 teaspoon salt

SWISS CHARD
2 bunches Swiss chard (about 2 pounds)
1 tablespoon unsalted butter
2 tablespoons olive oil
6 green onions, chopped
2 tablespoons balsamic vinegar
1 teaspoon salt
Freshly ground black pepper, to taste

Rinse rice in strainer and shake to remove excess water. Rice should be as dry as possible.

Melt butter in heavy saucepan over high heat and quickly brown the shallot. Add rice, stirring constantly to coat rice with melted butter, and combine with shallot. Add water and bring to a boil. Do not stir. Lower heat, loosely cover pot, and simmer for 35 to 40 minutes. The rice will be puffed and most of the liquid will be absorbed. Remove from heat. Fluff rice with a fork, cover tightly, and let rice stand for 5 to 7 minutes. Drain any excess water.

To make Swiss chard: Wash the Swiss chard, shaking off the excess water. Cut off and discard stems. Tear into pieces and reserve.

Melt butter and oil in heavy skillet over medium heat. When it starts to sizzle, add green onions and sauté until colored, 3 to 5 minutes. Add chard and toss, mixing chard with green onions and coating with butter-oil mixture.

Raise the heat, add the drained, cooked rice, and mix well, allowing rice to absorb any cooking liquids without getting soggy.

Season with salt and pepper and serve.

SERVES 6

ORZO AND RICE PILAF

2 tablespoons unsalted butter
1/4 cup orzo
1/2 teaspoon crushed red pepper
1 cup basmati rice
2 cups low-sodium beef stock , brought to a boil and kept hot

Melt butter in medium saucepan over low heat. When butter is melted, raise heat slightly, stirring in orzo and crushed red pepper. Cook for 2 to 3 minutes, until orzo takes on a golden color.

Add rice, stirring to combine, and slowly add hot beef stock. Bring to a boil. Reduce heat, cover pot tightly, and simmer for 18 to 20 minutes. Remove from heat but do not uncover. Let sit for a few minutes and fluff with fork.

SERVES 4

MIXED WILD AND LONG-GRAIN RICE

This could also become the basis of a stuffing for chicken or turkey.

1½ cups long-grain rice
½ cup wild rice
2 tablespoons unsalted butter
4 ounces andouille sausage, removed from
  casing and chopped
¼ cup finely chopped red bell pepper
¼ cup finely chopped green bell pepper
¼ cup finely chopped red onion
¼ cup finely chopped zucchini
¼ cup finely chopped yellow squash
¼ teaspoon salt
¼ teaspoon freshly ground black pepper
⅔ cup Chicken Stock (page 41)

Preheat oven to 250 degrees. Grease a 4-quart ovenproof casserole.

Boil the long-grain rice as directed on page 170 until tender. Drain, rinse, and set aside.

Cover wild rice with 1½ cups well-salted water. Bring to a boil over high heat. Turn heat down to a slow boil and cook until tender, 12 to 15 minutes. Drain, rinse, and combine with white rice. Set aside.

Melt butter in large skillet and add sausage. Cook over medium heat, stirring, until browned, about 3 minutes. Add vegetables and continue to cook, tossing lightly, until softened, about 3 minutes.

Reheat rices by putting them in a strainer and immersing in boiling water, off the heat, for 1 minute. Drain. Mix rices with sausage and vegetables. Add salt and pepper. Put into greased casserole and add stock. Cover and bake for 20 minutes.

SERVES 6 TO 8

WILD RICE WITH PEPPERS

To hold this dish, place a tea towel over the pot and then replace the lid. This keeps steam from collecting under the lid and dripping back into the finished rice.

1 cup wild rice
2 cups Chicken Stock (page 41), boiling
1 tablespoon unsalted butter
¼ cup finely chopped green bell peppers
½ teaspoon salt
1 teaspoon coarsely ground black pepper

Place all ingredients in top of double boiler, cover, and cook over medium heat for 1 hour, or until liquid is absorbed and rice is fluffy. Fluff with a fork before serving.

SERVES 6

DIRTY RICE

Dirty rice is about as Southern a dish as there is.

1/2 pound chicken livers
1 medium onion, very coarsely chopped
3 celery ribs, very coarsely chopped
1 medium green bell pepper, very coarsely chopped
3 fresh medium tomatoes, very coarsely chopped
1 cup very coarsely chopped fresh Italian flat-leaf parsley
4 tablespoons (1/2 stick) unsalted butter
1/2 teaspoon salt
1/2 teaspoon freshly ground black pepper
1/2 teaspoon dried thyme
1 large bay leaf
2 cups long-grain rice (not instant)
4 cups Chicken Stock (page 41), boiling

In a food processor fitted with a steel blade, purée livers, onion, celery, green pepper, tomatoes, and parsley. Melt butter in large heavy saucepan, and add purée, salt, pepper, thyme, and bay leaf. Cook, stirring often, over medium-low heat for 30 minutes. Add rice and sauté over medium heat for 2 minutes, stirring with a fork. Add boiling stock, stir, and cover. Cook over low heat for 15 minutes, then remove from heat and allow rice to steam, covered, for 20 minutes. Remove bay leaf, fluff with a fork, and adjust seasoning if necessary.
SERVES 8

OKRA PILAF

1 teaspoon salt, or to taste
1 cup plus 3 tablespoons long-grain rice
2 1/3 cups Chicken Stock (page 41)
1 tablespoon unsalted butter, or more to taste
2 cups sliced okra

Add salt and rice to stock and bring to a boil in medium saucepan. Reduce the heat, cover, and simmer for 18 to 20 minutes, or until rice is tender and liquid has been absorbed. Toss with 1 tablespoon butter.

While rice is cooking, steam okra about 5 minutes, until tender. Toss with rice, adding more salt and butter if you like.
SERVES 6

RICE WITH EGGS AND VEGETABLES

This rice concoction resembles Chinese fried rice and can be cooked to any degree of doneness if the vegetables have been slightly wilted first.

2 tablespoons safflower oil
3/4 cup finely chopped red bell pepper
3/4 cup finely chopped green onions, with some of the green
4 cups cooked rice
3 large eggs
1/2 teaspoon salt
Freshly ground black pepper, to taste
2 tablespoons clarified unsalted butter
1/4 pound parmesan, grated

Heat 1 tablespoon of safflower oil in large skillet and add bell pepper and green onions. Sauté slowly until just wilted. Add rice and mix.

In large bowl, beat eggs and add salt and pepper. Add rice and vegetable mixture and mix well.

Wipe out the skillet and return to heat with the remaining oil and the butter. When foamy, add the egg and rice mixture and cook, turning until the eggs are set. Make sure it is turned and separated so that all the egg has a chance to cook. Heap onto a serving plate and serve with parmesan on the side.
SERVES 6

BAKED WILD RICE AND PORCINI MUSHROOMS

Because wild rice is so expensive, I stretch it a bit by mixing it with regular rice. You still get the distinctive taste and texture of wild rice, but at half the cost.

Sometimes inverting the rice onto a platter can be temperamental. In that case, pack it back into the casserole to serve.

3/4 cup wild rice, washed carefully
3/4 cup long-grain white rice
Chicken Stock (page 41)
1 ounce dried porcini mushrooms
1 tablespoon unsalted butter
1/4 cup sherry

Preheat oven to 350 degrees. Generously butter a deep-sided casserole or soufflé dish.

Bring 3 cups salted water to a boil. Stir in the wild rice. Turn heat down to a simmer and cook, uncovered, for 40 minutes. (Or if you have a favorite method of cooking this kind of rice, use it.) Meanwhile, in another pot cover the white rice with chicken stock to about an inch above the rice. Bring to a boil and turn heat down to a simmer, stirring occasionally. Cook for 10 minutes. Drain in a colander and rinse with hot water. Set aside.

Cover dried mushrooms with hot water. After about 20 minutes drain them, reserving the liquid for another use, and chop coarse. Sauté for 3 or 4 minutes in butter and then pour in sherry. Simmer until the liquid evaporates. Combine mushrooms with white rice. Drain off any excess liquid from wild rice. Drain off any excess liquid from wild rice. Mix it with the other ingredients and pour into the casserole. Bake set in a pan of hot water for 20 minutes. Let it sit for a few minutes after removing it from the oven. Loosen the edges with a knife and invert onto a serving plate.

Note: Mushroom liquid, after being strained through a doubled piece of cheesecloth or a coffee filter, may be used in soup or sauces.

SERVES 6 TO 8

RICE LOAF

1 1/2 cups water
1/3 cup basmati rice
1/3 cup bulgur
5 tablespoons unsalted butter
1 medium onion, finely chopped
1 cup finely chopped fresh Italian flat-leaf parsley
2 tablespoons finely chopped canned jalapeños
1 jar (4 ounces) mild green chilies, chopped
2 cups grated sharp cheddar
1 cup milk
2 eggs

Preheat oven to 350 degrees and lightly grease an 8½ × 4½-inch loaf pan.

Bring ½ cup water to a boil in a small saucepan. Add rice, cover, and simmer over low heat for 15 minutes. Set aside to cool.

Meanwhile, bring the remaining 1 cup water to a boil in a separate saucepan. Add bulgur and stir. Cover and simmer over low heat for 10 minutes. Remove from heat and leave covered for 15 minutes. Drain if necessary. Set aside to cool.

Melt 1 tablespoon of the butter in a small cast-iron skillet over medium-high heat. Once the pan is hot, add onion and sauté, stirring occasionally, until it just begins to brown, about 6 or 7 minutes. Remove from heat, add parsley, and stir.

In large mixing bowl, combine rice, bulgur, jalapeños, green chilies, and sautéed onion and parsley. Stir to combine. Add cheese and mix well.

Melt remaining 4 tablespoons butter and combine with milk and eggs. Add this to the rice mixture and stir.

Spoon the mixture into the pan and bake for 45 to 50 minutes, until golden brown.

SERVES 4

RICE SALAD

Like other salads, this may have as many ingredients as strike your fancy. Also, it may have as much dressing as you like. Some people like it very soupy and others don't.

The only thing to know about this salad is that it does not last very well in the refrigerator, so just make what you will serve at one sitting. It isn't that the salad spoils, but the texture of the rice and the overall flavor deteriorate in five to six hours.

> 1 cup rice
> 2 cups Chicken Stock (page 41)
> 3/4 cup fresh or canned green peas, drained
> 2 medium red bell peppers, roasted, peeled, and seeded (see Note, page 74), cut into strips
> 3 large green onions, with some of the green, sliced into medium rings
> 1 tablespoon small capers, rinsed and drained
> 2 tablespoons chopped sweet pickle
> 2 tablespoons snipped fresh chives
> 2 tablespoons chopped fresh dill
> 2 tablespoons mayonnaise
> White Wine Vinaigrette (page 44)

Cover rice with stock in a small pan and bring to a boil. Reduce heat and simmer for 10 minutes, stirring occasionally. Test for doneness. If not done, let it cook for another minute or two. Rinse with very hot water, drain, and set aside. You may do this several hours in advance.

When ready to serve, fluff up the rice and toss in peas, half of the bell pepper, the green onions, capers, pickle, chives, and dill. Set aside.

Stir mayonnaise into vinaigrette, mixing well. Toss into the salad. Correct the seasoning if necessary. Garnish with remaining strips of bell pepper.

SERVES 6

RED BEAN AND RICE SALAD

VINAIGRETTE
> 1/3 cup cider vinegar
> 2 tablespoons Worcestershire Sauce
> 2 tablespoons Tabasco Sauce
> 1 teaspoon grainy mustard
> 3/4 cup olive oil
> 1/4 cup vegetable oil
>
> 1 small onion, peeled and cut in half
> 2 bay leaves
> 3 garlic cloves, smashed
> 6 black peppercorns
> 6 whole allspice
> 6 whole cloves
> 1 pound small red kidney beans, soaked overnight
> 2 celery ribs
> Salt and freshly ground black pepper, to taste
> 4 cups cooked basmati rice
> 1 pound smoked chicken breast, diced into medium pieces (about 2 cups)
> 1/2 pound chorizo, quartered lengthwise and chopped into small pieces (about 1 1/2 cups)
> 1 green bell pepper, cored, seeded, and diced (about 1 cup)
> 1 bunch of green onions, coarsely chopped (about 1 cup)

To make vinaigrette: Combine cider vinegar, Worcestershire, Tabasco, and mustard. Gradually add oils, whisking constantly to emulsify.

Place onion, bay leaves, garlic, peppercorns, allspice, and cloves into a square of cheesecloth and tie together to form a bag.

Drain and rinse soaked beans. Cover with fresh water. Add celery and the spice bag. Bring to a boil, reduce heat, and simmer until beans are tender but still a little firm, about 45 minutes.

Rinse and drain the beans, discarding the celery and the spice bag. While they are still warm, toss beans with vinaigrette. Season with salt and pepper.

Combine beans with cooked rice, chicken, chorizo, green pepper, and green onions and mix well. Correct seasoning and serve.

SERVES 6

WHITE AND WILD RICE SALAD WITH VEGETABLES

Here's another combination of vegetables and rice to please your fancy.

1 cup white rice
1/2 cup wild rice
1 1/2 cups broccoli florets
1/2 cup shredded cabbage
1/3 cup thinly sliced carrots
1/4 cup minced red onion
1/4 cup minced fresh Italian flat-leaf parsley
1/3 cup rice wine vinegar
2 tablespoons white wine vinegar
1/3 cup vegetable oil
1/2 teaspoon salt
1/2 teaspoon freshly ground black pepper

Boil the white rice as directed on page 170 until tender, about 12 to 15 minutes. Drain and immediately wash with cold water. Set aside. Do the same with the wild rice, which will take slightly longer to cook. Mix the two rices together in a bowl and set aside.

Blanch broccoli, cabbage, and carrots for 1 minute in boiling salted water. Drain and plunge into ice water. Dry and add to rice along with red onion. Toss and set aside.

In a small bowl, whisk all the other ingredients together and pour over rice and vegetable mixture. Toss.

SERVES 8

BASMATI AND WILD RICE SALAD

2/3 cup wild rice
1 teaspoon salt
1 cup basmati rice
1 tablespoon vegetable oil
1 cup frozen petit pois
1 medium red bell pepper, roasted, peeled, and seeded (see Note, page 74), coarsely chopped
1 cup finely chopped green onions
1/4 cup diced dill pickle
3 tablespoons mayonnaise
Red Wine Vinaigrette (page 44)

Bring 3 cups water to a boil. Add wild rice and 1/2 teaspoon of the salt. Bring back to a boil, reduce heat to a simmer, and cook for about 50 minutes, until the rice has expanded and is tender. Drain rice and set aside to cool completely.

Bring 1 3/4 cups of water to a boil. Add basmati rice, oil, and remaining 1/2 teaspoon of salt. Return to a boil, reduce heat, and cover. Cook for 15 minutes. Remove from heat and fluff the rice with a fork. Let cool completely.

Defrost the frozen peas by placing them in a small bowl of warm water. Let sit for several minutes until soft and tender. Drain.

In large mixing bowl, combine wild and basmati rices, petit pois, red bell pepper, green onions, and pickle. Toss. Stir the mayonnaise into the vinaigrette, mixing well. Add to the salad and mix well.

SERVES 6

BAKED GREEN RICE

This loaf will be easy to slice when it really cools down and the cheese has had a chance to set.

2 cups cooked rice
1 can (4 ounces) chopped green chilies
1 small onion, chopped fine
2 cups grated cheddar
1 cup finely chopped fresh Italian flat-leaf
  parsley
8 tablespoons (1 stick) unsalted butter,
  melted
2 large eggs
1 cup milk

Preheat oven to 350 degrees. Grease a 5 × 4-inch ceramic pâté loaf pan lightly and line the bottom with wax paper, then grease paper lightly.

Combine rice, chilies, onion, cheese, and parsley. Mix well. Add melted butter and mix. Beat eggs lightly and add milk. Stir and add to the other ingredients. Mix thoroughly.

Pour into the pan and bake for 40 to 45 minutes. Allow to cool completely, loosen sides, and turn out. Remove wax paper. Use a very sharp knife and cut into slices.
SERVES 6

POTATOES

BUTTERED POTATOES

1 1/4 pounds medium new potatoes, peeled
Salt, to taste
1 tablespoon unsalted butter
1/2 teaspoon white pepper, or to taste

Simmer potatoes in well-salted water until just tender, 10 to 12 minutes. Drain well. To serve, put them in a skillet over medium heat with the butter. Toss and season with salt and white pepper.
SERVES 6

SKILLET NEW POTATOES

Here is one of the best ways I know of cooking new potatoes. It is quick and easy and in one process gives you bits of crispy peel and a soft creamy interior.

2 pounds small new red potatoes
8 tablespoons (1 stick) unsalted butter
3 tablespoons water
2 teaspoons salt
1/2 teaspoon freshly ground black pepper

Scrub potatoes and peel a strip around the center of each. Melt butter in deep skillet. Add potatoes, water, salt, and pepper. The potatoes should be in one layer. Cover and cook over medium to low heat for 25 minutes, shaking the pan occasionally or turning by hand to keep from sticking. If liquid remains in pan at the end of cooking time, reduce so that the potatoes are coated with butter.
SERVES 6

BOILED NEW POTATOES

For 4 people, buy 1 pound of the smallest red new potatoes you can find. Try to get them of a more or less consistent size. Scrub their skins well, and put in a pot of boiling salted water. Test for doneness after 15 minutes by pricking with the point of a knife. (When testing, go for the largest potato.) Drain and serve potatoes in their skins with good unsalted butter, salt, and freshly ground black pepper.

NEW POTATOES AND GREEN BEANS

This is a really old-fashioned dish.

*1 pound green beans, snapped with tips and
    ends removed*
4 slices bacon
2 cups coarsely chopped onions
8 cups water
16 very small new potatoes, scrubbed

Wash beans and set aside. In a large heavy pot, fry bacon over low heat for 8 minutes. Add onions and beans, and fry on low, stirring, for another 10 minutes, until beans are bright green. Add the water and potatoes, and simmer over low heat for 2 hours. Remove vegetables from liquid with a slotted spoon and serve hot.

SERVES 6

OVEN-BAKED POTATO CHIPS

To tell the truth, I wouldn't do these potatoes if I didn't have a food processor to slice them.

*7 baking potatoes, peeled and cut to fit into
    the feed tube of a food processor*
6 tablespoons unsalted butter, melted
Salt

Preheat oven to 500 degrees and generously oil 2 baking sheets.

   Peel potatoes and slice in the food processor into ⅛-inch-thick rounds. Arrange them in a single layer on the sheets and brush very generously with butter. Put pans on separate racks in the oven and bake for 10 minutes. Reverse the position of the pans and bake 10 minutes more. Remove from oven and sprinkle with salt. Push chips off sheets with a pancake turner. Put a tea towel over them if they have to wait.

SERVES 6

SPICY BOILED NEW POTATOES

Often when shrimp or crabs are boiled in that potent mix of herbs and spices favored along the Gulf Coast, small red new potatoes are added to the pot. Cooked this way, potatoes have a delicious bite.

1 large garlic clove, crushed
Several large shallots, peeled and cut in half
1 small onion, peeled and cut in half
½ large lemon, cut in half
2 large bay leaves, broken into pieces
1 teaspoon cayenne
1 tablespoon crushed black peppercorns
1 teaspoon mustard seeds
1 teaspoon celery seeds
½ teaspoon dried dill
½ teaspoon ground allspice
½ teaspoon ground nutmeg
10 whole cloves
Salt, to taste
2 pounds new potatoes
1 to 2 tablespoons unsalted butter

Pour water into a pot that will accommodate the potatoes snugly. Put in all the ingredients except the potatoes and butter. Bring to a boil. Cover and simmer for 5 to 10 minutes. Add the potatoes (and more water if necessary to cover). Return to a boil and turn the heat down to a simmer. Cook, uncovered, for 15 minutes or until the potatoes are done. Do not undercook.

   Drain and toss with butter. Serve hot.

SERVES 6

SCOTTISH SKILLET POTATOES

I don't know why these are called Scottish potatoes, but the person who told me how to make them called them that, and the name stuck in my head.

1 slice of thick bacon, cut into small pieces
1 medium onion, thinly sliced
2 tablespoons unsalted butter
2 pounds potatoes, peeled and cut into 1/2-inch slices
1 teaspoon salt in 1 cup hot water
1/4 teaspoon freshly ground black pepper

In a very large skillet with a lid that will hold the potatoes in one layer, sauté bacon until it is almost done. Add onion, and when it has wilted, add butter, potatoes, and salted water. Sprinkle on the pepper and cover. Bring to a boil and cook over very low heat for 20 minutes. Uncover and continue cooking for another 12 to 15 minutes, shaking the pan occasionally. At the end most of the liquid should be gone and the bottoms of the potatoes turning golden. Let them rest for an additional 10 minutes, covered, before serving.
SERVES 6

OVEN-ROASTED COTTAGE FRIES

You'll love these no-fat French fries.

6 baking potatoes, scrubbed and dried
1 tablespoon salt
Freshly ground black pepper, to taste

Preheat oven to 475 degrees.

Leaving the skins on, cut each potato in half lengthwise, and then in thirds lengthwise. Bake right on the oven rack. No pan is necessary. In 15 to 20 minutes, the potatoes will puff up and be browned on all sides. Sprinkle liberally with salt and pepper to serve.
SERVES 6

SKILLET POTATOES AND EGGS WITH CHILI AND HAM

You may want to sprinkle grated cheese on top just as the potatoes go under the broiler.

2 medium potatoes, peeled
2 tablespoons vegetable oil
1/2 teaspoon salt, or to taste
Freshly ground black pepper, to taste
8 large eggs, lightly beaten
2 tablespoons unsalted butter
1 cup medium to small cubes of cooked ham
3/4 cup chopped drained mild green chilies (canned)

Boil potatoes in well-salted water. When medium-tender, drain them and let cool. Dice into medium to small chunks. Heat oil in a medium skillet. Sauté potatoes until they begin to brown, about 5 minutes. Remove to a plate and wipe out skillet.

Preheat the broiler. Add salt and pepper to the eggs. Mix well. Add clarified butter to skillet and heat over medium heat. When bubbly, add eggs. Stir lightly as they begin to set. Sprinkle in the potatoes, ham, and chilies while the eggs are still liquid. Mix very lightly.

Run under the broiler for a minute or so until puffed and golden.
SERVES 4 TO 6

OVEN POTATO SLICES

This is an easy way to get crispy and perfectly cooked potato slices. Unfortunately, the timing on them is a little difficult to gauge. Sometimes they require a bit of extra cooking to get them lightly browned. So try to plan to have a fifteen-minute leeway. If you can't manage this, the potatoes will taste perfectly good even if they are not as brown as you might wish.

3 to 4 tablespoons unsalted butter
*5 unpeeled medium red potatoes (about 2
pounds, of more or less uniform size, if
possible), washed and cut into ¼-inch
slices*
Kosher salt
Freshly ground black pepper
Rosemary (optional)

Preheat oven to 425 degrees.

Melt butter and pour half of it into a large
shallow baking pan, making sure it covers the
entire bottom. Layer potato slices in rows, with
each slice slightly overlapping the next.
Sprinkle with salt, pepper, and rosemary, if
desired. Drizzle the remaining butter over all
and bake, uncovered, for 45 minutes, or until
the potatoes begin to crisp and turn golden.
SERVES 6

STUFFED BAKED POTATOES

*6 large baking potatoes, washed, dried, and
pierced with a fork*
*2 tablespoons unsalted butter, slightly
softened*
6 tablespoons half-and-half
*6 tablespoons coarsely shredded sharp
cheddar*
*6 tablespoons finely chopped fresh Italian
flat-leaf parsley*
1 teaspoon salt
1 tablespoon freshly ground black pepper

Preheat oven to 450 degrees.

Bake potatoes for 45 minutes to 1 hour,
until they are tender throughout. Set aside
until cool enough to handle. Lower oven temperature to 350 degrees.

Turn each potato on its side and, using a
serrated knife, cut lengthwise across the top.
This will make an oval opening.

Scoop out potato from the oval opening,
making sure you do not tear the skin. Place the
shell of the potato in a shallow baking dish.

Mash potato with butter and half-and-half
until smooth. Fold in cheese and parsley.
Season with salt and pepper. Restuff each
potato shell and bake until golden brown and
puffy, about 15 minutes.
SERVES 6

CRISPY ROSEMARY POTATOES WITH PARMESAN

⅓ cup olive oil
*3 pounds baking potatoes (about 6 large),
peeled and sliced ⅛ inch thick*
¼ cup coarsely chopped fresh rosemary
1 teaspoon salt
Freshly ground black pepper, to taste
1 cup freshly grated parmesan

Preheat oven to 400 degrees.

Oil the ring of a 9½-inch springform pan
and place it on a well-oiled baking sheet with a
rim. Toss the potatoes in all the remaining oil
and the rosemary, salt, and pepper. Beginning
with the potatoes, alternate layers of potatoes
and cheese, finishing with potatoes. Bake 1
hour or until top potatoes turn medium brown
and crispy. Let cool before running a knife
around rim and removing ring. Cut into
wedges to serve.
SERVES 6

ROASTED POTATOES

Crunchy on the outside and smooth within.

1 tablespoon vegetable oil
1 tablespoon unsalted butter
12 whole small white potatoes, peeled
Salt, to taste

Preheat oven to 400 degrees.

In an ovenproof skillet large enough to hold all the potatoes in a single layer, heat oil and butter over high heat. Add potatoes and roll them around to coat. Place pan in the oven and roast about 15 minutes, until done. Shake pan frequently to make sure potatoes brown evenly. Season with salt.

SERVES 6

ROASTED RED POTATOES

These are a perfect foil for roast chicken or duck.

2 pounds new red potatoes of approximately
 the same size, quartered but unpeeled
Salt
2 tablespoons unsalted butter
1 tablespoon minced garlic
1/2 teaspoon white pepper

Preheat oven to 375 degrees.

Cover potatoes with salted water and bring to a simmer; cook until just tender, about 12 minutes (boiling the potatoes too rapidly will dislodge the skin). Drain. In a large ovenproof skillet over medium-high heat, sauté potatoes in butter for about 6 minutes, turning carefully. Sprinkle with garlic and toss.

Place in the oven and roast until nicely browned, about 12 to 15 minutes. Toss with 1 teaspoon salt and the pepper.

SERVES 6

GRILLED POTATO POCKETS

24 very small red potatoes, scrubbed, dried,
 and pricked with the tines of a fork
2 tablespoons olive oil
2 teaspoons kosher salt
1 tablespoon freshly ground black pepper
6 fresh rosemary sprigs

Prepare an outdoor grill.

Place 4 potatoes in the middle of a large square of aluminum foil. Drizzle with olive oil, sprinkle with salt and pepper, and place one sprig of rosemary across the potatoes. Fold the foil tightly so no air will escape. Continue to form 5 additional pockets with the remaining ingredients.

Place the potato pockets on the grill, cover, and cook until tender, turning occasionally, about 40 minutes. Do not unwrap but place one pocket on each individual plate to serve.

SERVES 6

NEW POTATOES BAKED IN CHICKEN STOCK

Although these potatoes are best served about ten minutes out of the oven, they can be reheated if necessary. They are even good the next day. Don't peel the potatoes—it's what makes them so good.

4 tablespoons (1/2 stick) unsalted butter
3 pounds new potatoes, well scrubbed and
 cut into 1/8-inch slices
3/4 teaspoon salt
1/4 teaspoon freshly ground black pepper
3 large garlic cloves, peeled and minced
1/2 pound emmentaler, shredded
1 1/3 cups Chicken Stock (page 41), hot

Preheat oven to 375 degrees. Use 2 tablespoons of butter to grease a 13 × 9-inch casserole. Place sliced potatoes in cold water for about 30 minutes.

Drain potatoes and dry them with paper towels. Place one quarter of the potatoes in the casserole. Season with salt and pepper and sprinkle with one third of the garlic and one quarter of the cheese. Dot with butter. Make 3 more layers the same way (no garlic goes on top). Pour the stock over the potatoes. Bake for 1½ hours, covering loosely with foil for the last 15 minutes if the top is getting too browned. Allow to rest for about 10 minutes before serving.

SERVES 6

ROASTED GARLIC MASHED POTATOES

These are sinfully good!

2 medium garlic heads
2 tablespoons olive oil
4 large baking potatoes (abut 3½ pounds), peeled
6 tablespoons (¾ stick) unsalted butter
¼ cup heavy cream
½ teaspoon kosher salt
Freshly ground white pepper, to taste

Preheat oven to 375 degrees.

Cut bottoms off the heads of garlic, place each head on a square of aluminum foil, and drizzle olive oil over them. Wrap and bake for 1 to 1½ hours, until garlic is very soft. Squeeze pulp out of each garlic head. Set aside.

Cut potatoes into large cubes, place in medium saucepan, and cover with cold water. Over medium heat, bring quickly to a boil and reduce to a simmer. Simmer until potatoes are very soft, about 20 minutes. Drain and place in large mixer bowl with garlic pulp, butter, cream, salt, and pepper. Mash briefly, just until smooth. Do not overbeat.

SERVES 6 TO 8

MASHED POTATOES AND CAULIFLOWER

Of course, you can boil the potatoes for this, but I bake them, which I like better. I save the skins (sliced into strips), and at a later date butter and salt them and toast them for hors d'oeuvres.

3 pounds russet potatoes, scrubbed, dried, and rubbed with oil
2 cups cauliflower florets and tender stems
Low-fat milk
1 large head roasted garlic (see left)
6 tablespoons unsalted butter
Salt and freshly ground black pepper, to taste

Preheat oven to 425 degrees. Bake potatoes for 40 minutes to 1 hour, depending on size. When potatoes are done, remove and reduce oven temperature to 325 degrees.

Cover cauliflower with milk in large saucepan. Bring to a boil, being careful not to let it cook over. Turn back to slow boil and cook until just tender, about 10 minutes.

Scoop out hot potato flesh into large warm bowl. Squeeze soft garlic pulp into potatoes, using as much or as little as you like. Cut butter into pieces and mash in with a hand masher (do not use an electric mixer, as it will make the mixture glutinous). Drain cauliflower, reserving milk. Mash in with potatoes, adding about ¾ cup of cauliflower milk. Add a little more milk if you would like the potatoes creamier. Add salt and pepper.

Butter a casserole and scrape the mixture in. Smooth the top and rub with a bit of butter to make a thin film on top. (This may be done an hour before dinner. To hold, set aside, covered with a tea towel, until ready to reheat.) Put into oven, uncovered, for 20 minutes.

SERVES 8

MASHED POTATOES AND ONIONS

Potatoes can be successfully combined with many other vegetables, from celery root to turnips, or combinations of several. When this is done, they are usually boiled or steamed separately and then mashed together. Here the onions are sautéed in butter first, which gives them a marvelous flavor (this is my friend J.R.'s idea).

*9 medium white potatoes, peeled and
   quartered*
1 teaspoon salt
3 cups finely chopped onions
6 tablespoons unsalted butter
*³⁄₄ cup milk or a combination of milk and
   light cream*

Put potatoes in water to cover and add the salt. Bring to a boil, then turn down to a simmer. Test potatoes for doneness after 20 minutes.

While potatoes are cooking, sauté onions carefully in 3 tablespoons of the butter until translucent and just turning golden. Set aside. In another saucepan, melt remaining butter and add milk to it. Set aside and keep warm.

When potatoes are done, drain them and put back into the pan. Cover pan with a folded tea towel and set over the lowest possible heat for 5 minutes to dry out somewhat. Shake once or twice to prevent sticking. Mash potatoes with the butter–milk mixture (I think a hand masher gives the best results) and then fold in onions. Add more salt if necessary. This can sit in a pan of hot water for a few minutes, but don't make it wait too long.

SERVES 6

SCALLOPED POTATOES

Everyone seems to love scalloped potatoes.

*6 cups peeled and thinly sliced potatoes
   (¹⁄₈-inch slices)*
¹⁄₂ small garlic clove
4 tablespoons (¹⁄₂ stick) unsalted butter
1 teaspoon salt
¹⁄₂ teaspoon freshly ground black pepper
1¹⁄₂ cups grated swiss or gruyère cheese
1 cup milk

Preheat oven to 425 degrees. Keep potato slices in a bowl of cold water until ready to use.

Rub a 10-inch round baking dish that is 2 inches deep with the garlic and then generously grease. Drain and dry the potatoes. Layer them in the dish and divide butter, salt, pepper, and cheese among layers, reserving enough cheese for a top layer. Bring milk carefully to a boil and pour over all. Top with the last layer of cheese. Place in the oven and bake 30 minutes or more, until tender when pierced with the point of a knife and cheese is lightly browned.

SERVES 8

GOAT CHEESE MASHED POTATOES

This dish has a very subtle flavor.

*2 pounds large red potatoes, peeled and cut
   into large cubes*
3 tablespoons unsalted butter
¹⁄₂ cup half-and-half or milk, or to taste
7 ounces creamy goat cheese
2 teaspoons salt
³⁄₄ teaspoon white pepper

Cover potatoes with cold water. Bring to a boil and cook until fork-tender, about 12 minutes.

Meanwhile, heat together butter, half-and-half, and goat cheese. Stir until cheese melts. Set aside.

Drain potatoes and return to pot. Cover with a tea towel and shake pan over medium heat for about 30 seconds to dry out.

Pour in goat cheese mixture and mash with a hand masher until smooth, adding salt and pepper along the way.

Add more warm half-and-half or milk if you want these to be less thick.

SERVES 6

POTATO AND CABBAGE GRATIN

This may also be topped with parboiled cubes of bacon before it is baked.

6 cups finely shredded green cabbage
Salt
2 cups Light Béchamel Sauce (see below)
3 cups cooked, peeled, and sliced red
*   potatoes*
1 cup shredded gruyère
Freshly ground black pepper, to taste
2 tablespoons unsalted butter

Place cabbage in a large saucepan of salted water and boil over medium heat for 2 minutes. Drain and cover with cold water, bring back to a simmer (this takes about 20 minutes), and cook for 30 minutes over medium heat.

Meanwhile, preheat oven to 350 degrees and lightly grease an 8-inch round gratin dish.

Spread ⅔ cup of the béchamel in the bottom of the dish. Layer half of the cooked cabbage and top with half the potato slices and half of the gruyère, sprinkling each layer with salt and pepper as you go. Pour over another ⅔ cup of the béchamel. Make a final layer using balance of the ingredients and ending with béchamel. Dot with butter, cover with foil, and bake for 15 minutes. Remove foil and bake until light golden and bubbly, 30 to 40 minutes more.

SERVES 8

LIGHT BÉCHAMEL SAUCE

This recipe calls for less milk and butter than the usual béchamel sauce.

2 tablespoons unsalted butter
2 tablespoons minced shallots
1½ to 2 tablespoons all-purpose flour
2 cups low-fat milk, or half milk and half
*   Chicken Stock (page 41)*
½ teaspoon salt, or to taste
¼ teaspoon freshly ground black pepper, or
*   to taste*

Melt butter over medium-high heat and sauté shallots, stirring, until they begin to brown, 2 to 3 minutes. Stir in flour and cook, stirring constantly, for about 1 minute. Meanwhile, heat the 2 cups of liquid. Whisk into the butter–flour roux, and add the salt and pepper. Bring to a boil, then turn heat back to medium and continue cooking, whisking, until it begins to thicken, about 5 minutes. You want a pourable sauce about the consistency of heavy cream; add more liquid if it is too thick.

MAKES 2 CUPS

187

SWEET POTATOES

PAN-ROASTED SWEET POTATOES

2 pounds sweet potatoes
2 teaspoons unsalted butter, softened
1 teaspoon salt
Freshly ground black pepper, to taste
$^{1}/_{2}$ teaspoon herbes de Provence

Preheat oven to 375 degrees.

Peel potatoes, cut into 1½-inch chunks, and rub with butter to prevent discoloration.

Put sweet potatoes in a shallow roasting pan and season with salt, pepper, and herbes de Provence. Roast about 45 minutes, stirring and turning occasionally to prevent sticking.
SERVES 6

VARIATION

To roast with a chicken or turkey, add sweet potatoes to the roasting pan during the last 45 minutes. Baste occasionally with pan juices.

SWEET POTATO CHIPS

These come out a wonderful color and remain surprisingly crisp as they cool. The trick is not to try to fry too many at one time and to be sure the potatoes are sliced thin enough.

6 medium sweet potatoes, peeled
2 to 3 quarts vegetable oil, for deep-frying
Salt, to taste
Sugar, to taste
Cayenne, to taste

Slice sweet potatoes as thin as possible. Use a small meat slicer or a food processor fitted with the thinnest blade.

Immerse slices in cold water for about 10 minutes. Drain, pat with towels, and let dry.

Heat oil to 350 degrees in a large, deep pot or a deep-fat fryer. Use a candy thermometer to make sure the oil doesn't get too hot. Fry chips a few at a time for 1¼ minutes, or until bright golden. Drain and sprinkle with salt, sugar, and cayenne.
SERVES 6

VARIATION

Sprinkle with cinnamon sugar instead of salt, sugar, and cayenne.

SPICED SWEET POTATOES

6 medium sweet potatoes, boiled, peeled,
   and cut into $^{1}/_{2}$-inch-thick slices
$^{1}/_{2}$ teaspoon ground cinnamon
$^{1}/_{2}$ teaspoon ground ginger
$^{1}/_{2}$ teaspoon freshly grated nutmeg
$^{1}/_{2}$ teaspoon ground cloves
$^{1}/_{2}$ teaspoon salt
4 tablespoons ($^{1}/_{2}$ stick) unsalted butter, cut
   in pieces
3 tablespoons honey

Preheat oven to 375 degrees. Butter a 10-inch-round, 2-inch-deep baking dish.

Set out sweet potatoes. Combine spices and salt. Layer potatoes in the dish, sprinkling each layer with some of the spice mixture, dotting with butter, and drizzling with honey. Bake, uncovered, for 20 minutes, until heated and ingredients are well combined.
SERVES 8 TO 10

VARIATION

Substitute light brown sugar for the honey.

SWEET POTATO CAKES

Don't forget these luscious little cakes when the holidays roll around.

2 to 2¹/₄ pounds sweet potatoes, scrubbed,
    dried, and baked
2 tablespoons unsalted butter
¹/₂ teaspoon salt
¹/₄ teaspoon freshly ground black pepper
3 egg whites
6 tablespoons fresh fine white bread crumbs
3 teaspoons brown sugar

When the potatoes are cool enough to handle, peel and place in a bowl with butter, salt, and pepper. Mash smooth with a fork or a hand mixer. Stir in egg whites and set aside.

Preheat oven to 400 degrees.

Sprinkle bread crumbs in a large heavy ovenproof skillet. Bake for 7 or 8 minutes, until crumbs start to turn dark golden. Remove skillet and quickly drop heaping tablespoons of the potato mixture onto the crumbs, leaving a little space between. You should have about 12 cakes.

Bake for 10 minutes. Remove skillet and turn oven to broil. Using the blade of a knife, lift some of the crumbs from the bottom of the pan and sprinkle over each cake, then sprinkle each with a bit of the brown sugar.

Run under the broiler just long enough to melt the sugar. Allow to rest for 3 to 4 minutes before lifting cakes onto dinner plates with a spatula.

Note: To bake sweet potatoes, preheat oven to 350 degrees and bake the potatoes 1 to 1¹/₄ hours, or until tender.

SERVES 6

WHIPPED SWEET POTATOES

The simpler sweet potatoes are, the better.

6 medium sweet potatoes, baked until soft
¹/₂ cup unsalted butter
1¹/₂ teaspoons salt
³/₄ teaspoon freshly ground black pepper

Peel potatoes while they're hot. Mix with butter, salt, and pepper. Use a hand mixer to beat until smooth. May be rewarmed, covered, in a low oven.

SERVES 6 TO 8

SWEET POTATO PANCAKES

4 cups shredded peeled sweet potatoes
1 medium onion, grated
1 teaspoon salt
¹/₂ teaspoon freshly ground black pepper
3 tablespoons flour
2 large eggs
3 tablespoons unsalted butter
3 tablespoons safflower oil

Place shredded potatoes and onion in a small bowl and toss. Add salt and pepper and toss again. Sprinkle flour over all and mix. Stir in eggs.

Heat butter and oil in a large skillet over medium heat. When hot, divide potato mixture into 12 portions and slide each carefully into hot fat. Flatten slightly with a pancake turner and cook until lightly golden without turning, 3 minutes or less. Turn and cook other side, flattening again slightly, until golden, about 2 minutes.

Drain on paper towels.

MAKES 12 PANCAKES

POTATO SALAD

RED POTATO SALAD

2 1/2 pounds small red potatoes
Salt
1 tablespoon lemon juice
1/2 cup sour cream
1/2 cup mayonnaise
1/4 cup fresh basil, cut into thin strips
1/4 cup minced fresh Italian flat-leaf parsley,
    no stems
1 medium garlic clove, minced
2 tablespoons vinegar
1 teaspoon Worcestershire Sauce
1/2 teaspoon Dijon mustard
1/4 teaspoon freshly ground black pepper
1/2 teaspoon salt

Cover potatoes with lightly salted water and add lemon juice. Bring rapidly to a boil and turn heat down to just a rolling boil. Cook potatoes until tender when pierced with the point of a knife, about 12 minutes or more. Drain and cool.

Meanwhile, whisk together all other ingredients to make a dressing.

Cut cooled potatoes into small chunks, leaving the skins on, and toss with the dressing. Refrigerate until time to serve.
SERVES 6 TO 8

WARM VINEGAR POTATO SALAD

This has always been one of my favorite potato salads. I try to make it in batches just large enough for the meal, as I never like the flavor of it as well after it has been refrigerated.

2 thick bacon slices, cut into small pieces
1 large onion, thinly sliced
2 tablespoons unsalted butter
2 pounds potatoes, peeled and cut into cubes

1 teaspoon salt
1 cup Chicken Stock (page 41), hot
1/4 teaspoon freshly ground black pepper
1/4 cup apple cider vinegar, or more to taste

Using a very large skillet with a lid, fry bacon until almost done. Add onion and cook slowly until it is wilted and starting to turn color. Add butter, and when it has melted spread potatoes on top evenly. Sprinkle with salt and add stock. Bring to a boil, then turn the heat down to a simmer. Sprinkle on the pepper and cover. Cook, covered, for 20 minutes. Uncover and cook for 12 to 15 minutes more, shaking the pan occasionally. By the time you finish cooking this there should be almost no liquid in the pan.

Add vinegar and carefully move potatoes around to mix thoroughly but gently. Cover and let sit for 10 more minutes before serving.
SERVES 6

WARM POTATO SALAD WITH SHERRY VINAIGRETTE

1 1/2 pounds small whole red potatoes,
    scrubbed
Sherry Vinaigrette (page 49)
1 teaspoon caraway seeds
1 teaspoon kosher salt
2 teaspoons cracked black pepper
6 cups mixed greens

Place potatoes in a large pot, cover with water, and bring to a boil over medium heat. Boil gently until barely fork-tender, about 12 minutes. Drain but do not rinse.

While the potatoes are still hot, halve them roughly by inserting a fork and breaking the potato apart. Toss with vinaigrette, caraway seeds, salt, and pepper. Let sit for several minutes to absorb dressing.

Serve warm on a bed of greens.
SERVES 6

NEW POTATO, RED BELL PEPPER, AND CORN SALAD

*2 pounds small red new potatoes, with skins
    left on, washed and dried*
1 tablespoon olive oil
1 teaspoon salt
1 tablespoon freshly ground black pepper
1/2 cup diced red bell pepper
*3/4 cup corn kernels, cut and scraped from
    the cob (about 1 large ear)*
1 bunch of fresh chives, finely chopped

Preheat oven to 450 degrees.

Toss potatoes with olive oil, salt, and pepper and place on a baking sheet. Roast until tender, about 12 to 20 minutes, depending on the size of the potatoes, turning occasionally to prevent sticking.

Transfer to a serving bowl and toss with red bell pepper, corn, and chives.
SERVES 6

POTATO SALAD

This is similar to German potato salad, but is served at room temperature and spiced up with Louisiana Hot Sauce.

*2 pounds boiling potatoes, peeled and cut
    into 3/4-inch dice*
Salt
1/4 pound thick-sliced bacon
1 large red onion, minced
*1 medium green bell pepper, cut in small
    dice*
1 tablespoon brown sugar
1/3 cup cider vinegar
1/4 cup minced fresh Italian flat-leaf parsley
1/4 cup vegetable oil
1/4 teaspoon freshly ground black pepper
1/4 cup mayonnaise
1 teaspoon Louisiana Hot Sauce
4 hard-cooked eggs, chopped coarse
5 green onions, sliced

Cover potatoes with well-salted water and bring quickly to a boil over high heat; turn heat down so water is just boiling lightly. Cook until tender, about 11 to 12 minutes. Drain, wash with cold water, and drain again. Set aside.

Fry bacon in skillet until golden and remove with slotted spoon to drain. Pour out all but 2 or 3 tablespoons of the fat and sauté onion and green pepper for 1 minute, over medium heat. Add brown sugar and vinegar, and stir over heat to dissolve the sugar.

Place potatoes in a bowl, pour in the skillet mixture, and toss lightly. Mix parsley, oil, 1/4 teaspoon salt, pepper, mayonnaise, and hot sauce. Add this and the bacon; toss again lightly. Garnish with eggs and green onions.
SERVES 8

BEANS

PINTO BEANS

*2 cups dried pinto beans, soaked overnight
    or by the quick-soak method (see Note,
    page 25)*
2 cups water
1 pound ham hock, roughly cut
1 teaspoon dried oregano
1 teaspoon ground cumin
1 tablespoon pure chili powder
1 teaspoon salt

Drain beans and put in a pot along with the water, ham hock, oregano, cumin, and chili powder.

Bring to a boil, reduce to a simmer, and cook, simmering until tender, 2 1/2 to 3 hours. Add more water if needed to keep beans covered. Add salt and serve.
SERVES 6 TO 8

RED BEAN SUCCOTASH

1/2 pound dried red beans, soaked overnight
  or by the quick-soak method (see Note,
  page 25)
1 large bay leaf
2 tablespoons olive oil
1/2 medium red onion, diced
1/2 large green bell pepper, diced
1/2 cup fresh corn kernels, cut and scraped
  from the cob
3/4 cup 1/2-inch rounds of okra
1 medium-size ripe tomato, peeled, seeded,
  and diced
3/4 teaspoon salt
1/4 teaspoon freshly ground black pepper
Pinch of cayenne

Drain beans and cover with about 2 inches of water. Add bay leaf and bring quickly to a boil. Turn heat down to a simmer and cook until just done but not mushy, about 1 hour. Discard bay leaf and set beans aside to cool in the liquid.

Heat oil in a medium skillet over medium heat, and sauté onion and pepper until wilted, about 5 minutes. Stir in corn and okra. Cook another minute or two, stirring occasionally. Toss in tomato and remove from the heat. Drain beans and put into a large bowl. Toss in other vegetables and season with salt, pepper, and cayenne.
SERVES 6

WARM WHITE BEANS WITH RED ONIONS

2 cups cooked white beans, drained
6 tablespoons chopped red onion
3 tablespoons olive oil
1 tablespoon raspberry vinegar
2 garlic cloves, roasted (optional)
Freshly ground black pepper, to taste

Toss beans and onion together. Whisk together olive oil, vinegar, and squeezed-out pulp of the garlic, if using. Pour over beans and mix in a generous grind of black pepper.
SERVES 4

CUBAN BLACK BEANS

Some method of cooking these beans call for all sorts of herbs, but I have found the beans really don't require too much enhancing.

1 pound dried black beans, soaked
  overnight or by the quick-soak method
  (see Note, page 25)
1 onion, coarsely chopped
1 small garlic clove, crushed
2 parsley sprigs (optional)
2 tablespoons olive oil
1 to 2 cups Chicken Stock (page 41), hot
1 teaspoon salt, or to taste
1/4 cup dark rum or red wine, or to taste

Drain beans and combine with onion; garlic; parsley, if using; olive oil; and enough stock (about 1 cup) to just cover. Simmer, uncovered, for 1 1/2 hours, or until beans are tender. Add a small quantity of hot stock during the cooking time if necessary. Add salt and rum.
SERVES 6 TO 8

WHITE BEANS

1 pound dry white beans, soaked overnight
  or by the quick-soak method (see Note,
  page 25)
1 small yellow onion
2 fresh rosemary sprigs
4 bay leaves
3 garlic cloves, smashed
8 black peppercorns
3 whole cloves
1/2 teaspoon whole mustard seed
Salt, to taste

Drain and rinse soaked beans, place in a large pot, and cover with water. Place onion, rosemary, bay leaves, garlic, peppercorns, cloves, and mustard seed in a square of cheesecloth and tie together to form a bag. Add spice bag to the pot and bring to a boil over high heat. Reduce heat and simmer until beans are tender but still a little firm, about 45 minutes. Remove spice bag, drain beans, and season with salt. Serve hot or at room temperature.

SERVES 6

WHITE BEANS VINAIGRETTE

You could add any number of crunchy or aromatic vegetables to white beans and dress them simply with olive oil and wine vinegar, but this is my favorite combination. You could also add green bell pepper, green onions, and peeled and seeded cucumber.

1 pound dried navy beans, soaked overnight or by the quick-soak method (see Note, page 25)
1 medium onion, peeled and stuck with 4 cloves
1 bay leaf
1 piece salt pork (1 inch)
Salt and freshly ground black pepper, to taste
1 red bell pepper, roasted, peeled, and seeded (see Note, page 74), chopped
3 or 4 fresh Italian flat-leaf parsley sprigs, finely chopped
Red Wine Vinaigrette (page 44)

Drain beans well. Cover with fresh water and add onion, bay leaf, salt pork, salt, and pepper. Simmer uncovered until done, approximately 1½ hours. Drain, discarding everything but the beans. Let cool.

Combine the red pepper and parsley with the beans and toss with vinaigrette. Serve at room temperature. Store in refrigerator.

SERVES 6

WHITE BEAN AND WALNUT SALAD

1 medium cucumber, peeled, seeded, and cut into thin half-moons
Salt
1 can (16 ounces) small white beans
½ cup walnut pieces
1 very small garlic clove
1 tablespoon red wine vinegar
3 tablespoons cold water
Freshly ground black pepper, to taste
Cayenne (optional)
1 tablespoon finely chopped onion
2 tablespoons finely chopped fresh Italian flat-leaf parsley
2 tablespoons finely chopped fresh coriander (optional)
1 medium to large tomato, peeled, seeded, and coarsely diced

Put cucumber in a bowl and salt it to draw out a bit of water. Set aside. Drain beans in a sieve and run a bit of water over them. Let rest in the sieve.

Grind walnuts and garlic to a paste in a food processor or mortar and pestle. Stir in the vinegar and water. Add salt and black pepper and cayenne, if using. Mix in a medium bowl with onion, parsley, and coriander, if using. Drain cucumbers, pat dry with paper towels, and add. Dry the tomato dice, if they have given up any liquid, and add; mix in well.

SERVES 4 TO 6

WHITE BEAN SALAD
WITH TUNA

Bean salads are marvelous in the warm weather, either as part of a larger meal or as a meal in themselves. They may be as simple as white beans tossed with olive oil, a grind of black pepper, and a squeeze of lemon, or they may have as many more ingredients as you like.

1 pound dried white beans, soaked
  overnight or by the quick-soak method
  (see Note, page 25)
1 large onion, peeled and cut in half
Freshly ground black pepper, to taste
1/4 cup good-quality olive oil, or more to taste
1 can (6 1/2 ounces) Italian tuna in oil,
  drained and flaked
1 small green bell pepper, finely chopped
1 small red onion, finely chopped
Juice of 1/2 small lemon
Salt, to taste
Lemon wedges

Drain beans and add the halved onion. Cover with water to about 1 inch above beans. Add pepper. Simmer until tender. The time will vary according to the age of the beans.

Pour off any excess liquid and let cool for a few minutes. Pour the olive oil over the beans and toss lightly. Let cool completely and add all the remaining ingredients, except the lemon wedges, and more oil if you like. Correct the seasoning.

Serve with wedges of lemon.

SERVES 6 TO 8

WHITE BEAN AND PASTA
SALAD

I like white bean salads bound together with a slightly mayonnaisey dressing that has just a bit of ketchup in it. However, a simple mustard vinaigrette can be just fine.

2 cups cooked white beans, drained
2 cups cooked small elbow macaroni
1 cup fresh small green peas
1/2 to 3/4 cup medium-chopped red onion
1/4 cup thinly sliced dill pickle or cornichon
1 4-ounce jar chopped pimientos, drained
1 1/2 cups coarsely chopped cooked pork
  sausage

KETCHUP MAYONNAISE
1 teaspoon salt
1/2 teaspoon freshly ground black pepper
1 teaspoon sugar
3 tablespoons red wine vinegar
6 tablespoons olive oil
1/4 cup prepared mayonnaise
2 teaspoons ketchup

Toss together beans, pasta, peas, red onion, pickle, pimientos, and sausage in large bowl.

In small bowl, combine salt, pepper, sugar, and vinegar. Mix well with a fork. Whisk in olive oil, mayonnaise, and ketchup. Pour over salad and toss to coat all ingredients.

SERVES 8

LENTILS WITH GOAT CHEESE

*1/2 pound dried brown lentils, rinsed and
 picked over*
1 small onion, chopped
1 large shallot, chopped
Chicken Stock (page 41), hot
1 tablespoon good mild olive oil
*3 to 4 ounces goat cheese (preferably montra-
 chet) crumbled or cut into small bits*

Cover lentils with boiling water and soak for
about 1 1/2 hours. Drain and put in a pot with
onion and shallot. Add hot stock to just cover
and bring to a simmer. Cook gently for 15 minutes, or until tender. Do not overcook. If the
liquid is too low, add a small amount of hot
stock. At the end of the cooking time, all liquid
should be absorbed.

Before serving, stir in olive oil carefully and
put in a serving bowl, topped with cheese.
Serve warm.
SERVES 4

LENTIL SALAD

*1 pound dried brown lentils, rinsed and
 picked over*
1 large onion, chopped
2 large shallots, chopped
Chicken Stock (page 41), hot
4 to 6 drops of Tabasco Sauce
2 tablespoons good-quality olive oil
*1/2 cup finely chopped celery (with some ten-
 der yellow leaves)*
*Salt and freshly ground black pepper, to
 taste*

Cover lentils with boiling water to cover by
about 1 inch and soak for 1 1/2 hours. Drain and
put in a pot with onion and shallots. Add stock
and bring just to a simmer. Cook very gently

for about 10 minutes, until just tender, adding
more stock if necessary. Do not overcook. Stir
Tabasco into olive oil and mix into lentils. Let
cool.

To serve, mix in celery and season with salt
and pepper.
SERVES 6 TO 8

BLACK BEAN AND JICAMA SALAD

The proportion of ingredients added to the
beans is fairly flexible, so feel free to add or
subtract after you taste this.

*2 cups dried black beans, soaked overnight
 or by the quick-soak method (see Note,
 page 25)*
6 cups cold water
3/4 teaspoon salt
1/2 teaspoon freshly ground black pepper
3/4 teaspoon ground cumin
1 bay leaf
1 cup peeled and diced jicama
*1 medium tomato, cored, seeded, and
 chopped*
*1/4 cup green onions, with some of the green,
 cut into small rings*
2 tablespoons minced fresh cilantro
Sherry–Red Wine Vinaigrette (page 45)

Drain beans. Combine with the cold water, salt,
pepper, cumin, and bay leaf in a pot and bring
to a boil over high heat. Turn back to a slow
boil and cook until tender, at least 50 minutes.
Remove from heat and let cool to room temperature. Remove bay leaf.

Toss jicama, tomato, green onions, and
cilantro together with beans in large bowl. Add
5 or 6 tablespoons of the vinaigrette and toss
again. Use all the vinaigrette if you need it, but
do this by taste.
SERVES 6 TO 8

POULTRY AND GAME BIRDS

ALMOST NOBODY DOESN'T LIKE CHICKEN. AND SINCE IT'S THE one thing that seems to please every crowd, it's probably your safest bet to build a meal around. I like to use boned chicken breasts because they are quick and easy to cook and, unlike a  whole roasted chicken, require no slicing and even less fussing with. There are many other options to consider utilizing chicken, some new and some old-fashioned. One of my favorites among the older ones is chicken pot pie, which has always been a wonderful party dish for me.

✦ I'm glad to see capon and turkey on everyday menus and not just reserved for special occasions. And on the subject of game birds, I'm reminded of the fall days when my father would return from a hunting trip with a bag of ducks, or with my very favorite, wild quails. We used to have these sautéed in butter for Sunday breakfast—talk about sublime.

CHICKEN

GARLIC CHICKEN

These chickens may be cooked on an oven rotisserie—if you have such a contraption. The garlic oil would be great to use for a sharp vinaigrette.

1 tablespoon Creole Seasoning
2 tablespoons minced garlic
3 small chickens (2¹/₂ pounds each)
1 large onion, cut into chunks
2 large celery ribs, cut into large pieces
3 small carrots, scraped and cut into large pieces
Garlic Oil (recipe follows)

Preheat oven to 350 degrees.

Mix seasoning and garlic together and rub chickens with it inside and out. Divide vegetables into 3 portions and stuff each chicken. Truss and place breast side down on the rack of a roasting pan.

Bake, basting every 10 to 15 minutes with garlic oil, until juices run clear when thigh is pierced with the point of a knife, about 1 hour and 10 minutes.

Let rest a few minutes before cutting into serving pieces with poultry shears.

SERVES 6 TO 8

GARLIC OIL
4 large garlic cloves, minced
1 cup olive oil

Put garlic and oil together in a jar. Shake well, then allow to sit for several hours before using.

MAKES 1 CUP

GREEK LEMON CHICKEN

LEMON BUTTER
1 cup dry white wine
1 cup Beef Stock (page 42)
3 tablespoons minced shallots
3 tablespoons lemon juice
¹/₂ teaspoon salt
8 tablespoons (1 stick) unsalted butter, softened, plus 2 tablespoons
3 teaspoons grated lemon zest

6 medium chicken breasts, boneless and skinless (about 2¹/₂ pounds), slightly flattened
Flour
2 large eggs, lightly beaten
2 tablespoons olive oil

Place wine, stock, shallots, and lemon juice in a small pot and reduce to about ¹/₄ cup over high heat, about 25 minutes. Stir in salt and let cool. When slightly warmer than room temperature, whisk in the softened butter, a few tablespoons at a time, until mixture is the consistency of mayonnaise. Beat in lemon zest and set aside.

Dredge flattened chicken breasts in flour, shaking off excess, then place in the beaten egg, allowing excess to drain off, then once more in flour. Shake off any excess. Set aside carefully. Heat the remaining 2 tablespoons butter and the olive oil in a large heavy skillet. Over medium-high heat, sauté chicken breasts until golden on both sides, about 5 minutes in total. Transfer to a warm plate and spread some of the lemon butter over the top of each.

Note: The amount of Lemon Butter in this recipe makes enough for 12 or more servings of chicken. Any leftover may be refrigerated, covered. Let return to room temperature before using again.

SERVES 6

SPICY MILK-FRIED CHICKEN WITH PAN GRAVY

I understand that the Louisiana Hot Sauce used in the marinade is regularly available in stores throughout the country. It is not as hot as the fiery Tabasco, although surely no slouch in the heat department.

4 cups milk
1 cup Louisiana Hot Sauce
3 tablespoons salt
2 medium frying chickens, cut into small serving pieces
1 pound all-purpose flour
Vegetable oil, for frying
About 1 cup Chicken Stock (page 41)
Freshly ground black pepper

Mix milk and hot sauce in small pitcher and stir in about 1 tablespoon of the salt. Place chicken pieces in a shallow pan and pour mixture over. Turn once and marinate for 30 minutes.

Meanwhile, put half of the flour and remaining salt in a brown paper bag and tear off several large sheets of wax paper. Place the paper conveniently on the counter next to the stove. Lift chicken out of milk mixture and allow to drain slightly before putting in the flour bag. Do this in batches. Shake chicken to coat well. Lift out, shake off excess flour, and place on the wax paper. Repeat until all the chicken is coated, using more salted flour as necessary.

Pour at least 2 inches vegetable oil in a deep skillet. Heat to 300 degrees. (I use a candy thermometer but a thermostat-controlled deep-fat fryer, such as a Fry Daddy, is also a good idea.) Put chicken in, but do not crowd. Fry, adjusting the heat to keep flour from burning, 15 minutes, turning a couple of times. Place on a cooling rack to drain, underneath which you have placed double sheets of paper towels. Keep an eye on the skillet so flour does not burn, and continue until all the chicken is cooked. You may want to do this in 2 large skillets.

To make pan gravy, carefully pour off all the oil from the browned flour and chicken bits left in the pan. Add stock and simmer a few minutes, until thickened. Adjust seasoning with salt and a generous amount of black pepper.

SERVES 6

SOUTHERN FRIED PECAN CHICKEN

2 pounds boneless and skinless chicken breasts
1 1/2 cups buttermilk
2 cups pecans
1 1/3 cups all-purpose flour
1 1/2 teaspoons salt
1/2 teaspoon freshly ground black pepper
Olive oil, for frying

Cut each chicken breast lengthwise into 4 strips.

Place chicken in a bowl, cover with buttermilk, and marinate for 30 minutes.

Place all dry ingredients into the bowl of a food processor. Pulse mixture until nuts are roughly chopped. Place this mixture into a bowl. Dip chicken pieces into nut mixture, pressing it onto chicken to coat it well. Set coated pieces on a plate, cover with plastic wrap, and refrigerate for at least 30 minutes.

Fill a cast-iron skillet halfway with oil and heat over medium-high heat until hot, not smoking. Drop in chicken and cook on each side until golden brown, approximately 4 minutes per side. Drain chicken on paper towels.

SERVES 6

BUTTERMILK CHICKEN WITH DEEP GRAVY

In the South when they say something is served with deep gravy, they mean with lots of gravy so you can have some to put on your biscuits if you like.

6 large chicken thighs
1 large chicken breast, cut into 4 pieces
4 cups buttermilk
1³/₄ cups all-purpose flour
Salt
1¹/₂ teaspoons paprika
1¹/₂ teaspoons freshly ground black pepper
Canola oil, for frying
1¹/₂ cups minced onion
1 cup minced green bell pepper
³/₄ cup minced celery
4 cups Chicken Stock (page 41), hot

Preheat oven to 375 degrees.

Place chicken pieces in a bowl and cover with buttermilk. Soak for about 1 hour.

In the meantime, mix 1½ cups flour, 1½ teaspoons salt, paprika, and 1 teaspoon of the pepper. Drain chicken but do not wipe. Dredge well in the seasoned flour and set on a plate. Over high heat, warm about 1 inch of oil in a large skillet. Quickly brown chicken on both sides, about 1 minute. Place chicken pieces in a single layer in an ovenproof pan. Set aside.

Meanwhile, in another medium skillet combine remaining ¼ cup flour with ¼ cup oil. Make a dark roux over medium-high heat, stirring constantly with a spatula or pancake turner, about 10 minutes. When the roux is dark, add onion and brown lightly, about 4 to 5 minutes. Add green pepper and celery and cook long enough to wilt slightly, a minute or so, stirring constantly. Remove from the heat.

Carefully pour out all oil from the skillet in which you browned the chicken but retain any browned bits of flour. Scrape the roux and vegetables into this skillet and stir in stock. Also rinse out the roux skillet with a little of the stock and pour it in with the other mixture. Add salt and remaining ½ teaspoon pepper. Simmer to thicken. Pour around the chicken and bake, lightly covered, 30 minutes, or until chicken is done.

SERVES 6 TO 8

GRILLED MARINATED CHICKEN BREASTS

Not only does this marinade give the chicken a zesty flavor, but the breasts require very little cooking time.

6 very small whole chicken breasts, boned,
*   or 3 large, each cut in half*
3 medium garlic cloves, crushed
1¹/₂ teaspoons salt
¹/₂ cup packed brown sugar
3 tablespoons grainy mustard
¹/₄ cup cider vinegar
Juice of 1 lime
Juice of ¹/₂ large lemon
6 tablespoons olive oil
Freshly ground black pepper, to taste
Endive leaves
Watercress

Put chicken breasts in a shallow bowl. Mix garlic, salt, sugar, mustard, vinegar, and lime and lemon juices. Blend well. Whisk in the olive oil and add pepper. Pour over the chicken and refrigerate overnight, covered. Turn once.

Remove from refrigerator an hour before you want to cook it and let come to room temperature. Prepare an outdoor grill or a stovetop grill pan.

Grill the breasts for approximately 4 minutes per side, or until done. Be careful not to overcook, as this will toughen them.

You may also do these under the broiler for the same amount of time.

Garnish with endive and watercress.

SERVES 6

ITALIAN CHICKEN CUTLETS

These are best served at room temperature.

*3 cups fresh bread crumbs, made from 9
    slices firm white bread
5 medium chicken breasts, boneless and
    skinless, cut in half and flattened (see
    Note)
All-purpose flour for dusting
1/2 cup milk
3 eggs
1/2 cup mild olive oil, or more to taste
Salt, to taste
Freshly grated parmesan
Lemon wedges*

Preheat oven to 350 degrees.

Put bread, including crusts, into a food processor or blender and process into fine crumbs. Spread crumbs on a baking sheet and place in oven to dry out for 5 minutes, stirring once or twice.

Dust each piece of chicken with flour and set aside on a sheet of wax paper. Whisk milk and eggs together. Leaving the bread crumbs on the baking sheet on which they were dried, first dip the floured chicken in the egg (allow to drain off) and then into the crumbs. Press slightly to make crumbs adhere. Transfer to the wax paper as you finish. Refrigerate breaded cutlets for an hour to make sure the coating sticks. Remove from the refrigerator 15 minutes before you want to cook them.

Heat 1/2 cup oil in a heavy skillet until it is hot but not smoking. Sauté cutlets in batches, for 45 seconds on each side, adding more oil as necessary. Drain on paper towels. Sprinkle with salt and parmesan while they are still hot. Cut into "fingers" to serve, accompanied by lemon wedges.

SERVES 6

SESAME CHICKEN BREASTS

I am very fond of the flavor of sesame oil, but it has to be used sparingly because it is so potent. This recipe was devised by photographer Joshua Greene.

*6 tablespoons soy sauce
1/4 cup water
2 tablespoons sesame oil
Juice and scrapings from grating of 3-inch
    piece of ginger root, unpeeled (use the
    fine grating side)
Juice of 2 1/2 lemons
3 large chicken breasts, skinless and bone-
    less, cut in half
Toasted sesame seeds (enough to make single
    layer on baking sheet)
Lemon slices*

Mix soy sauce, water, sesame oil, ginger juice and scrapings, and lemon juice in a glass bowl large enough to hold the chicken breasts comfortably. You should have 6 ounces or more of marinade. If not, add enough water to make up the difference. Put the chicken into the mixture, cover with plastic wrap, and refrigerate for at least 1 hour. Turn a few times if the marinade doesn't quite cover the breasts.

Preheat broiler. Broil chicken for approximately 8 to 10 minutes per side. This will vary with the thickness of the meat. Baste with the marinade a few times during the cooking. Test for doneness by cutting into one of the pieces. Remove to a platter. Discard remaining marinade.

Spread a layer of toasted sesame seeds on a sheet of wax paper and roll the cooked breasts in them, carefully coating both sides. Serve at room temperature, garnished with lemon slices. Do not refrigerate.

SERVES 6

CHICKEN SAUCE PIQUANT

If you like your chicken with a very flavorful sauce, this is for you. I love it.

1 cup safflower oil
2 large chicken breasts, split, with each half cut in half
12 chicken thighs
1½ cups coarsely chopped onion
2 cups coarsely chopped celery
1 very large green bell pepper, coarsely chopped
¾ cup all-purpose flour
4 cups crushed canned tomatoes with juice
4 tablespoons tomato paste
1 teaspoon Tabasco Sauce, or to taste
4 cups Chicken Stock (page 41)
1 tablespoon lemon juice
2 large bay leaves
2 large garlic cloves, minced
1 teaspoon salt
½ teaspoon freshly ground black pepper
2 tablespoons chopped green onion tops
2 tablespoons finely chopped fresh Italian flat-leaf parsley
12 stuffed olives, sliced (optional)

Place oil in a deep skillet or Dutch oven and brown chicken on all sides, in several batches if necessary. Set aside as browned. Add onion, celery, and bell pepper to oil and cook until vegetables are wilted but not browned, about 5 minutes. Remove with a slotted spoon, draining carefully. Set aside.

Add flour to oil and stir over medium heat using a pancake turner, scraping flour from bottom of pan as it browns (you are making a roux—see Note). When dark brown, stir in tomatoes, tomato paste, Tabasco, chicken stock, lemon juice, bay leaves, garlic, salt, pepper, and reserved vegetables. Bring to a simmer and add the chicken. Simmer, uncovered, for about 1 hour or until chicken is tender and sauce is reduced and thick. When the oil begins to rise and collect on top of the sauce, skim it off and discard.

Mix in green onion tops, parsley, and olives a few minutes before serving.

Note: You should have the tomatoes with their juice and the other liquid ingredients measured and ready to add here. When a roux begins to brown, it burns very quickly; and it will continue to cook—even off the heat—if liquid is not added right away.

SERVES 6 TO 8

GRILLED CHICKEN BREASTS WITH TABASCO–HONEY GLAZE

This chicken can be cooked under the broiler instead of on the grill.

6 small chicken breasts, skinless, cut in half
6 small chicken thighs, skinless

MARINADE
⅓ cup olive oil
2 tablespoons chopped fresh sage
2 tablespoons fresh lemon juice
3 tablespoons honey

GLAZE
⅓ cup honey
2 tablespoons lemon juice
6 dashes Tabasco Sauce

Place chicken in a bowl. Mix marinade ingredients. Pour over chicken, cover, and refrigerate for at least 3 hours.

Prepare grill so coals are ash-covered. Drain and discard marinade. Grill chicken over charcoal for 5 minutes per side. Meanwhile, whisk together ingredients for the glaze, remove chicken pieces, and paint tops. Grill for 2 minutes, turn and paint other side, and grill another 2 minutes.

SERVES 6 TO 8

LEMON CHICKEN WITH SOUR CREAM SAUCE

The lemon zest and dry roux in this recipe give it its special rich flavor. In total it takes about 45 minutes to complete once you understand the process.

This recipe serves 6 but can easily be increased to serve 8 by adding another chicken breast, cut in half. There'll be plenty of sauce.

> Salt and freshly ground black pepper, to taste
> 4 whole chicken breasts, skinless and boneless, each cut in half (about 2¾ pounds)
> All-purpose flour
> 2 tablespoons olive oil
> 1 tablespoon unsalted butter
> 1½ cups diced onion
> 1½ cups diced green bell pepper
> 2 garlic cloves, thinly sliced
> ½ teaspoon dried rosemary leaves
> 2 tablespoons dry roux (see Note)
> 3 cups Chicken Stock (page 41)
> 2 tablespoons minced lemon zest
> ¼ cup sour cream substitute

Salt and generously pepper the breast halves and dredge in the flour. Shake off any excess and set aside.

Heat oil and butter in a large heavy skillet with a lid. Brown chicken over high heat, about 5 minutes per side. Remove and set aside. Add onion and bell pepper to the skillet. Turn the heat to medium and cook until onion is golden, about 8 minutes.

Add garlic, rosemary, and dry roux; stir to mix. Stir in stock. Return chicken and any juice to the skillet. Cover and simmer for 20 minutes, turning once.

Remove breasts to a warm platter. Add lemon zest to the sauce, increase heat to high, and cook for 10 minutes to reduce the sauce. Return the cooked breasts to the pan and simmer for another minute or two, just long enough to heat them through. (If you are pausing here and completing the dish later, add the breasts, cover, and set aside off the heat.) Remove from the heat and stir in the sour cream substitute. Serve with some of the sauce spooned over each portion.

To reheat, simmer just until the breasts are heated through, several minutes, before stirring in the sour cream substitute.

Note: Dry roux is very handy, easy to prepare, and keeps for months. Place a cast-iron skillet over high heat until hot. Sprinkle in about ½ cup all-purpose flour, and working quickly, stir the flour around with the edge of a pancake turner. If the flour is browning too quickly, remove the skillet from the heat momentarily and continue to stir. Cook until the flour is dark gold, about 4 minutes. Do not allow to burn. Remove the dry roux to a bowl as soon as the desired degree of doneness is reached; the flour will continue to cook if left in the hot skillet. When cool, store in a tightly sealed jar. No refrigeration is needed.

SERVES 6

CHICKEN WITH RASPBERRY VINEGAR

Here is a very easy recipe for making plain roast chicken more tasty.

> 4 tablespoons (½ stick) unsalted butter
> 4 tablespoons safflower oil
> 12 small chicken thighs
> 2 whole chicken breasts, split in half
> ¾ cup finely chopped onion
> 3 tablespoons finely chopped shallot
> ¾ cup raspberry vinegar
> 1½ tablespoons Italian tomato paste
> (or 1 small tomato, peeled, seeded, and chopped)
> ¾ cup Chicken Stock (page 41)
> 1 tablespoon chopped fresh Italian flat-leaf parsley
> ½ cup crème fraîche
> Salt and freshly ground black pepper, to taste
> Fresh raspberries

Preheat oven to 350 degrees.

Heat 2 tablespoons of the butter and all the oil in a skillet large enough to hold all the chicken pieces. Carefully brown pieces in two batches. Be careful not to burn them. When both batches are finished, fit chicken pieces snugly in pan. Lay a sheet of foil loosely over the top. Bake for just 1 hour.

Remove chicken and keep warm. Pour out the fat from skillet, then add remaining butter. Add onion and shallot and sauté until wilted. Add vinegar and cook at high heat until the mixture is reduced to a syrupy consistency. Dissolve tomato paste in stock. Add with parsley to the vinegar mixture and simmer for a few minutes. (If using fresh tomatoes, instead of paste, reduce the mixture by cooking it very slowly for about 5 minutes.) Stir in crème fraîche. Season with salt and pepper.

Fit all the chicken pieces back into the pan and simmer for another few minutes, spooning the sauce over them continually or turning them several times.

Serve garnished with fresh raspberries.

SERVES 6

CHICKEN WITH PRUNES AND HOT PEPPERS

Prunes, hot peppers, and ground almonds are traditional ingredients in many chicken dishes from North Africa. Doubling this recipe to serve a dozen people works fine. It's a perfect buffet supper.

16 pitted prunes
¼ cup olive oil
2 pounds whole chicken breasts, each cut into 4 parts
2 pounds chicken thighs
4 large onions, peeled and coarsely chopped
1 hot red chili pepper, about 4 inches long, seeded and coarsely chopped
5 tablespoons unblanched almonds, finely ground
¾ cup Chicken Stock (page 41), hot

The night before, put prunes in a bowl and cover with boiling water.

In a large heatproof casserole, heat oil until almost smoking. Brown the chicken pieces in batches, setting them aside as they are finished.

Preheat oven to 350 degrees.

When all the chicken is browned, pour off all but ¼ cup of the rendered fat and add onions and hot pepper to the casserole. Lower heat and cook for 15 minutes. When onions are nicely wilted, stir in ground almonds and add the chicken pieces. Drain prunes and add them. Pour in stock. Cover tightly with foil and make half a dozen holes in the top. (This dish can be set aside for several hours at this point. Reheat it on top of the stove very slowly for a few minutes before putting it in the oven.)

Bake chicken for 1 hour and 15 minutes. If your chicken pieces are fairly large or thick, remove one of the biggest and make an incision down to the bone with the point of a sharp knife to make sure it is cooked through. If not, give it another 10 minutes. Remove chicken and prunes to a warm platter. If the sauce is too thin, reduce it for a few minutes over low heat. Pour over chicken.

Note: Be sure to use gloves when handling hot peppers.

SERVES 6 TO 8

CHICKEN AND WALNUT ENCHILADAS WITH ROASTED GREEN CHILI SAUCE

The sauce is rather mild, so if you like yours hot, add more jalapeño. Serve these as the centerpiece of any supper.

GREEN CHILI SAUCE
20 to 25 tomatillos (3 to 3¼ pounds)
2 tablespoons olive oil
2 cups coarsely chopped onions
2 cans (7 ounces each) diced roasted green chilies, drained and diced
3 medium garlic cloves, minced
2 teaspoons dried oregano
2 cups Chicken Stock (page 41)
2 medium bay leaves
1 tablespoon sugar
Salt and freshly ground black pepper, to taste

FILLING
1 chicken (3 to 4 pounds)
1 cup shredded mild cheddar
1½ cups shredded Monterey Jack
1 cup shelled walnuts, roasted and chopped
1 tablespoon dried oregano
Salt and freshly ground black pepper, to taste

ASSEMBLY
1 cup vegetable oil
12 corn tortillas
2 cups shredded Monterey Jack
2 large tomatoes (about 1 pound), coarsely diced
2 medium avocados, peeled, pitted, sliced, and rubbed with lemon juice
1 cup sour cream
6 ounces black olives packed in brine, drained
12 cilantro sprigs, chopped
1 cup shelled, roasted pumpkin seeds (see Note)

To make green chili sauce: Remove husks and stems from tomatillos. Place in a saucepan and cover with water. Bring rapidly to a boil and cook over medium-high heat until tender, about 5 minutes. Drain and rinse. Set aside. Place olive oil in a medium skillet over medium-high heat, add onions, and sauté until translucent, about 3 minutes, stirring. Transfer to a food processor with the tomatillos, chilies, garlic, oregano, and 1 cup of the stock. Process a few seconds until coarse. Return to the saucepan and stir in remaining stock, bay leaves, sugar, salt, and pepper. Bring to a boil and simmer for 30 minutes. Remove bay leaves and discard. Set sauce aside.

To make filling: Place chicken in a large pot and cover with water. Bring quickly to a boil, cover, reduce heat, and simmer until very tender, 1½ to 2 hours. Cool chicken in liquid. Discard skin and bones and shred meat. Combine shredded chicken with the cheeses, walnuts, oregano, salt, and pepper. Set aside.

To assemble: Preheat oven to 350 degrees.

Heat oil in a large skillet over medium heat and quickly cook tortillas, one at the time, for a few seconds. Drain as you remove them from the oil. Dip each into the green chili sauce and lay flat in a large baking dish. Spoon ½ cup chicken filling onto tortillas and roll, placing seam side down. Continue until all tortillas are used. Spoon remainder of the sauce over the top. Cover with foil and bake until heated through, 15 to 20 minutes. Remove the foil and sprinkle with Monterey Jack cheese. Return dish to oven and bake until cheese melts, 5 to 10 minutes.

Serve 2 enchiladas on a warm plate, garnished with diced tomatoes, avocado slices, sour cream, olives, and cilantro. Sprinkle roasted pumpkin seeds over the top.

Note: To roast pumpkin seeds, spread them on a baking sheet and place in a moderate oven until golden, 5 to 8 minutes.

SERVES 6

CHICKEN ENCHILADAS WITH ANDOUILLE SAUSAGE

You can also make this with leftover roast chicken.

SAUCE

1/4 cup olive oil
2 1/4 cups roughly chopped onions
1 tablespoon roughly chopped garlic
2 cans (28 ounces each) whole peeled tomatoes
1/2 teaspoon salt
1/2 teaspoon freshly ground black pepper
1/2 teaspoon dried oregano
1 teaspoon dried basil
1 tablespoon minced canned chipotle chilies

ASSEMBLY

1 1/2 cups roughly chopped onions
Vegetable oil
10 10-inch flour tortillas (6 1/2-inch tortillas can be substituted)
2 1/2 cups shredded cooked chicken breast
6 ounces andouille sausage, cut into quarters lengthwise, then into 1/4-inch pieces
1 pound Monterey Jack, grated
1 pound cheddar, grated

To make sauce: Put olive oil into a large cast-iron skillet, add onions, and cook over medium-high heat until translucent, about 4 or 5 minutes. Add garlic and cook for an additional minute. Add tomatoes, salt, pepper, oregano, and basil. Bring to a boil, then break up tomatoes with a potato masher. Reduce heat and simmer for 30 to 40 minutes. Run sauce through a food mill using the coarse disk. Measure the sauce and if you need to, reduce until you have about 5 1/2 cups. Stir in the chopped chilies. Set aside.

To assemble casserole: Heat a cast-iron skillet over very high heat until hot. Add enough onions to just cover the bottom of the pan. Stir and turn the onions with the edge of a metal spatula for approximately 10 minutes, until well browned. Set aside. Repeat with the remaining onions.

Use a paper towel to lightly oil a skillet with vegetable oil and place it over high heat. Place 1 tortilla in the skillet for several seconds and then flip it and heat the other side. Remove each tortilla as it is heated, stacking them on top of each other until all are done.

Preheat oven to 350 degrees. Combine shredded chicken with andouille sausage. In a large bowl, combine both grated cheeses.

Place 1/4 cup sauce, 1/3 cup chicken mixture, 1 tablespoon caramelized onions, and 1/4 cup cheese on each tortilla. (If you are using small tortillas, they will be quite full. This is fine.) Roll each tortilla and place it seam side down into a large casserole dish. When all are assembled and lined up in the casserole dish, cover them all with the remaining sauce and the remaining cheese. Bake uncovered for 40 to 45 minutes, until golden brown and bubbly.

SERVES 6 TO 8

ROASTED CHICKEN BREASTS WITH PAN GRAVY

The important thing about this recipe is that you use whole boned chicken breast *with* the skin. You may have to ask your butcher to do this because prepackaged boned breasts are often skinned.

> 3 whole chicken breasts, boned, split, with the skin left on (about 3 pounds)
> 3 tablespoons butter, slightly softened
> 1 teaspoon salt
> 1 teaspoon freshly ground black pepper
> 1 1/2 cups Chicken Stock (page 41), warm
> 3/4 teaspoon cornstarch dissolved in 1 tablespoon water

Preheat oven to 425 degrees.

Rub chicken breasts on all sides with butter and sprinkle with salt and pepper. "Reassemble" to whole chicken breasts by stacking two breasts together, skin side out, and stretching skin to cover as much surface as possible. Hold the pairs together by running two wooden skewers through each. (You will now have what looks like three whole chicken breasts.)

Place chicken on a roasting rack in a pan and bake until internal temperature is 155 to 160 degrees, about 30 minutes. Remove to a cutting board and cover loosely with foil.

To deglaze the roasting pan, pour stock into the pan, scraping any browned bits up from the bottom. Pour liquid into a fat separator and allow fat to rise. Remove fat and discard. Pour remaining liquid into a saucepan and reduce at a rapid boil to approximately 3/4 cup. Thicken with dissolved cornstarch.

Cut each doubled breast into six slices, discarding skin if you wish. Arrange on individual plates and top with sauce to serve.

SERVES 6

GUMBO YA YA

The classic.

> 1/4 cup vegetable oil
> 3 chickens (3 pounds each), chopped into large pieces
> 2 tablespoons Creole Seasoning
> 2 1/4 cups peanut oil
> 3 cups flour
> 2 pounds onions, peeled and cut into medium dice
> 1 pound celery ribs, cut into medium dice
> 3 tablespoons minced garlic
> 5 quarts boiling water
> 3 tablespoons salt
> 1 tablespoon cayenne pepper
> 1 pound andouille sausage, cut into 1/4-inch rings
> 1 tablespoon gumbo filé
> Louisiana Hot Sauce

Heat vegetable oil in large saucepan. Rub chicken pieces with Creole Seasoning. Add to the oil and brown, turning, several minutes. Set aside off the heat.

In heavy skillet, combine peanut oil and flour. Make a dark roux (see page 34). When about as dark as a roasted pecan, scrape the roux immediately into a 10-gallon stockpot. Stir in vegetables and mix. Carefully pour in the water. Stir to dissolve roux. Add the seasonings and the chicken along with any juices it has given up. Simmer over low heat for 45 minutes. Along the way, skim off and discard any oil that may rise to the top. Add sausage and simmer another 12 minutes. Whisk in the filé.

Serve with hot sauce on the side.

SERVES 12 OR MORE

CHICKEN AND OKRA GUMBO

There are dozen of recipes for gumbo using various methods. The one thing they all have in common is the roux, which gives the soup its distinctive flavor. This particular recipe uses quite a large quantity of this robust element.

2 pounds chicken breasts, cut into 4 parts
2 pounds chicken thighs
Salt and freshly ground black pepper, to
*   taste*
Cayenne, to taste
Oil for frying
1 cup chopped onion
1 cup chopped celery
4 garlic cloves, crushed
Up to 1 cup oil
1 cup flour
2 quarts hot water
1 pound okra, tops and stems removed, cut
*   into rings*
6 cups cooked rice
¼ cup chopped green onions

Skin and season all the chicken pieces generously with salt, pepper, and cayenne. Brown them in about ½ inch of heated oil (vegetable or a combination of vegetable and bacon drippings). Remove to a large pot. Pour oil left after browning the chicken into a measuring cup. Add onion and celery to the pan and cook slowly until onion wilts. Add a little of the drained oil if necessary.

Scrape vegetables into pot with the chicken and add garlic.

Add enough oil to that which was left over from cooking the chicken to measure 1 cup. Pour it, along with the flour, into a skillet to make the roux. Mix the flour together with the oil over medium heat. Use the reverse side of a flat-ended spatula to scrape the mixture from the bottom as it begins to brown. Keep it constantly moving. When it starts to brown it can go very quickly, so keep scraping it from the bottom and mixing. As the roux darkens you can lift the skillet from the heat and let it continue to cook from the retained heat. Remember that the browning process does not immediately stop when the skillet is removed from heat, so it is necessary to keep stirring. When the roux is about as dark as bread crust, it is almost ready. Darken it a bit more and immediately pour into the pot with the chicken and vegetables.

Pour 2 quarts hot water over all, and simmer slowly until the chicken is tender, testing after 1 hour. During the cooking, skim off any oil that rises to the surface. The soup should be rather thick, but thinner than pea soup. If it seems too thin, continue to simmer to reduce water content; if too thick, add a little more water and correct seasoning. When cooking is completed, allow soup to cool enough to remove the bones from the chicken. (The soup can be made up to this point several days in advance and refrigerated. Reheat to serve, adding okra during last 5 or 10 minutes. If it has been refrigerated, a bit more liquid may be needed.)

Return the soup to the heat and add okra. Cook 5 to 10 minutes, until okra is tender.

Put a scoop of rice into each of 6 bowls and pour the gumbo over it, making sure that everyone gets a few nice chunks of chicken and some okra. Sprinkle with the green onions.

Note: Peeled raw shrimp, oysters, or crabmeat may be added.

SERVES 6

CHICKEN WITH TUNA SAUCE

3 whole chicken breasts or 1 whole "oven roaster" breast (about 3¹/₂ pounds)
1 celery rib
1 medium onion, thinly sliced
1 medium bay leaf
1 teaspoon dried thyme
1 tablespoon salt
Dash of freshly ground black pepper
1 6-ounce can good-quality Italian tuna in oil, drained
3 flat anchovy fillets, drained
1 tablespoon capers, rinsed and drained
2 egg yolks
2 tablespoons fresh lemon juice
¹/₂ cup olive oil
³/₄ cup vegetable oil
Lemon wedges (optional)
Capers (optional)

Place chicken breasts in small saucepan and cover with cold water. Add celery, onion, bay leaf, thyme, salt, and pepper. Bring to a boil over high heat and immediately reduce the heat. Simmer 10 minutes for chicken breast, 17 minutes for roaster breast. Let cool in the liquid. When cool, skin and bone the chicken, then slice.

Place tuna, anchovies, capers, egg yolks, and lemon juice in a blender and process a few seconds before adding the oils in a steady stream, blending until smooth.

To serve, smear the bottom of the serving dish with some of the sauce and arrange a layer of the sliced chicken on top. Continue layering sauce and chicken, finishing with sauce.

Garnish with lemon wedges and capers, if desired.

SERVES 6

RIGODON

This custard dish originated in Burgundy. The ingredients make it related to quiche but it is easier to make because it doesn't require a crust. It also can utilize leftover meats, such as chicken, beef, lamb, or pork, but I prefer it made with freshly baked chicken.

4 to 5 small chicken thighs or 1¹/₂ cups cubed cooked chicken
Salt and freshly ground black pepper
1¹/₄ cups low-fat milk
³/₄ cup evaporated skimmed milk
1 slice bacon
1 green onion, with some of the green, chopped
1 tablespoon unsalted butter or margarine
1 tablespoon chicken fat
³/₄ cup cubed brioche
1¹/₂ tablespoons all-purpose flour
4 eggs
1 tablespoon chopped fresh Italian flat-leaf parsley
¹/₄ teaspoon salt
¹/₄ teaspoon freshly ground black pepper
Few drops of Tabasco Sauce or a pinch of cayenne
¹/₂ cup cubed mozzarella
1 tablespoon freshly grated parmesan

Preheat oven to 375 degrees.

Put chicken thighs skin side up in an 8 × 8-inch baking dish (or any dish in which they fit snugly) and salt and pepper very generously. Bake for 35 minutes and turn off the oven. You can leave them this way for several hours, as they finish cooking by retained heat. (This can be done the day before you plan to use them. You may use the same dish in which the chicken has been cooked for the rigodon. If you are planning to do this, make it an attractive dish. It is much easier to serve without trying to get it out in one piece to put on a platter.) Reserve chicken fat. Remove skin and cube chicken meat.

Preheat oven to 325 degrees.

In a small saucepan bring both milks to a boil, then turn off the heat.

Sauté bacon until crisp; drain, crumble, and set side. Pour out rendered fat from skillet and add green onion. Cook until wilted. Melt butter and chicken fat in with the onion. Add brioche cubes and toss. When they start to turn golden, switch off heat and set aside.

In a large bowl, whisk together flour and eggs until smooth. Add chicken, parsley, ¼ teaspoon salt, ¼ teaspoon pepper, and Tabasco and mix. Add milks and mix again. Pour into a greased 8 × 8-inch baking pan. (You can just wipe out the one you have cooked the chicken in, leaving some of the fat and gelatin.)

Sprinkle the mozzarella cubes evenly over the top, followed by the toasted brioche–onion mixture. They should sink slightly, or press them down lightly. Sprinkle with parmesan and crumbled bacon. Bake until set and lightly browned, about 30 minutes. Let cool at least 1 hour before serving.

SERVES 4 TO 6

VARIATIONS

Substitute whole milk and heavy cream for the low-fat milk and evaporated skimmed milk. Substitute plain bread cubes for the brioche.

CHICKEN AND WHITE BEAN CHILI

1 pound dried white beans, soaked overnight or by the quick-soak method (see Note, page 25)
4 cups Chicken Stock (page 41)
2 cups water
2 garlic cloves, minced
2 medium onions, chopped
1 tablespoon olive oil
2 cans (4 ounces each) chopped green chilies with liquid
2 teaspoons ground cumin
1½ teaspoons dried oregano
¼ teaspoon ground cloves
¼ teaspoon cayenne
1½ pounds chicken breasts, boneless, cut into 1-inch strips

Drain beans, place in a medium pot, and cover with cold water. Heat to boiling. Boil for 2 minutes. Turn off heat and let the beans stand for 1 hour. Drain.

In a medium (at least 6-quart) stockpot, combine drained beans, stock, water, garlic, and half of the chopped onions. Bring to a boil, reduce heat, and simmer, covered, until beans are almost tender, about 45 minutes.

Heat olive oil in a heavy skillet over medium heat and add remaining onions. Wilt but do not brown, 3 to 5 minutes. Add chilies, cumin, oregano, cloves, and cayenne to the onions and cook, stirring constantly, until the spices are a deep, rich color, about 5 minutes.

Stir this mixture into the beans and add the chicken pieces. Bring to a boil, reduce heat, and simmer, partially covered, for 1 hour, adding more water if needed. The chicken should be thoroughly cooked, but not tough.

SERVES 6

CHICKEN PANCAKES WITH PAPAYA SALSA

These are also good served with the more traditional sour cream or crème fraîche.

Salt and freshly ground black pepper
6 medium chicken thighs
1½ cups shredded potato, squeezed dry (see Note)
1 small onion, grated
2 tablespoons flour
Tabasco Sauce, to taste
Vegetable oil and butter for frying
3 medium eggs, lightly beaten
Papaya Salsa (page 357)

Preheat oven to 375 degrees.

Generously salt and pepper the chicken thighs and place them skin side up, in a pan into which they fit snugly. Make sure the skin is stretched over all. Bake without opening the door for 30 minutes and then turn off the oven. Leave to be baked by the retained heat for another 45 minutes or so without opening the door. This may be done in advance.

When ready to assemble pancakes, remove skin and bones from the chicken and discard. Chop the meat coarse. Set aside.

Mix potato with onion, flour, ¾ teaspoon salt, ¼ teaspoon pepper, and a drop or two of Tabasco, combining thoroughly.

Place a combination of oil and butter in a large skillet. While this is heating over medium-high heat, combine chicken with potato mixture and then add eggs. Mix quickly.

When oil is hot, drop rounded tablespoonfuls of the batter into the skillet. Allow to cook until golden, about a minute or so, before turning. Flatten slightly and cook until golden. Keep finished pancakes warm until all the batter is used. Serve with Papaya Salsa.

Note: To squeeze the potato dry, wrap it in a tea towel and twist out as much liquid as possible.

MAKES 18 TO 24 MEDIUM PANCAKES

CHICKEN LOAF

1½ pounds chicken breast, boneless and skinless
2 tablespoons olive oil
¾ cup finely chopped onion
¾ cup finely chopped shallots
3 tablespoons finely chopped fresh Italian flat-leaf parsley
¼ cup milk
1 egg
1 teaspoon dried tarragon
¼ teaspoon dried savory
½ teaspoon salt
¼ teaspoon freshly ground black pepper
1 cup fresh bread crumbs

Preheat oven to 375 degrees and lightly grease an 8½ × 4½-inch loaf pan.

Cut the chicken breast into chunks, then place in the bowl of a food processor. Pulse until finely chopped. Do not overwork. Place chicken into a large mixing bowl.

Heat oil in a large cast-iron skillet over medium-high heat until hot, not smoking. Add onion and shallots and sauté until tender, 6 to 8 minutes. Remove from the heat and stir in parsley. Let cool for several minutes, then add to chicken.

Combine milk, egg, tarragon, savory, salt, and pepper in a small bowl. Beat lightly with a fork, then add it to the chicken mixture. Mix by hand. Add bread crumbs and mix again.

Spoon the mixture into the pan and place it into a deep baking dish. Place the baking dish into the oven and then fill the baking dish with ½ inch of water. Bake for 1 hour. Remove from the oven, leaving the loaf pan in the baking dish. Let cool for at least 30 minutes. Loosen the sides of the loaf by running a sharp knife around the edge. Carefully drain off any excess liquid and then invert the loaf onto a plate to cool further.

SERVES 4

CHICKEN POT PIE WITH BISCUIT TOPPING

When I make chicken pot pie, I usually cook the chicken a day ahead.

12 celery ribs
16-pound hen
Generous 1½ cups sliced carrot
Generous 1½ cups diced potato (½-inch dice)
3 tablespoons margarine
3 tablespoons unsalted butter
¾ cup dry roux (page 34)
2 tablespoons all-purpose flour
1 teaspoon salt, plus extra for salting layers
½ teaspoon freshly ground black pepper
14 dashes Tabasco Sauce
1 very large onion, coarsely chopped and caramelized (see page 130)
1½ cups frozen baby lima beans

BISCUIT TOPPING
2½ cups all-purpose flour
1¼ teaspoons salt
2½ teaspoons baking powder
½ teaspoon baking soda
4 tablespoons (½ stick) unsalted butter
4 tablespoons (½ stick) margarine
1½ cups buttermilk

Break celery into pieces and stuff hen with some of them. Place hen in a deep pot just large enough to hold it and cover it with water. Add remaining celery. Cover and simmer for 1½ hours, or until tender.

Let hen cool in the stock and then refrigerate until well chilled. Degrease the stock. Remove the meat from the bones and set aside. Return bones to the stock in the pot and cook at a gentle boil until reduced to 6 cups, about 45 minutes to 1 hour. Set aside.

Put carrot slices in a small saucepan and cover with water. Bring to a simmer and cook for 4 minutes. Drain and set aside. Put the diced potato in a small saucepan, cover with salted water, bring to a boil, and cook for 7 minutes. Drain and set aside.

Preheat oven to 450 degrees. Grease a 12 × 9 × 2-inch baking dish and set aside. Strain the stock and reheat.

Combine margarine and butter in a large skillet over medium heat. Sprinkle in the roux and stir to mix well. Whisk in 5 cups of the hot stock. Put the flour in a small bowl. Add about 1 cup of the heated stock and whisk to make sure there are no lumps. Add this to the sauce and simmer, whisking, until thickened, about 5 minutes. When smooth add salt, pepper, and Tabasco. Simmer for 1 minute.

Put a layer of chicken in the bottom of the baking dish and top with one third of the carrots, potatoes, and onion. Sprinkle with salt (and a little pepper if you like). Continue layering until all the chicken and vegetables are used, finishing with the chicken. Top with lima beans. Pour the sauce over all.

To make biscuits: Mix flour, salt, baking powder, and baking soda in a large bowl. Cut in butter and margarine with 2 knives or a pastry blender to about the size of large peas. Quickly stir in buttermilk. Gather the dough into a ball and turn out onto a floured surface. Pat or roll out about ⅜ inch thick. Cut into about twenty 2½-inch biscuits with a floured cutter. Place the biscuits on the assembled pie, leaving space between each—4 across and 5 down.

Bake until the biscuits are golden and cooked, about 30 minutes. Put a foil-lined pan on the shelf below the baking dish as it sometimes bubbles over.

SERVES 8 TO 10

DOUBLE-CRUST CHICKEN AND DUMPLING PIE

You will need a deep baking dish that has a capacity of about five quarts, about the size of a small roasting pan. If all else fails, you can use a roasting pan; it just won't make as nice a presentation.

For those of you who are accustomed to small square or round dumplings, these are different; they are made in long strips.

DUMPLINGS AND CRUST

5 cups flour

9 teaspoons baking powder

1/2 teaspoon baking soda

1 teaspoon salt

1/2 pound (2 sticks) chilled unsalted butter, cut into 16 pieces

2 cups buttermilk

6 cups Chicken Stock (page 41)

3 1/2 to 4 pounds mixed chicken breasts and thighs, skin removed, the breast halves cut in two

Salt and freshly ground black pepper

1 1/2 cups finely chopped celery

1/2 cup finely chopped red onion

3 tablespoons unsalted butter or margarine

Preheat oven to 450 degrees. Lightly grease the pan and set aside.

Sift all the dry ingredients for the dumplings and crust into a large bowl. Cut in the butter with two knives or a pastry blender. Butter pieces should be the size of large peas when you finish the cutting in. Stir in the buttermilk and make a ball of dough. Turn it onto a floured surface and knead it for just a few minutes. Divide it into 2 equal parts. One ball will be used to line pan and make dumplings, the other for the double crust. Dust each with a little flour and cover with a tea towel.

To assemble the dish, put stock on to heat and roll out half of one of the balls of dough to about 1/4-inch thickness. With a pastry wheel, cut a long strip or two to fit around the sides of the pan, leaving the bottom unlined. You may want to press the dough along the top rim of the pan to hold it in place. Neatness is not important here, as this is temporary. Set aside any leftover rolled-out dough. Using half the chicken pieces, make a single layer in the bottom of the pan. Sprinkle with salt and pepper and half the celery and onion.

To make dumplings, roll out the other half ball of dough to 1/4-inch thickness. Cut it into strips 1 inch wide. Lay half of them lengthwise across the chicken parts in the pan. Gently place the remainder of the chicken on top of the strips of dough and sprinkle with salt and pepper and vegetables as before. Cover with remaining strips of dough, also as before.

To make the top crusts, divide the second ball of dough into 2 parts. Roll out one part to the size of the top of the pan. (If you like, cut out a paper pattern the size of the top of the pan before you start, to use as a guide.) Lay dough, which will be rather thin and elastic, over chicken and dumplings, covering the entire top. If you are apprehensive about picking up this large sheet of dough, you may cut it into 2 or 4 pieces and reassemble on the pie. The crust will be slightly below the top edge of the pan, to allow for it to float up when the liquid is added. To join the top to the sides, push the side strips so that they fall over onto the top crust. They will melt together slightly while baking.

Make a hole in the center of the top crust and using a funnel with a handle if possible, pour in the 6 cups of hot stock. The top crust will float up. Bake for 25 minutes until golden brown. About 5 minutes before this cooking time is up, melt butter.

To make the final crust, roll out the remaining piece of dough to the size of the top of the pan. Take pie from the oven and, using half the melted butter, paint the cooked crust with a pastry brush. Place the uncooked second crust over the top of the first, making sure it covers completely. Trim off any dough that may be hanging over. Carefully paint this last crust with the remaining butter. Return to the oven, turn it down to 250 degrees, and cook an additional 65 minutes. The total cooking time is 1½ hours.

To serve, cut a piece of the top (and side) crust and place on the plate first, then spoon out chicken and dumplings over it.

Note: The dough can be made the day before, divided into 2 parts, and refrigerated tightly wrapped in plastic wrap. If you do this, take it out of the refrigerator 30 minutes or so before you intend to use it. Because of the baking time, this pie should be in the oven when your guests arrive.
SERVES 6 TO 8

CHICKEN POT PIE WITH CORNBREAD CRUST

Chicken Pot Pie never fails to please. I've tinkered around with the combination of vegetables, the crust, and the sauce for many years. This recipe is my favorite on all scores—don't let that keep you from doing your own tinkering.

1 large hen (over 3 pounds)
10 celery stalks (with tops)
1 cup carrot slices
1 cup potato cubes
1 large onion (8 ounces), thinly sliced
6 tablespoons (¾ stick) margarine (or half butter and half margarine)
6 tablespoons flour
Salt, to taste
½ teaspoon white pepper
8 drops Tabasco Sauce
1 cup frozen baby lima beans

CRUST
1½ cups white cornmeal
1½ cups flour
2 tablespoons baking powder
3 tablespoons sugar
1½ teaspoons salt
1½ cups milk

2 eggs, lightly beaten
¼ cup safflower oil

Put the hen in a large kettle and just cover with water. Break up the celery and put it in the pot. Simmer for 1½ hours, or until chicken is tender. Skim if necessary. Let cool in the stock. When cool, take the chicken carefully from the stock and remove the meat, discarding the skin, but returning the bones to the pot. Measure out 4 very generous cups of chicken meat, cube, and set aside. (Refrigerate the rest of the meat for another use.) Simmer the stock for another hour to reduce it. Taste it to correct the seasoning. Discard the bones. If it does not have a pronounced enough flavor, bolster it with a few chicken bouillon cubes. Reserve 4 cups and cool and refrigerate the rest.

Put carrots in a saucepan and just cover with water. Simmer for 4 minutes. Drain. Set aside. Put potatoes on, just covered with water, and simmer for 7 minutes. Drain. Set aside.

Preheat oven to 450 degrees.

Sauté onion in margarine until wilted. Meanwhile, put the stock on to heat up. Stir flour into onion and mix well. Add the heated stock slowly, stirring or whisking constantly. When smooth, let simmer for a minute and add salt and pepper and the Tabasco.

To assemble the pie, put a layer of chicken in the bottom of a greased shallow 3-quart casserole. Sprinkle a third each of the frozen limas and cooked carrots and potatoes over it. Add salt and pepper. Repeat until all the chicken and vegetables are used. Pour the stock sauce over it all.

To make crust: Sift together cornmeal, flour, baking powder, sugar, and salt in a large bowl. Mix milk with eggs and safflower oil in a small bowl, and mix in with the dry ingredients. Pour over chicken and vegetables and bake for 25 minutes, or until golden brown.

Note: If a hen is not available, use a large chicken. It may take a little less time to be tender.
SERVES 8

MACARONI CASSEROLE WITH CHICKEN AND SPICY SAUSAGE

You'll need to start this casserole a day ahead, because it must be refrigerated overnight before baking.

2 tablespoons margarine
³/₄ pound chicken breast, boneless and skinless, cut into small chunks
¹/₂ pound andouille sausage or other cured spicy sausage, removed from the casings and coarsely chopped
2 cups tomato sauce (see pages 350 to 352)
¹/₂ pound elbow macaroni
1 cup low-fat cottage cheese
1 cup low-fat cream cheese, at room temperature
¹/₄ cup low-fat sour cream
¹/₂ cup minced onion
³/₄ cup minced red bell pepper
1 tablespoon unsalted butter

Place 1 tablespoon of the margarine in a large skillet over medium-high heat. When it starts to bubble, add chicken. Sauté, tossing from time to time, until chicken is done, about 5 minutes. Stir in sausage and tomato sauce. Set aside.

Cook macaroni according to package directions and drain. Place cottage cheese, cream cheese, and sour cream in a bowl and beat with an electric mixer until smooth. Combine with macaroni and blend well with a wooden spoon. Stir in onion and bell pepper. Melt the remaining 1 tablespoon margarine with the butter.

Grease a low-sided 2-quart rectangular baking dish. Cover the bottom of the dish with the macaroni mixture. Drizzle with the melted butter and margarine. Top with the meat–tomato mixture. Cover and refrigerate overnight.

To cook, preheat oven to 350 degrees. Remove the casserole from the refrigerator while the oven preheats. Bake for 40 minutes, until bubbly.
SERVES 8

TRADITIONAL CHICKEN SALAD

4 chicken breasts, boneless and skinless
Salt and freshly ground black pepper, to taste
6 tablespoons olive oil
¹/₂ cup finely chopped sweet pickle
¹/₂ cup finely chopped canned pimiento
¹/₂ cup finely chopped celery
2 tablespoons finely chopped green onion
2 tablespoons balsamic vinegar

Preheat oven to 400 degrees.

Divide breasts in half and sprinkle lightly with salt and pepper. Heat oil in a cast-iron skillet over high heat until hot, not smoking. Sear each breast until browned on both sides, about 2 minutes per side.

Place in the oven and bake for 5 minutes. Remove the chicken to a plate and let cool completely. Slice the breasts on the diagonal into ¹/₄-inch slices, then into chunks, and place in a mixing bowl.

Add the remaining ingredients to the chicken and toss well. Taste for salt and pepper.
SERVES 6

WARM SPICY CHICKEN SALAD WITH BACON-MOLASSES DRESSING

This salad can also be prepared with quail.

SALAD

1 teaspoon paprika
1 teaspoon ground cumin
1 teaspoon ground coriander
³/₄ teaspoon cayenne
4 tablespoons olive oil
1 whole chicken breast, boneless and skinless
1 medium head romaine or ruby lettuce, washed, dried, and torn into bite-size pieces
6 to 8 large white mushrooms, sliced
1 red or yellow bell pepper, seeded and sliced
1 bunch red radishes, tipped, stemmed, and cut into quarters lengthwise
1 medium carrot, grated
¹/₂ teaspoon toasted sesame seeds

DRESSING

¹/₂ pound bacon, finely diced
2 to 3 medium shallots, chopped
¹/₃ cup homemade or store-bought pesto
¹/₃ cup red wine vinegar
2 tablespoons molasses
¹/₄ to ¹/₂ cup olive oil

To make salad: Combine paprika, cumin, coriander, and cayenne with 2 tablespoons of olive oil. Cut chicken breast into ¹/₂-inch strips and coat with the spice mixture. Set aside. Place lettuce, mushrooms, bell pepper, and radishes in a large salad bowl. Set aside.

To make the dressing: Sauté bacon until golden brown. Remove to paper towels and reserve the fat in pan. Combine shallots, pesto, vinegar, and molasses in a blender and blend until puréed. Add enough olive oil to the bacon fat to measure 1 cup and add gradually to the blender. Blend well. Pour into a bowl and add bacon bits. Set aside.

Heat the remaining 2 tablespoons of olive oil in a medium sauté pan over high heat and sauté the chicken strips until golden brown, 2 to 3 minutes. Add ¹/₄ cup of the dressing and cook for 30 seconds. Add the chicken strips to the salad, and toss. Pour dressing over all and toss again quickly. Garnish with grated carrot and sprinkle sesame seeds on top.

SERVES 2 AS AN ENTRÉE OR 4 AS A FIRST COURSE

WARM CHICKEN SALAD WITH HAZELNUT VINAIGRETTE

1 small chicken breast, skinless, cut in half lengthwise
1 small garlic clove, crushed
5 tablespoons plus 1 teaspoon hazelnut oil
Salt and freshly ground black pepper, to taste
2 tablespoons white wine vinegar
³/₄ teaspoon Dijon mustard
1 teaspoon minced shallots
2 or more cups shredded salad greens

Flatten the chicken halves slightly between 2 sheets of wax paper, rub them with garlic, and then with 4 teaspoons of the hazelnut oil. Sprinkle with salt and pepper, cover, and refrigerate for at least 1 hour. Preheat the broiler or prepare coals for grilling.

Cook chicken in broiler or on grill very close to the heat for 3 to 4 minutes per side, or until done but not dry. Do not overcook.

Meanwhile, whisk together the remaining oil, the vinegar, mustard, salt, and pepper. Stir in the shallots.

Toss the greens with just enough vinaigrette to coat them well. Arrange on 2 large plates. Place grilled chicken on the greens directly from the grill and spoon a little extra vinaigrette over the top of each breast.

You may also sprinkle the chicken with crumbled bacon, toasted chopped hazelnuts, or cheese—or all three.

SERVES 2

CHIPOTLE CHICKEN SALAD

4 chicken breasts, boneless and skinless
Salt and freshly ground black pepper, to
taste
1 tablespoon olive oil
1 canned chipotle pepper
1/4 cup mayonnaise
1/4 cup sour cream

Preheat oven to 400 degrees.

Divide breasts in half and sprinkle lightly with salt and pepper. Heat oil in a cast-iron skillet over high heat until hot, not smoking. Sear each breast until browned on both sides, about 2 minutes per side.

Place in the oven and bake for 5 minutes. Remove chicken to a plate and let cool completely. Slice breasts on the diagonal into 1/4-inch slices and place in a mixing bowl.

Combine chipotle pepper, mayonnaise, and sour cream in the bowl of a food processor and process until pepper is finely minced. Spoon dressing over chicken and toss.

SERVES 6

TURKEY

TURKEY AND CHEESE ENCHILADA CASSEROLE

This is guaranteed to be a crowd pleaser.

TURKEY
1 4 1/2-pound whole turkey breast, with the
bone in
1 teaspoon salt
1 teaspoon freshly ground black pepper

TOMATO SAUCE
1/2 cup olive oil
4 1/2 cups roughly chopped onions
2 tablespoons roughly chopped garlic
4 cans (28 ounces each) whole peeled toma-
toes (without paste), drained
1 teaspoon salt
1 teaspoon freshly ground black pepper
1 teaspoon dried oregano
2 teaspoons dried basil
6 tablespoons hot chili powder

Vegetable oil
10 flour tortillas
1 pound cheddar, shredded
1 pound Monterey Jack, shredded
3 medium onions, roughly chopped and
caramelized (see page 130)

Preheat oven to 350 degrees.

To make turkey: Rub the breast inside and out with salt and pepper. Place on a rack in a roasting pan and roast until the internal temperature reaches 170 degrees, about 1 hour and 20 minutes.

Set the turkey aside to cool. When cool enough to handle, remove the skin and shred the meat. Measure out 3⅓ cups and reserve. Use any leftover turkey meat for another purpose.

To make tomato sauce: Heat oil in a very large deep sauté pan over medium-high heat. Add onions and cook until wilted, about 5 minutes. Add garlic and cook for another minute. Stir in tomatoes, salt, pepper, and herbs until combined. Gently crush the tomatoes with the back of a wooden spoon to release their juices; bring the sauce to a boil. Turn the heat back to a simmer and cook, uncovered, until reduced and thickened, 25 to 30 minutes. Let the sauce cool for a minute or two, then pass it through the coarse die of a food mill.

Measure out 5 cups of sauce and reserve. If you have much more, return the sauce to the skillet and reduce it to about 5 cups. Stir in the chili powder.

Preheat oven to 350 degrees.

Lightly oil a cast-iron skillet and set over high heat. Soften tortillas by cooking them for about 30 seconds on each side.

Mix the cheeses together in a bowl. Spread about ⅓ cup of the sauce over the bottom of an 11 × 9-inch casserole dish (you can use a foil one).

Place tortillas on the countertop and fill each with ¼ cup sauce, 2 tablespoons caramelized onions, ¼ cup of the mixed cheeses, and ⅓ cup shredded turkey meat. Roll the tortillas around the filling. Place the rolled enchiladas, seam side down, in a single layer in the prepared dish. Cover with the remaining sauce and sprinkle with the remaining cheeses. Bake until bubbly and very lightly browned on top, 40 to 45 minutes.

SERVES 8

ROASTED HERB TURKEY BREAST

Whole turkey breast, bone in (4 to 6 pounds)
1 tablespoon olive oil
1 tablespoon herbes de Provence
1 teaspoon salt
1 tablespoon freshly ground black pepper

Preheat oven to 325 degrees.

Place turkey breast on a heavy baking sheet with low sides. (A heavy-gauge 10 × 15-inch sheet is ideal.) Bring turkey to room temperature, coat with olive oil, and rub with herbs, salt, and pepper. Let the turkey sit for 30 minutes. Roast for 1½ to 2¼ hours. A meat thermometer inserted in the thickest part, away from the bone, should read approximately 170 degrees.

Remove to carving board and let rest for at least 10 minutes before slicing.

SERVES 6

BONED TURKEY BREAST WITH PEANUT SAUCE

Grilled turkey breast can also be done under a broiler, about 6 inches from the heat.

½ cup chunky peanut butter
¼ cup soy sauce
¼ cup sesame oil
1 large garlic clove, minced
2 teaspoons sugar
¼ cup cider vinegar
1½ tablespoons Oriental hot pepper oil
1 cup sour cream
Milk as needed
½ turkey breast (about 3 pounds), boned

Combine all the ingredients except the milk and turkey breast and mix well. Thin with a little milk if necessary to make the consistency of softly whipped cream. Set aside.

Gently loosen and remove skin and any fat from turkey breast. Cover with plastic wrap and flatten with a mallet or rolling pin to approximately 1 inch thick. Spread with half the peanut sauce and refrigerate, covered, for several hours or overnight.

Prepare outdoor grill. Grill turkey breast over a moderately hot fire for 15 minutes per side or until a slit in the middle reveals opaque meat. Slice and serve immediately with the remaining peanut sauce.

Note: This may be made in advance and refrigerated, along with the sauce, and served cold (or at room temperature).

SERVES 6 TO 8

ROAST TURKEY WITH PAN GRAVY

Be sure to order your turkey in advance, and order a fresh one—automatically guaranteeing a better flavor.

Next, remember that the legs and thighs are tougher than the breast meat and take longer to be tenderized by the heat. Also, drumsticks and wings tend to dry out while in the oven if they are not properly secured. So correctly trussing the turkey is important. Simple instructions for doing this may be found in almost any good basic cookbook. My father used to wrap slices of bacon around the lower part of each drumstick—a trick you might try. To keep the breast from drying out, start cooking the turkey with a piece of doubled cheesecloth, about 8 by 12 inches, dipped in melted margarine or butter, stretched over the breast. Leave this protection in place during the roasting period; just remove it for the last hour to allow the breast to brown.

I begin with a very hot oven, 450 degrees, to seal the meat. I reduce the heat to 325 degrees as soon as the turkey goes in. For a fifteen-pound bird, I figure about eighteen minutes a pound, and I baste every thirty minutes with pan juices and additional chicken stock. However, timing can be difficult to gauge because it may vary somewhat according to the age of the bird and heat loss from opening the oven door for basting (and the likelihood that the oven thermostat may be slightly off). For that reason, I use the traditional test of pricking the thighs to see how the juices look after all but about a half hour of the cooking time has elapsed. Juices must run clear, with no trace of pink, for the meat to be properly done. As an additional test, I use one of those small instant-read thermometers. The reading ought to register around 185 or 190 degrees. Remember a turkey continues to cook after it is removed from the oven.

Once out, leave it to rest for a half hour, which will make it easier to carve.

Don't worry about it getting cold; if the turkey is covered loosely with foil, you will be surprised by how hot it remains. The thirty-minute grace period after roasting will give you ample time to deal with all the other elements of the meal. Before you start the gravy, skim the fat off carefully. And don't use too much thickener—gravy tends to thicken more while being kept warm. And, finally, be sure to make enough!

Now, how to serve the turkey. Of course, you want everyone to see how beautifully cooked it is, but carving the whole thing at the table can be a nightmare without the proper know-how and technique. Even then I think it is still too messy. My solution is a compromise. In the kitchen, I cut off the legs and wings, carving the meat from the thighs while leaving the drumsticks and wings whole. (I do cut the joints of the wings with poultry shears to make them easier to eat.) Next, I remove the stuffing from the body cavity, but leave the stuffed neck untouched. Incidentally, if there is a time lag here, keep the meat and stuffing warm in the oven. When everything is ready to go, I put the turkey, minus its wings and legs, in the center of a warm platter and garnish with whatever strikes my fancy; the dark meat, wings, and drumsticks go around both sides. The breast is easy to carve in the dining room and everyone gets a chance to exclaim over the perfectly cooked bird.

No matter how you do it, by the time the last guests are served, the food will have cooled off a bit, making it doubly important for the gravy to be hot. Ideally, keep the gravy boat over a warming light, and warm the plates if you can. And personally, since a denuded turkey carcass is not the most edifying sight in the world, I think it is best to serve from a sideboard or a small table set up for that purpose, so everything will be more or less out of view while you are dining.

1 15-pound turkey
Cornbread Stuffing (recipe follows)

PAN GRAVY
3 tablespoons flour
3 tablespoons unsalted butter, softened
3 cups Turkey Stock (page 41)
Salt and freshly ground black pepper

Preheat oven to 450 degrees.

Stuff the cavity and neck of the turkey with cornbread stuffing and close the openings securely. Truss. Place the bird on a greased rack in a roasting pan and place in the oven. Turn the heat down to 325 degrees and roast for approximately 4¼ hours (about 18 minutes per pound).

To make gravy: Press the flour into the butter. Set aside. Heat the stock.

While the turkey is resting after being roasted, deglaze the pan with the heated stock. Skim off whatever fat rises to the top (I use a defatting cup, or gravy separator). Dissolve just enough of the flour–butter mixture into the liquid to begin to thicken it. Simmer for about 5 minutes.

Taste and correct seasoning if necessary. Pour into a saucepan and reserve. Reheat the gravy before serving.

Note: If you do not have enough turkey stock, add some canned chicken stock.

SERVES 10, WITH LEFTOVERS

CORNBREAD STUFFING
Skillet Cornbread (page 308)
1½ cups cubed toast (see Note)
8 tablespoons (1 stick) unsalted butter
1½ cups chopped green bell pepper
1½ cups chopped onion
1½ cups chopped celery
1 large bunch green onions, with some of the green, chopped
1 cup coarsely chopped toasted pecans
¼ cup finely chopped fresh Italian flat-leaf parsley
1 tablespoon salt, or to taste
1 teaspoon freshly ground black pepper
¼ teaspoon cayenne
¼ teaspoon dried thyme
2 to 4 hard-cooked eggs, coarsely shredded
2 large eggs, lightly beaten
1 cup Turkey Stock (page 41)

Crumble the cornbread and place it in a large mixing bowl with the toast. Melt half the butter in a large skillet and add green pepper, onion, celery, and green onions. Cook over very low heat to wilt the vegetables. Meanwhile, toss pecans, parsley, salt, pepper, cayenne, and thyme with the breads. When the vegetables are wilted, add them to the bread mixture and toss. Carefully mix in the hard-cooked eggs, then the raw eggs. Last, melt the rest of the butter, mix it with the turkey stock, and use this to dampen the stuffing.

Put any stuffing that doesn't fit into the turkey into a well-greased, shallow baking dish. Cover it with foil and bake it with the turkey for the last hour, or bake it separately at 350 degrees for 45 minutes.

Note: I use 5 slices of Pepperidge Farm Toasting White Bread, well toasted, to make the cubes.

SERVES 10, WITH LEFTOVERS

DUCK

ROAST DUCKLING WITH BLACKBERRY SAUCE

This may be done partially in advance—say, the morning of the day of the dinner—and finished later to serve. Make the sauce while the ducks are baking, so it will be ready to glaze them when they come out of the oven.

3 ducklings (4 to 4¹/₂ pounds each)
¹/₄ cup salt
2 tablespoons freshly ground black pepper
Blackberry Sauce (recipe follows)

Rinse ducks well with cold water and let sit in a bowl with the cold tap water running slowly over them for about 20 minutes to further rinse away any blood. Dry with paper towels. Mix salt and pepper together and rub all ducks inside and out with it. Place ducks on a tray, uncovered, in the refrigerator for several hours or overnight (this helps dry out the skin).

Preheat oven to 325 degrees.

Place ducks on a roasting rack and bake 40 minutes. Turn heat up to 400 and cook for another 10 to 15 minutes to brown nicely. Remove and let cool. Split the ducks, bone them, and cut into serving pieces. (You may prepare to this point and refrigerate for final roasting later.)

To finish, put duck pieces, skin side up, in a roasting pan and bake at 400 degrees 10 to 15 minutes, until skin is crisp.

Serve with the blackberry sauce.

SERVES 6

BLACKBERRY SAUCE
1 cup blackberries
1 cup port
2¹/₂ cups Chicken Stock (page 41) or demi-glace
1 teaspoon salt (optional)
¹/₂ teaspoon white pepper (optional)

Bring blackberries and port to boil in a nonreactive saucepan over high heat. Continue at a rolling boil until reduced by half, 10 to 12 minutes. Add stock and bring again to a boil. Strain, season, if desired, and serve with the heated duck.

MAKES ABOUT 3 CUPS

QUAIL

MANDARIN GRILLED QUAIL

1¹/₂ cups low-sodium soy sauce (tamari)
¹/₂ cup water
¹/₂ cup hoisin sauce
6 tablespoons dark brown sugar
3 tablespoons rice wine vinegar
4 medium garlic cloves, finely minced
2-inch piece fresh ginger, peeled, thinly sliced, and minced
2 medium shallots, finely minced
6 green onions, white and green parts, finely chopped
1 tablespoon hot sesame oil
24 small quail, butterflied

Mix the first 10 ingredients, stirring until the brown sugar dissolves. Place the quail in a shallow nonmetallic dish and cover with the marinade. Refrigerate, covered, turning occasionally, for at least 3 hours. (They are best if allowed to marinate overnight.)

Remove quail from marinade and pat dry. Grill over hot coals approximately 3 to 4 minutes per side. Or cook the quail under a preheated broiler for the same amount of time.

Note: When you buy quail, ask your butcher to remove the backbone and rib cage. Or cut them through the breast bone and cut out the backbone with poultry shears.

SERVES 12

SKILLET-COOKED QUAIL

I've been eating quail all my life and I've decided the more simply they are prepared, the better. This recipe fills that bill.

6 large quail, butterflied
Tabasco Sauce
Salt and freshly ground black pepper
Flour
3 tablespoons unsalted butter
3 tablespoons peanut oil

Flatten the birds slightly by placing them between 2 sheets of wax paper and giving them a few whacks with the side of a cleaver. Put a drop of Tabasco on each side of the quails and rub it in. Sprinkle well with salt and pepper. Dredge in flour, shaking off excess.

Heat 2 very large skillets and divide butter and oil between each. When bubbly, place quail halves in, skin sides down. Cook for about 3 minutes over medium-low heat. Turn and cook for another 3 minutes. Use a small heavy skillet to weight the quails down and cook an additional 2 minutes. Remove weights and turn, cooking until golden on the other side, about 3 minutes. If quails are not golden by this time, turn up the heat to finish them.

SERVES 6

BAKED QUAIL

Salt and pepper could be substituted for the Creole Seasoning here.

16 partially boned quail, rib cages removed
1 1/2 teaspoons Creole Seasoning
1 to 2 tablespoons unsalted butter, melted

Preheat oven to 350 degrees.

Rub quail with the seasoning and brush lightly with butter. Bake until golden, about 13 to 15 minutes.

SERVES 8

SQUABS

GRILLED HERBED SQUABS

Slipping herbs under the skin of the squabs gives them a strong and distinctive flavor. Fresh herbs must be used.

3 cups fresh oregano
2 tablespoons fresh thyme
2 medium garlic heads, roasted (page 185), pulp removed
1/2 cup olive oil
6 plump squabs

Prepare grill. Place oregano, thyme, and garlic pulp in a food processor. Process, adding the oil in a thin stream to form a paste. Slip the mixture under the breast skin of the birds. Thread stuffed birds onto a spit.

Grill for 30 to 40 minutes, to an interior temperature of 160 degrees.

Note: These may also be done in an oven by roasting them at 400 degrees until the desired temperature is reached, about 20 minutes. Turn once during the cooking time.

SERVES 6

POULTRY SAUSAGES

CHICKEN-APPLE SAUSAGE

Be sure to make this enough in advance—at least a day—so that the flavors will have time to blend together in the refrigerator.

1 pound skinless chicken meat, from the leg and thigh only, chilled and cut into large dice
4 ounces pork fat, chilled and cut into large dice
4 ounces pork meat (butt), chilled and cut into large dice
1½ tart apples (Pippin or Granny Smith), peeled, cored, and cut into large dice
1 small onion, cut into medium dice
1 tablespoon kosher salt
¼ teaspoon white pepper
1 teaspoon dried sage
2 tablespoons Calvados (apple brandy)

Toss all ingredients together and put through a grinder fitted with a medium-hole plate or place in a food processor and pulse until medium chopped. Do not overprocess. Divide into 8 patties and refrigerate overnight.

Grill until cooked through but not dry, about 5 minutes or less on each side.

SERVES 6 TO 8

CHICKEN SAUSAGE PATTIES

These sausages are very simple. They should be made a day in advance and refrigerated uncooked to give the flavors a chance to develop. After you have made the sausages once, you might want to try varying the seasonings to find a taste that is uniquely your own. Make small batches and pinch off a bit of the finished mix and fry it to see if it needs adjusting.

1 cup uncooked, noninstant rice
Grated zest of ½ large lemon
¾ teaspoon ground dried sage
¾ teaspoon ground dried thyme
¾ teaspoon poultry seasoning
¾ teaspoon freshly ground black pepper
Dash of cayenne
1 teaspoon salt
½ cup clarified unsalted butter, cooled
2 pounds boned chicken breast, coarsely ground

Safflower oil

Cook rice according to directions. You should have 2 cups. Drain well and run hot water over to rinse off excess starch. Put in a crockery bowl and add lemon zest, herbs, pepper, cayenne, and salt. Pour the clarified butter over. Toss lightly. Add chicken and mix with your hands. Divide into 2 equal portions and shape into rolls. Wrap tightly in foil. Refrigerate at least 24 hours before using.

To cook, cut each roll into 8 patties and put in a warm skillet that has been rubbed with a few drops of safflower oil. Turn up heat and brown on each side. The patties cook very fast, the whole cooking time being about 8 minutes. Put on a platter and pour over any butter that may have rendered out. Keep warm.

SERVES 6 TO 8

DUCK AND ORANGE SAUSAGE

California sausage maker Bruce Aidells very generously gave us this recipe. His sausages are available from the Aidells Sausage Company.

1 pound duck breast meat, including skin, cut into 2-inch pieces
1 pound (approximately) duck meat from 2 deboned duck legs, including skin, cut into 2-inch pieces
1/4 pound smoky bacon, chilled in the freezer for 30 minutes, then cut into 2-inch cubes
2 teaspoons kosher salt
2 teaspoons coarsely ground black pepper
1 teaspoon finely chopped garlic
1 teaspoon Hungarian sweet paprika
1/4 teaspoon ground dried sage
1/2 teaspoon whole dried thyme
1/4 teaspoon whole dried savory
1/2 teaspoon cayenne
Pinch of ground allspice
1 teaspoon sugar
1/4 cup orange-flavored liqueur, such as Grand Marnier or Curaçao
1/4 cup water
5 to 6 feet medium hog casing, rinsed

Place duck meat, skin, and bacon in a grinder fitted with a 1/4-inch plate and grind. Place in a bowl and sprinkle other ingredients, except hog casing, over all. Blend well with your hands, kneading and squeezing as you mix, but do not overmix because the fat will begin to melt and the sausage will turn white. Stuff into hog casings and tie off in 5-inch links. (Sausages will keep 3 days refrigerated or 2 months frozen.)

To cook, prick casings and place links in a cold skillet over medium heat. Cook 15 to 18 minutes, turning occasionally, until evenly browned.

MAKES 2½ POUNDS, OR 12 TO 15 LINKS

DUCK AND PORK RILLETTES

Rillettes are usually made with pork only, but the duck is a pleasant change.

2 pounds boneless salt pork (no rind), cut into 1/2-inch cubes
1 pound lean pork, cut into large cubes
1 pound boned duck meat and neck
1 teaspoon freshly ground black pepper
1 teaspoon dried rosemary
1/2 teaspoon dried thyme
1 cup water
1/4 cup cognac
Bouquet garni of 3 large peeled shallots, 1 crushed large garlic clove, 1 large bay leaf, 1 tablespoon juniper berries
1 bay leaf (optional)

Preheat oven to 350 degrees.

Cover salt pork cubes with cold water and blanch for 5 minutes. Drain.

Place all ingredients, including salt pork, in a cast-iron pot and bring to a boil on top of the stove. Skim foam and cover tightly. Bake in the oven, covered, for 3 to 3½ hours. Uncover and continue baking until all the liquid has evaporated, leaving only the meat and fat; this should take an additional 25 to 30 minutes.

Drain off fat, pressing it out of the meat lightly. When cool enough to handle, pull meat apart, discarding any bone and skin. Discard bouquet garni. Process the meat in small batches very briefly in the food processor. You want this to be chunky. Pack into a crock and chill. Heat fat and pour over chilled meat. Place a bay leaf in the fat for decoration, if you like.

Keeps in the refrigerator for up to 1 month if tightly sealed and covered with fat.

Serve with Melba Toast (page 327).

MAKES ABOUT 2 POUNDS

223

DUCK SAUSAGE AND NEW POTATOES

Sausage making can be fun and is easy to personalize when you alter the kind, quantities, and proportions of herbs used. Always make this far enough in advance to give it a day or so in the refrigerator for the flavors to develop.

> 1 pound duck meat (no skin or fat), cut into
>   large cubes
> 4 ounces duck fat (see Note)
> 10 juniper berries, crushed
> 1/2 teaspoon ground dried thyme
> 1/8 teaspoon ground dried sage
> 1/2 teaspoon coarsely ground black pepper
> 1 teaspoon salt
> 18 small new potatoes, scrubbed and boiled
> Butter

Place duck meat and fat in a food processor and chop coarsely. Do not overprocess. Mix in other ingredients, except potatoes and butter, with your hands, being sure they are well combined. To check seasoning, fry a small amount of the sausage, starting it in a cold skillet. Refrigerate overnight, covered, to allow flavors to meld.

Form into patties and fry as above.

Serve with new potatoes, buttered.

Note: If you come up short on duck fat, add chicken fat to make up the difference.

SERVES 6

SMOKING METHOD

Soak 3 to 4 cups of wood chips or 6 to 8 wood chunks in water for at least 30 minutes. Mound 10 to 15 briquettes to one side of a barbecue kettle with cover. Once the coals are hot, allow them to burn down to medium-low. This takes about 30 minutes and they should be covered with gray ash. Spread the coals in a single layer to one side of the barbecue. Sprinkle the chips or chunks over the coals. Place a pan half full of hot water next to the coals. Replace grill rack and spread sausages on the grill on the side opposite from the coals and over the pan of water. Cover the grill, making sure the vent in the lid is directly over the sausages. Open the top and bottom vents about 1/4 inch. Smoke the sausages at 180 to 280 degrees. This temperature can be measured by inserting an instant thermometer into the partially opened top vent. Add more wood or charcoal if needed. Smoke the sausages for 1 1/2 to 2 hours, turning every 30 minutes, until the internal temperature of the sausages is 160 degrees.

MEATS

MEATS BEING SERVED NOWADAYS ARE DIFFERENT FROM what was in demand only a decade ago. There is a change in attitude about what a meat course should be and how it should be cooked. What's also new is that game, especially venison—which, incidentally, is as low in calories and cholesterol as chicken—has become more popular and available. ✦ When it comes to beef, people want leaner cuts that have all the familiar flavor without the familiar unhealthy stuff. Gone are the bad good-old-days of heavily marbled roasts and steaks. And I say good riddance. Now even tradi-

tional dishes like classic boiled beef are trimmed before serving. Portions are smaller and the accompaniments more appetizing. ✦ Pork and lamb have also undergone transformations and emerged trimmed, leaner, and maybe best of all, not cooked to death. All the news is good.

BEEF

GARLIC SMOKED TENDERLOIN OF BEEF

This recipe, or method, came from Barbara Rodriguez, who is noted for her smoked tenderloin in Natchez. Obviously, when you smoke meat you have to become familiar with the equipment you are using and make a few test runs with it first. Following are her comments:

"Build a fire with 5 pounds of charcoal in a small pit or 10 pounds of charcoal in a larger one. Allow your fire to burn off all starter fluid before putting meat on. When coals are white, close the pit to allow it to heat evenly. Adjust vents to begin smoking and allow fire to remain steady. Do not allow fire to flame. The meat should be about 1 foot from the coals or, if the pit is smaller, you may adjust the heat to a lower temperature to prevent meat from crusting. Cook meat for 15 minutes and turn. Cook for another 15 minutes. Each pit cooks differently, and you will be able to judge if the pit is cooking too fast and you need to adjust the heat accordingly. I do not use any type of wood for flavoring, just plain charcoal, but you could add wood chips if you like."

5- to 7-pound beef tenderloin, trimmed
2 large garlic cloves, crushed
2 tablespoons freshly ground black pepper
1 teaspoon salt

Rub meat with crushed garlic, spreading it evenly on both sides, then do the same with pepper and sprinkle with salt. Allow meat to absorb seasonings while preparing the fire.

Barbara's directions will produce a rare tenderloin. Use an instant-read thermometer to test for doneness. If you prefer medium, cook it for another 15 minutes. For well done, cook for 1 hour, turning every 15 minutes.

SERVES 10 TO 12

ROAST BEEF TENDERLOIN STEAK

This cut of beef from the center of the tenderloin is referred to as a chateaubriand.

1 thick beef tenderloin steak (3 to 4 pounds)
Salt and freshly ground black pepper, to taste

Preheat oven to 450 degrees.

Put a heavy skillet, large enough to accommodate the meat comfortably, onto high heat. Meanwhile, season meat very well with salt and a generous amount of pepper. When the skillet is very hot, put the steak in and brown quickly on both sides. Transfer to a baking sheet with low edges, and roast for about 20 minutes, or until 120 degrees in the center for rare.

Remove meat to a cutting board and allow to rest for 10 minutes before slicing and serving with juices.

SERVES 8

ROAST TENDERLOIN OF BEEF WITH SHALLOT BUTTER

Also called filet of beef, this cut of beef is always served either rare or medium-rare, never well done. Be sure meat is close to room temperature when you start.

2½ pounds tenderloin of beef
2 teaspoons soy sauce
4 teaspoons freshly ground black pepper
2 tablespoons olive oil
3 tablespoons unsalted butter, softened
2 tablespoons minced shallots

Preheat oven to 450 degrees.

Cut tenderloin across into 2 pieces. Rub with soy sauce and press black pepper into all sides. Heat oil in a heavy skillet over high heat. Sear meat on all sides, about 3 minutes. Roast for 18 to 20 minutes, turning meat once halfway through the cooking time for medium-rare. Test it after 18 minutes, as this timing can vary by several minutes depending on the thickness of the meat. The internal temperature should be about 120 degrees.

Mash the butter and shallots together. Put a dab on each serving.

SERVES 6

SLOW OVEN-BARBECUED BRISKET

This is a meat dish that reheats very well. Don't let the brisket dry out, for moistness is one of this method of cooking's most appealing qualities.

7- to 9-pound beef brisket
1 teaspoon minced garlic
1 teaspoon celery seeds
Freshly ground black pepper, to taste
1 teaspoon ground ginger (optional)
4 large bay leaves, crumbled
1 can (6 ounces) tomato paste
1 cup soy sauce
1 cup Worcestershire Sauce
1/2 cup tightly packed dark brown sugar
2 medium onions, thinly sliced

Preheat oven to 350 degrees. Tear off 2 large pieces of foil, enough to completely enclose and seal in the brisket. Place the meat on the double sheets of foil and rub it on all sides with the garlic.

Combine celery seeds, pepper, ginger, if using, and crushed bay leaves, then sprinkle on all sides. Mix tomato paste, soy sauce, Worcestershire, and brown sugar, and smear this on the meat.

Score the fat side of the brisket and place the onions on top. Wrap in the foil and carefully seal by folding it down well. Place fat side up on a rack in a roasting pan. Cook in the foil for 4 hours.

Open the foil to expose the onion-covered top and cook for another hour.

Remove meat to a heated plate and keep warm. Meanwhile, degrease the sauce, add a bit of water if you like, then reduce. To serve, slice thin against the grain and top with a spoonful of sauce. Pass remaining sauce.

SERVES 8 TO 10

BOILED BRISKET OF BEEF

Brisket is generally available most places, but it's a good idea to call ahead of time and arrange to have your butcher get one for you. You can either use the first cut, which is thinner and leaner, or the second, which is thick and contains more fat. This recipe calls for six pounds of meat, but if you are planning on leftovers you might want to use more.

6-pound beef brisket
2 medium onions, peeled
2 carrots, scrubbed and broken into several
  pieces
1 tablespoon kosher salt
4 celery ribs, washed and broken into several pieces
2 bay leaves
4 parsley stems
Sprigs of fresh thyme (or 1 teaspoon dried thyme)

Put meat in a Dutch oven or other deep pot with a lid and barely cover with water. Add all the other ingredients. Bring quickly to a boil over high heat. Turn back to a simmer (the surface of the water should barely bubble) and cook, covered, until fork-tender, 3 to 4 hours. Check it periodically and use a slotted spoon to skim off any of the scum that rises to the surface. Add more boiling water as needed. Leave the meat in the cooking liquid until you're ready to serve it.

To serve, remove the beef from the cooking liquid and slice it across the grain.

SERVES 6

OVEN-BARBECUED SIRLOIN

2 pounds sirloin steak
1 teaspoon minced garlic
1 teaspoon salt
1 tablespoon freshly ground black pepper
½ teaspoon ground ginger
2 bay leaves, crushed
1 can (6 ounces) tomato paste
½ cup soy sauce
¼ cup Worcestershire Sauce
½ cup packed dark brown sugar
⅓ cup flour
¼ cup olive oil
1 cup chopped onion
1 can (15 ounces) cannellini beans, drained

Preheat oven to 400 degrees. Trim meat and cut into 1-inch cubes. Combine garlic, salt, pepper, ginger, and bay leaves. Rub this mixture all over the meat. Set aside.

In a small saucepan, combine tomato paste, soy sauce, Worcestershire, and brown sugar. Place over low heat, stirring until the sugar is dissolved. Keep warm.

Dredge the seasoned meat in flour. Shake off any excess. Add enough olive oil to cover the bottom of a large cast-iron skillet and heat over medium-high heat until oil is hot but not smoking. Brown meat on all sides in batches—don't crowd it in the skillet—about 10 minutes per batch. Use a slotted spoon to remove the meat when done. Place in a 2-quart casserole with a tight-fitting lid. If necessary, add more oil to the skillet to brown the remaining meat.

Add onion to the hot skillet and sauté, stirring occasionally, until tender, 6 to 8 minutes. Spoon onion over meat in the casserole. Add the warm sauce, stir to combine, cover, and bake for 1 hour. Add the beans and cook until the meat is tender and the beans warmed through. Let stand for 15 minutes. Remove fat from surface, taste for seasoning, and serve.

SERVES 6

BEST BEEF STEW

This really should be made the day before. That way it will be easy to degrease. Besides, the flavor will be much enhanced.

4 pounds boneless sirloin, cut into 1 × 2-inch chunks
2 cups hearty red wine
½ pound slab bacon (not smoked), cut into ¼-inch dice
2 tablespoons olive oil
2 large onions, thinly sliced
2 small carrots, scraped and thinly sliced
¼ cup unsalted butter
¼ cup all-purpose flour
3 cups Beef Stock (page 42) or veal stock, hot
2 large garlic cloves, thinly sliced
2 teaspoons tomato paste
1½ teaspoons salt
½ teaspoon freshly ground black pepper

Put beef in a crockery bowl, add wine, cover, and marinate, refrigerated, for 3 hours.

Preheat oven to 325 degrees.

Cover bacon pieces with water, bring to a boil, and simmer for 10 minutes. Drain and dry.

Put olive oil in a Dutch oven and add bacon. Sauté until golden. Remove with a slotted spoon.

Drain the sirloin, reserving the marinade. Dry the meat well and brown it in batches over high heat. Set aside.

Add onions and carrots to the Dutch oven and sauté until wilted and beginning to brown, about 7 minutes. Remove with a slotted spoon.

Pour out any oil that may be in the Dutch oven. Melt butter over medium heat in the Dutch oven and stir in flour. Cook, scraping the bottom of the pan, until the roux turns a dark golden brown. Stir in the hot stock. This will foam up, so stand back. Simmer a minute or two, then stir in the garlic, tomato paste, salt, and pepper. Add the sautéed vegetables, meat,

228

bacon, and reserved marinade. Bring to a boil quickly on top of the stove. Cover and bake until tender, about 2 hours. Let cool, then refrigerate overnight.

Remove the stew from the refrigerator an hour before reheating. Lift off the congealed fat and discard. Reheat in a preheated 325 degree oven until bubbly, about 45 minutes.

If the sauce has reduced and is a bit too thick, thin it with an extra cup of hot chicken stock.

SERVES 8

LEMON STROGANOFF

This is a very simple version of an old standby. Too often I've noticed that as classic dishes become more publicized they tend to pick up extra (and extraneous) ingredients and unnecessary preparation steps along the way.

1 cup all-purpose flour, or more as needed
1 teaspoon salt
4 pounds round or chuck, cut in 3/4-inch cubes
8 tablespoons (1 stick) unsalted butter
4 very large onions, coarsely chopped
2 1/2 teaspoons crushed red pepper
2 bay leaves
Lemon zest, chipped with a sharp paring knife into pieces the size of a small fingernail, from 1 1/4 large lemons
1/2 pound mushrooms, sliced
1 1/2 cups sour cream
Beef Stock (page 42), if needed

Put flour and salt in a medium-size paper bag. Working in batches, drop in meat cubes and shake to coat them; brush off any excess. Melt 6 tablespoons of the butter in a large skillet and carefully brown the meat, setting the cubes aside as they finish. (Do not crowd the pan and be careful not to cook this at too high a heat, because it is easy to burn the flour.) Add a little safflower oil if the pan dries out.

When you have browned the last batch, leave it in the skillet, add onions, and wilt them a bit. Add the rest of the meat, crushed red pepper, bay leaves, and lemon chips. Cover tightly and cook over the lowest possible heat for 1 1/2 hours. Use a heat diffuser such as a Flame Tamer. Check every 15 minutes, and scrape the bottom to keep it from scorching (see Note).

Sauté mushrooms until wilted in the remaining 2 tablespoons butter. Add mushrooms and their juice to the meat and mix. Add sour cream and mix thoroughly. Remove from the heat. Take out the bay leaves. Rewarm over low heat for an additional 5 minutes; you do not want to cook the sour cream, only heat it. If the stroganoff seems too thick, thin with hot stock to the desired consistency.

Note: You can prepare up to this point a day in advance. If you would like to hold it here, let cool and refrigerate. (Incidentally, if you taste it you will find it very hot because of the crushed red pepper. Don't be alarmed; it will be considerably diluted with sour cream and stock when you finish.) To complete, remove from the refrigerator an hour or so before serving and add a little hot stock. Give it a stir and put, covered, in a 200-degree oven to wait. Twenty minutes before serving, reheat the meat over low heat and proceed with the recipe.

SERVES 8 TO 10

BEEF STEW WITH RUM AND OLIVES

This stew is fairly juicy, so use a slotted spoon to serve it and use a small ladle for the sauce. If you plan to make this the day before, remove the orange zest, bay leaves, and parsley from the pot before allowing to cool.

> *¹/₄ pound thick-sliced bacon, cut into 1-inch pieces*
> *5 pounds chuck or round, cut into 1-inch cubes*
> *1¹/₂ cups coarsely chopped onion*
> *³/₄ cup coarsely chopped green onion, with some of the green*
> *4 large garlic cloves, crushed*
> *1 can (35 ounces) tomatoes (without paste), drained (reserve 1 cup of the juice)*
> *²/₃ cup dark rum*
> *4 3 × 1-inch strips of orange zest*
> *1 2 × 1-inch strip of lemon zest*
> *Bunch of fresh Italian flat-leaf parsley, tied together*
> *2 large bay leaves*
> *¹/₄ teaspoon dried thyme*
> *2 cups pimiento-stuffed green olives*
> *Chopped fresh Italian flat-leaf parsley*

Cook bacon in a deep casserole until crisp. Remove and set aside. Working in small batches, brown beef cubes in the bacon fat over medium-high heat and set aside.

Preheat oven to 300 degrees.

Pour off all but about 2 tablespoons of fat and sauté onions over moderate heat until wilted. Add garlic and stir. Chop tomatoes and add. Add reserved tomato juice, rum, orange zest, lemon zest, parsley, bay leaves, and thyme. Bring to a simmer and add the beef and bacon. Cover tightly and cook in the oven until tender, about 1 hour.

Remove casserole from the oven and take out the orange zest, lemon zest, bay leaves, and parsley sprigs. Add olives and simmer over moderate heat to reduce sauce. Serve decorated with chopped parsley.

Note: If cooking this stew in advance, add the olives and reduce the sauce just before serving.

SERVES 10 TO 12

BEEF SALAD

Spicy Pickapeppa Sauce is available in specialty food shops.

> *2 teaspoons olive oil*
> *1 pound beef tenderloin*
> *Salt and freshly ground black pepper, to taste*
> *1 tablespoon chopped green bell pepper*
> *1 tablespoon grated carrot*
> *1 tablespoon finely chopped green onion*

DRESSING
> *1 tablespoon yellow mustard*
> *2 tablespoons prepared horseradish*
> *2 teaspoons Worcestershire Sauce*
> *1 tablespoon mayonnaise*
> *2 tablespoons sour cream*
> *1 tablespoon olive oil*
> *1 tablespoon red wine vinegar*
> *1 teaspoon Pickapeppa Sauce*

Preheat oven to 400 degrees.

Heat olive oil in a cast-iron skillet over high heat until hot, not smoking. Season beef with salt and pepper and sear it until dark brown on all sides. Place it in the oven for 9 minutes. Remove it to a plate and let cool completely. Once the meat has cooled, slice it into ¹/₂-inch slices, then into ¹/₂-inch strips. Put in a medium bowl and toss with the green pepper, carrot, and green onion.

Whisk together the dressing ingredients. Pour some of the dressing over the beef and toss. (You may not want to use all the dressing. Refrigerate any that is left over.)

SERVES 6

230

BEEFSTEAK FLORENTINE

3 to 3½ pounds boneless sirloin steak, at
    room temperature
3 tablespoons olive oil
2 tablespoons salt
2 tablespoons freshly ground black pepper

Preheat oven to 400 degrees.

Rub steak with 2 tablespoons of the oil and
season with salt and pepper. Let stand at least 1
hour at room temperature.

Put remaining tablespoon of oil in a heavy
skillet over high heat and heat until smoking.
Pour off excess oil and carefully place steak in
hot skillet to sear, turning only once, approximately 3 minutes on each side.

Place seared steak on ungreased baking
sheet (with low sides) and roast 18 to 20 minutes for rare, 20 to 25 minutes for medium-
rare. Remove to cutting board and let rest for
at least 15 minutes before slicing.

SERVES 6

VEAL

ROAST VEAL

This simple method of pot roasting veal is of
French origin. You might want to add a bit of
stock to the roasting pot if the veal seems to be
too dry. Keep a close watch on your meat thermometer, because the cooking time can vary
depending on the thickness of the meat. Use a
casserole into which the meat fits rather
closely. There should be a bit of room between
the meat and the pot cover.

2 tablespoons unsalted butter
2 tablespoons vegetable oil
3 pounds boneless veal rump, shoulder, or
    loin roast wrapped and tied in a very
    thin layer of fat (see Note)
2 medium carrots, thinly sliced
2 medium onions, thinly sliced
½ teaspoon salt
Freshly ground black pepper
4 fresh Italian flat-leaf parsley sprigs and 1
    bay leaf, tied together
½ teaspoon dried thyme

Preheat oven to 325 degrees.

Put butter and oil in a heavy casserole, and
when they begin to foam add veal. Brown it
lightly on all sides. Remove meat and add carrots and onions to the pot. (If the butter has
darkened too much you should discard it and
add more to the pot before doing the vegetables.) Sauté for about 10 minutes, or until
onions are wilted and carrots have softened.
Put meat back in the casserole and sprinkle salt
over it, along with a bit of black pepper and the
herbs. Insert the meat thermometer so that
you can read it easily when you baste, every 20
minutes, with a bulb baster. Cover and roast
until the thermometer reads 175 degrees,
about 1½ hours (or use an instant-read thermometer).

Remove roast to a warm platter. Strain the
juice and skim off fat. Discard parsley and bay
leaf and press vegetable pulp through a
strainer into the degreased juice. Simmer a few
minutes and correct seasoning. Pour a few
spoonfuls over each serving.

*Note: If the veal has no fat covering, wrap it
in 2 thick slices of bacon that have been blanched
10 minutes.*

SERVES 6 TO 8

COUNTRY VEAL SHANKS

This is my Cajun version of osso buco. I call it that because almost all Cajun meat dishes start with onions, bell peppers, garlic, and celery. I veer off by adding wine, chicken stock, and thyme, but the typical flavor is established by the vegetables.

You can make this a day in advance. To reheat it, put the veal in a very low oven (200 degrees) for about 30 minutes to warm it through. Then, right before serving turn the heat up to 350 degrees for about 20 minutes.

6 tablespoons (3/4 stick) unsalted butter
6 tablespoons safflower oil
Flour
6 slices of veal shank, cut 1 1/2 inches thick, tied
1 medium to large onion, coarsely chopped
1 large red bell pepper, coarsely chopped
1 large celery stalk, coarsely chopped
1 medium carrot, scraped and coarsely chopped
1 1/2 cups dry white wine
1 cup Chicken Stock (page 41)
1 large garlic clove, crushed
3/4 teaspoon dried thyme
1/2 teaspoon salt
1/4 teaspoon freshly ground black pepper

Melt 3 tablespoons each of the butter and oil in a heavy casserole or deep skillet with a lid. Lightly flour both ends of the tied veal slices and brown them in the hot butter and oil. Do not turn the heat up so high as to burn the butter. Set the meat aside, and if the butter has darkened too much, pour it out and wipe out the skillet. Add the remaining butter and oil. When hot, add all the vegetables and cook for 10 minutes, until wilted but not browned. Add the wine and simmer for another 20 minutes.

Meanwhile, reduce chicken stock to 1/2 cup. Add it and the remaining ingredients to the vegetables.

Last, place meat in a single layer on top and cover tightly. Simmer for 45 minutes, turn, and cook for another 30 minutes, covered. Remove the veal to a warm platter. Strain out the vegetables and put them through a ricer or purée in a food processor. Return the liquid to the pan and boil briskly to reduce slightly. To serve, spoon some sauce over each serving of meat and pass the rest.

SERVES 6

GRILLED VEAL CHOPS

If you don't have time to make a sauce, use this simple method.

6 rib veal chops, about 1 inch thick, trimmed
Olive oil
Balsamic vinegar
Salt and freshly ground black pepper
6 lemon wedges

Rub the chops with olive oil, vinegar, salt, and a liberal amount of pepper. Place on the grill or under a preheated broiler. Broil about 5 minutes per side until just slightly pink inside.

Serve with a little extra olive oil and balsamic vinegar drizzled on top. Garnish with a wedge of lemon.

SERVES 6

MARINATED ROAST LOIN OF VEAL IN PORT WINE AND ORANGE

This unusual method calls for marinating the loin and placing the tenderloin inside it.

2 to 3 pounds loin and tenderloin of veal
1 bottle port wine
3 medium oranges, juiced, with the zest finely chopped
1 cup coarsely chopped fresh basil
1 tablespoon freshly ground black pepper
Salt, to taste
1 cup Beef Stock (page 42)

Trim the loin of all fat and sinew. In a deep roasting pan, combine wine, orange juice and zest, basil, pepper, and salt. Add the loin, cover, and marinate in the refrigerator for 24 hours.

Preheat oven to 350 degrees.

Remove the loin from the marinade, make a cut three-fourths through the width of the loin, spread out, and place the tenderloin in the center of the loin. Close to form a cylinder and tie securely with kitchen string.

Roast the meat on a rack until a meat thermometer inserted in the center of the roast registers between 135 and 140 degrees, about 1¼ hours. Let rest for 10 minutes with a foil tent loosely over it.

While roast is in the oven, strain 3 cups of the marinade into a nonreactive pan. Boil over high heat until reduced to 1½ cups, about 20 minutes. Add stock and cook over medium-high heat until sauce is reduced to about 1 cup and is just slightly thickened, about 12 minutes. Season with salt and pepper. Reheat, if necessary, before serving.

To serve, slice roast about ½ inch thick and drizzle sauce over all.

SERVES 6

ROAST TENDERLOIN OF VEAL WITH NATURAL SAUCE

This meat has a very gentle flavor. I like it with a hint of tarragon. The veal should be at room temperature when you start to cook it.

2½ pounds veal tenderloin
Salt and white pepper, to taste
1 small onion, thinly sliced
1 small carrot, thinly sliced
1 teaspoon dried tarragon
2 cups Beef Stock (page 42)
2 tablespoons plus 1 teaspoon unsalted butter, softened
1 tablespoon vegetable oil
1 teaspoon flour

Preheat oven to 450 degrees.

Season veal with salt and pepper. Set aside. Meanwhile, combine onion, carrot, tarragon, and stock. Bring to a boil, then simmer over medium-low heat for about 8 minutes. Set aside.

Put 2 tablespoons of the butter and the vegetable oil in a heavy skillet and sear veal over high heat until browned on all sides, about 2 minutes. Place in the oven and roast 7 to 9 minutes, turning once, until light pink inside. Test for doneness after 8 minutes.

Remove to a cutting board and cover lightly with foil.

Strain stock and discard vegetables. Pour out any fat and deglaze pan with liquid. Mash flour and remaining teaspoon of butter together and stir into sauce. Simmer for several minutes.

Serve veal slices with a few spoons of the sauce over each.

SERVES 6

VEAL CHOPS WITH BLACKBERRIES

Veal chops can be broiled or baked, but they need a little sauce of some sort. There are many simple ways to cook veal chops using the basic method in this recipe. You might experiment with different berries or even other kinds of fruit. You might also add a bit of cream to the sauce at the end of the cooking time.

1 1/2 tablespoons unsalted butter
1 1/2 tablespoons safflower oil
Flour
6 loin veal chops, cut 1 inch thick, trimmed
Salt
Freshly ground black pepper
5 large shallots, chopped
2 small carrots, scraped and coarsely
*   shredded*
1/2 cup dry white wine
1 cup Chicken Stock (page 41)
1 cup frozen blackberries

Preheat oven to 325 degrees.

Put butter and oil in a deep skillet or casserole (with a cover) large enough to hold all the chops in one layer. Turn on the heat under it, and while it is slowly heating, flour the chops on both sides and shake off the excess. Sprinkle with salt and pepper. Carefully brown chops on both sides; do not let butter burn. Transfer to a platter and set aside.

Put shallots and carrots in the pan and sauté for a couple of minutes, until wilted. Add wine and let it bubble up for a few minutes before adding stock. When stock is simmering, put in chops and baste them before covering the pan.

Bake for 1 hour. Remove the chops to a heated platter and very quickly boil the liquid to reduce it slightly, adding the blackberries in the last few minutes. Correct the seasoning if necessary. Spoon the sauce over the chops and pass the extra sauce.

SERVES 6

GRILLED VEAL CHOPS WITH SMOKED TOMATO SAUCE

6 veal chops, cut 1 inch thick
2 tablespoons unsalted butter, melted
Salt and freshly ground black pepper, to taste
Smoked Tomato Sauce (recipe follows)

Preheat the grill or oven broiler. Brush all sides of the chops with butter and season with salt and pepper. Grill for 8 to 10 minutes, turning once. Serve with the tomato sauce.

SERVES 6

SMOKED TOMATO SAUCE
6 to 7 medium vine-ripened tomatoes,
*   smoked (see page 143)*
1 1/2 teaspoons minced fresh thyme
1 1/2 medium bay leaves
1/4 teaspoon Creole Seasoning
1 tablespoon plus 3/4 teaspoon paprika
1 teaspoon minced garlic
Pinch of cayenne or dash of Tabasco Sauce
2 tablespoons Chicken Stock (page 41)
2 tablespoons rice wine vinegar
2 tablespoons heavy cream
1/2 to 3/4 cup (1 to 1 1/2 sticks) unsalted butter,
*   chilled and cut into bits*

Place a fine strainer over a bowl. Holding the tomatoes over it, slip the skins off and squeeze the seeds out. Put skinned and seeded tomato pulp, and the tomato liquid that has been strained of seeds, in a medium saucepan along with the herbs and seasonings. Simmer over medium-low heat for 5 or 6 minutes to reduce and thicken slightly.

Remove from the heat, discard bay leaves, and purée the mixture. Return it to the saucepan and stir in stock and vinegar. Simmer another 6 to 8 minutes to thicken. Off the heat, whisk in cream and then bits of butter until well emulsified. Serve immediately.

MAKES ABOUT 2 CUPS

CLASSIC LIVER AND ONIONS

1 1/2 pounds yellow onions, thickly sliced
6 tablespoons unsalted butter
1 teaspoon sugar
3/4 cup water
3/4 teaspoon salt
1/2 teaspoon freshly ground black pepper
2 1/4 pounds calf liver
All-purpose flour, for dredging
3 tablespoons vegetable oil
3 tablespoons Marsala wine
1 1/4 cups Beef Stock (page 42)

Put onions, 3 tablespoons of the butter, the sugar, water, salt, and pepper in a small saucepan. Cover and bring to a boil over high heat. Reduce the heat to low, cover, and simmer for 2 minutes. Remove the lid and simmer, shaking occasionally, until the liquid is reduced and browned.

Wash liver and dry with paper towels. Sprinkle lightly on both sides with salt and pepper. Put some flour into a plastic bag, add the liver, and shake to coat well. Remove the liver, shaking off any excess flour.

In a large, heavy skillet set over medium heat, melt the remaining 3 tablespoons butter with the oil until almost shimmering. Sauté liver in batches, turning when browned on the outside and still pink on the inside, about 1 1/2 minutes on each side. Remove to a platter and cover to keep warm until all of the liver is cooked.

Add Marsala and stock to the pan, and cook over high heat, stirring up any browned bits from the bottom of the pan, until the sauce thickens, 2 to 3 minutes. Add onions and stir to combine. Cover liver with sauce. Serve at once.

SERVES 6

LAMB

ROASTED LAMB LOIN WITH CABERNET WINE SAUCE

CABERNET WINE SAUCE
1 bottle cabernet sauvignon
1 medium onion, finely chopped
2 medium garlic cloves, coarsely chopped
3 medium shallots, thinly sliced
1 to 2 small carrots, thinly sliced
3 fresh Italian flat-leaf parsley sprigs
1 medium bay leaf
2 fresh thyme sprigs, or 1 teaspoon dried
3 cups lamb or veal stock or Chicken Stock (page 41)
8 tablespoons (1 stick) chilled unsalted butter, cut into small pieces

4 lamb loins (about 8 ounces each)
Salt and freshly ground black pepper
6 tablespoons (3/4 stick) unsalted butter

For the sauce, combine wine, onion, garlic, shallots, carrots, and herbs in a nonreactive saucepan and bring rapidly to a boil. Boil until reduced to 1 1/2 cups of liquid, about 20 minutes. Add stock and reduce to about 2 cups of liquid, about 30 minutes. Pass through a sieve into a fresh saucepan and whisk in the butter piece by piece over low heat. Keep warm.

Preheat oven to 450 degrees. Generously coat meat with salt and pepper. Heat a large, heavy ovenproof skillet to very hot over high heat, add butter, and as soon as it has melted and starts to brown slightly, sear the lamb on all sides until nicely browned, about 3 minutes to a side. Leave loins in the skillet and place in the oven and bake for 7 to 10 minutes for medium rare; 12 minutes for medium.

Serve with wine sauce.

SERVES 6 TO 8

CHARCOALED BOURBON-MARINATED LAMB STEAKS

I order a medium-size leg of lamb for this and have the butcher cut ½-inch steaks from it (across the bone). The number you get depends on the size of the leg, but it is always enough to serve eight, and sometimes a little more. But cook them all, because they are good cold, sliced thin. There should be enough marinade to cover all the meat. If there isn't, slightly increase the amount called for.

> 1 medium leg of lamb (approximately 8 pounds), cut into ½-inch steaks
> 1½ cups of bourbon
> ¾ cup soy sauce
> ¾ cup olive oil
> 3 large garlic cloves, chopped
> 3 large onions, thinly sliced
> Chutney
> Mustard
> Slivered green onions

Put lamb steaks in a glass or plastic container large enough to hold them comfortably. Combine bourbon, soy sauce, olive oil, garlic, and onions and pour over the lamb. Cover and refrigerate for 24 hours, or a little longer. Now and then give the steaks a turn.

About an hour before you want to start cooking, take the steaks out of the refrigerator and let them come to room temperature.

Arrange the charcoal in the grill so that you have a large even bed. After it is lighted, give it 30 to 40 minutes, so that all the coals are covered with a good gray ash. Put the meat on and set your timer for 7 minutes. Turn the steaks and give them another 7 minutes. They will be slightly pink inside, but not bloody. For pinker meat, cook 5 minutes per side.

Serve with chutney, mustard, and green onions on the side.

SERVES 8

LAMB SHANKS WITH BLACK OLIVES AND ORANGE ZEST

> 6 lamb shanks (have butcher saw crosswise, into thirds)
> ¼ cup flour for dredging
> 6 tablespoons olive oil
> 3 onions, chopped (about 2½ cups)
> 4 large shallots, minced
> 6 garlic cloves, minced
> 12 small carrots, peeled and chopped (about 4 cups)
> 1 cup Chicken Stock (page 41) mixed with 5 cups water and 1½ cups orange juice
> 1 teaspoon ground cloves
> 1 teaspoon freshly grated nutmeg
> ½ teaspoon cayenne
> 1½ cups Greek or Moroccan oil-cured black olives, pitted and chopped
> 6 tablespoons orange zest
> ½ cup chopped fresh Italian flat-leaf parsley
> 6 ripe tomatoes, roughly chopped
> 2 teaspoons salt
> 1 tablespoon freshly ground black pepper

Preheat oven to 350 degrees.

Dredge lamb in flour and shake off excess. Set aside.

In a heavy, flameproof pot (with tight-fitting lid), heat oil over medium heat. Brown lamb in hot oil, turning to make sure all sides are seared. This is a messy but important step. Much of the flavor of the sauce depends on this procedure. Remove and set aside.

In the same pot, sauté onions, shallots, garlic, and carrots, stirring frequently to scrape up any browned bits of meat.

Add liquids, cloves, nutmeg, and cayenne, scraping the pot and stirring to combine. Bring this mixture to a boil and remove pot from heat. Carefully add lamb shanks, cover, and bake for 45 to 50 minutes.

While lamb is cooking, combine olives, orange zest, and parsley, and let mixture stand at room temperature until needed.

Uncover lamb and cook for an additional 30 minutes. Remove the pot from oven. Transfer lamb shanks to serving platter and set aside.

Over medium-high heat, bring cooking liquid to a boil. Add tomatoes and simmer uncovered for 10 to 12 minutes. Reduce heat, add olive mixture, season with salt and pepper, and cook, stirring frequently, for another 5 minutes.

Arrange lamb shanks on individual plates and ladle sauce over them, reserving some sauce to pass separately.

SERVES 6

OUZO LEMON LAMB WITH YOGURT

The lemon zest in this dish gives it a nice zing and the cayenne a bit of bite. A good combo.

3 pounds boneless lamb, cut from the leg

MARINADE
1/2 cup ouzo
1 cup Beef Stock (page 42)
2 medium garlic cloves, crushed
1 small onion, coarsely chopped 6-inch sprig of rosemary, leaves stripped off, or 1 tablespoon dried rosemary
2 medium bay leaves, broken into several pieces
24 fresh mint leaves, coarsely chopped
3 tablespoons fresh lemon juice
1 teaspoon salt
1 teaspoon freshly ground black pepper

TO COMPLETE THE DISH
3/4 teaspoon salt
3/4 teaspoon freshly ground black pepper
2 tablespoons olive oil
2 tablespoons unsalted butter

2 cups chopped onions
2 tablespoons flour
2 cups Beef Stock
3 tablespoons coarsely chopped lemon zest
Pinch of cayenne
1 teaspoon paprika
1 cup plain yogurt
Lemon zest strips (optional)
Mint sprigs (optional)

To marinate lamb: Cut lamb into 2¾-inch cubes. Carefully trim off all gristle, fat, and connective tissue. You should wind up with about 2 pounds of trimmed lamb. Set aside.

Combine all the ingredients for the marinade in a large glass or ceramic bowl and shisk together. Add lamb, tossing lightly and pressing down gently so that it is completely covered with the liquid. Cover tightly and marinate overnight in the refrigerator.

To complete dish: Remove lamb from marinade and pat dry. Discard marinade, then generously salt and pepper the lamb. Set aside.

In a large, heavy skillet, heat oil and butter together over high heat. When very hot, quickly brown meat on all sides, placing it in a large pot as it is finished. When all meat is browned, add chopped onions and sauté, over medium-high heat, until wilted and beginning to brown, about 2 minutes. Sprinkle with flour and mix. Continue to cook, moving mixture around with a spatula, until flour turns golden, another 3 minutes. Scrape mixture into pot with lamb. Deglaze skillet with stock and add to pot. Bring to a simmer and add lemon zest, cayenne, and, if necessary, salt and pepper. Simmer until lamb is tender, about 15 minutes. Stir in paprika and yogurt and serve over a bed of rice. Garnish with lemon zest strips and sprigs of mint, if using.

SERVES 6

LAMB AND PORK WITH WALNUTS, PUMPKIN, PRUNES, AND BEANS

People in the Caucasus like lamb skewered, ground, roasted, barbecued, and fried—but mostly they like it stewed. Their marvelously hearty stew starts very much like any other stew, with the meat and a few onions being braised and a liquid. From then on anything handy can be added: potatoes, pumpkins, greens, eggplant, okra, carrots, onions, and beans—as well as fresh and/or dried fruit. Walnuts are popular too. My version includes a little pork, which isn't authentic but which suits my Southern background.

> 5 tablespoons unsalted butter
> 1½ to 2 pounds lamb from the leg, cut into
>   1-inch cubes
> ¾ pound pork cut into smaller cubes
> 2 cups coarsely chopped onions
> 2 teaspoons salt
> ½ teaspoon freshly ground black pepper
> 2 tablespoons sugar
> 1 can (13½ ounces) beef broth
> 16 large pitted prunes
> 2 cups peeled and cubed pumpkin
> 1 cup walnuts, chopped fine
> 1 can (20 ounces) cannellini beans,
>   drained
> 2 tablespoons chopped fresh cilantro
>   (optional)

Put butter in a heavy pot (with a lid) and when it is bubbling, add lamb, in two batches, and brown it. Set aside and add pork. When this is browned, remove and add onions. When these are wilted, over medium heat (about 5 minutes), add salt, pepper, sugar, and broth. Bring to a simmer and add the meats. Simmer, covered, for 30 minutes.

Remove cover and add prunes and pumpkin. At this point if you have other things to attend to you may switch off the heat and let the dish sit for an hour or so before finishing it.

(Should it have to sit longer, do not add the pumpkin and prunes until you restart.) To finish, simmer, covered, for 20 minutes, then test pumpkin for doneness. If it is getting soft, stir in the walnuts and add the beans. Simmer for an additional 10 minutes, covered. If pumpkin is still firm, simmer an additional 10 minutes before adding the walnuts and beans.

After it is done, the stew can sit off the heat for 30 minutes if it must. Sprinkle the finished dish with coriander before serving, if you like.

SERVES 8 TO 10

VARIATION

Substitute butternut squash for the pumpkin. Peel away a good bit of the harder part just under the rind. Then the softer center will not overcook by the time the firmer outer edge is done.

BROILED LAMB MEDALLIONS

The marinade gives the lamb just the right amount of seasoning.

> 1½ pounds boned lamb loin
> ¼ cup Dijon mustard
> 2 tablespoons fresh rosemary leaves
> 2 tablespoons dry white wine
> 2 tablespoons white wine vinegar
> Freshly ground black pepper, to taste
> 1 to 2 tablespoons unsalted butter, melted

Trim all fat from lamb and place in a shallow dish. Mix together all the other ingredients except butter and pour over meat, turning it to make sure all surfaces are well coated. Cover and refrigerate overnight, turning once or twice.

To cook, remove lamb from the refrigerator at least an hour before you preheat the broiler. Blot off excess marinade. Cut lamb into 1¼-inch slices and brush the slices with melted butter. Broil about 3 inches from the

flame for 2 to 3 minutes per side, brushing
with butter as you turn meat.
SERVES 6

LAMB AND ZUCCHINI PIES

1 recipe All-Shortening Pie Pastry
  (page 405)
1/2 pound ground lamb
2 tablespoons olive oil
1/2 medium zucchini, grated
5 large green onions, with some of the green,
  coarsely chopped
1 large garlic clove, finely chopped
2 teaspoons unsalted butter
1 tablespoon tomato paste dissolved in 1 tea-
  spoon warm water
1/2 teaspoon salt
1/4 teaspoon freshly ground black pepper

Preheat oven to 350 degrees.

Sauté lamb in olive oil until it turns color.
Pour out the oil and reserve the meat. Sauté
zucchini, green onions, and garlic together in
butter until the zucchini gives up its water and
the vegetables are wilted but not browned.
Add meat, tomato paste, salt, and pepper.
Simmer for just a minute.

Roll out the pastry and cut into 4- to 5--inch
squares. Put 2 tablespoons of filling in a line
down the middle. Dampen the edges of the
square with water. Fold over to make a cigar
shape and seal the three sides with the tines of a
fork. Transfer to a greased baking sheet and
bake for 25 to 30 minutes.
MAKES ABOUT 12 PIES

VARIATION
Substitute ground beef or pork for the lamb.

PORK

ROAST TENDERLOIN OF PORK WITH MUSTARD WINE SAUCE

As you probably know already, pork may be
served slightly pink, which makes it less dry.
Start out with the meat at room temperature.

2 1/2 pounds pork tenderloin
Salt, to taste
2 teaspoons freshly ground black pepper
1 teaspoon dried thyme
2 tablespoons olive oil
1 medium garlic clove, minced
3 medium shallots, minced
1/3 cup dry red wine
1 1/2 tablespoons Dijon mustard
1 cup Beef Stock (page 42)
5 tablespoons heavy cream
2 tablespoons unsalted butter

Preheat oven to 450 degrees.

Sprinkle pork with salt and press in pepper
and thyme. Place oil in a heavy ovenproof skillet and sear meat over high heat for about 3
minutes, browning all sides. Place in the oven
and roast, turning once, until the internal temperature is 160 degrees, about 16 minutes.

When the meat is done, remove to a cutting
board and cover lightly with foil. Pour fat from
the skillet and add garlic and shallots and cook
for several minutes over medium-low heat
until lightly brown. Add wine and increase
heat to high; simmer for 1 minute. Stir in mustard, stock, and cream and bring to a boil.
Reduce heat and simmer until reduced to 1
cup, about 6 minutes. Reduce heat to low and
stir in butter.

Top each serving with a few teaspoons of
the sauce.
SERVES 6 TO 8

MOCK BOAR ROASTED WITH A MUSTARD COATING

ROAST AND MARINADE

2 tablespoons olive oil
3 medium carrots, roughly chopped
1 large onion, roughly chopped
2 large shallots, chopped
3 medium garlic cloves, minced
5 cups hearty red wine
1/2 cup good red vinegar
4 medium bay leaves
*6 fresh Italian flat-leaf parsley sprigs,
    roughly chopped*
16 juniper berries
2 teaspoons salt
12 black peppercorns
*5 to 6 pounds boneless center-cut loin of pork
    with fat removed to 1/4 inch of the meat*

MUSTARD COATING

3 large garlic cloves, roughly chopped
1/3 cup coarsely chopped green onions
1/4 cup dry white wine
1/2 teaspoon dried sage
1/2 teaspoon dried thyme
1 cup Dijon mustard
1/4 cup olive or light salad oil
1 teaspoon salt
1/2 teaspoon freshly ground black pepper

2 tablespoons olive oil

To make marinade: Heat oil over medium heat and cook vegetables until lightly browned, 3 to 4 minutes. Add wine, vinegar, and seasonings, then bring to a boil. Simmer for 10 minutes and let cool. Place meat in a ceramic bowl and cover with the marinade. Refrigerate for 2 to 3 days, turning once or twice.

To make coating: In a food processor, quickly process garlic, green onions, wine, and herbs until smooth. Add remaining ingredients and process just until combined. Mixture should be very thick.

To roast, preheat oven to 400 degrees. Remove meat from marinade. Pat dry. Heat the 2 tablespoons of olive oil in a large skillet over medium to high heat and lightly brown pork on all sides, about 5 minutes or more. If you don't have a skillet large enough to do this, cut meat into 2 equal pieces. Place roast on a rack in a baking pan and coat well with mustard mixture. Bake until just done, 1 to 1½ hours, or until juicy and slightly pink, with an internal temperature of 160 degrees. Let rest 10 minutes before serving.

SERVES 12 TO 15

ROAST LOIN OF PORK WITH NATURAL GRAVY

You may dredge the pork in flour mixed with herbs, shaking off the excess; this gives it a crustier surface.

1 teaspoon salt
1 teaspoon freshly ground black pepper
1 teaspoon dried thyme
1 teaspoon paprika
1/2 teaspoon mace
1/4 teaspoon ground cumin
4 to 5 pounds boneless loin of pork
1 medium onion, thinly sliced

Preheat oven to 450 degrees.

Mix salt, pepper, thyme, and spices. Sprinkle evenly on all sides of roast. Place onion slices in the bottom of a roasting pan and put roast, fat side up, on them. Insert a meat thermometer. Sear in the hot oven for 15 minutes, then turn heat down to 325 degrees. Bake for 1 hour, cover with foil, and bake another 45 minutes to an hour, until internal temperature is 160 degrees. Remove and let rest for 10 minutes.

Slice pork and serve with a spoonful of the pan gravy.

SERVES 10 TO 12

PORK ROASTED IN MILK

Pork was often served in our family when I was a child. Over the years, as I have become more diet- and cholesterol-conscious, I've tended to serve it less. The good thing about this self-imposed restriction is that when I do have it, it is a great treat.

> 3½ pounds boneless loin of pork
> 3 large garlic cloves, crushed
> 1 teaspoon dried thyme
> Few drops of Tabasco Sauce
> Flour
> 2 tablespoons safflower oil
> 2 tablespoons unsalted butter
> 4 cups milk, heated
> 2 bay leaves

Preheat oven to 325 degrees.

Smear pork with crushed garlic and sprinkle on thyme and Tabasco. Dust very lightly with flour.

In a heavy pot with a lid, heat oil and butter together. Sear meat carefully on all sides. Do not have the heat so high that you burn the butter. When it is browned, pour out the oil and add heated milk and bay leaves. Insert a meat thermometer in the pork and place it in the oven with the lid slightly ajar. Bake for 1 hour.

Turn up the heat to 375 degrees and remove the lid. Continue to cook for another 45 minutes or more, until the thermometer registers 150 to 160 degrees.

When the pork is done, remove it from the cooking liquid—which should be considerably reduced—and skim the fat from the milk. You may boil it down for a few minutes. And since the milk will have curdled, you should either put it through a fine sieve or give it a few whirls in a food processor to smooth it out. It will still be very liquid, but tasty. Correct the seasoning if necessary—but it shouldn't be.

SERVES 8 TO 10

ROASTED PORK LOIN WITH PAN JUICES

Be sure you start out with the meat at room temperature.

> 2½ pounds boneless loin of pork
> Salt, to taste
> 1 teaspoon freshly ground black pepper
> 1 tablespoon olive oil
> 2 cups Chicken Stock (page 41)
> 2 tablespoons all-purpose flour
> 1 tablespoon butter, softened

Preheat oven to 450 degrees.

Sprinkle loin with salt and pepper. Heat oil in a heavy ovenproof skillet over medium-high heat. Brown the meat on all sides. Place in the oven. Roast until an internal temperature of 155 degrees is reached, 30 to 35 minutes, turning once. Remove it to a cutting board and cover it loosely with foil.

While the meat is roasting, heat stock and mash flour and butter together in a small bowl.

Place the skillet you cooked the pork in over medium-high heat. Add the stock to deglaze the skillet, stirring to dissolve any browned bits. When the sauce has come to a boil, add bits of the butter-flour mixture, stirring, to thicken the sauce.

To serve, cut the meat into thick slices and top with a spoonful or two of the sauce.

SERVES 6

BAKED COUNTRY-STYLE RIBS

These are almost a meal in themselves.

10 country-cut spare ribs
3 tablespoons pure chili powder
1 large onion, sliced thin
3 medium garlic cloves, minced
1/2 cup chopped celery
2 cups Red Chili Sauce

Place ribs in a large pot and cover with water. Bring to a boil, reduce to a simmer, and cook for 30 minutes to remove some of the fat.

Preheat oven to 300 degrees.

Drain ribs and place in a roasting pan. Sprinkle with all the seasonings and aromatics and top with 1 cup of the chili sauce. Bake, basting with the pan juices every 30 minutes or so. After 1½ hours, add the remaining cup of chili sauce. Bake until meat is tender and falling off the bone. Total cooking time is 2½ to 3 hours.

SERVES 8 TO 10

FRESH HAM WITH PAN GRAVY

Leftover fresh ham and gravy can become the main ingredients for a pot pie. However, if this is not your plan, don't buy a whole ham. Remember Dorothy Parker's definition of eternity: "Two people and a ham."

½ fresh ham (8 to 9 pounds)
Salt and freshly ground black pepper
Flour (optional)
1½ cups Chicken Stock (page 41)
8 tablespoons (1 stick) unsalted butter, melted
¾ teaspoon dry mustard
1 tablespoon fresh lemon juice
¼ teaspoon dried thyme
1 tablespoon unsalted butter, at room temperature (optional)

Preheat oven to 325 degrees.

Place ham on a rack and salt and pepper generously. You may also dust lightly with flour. Put in the oven. Cook 25 minutes to the pound and baste every 30 minutes or so with ½ cup of stock and a mixture of butter, mustard, lemon juice, and thyme.

Pour off all the grease from the pan and pour in the remaining 1 cup stock and deglaze the pan. You may also add any leftover basting liquid. Simmer a few minutes. If desired, thicken the gravy by using 2 tablespoons flour made into a paste with 1 tablespoon soft butter. Simmer for 15 minutes if you do this, and correct seasoning.

SERVES 8 TO 10

PORK CHOPS WITH RASPBERRY SAUCE

I like the flavor of something slightly sweet with pork, so raspberries come in handy for this delicious little sauce. When I make chops this way I let them be the star of the meal, accompanied only by buttered pasta and followed by a watercress salad.

5 tablespoons unsalted butter
3 tablespoons safflower oil
6 thick pork chops, trimmed of fat (about 3 pounds)
Salt and freshly ground black pepper
Flour, for dredging
3 medium onions, thinly sliced
2½ cups Chicken Stock (page 41)
1 tablespoon raspberry vinegar
1 cup fresh raspberries

Preheat oven to 350 degrees.

Put 3 tablespoons butter and the safflower oil in a skillet large enough to hold the chops in one snug layer. Salt and pepper them and dredge on both sides with flour. Brown them in the butter and oil. Remove the chops and pour out the fat. Wipe out the skillet and cover the bottom with an even layer of sliced onions. Put the pork chops on top. Pour in enough stock to come up about ¼ inch. Cover and bake for 1 hour and 15 minutes. Check after about 45 minutes to make sure stock has not boiled away. The onions should get dark golden but not burn. Add more stock if necessary.

When done, remove chops to a warm platter and degrease the pan with the remaining stock, simmering for a minute or two. Add vinegar and whip in the 2 remaining tablespoons of butter. Add berries and mash them gently. Reduce until slightly thickened. Correct the seasoning; you should not need to add more salt. Spoon the sauce over the chops as they are served, and garnish with a few fresh berries if you like.

SERVES 6

PORK MEDALLIONS WITH PRUNES AND PORT

You'll find this elegant little dish fast and easy.

1½ pounds trimmed boneless pork loin
Salt and freshly ground black pepper
Flour, for dredging
2 tablespoons butter
¾ cup Chicken Stock (page 41)
¾ cup port
12 pitted prunes, cut in half

Preheat oven to 200 degrees.

Cut pork into 12 slices. Season with salt and pepper and then dredge in flour, shaking off excess.

Heat butter in a skillet over medium-high heat and brown pork a minute on each side, turning only once. Remove to a platter and keep warm in the oven.

Deglaze the pan with stock and port. Add the prunes and increase heat to high. Reduce, stirring, until the sauce coats the back of a spoon, 6 to 8 minutes.

Arrange 3 pork medallions on each plate and spoon some sauce over each. Top with 2 prune halves.

SERVES 4 TO 6

PORK CHOPS AND RICE

6 thin boneless pork chops (about 2¼ pounds)
Salt and freshly ground black pepper
Flour, for dredging
3 tablespoons olive oil
3 cups diced onions
2 cups Chicken Stock (page 41), hot
2 cups diced green bell peppers
1 cup white rice
Chopped fresh Italian flat-leaf parsley

Preheat oven to 400 degrees.

Season pork chops with salt and pepper to taste. Dredge in flour and shake off excess. Heat a large cast-iron skillet over medium-high heat and add 1 tablespoon of the olive oil. Sear pork chops on both sides until browned, about 1½ minutes per side. Remove chops to a plate.

Add remaining 2 tablespoons olive oil to the skillet and then add onions. Cook, stirring from time to time, until translucent, about 5 minutes. Put onions in the bottom of a large casserole dish that has been greased or sprayed with nonstick spray. Add stock to the skillet and cook over medium-high heat, stirring occasionally, until it begins to boil. Add bell peppers and rice to the onions and stir to combine. Once the stock has come to a boil, pour over rice mixture. Top with pork chops and bake, covered, for 45 minutes.

Garnish with chopped parsley just before serving.

SERVES 6

CABBAGE STUFFED WITH PORK AND APPLE

Since there is nothing in this stuffing to bind it together, such as egg, it remains very light and crumbly in spite of the fact that it is packed very tightly into the cabbage head. To serve it, spoon out a bit of the meat mixture first and then cut a portion of the cabbage. Top with the tomato sauce.

1 large head cabbage
1 pound sausage meat (I use Jones Country)
1 pound ground pork
1 pound cooked ham, diced
4 tablespoons safflower oil
2 cups chopped onions
1 cup chopped celery
2 cups cooked rice
2 large garlic cloves, crushed or finely
*   chopped*
1 medium cooking apple
1½ teaspoons salt
1½ teaspoons dried thyme
¼ teaspoon cayenne
½ teaspoon freshly ground black pepper
4 tablespoons chopped fresh Italian flat-leaf
*   parsley*

TOMATO SAUCE
2 tablespoons unsalted butter
2 tablespoons olive oil
2 large onions, peeled and coarsely chopped
3 medium garlic cloves, peeled and cut into
*   large chunks*
1 can (28 ounces) tomatoes with purée
*   (without basil)*
Salt and freshly ground black pepper, to
*   taste*
4 or 5 fresh tarragon leaves
1 handful of fresh Italian flat-leaf parsley,
*   washed and stemmed*

Peel off large outer leaves of cabbage head. If they are in good condition, wash them and set aside to decorate the dish. Cut off core end of cabbage. Remove core without disturbing outer walls, and discard. Using a small pointed paring knife, and making short, slashing, crosshatch motions, hollow out the entire cabbage head, leaving a thin outer wall intact. This chopped cabbage can be reserved and used for another meal. Set aside.

Cook sausage meat in small batches until lightly browned and discard any fat. Do the same with the pork, then the ham. Put meats into a large mixing bowl and set aside.

Heat oil in a skillet and cook onions and celery until just wilted. Add these to the cooked meats along with rice and garlic. Combine well. Peel and core apple and chop into medium pieces. Add to rice–meat mixture and combine. Add remaining seasonings and parsley and mix well.

Place the cabbage head into a cheesecloth tube with one end knotted. Pack the stuffing into the cabbage very tightly. It may seem that you have too much stuffing, but keep packing it in and mound it very high over the top, pressing down. Tie the open end of the tube with a string so that the cabbage and stuffing are held securely in place. Put in a large steamer pot (I use a pasta pot with a removable perforated insert) and steam for 2 hours. It can rest here for a bit while you prepare the other elements of the dinner.

To make tomato sauce: Put butter and oil in skillet. Add onions and sauté lightly. Add garlic and tomatoes, salt, pepper, and tarragon. Simmer about 45 minutes. Add parsley. Cook about 15 minutes more. Put entire mixture into a food processor and purée.
SERVES 8

244

MEXICAN PORK STEW

This pork stew is good served with brown rice.

1 pound fresh tomatillos, husked and washed
   (or 3 cups drained canned tomatillos)
1/4 cup corn oil
1 large white onion, diced
1 tablespoon thinly sliced garlic
2 medium jalapeños, stemmed, seeded, and
   minced
2 tablespoons minced fresh cilantro
3/4 cup coarsely chopped and loosely packed
   romaine
2 cups Chicken Stock (page 41)
3 pounds boneless pork butt, well trimmed
   and cut into 1-inch cubes
1/2 teaspoon dried oregano
Flour, for dredging
Salt, to taste

Poach fresh tomatillos in hot water until tender, about 10 minutes. Drain and set aside.

Place 2 tablespoons of the oil in a large heavy saucepan over medium heat and cook onion, garlic, and jalapeños until limp and golden, about 10 minutes. Add cilantro, romaine (which adds color but not much flavor), and stock. Heat to a boil, 3 to 5 minutes. Pour into a food processor and purée. Add tomatillos and process until smooth. Pour out into a bowl and set aside.

Place pork cubes in a single layer on a baking sheet and sprinkle with oregano. Sprinkle with flour and roll cubes around to coat completely.

Place remaining 2 tablespoons oil in the same skillet in which you cooked the vegetables and brown the pork cubes in a single layer over high heat. When pork is browned, add tomatillo sauce, scraping the bottom of the pan to incorporate any brown bits. Bring quickly to a boil, then turn back to a simmer. Cook for 45 minutes to 1 hour, until meat is tender. Add more stock if sauce becomes too thick. Stir occasionally. Correct seasoning with salt if necessary.

SERVES 8

RILLETTES

I make this pâtélike concoction from a recipe given to me by Susan Costner and included in her book *Gifts of Food*.

1 1/4 pounds lean pork, cut into cubes
3/4 pound pork fat, diced, and 1/2 pound
   country-style bacon, diced (or any combination of fat and bacon totaling 1 1/4
   pounds)
1/4 teaspoon salt
Freshly ground black pepper, to taste
Pinch of nutmeg
1 teaspoon herbes de Provence
1/2 teaspoon fresh thyme
1 teaspoon juniper berries
1 teaspoon coriander seeds
3 or 4 shallots, cut in half
1 bay leaf
1 garlic clove
6 to 8 fresh Italian flat-leaf parsley sprigs
1/2 cup water
1/4 cup cognac
Bay leaves for decoration

Preheat oven to 325 degrees.

Put pork, pork fat, and bacon in a large mixing bowl. Add salt, pepper, nutmeg, herbes de Provence, and thyme. Toss together and put the mixture in a deep enameled flameproof casserole.

Tie juniper berries, coriander seeds, shallots, bay leaf, garlic, and parsley in a square of cheesecloth with a string attached for easy removal. Add this bouquet garni, the water, and the cognac to the casserole and bring to a boil on top of the stove.

Cover the casserole and bake in the oven for 3 1/2 to 4 hours. Remove the bouquet garni after 3 hours. The liquid will evaporate and the meat should brown slightly. If the meat browns too quickly, reduce the heat to 300 degrees.

Transfer the meat to a strainer lined with cheesecloth, set over a large bowl to catch the fat. Reserve the fat.

After the meat has cooled, shred it either with your hands or with two forks. Put the meat in a 4- to 5-cup earthenware container, or divide it among several small ramekins. Press down to compress the meat slightly, but do not pack it too tightly. Use three quarters of the reserved fat to cover the rillettes so that no meat is exposed to the air. Cover and refrigerate until the fat is set.

Remove the rillettes from the refrigerator and make an additional thin layer with the remaining fat. If there is not enough fat left from the cooking, render additional pork or bacon or use melted lard. Gently press the bay leaves into a pattern on top of the fat and refrigerate until hard. Sealed with the fat, this will keep for several months in the refrigerator.

MAKES 4 CUPS

JULIENNED PORK IN MUSHROOM BROTH WITH PASTA SHELLS

This dish may be made with beef or veal, too.

4 cups thinly sliced white mushrooms, including stems
1½ cups thinly sliced shallots
3 cups thinly sliced onions
3 large garlic cloves, thinly sliced
4 cups water
Salt and freshly ground black pepper, to taste
1¼ to 1½ pounds boneless pork loin, trimmed of all fat and cut into ¼-inch-thick slices
3 tablespoons flour
4 tablespoons olive oil
4 cups Chicken Stock (page 41)
1 tablespoon lemon juice
½ pound small pasta shells

Place mushrooms, shallots, onions, and garlic in a large, heavy skillet, preferably nonstick without any oil, and cook over medium-high heat, stirring, for about 5 minutes, until mushrooms begin to give up liquid. Continue to cook over medium heat, stirring, for another 15 minutes to reduce. Do not allow to burn. Add water and reduce over medium heat for another 30 minutes. Strain out solids, reserving ½ cup and discarding the rest. You should have about 1¼ to 1⅓ cups of liquid. Refrigerate mushroom liquid and reserved solids separately until ready to use. This may be done several days in advance.

Place reserved mushroom solids and liquid in a food processor and purée mixture. Set aside.

Salt and generously pepper the pork slices and then dredge them in flour, shaking off excess. Heat olive oil in a large skillet and fry pork slices about 3 minutes per side, until turning golden (add another tablespoon of olive oil if necessary). Cut pork into ¼-inch julienne strips and set aside.

Pour out any oil remaining in the skillet and deglaze with stock, scraping and dissolving pan solids. Stir in mushroom purée and heat. Correct seasoning with additional salt and pepper, and lemon juice. Add pork julienne and set aside off heat.

Cook the pasta shells until tender and drain. Divide among 6 warm soup bowls. Reheat the pork and mushroom broth quickly and ladle over the pasta shells.

SERVES 6

HAM

BAKED HAM

MOLASSES GLAZE
¾ cup unsulfured molasses
¼ cup white wine vinegar
2 tablespoons soy sauce
3 tablespoons cracked black pepper

1 boneless cured ham (5 to 6 pounds)

Preheat oven to 250 degrees.

Mix the glaze ingredients together in a small saucepan and heat. Place ham on a rack in a roasting pan. Bake for 1½ to 2 hours, basting every 10 to 15 minutes with glaze, until well glazed.

Cool and slice thin.

SERVES 18 OR MORE

VARIATION

For a maple glaze, combine and heat ½ cup maple syrup, ¼ cup apple juice, and 2 tablespoons dark brown sugar.

HAM SALAD

Mango chutney is readily available, but you might want to substitute some other fruit chutney here.

3 pounds boneless ham steak
1 cup finely chopped onion
1 cup finely chopped celery
¾ cup finely chopped green onions
6 tablespoons finely chopped fresh Italian flat-leaf parsley
3 ounces cream cheese, softened
3 ounces mango chutney

Preheat broiler.

Broil ham steak for 6 minutes on each side. Remove and let cool. Chop into bite-size pieces and place in a bowl.

Add onion, celery, green onions, and parsley to the chopped meat and stir. Place cream cheese and chutney in the bowl of a food processor and process until smooth. Stir into the salad.

SERVES 8 TO 10

BAKED MARINATED HAM STEAKS

Not only are these wonderfully flavorful and moist, baked ham steaks solve the dilemma of what to do with all that leftover meat baking a whole or half ham leaves you with.

Two 1-inch-thick ham slices, with bone left in (about 3½ pounds)
½ cup port
½ cup safflower oil
¼ cup water
1 large garlic clove, crushed
2 bay leaves
6 drops Tabasco Sauce
½ teaspoon salt
1 tablespoon fresh lemon juice
¼ teaspoon freshly ground black pepper
4 tablespoons Worcestershire Sauce
2 tablespoons tomato paste

Put ham slices in a single layer in a glass baking dish. Combine remaining ingredients in a medium saucepan. Bring the mixture to a boil, then turn off the heat and let cool. Pour it over the ham and refrigerate, covered, overnight.

The next day, let the steaks return to room temperature in the marinade. Preheat oven to 375 degrees.

Bake in the marinade for 45 minutes to 1 hour. Turn the steaks once during the cooking. Cut into serving portions.

SERVES 6 TO 8

BOILED SMOKED PORK BUTT WITH VEGETABLES

This dish can be done in two parts. The meat can be boiled first and reheated just before serving time and the vegetables put in for their 15 minutes at the end.

2 small smoked pork butts
2 bay leaves
3 medium white potatoes, cut into 1-inch
* cubes*
3 medium sweet potatoes, cut into 1-inch
* cubes*
2 kohlrabies, cut into ¹/₂-inch rings
2 parsnips, cut into ¹/₂-inch rings
12 small white onions, skinned (see Note)
2 turnips, cut into 1-inch cubes
1 small head cabbage, cut into 8 wedges
8 small tender pieces of celery, trimmed and
* left whole*
4 tablespoons (¹/₂ stick) unsalted butter

Cover pork butt with water, add bay leaves, and simmer for 1 to 1¹/₂ hours, or until fork-tender. Remove meat to a platter and keep warm.

Return liquid to a boil. Put vegetables in the boiling liquid, finishing with the cabbage and celery on top. Be careful not to separate the cabbage. Steam and simmer for 15 to 20 minutes, until done, being careful not to overcook.

While vegetables are steaming, melt butter. Arrange sliced meat and vegetables on a platter, pour butter over the vegetables, and serve.

Note: The best way to peel white onions is to simmer them in boiling water for a couple of minutes. Remove and cut off root and the skins will slide off.

SERVES 8 TO 10

MEATLOAF

BEST YANKEE MEATLOAF WITH OVEN-CURED TOMATOES

This meatloaf has a fine texture, and I think it's best sliced fairly thin. Of coarse, leftovers are great for sandwiches. Use a good sandwich loaf for the bread crumbs, don't trim off the crusts, and don't make the crumbs too fine. I usually make the Oven-Cured Tomatoes ahead in fairly large batches because they have many uses.

1 pound ground beef
1 pound ground pork
1 pound ground veal
1¹/₂ cups chopped shallots
1¹/₂ cups chopped celery
1 tablespoon margarine
1 tablespoon vegetable oil
4 large garlic cloves, minced
4 large eggs, lightly beaten
2 tablespoons Worcestershire Sauce
2 teaspoons soy sauce
2 tablespoons Dijon mustard
1 tablespoon chili powder
³/₄ teaspoon dried thyme
1 teaspoon salt
Freshly ground black pepper, to taste
2 cups fresh bread crumbs, dampened
* slightly with 2 tablespoons red wine or*
* water*
1 pound bacon, blanched 3 minutes
Oven-Cured Tomatoes (page 142)

Preheat oven to 375 degrees.

Combine meats well with your hands and set aside. In a medium skillet, sauté shallots and celery in margarine and oil until just beginning to wilt, about 2 to 3 minutes. Add garlic and cook another minute. Cool slightly and combine with meats. Mix eggs, Worcestershire, soy sauce, mustard, chili powder, thyme, salt, and pepper. Pour over meats and mix. Mix in bread crumbs.

Lay about two thirds of the bacon across the bottom of a large, low-sided pan. Pat the meatloaf mixture into the pan, mounding it slightly in the middle, and bring side bacon strips up and onto the top, pressing in place. Use the rest of the bacon to cover the top of the meatloaf. Bake for 1½ hours, or until browned.

Let rest for 10 minutes before slicing. Top each serving with an oven-cured tomato.

SERVES 8 TO 10

VARIATIONS

Omit the bacon.

Omit the chili powder.

Top with a tomato sauce of your choice instead of Oven-Cured Tomatoes.

Top with bay leaves and tomato wedges drizzled with olive oil and softened for 3 minutes in the microwave instead of Oven-Cured Tomatoes.

Bake in a 9 × 5-inch loaf pan.

SAUSAGE

ITALIAN SAUSAGE AND RATATOUILLE

If you have a favorite recipe for ratatouille, just add sliced baked sausages to it for this sandwich filling.

½ pound sweet Italian sausages
1 pound eggplant, peeled and cubed
Salt
5 tablespoons olive oil
2 medium onions, minced
2 medium green bell peppers, cored, seeded, and coarsely chopped
1 pound canned Italian plum tomatoes, drained and coarsely chopped

1 large garlic clove, minced
1 bay leaf
½ teaspoon dried tarragon
½ teaspoon dried thyme
½ teaspoon freshly ground black pepper
3 tablespoons minced fresh Italian flat-leaf parsley
2 tablespoons freshly grated parmesan

Put sausage in a pan lined with foil in a cold oven. Turn on to 350 degrees. Bake for 45 minutes, turning and pricking the skins several times. Drain and set aside.

Sprinkle eggplant with salt and let drain for 15 minutes or more.

Heat 2 tablespoons of the olive oil in a large skillet and wilt onions and peppers, about 5 minutes. Add the rest of the oil and heat. Pat the eggplant dry and sauté in the pan for 3 minutes. Add tomatoes, garlic, bay leaf, herbs, 1½ teaspoons salt, and pepper. Cook for 20 minutes, stirring occasionally. Remove from the heat and stir in parsley and parmesan. Slice sausages into rings and combine with ratatouille.

SERVES 4

MEDITERRANEAN PATTIES

1 pound ground beef
1 pound ground lamb
1 cup grated onion
¼ cup chopped fresh Italian flat-leaf parsley
¼ cup chopped fresh mint
¼ teaspoon ground cumin
¼ teaspoon ground allspice
1 teaspoon salt
2 teaspoons freshly ground black pepper

Combine all ingredients until well mixed. Shape into 8 patties. Grill for approximately 6 to 8 minutes per side, until brown on the outside and slightly pink in the center.

SERVES 8

CHILI SAUSAGE

Chili sausage is hot and spicy—and very simple to make. You learn about sausage seasoning only by doing it, so try it this way the first time. Then add more or less of the ingredients to suit your own taste next time.

The sausage mixture should be made a day or two in advance and refrigerated so the flavors have a chance to mature.

1 onion coarsely chopped
1 small garlic clove, cut into several pieces
1 bay leaf, crumbled
1 pound lean pork
1/2 pound pork fat
1/2 teaspoon salt
1/2 teaspoon freshly ground black pepper
1/4 teaspoon ground cumin
1/4 teaspoon dried oregano
1/4 teaspoon cayenne
1/4 teaspoon dried thyme
1/4 teaspoon ground allspice
1/4 teaspoon fennel seeds

Tear off an 18-inch piece of wax paper and another of foil. Set aside. Put onion, garlic, and bay leaf in a food processor and purée. Scrape down the sides a time or two. Add pork and pork fat and pulse on and off for just a second or two. Do not overprocess. Add all the remaining ingredients and process to about the texture of ground hamburger. This will make a very sticky mass because of all the pork fat.

Pour and scrape the sausage meat out onto the wax paper and pat into a log shape. Roll it onto the foil and then roll the foil around it. Refrigerate.

To cook, cut off rounds (this will still be a bit sticky) about ¾ inch thick, put them in a cold skillet, and cook over medium to low heat until well done, flattening them slightly during the cooking process. They will give up a great deal of fat. Do not cook them too fast, or they will burn on the outside without cooking properly in the middle. Drain them on paper towels.
SERVES 4 TO 6

ROASTED MIXED SAUSAGES

To tell the truth, I think sausages are best pan-fried, but doing them that way is so much more trouble than baking that I invariably wind up with them in the oven instead of the frying pan.

6 sweet pork sausages
6 veal sausages
3 hot pork sausages

Finely chopped fresh Italian flat-leaf parsley (optional)
Sweet mustard (optional)

Preheat oven to 350 degrees.

For the most attractive presentation, make three diagonal slashes in each sweet pork sausage and cut the veal sausages down the middle lengthwise and flatten them out, leaving the halves joined.

Put the hot and sweet sausages on a foil-lined pan in the oven. After they have cooked for 10 minutes, turn them and put in the veal sausages, in a separate pan. Continue to turn them every 10 minutes, for a total cooking time of 40 minutes.

Transfer to a platter and cut the hot sausages into 2 or 3 pieces. Sprinkle with parsley and serve with mustard, if you like.
SERVES 6

SPRING SAUSAGE WITH SAUTÉED ONIONS

Pinch off a small piece of sausage and fry it to check the seasoning before doing the whole batch.

2 pounds ground pork
1 pound pork fat
1/4 teaspoon cayenne
1/4 teaspoon coarsely ground black pepper
1/8 teaspoon dried sage

¹/₈ teaspoon dried thyme
¹/₈ teaspoon ground allspice
¹/₄ teaspoon ground mace
1 teaspoon dark brown sugar
1¹/₂ tablespoons salt
1 garlic clove, minced
¹/₄ cup minced onion
¹/₄ cup chopped pecans
2 tablespoons Grand Marnier (optional)
Sautéed Vidalia Onions (page 131)

Place meat and fat in a bowl and sprinkle with sausage ingredients. Mix well by hand, lifting, not mashing; if you overwork this it will pack and become tough.

Wrap well and refrigerate for 12 to 24 hours to allow flavors to marry.

Form into patties. Start in a cold skillet and fry about 10 minutes, until browned on both sides and done in middle. Serve with Sautéed Vidalia Onions.

SERVES 6

GAME

CHAMPAGNE RABBIT WITH APPLE AND GREEN PEAR CHUTNEY

This recipe allows for very small portions. If you would like to serve the rabbit accompanied simply by a first course or salad, double the recipe.

1 rabbit (2 to 3 pounds), cut into 6 or more
*   serving pieces*
Flour, for dredging
2 tablespoons vegetable oil
3 tablespoons unsalted butter, softened
2 tablespoons finely chopped shallots
1¹/₂ cups champagne
1 tablespoon light brown sugar

Juice and grated zest of 1 medium lemon
1 tablespoon all-purpose flour
6 slices French bread, ³/₄-inch thick, cut on
*   a diagonal to make them long enough to*
*   accommodate individual servings of*
*   rabbit*
Melted butter or olive oil
¹/₄ cup pine nuts, lightly browned in 1 table-
*   spoon butter*
Chopped fresh Italian flat-leaf parsley, for
*   garnish (optional)*
Apple and Green Pear Chutney (page 357)

Snip off any protruding bones and trim pieces of rabbit. Dredge with flour, shaking off excess, and set aside.

Heat oil and 2 tablespoons of the butter in a large, heavy skillet over medium heat. Lightly brown rabbit pieces, 8 to 10 minutes. Add shallots, sauté another minute, and add champagne, brown sugar, lemon juice, and lemon zest. Cover and simmer over low heat until rabbit is tender, about 45 minutes.

Meanwhile, make a beurre manié by combining the tablespoon of flour and the remaining tablespoon of butter. When the rabbit is done, remove pieces to a serving platter and keep warm. Stir the beurre manié into the simmering sauce. Continue to simmer, stirring, until it reaches the consistency of heavy cream, 2 to 3 minutes.

Brush the slices of French bread with melted butter or olive oil and fry until golden.

To serve, place a piece of rabbit on a slice of the fried bread (a crouton) and top with the sauce and a sprinkling of pine nuts. Garnish with parsley if you like and a spoonful of chutney.

SERVES 6

VARIATION

Substitute 1 small chicken (2¹/₂ pounds) for the rabbit.

VENISON WITH GRAINY MUSTARD SAUCE

2 tablespoons olive oil
1 tablespoon kosher salt
2 tablespoon freshly ground black pepper
Venison loin (2^1/2 to 3 pounds), at room
  temperature

GRAINY MUSTARD SAUCE
  ^{1}/2 cup red wine
  1 cup Beef Stock (page 42) or low-sodium
    canned broth
  2 tablespoons unsalted butter
  1 tablespoon olive oil
  1 shallot, minced
  2 garlic cloves, minced
  ^{1}/4 cup grainy mustard
  3 tablespoons heavy cream
  1 tablespoon green peppercorns (canned,
    drained of brined)
  ^{1}/4 teaspoon dried tarragon, crumbled

Preheat oven to 400 degrees.

In a small mixing bowl, combine oil, salt, and pepper to make a paste. Rub paste on all sides of venison. Place prepared meat on a baking sheet with low sides (to allow maximum browning surface). Roast for 25 to 35 minutes, checking with internal meat thermometer, until meat is 115 to 120 degrees. Remove and let rest for at least 15 minutes before slicing.

To make Grainy Mustard Sauce: In a heavy pot over medium heat, combine red win and stock. Bring to a boil and reduce by half.

In a small skillet, melt butter and oil to combine and sauté shallots and garlic, stirring frequently, for about 3 minutes. Remove from heat and place in a small mixing bowl. Stir in mustard, cream, green peppercorns, and tarragon.

When stock and wine have reduced, whisk 3 tablespoons into the mustard mixture to form a liaison and return this slowly to the hot stock and wine combination. Whisk until smooth. Remove from heat and keep warm until ready to serve. This can be reheated in a double boiler.

SERVES 6 TO 8

PEPPERED LOIN OF VENISON WITH RED WINE SAUCE

This is absolutely delicious and very easy to prepare.

  6 cups Beef Stock (page 42)
  2 pounds trimmed axis venison loin or
    Denver cut
  Salt
  Whole black peppercorns, to taste
  Olive oil
  16 to 24 cipolline onions, pearl onions, or
    shallots
  1^1/4 cups cabernet
  1 tablespoon cornstarch
  3 tablespoons cold water
  2 tablespoons unsalted butter, cut into bits
    (optional)

Bring stock to a slow boil and reduce to 3 cups. This can take up to 45 minutes, so allow time for it. Season venison lightly with salt. Set aside. Coarsely crush peppercorns with a rolling pin, then pat crushed pepper on all sides of the venison.

Heat a large, heavy skillet or casserole until very hot. Add enough olive oil just to coat the bottom of the pan. Sear all sides and ends of the venison quickly, until well browned. Place a rack on a baking sheet and put venison on the rack. Set aside.

Reheat skillet and add onions; toss to sear until browned in spots. Reduce heat, then add wine and stock. Cover pan tightly and simmer gently until onions are tender, 15 to 20 minutes. Remove onions with a slotted spoon and set aside, lightly covered. Reduce sauce until you have 1^1/2 cups, about 10 minutes. Stir cornstarch and cold water together in a small bowl, whisk into sauce, and cook over medium heat until sauce thickens. Whisk in butter, if using. Return onions to pan.

Meanwhile, preheat oven to 450 degrees. Roast venison 7 to 10 minutes, to desired degree of doneness. Let rest 5 minutes before slicing. Place each serving of venison on about 3 tablespoons of the sauce with several onions.

Note: Venison is becoming available in more and more markets. But if you can't find it near you, order it from the Texas Wild Game Co-operative.

SERVES 6 TO 8

ROAST TENDERLOIN OF VENISON WITH CABERNET SAUCE

This red meat has as few calories and as little cholesterol as chicken.

2¹/₂ pounds axis venison loin or Denver cut (see Note)
2 large garlic cloves, minced
Salt and freshly ground black pepper, to taste
2 tablespoons olive oil
1¹/₂ cups cabernet sauvignon
¹/₂ cup coarsely chopped shallots
1 small carrot, thinly sliced
1 bay leaf
2 fresh Italian flat-leaf parsley sprigs
1 cup Beef Stock (page 42)
1 tablespoon unsalted butter, chilled

Preheat oven to 450 degrees.

Rub venison with garlic and sprinkle with salt and pepper. Put olive oil in a heavy skillet. Add venison and sear over high heat until browned on all sides, about 3 minutes. Place in oven and roast for about 16 minutes, turning once, until medium-rare.

Meanwhile, combine wine with vegetables and herbs and bring to a boil. Reduce by half over medium heat, about 8 minutes. Strain out vegetables and discard. In a saucepan reduce stock by half, about 7 minutes over high heat. Combine the liquids.

When meat is done, remove to cutting board and cover loosely with foil. Pour any fat from the pan and deglaze with the reduced liquids. Whisk in butter and add salt and pepper.

Spoon a bit of the sauce over each serving of meat.

SERVES 6 TO 8

GRILLED VENISON AND WILD BOAR SAUSAGE

Serve these sausages with a good mustard and an assortment of chutneys.

¹/₂ cup freshly grated parmesan
¹/₂ cup freshly grated romano
1 teaspoon minced fresh basil
¹/₂ teaspoon freshly grated nutmeg
¹/₂ teaspoon ground coriander
2 teaspoons grated orange zest
2 teaspoons grated lemon zest
2 teaspoons salt
4 teaspoons Butter Buds
3 pounds venison, cubed
1 pound wild boar, 50% fat and 50% meat

Combine all ingredients except meat and mix thoroughly. Mix the meat and the seasonings together. Chill. Put through a meat chopper fitted with the coarse plate. Chill again for a few minutes in the freezer, then mix it and put it through the chopper a second time. Stuff into casings or make patties.

Let sit a few days in the refrigerator before using for flavors to meld.

Cook sausages, starting them in a cold skillet, broiler, or grill.

Note: Venison and wild boar sausages come ready to grill or broil from Broken Arrow Ranch in Ingram, Texas.

SERVES 8 TO 10

VENISON SAUSAGE AND VEAL CASSEROLE

Use a light rye bread to make the bread crumbs for this tasty casserole.

> 13 ounces venison sausage, quartered
>   lengthwise and cut into $1/4$-inch pieces
> $1/2$ pound boneless veal steak, cut into $1/2$-
>   inch cubes
> 2 teaspoons salt
> 2 teaspoons freshly ground black pepper
> $1/3$ cup flour
> 6 tablespoons unsalted butter
> 1 pound mushrooms, roughly chopped
> 2 cups roughly chopped onions
> 1 teaspoon minced garlic
> 2 tablespoons water
> 16 ounces low-fat sour cream
> 2 tablespoons Worcestershire Sauce
> $1/2$ teaspoon freshly ground nutmeg
> 1 cup fresh rye bread crumbs
> 6 ounces egg noodles, cooked according to
>   package directions

Preheat oven to 375 degrees.

Heat a large cast-iron skillet over medium-high heat. Add venison sausage and brown it, stirring occasionally. Pour off fat as it accumulates. When brown, remove to a bowl.

Sprinkle veal pieces with salt and pepper. Dredge in flour and shake off any excess. Heat 1 tablespoon butter over high heat in the skillet that was used for the sausage and brown the veal in batches—do not crowd the meat, and use 1 tablespoon butter for each batch of meat. As the meat is browned, remove it from the pan and add to the sausage. Scrape any bits of meat out of the pan and add them to the rest of the meat.

Add 1 tablespoon of butter to the same pan and sauté mushrooms over high heat until they give up their liquid and reduce slightly, 5 to 7 minutes. Remove mushrooms to the bowl with the sausage and veal. Add 1 tablespoon butter to the pan and cok onions, stirring occasionally, over medium-high heat until translucent, 4 or 5 minutes. Add garlic and cook an additional minute. Add the water to the pan and stir for a minute or so, scraping the bottom of the skillet to deglaze it. Place the onion and garlic mixture in the bowl with the sausage, veal, and mushrooms.

In a small bowl, combine sour cream, Worcestershire, and nutmeg. Add to the meat mixture and stir to combine.

Sauté bread crumbs in 1 tablespoon butter until golden brown. Set aside.

Combine noodles with the sausage and veal mixture. Stir well to combine. Grease a large casserole dish, or spray it with nonstick spray. Place the mixture into the casserole dish and sprinkle the top with the toasted crumbs. Cover with foil or a tight-fitting lid and bake for 45 minutes.

SERVES 6

254

SEAFOOD AND FISH

GROWING UP LANDLOCKED AND SURROUNDED BY SUGARCANE, I may not have known the pleasures of lobster thermidor or clams on the half shell, but that doesn't mean I didn't know the seductive flavors of seafood—far from it. We had plump oysters, big blue crabs, Gulf and freshwater shrimp plus Louisiana crawfish fresh from the bayous—and you can bet we made the most of this abundance. As you can guess, this initiation had a lasting effect on me— I'm still likely to choose backfin lump crabmeat over lobster and

 gumbo over chowder. I find the likes of lobster thermidor overkill. And when I do have lobster I want it straightforward—boiled or broiled, with plenty of dipping butter. ✦ As for cooking fish, I'm convinced the less you tart it up the better. My formula is pretty simple: the fish is filleted, sprinkled with aromatic herbs, dotted with butter, and quickly baked or broiled. Add a lemon wedge and sprig of garnish.

CRABS

SOFT-SHELL CRABS WITH LEMON BUTTER SAUCE

These are easy to make, and they look very impressive. Ask your fishmonger to trim the crabs or do it yourself by removing eyes, tail, and gills under the top shell, leaving a small cavity.

STUFFING

4 ounces claw crabmeat, picked over
1 egg
3/4 cup diced green bell pepper
2 tablespoons mayonnaise, preferably home-
    made (see page 348)
1/2 cup dry bread crumbs
1 teaspoon Creole Seasoning

6 soft-shell crabs, washed and trimmed

COATING

1/2 cup cornmeal
1 cup all-purpose flour
1/2 cup cornstarch
Freshly ground black pepper, to taste
1/2 teaspoon salt
1/2 teaspoon garlic powder
1 teaspoon paprika
1 teaspoon Creole mustard
2 eggs
1 1/2 cups milk

Vegetable oil for deep-frying
Lemon Butter Sauce (recipe follows)

Wash and trim the crabs.

To make stuffing: Mix together all the ingredients for the stuffing and stuff the crabs.

To make coating and fry: Mix all dry ingredients together with mustard in a bowl; beat together eggs and milk in a separate bowl. Dust stuffed crabs carefully in flour mixture; dip them in the egg wash and coat once more in the flour mixture.

Heat oil in a deep-fryer to 375 degrees. Fry crabs until golden, about 4 minutes. Serve with Lemon Butter Sauce.

SERVES 6

LEMON BUTTER SAUCE

2 tablespoons cream
12 tablespoons (1 1/2 sticks) unsalted butter,
    chilled and cut into bits
2 tablespoons fresh lemon juice
Salt and freshly ground black pepper, to
    taste

In a small heavy saucepan, heat cream over low heat until boiling; whisk in half the butter. Remove from heat and whisk in remaining butter, and lemon juice and seasonings. Serve warm.

MAKES ABOUT 1 CUP

FRIED SOFT-SHELL CRABS

Flour, for dredging
6 soft-shell crabs, washed and trimmed
1 teaspoon salt
2 teaspoons freshly ground black pepper
3 tablespoons unsalted butter
3 tablespoons olive oil
1 lemon, cut in half
1/4 cup chopped fresh Italian flat-leaf parsley

Put flour in a pie pan. Dredge crabs one at a time, coating as evenly as possible. Season with salt and pepper.

Melt butter and oil in a large, heavy skillet, preferably cast-iron, over medium-high heat. Sauté crabs until golden brown, about 2 to 3 minutes per side. Remove from heat, squeeze lemon over hot crabs, and sprinkle with parsley. Serve immediately.

SERVES 6

256

TOMATO ASPIC WITH CRABMEAT SALAD

I've often wondered why tomato aspic never became a traditional dish in any part of the United States except the South. I have probably eaten half my weight in it over the years and still love it—even though lots of people seem to think of it as being rather "tea-roomy."

I serve it with crabmeat, but any mayonnaise-dressed concoction (tuna, chicken) could be substituted.

1½ envelopes unflavored gelatin
½ cup cold water
3½ cups crushed canned tomatoes or canned tomato pulp, coarsely chopped
3 tablespoons grated onion
3 tablespoons grated green bell pepper
1 teaspoon Worcestershire Sauce
2 dashes Tabasco Sauce
2 tablespoons red wine vinegar or fresh lemon juice
¼ teaspoon freshly ground black pepper
1½ teaspoons salt, or to taste
3 cups picked-over fresh crabmeat, chilled
Homemade Mayonnaise (page 348)
Fresh lemon juice

Sprinkle gelatin over water in a saucer. Meanwhile, heat crushed tomatoes in a saucepan. Stir softened gelatin into the tomatoes off the heat. Add onion, green pepper, Worcestershire, Tabasco, vinegar, pepper, and salt. Mix thoroughly and pour into a 6-cup ring mold. Refrigerate for several hours, or until thoroughly set.

To serve, loosen the aspic by placing the mold briefly in a pan of hot water. Then turn it onto a serving plate, making sure it is centered. Re-refrigerate until it has set again.

Toss crabmeat with mayonnaise and a bit of lemon juice, and heap into the middle of the aspic ring. The crabmeat salad should not be too seasoned because the aspic is very spicy.

SERVES 6 TO 8

BAKED CRABMEAT CAKES

Baked crabmeat cakes are one of everyone's favorites.

1 pound back-fin lump crabmeat
3 tablespoons unsalted butter
½ cup finely chopped onion
½ cup finely chopped celery
1 garlic clove, minced
½ cup chopped green onion tops
2 tablespoons minced fresh Italian flat-leaf parsley
⅓ cup mayonnaise
Pinch of cayenne
¼ teaspoon freshly ground black pepper
1 teaspoon dry mustard
¼ teaspoon baking soda
1 teaspoon salt
1½ cups fresh saltine cracker crumbs

Preheat oven to 450 degrees.

Carefully pick over and drain the crabmeat. Set aside. Melt butter in a medium skillet over medium heat.

Sauté onion, celery, garlic, and green onion tops until wilted, about 5 minutes. Do not brown. Remove from heat and stir in parsley and then the crabmeat. Mix mayonnaise, cayenne, pepper, mustard, baking soda, and salt. Stir into the crabmeat mixture. Mix in ⅓ cup of the cracker crumbs.

Form into 12 medium patties and roll in remaining crumbs. Place in a well-oiled or buttered pan and bake for 10 minutes. Turn and bake for another 15 minutes.

SERVES 6

MARYLAND CRAB CAKES

This is a favorite of my Aunt Freddie, who lives in Natchez, Mississippi, not Maryland. Most recipes for crab cakes contain—along with the crabmeat—eggs and bread or bread crumbs to bind them together and bread crumbs to coat them. Seasonings and other ingredients vary and are a matter of local or personal taste. These crab cakes are baked rather than fried.

1 pound fresh crabmeat, preferably lump
8 tablespoons (1 stick) unsalted butter
1 cup finely chopped onion
1 cup finely chopped celery
½ cup finely chopped green onion, with
*   some of the green*
6 slices stale bread, torn into 1-inch pieces
1 cup evaporated low-fat milk
3 eggs, lightly beaten
⅓ cup chopped fresh Italian flat-leaf parsley
½ teaspoon freshly ground black pepper
Salt, to taste
1½ tablespoons Worcestershire Sauce
*   (optional)*
½ teaspoon Tabasco Sauce (optional)
2 cups fresh bread crumbs, dried in the oven

Preheat oven to 375 degrees.

Place crabmeat in a large bowl and pick out any cartilage or shell. Set aside. Heat butter in a large skillet and when it is foaming, add onion, celery, and green onion and sauté until onion is wilted. Add vegetables to the crabmeat.

While vegetables are cooking, put bread slices in the milk to soak. Squeeze most of the milk out of the bread and add bread (reserving the milk) to the crabmeat and mix carefully. Add all other ingredients except the bread crumbs. Combine and form into patties. Use a little of the reserved milk if it is not moist enough. Discard what milk you don't use.

Butter a baking sheet. Roll patties in the bread crumbs and place on the sheet.

Bake for 10 to 12 minutes until golden.
SERVES 4 TO 6

DUNGENESS CRAB CAKES WITH JALAPEÑO–LIME MAYONNAISE

¼ cup peanut oil
4 tablespoons (½ stick) unsalted butter
1 cup finely diced white onion
1 cup finely diced celery
1 pound fresh crabmeat, preferably
*   Dungeness*
1 egg, lightly beaten
1½ tablespoons Dijon mustard
1 tablespoon roughly chopped fresh Italian
*   flat-leaf parsley*
1 tablespoon finely chopped fresh thyme
Salt and freshly ground black pepper, to
*   taste*
Cayenne to taste
¾ pound fresh, fine white bread crumbs
Jalapeño–Lime Mayonnaise (page 349)

Heat half the oil and 2 tablespoons of the butter in a small skillet and cook onion and celery over medium heat until tender, about 5 minutes. Place in a food processor and pulse a few times to make mixture finer. Put crabmeat in a mixing bowl and pick over carefully. Add sautéed vegetables. Mix lightly and add egg and mustard. Mix again very lightly and add parsley, thyme, salt, pepper, cayenne, and half the bread crumbs. Toss but do not overmix. Form into 12 small cakes, handling as little as possible, and roll in the remaining bread crumbs.

Preheat oven to 350 degrees. Heat remaining oil and butter in a large cast-iron skillet over medium heat. Lightly brown crab cakes on each side, 2 to 3 minutes, turning once. Place in the oven for about 3 minutes to finish cooking. Serve with Jalapeño–Lime Mayonnaise.
SERVES 12 AS AN APPETIZER OR 6 AS AN ENTRÉE

MIXED SEAFOOD CAKES WITH JALAPEÑO TARTAR SAUCE AND THIN FRIED ONIONS

For this dish, I prefer the seafood in chunks rather than minced. I find the individual flavors come through better.

> *4 tablespoons (1/2 stick) unsalted butter*
> *1/2 cup coarsely chopped onion*
> *1/2 cup coarsely chopped celery*
> *2 cups coarsely chopped mixed seafood (such as shrimp, crabmeat, lobster, and poached fish, in any proportion)*
> *1 tablespoon mayonnaise*
> *1 large egg*
> *1 tablespoon Worcestershire Sauce*
> *1 teaspoon dry mustard*
> *1/4 teaspoon salt*
> *Dash of freshly ground black pepper*
> *1/2 teaspoon paprika*
> *3 cups coarse fresh, bread crumbs*
> *2 tablespoons vegetable oil*
> *Fried Thin Onion Rings (page 132)*
> *Jalapeño Tartar Sauce (page 349)*

Heat 1 tablespoon of the butter in a small skillet and sauté onion and celery over medium heat until wilted, about 5 minutes. Meanwhile, toss together mixed seafood in a glass bowl. Toss in wilted onion and celery.

In another small glass bowl combine mayonnaise, egg, Worcestershire, mustard, salt, pepper, and paprika. Beat with a fork until well mixed. Pour into the seafood and mix lightly. Melt another tablespoon of the butter and pour over all. Mix, being careful not to break up the chunks of crab and fish. Mix in 1 cup of the bread crumbs. Set aside.

Pour the remaining bread crumbs onto a sheet of wax paper. Form the seafood mixture into 12 small balls and roll in the crumbs to coat. Place on a plate and flatten slightly. Refrigerate for at least 1 hour.

To cook, heat the vegetable oil and the 2 remaining tablespoons of butter in a large skillet over medium heat. When hot, slide seafood cakes in, being careful not to crowd. After they have cooked for about 30 seconds, flatten and gently loosen them from the bottom of the pan. When golden underneath, about 2 minutes, carefully turn and brown the other side, about 2 minutes. Drain on paper towels.

Serve topped with Fried Thin Onion Rings and Jalapeño Tartar Sauce on the side.
SERVES 6

CRAB WITH RAVIGOTE SAUCE

Here's one way to serve New Orleans back-fin lump crabmeat. Another way is to place a scoop of it in the center of a plate, surround that with slices of Creole tomatoes and hard-cooked eggs, and dress it with homemade mayonnaise and lemon wedges.

> *1 cup mayonnaise, preferably homemade (see page 348)*
> *1/3 cup Creole mustard*
> *1/4 cup prepared horseradish, drained*
> *1 tablespoon minced green onion, with some of the green*
> *1 tablespoon finely minced fresh Italian flat-leaf parsley*
> *1 hard-cooked egg, finely chopped*
> *1 tablespoon fresh lemon juice*
> *1 1/2 teaspoons minced capers, plus extra whole capers for garnish*
> *4 or more cups mixed salad greens, cut into thin strips*
> *3 cups back-fin lump crabmeat, picked over*
> *1 lemon, cut into 6 wedges*

Mix mayonnaise, mustard, and horseradish well, then add green onion, parsley, egg, lemon juice, and minced capers. Mix well.

To assemble, place shredded greens on individual plates with a serving of crabmeat in the center of each. Top with sauce and a sprinkling of whole capers and a lemon wedge.
SERVES 6

STONE CRAB CLAWS WITH HOT KETCHUP MAYONNAISE

Other large crab claws could be substituted for the colorful stone crab claws. Allow two stone crab claws per person. As for the Tabasco, I like this hot.

HOT KETCHUP MAYONNAISE

1 cup mayonnaise, preferably homemade (see page 348)
2 tablespoons prepared horseradish
1 tablespoon fresh lemon juice
1 tablespoon ketchup
4 to 5 dashes Tabasco Sauce, or to taste
1 teaspoon Dijon mustard

12 cooked stone crab claws
Lemon wedges

Mix ingredients for the ketchup mayonnaise.
   Serve the hot mayonnaise with crab claws, garnished with lemon wedges.
SERVES 6

CRAWFISH

SMOTHERED CRAWFISH WITH HAM STUFFING

24 crawfish, steamed (see Note)

HAM STUFFING

4 tablespoons (1/2 stick) unsalted butter
1/4 cup finely chopped onion
1/4 cup finely chopped green bell pepper
1/4 teaspoon dried thyme
1/4 teaspoon dried marjoram
1/4 teaspoon cayenne
1/4 cup finely chopped ham
1/2 cup soft bread crumbs
1/4 cup beer, approximately

SMOTHERED CRAWFISH

8 tablespoons (1 stick) unsalted butter
4 cups coarsely chopped onions
2 large garlic cloves, minced
2 cups coarsely chopped green bell peppers
3 cups coarsely chopped celery, with some tops
2 pounds peeled crawfish tails, with fat from heads (see Note)
1/2 cup coarsely sliced green onions, with some of the green
1/2 cup chopped fresh Italian flat-leaf parsley
1/2 teaspoon cayenne
1/2 teaspoon freshly ground black pepper
3/4 teaspoon salt
1 teaspoon Tabasco Sauce
1 teaspoon Worcestershire Sauce
1 teaspoon paprika
1/2 cup beer

Boiled Rice (page 170)

Separate the crawfish heads from the tails. Peel tails and set aside for the main dish. Clean out the heads, leaving the claws attached.
   To make stuffing: Melt butter in a small skillet and add onion, green pepper, thyme, marjoram, and cayenne. Sauté over medium-low heat about 5 minutes, or until wilted but not browned. Put ham and bread crumbs in a bowl and add sautéed vegetables. Toss to mix, adding beer to moisten. Stuff each crawfish head with 1 to 2 tablespoons of the stuffing, and set them aside.
   To make main dish: Melt butter in a large Dutch oven and add onions, garlic, green peppers, and celery. Sauté over medium-low heat for about 20 minutes until soft. Mix in the crawfish tails, plus the tails set aside from the stuffing, the crawfish fat, and then the green onions, parsley, cayenne, black pepper, salt, Tabasco, Worcestershire, paprika, and beer. Fold together well. Place the stuffed heads on top of this mixture and cook, covered, for 10 more minutes. Turn heat down to very low

and continue cooking for an additional 20 minutes, moving mixture around to make sure it doesn't scorch.

Remove the stuffed heads before serving and stir mixture well.

Serve over boiled rice in a soup bowl, garnished with the stuffed heads.

Note: If you can't get whole crawfish, substitute very large escargot shells to stuff. If you would like a little more sauce in the main dish, or if the sauce is too thick, thin it with a little chicken stock.

SERVES 6

CRAWFISH WITH SPICY TOMATO SAUCE

Since all you eat of these delicious little crustaceans is their tails, it takes a fairly large quantity to keep your guests happy.

> 3 quarts Chicken Stock (page 41) or canned chicken broth
> 3 large bay leaves
> 1 large sweet red onion, cut in quarters
> 1 tablespoon black peppercorns
> 1 teaspoon salt
> 2 large celery ribs with leaves
> 5 pounds live crawfish
> Fresh dill
> Lemon wedges
> Spicy Tomato Sauce (page 352)

Place stock, bay leaves, onion, peppercorns, salt, and celery into a large pot. Bring to a hard boil and add one fourth of the crawfish. Cook until bright red, only a few minutes. Remove with a wire sieve and let cool. Repeat until all are cooked.

Arrange neatly on a long serving platter garnished around the edges with fresh dill and lemon slices. Serve with the tomato sauce.

SERVES 12 TO 15

CRAWFISH FETTUCCINE

Luckily, cooked and peeled crawfish tails are sold frozen in many specialty markets today.

> 10 tablespoons (1¼ sticks) cold unsalted butter, cut into 5 or 6 pieces
> ½ cup diced green bell pepper
> ½ cup diced red bell pepper
> 1 cup diced onion
> 1½ pounds cooked and peeled crawfish tails
> ½ teaspoon Creole Seasoning
> ¼ teaspoon crushed red pepper
> ½ teaspoon salt
> 1 cup peeled, seeded, and diced tomato
> 6 tablespoons thinly sliced green onion
> 12 ounces dried fettuccine
> 6 whole cooked crawfish (optional)

Put up a large pot of salted water to boil while you prepare the sauce.

In a large skillet, melt 2 tablespoons of the butter and sauté peppers and onion over high heat, stirring, for 2 or 3 minutes, until well wilted. Add crawfish tails, Creole Seasoning, crushed red pepper, and salt. Turn down heat and cook for 2 to 3 minutes. Add tomato and green onion and continue to cook. Stir in the bits of butter one by one. When all is incorporated, turn off heat.

Cook fettuccine until al dente.

Place fettuccine on individual plates. Surround and top with the sauce. Garnish with a whole crawfish if you like.

SERVES 6

CRAWFISH-STUFFED EGGPLANT "TORTILLAS" WITH TOMATILLO SAUCE

Although it wouldn't be the same, because crawfish have such a different flavor, you could substitute shrimp here. Don't be daunted by the length of this recipe. There are simply a number of quick and simple steps to explain. Start off by reading this through so you'll know what you're doing, then begin by making the sauces and accompaniments.

TOMATILLO SAUCE
1 pound tomatillos, husked, washed, and coarsely chopped
$^1/_4$ medium onion, chopped
2 teaspoons minced garlic
1 teaspoon minced jalapeño
1 tablespoon vegetable oil
$^1/_2$ cup water
$^1/_2$ teaspoon salt
$^1/_4$ teaspoon sugar

SALSA
2 cups finely diced ripe tomatoes
3 tablespoons diced red bell pepper
3 tablespoons diced green bell pepper
3 tablespoons minced white onion
3 tablespoons minced jalapeño
1 tablespoon minced fresh cilantro
1 teaspoon salt
$^1/_2$ teaspoon white pepper

"TORTILLAS"
6 $^1/_8$-inch-thick slices of eggplant (cut from the center of a large eggplant)
1 cup flour
2$^1/_2$ teaspoons Creole Seasoning
2 eggs
$^1/_2$ cup milk
1 cup toasted bread crumbs
$^1/_2$ cup vegetable oil

FILLING
1 tablespoon vegetable oil
3 tablespoons diced red bell pepper
3 tablespoons diced green bell pepper
2 teaspoons minced garlic
3 tablespoons minced white onion
$^3/_4$ pound peeled crawfish tails
1 teaspoon Creole Seasoning
2 teaspoons Tabasco Sauce
2 teaspoons Worcestershire Sauce
6 ounces jalapeño cheese, shredded
2 tablespoons finely chopped green onion tops

$^1/_2$ cup sour cream
$^1/_2$ cup snipped fresh chives

To make sauce: Purée tomatillos, onion, garlic, and jalapeño in a food processor.

Heat oil in a nonreactive skillet over medium heat. Add purée and bring to a boil. Reduce heat and simmer for 10 minutes. Add water, salt, and sugar and cook for another 12 to 15 minutes. Reserve.

To make salsa: Mix all the ingredients together and let marinate for at least an hour before serving. You can refrigerate this, but allow it to come back to room temperature.

To make "tortillas": Pat the eggplant slices dry. Mix flour with 2 teaspoons of Creole Seasoning and spread out on a piece of wax paper. In a flat bowl, whisk eggs and milk. Sprinkle the eggplant with $^1/_2$ teaspoon Creole Seasoning. Dip the slices first in the flour, then into the egg wash, and then into the bread crumbs. Set aside on a tray.

Heat oil to almost smoking in a large skillet over high heat. Fry eggplant quickly until golden on both sides. Set aside to drain on paper towels.

To make filling: Heat a skillet over high heat. Add oil, peppers, garlic, and onion and sauté for a minute or so. Add the crawfish, Creole Seasoning, Tabasco, and Worcestershire and continue to sauté, stirring, for another 3 or 4 minutes. Remove from heat and stir in cheese and green onion.

Preheat oven to 350 degrees.

Oil a small pan just large enough to hold the stuffed tortillas. Spread about 2 tablespoons of the filling over half of an eggplant slice; fold the slice over carefully and transfer it to the prepared pan. Repeat. (You can cover this dish with a damp cloth and hold it for about an hour.) Bake until heated through, 5 to 10 minutes.

To serve: Mix sour cream and chives. Heat the tomatillo sauce. Spread a slick of sauce on individual plates and top with a tortilla. Garnish with salsa and sour cream.

SERVES 6

LOBSTER

SEAFOOD RISOTTO

Use Arborio rice, or another Italian medium-grain rice, for best results.

4 tablespoons (1/2 stick) unsalted butter
2 tablespoons margarine
3 tablespoons olive oil
1 large carrot, scraped and finely minced
1 large celery rib, finely minced
1 medium to large onion, finely minced
1 teaspoon fennel seed
1 garlic clove, mashed
1 cup chopped fresh Italian flat-leaf parsley
About 4 cups Fish Stock (page 42), hot
1 1/2 cups Arborio rice
3/4 cup dry white wine
1/2 teaspoon saffron threads
1/2 cup hot water
Freshly ground black pepper, to taste
Salt (optional)
1/2 pound cooked lobster (or crabmeat), cut into large pieces
1/2 pound cooked shrimp, cut into large pieces
12 steamed littleneck clams
Lemon slices
Fresh Italian flat-leaf parsley, minced

In a large pot, melt 2 tablespoons of the butter and the margarine along with the olive oil. When it bubbles, add carrot, celery, onion, and fennel seed. Sauté gently for about 10 minutes. Add garlic and continue cooking for a minute, then add parsley. Stir and cook for another minute or two.

Put on the fish stock to heat up.

Add rice to the vegetables and stir until it is well coated. Cook, stirring, for several minutes, until rice begins to turn white. Add white wine and cook over medium heat until it has all been absorbed.

Begin adding fish stock, just enough each time to barely cover the rice. Let it simmer, not boil. Stir occasionally to keep rice from sticking to the bottom of the pot. It is better for it to cook too slowly than too fast. Continue this process until about three quarters of the stock is used. When rice starts to become al dente, dissolve the saffron in the hot water and add. Keep stirring. The rice is done when it is al dente, tender but still a bit chewy. Add pepper and salt, if using. (Sometimes fish stock is very salty, making additional salting unnecessary.)

Quickly sauté the cut-up lobster and shrimp in the remaining butter and then carefully mix it in with the rice, using a fork. A couple of the steamed clams in their opened shells should be put on each individual plate. Garnish with lemon slices and parsley. Serve immediately.

This ought to be eaten *without* parmesan cheese.

SERVES 6

LOBSTER WITH TARRAGON MAYONNAISE

The palate-teasing flavor of this salad is very dependent on fresh tarragon leaves—dried won't do. Luckily, fresh herbs now seem also to be available in specialty markets for most of the year.

3 cups cooked lobster meat, cut into large cubes
1 tablespoon minced shallots
1 tablespoon snipped fresh tarragon leaves
Zest of 1 lemon
2 tablespoons tarragon vinegar
3 tablespoons crème fraîche
½ cup Homemade Mayonnaise (page 348)
Salt and freshly ground black pepper, to taste
Bibb lettuce leaves
Lemon wedges
4 hard-cooked eggs, quartered

Place lobster, shallots, tarragon, lemon zest, and tarragon vinegar in a large bowl and toss. Let marinate briefly. Mix crème fraîche and mayonnaise and fold into the salad. Correct seasoning.

Serve garnished with Bibb lettuce leaves, lemon wedges, and quartered hard-cooked eggs, if desired.

SERVES 6

SHRIMP

SHRIMP RÉMOULADE

An evergreen favorite revisited.

1 large celery rib, coarsely chopped
2 large green onions, with some of the green, coarsely chopped
½ cup coarsely chopped fresh Italian flat-leaf parsley
⅛ lemon (1 wedge)
3 eggs
¼ cup prepared horseradish
¼ cup Creole mustard
¼ cup yellow mustard
½ cup ketchup
1½ teaspoons salt, or to taste
2 teaspoons paprika
¼ cup Worcestershire Sauce
1½ cups vegetable oil
¼ cup white wine vinegar
2 cups shredded lettuce
36 medium shrimp, peeled and deveined, boiled
6 lemon wedges
12 toast points

Purée celery, green onions, parsley, and lemon wedge together in a food processor. Scrape out into a bowl and mix in eggs, horseradish, mustards, ketchup, salt, paprika, and Worcestershire. Drizzle in oil, whisking. Stir in the vinegar. Correct seasoning if needed.

To assemble, place a bed of shredded lettuce on 6 individual small plates or in small bowls. Divide shrimp among them and top with sauce. Serve with a lemon wedge and slices of thin toasted bread. Pass the extra sauce.

SERVES 6

NEW ORLEANS SHRIMP AND CRAWFISH CREOLE

The reason shrimp Creole has endured so long is that it is so simple to make—and so delicious—a hard-to-beat combo. As you can imagine, there are dozens of recipes for this New Orleans classic. This one is based on a recipe from Commander's Palace restaurant.

2 tablespoons margarine
1 cup minced onion
1 cup minced green bell pepper
2 celery ribs, minced
2 large garlic cloves, thinly sliced
1 bay leaf
2 tablespoons paprika
2 cups peeled, seeded, and diced fresh tomatoes or drained canned tomatoes
1 cup thick tomato juice
4 teaspoons Worcestershire Sauce
4 teaspoons Louisiana Hot Sauce or Tabasco Sauce
1 1/2 tablespoons cornstarch
1/2 cup cold water
3 tablespoons unsalted butter
1 1/2 pounds shrimp, peeled and deveined
1 1/2 pounds peeled crawfish tails, fresh or frozen

Boiled Rice (page 170)

In a large skillet, melt margarine over medium heat. Add onion, bell pepper, celery, and garlic and cook for a minute or two, until wilted. Add bay leaf, paprika, tomatoes, and tomato juice. Stir well and add Worcestershire and hot sauce. Stir again and simmer over medium-low heat until reduced by a quarter, about 30 minutes.

Mix cornstarch and water together to dissolve any lumps and stir into the sauce. Cook, stirring, for about 2 minutes to thicken the sauce slightly.

Melt butter in a large skillet over medium-high heat. Add shrimp and crawfish and cook, tossing, until pink, about 5 minutes. If your crawfish is already cooked, add it once the shrimp is done and just heat it through. Add the seafood to the sauce and cook for a minute.

Serve over rice.

SERVES 6 TO 8

MARINATED SHRIMP WITH GREEN CHILI POLENTA AND ROASTED CORN SALSA

What a tempting combination of flavors this is.

18 large shrimp or prawns, peeled and deveined with tails left on
Grated zest of 1/2 medium lemon
5 medium garlic cloves, minced
1 medium serrano chili, seeded and minced
1/4 cup loosely packed fresh cilantro
1/4 cup olive oil
Salt and freshly ground black pepper, to taste
Green Chili Polenta (page 170)
Roasted Corn Salsa (page 355)

Toss shrimp, lemon zest, garlic, chili, cilantro, oil, and seasonings together in a glass bowl. Cover tightly with plastic wrap and marinate for at least 1 hour. Drain the shrimp and grill until opaque, about 3 minutes per side, sprinkling with more salt and pepper. (Shrimp may also be cooked under a preheated broiler.)

Serve with Green Chili Polenta and Roasted Corn Salsa.

SERVES 6 TO 8

SEAFOOD STUFFED ARTICHOKES

These taste as good as they look.

*6 large artichokes, stem and top 1 inch of
  leaves cut off*
1 large lemon, cut in half
2 tablespoons salt
2 bay leaves
1 cup Shallot Vinaigrette (page 355)

STUFFING
36 small shrimp, cooked and peeled
¹/2 pound lump crabmeat, picked over
*¹/2 pound poached firm-fleshed fish such as
  tuna or trout, broken into medium pieces
  (see Note)*
*2 carrots, scraped and cut into 3 × ¹/8-inch
  julienne*
*2 small yellow squash, trimmed, seeded,
  and julienned as above*
*2 small zucchini squash, trimmed, seeded,
  and julienned as above*
*1 medium onion, cut into thin strips
  lengthwise*
1¹/2 cups Shallot Vinaigrette
Salt and freshly ground black pepper, to taste

Place trimmed artichokes in a large pot. Pour in enough water to just cover. Remove artichokes and set aside. Squeeze the lemon halves into water and drop them in, add salt and bay leaves, cover, and bring to a boil over high heat. Drop in the artichokes, and weight them with a plate to keep them submerged. Boil gently over medium-low heat until tender (test by piercing bottom with a sharp knife; the knife should meet with a little resistance), about 15 minutes. Do not overcook. Drain the artichokes, refresh them in ice water, then drain upside down on a towel. Remove the choke from the artichokes and discard. Place artichokes right side up and pour the vinaigrette over them. Reserve.

To make stuffing: Combine all the ingredients and toss gently.

To serve, stuff the cavities of the artichokes. Then, working outward, separate the leaves and stuff more of the mixture in between them, forcing the leaves out like petals of a flower.

Note: You may simply place fish fillets in a shallow baking dish. Sprinkle in some herbs, a squeeze of lemon, salt, and pepper, then pour a mixture of white wine and water. Cover with foil and bake in a 350-degree oven until flaky, about 10 minutes. Or you could poach it in a traditional Court-Bouillon (recipe follows). Or, substitute lobster or more crabmeat.

SERVES 6

COURT-BOUILLON
1 cup dry white wine
Juice of ¹/2 lemon
2 medium carrots, scraped and thinly sliced
1 medium onion, chopped
2 celery ribs, thinly sliced
1 bay leaf
8 cups water

Combine all ingredients in a stockpot. Bring slowly to a boil and simmer 30 minutes. Court-bouillon is ready for poaching fish. Add desired fish and simmer for about 10 minutes per inch of thickness.

MAKES 3 QUARTS

SHRIMP, WHITE BEANS, AND ROASTED RED PEPPERS

I am very fond of this combination and use it often.

2 cups dried white navy beans, soaked overnight or by the quick-soak method (see Note, page 25)
1 medium onion, coarsely chopped
1 large garlic clove, minced
1 large bay leaf
1/4 teaspoon dried thyme
Salt and freshly ground black pepper, to taste
2 tablespoons olive oil
2 or 3 large red bell peppers or a combination of red and yellow peppers, roasted, peeled, and seeded (see Note, page 74), cut into strips
30 cooked medium shrimp, peeled but with the tails left on
Lemon wedges

Drain beans and cover with several inches of fresh water. Bring to a simmer and add onion, garlic, bay leaf, and thyme. Simmer, skimming off foam, until water is reduced and beans begin to get tender, about 1 hour. Add more hot water in small amounts if necessary, to keep beans covered. When beans are done, season with salt and pepper, remove bay leaf, and stir in the olive oil.

To serve, place warm beans in a bowl on a large platter. Surround beans with strips of roasted pepper. Sprinkle these with additional olive oil and grind black pepper over all. Arrange cooked shrimp on the side of the platter or around the bowl.

Each serving should have a bit of all the ingredients. Garnish with lemon wedges.
SERVES 6

BARBECUED SHRIMP AND CAPELLINI WITH SHRIMP SAUCE

To do this right, plan to cook the shrimp in batches. Even that way, it doesn't take too long.

2 to 3 pounds large shrimp in the shell with heads on
4 1/2 teaspoons freshly ground black pepper
4 1/2 teaspoons cracked black pepper
1 tablespoon Creole Seasoning
9 tablespoons Worcestershire Sauce
1 tablespoon minced garlic
1/2 pound (2 sticks) unsalted butter
Juice of 3 lemons
8 ounces capellini

Preheat oven to 450 degrees.

Place half the shrimp in a large, heavy oven-proof skillet, about 12 inches (they should fit in a single layer). Sprinkle with half the peppers, Creole Seasoning, Worcestershire, and garlic. Dot with half a stick of the butter. Place in the oven. Cook for 2 minutes, turn, and cook for another 2 minutes. Remove to the top of the stove and continue to cook for another 4 minutes, tossing lightly, over medium-high heat. Off the heat, stir in the juice of 1 1/2 lemons and 1 tablespoon plus 1 1/2 teaspoons of the water. Then stir in another half stick of butter, cut into pieces. When butter is melted, lift the shrimp out with a slotted spoon into a large bowl, cover with a tea towel to keep warm, and pour sauce into a small saucepan.

Repeat with the remaining shrimp and other ingredients.

To serve, cook pasta in lightly salted water until al dente. Reheat the sauce and lightly coat the shrimp with it. Toss pasta with a bit of the sauce and serve the balance of the sauce on the side.
SERVES 6

GULF SHRIMP, CRAB, AND OYSTER STEW

Many people make the fish base for this dish in large quantities and freeze it in batches large enough to prepare dinner for six or eight. Use as many of the garnish vegetables as you like.

FISH BASE

$1^{1}/_{4}$ pounds onions, coarsely chopped
$^{1}/_{4}$ cup olive oil
$^{1}/_{4}$ pound garlic, peeled, cloves left whole
3 pounds fresh tomatoes, seeded and
    chopped
$1^{1}/_{2}$ teaspoons dried thyme
$1^{1}/_{2}$ teaspoons dried oregano
1 tablespoon dried basil
2 bay leaves
Pinch of saffron
4 cups Fish Stock (page 42), oyster liquor,
    or bottled clam juice
$2^{1}/_{2}$ teaspoons salt

ASSEMBLY

3 tablespoons olive oil
1 tablespoon minced garlic
1 pound shrimp, peeled and deveined
1 pound shucked oysters
1 pound crabmeat, picked over
1 leek, white part only, carefully washed
    and cut into thin julienne (optional)
1 small carrot, cut into thin julienne
    (optional)
$^{1}/_{2}$ red bell pepper, cut into thin julienne
    (optional)
$^{1}/_{2}$ yellow bell pepper, cut into thin julienne
    (optional)
Zest of 1 lemon in long strips (optional)

To make fish base: In a large skillet, sauté onions in olive oil until quite soft, about 8 to 10 minutes. Add all other ingredients except stock and salt. Cover, bring to a simmer, and cook 20 minutes. Add stock and bring to a boil, reduce heat, and simmer another 20 to 30 minutes.

Purée the mixture, then strain it, pressing out as much liquid as possible. Add salt.

To assemble: Heat 2 tablespoons of the oil in a deep saucepan and cook garlic over medium heat until wilted and beginning to brown, about 4 minutes. Add shrimp. Cook for 1 minute and add the fish base. Simmer 3 to 4 minutes. Add oysters and crabmeat. Cook for another 1 to 2 minutes until oysters begin to curl. This makes a very thick stew, which could be thinned out with more liquid (water or fish stock) if desired.

Meanwhile, heat the remaining tablespoon of oil in a small skillet and sauté the julienned garnish vegetables until barely wilted, about 3 minutes.

Serve stew in large bowls garnished with the julienned vegetables and the lemon zest.
SERVES 6 TO 8

GRILLED PRAWNS WITH PAPAYA SALSA

Papaya Salsa makes an interesting complement to the grilled prawns.

18 jumbo prawns, peeled except for the tail
    and deveined
$^{1}/_{4}$ cup vegetable oil
Juice of 1 medium lime
$^{1}/_{2}$ cup chopped fresh cilantro
4 green onions with some of the green,
    coarsely chopped
3 small avocados, peeled, pitted, and thinly
    sliced
Papaya Salsa (page 357)

Place prawns in a glass bowl. Whisk together oil, lime juice, cilantro, and green onions, and pour the mixture over them. Cover and marinate for 1 hour at room temperature.

Prepare grill so coals are ash-covered.

Grill prawns 4 inches from coals until opaque, about 2 minutes per side.

To serve, fan out avocado slices on individual plates, add a line of prawns, and garnish with salsa.
SERVES 6

GUMBO

There are basically two methods of making gumbo; they both include that key ingredient, roux, but the amount of roux and the use of a stock instead of water makes the difference. My father used quite a lot of roux for his soup, which is the way in the recipe that follows. To it he added either chicken, duck, or seafood—or a combination of all of them.

For a less thick soup, make the roux from only two tablespoons each of flour and oil, and use fish stock instead of plain water. Ham or sausage is often a part of this version as well as canned peeled tomatoes. Once you understand the basic taste of gumbo, you can make any variation you like.

1 cup safflower oil
1 cup coarsely chopped onion
1 cup coarsely chopped celery, with leaves
¾ cup coarsely chopped green bell pepper
4 large garlic cloves, minced
¼ cup chopped fresh Italian flat-leaf parsley
8 cups water or Fish Stock (page 42)
¾ cup all-purpose flour
Salt and freshly ground black pepper, to taste
Cayenne, to taste
Worcestershire Sauce to taste (optional)
1 pound okra, tops and stems removed, cut into rings
1 pound shrimp, peeled, or more to taste
1 pint shucked oysters and their liquid, or more to taste
Boiled white rice
Chopped green onions, with some of the green

Put ¼ cup of the oil in a deep heavy pot. When hot, add onion, celery, and green pepper. Sauté until wilted and starting to brown. Add garlic and parsley. Set aside.

Have the water heating while you mix the remaining oil and the flour in a heavy skillet. Using the reverse side of a flat-end spatula (or pancake turner), keep the mixture moving as it begins to brown, scraping from the bottom. This is not a difficult process, but when the roux begins to brown it will do so very quickly and will continue to darken off the heat, so it is necessary to continue scraping. You want the roux to be a very dark brown. When the proper color is reached, add 1 cup of the hot water, stirring constantly. Pour this paste into the pot with the vegetables and add the remaining water. Add salt, pepper, cayenne, and Worcestershire, if using. This sauce should be very spicy and hot with pepper.

Simmer for about 45 minutes. At the end of this cooking time, the oil will begin to rise to the top. Carefully skim it off and discard. Add more water if the mixture has become too thick, but this version of gumbo should be a bit thicker than the kind made with less roux. The soup may be put aside at this point.

To serve: Add okra and cook until just tender, 5 or 10 minutes. Add the shrimp and oysters. Cook until shrimps turn pink, 5 to 10 minutes more. Serve over rice, topped with chopped green onions over all.

SERVES 6 TO 8

VARIATION

To make chicken gumbo, generously salt and pepper a 4- to 5-pound chicken, cut into serving pieces, and brown in the oil. Use the pot in which you intend to sauté the vegetables. Remove and reserve the chicken and continue with the recipe, adding the chicken when you start simmering the roux–vegetable mixture. Continue simmering until the chicken falls off the bones. Remove and discard bones and skin. Okra should be added at the end of the cooking time, but shrimp, oysters, and cooked crabs are optional. Serve as above.

WARM SHRIMP, WHITE BEAN, AND TOMATO SALAD

The marinade gives the shrimp a distinctive flavor. You'll also end up with more beans than you need for the salad, but I like them in composed salads and as a side dish, peppered, dressed with olive oil, and served at room temperature.

1½ cups Great Northern Beans, soaked overnight or by the quick-soak method (see Note, page 25)
6 cups Chicken Stock (page 41)
2 bay leaves
1 small onion, chopped
1 tablespoon chopped fresh ginger
4 large garlic cloves, mashed
2 large green onions, white and green parts, chopped
½ cup fresh lemon juice
¼ cup soy sauce
2 tablespoons honey
30 large shrimp, peeled and deveined
1 large head Boston lettuce, washed, dried, and cut into ¼-inch strips
Salt and freshly ground black pepper
¼ cup minced red onion
Balsamic Vinaigrette (page 44)
1 large tomato, peeled, seeded, chopped coarse, and salted

Drain beans and put them in a deep pot. Add stock and bay leaves and bring to a boil. Reduce heat and simmer very slowly, uncovered, until beans are tender, about 1½ hours. Discard the bay leaves.

Combine onion, ginger, garlic, green onions, lemon juice, soy sauce, and honey in a large bowl. Add shrimp, combine well, and marinate for 30 minutes. Place shrimp on skewers.

Preheat the broiler.

Cover 6 luncheon plates with lettuce. Sprinkle with a little salt and pepper. Measure out 4 cups of drained beans. (If they are sticking together, place them in a strainer and wash quickly with hot water.) Toss the beans with the onion and ¼ cup of the vinaigrette. Divide beans equally among the plates. Sprinkle chopped tomato over beans, dividing among the plates.

Broil shrimp for 3 minutes per side. Top each salad with 5 shrimp. Top with a good grind of black pepper and spoon a little of the vinaigrette over the shrimp.

SERVES 6

NATCHEZ SEAFOOD SALAD

You could add or substitute scallops or lobster in this recipe if you live in an area where they are plentiful. Should you do this, though, remember to cook and marinate one of the ingredients as the shrimp are here.

SHRIMP

6 quarts water
½ cup salt
4 fluid ounces Zatarain's Crab Boil
1 tablespoon black peppercorns
6 lemons, halved
2 medium onions, quartered
¾ pound fresh medium shrimp

MARINADE

¼ cup rice wine vinegar
¼ cup German riesling wine
2 teaspoons chopped fresh basil
½ teaspoon minced garlic
1 teaspoon Dijon mustard
½ teaspoon salt
½ teaspoon freshly ground black pepper
1 cup olive oil
½ cup chopped sweet red or Vidalia onion

CRAWFISH
Salt, to taste
3 lemons
1 pound peeled crawfish tails

ASSEMBLY
1 pint fresh back-fin lump crabmeat, carefully picked over
Capers, grated hard-cooked egg, minced green onion tops, or minced chives (optional)
Homemade Mayonnaise (page 348)

To cook shrimp: Boil water, salt, spices, lemons, and onions for 30 minutes. This is a strong concoction so I advise not only turning on the vent but vacating the kitchen until the 30 minutes are up. People here often do this in the yard. Add shrimp and cover the pot. Remove from heat immediately. Allow to steep for 5 minutes, then pour shrimp into a colander and cover with ice to stop the cooking. Peel and devein when cool.

To make marinade: Purée vinegar, wine, basil, garlic, mustard, salt, pepper, and olive oil in a food processor or blender. Place shrimp in a bowl and toss with chopped onion. Pour marinade over all and cover. Refrigerate overnight.

To steam crawfish: Fill the bottom of a small steamer with water and salt. Cut lemons in half and add to water. Place crawfish tails in the top of the steamer and cover. Bring to a boil and steam for 10 minutes. Cool.

To assemble salad: Drain marinade from shrimp and toss shrimp with crawfish and crabmeat. Add a few capers and, if you like, grated hard-cooked egg and minced green onion tops or chives on top. Serve with mayonnaise on the side.

SERVES APPROXIMATELY 8

SHRIMP AND PASTA SALAD

Tiny green peas are also good in this.

1 pound shell pasta
2½ cups cold water
1 lemon
½ teaspoon crushed red pepper
2 medium bay leaves
1 tablespoon salt
1 tablespoon paprika
½ teaspoon chili powder
½ pound medium shrimp, peeled and deveined
¼ cup ketchup
1 cup mayonnaise
2 tablespoons rice wine vinegar
⅓ cup diced pineapple
1 teaspoon Louisiana Hot Sauce
⅓ cup diced red bell pepper
⅓ cup diced green bell pepper
⅓ cup diced red onion
¼ cup minced fresh Italian flat-leaf parsley
¼ teaspoon salt
¼ teaspoon freshly ground black pepper

Cook pasta according to package directions. Drain, rinse in cold water, and set aside.

In a saucepan, bring the 2½ cups water to a boil. Cut the lemon in half. Squeeze in the juice and drop in the rinds. Add crushed red pepper, bay leaves, salt, paprika, and chili powder. Simmer for 3 minutes, then add the shrimp. When water comes back to a boil, remove from heat and let shrimp rest in the water for 5 minutes. Drain, cool, and cut shrimp in half. Toss with the pasta.

In a small bowl, combine ketchup, mayonnaise, vinegar, pineapple, and hot sauce. Toss in with pasta–shrimp mixture. Toss in peppers, onion, parsley, salt, and black pepper. Adjust seasoning if necessary. Chill before serving.

SERVES 8

BOILED CRAB, CRAWFISH, SHRIMP, CORN, AND POTATOES

This brew is potent, fiery stuff—just the way they like it around New Orleans. And it's designed for a big crowd.

15 quarts water
8 lemons
3 pounds onions, peeled and sliced thick
4 bags Zatarain's Seafood Boil
3 cups kosher salt
2 cups Louisiana Hot Sauce
1/2 cup cayenne
3 heads garlic, halved crosswise
6 bay leaves
2 cups peppercorns
4 pounds small new potatoes, scrubbed and unpeeled
12 ears corn, shucked and broken in two
18 live crabs
4 pounds fresh shrimp in their shells
15 pounds live crawfish

Put the water in a 20-gallon pot. Cut lemons in half, squeeze their juice into the water, and drop in the rinds. Add onions and seasonings. Bring to a boil and cook for several minutes. When the boil tastes very hot and salty, it's ready.

Add potatoes and boil for 4 to 5 minutes. Add corn and bring back to a boil. Add crabs and bring back to a boil. Then add shrimp and crawfish and bring back to a final boil. Remove from the heat and let stand for 10 minutes. Drain and serve on large trays with sauces on the side.

SERVES 18 TO 24

CLAMS

BAKED CLAMS

Rock salt
Tabasco Sauce
36 cherrystone clams, scrubbed, shucked, and left on the half shell
6 tablespoons unsalted butter, softened
1/4 cup minced fresh chives
1/4 cup minced fresh Italian flat-leaf parsley
1/4 cup minced green bell pepper
1 tablespoon minced garlic
6 slices bacon, each cut into 6 pieces
12 lemon wedges

Preheat oven to 450 degrees. Cover the bottom of a low-sided baking sheet with rock salt and put in the oven.

Put a drop of Tabasco on each clam on its half shell and slip a teaspoon of butter under each clam. Set aside.

Toss together chives, parsley, green pepper, and garlic. Set aside.

Fry bacon squares over low heat until translucent but not browned, several minutes, and drain on paper towels.

Remove the pan from the oven and arrange the clams on it. Sprinkle each with the chive mixture and top with a square of bacon. Bake until the bacon crisps, about 5 minutes.

Serve with lemon wedges.

SERVES 6

OYSTERS

MANDICH OYSTERS

These oysters get their name from Mandich Restaurant in New Orleans, where they are a house specialty. The dish is the inspiration of Joel English, who, together with her husband Lloyd, runs the popular family-style place out near fabled Desire Street in the Crescent City.

1/4 cup olive oil
3/4 cup safflower oil
3 tablespoons coarsely chopped garlic
1/4 cup minced green onions
3/4 teaspoon salt
1/8 teaspoon freshly ground black pepper
2 tablespoons dry sherry
4 cups vegetable oil for deep-frying
2 eggs
1 cup all-purpose flour
1 tablespoon paprika
2 to 3 dozen medium oysters, shucked, with deeper half of the shell reserved and washed
2 tablespoons chopped fresh Italian flat-leaf parsley
Lemon wedges

Place olive and safflower oils in a medium saucepan and add garlic, green onions, salt, and pepper. Simmer very gently or until garlic is tender but not browned. Off the heat, stir in sherry and set aside.

Heat vegetable oil to 425 degrees in a deep pot.

While oil is heating, beat eggs in a small bowl. In a shallow dish combine flour and paprika. Drain oysters and, one at a time, dip them first in flour, then in the egg (allow excess to drain off), and then dredge in flour mixture again. Shake off excess flour. Working in batches, fry the oysters until crisp, about 15 to 20 seconds.

Place 2 oysters (or more) in each reserved half shell and spoon about 1 teaspoon of the sauce over each. Sprinkle with parsley and garnish with lemon.
SERVES 6

OYSTER TARTARE WITH SPARKLING WINE SAUCE

This may be made in advance and be ready and waiting in the refrigerator.

24 oysters, shucked, shells reserved
1/2 cup champagne vinegar
1/4 cup sparkling white wine
2 teaspoons minced shallot
1 teaspoon minced fresh tarragon
Freshly ground black pepper, to taste
4 hard-cooked eggs, peeled with yolks and whites separated and finely chopped
Fresh tarragon sprigs, for garnish (optional)

Remove the tough muscles from the oysters and chop oysters into fine dice. Wash and refrigerate empty bottom shells.

Blend vinegar, wine, shallot, tarragon, and black pepper. Set aside.

Spoon the oyster tartare back into the shells, dividing as evenly as possible. Top each with a teaspoon or more of the sauce. Chill the oysters well and then serve in shells over crushed ice. Garnish each with a bit of egg yolk and white and a sprig of tarragon.
SERVES 4 TO 6

273

OYSTER SALAD WITH RADISH RELISH

You could substitute large shrimp or crawfish tails for the oysters and come up with a tasty variation. You might want to make the salad before you fry the oysters, because the sooner you eat the oysters, the better you'll like them.

OYSTERS
36 freshly shucked oysters, drained
¼ cup Creole Seasoning
1 cup all-purpose flour
1 cup masa harina (see Note)
Oil for deep-frying

ASSEMBLY
1 medium head radicchio, cleaned and torn into bite-size pieces
1 medium head green leaf lettuce, cleaned and torn into bite-size pieces
Garlic Mayonnaise (page 348)
36 medium asparagus spears, trimmed and blanched for 2 minutes
12 Belgian endive leaves
Radish Relish (page 360)

To fry oysters: Sprinkle oysters with 3 tablespoons of Creole Seasoning. Set aside. Toss together flour, masa harina, and remaining Creole Seasoning.

Heat oil in a deep-fryer to 350 degrees.

Dredge oysters in the flour mixture, coating them well and shaking off the excess. Fry until golden, about 2 to 3 minutes. Drain on paper towels.

To assemble salad: Divide the greens among 6 large plates. Top each salad with 6 oysters and garnish with asparagus, endive, and radish relish. Add a dollop of mayonnaise and serve immediately.

Note: Masa harina is flour made from dried corn and used to make tortillas. It is available in many specialty food stores and supermarkets.

SERVES 6

CORNMEAL FRIED OYSTERS

Flour, cracker crumbs, and meal, separately or in combination, are used to coat oysters for frying. I have tried most of them, but for my money, you just can't beat plain cornmeal. It creates the perfect thin, crunchy casing for these delicious little morsels.

Safflower or corn oil for frying
About 3 cups yellow cornmeal
1 tablespoon freshly ground black pepper
1 teaspoon salt
6 dozen medium oysters, shucked and drained

Put the oil in a deep-fryer with a wire basket and heat to very hot. If you have a frying thermometer, the temperature should be 375 degrees.

While oil is heating, mix cornmeal, pepper, and salt on a long sheet of wax paper, placed next to the stove if possible. Roll oysters in the mixture, coating well. Put the coated oysters in a single layer in the wire basket and lower it into the hot oil. Fry a batch at a time this way for about 2 minutes, until golden. Drain on paper towels. Continue until all are fried. Keep the oysters warm on a baking sheet in the oven (in one layer) until you finish them all. Serve immediately on a warm platter. Let the oil reheat for a few seconds between batches.

SERVES 6

BAKED JALAPEÑO OYSTERS

A delicious new take on traditional baked oysters.

4 ounces slab bacon, cut into small dice
½ cup minced red onion
¼ cup seeded and minced jalapeño
½ cup diced red bell pepper
½ cup diced green bell pepper
7 tablespoons unsalted butter
6 tablespoons all-purpose flour
2 cups milk
1 cup heavy cream
½ teaspoon salt
½ teaspoon white pepper
1¼ cups peeled, seeded, and chopped
*   tomato*
¼ cup grated romano
¼ teaspoon Louisiana Hot Sauce
⅓ cup dry bread crumbs
1 pound fresh spinach, stemmed and torn
*   into large pieces*
18 oysters, shucked, shells reserved
Rock salt

In a medium skillet, cook bacon over medium heat until crisp. Pour out all but 2 tablespoons of the fat. Add onion, jalapeño, and bell peppers. Cook over medium heat until wilted, about 5 minutes. Set aside.

Melt 6 tablespoons of the butter in a medium saucepan over low heat; stir in flour and turn heat up to medium. Whisk in milk and cream and continue to cook, whisking, for 8 minutes. Stir in vegetables and continue to cook until thickened, another 6 to 8 minutes. Add salt, pepper, and chopped tomato and cook, stirring, another 2 minutes. Off the heat, stir in half the cheese and the hot sauce. Taste for seasoning and add more salt, pepper, or hot sauce. Mix the remaining cheese with the bread crumbs. Set aside.

Preheat oven to 450 degrees.

Rinse spinach and shake off water. Melt remaining tablespoon of butter in a large skillet and add spinach. Cover, shaking pan, until wilted slightly.

Scrub 18 of the reserved shells. To bake, cover bottom of a rimmed baking sheet with rock salt and arrange shells on it. Divide spinach among the shells and top each with an oyster. Sprinkle oysters with half the cheese–crumb mixture. Top each with a generous tablespoon of the sauce and sprinkle with the remaining cheese–crumb mixture. Bake for 8 to 10 minutes. Turn on broiler and cook for about another minute to brown tops lightly.
SERVES 6

SCALLOPS

SCALLOP SEVICHE

Quick and simple and delicious.

1½ pounds sea scallops
Juice of 4 limes
¼ cup finely diced red onion
4 medium tomatoes, peeled, seeded, and
*   diced small*
2 tablespoons finely chopped fresh cilantro
6 tablespoons olive oil
Freshly ground black pepper, to taste
6 fresh cilantro sprigs

Remove the small muscle from the side of each scallop and discard. Marinate scallops in lime juice for 3 hours, refrigerated.

Drain and thinly slice the scallops. Arrange in a circle, slices overlapping, on individual plates. Heap some diced onion in the center of each circle and arrange tomato pieces around scallops. Sprinkle with cilantro. Drizzle a tablespoon of olive oil over each serving and top with a grinding of black pepper. Garnish with cilantro sprigs.
SERVES 6

BROILED SCALLOPS
WITH BEGGARS' PURSES

If you can only find large sea scallops, cut them in half.

> 1 1/2 pounds small sea scallops, washed and
>   trimmed
> 2 tablespoons olive oil
> 5 tablespoons vegetable oil
> 1/2 cup snipped fresh chervil
> Freshly ground black pepper, to taste
> Salt
> 8 ounces crabmeat, picked over
> 3 tablespoons minced red bell pepper
> 1 1/2 tablespoons minced fresh chervil, plus
>   extra for garnish
> 3 tablespoons mayonnaise
> 2 teaspoons fresh lemon juice
> 1/2 teaspoon white pepper
> 12 squares phyllo dough, about 6 × 6
>   inches each
> 8 tablespoons (1 stick) unsalted butter,
>   melted
> 6 long strips of chives
> Lemon Butter Sauce (page 256)
> Lemon wedges (optional)

Place scallops in a bowl with oils and the 1/2 cup chervil. Sprinkle with black pepper and 1/2 teaspoon salt. Mix with your hands or 2 forks to coat thoroughly and let marinate at room temperature for 1 hour.

Meanwhile, mix together crabmeat, red bell pepper, the 1 1/2 tablespoons minced chervil, mayonnaise, lemon juice, salt, and white pepper.

Brush one phyllo square lightly with the melted butter (keep remainder covered with a damp cloth). Place a second square on top at a 45-degree angle (this will look like an 8-pointed star) and brush lightly with butter. Put a heaping tablespoon of the crab mixture in the center. Pull up the dough and gather it together to enclose the filling. Squeeze it slightly to make a little neck, leaving the points sticking up. Soak chives in hot water for about 30 seconds to make them pliable and knot the neck closed with one. Place on a metal pie tin. Repeat the process to make 5 more purses (these may be made up to 2 hours in advance).

Preheat oven to 375 degrees. Bake beggars' purses until heated through and just beginning to turn golden, about 10 to 12 minutes.

Meanwhile, place marinated scallops in a single layer on a low-sided broiler pan (do not crowd). As soon as the purses come out of the oven, turn on broiler and cook scallops for 2 to 3 minutes, just to heat through. Do not let brown.

To serve, place a purse in the middle of a plate and surround with scallops. Serve with Lemon Butter Sauce and garnish with a lemon wedge, if desired.

SERVES 6

FROGS' LEGS

FROGS' LEGS WITH
PARSLEY BUTTER

In Natchez, frogs' legs are often served broiled. You could do them that way for this recipe after they have been marinated (and patted dry), if you prefer.

> 12 pairs frogs' legs
> 4 cups milk
> 4 garlic cloves, crushed
> 2 teaspoons Tabasco Sauce
> Oil for deep-frying
> 4 eggs
> 2 1/2 cups all-purpose flour
> 1 tablespoon salt
> 1 tablespoon freshly ground black pepper
> Parsley Butter (page 350)

Divide the legs by cutting along the joint at the top of the thigh. Place legs in a large bowl with

276

milk, garlic, and Tabasco. Cover and marinate, refrigerated, overnight.

Heat oil to 400 degrees, preferably in a thermostatically controlled fryer. Place eggs in a bowl and beat lightly. Set aside. Mix flour, salt, and pepper in a plastic bag. Dip legs in egg, then allow excess to drain off. Shake in flour. Fry for 5 to 8 minutes (depending on their size). Legs will float, and bubbling will die down when done. They should be light brown with dark flecks. Serve topped with a dab of Parsley Butter.

SERVES 6 TO 8

CATFISH

PAN-SAUTÉED CATFISH FILLETS WITH PARSLEY-PECAN SAUCE

Many of the catfish you buy now are farm raised and seem to me to be somewhat sweeter than those we used to catch in the rivers and bayous. Maybe that is my imagination, but anyway I like farm-grown catfish better.

2 cups all-purpose flour
1 tablespoon cayenne
1 tablespoon plus 1 teaspoon salt
6 catfish fillets (5 to 6 ounces each)
2 or more tablespoons vegetable oil
2 or more tablespoons unsalted butter
Parsley-Pecan Sauce (page 347)

Mix flour, cayenne, and salt (you can shake this in a bag). Spread it on a large platter and dredge each fillet, shaking off excess. Set aside on a sheet of wax paper.

Heat half the oil and butter in a skillet large enough to accommodate 3 fillets at a time. When butter is foaming but not brown, add fillets and sauté on one side for about 4 minutes,

until light golden. Turn fillets and spread the browned side with sauce; continue to sauté until underside is nicely browned, about another 4 minutes. Cover the skillet for a few minutes of the cooking time to melt the sauce. Remove fish to a platter.

Add the balance of the oil and butter and cook the remaining fillets.

You may reheat these slightly under the broiler just before serving if you like.

SERVES 6

CATFISH FINGERS WITH TOMATO TARTAR SAUCE

Of course, if you prefer you could substitute your favorite tartar sauce for the one here.

1½ pounds catfish fillets
3 tablespoons Creole mustard
2 tablespoons dry white wine
½ teaspoon salt
¼ teaspoon freshly ground black pepper
Peanut oil for frying
1 cup yellow cornmeal
½ cup corn flour
⅓ cup cornstarch
1 tablespoon Creole Seasoning
Tomato Tartar Sauce (page 350)

Cut catfish fillets into ½ × 2-inch strips. Combine mustard, wine, salt, and pepper. Add catfish strips and toss to coat well. Cover and marinate for 1 hour.

Heat oil in a deep-fryer to 350 degrees.

Mix together the cornmeal, corn flour, cornstarch, and Creole Seasoning. Spread out on a sheet of wax paper. Roll the marinated strips in the mixture, lightly shaking off any excess. Fry until golden, about 4 minutes. Drain on paper towels and serve with tomato tartar sauce.

SERVES 6

GROUPER

COLD POACHED GULF FISH WITH FRESH CUCUMBER SAUCE

Choose any firm mild fish, such as red grouper. If you don't have a fish poacher, use a roasting pan and cover it securely with foil.

2 cups dry white wine
Juice of 1 large lemon
4 quarts cold water
2¼ cups scraped and thinly sliced carrots
1¾ cups thinly sliced celery
2 medium onions, coarsely chopped
3 bay leaves
6 pounds grouper, cleaned, with head and
  tail on
1 red bell pepper, roasted, peeled, and
  seeded (see Note, page 74), cut into strips
1 yellow bell pepper, roasted, peeled, and
  seeded, cut into strips
Lettuce leaves
4 hard-cooked eggs
12 green onions, trimmed
3 lemons, cut into wedges
Fresh Cucumber Sauce (recipe follows)

Combine wine, lemon juice, water, carrots, celery, onions, and bay leaves in a fish poacher. Bring to a boil and simmer for 30 minutes. Wrap the fish well in several thicknesses of cheesecloth and carefully lower it into the court-bouillon. Cover and barely simmer for 20 minutes, or until flesh is firm and white. Cool and chill in the liquid.

To serve, drain fish, pat dry, and carefully scrape off the skin. You may also remove and discard the head and tail if you choose. Garnish with roasted red and yellow peppers, lettuce, hard-cooked eggs cut into eighths, green onions, and lemon wedges.

Serve with cucumber sauce.

SERVES 6 TO 8

FRESH CUCUMBER SAUCE

1 cup low-fat sour cream
1 teaspoon salt
1 teaspoon Dijon mustard
2 teaspoons red wine vinegar
2 tablespoons coarsely chopped sweet pickle
1 teaspoon sweet pickle juice
2 medium cucumbers, peeled, seeded, and
  diced small
Paprika, to taste (optional)

Whisk together all the ingredients except the cucumber and paprika. Just before serving, drain and dry the cucumber and fold it into the sauce. Sprinkle the top with paprika if you like.

MAKES ABOUT 2 CUPS

MONKFISH

BAKED MONKFISH

M. F. K. Fisher is responsible for this recipe, because I read once that she said she almost always rubbed fish with soy sauce before baking it. It seemed like a good idea, so I tried it. Now I do the same.

3 pounds monkfish
Soy sauce
2 tablespoons unsalted butter
Fresh lemon juice
Lemon slices

Preheat oven to 450 degrees.

Rub the fish very generously all over with soy sauce and let it come to room temperature. With foil, line a pan large enough to hold all the fish in one layer. Grease the foil lightly. Place the fish in the pan and bake for 7 minutes for each half inch of thickness.

Meanwhile, melt the butter. When the fish is done, squeeze lemon juice liberally over all and then pour on the butter. Baste with some of the pan juices.

Serve with lemon slices.

SERVES 6

POMPANO

GRILLED POMPANO WITH THYME AND GARLIC BUTTER

Any firm, mild, white fish may be substituted.

6 pompano fillets (5 to 6 ounces each)
2 teaspoons salt
1/2 teaspoon freshly ground black pepper
Olive oil
8 tablespoons (1 stick) unsalted butter
1 1/2 tablespoons finely minced garlic
1 tablespoon Worcestershire Sauce
Juice of 2 lemons
1 1/2 tablespoons coarsely chopped fresh thyme
1/2 teaspoon white pepper
Pan-Roasted Shallots (page 138), optional

Preheat grill or broiler for at least 20 minutes.

Lay fillets out on a tray. Mix together 1 teaspoon of the salt and the black pepper and rub the fish with it.

Brush the grill or broiler with a little olive oil and cook fish about 1 1/2 to 2 minutes per side, depending on thickness, until it is just beginning to flake.

Meanwhile (or before you start the fish), melt butter in a medium skillet over high heat. Add garlic, stirring and continuing to cook until garlic just begins to brown lightly, about 1 minute. Add Worcestershire, lemon juice, and remaining teaspoon of salt. The mixture should be a light caramel color. Add thyme and remove from heat. Stir in white pepper.

Brush fish lightly with the infused butter as it is served. Garnish with Pan-Roasted Shallots.

SERVES 6

SALMON

BAKED THIN-SLICED SALMON

I'm very partial to this method of cooking salmon. You can even do it directly on the dinner plates if they are ovenproof.

1/2 cup fresh dill, no stems
1/4 cup fresh lemon juice
1/2 cup olive oil
3 tablespoons Dijon mustard
1 salmon fillet, 1 1/2 to 2 pounds, in 1 piece
Fresh chopped herbs (optional)
Lemon slices (optional)

Combine the dill, lemon juice, olive oil, and mustard in a food processor and process until smooth. This will have the consistency of mayonnaise.

Wrap the salmon in plastic and put in the freezer for 10 minutes. Unwrap and cut at an angle against the grain into 1/4-inch-thick slices —as if you were slicing smoked salmon. This should give you 12 slices.

Place slices in a dish and combine with the dill mixture making sure all surfaces are coated. Cover and marinate 4 to 6 hours, refrigerated.

Preheat oven to 450 degrees. Coat 2 baking sheets with vegetable spray and arrange 6 slices on each. Smooth the marinade with a spatula. Bake in the center of the oven for 2 1/2 to 3 minutes, until flaky. Remove to warmed plates with a spatula. May be garnished with fresh herbs or lemon.

SERVES 6

BAKED SALMON FILLET WITH WASABI CRUST AND ORANGE–ANAHEIM CHILI SAUCE

This dish could be made lighter by serving the salmon with a salsa flavored only with oranges.

> 1 teaspoon wasabi powder (Japanese horseradish)
> ½ cup water
> 1½ cups bread crumbs, toasted
> ¼ cup mayonnaise
> 1 tablespoon honey
> ¼ teaspoon salt
> 2 tablespoons sesame seeds
> 6 salmon fillets, 4 to 6 ounces, with any remaining bones removed
> 1 tablespoon cold unsalted butter, cut into bits
> Orange–Anaheim Chili Sauce (page 361)

Preheat oven to 425 degrees.

Mix wasabi with enough of the water to form a paste. Let it rest for 20 minutes.

Put the wasabi paste, rest of the water, bread crumbs, mayonnaise, honey, salt, and sesame seeds in a small bowl and combine with your hands to make a moist mixture.

Put several tablespoons of water in a rimmed baking sheet to prevent sticking (you want a film of water in the pan) and lay the fillets on it. Pat mixture on top of each fillet to about ¼-inch thickness. Dot with the butter and bake for 6 to 7 minutes. Center of fish should be slightly undercooked.

Serve with Orange–Anaheim Chili Sauce.

SERVES 6

COLD KING SALMON WITH ASPIC AND HERB SAUCE

This is a dish for a special occasion because it takes a bit of doing, but the result is well worth it. You will need a deep 24-inch lidded fish poacher with a rack with handles. In a pinch you could improvise with a deep roasting pan, wrapping the fish in several layers of cheesecloth in order to lift it out.

This dish should be made a day ahead to give the fish time to chill thoroughly.

FISH
> 2 cups chardonnay or other dry white wine
> 2 medium onions, finely sliced
> 2 medium carrots, thickly sliced
> 1 large celery rib, thickly sliced
> 2 tablespoons black peppercorns
> 2 tablespoons salt
> 3 large bay leaves
> 1 cleaned king salmon with head, tail, and skin intact, but with gills removed (5 to 7 pounds)

ASPIC
> 5 envelopes unflavored gelatin
> ½ cup cold water
> 3 cups poaching liquid

ASSEMBLY
> 1 medium carrot, cut into thin rounds
> 1 pitted black olive
> Fresh dill, blanched for 5 seconds and dried
> Fresh tarragon, blanched for 15 seconds and dried
> 1 medium leek, carefully washed and cut into julienne, blanched for 40 seconds, and dried
> Ice cubes
> 1 medium cucumber, washed

To poach fish: Make a court-bouillon by combining all the ingredients except fish in the poacher and bringing it to a boil over 2 heating units at high heat. Turn back heat and simmer for 1 hour.

The cooking time for the fish is calculated by its thickness (not weight), so measure the salmon at its widest point. Rinse salmon carefully and be sure the red vein along the inner backbone is removed (this is actually the fish's kidney). Slide the fish into the poacher on its side. Add boiling water to court-bouillon so that the fish is just covered by the poaching liquid. Return heat to high and when boiling, lower heat so that liquid barely moves in the covered poacher. Poach for 13 minutes for each inch of thickness (see Note).

Let the fish cool in the liquid, uncovered at room temperature. Then cover it and refrigerate overnight.

Carefully lift the fish out of the poaching liquid and let drain. Slide gently onto a serving platter. With the point of a sharp knife, cut through the skin along the sides of the gill plates and along the backbone. Peel the skin away, cutting a neat curve where it joins the tail. Gently scrape away any brown meat on the sides until only pink is showing. Clean the platter around the fish.

To make aspic: Soften the gelatin in the water for several minutes. Strain the poaching liquid through a thickness or two of cheesecloth and add to the gelatin. Bring to a simmer, stirring constantly, then remove from heat.

To assemble: Dip a carrot round in warm aspic and place over fish's eye. Cut a slice of black olive, dip it in the aspic, and place on the carrot as the "pupil." Decorate the sides of the fish with the blanched dill, tarragon, and leek, again dipping them into the warm aspic first.

Place the pot with the remaining aspic into a large bowl filled with ice cubes. Stir the aspic as it thickens. When it is somewhat thicker than heavy cream ladle it on the fish in long, smooth strokes from head to tail. Work very rapidly since aspic will continue to thicken and get lumpy. If you do have a few lumps, heat the blade of a wooden-handled knife over a flame and smooth them out.

Finish the decoration by cutting a dorsal fin from a length of cucumber and "gluing" it along the backbone with aspic.

Serve with the herb sauce.

Note: To serve the salmon hot, poach it 15 minutes to the inch. This extra time is because it will be lifted from the poaching liquid as soon as it is done.

SERVES 8 TO 12

VARIATION

You can also bake the salmon. To do so, tear off a large sheet of foil and place it in a deep poacher with enough extra to seal it on top. Put the fish on its stomach on a bed of finely sliced onion, curving it in the foil and against the sides of the pan so it has a graceful shape. You could prop the fish's mouth open with a broken off toothpick.

Dot with 3 tablespoons of unsalted butter and tuck sprigs of dill, sorrel, or tarragon along and around the sides of the salmon. Squeeze a lemon over, pour on a cup of dry white wine, and carefully seal foil, making sure entire fish is enclosed. Cook in a preheated 325 degree oven.

Let fish cool and then refrigerate. To serve, gently slide fish onto the platter and carefully peel away the foil and cooked vegetables. Continue with instructions for cleaning and decorating.

CORN AND SALMON CROQUETTES

I've used the minimum of filler with these so they are very tender. They are easy to make and cook, but care should be taken when frying them. When they first start to brown, nudge them slightly to keep them from sticking, then let them brown a bit before moving them around and turning them over.

1 cup fresh corn kernels, cut and scraped
   from the cob (about 2 medium ears)
1 cup skinned, boned, and coarsely chopped
   fresh salmon
3 tablespoons unsalted butter
1/2 cup minced shallots
3/4 cup minced celery
1 1/2 cups soft bread crumbs
2 eggs, lightly beaten
1 1/2 teaspoons salt
1/2 teaspoon freshly ground black pepper
1 tablespoon Dijon mustard
1 tablespoon Worcestershire Sauce
All-purpose flour
3 tablespoons vegetable oil

Put corn into a food processor and pulse a few times. Place corn and salmon in a medium mixing bowl and set aside.

Melt 1 tablespoon of the butter in a small skillet and add shallots and celery. Sauté over medium heat until wilted, about 5 minutes. Add to the corn and salmon and toss. Mix in the bread crumbs and enough egg to make a moist mixture. Add the salt, pepper, mustard, and Worcestershire.

Divide the mixture into 12 portions and form into cylinders. Roll lightly in flour to coat, dusting off excess.

Heat the remainder of the butter and the vegetable oil in a skillet over high heat. When hot, add the croquettes. Turn heat back slightly and fry until golden, about 1 to 1 1/2 minutes, depending on the size. Turn carefully with 2 spatulas and fry other side until golden. Reduce heat slightly and continue to cook until done but not dry, 1 1/2 to 2 additional minutes per side. Turn again if necessary.
SERVES 6

SALMON SALAD

1 lemon, quartered
3 medium carrots, cut into rough pieces
4 celery stalks, cut into rough pieces
12 black peppercorns
3 to 4 cups cold water
1 pound salmon fillet, skin removed
2 tablespoons sour cream
3 tablespoons mayonnaise
3 tablespoons minced shallots
2 tablespoons finely chopped fresh dill
1/2 teaspoon grated lemon zest
1 teaspoon white wine vinegar
2 teaspoons capers, rinsed and drained
2 tablespoons finely chopped green onion
1 hard-cooked egg, mashed

Place lemon, carrots, celery, and black peppercorns in a medium saucepan and add cold water. Bring to a boil over medium-high heat. Add the fish and bring it back to the boil. Turn off the heat and allow the fish to cool in the poaching liquid, 1 to 1 1/2 hours.

Combine sour cream, mayonnaise, shallots, dill, lemon zest, vinegar, capers, green onion, and egg in a large bowl. Flake the salmon into the dressing and toss gently.
SERVES 4

282

SNAPPER

WHOLE RED SNAPPER

3 whole red snappers (about 1½ pounds each), scaled, cleaned but with head and tail on, rinsed and patted dry
2 teaspoons salt
1 tablespoon freshly ground black pepper
3 small bunches of fresh chervil
3 small bunches of fresh chives
3 tablespoons olive oil
3 tablespoons fresh lemon juice

Preheat oven to 375 degrees.

Season the fish, inside and out, with salt and pepper. Stuff with fresh herbs and place in a shallow baking dish that will hold them snugly. Drizzle with olive oil and lemon juice.

Bake, uncovered, for 25 to 30 minutes, basting occasionally. Final cooking time will be determined by the thickness of the fish. When done, it should be opaque.

Remove from oven and let rest until the fish has cooled sufficiently to fillet.

Fillet by sliding a wide-blade, thin knife just above the backbone of the fish (along the width) and then down each length. This frees the fillet from the bone frame. Lift the fillet and place on a warm serving dish.

Remove the bone frame from the fish and lift the bottom fillet to another serving plate. Repeat until you have served all the fish.

SERVES 6

GRILLED TERIYAKI SNAPPER

You can substitute any firm fish fillet in this dish if snapper isn't available.

⅓ cup soy sauce
1 thick slice of fresh ginger, peeled and chopped
2 tablespoons dry sherry
1 tablespoon sugar
2 garlic cloves, minced
2½ pounds snapper fillet, 1 inch thick, cut into 6 pieces
3 tablespoons unsalted butter, cut into 6 pieces

Preheat the broiler.

In a small bowl, whisk together soy sauce, ginger, sherry, sugar, and garlic. Place the fish in a single layer in a shallow dish and pour the marinade over the fish. Set aside, covered, for 30 minutes, turning the fish several times.

Broil the fish about 5 minutes per side, until well browned and flaky, basting once on each side with the marinade. Discard any unused marinade.

Place the fish on individual plates and top each serving with a bit of butter.

SERVES 6

SWORDFISH

SWORDFISH STEAK SALAD

TOMATO VINAIGRETTE
¼ cup red wine vinegar
1 tablespoon grainy mustard
½ teaspoon salt
1 teaspoon freshly ground black pepper
¼ cup olive oil
½ cup vegetable oil
*½ medium tomato, peeled, seeded, and
    finely chopped (approximately 4
    tablespoons)*

1½ pounds small red new potatoes
4 tablespoons olive oil
1 teaspoon salt
2 teaspoons freshly ground black pepper
*4 tablespoons coarsely chopped fresh
    rosemary*
2 tablespoons coarsely ground black pepper
6½ pounds swordfish pieces
6 cups mixed greens

To make tomato vinaigrette: Combine the vinegar, mustard, salt, and pepper. Whisk in oils to emulsify. Add the chopped tomato and allow to sit for at least 30 minutes.

Preheat oven to 400 degrees.

Wash and dry potatoes (quarter, if large). Toss with 2 tablespoons of the olive oil, salt, and 2 teaspoons pepper and transfer to a sheet pan. Roast until golden brown, turning occasionally to avoid sticking, about 30 minutes. Set aside to cool until needed.

Place rosemary, 2 tablespoons pepper, and 1 tablespoon of the olive oil in a bowl and combine well, using your hands. Rub the rosemary mixture on the fish and allow to stand for at least an hour.

In a heavy skillet over high heat, heat the remaining 1 tablespoon of olive oil until almost smoking. Sear the swordfish on each side for approximately 3 to 5 minutes. The fish should form a crust but still be pink in the center. Cool just slightly. Serve warm.

Divide the greens and potatoes onto 6 over-sized plates. Flake the fish over the top and drizzle with tomato vinaigrette.
SERVES 6

TROUT

OAK-GRILLED STEELHEAD TROUT WRAPPED IN VINE LEAVES

If vine leaves are not handy, you can substitute romaine or savoy cabbage leaves.

*6 whole boned steelhead trout with heads
    and tails left on (12 ounces each)*
6 tablespoons olive oil
*Salt and freshly ground black pepper, to
    taste*
24 thin slices lemon
24 fresh thyme sprigs
24 blanched vine leaves

Prepare grill to have ash-covered coals (see Note).

Place trout skin side down on a cutting board. Drizzle 1 tablespoon of the olive oil in the cavity of each, sprinkle with salt and pepper, then lay 4 lemon slices and 4 sprigs of thyme in each cavity. Close the fish and wrap them individually in vine leaves. Use wooden skewers to hold fish closed.

Place on a moderately hot grill for about 3 minutes per side, then remove fish to the edge of the grill to finish cooking more slowly. This will take several minutes, depending on how hot the fire is. Flesh should be flaky. Remove skewers before serving.

Note: If you don't have a grill or would rather sauté these, first preheat the oven to 350 degrees. Place a slick of olive oil in 2 large oven-proof skillets and place over high heat. Sear fish on both sides and place pans in the oven for 6 to 8 minutes.

SERVES 6

TROUT IN A SHOESTRING POTATO CRUST

This method works with any kind of firm fish fillet.

6 trout fillets (4 to 5 ounces each)
2 teaspoons salt
1 teaspoon white pepper
1 cup all-purpose flour
8 cups shredded or shoestring potatoes
    (about 6 medium)
¾ cup olive oil
Tomato Coulis (page 353)
Caramelized Onions (page 130)
4 pieces pickled okra, cut into rings
    (optional)
1 lemon, cut into wedges (optional)

Lay fillets out on a sheet of wax paper. Mix salt and pepper and sprinkle the fish. Mix leftover salt and pepper with the flour. Dredge fillets well in the flour and shake off excess. Place on a plate and cover lightly with wax paper. Refrigerate for at least 30 minutes.

Put shredded potatoes in a shallow bowl and carefully place each fillet on them, pressing down to make potatoes adhere on both sides—don't worry, it will look messy. (During refrigeration, the flour will have combined with moisture from the fish, making its surface sticky.) Put each coated fillet aside on a tray as it is finished.

Heat oil in a very large skillet over high heat. When very hot, carefully place 3 fillets in the pan, skin side down. Turn the heat down slightly and let cook undisturbed for a minute or two. Beginning with the two ends, gently slide a spatula under the cooking fillets to loosen any points that may be sticking; after about 3 minutes, lift an end to check that they are not browning too quickly. When golden, 4 to 6 minutes, turn carefully and repeat the process. Before turning, you may sprinkle a few more shredded potatoes on top and press them down lightly. Hold the potatoes in place with your hand while you turn the fish with the spatula.

Add more oil if necessary to cook the second batch.

To serve, spread a generous slick of the tomato coulis on individual plates and sprinkle with the caramelized onions. Top with a fillet and garnish if desired, with rings of pickled okra and a lemon wedge.

SERVES 6

TUNA

GRILLED TUNA, SALMON, AND STURGEON

Actually, any combination of fish would be fine here, but this is an especially pleasing threesome.

1¼ pounds fresh tuna fillets
1¼ pounds fresh salmon fillet, cut into
*   serving-size pieces*
1¼ pounds fresh sturgeon fillet, cut into
*   serving-size pieces*
Olive oil
Salt and white pepper, to taste
Fresh Tomato Sauce (page 92)

Start the coals in an outdoor grill and place the grill rack 4 to 6 inches above the ash-covered coals (allow the rack to heat thoroughly before putting the fish on).

Brush fish generously on all sides with olive oil and season with salt and pepper. Place salmon on first and cook until just flaky, about 2 minutes for each side. Remove to a warm platter. Place the tuna and sturgeon on next and cook the tuna about 2¼ minutes per side so it will be rare in the center; cook the sturgeon about 3 minutes per side, until flaky but still firm. Remove to a warm platter. (You can also cook the fish in a preheated oven broiler with the rack set 4 to 6 inches from the heat.)

Arrange the sturgeon and salmon around the tuna fillet. Serve with sauce.
SERVES 8 TO 10

WARM YELLOWFIN TUNA SALAD

You may use as many of the garnishes here as you have time for or want.

1 pound angel hair pasta
¼ cup vegetable oil
¼ cup plus 1 teaspoon rice wine vinegar
½ cup drained chopped canned pimiento
Green end of 6 green onions, chopped
¾ teaspoon salt
¼ teaspoon white pepper
12 small broccoli florets
1 medium cucumber, peeled, seeded, and
*   cut into 2 × ¼-inch strips*
1 teaspoon toasted sesame seeds

WASABI DRESSING
2 teaspoons wasabi powder
¼ cup water
1 egg yolk
2 cups vegetable oil
¼ cup rice wine vinegar
¼ teaspoon salt
⅛ teaspoon white pepper

ASSEMBLY
1 pound yellowfin tuna cut into ½-inch-
*   thick medallions*
¼ cup soy sauce
6 Bibb lettuce leaves
6 radicchio leaves
3 medium ripe tomatoes, cut into wedges

Cook pasta in salted water until al dente. Rinse in cold water and drain. Toss with oil, ¼ cup of the vinegar, pimiento, green onion tops, ½ teaspoon of the salt, and white pepper. Set aside.

Blanch broccoli florets in boiling salted water for 1 minute and immediately immerse in cold water. Drain and set aside. Toss cucumber with the remaining teaspoon of vinegar and ¼ teaspoon of salt. Sprinkle with sesame seeds, toss, and set aside.

To make dressing: Blend wasabi with

enough water to make a paste. Set aside for 15 minutes. Whisk egg yolk and add oil in a thin steady stream, whisking until all the oil is incorporated and mixture is the texture of mayonnaise. Stir in vinegar, salt, and pepper. Mix in wasabi.

To assemble salad: Preheat broiler and rub medallions with soy sauce. Let rest for 5 minutes. Meanwhile, arrange pasta, lettuces, tomatoes, cucumber, and broccoli as you wish on individual plates.

Put tuna on a baking sheet and broil for 1 minute on each side. Immediately place equal portions of tuna on each serving of pasta. Drizzle wasabi dressing over top. Serve extra on the side.

SERVES 6

FRESH TUNA SALAD

1 lemon, cut into 8 wedges
4 celery stalks, halved
4 medium carrots, peeled and cut into 4
    pieces each
10 black peppercorns
1 pound fresh tuna
1/2 cup plus 2 tablespoons chopped red onion
2 tablespoons capers, rinsed and drained
1/4 cup plus 2 tablespoons mayonnaise
1/2 cup plus 2 tablespoons chopped sweet
    pickles
Freshly ground black pepper

Put lemon, celery, carrots, and peppercorns in a large saucepan. Cover with cool water and bring to a boil. Add fish and bring back to the boil. Turn off heat and let sit until cool, 1 to 1½ hours.

Drain and place the tuna in a bowl, then shred with a fork. Discard lemon, celery, carrots, and peppercorns. Add remaining ingredients and toss to mix well.

SERVES 4

PASTA AND SEAFOOD SALAD

1/2 pound tubettini pasta
1 tablespoon plus 1 teaspoon olive oil
1 lemon, cut into 8 wedges
3 garlic cloves, roughly chopped
3/4 pound medium shrimp
3/4 pound fresh tuna
1 large onion, roughly chopped
1/2 cup finely chopped green onions (green
    part only)
1 cup minced dill pickle
Red Wine Vinaigrette (page 44)

Cook pasta until just tender. Drain, then run the pasta under cold water and drain again thoroughly. Place in a large bowl and toss with 1 teaspoon olive oil.

Place lemon and garlic in a saucepan and add 2 cups cold water. Bring to a boil, add shrimp, and cook until shrimp are bright pink, cooked through but still tender, about 3 minutes. Remove shrimp to a colander with a slotted spoon and run them under cold water. Drain well. Peel and devein the shrimp and add to the pasta.

Bring the cooking liquid back to a boil and add tuna. Return to a boil, then turn off heat. Leave tuna in the cooking liquid for 15 minutes, then remove it to a plate and let it cool.

Heat remaining 1 tablespoon olive oil in a cast-iron skillet over medium-high heat until hot but not smoking. Add onion and cook, stirring occasionally, until dark golden brown, 10 to 12 minutes. Set aside to cool.

Use a fork to shred the tuna. Add it, along with the onion, green onions, and pickle, to the pasta.

Pour about 4 tablespoons of the vinaigrette over the salad ingredients and toss.

SERVES 6 TO 8

TUNA AND SHRIMP SALAD

1 lemon, cut into 8 wedges
3 garlic cloves, roughly chopped
2 cups cold water
1½ pounds medium shrimp
1½ pounds fresh tuna
2 tablespoons capers, rinsed and drained
¼ cup coarsely chopped dill pickle
6 tablespoons chopped red onion

DRESSING
3 tablespoons minced red onion
3 tablespoons minced fresh dill
2 tablespoons minced dill pickle
3 tablespoons minced capers, plus 1 table-
    spoon brine
6 tablespoons olive oil
3 tablespoons red wine vinegar
1 teaspoon salt
¾ teaspoon black pepper
6 dashes Tabasco Sauce

Place lemon and garlic in a saucepan and add the cold water. Bring to a boil, add the shrimp, and cook until shrimp are bright pink, cooked through but still tender, about 3 minutes. Remove shrimp to a colander with a slotted spoon and run under cold water. Drain well. Peel and devein shrimp and place them in a large bowl.

Bring cooking liquid back to a boil and add tuna. Return to a boil, then turn off heat. Leave tuna in the cooking liquid for 15 minutes, then remove it to a plate and let it cool. Once cooled, flake the tuna and add it to the shrimp along with capers, pickle, and onion.

To make dressing: Combine ingredients in a jar with a tight-fitting lid. Shake well to combine. Pour dressing over salad ingredients and toss.

SERVES 6 TO 8

GRILLED TUNA STEAKS

The popularity of Japanese sushi bars in eastern cities must certainly have something to do with the fact that fresh tuna is becoming more readily available in our fish markets. I prefer red tuna.

6 tuna steaks, cut 1 inch thick (about
    2½ pounds)
Soy sauce
Safflower oil
Unsalted butter, at room temperature
Creole Sauce (page 346)
Lemon wedges and thin lemon slices

Put broiler rack at its lowest level and allow it to preheat for at least 15 minutes. This will help to prevent the fish from sticking to rack's surface when it is grilled. Meanwhile, rub both sides of the steaks liberally with soy sauce and then with safflower oil. Allow them to come to room temperature while the grill is heating.

When ready to cook, put fish on the hot rack and broil for 4 minutes. Carefully turn the steaks, using a wide spatula. Spread the uncooked side with softened butter and broil for another 4 minutes. Remove to a hot platter and serve with the Creole sauce, garnished with lemon wedges and slices.

SERVES 6

FILLETS

PISTACHIO-COATED FISH

Here is my Greek version of Louisiana nut-coated fish.

6 white fish fillets, ¹/₂ inch thick (about
*   2 pounds)*
Milk to cover
Salt and freshly ground black pepper, to
*   taste*
All-purpose flour for dredging
1 large egg, beaten with 3 to 4 tablespoons
*   milk*
1 cup fresh soft bread crumbs
1 cup coarsely ground pistachio nuts
3 tablespoons unsalted butter
1 tablespoon vegetable oil
Cucumber Sauce (page 7)
Lemon wedges

Place fish in a shallow bowl and cover with milk. Refrigerate, covered, for several hours.

Drain off milk and pat fillets dry. Salt and pepper on all sides and set aside.

Set up a little assembly line. Put about 1 cup of flour onto a sheet of wax paper, beside that a low bowl holding the beaten egg, and finally another sheet of wax paper with the bread crumbs and nuts tossed together. Next to these have another sheet of wax paper or a platter to hold the coated fillets.

Dredge each fillet in flour, shaking off excess. Next dip it into the egg mixture, letting excess drain off, and then put it into the nut mixture, coating it well by pressing it lightly. Carefully transfer to the platter.

Heat half the butter and oil in a large skillet over medium heat. When hot, slide in the first 3 fillets and brown on both sides, cooking until done, about 3 to 4 minutes in total. It is best not to turn these more than once so as not to break

off the crust. Add the remaining butter and oil and quickly cook the other 3 fillets, while keeping the first batch warm in a low oven.

Serve immediately with the sauce and lemon wedges.

SERVES 6

STEAMED AND SEARED WHITE FISH FILLETS

This method of cooking gives fish a marvelous flavor.

2 pounds flounder fillets
¹/₂ cup peanut oil
3 bunches green onions, with some of the
*   green, chopped in rings*
2 or more tablespoons soy sauce

Oil the surface of the poaching cradle of a long fish poacher and put a piece of foil in it, allowing the foil to extend over the sides so that you can get a hold on it. Grease this. Arrange the fillets in a layer, not thicker than 1¹/₂ inches. Make a long fish shape. Put in steamer over an inch of water. You can set the cradle on a couple of little custard cups or any other low heat-proof objects that will support it. Steam for about 15 minutes, or until fish is done in the middle.

While this is cooking, start heating the oil and have the serving platter, onions, and soy sauce ready. When the fish is done, slide it off the steamer tray onto the serving platter. You are more likely to be able to keep the fish intact if you slide it onto the dish with the foil underneath and then slide foil out. Turn up heat under oil; it must be smoking. If fish gets a little disarranged, pat back into shape. Drain off any water that might have accumulated in the platter. Sprinkle fish very generously with soy sauce (at least 2 tablespoons) and onions. Pour the smoking oil over the length of the fish and serve immediately with extra soy sauce on the side. To serve, cut fish into chunks.

SERVES 6

OVEN-FRIED FISH FILLETS

You may use almost any kind of firm white fish for this, from fluke to bass. I think the breading of the fillets is best done just before you cook them—although some people say that the fish may be breaded in advance and refrigerated.

Flour for dredging
1 egg, lightly beaten with 3 tablespoons milk
Fresh bread crumbs
6 white fish fillets (2 pounds)
Salt, to taste
Freshly ground black pepper, to taste
8 tablespoons (1 stick) unsalted butter,
*   melted*
Capers, rinsed and drained
Lemon slices

Preheat oven to 500 degrees.

Lay out a piece of wax paper and put the flour for dredging on it. Next to it put a shallow plate for the egg–milk mixture. Last, lay out another sheet of wax paper for the bread crumbs. Dredge fillets in the flour, shaking off any excess. Dip them in the egg mixture and let the excess drain off. Finally, coat with bread crumbs, pressing gently to make them adhere. Salt and pepper the top of the fish generously.

Line with foil a pan that is large enough to hold all the fillets in one layer. Put half of the butter in it and place in the oven. Let it heat for 4 or 5 minutes. Do not let it burn. Remove the pan from the oven and immediately place the fillets in it, seasoned side down. Pour the remaining butter over all. Salt and pepper the top. Bake for about 10 minutes, or until the fish flakes easily and is lightly browned. If you like it browner, run it under the broiler for just a couple of minutes—watching it all the while so it does not burn.

Garnish with a sprinkling of capers and the lemon slices.

SERVES 6

BROILED FISH WITH ONION–HOT PEPPER TOPPING

The oil in the pan is to keep the fish from sticking or burning on top, and the soy sauce should coat the fillets evenly on both sides. The quantity of herbs may be varied to suit your taste. Same with the butter. I don't use any salt because there's enough in the soy sauce.

2 tablespoons safflower oil
6 white fish fillets (about 2 pounds)
1/4 cup light soy sauce
1/4 cup coarsely chopped green onions, with
*   some of the green*
1 1/2 tablespoons coarsely chopped fresh
*   Italian flat-leaf parsley*
1 1/2 tablespoons coarsely chopped fresh dill
Juice of 1/2 lemon, plus wedges for garnish
3 tablespoons unsalted butter
Freshly ground black pepper, to taste
Lemon wedges
Onion–Hot Pepper Topping (page 360)

Preheat the broiler and place the tray on the lowest rung.

Line a shallow pan large enough to hold the 6 fillets in one layer with foil. Spread oil evenly in the pan, then add the fillets, turning and coating both sides. Rub both sides with soy sauce. Arrange fish skin side down. Sprinkle with green onions, parsley, and dill. (It's better to have too much of this herb mixture than too little.) Squeeze the lemon over all. Dot with butter and add pepper.

Broil without turning until fish just flakes, 3 to 5 minutes depending on its thickness. The herbs may blacken slightly in spots, but that is all right. Lift directly onto the individual warmed dinner plates with a spatula. Garnish with lemon wedges and serve with the Onion–Hot Pepper Topping.

SERVES 6

BAKED FISH FILLETS

When you test fish for doneness, be sure you test the thickest part of the largest fillet you are cooking. A minute or two can make the difference between a properly cooked fish and an underdone one.

6 mild white fish fillets, such as lemon sole
(about 6 ounces each)
6 tablespoons soy sauce
1 tablespoon canola oil
Freshly ground black pepper, to taste
1/4 cup finely chopped green onion
1/4 cup coarsely chopped fresh dill
3 tablespoons cold unsalted butter, cut into
18 or more small pieces
Fresh lemon juice
Lemon wedges

Preheat oven to 350 degrees. Line 2 low-sided baking pans with foil and spray with vegetable oil spray.

Place fillets, skin side down, on a sheet of wax paper and rub each generously with soy sauce, using about 1 tablespoon of soy on each. Rub lightly with the oil. Place fillets, skin side down, in the prepared baking pans and season with pepper. Toss the green onion and dill together and sprinkle each fillet with an equal amount. Dot with butter, then squeeze a little lemon juice over each.

Bake for about 15 minutes, or until the fish just starts to flake. Serve on heated plates with a wedge or two of lemon.

SERVES 6

SMOKED AND CURED FISH

SMOKED FISH CAKES WITH CAPER SAUCE

This is one of those first courses that could easily become a main course. You might want to use a fruit salsa with it instead of the Caper Sauce called for here.

20 to 24 ounces smoked white fish, such as
mahi mahi
1 1/2 teaspoons Creole Seasoning
1 tablespoon Creole mustard
3 tablespoons mayonnaise
1 teaspoon chopped rinsed and drained
capers
2 tablespoons chopped green onion tops
1 egg
2 tablespoons dried bread crumbs
1/4 teaspoon salt
1/4 teaspoon white pepper
Caper Sauce (page 346)

Preheat oven to 350 degrees.

Crumble fish, discarding any skin or bones, into small chunks (do not crumble too fine). In a small bowl mix together the Creole Seasoning, mustard, mayonnaise, capers, and green onion. Add fish and mix lightly. Break the egg over mixture. Sprinkle bread crumbs, salt, and pepper over all and mix lightly with your hands. Form into 6 cakes about 2 inches in diameter and 1 inch thick. Do not compress; just pat together.

Place on an ungreased baking sheet and bake for 10 to 12 minutes, until set and just barely beginning to turn color.

Serve hot from the oven with the sauce.

MAKES 6

SMOKED FISH WITH ROASTED PEPPERS AND ZUCCHINI

I am very fond of this sort of "composed" first course. You really could use any vegetable you like for this, from grilled asparagus to small new potatoes boiled in their skins. Pickles and olives may also be added.

3/4 to 1 pound smoked trout or other white
  fish, including head and tail
3 tablespoons prepared horseradish or
  mayonnaise
1 tablespoon light cream
Lemon juice, to taste
Grated lemon zest, to taste
3 small zucchini, split in half lengthwise
Olive oil
Freshly ground black pepper
Freshly grated parmesan
1 large red bell pepper, roasted, peeled, and
  seeded (see Note, page 74), cut into 6
  wide strips
Endive leaves (optional)
Lemon wedges, seeded (optional)

Slice fish across the backbone into sections several inches wide, discarding head and tail. Remove skin and place fish slices on individual plates. Mix horseradish and cream. Add lemon juice. Top each section of fish with a dab of horseradish sauce and sprinkle with grated zest.

Meanwhile, score cut zucchini and smear with olive oil. Sprinkle with black pepper. Place under the broiler, and when they start turning golden, sprinkle with parmesan. Place under broiler again until golden. Set aside. These should be served at room temperature.

To serve, put half a zucchini on each plate with the fish and top with a strip of roasted pepper. Garnish with endive and lemon wedges, if desired.

SERVES 6

SMOKED SALMON SALAD

8 ounces pre-sliced smoked salmon
3 heads Belgian endive, trimmed, halved,
  and julienned (about 3 cups)
2 cups arugula leaves, washed and dried
1/2 cup julienne hothouse cucumber
3 tablespoons olive oil
5 tablespoons lemon juice
Freshly ground black pepper, to taste
3 tablespoons finely snipped fresh chives or
  minced green onion

Do not stack the salmon, but separate each slice and cut into strips approximately 3/8 inch thick.

Put endive, arugula, and cucumber in a large mixing bowl. Using a small jar with a tight-fitting lid, mix olive oil, lemon juice, and pepper, shaking vigorously to combine. Toss salad greens with dressing, add three quarters of the salmon, and toss again. Divide onto individual plates and garnish with chives and remaining strips of salmon.

SERVES 6

BREADS, ROLLS, BISCUITS, AND MUFFINS

TRUTH TO TELL, I'VE NEVER BEEN interested enough to experiment more than a couple of time with bread making—and now that really good breads are available in most markets, I know I'll probably never get around to it. But I'm delighted that others do. This focus on quality breads is one of the best recent contributions to the pleasures of baked goods—and while they've been at it, bakers have extended their interest to include rolls and muffins as well, both sweet and plain. ✦ I may not bake bread, but like any son of the South, I'm a biscuit-maker by heritage. And the same goes for cornbread, spoon bread, and simple rolls —and those easy-to-stir-up muffins, both savory and sweet. If I were pressed to venture a prediction, it would be that the muffin market—along with this whole category—is ripe for a whole lot of innovation and experimentation.

BREAD

SOURDOUGH BREAD

You must make the sourdough mix for this bread at least twenty-four hours in advance. The only thing hard about this recipe is explaining how to handle the dough, which is very sticky—and that's not even crucial. You might also make this into a round loaf, baking it on an oiled baking sheet.

> 1 cup warm water (105° to 105° F.)
> 1 package active dry yeast
> 1/2 teaspoon sugar
> Olive oil
> 3 cups unbleached all-purpose flour, plus extra for dusting
> 2 teaspoons salt
> 2 tablespoons vegetable oil
> 1 cup Wild Sourdough Starter (see page 318)

Put the water in a small bowl, sprinkle yeast over, and stir in sugar. Let stand until foamy, about 5 minutes.

Generously oil two 8½ × 4½-inch loaf pans with olive oil. Set aside.

Pour yeast into a large bowl and mix with all other ingredients. When well combined, spread additional flour on a clean surface and turn the dough out onto it. Sprinkle the flour over the top and work a bit more into the sides. Roll it around to make a long sausage shape approximately the length of the oiled pans. Brush off excess flour, divide dough in half, and place in the 2 pans. The dough is very damp so you aren't really kneading it in the conventional sense, but rather just pressing a bit of flour into it and flopping it around.

Let dough in the pans rise in a warm, draft-free spot until it comes near the tops of the pans, about 30 minutes or more. If you have an oven kept warm by a pilot light, that is a good place in which to let the dough rise.

Preheat oven to 400 degrees and bake loaves until golden brown on top, about 30 minutes.

MAKES 2 LOAVES

MONKEY BREAD

Texans love this simple bread, and you'll love it too.

> 1 cup milk
> 1/2 cup plus 5 tablespoons unsalted butter
> 1/4 cup sugar
> 1 teaspoon salt
> 1 package active dry yeast
> 3½ cups unbleached all-purpose flour

Place milk, ½ cup butter, sugar, and salt in a small saucepan. Warm over low heat just until butter melts. Set aside to cool down to about 110 degrees, then stir in yeast. Put flour in a large bowl and pour in yeast mixture. Stir to combine. Cover with a clean kitchen towel and let rise until doubled in bulk in a warm, draft-free spot, about 1 hour and 15 minutes.

Melt the remaining butter. Punch down the dough and roll into golf-ball-size balls. Roll each in the melted butter and place in a 10-inch tube pan. Cover and let rise 45 minutes, until doubled in bulk.

Preheat oven to 400 degrees.

Bake for 25 minutes, or until golden on top. Let cool for about 5 minutes before turning out onto a warmed serving plate.

SERVES 8 TO 12

NEW ORLEANS FRENCH BREAD

Here it is, folks—a proven winner! Special thanks to the folks at the G. H. Leidenheimer Baking Company for this recipe.

2 cups warm (105° to 110° F.) water
2 tablespoons sugar
2 packages active dry yeast
2 tablespoons solid vegetable shortening
6½ cups bread flour
1 tablespoon salt

Place the water in the bowl of a heavy-duty electric mixer fitted with a dough hook. Add 1 tablespoon sugar and sprinkle with the yeast. Let sit for about 15 minutes, until the mixture is bubbling. Add the remaining 1 tablespoon of sugar, the shortening, and 5 cups of flour. Mix until a dough starts to form. Add the salt and the remaining flour as needed until the dough forms a ball and pulls away from the sides of the bowl. Continue to knead with the dough hook for 10 minutes.

Turn the dough out onto a lightly floured board and knead by hand for a minute or two, until dough is smooth and elastic. Return it to the mixing bowl, cover with plastic wrap, and set in a warm, draft-free corner to rise for 1½ hours, or until doubled in size.

Punch the dough down, then divide it into four balls. Cover these with a clean kitchen towel and let them rest for 15 minutes. Form each ball into a 16 × 3-inch loaf. Place the loaves on baking sheets, cover them with a damp cloth, and set aside to rise for 1½ hours.

Preheat oven to 375 degrees.

Make 3 diagonal slashes on the top of each loaf. Place in the oven and bake for about 30 minutes, until golden brown. Cool on racks.

MAKES 4 LOAVES

GARLIC BREAD

This is how they make garlic bread at the famous Commander's Palace restaurant in New Orleans. It has been a favorite there for years.

1 loaf French bread
8 tablespoons (1 stick) unsalted butter (or a
    combination of butter and margarine)
2 garlic cloves, mashed to a purée
¼ cup finely chopped fresh dill
¼ cup freshly grated parmesan

Preheat oven to 375 degrees.

Slice bread lengthwise. Melt butter in a small skillet, add garlic, and heat gently for 2 minutes. Do not brown. Brush the garlic–butter mixture generously over the cut sides of the bread halves. Sprinkle with the dill and cheese. Place on a baking sheet and bake until golden, 5 to 8 minutes. Cut each half crosswise into 1-inch slices.

SERVES 6

ENGLISH MUFFIN LOAF

George Bay of the famous Bay's English Muffins in Chicago had his kitchen create this recipe for me. It is as delicious as their muffins.

¼ cup instant mashed potato flakes
2 cups milk, scalded
1 package active dry yeast
½ cup warm water (105° to 115° F.)
Pinch of sugar
6 cups bread flour
2 tablespoons sugar
1 tablespoon salt
4 tablespoons (½ stick) unsalted butter,
  melted and cooled
White cornmeal

Place instant potatoes in a small bowl, add scalded milk, and stir to dissolve. In another bowl, combine yeast, water, and the pinch of sugar. Stir well and set aside.

In a large mixer bowl, combine flour, sugar, and salt. Add potato mixture, yeast mixture, and butter. Stir with a spatula until flour is moistened. Using a mixer dough hook, knead mixture for 10 minutes. It should form a ball and pull away from the bottom of the container. Place dough in a fresh, buttered bowl. Cover tightly and let rise in a warm place until doubled in volume, about 1 hour.

Thinly butter two 8 × 4-inch loaf pans. Add a small amount of the cornmeal to the pans and rotate to evenly coat the interiors. Knock out any excess. Set aside.

Punch down and divide dough into 2 equal pieces. On a sparingly floured board, roll out one piece of dough into an 8 × 14-inch rectangle. Brush off any excess flour, then, starting at the narrow end, roll into a loaf shape, pinching bottom seam to seal. Place dough, seam side down, in prepared pan. Repeat with remaining dough. Cover with plastic wrap and let rise in a warm place until dough extends 2 inches above pan.

Meanwhile, preheat oven to 375 degrees.

Bake loaves for 35 to 40 minutes or until golden brown. Loaves should make a hollow sound when tapped. Let cool on a wire rack.

MAKES 2 LOAVES

SUNFLOWER BREAD

The recipe for this nutty-tasting bread came from my cohort Lee Klein.

½ cup cracked wheat or bulgur
½ cup rolled oats
¼ cup firmly packed light brown sugar
2 teaspoons salt
2 tablespoons solid vegetable shortening
¾ cup boiling water
2 packages active dry yeast
1 cup warm milk (100° to 115° F.)
2 tablespoons sesame seeds, toasted
2 tablespoons poppy seeds, toasted
1 cup raw sunflower seeds, toasted
¼ cup instant polenta or yellow cornmeal
1 cup whole wheat flour
1½ cups unbleached all-purpose flour

Put cracked wheat, oats, brown sugar, salt, and shortening in a large mixing bowl. Pour the boiling water over this and stir to melt the shortening. Set aside.

Sprinkle yeast over the warm milk in a small bowl and set aside for a few minutes to proof. Add the yeast to the cracked wheat mixture and stir in the seeds and polenta. Mix well. Add whole wheat flour and mix well. Add 1¼ cups of all-purpose flour and mix until incorporated. The dough will still be a bit sticky.

Sprinkle some of the extra flour on a board and turn the dough out onto it. Knead, gradually incorporating remaining flour, until dough is elastic, about 10 to 15 minutes. Gather into a ball and put in an oiled bowl. Cover with a clean kitchen towel or plastic wrap and let rise in a warm, draft-free spot until doubled in bulk, about 45 minutes.

Preheat oven to 350 degrees.

Punch down dough. Turn out onto a board and roll into a rectangle about 7 × 12 inches. Starting at the narrow end, roll the dough. Fit it into an oiled 9 × 5 × 3-inch bread pan. Cover and let rise again until dough is above sides of the pan, about 20 minutes.

Bake for about 1 hour. Loaf will be light golden and will sound hollow when rapped with your knuckle. Turn it out of the pan immediately and cool on a rack.

MAKES 1 LOAF

CAJUN THREE-PEPPER BREAD

This spicy bread is wonderful when buttered and served with soup.

8 cups unbleached all-purpose flour or bread flour
3/4 cup polenta or coarse cornmeal, plus extra for sprinkling
2 tablespoons dried parsley flakes
2 tablespoons granulated garlic
2 tablespoons active dry yeast (rapid-rise, if possible)
1 3/4 tablespoons salt
1 teaspoon freshly ground black pepper
1 cup finely chopped roasted, peeled, and seeded red bell pepper (see Note, page 74)
1/4 cup Tabasco Sauce or Louisiana Hot Sauce
Approximately 3 cups water

Combine flour, polenta, parsley flakes, garlic, yeast, salt, and pepper. Add 2 1/2 cups water and mix well. Stir in red bell pepper and Tabasco. Knead for about 8 minutes, or until a soft tacky dough if formed, using the remaining 1/2 cup water if needed. Dough should be tacky by not sticky.

Place dough in a clean greased bowl, cover with plastic wrap, and let rise approximately 1 1/2 hours in a warm, draft-free spot. Punch down and let rise again for another hour.

Divide the dough into 4 balls and roll out into rectangles. Fold each into thirds, pinching seams closed, and turn over, seam side down. Roll out again and fold again. The rectangles should be getting longer. Repeat one more time and pinch off seam carefully. You should have 4 baguette shapes. Sprinkle polenta or cornmeal on 2 baking sheets and put 2 loaves on each, at least 2 inches apart. Let rise 1 hour, lightly covered with a clean kitchen towel.

Preheat oven to 425 degrees.

Make 3 diagonal slashes across the top of each loaf with a serrated knife. Spray tops with cold water from a flower mister. Place loaves in the oven and spray 3 more times, every 2 minutes. Bake, checking in about 10 minutes after the last spraying. Bread should turn deep golden; when it does, turn heat off and let cool for 10 minutes more in the oven. Remove from oven and let rest at least 15 minutes before cutting.

MAKES 4 LOAVES

VARIATION

For Oreganato Bread, omit the bell pepper and Tabasco and add 3 tablespoons dried oregano. Follow the directions for Cajun Three-Pepper Bread.

297

SCOTCH UNKNEADED BREAD

Margaret Brown, a British friend of mine, gave me this recipe. It is an easy way to make bread because it requires no kneading and not much rising time. The bread is dense and very good toasted.

1/2 pound (about 1 3/4 cups) whole wheat flour
1/2 pound (about 1 3/4 cups) unbleached all-purpose flour
2 teaspoons salt
2 packages active dry yeast
1 tablespoon sugar
2 tablespoons dark molasses
1 cup hot water
1/2 cup chopped walnuts

Stir flours, salt, yeast, and sugar together. Dissolve molasses in the hot water and stir into the flour mixture. Add walnuts and mix well to form a ball. Put in a greased bowl, lightly covered with a clean kitchen towel, and place in a warm, draft-free spot. Let rise to about half again its original bulk, approximately 45 minutes.

Preheat oven to 400 degrees. Grease an 8 × 4-inch loaf pan.

Turn into loaf pan and bake for about 35 minutes. Brush with water and bake until set and very lightly golden, another 5 minutes.

MAKES 1 LOAF

SESAME BREADSTICKS

These are fun to do.

1 1/2 teaspoons active dry yeast
1 cup warm water (105° to 115° F.)
1 teaspoon sugar
1/2 teaspoon salt
2 1/2 cups unbleached all-purpose flour, approximately
White sesame seeds
1 large egg white
1 1/2 teaspoons water

Place yeast, warm water, and sugar in a large bowl. Mix. When yeast has dissolved, add salt and 2 cups of the flour. You want a fairly stiff dough. If mixture is still sticky, add the balance of the flour a little at a time. Turn out onto a floured surface and knead for 7 or 8 minutes, or knead in a mixer with a dough hook. Return to bowl and cover with plastic wrap. Let triple in bulk in a warm, draft-free place; it will take several hours.

Punch down and let rise for another 30 minutes.

Preheat oven to 450 degrees. Generously grease 2 baking sheets.

Divide dough into 8 parts, and roll each into a stick about 16 to 18 inches long. If you mess up one of them, form dough into a ball and start over. Cut each stick in half crosswise. Sprinkle very generously with seeds and press them in, or roll the sticks in the seeds. Place breadsticks on baking sheets and let rest, covered by clean kitchen towels, for 30 minutes.

Just before baking, mix egg white and water, and paint the top of each stick. (This is really optional, but will make the sticks browner.) Bake until golden, about 15 to 17 minutes.

MAKES ABOUT 16 BREADSTICKS

TOMATO GOUGÈRE

People who have never made or had this bread are amazed when they discover how uncomplicated it is to prepare. Delicious and impressive for a cocktail party!

2 ounces Oven-Dried Tomatoes (page 142)

PÂTE À CHOUX
   8 tablespoons (1 stick) unsalted butter
   Pinch of salt
   1 cup sifted unbleached all-purpose flour
   4 eggs, at room temperature

   4 ounces gruyère, cut into small dice (about ⅔ cup)

Preheat oven to 425 degrees and grease a baking sheet.

   Cover tomatoes with hot water and soak for about 10 minutes. Drain, dry, and chop fine. Set aside.

   To make pâte à choux: Put 1 cup water, the butter, and salt in a saucepan. Bring to a boil. Dump in the flour all at once and stir vigorously over medium heat until the paste begins to pull away from the sides of the pan. Off the heat, beat in eggs, one at a time.

   Stir in the tomatoes and cheese. Place heaping tablespoons of dough just touching in a small circle on the baking sheet. Keep adding to the outside of the circle until all of the dough is used. Bake for 10 minutes and turn the heat down to 350 degrees. Continue to bake until golden, about 20 more minutes. Serve warm.
SERVES 8

DEEP-FRIED SCALLION BREAD

The only thing to remember about breads of this sort is that they toughen up as they stand, so plan to serve this hot. Fortunately, this dough can be prepared ahead and then refrigerated, to be used when you are ready to cook. I have left it at this point for up to five hours.

   10 ounces (2 cups) unbleached all-purpose flour
   1 teaspoon salt
   1 teaspoon freshly ground black pepper
   1 cup boiling water
   1 cup chopped green onions, with some of the green
   Safflower oil for frying

Place flour, salt, and pepper in a food processor with a metal blade. Turn on machine and pour boiling water through the top in a steady stream. Continue to process for about another minute. The dough should be shiny and elastic. Wrap tightly in plastic wrap and let rest at room temperature for about 30 minutes.

   Meanwhile, sauté green onions in a tablespoon of oil until they are wilted, about 5 minutes.

   Turn dough out onto a floured surface and roll out with a floured pin into a rectangle approximately 14 × 16 inches. Spoon green onions evenly over dough and roll up jelly roll fashion. Cut into 12 rounds and flatten each with the heel of the hand. (These can be refrigerated at this point to be fried later.)

   Heat 1 inch of safflower oil in a heavy skillet until it is very hot but not smoking and fry each round until golden. Turn once. These cook very quickly, so be careful not to burn them.
MAKES 12 PUFFS

PARMESAN ONION PUFFS

Considering how impressive these little puffs look, they are remarkably easy to prepare.

2 cups coarsely chopped onions
4 tablespoons (¹/₂ stick) unsalted butter
Pâte à Choux (page 299)
1 cup freshly grated parmesan
Milk
Additional grated parmesan for topping

Preheat oven to 400 degrees and grease 2 baking sheets.

Sauté onions in butter until wilted, about 5 minutes. Set aside.

Make the pâte à choux as directed. Combine the parmesan with the dough and mix in the sautéed onions.

Drop heaping tablespoons of dough onto the baking sheets. Brush tops with milk and then sprinkle with additional parmesan. Bake until golden and puffy, about 35 to 40 minutes.

MAKES ABOUT 18 PUFFS

SKILLET PEPPER BREAD

2 cups unbleached all-purpose flour
1 teaspoon baking soda
1 teaspoon salt
³/₄ teaspoon finely ground black pepper
1 cup milk, approximately
Several tablespoons unsalted butter, slightly softened

Sift flour, baking soda, salt, and pepper into a large bowl. Stir in ³/₄ cup of the milk. Mix well; you want to wind up with a stiff dough, so add the balance of the milk a little at a time. Use it all or just a portion of it.

Heat an ungreased iron skillet or a griddle.

Pinch off walnut-size pieces of dough and roll them out until thin on a floured surface. Spread the center of each rolled-out circle with butter. Fold circle over and roll out thin again.

Test the skillet or griddle by sprinkling it with a few pinches of flour. If the flour immediately begins to brown, it is ready. Add circles of dough, allowing room to turn them. Keep turning until the dough puffs and browns. These will brown unevenly. Serve hot.

MAKES 16 TO 18 PUFFS

ROLLS

QUICK BUTTERMILK ROLLS

This recipe came to me from my friend Ann Criswell of *The Houston Chronicle*.

1 package active dry yeast
2 tablespoons warm water (about 110° F.)
³/₄ cup buttermilk, heated to lukewarm
2 tablespoons sugar
¹/₄ cup melted vegetable shortening or vegetable oil
¹/₂ teaspoon salt
2¹/₄ cups unbleached all-purpose flour
¹/₄ teaspoon baking soda
2 tablespoons unsalted butter

Combine yeast and water and set aside to proof. Mix the warmed buttermilk, sugar, shortening, and salt. Sift flour with the baking soda into a large bowl. Stir yeast into the buttermilk mixture and pour onto the flour. Stir to mix well and let rest 10 minutes covered with a clean kitchen towel. Roll out to ¹/₂ inch thick and form into desired shapes.

Preheat oven to 425 degrees. Melt butter in a baking pan and place rolls in, turning to coat the tops. Let rise 30 minutes.

Bake until golden, about 10 to 12 minutes.

MAKES ABOUT 24 ROLLS

FRENCH ROLLS

The French call these *petits pains*—little breads. Make the dough for these in the food processor.

1½ packages active dry yeast
1¼ cups warm water (about 105° to 110° F.)
2 tablespoons unsalted butter
3½ cups unbleached all-purpose flour
1 teaspoon salt

Blend yeast with ¼ cup of the warm water. Set aside. Heat the remaining 1 cup water and the butter together in a small saucepan until butter melts. Set aside to cool slightly.

Meanwhile, place flour and salt into a food processor and pulse a few times. Add the dissolved yeast and the butter mixture. Process until dough forms a ball.

On a lightly floured surface, knead dough for several minutes, then place in a lightly buttered, straight-sided bowl. Cover with a clean kitchen towel and let rise for 1 hour in a warm, draft-free spot until doubled in bulk.

Turn out dough onto a floured surface and knead gently a few minutes. Return to the bowl and let rise again, for 1 hour, or until doubled in bulk.

Punch dough down and turn out once more, dividing into 10 equal balls. Flatten each ball to make a circle about ¼ inch thick. Fold one side of the circle about two thirds of the way over the other side. Give the folded dough a quarter turn and fold *that* side two thirds of the way over the opposite side. Repeat until you have gone all the way around and have a small, fat circle of dough. Place folded side down on a baking sheet. Repeat with other circles, placing them several inches apart on the sheet. Handle dough quickly and lightly. Cover and let rise for 1½ hours.

Preheat oven to 450 degrees. Place rolls in the oven and, after a minute, toss 4 or 5 ice cubes onto the bottom of the oven to give you a bit of steam. After another 5 minutes, toss in another 4 ice cubes. Bake for another 10 minutes, then turn heat back to 400 degrees and bake for an additional 20 minutes, until tops are golden.

MAKES 10 ROLLS

GREEN PEPPERCORN MUSTARD ROLLS

The hint of green peppercorn mustard gives these rolls a nice snap. They are good with any hearty flavored soup.

1 package active dry yeast
1 teaspoon sugar
1 cup warm water (105° to 115° F.)
⅔ cup green peppercorn mustard
4 cups unbleached all-purpose flour
1½ teaspoons salt
Melted butter

Put yeast and sugar in a small bowl with the water. When dissolved, stir in mustard and 1 cup of the flour to make a paste. Mix well. Add the rest of the flour and salt, mixing as you go. Turn out onto a floured surface and knead dough until smooth and elastic, about 7 minutes.

Grease a large crockery bowl and place the dough in it. Cover with a clean kitchen towel. Let dough rise in a warm, draft-free spot until at least doubled in bulk, about 1 hour.

Punch the dough down and form it into 18 round balls. Place them on a greased baking sheet and let rise once again, covered, until doubled in size.

Meanwhile, preheat oven to 350 degrees.

Bake rolls until golden, about 20 minutes. The rolls can be brushed with melted butter during the last few minutes of baking to make them browner.

MAKES 18 ROLLS

CLOVERLEAF ROLLS

1/4 cup instant mashed potato flakes
2 cups milk, scalded
1 package active dry yeast
1/2 cup warm water (105° to 115° F.)
Pinch of sugar
6 cups bread flour
1 tablespoon salt
4 tablespoons unsalted butter, melted and
*   cooled*
White cornmeal

Place instant potatoes in a small bowl. Add scalded milk and stir to dissolve. In another bowl, combine yeast, water, and sugar. Stir well and set aside to proof until frothy, 6 to 8 minutes.

In the bowl of a heavy-duty electric mixer fitted with a dough hook, combine flour and salt, then add the potato mixture, yeast mixture, and butter. Stir with a rubber spatula until the flour is moistened. Work the dough at medium speed with the dough hook for 10 minutes. It should form a ball and pull away from the bottom of the bowl. Place the dough in a clean, lightly oiled bowl. Cover with a clean kitchen towel and set aside in a warm, draft-free place to rise until doubled in volume, about 1 hour.

Lightly butter the insides of 24 large muffin cups. Sprinkle a small amount of the cornmeal in the cups and rotate to evenly coat the interiors.

Punch the dough down; break off small pieces and roll them into small balls. Place 3 small balls of dough into each buttered muffin tin. Cover loosely with plastic wrap and set aside in a warm place to rise until almost doubled, about 1 hour.

Preheat oven to 375 degrees.

Bake rolls for 35 to 40 minutes or until golden brown. Remove rolls from muffin tins and let cool on a wire rack.

MAKES 24 LARGE ROLLS

VARIATION
Stir in 4 cups sautéed diced onions with the potato and yeast mixtures.

ICEBOX ROLLS
Soft dinner rolls were very popular when I was growing up. They are easy to prepare, and the leftover dough can be refrigerated and used for up to three to four days.

1 package active dry yeast
1 cup warm water (about 105° to 110° F.)
1/2 cup butter, margarine, or a combination
1/4 cup sugar
1 egg
1 teaspoon salt
3 cups unbleached all-purpose flour

Preheat oven to 350 degrees.

Dissolve yeast in warm water. Cream shortening with sugar and beat in egg. Add yeast mixture and beat. This will not combine completely but mix well. Add salt and flour, working in until a smooth dough is formed. Knead for a very few minutes. Grease the surface of the dough with a little melted shortening, cover very tightly with plastic wrap, and put in refrigerator.

When ready to use dough, pull off 12 golf-ball-size pieces and roll to make balls. Refrigerate rest of dough to use another time. Put on greased baking sheet, cover lightly, and let rise for up to 1 1/2 hours in a warm place. Bake for 15 minutes.

MAKES 12 ROLLS

BISCUITS

BISCUITS

2 cups all-purpose flour
4 teaspoons baking powder
¹/₄ teaspoon salt
1 teaspoon sugar
5 tablespoons solid vegetable shortening,
    chilled
³/₄ to 1 cup cold milk, plus additional for tops

Preheat oven to 450 degrees.

Put all the dry ingredients in a food processor and give it a few whirls to mix. Add shortening and process, turning off and on a few times, until mixture is the texture of coarse meal. (You may also cut in the shortening with a pastry blender or 2 knives if you don't have a food processor.) Pour in milk through the feed tube with the motor running, until mixture forms a ball. Stop immediately and roll dough out on a floured surface with a floured rolling pin to a thickness of about ¹/₄ inch. Cut into 2-inch biscuits. Gather up the scraps and form into a ball, flatten, and cut more biscuits until all dough is used.

Place on ungreased baking sheets and paint tops with milk, if you like, to make them brown more. Bake for 15 minutes or until golden brown.

These are usually split and buttered in the kitchen while they are still very hot. (If you don't serve them right away, keep in a warm oven.)

MAKES 36 BISCUITS

BEATEN BISCUITS

The name of these biscuits comes from their method of preparation. It is quite tedious to do by hand, so I use a food processor. I would not even suggest making them if you do not have such a machine.

3 cups all-purpose flour
2 teaspoons salt
12 tablespoons (1¹/₂ sticks) unsalted butter,
    cut into small pieces
³/₄ cup ice-cold milk

Preheat oven to 350 degrees.

Combine flour and salt in the container of a food processor fitted with a metal blade. Put butter in with the dry ingredients. Process until the mixture resembles coarse cornmeal. Remove top of machine and sprinkle the milk in. Process until the mixture makes a ball. Continue processing for 2 more minutes. This will shake the machine around a bit because of the volume of the dough.

At the end of the processing time, remove the dough, which should be shiny and elastic, to a well-floured surface. Turn to flour both sides. Roll out to ¹/₄-inch thickness using a floured rolling pin. Smooth flour evenly onto the rolled-out dough and then fold it over on itself. Make sure there is still flour on the surface under the dough. Cut into 1¹/₂-inch biscuits and place on an ungreased baking sheet. Prick the tops with a fork. Bake for 25 minutes, until golden brown.

Note: The reason for folding the dough over on itself before cutting is so that the baked biscuits will come apart easily for buttering.

Leftover biscuits are good cold with a bit of mustard and ham sandwiched in them.

MAKES ABOUT 24 BISCUITS

SHORTCAKE BISCUITS I

Butter these lightly when you split them.

2 cups all-purpose flour
2½ teaspoons baking powder
1 teaspoon salt
6 tablespoons cold unsalted butter, cut into
*   small pieces*
¾ cup milk

Preheat oven to 450 degrees.

Mix dry ingredients in a bowl and cut in butter with 2 knives or a pastry blender until mixture has a coarse texture. Stir in milk all at once, mixing quickly and well. Turn out onto a floured surface and knead briefly. Roll out ½ inch thick on a floured surface. Cut into eight 3-inch rounds and place on an ungreased baking sheet. Bake until golden, about 13 to 15 minutes.

MAKES 8 BISCUITS

SHORTCAKE BISCUITS II

2 cups all-purpose flour
2 tablespoons sugar
¼ teaspoon salt
4 teaspoons baking powder
2 large eggs, lightly beaten
4 tablespoons cold unsalted butter, cut into
*   small pieces*
⅓ to ½ cup heavy cream

Preheat oven to 400 degrees.

Mix dry ingredients quickly. Stir in eggs. Cut in the butter with a pastry blender or 2 knives, then mix in enough cream to make a dry dough. Roll out ½ inch thick on a floured surface and cut into 8 biscuits. Place on an ungreased baking sheet and bake until golden, about 12 to 15 minutes.

MAKES 8 BISCUITS

BUTTERMILK BISCUITS

A Texas friend, David Tiller, passed this recipe on to me; it was his mother's. The baking method—in a preheated dish—gives them a wonderfully crisp crust, perfect with gravy.

2 cups all-purpose flour
1 tablespoon baking powder
1 teaspoon salt
½ teaspoon baking soda
8 tablespoons butter, margarine, or a
*   combination*
1 cup buttermilk

Preheat oven to 450 degrees. Coat 2 glass baking dishes with vegetable spray and put them in to heat.

Combine dry ingredients in a large bowl. Cut in the butter with a pastry blender or 2 knives. Mix in buttermilk. Place on a floured surface and pat down to ½ inch thick. Cut into 12 biscuits, gathering up the scraps and patting them down again to make the final cuts. Remove heated dishes from the oven. Put biscuits in, touching one another, and bake until golden, about 12 to 15 minutes.

MAKES 12 BISCUITS

DROP BUTTERMILK BISCUITS

These biscuits are simple to prepare because they do not require rolling out and cutting before being baked. After the butter has been cut in, they only need a few quick strokes and they are ready to be dropped onto a baking sheet.

2 cups all-purpose flour
1 teaspoon salt
2 teaspoons baking powder
½ teaspoon baking soda
6 tablespoons (¾ stick) cold unsalted butter,
*   cut into 6 pieces*
1½ cups buttermilk

Preheat oven to 450 degrees.

Sift together into a bowl the flour, salt, baking powder, and baking soda. Add butter and blend with a pastry blender or 2 knives until butter is the size of peas. Add buttermilk all at once and stir just enough to mix.

Drop by tablespoonfuls onto an ungreased cookie sheet. Bake for 12 to 15 minutes, until golden brown.

MAKES 18 BISCUITS

ANGEL BISCUITS

These biscuits are just a variation of the old Icebox Rolls (page 302). The dough can be used this way or to make sweet rolls. If these taste too sweet, leave out all but one tablespoon of the sugar next time.

1 package active dry yeast
2 tablespoons warm water
5 cups all-purpose flour
4 tablespoons sugar
1 teaspoon baking powder
1 teaspoon baking soda
1 1/2 teaspoons salt
8 tablespoons (1 stick) unsalted butter
8 tablespoons (1 stick) margarine
2 cups buttermilk
Extra melted butter

Sprinkle yeast over warm water in a small bowl. Sift together flour, sugar, baking powder, baking soda, and salt. In the meantime, melt butter and margarine over very low heat or a "flame tamer"— you do not want it to brown.

Put sifted dry ingredients in a large bowl and add the yeast. Mix. (This will not mix very well, but that is all right.) Next add the butter–margarine and buttermilk. Mix carefully. You will wind up with a very sticky dough. Cover this with a clean kitchen towel and refrigerate until you are ready to use it.

Preheat oven to 400 degrees.

Take out a third of the dough and knead it on a floured surface for about 10 minutes. This is important, because the kneading heats up the dough and starts the yeast working.

Roll out as you would ordinary biscuits, to about 1/2 inch thick. Fold each one over and pinch it shut. Brush with additional melted butter and place on a generously greased baking sheet. Bake for about 12 minutes until golden. Continue with remaining dough.

MAKES SLIGHTLY MORE THAN 3 DOZEN BISCUITS

COTTAGE CHEESE BISCUITS

This recipe makes a very soft and doughy biscuit, which is marvelous toasted.

2 cups all-purpose flour
1 teaspoon salt
2 1/2 teaspoons baking powder
6 tablespoons (3/4 stick) cold unsalted butter
1 1/2 cups small-curd cottage cheese

Preheat oven to 450 degrees.

Sift flour, salt, and baking powder into a large bowl. Cut butter in with a pastry blender or 2 knives until it is the size of small peas. Stir in cottage cheese all at once.

Drop by generous tablespoons onto an ungreased baking sheet. Bake until golden, about 15 minutes.

MAKES ABOUT 18 BISCUITS

FLAKY BISCUITS WITH PARSLEY BUTTER

Increasing the butter in biscuits makes them tenderer and flakier as well as more flavorful.

> *2 cups sifted all-purpose flour*
> *1/4 teaspoon salt*
> *3 teaspoons baking powder*
> *6 tablespoons (3/4 stick) cold unsalted butter, cut into 6 pieces*
> *2/3 cup milk, plus extra for brushing tops*
> *Parsley Butter (page 350)*

Preheat oven to 450 degrees.

Sift dry ingredients together into a bowl. Cut in the butter with 2 knives or a pastry blender. The butter should be the size of small peas. Add the milk and mix quickly. Turn out onto a floured surface and roll with a floured pin or flatten with the heel of your hand to about 3/8-inch thickness. Cut with a biscuit cutter or a water glass. Set apart on a heavy baking sheet znd brush the top of each with a little milk. Bake for 10 minutes or more, until golden.

Serve with the Parsley Butter.

MAKES ABOUT 18 BISCUITS

SAUSAGE AND CHEESE DROP BISCUITS

The flavor of these delicious little biscuiuts holds even when they are just warm—fine to take on a picnic.

I thought they might be the sort of thing that would freeze well, but although the flavor is passable when thawed, it is nothing to compare with the way they taste before being frozen. So freezing should be a last resort.

> *1 1/2 cups sifted all-purpose flour*
> *3/4 teaspoon salt*
> *1 1/2 teaspoons baking powder*
> *1/4 teaspoon baking soda*
> *4 1/2 tablespoons unsalted buter*
> *1 cup plus 2 tablespoons buttermilk*

> *8 ounces sharp cheddar, grated*
> *3/4 pound sausage meat*

Preheat oven to 425 degrees.

Mix all the dry ingredients and cut in the butter with a pastry blender or 2 knives. When the mixture has the texture of small peas, add buttermilk and blend. Add cheese and sausage meat, making sure they are dispersed throughout.

Drop large tablespoonfuls onto a greased baking sheet. Bake for 18 to 20 mintes, until well browned.

MAKES ABOUT 18 BISCUITS

MOZZARELLA BISCUITS

If you have any of these easy little biscuits left over, you can warm them by placing them directly on the oven rack (not in a pan), so that the bottoms get crispy. I like them almost as well this way as I do when they first come out of the oven.

> *2 cups sifted all-purpose flour*
> *1 teaspoon salt*
> *2 teaspoons baking powder*
> *1/2 teaspoon baking soda*
> *6 tablespoons (3/4 stick) cold unsalted buter, cut into pieces*
> *1 1/2 cups buttermilk, approximately*
> *1 cup coarsely shredded mozzarella*

Preheat oven to 450 degrees.

Sift together flour, salt, baking powder, and baking soda. Cut in butter with a pastry blender or 2 knives. Add enough buttermilk to make a thick dough. Stir in cheese. The dough should be thick enough so that it will just drop from a spoon with a little nudge.

Drop onto a well-greased baking sheet by the tablespoonful and bake for about 15 to 18 minutes. Remove with a spatula as soon as they come from the oven.

MAKES ABOUT 18 OR MORE BISCUITS

CORNBREAD, CORNSTICKS, AND CORN MUFFINS

BACON AND ONION CORN MUFFINS

6 strips thick-cut bacon, diced
1½ cups diced onion
1 cup buttermilk, at room temperature
½ cup plus 2 tablespoons yellow cornmeal
2¼ cups all-purpose flour
1 teaspoon baking soda
2 teaspoons baking powder
4 tablespoons (½ stick) unsalted butter,
*   softened*
4 tablespoons solid vegetable shortening,
*   softened*
2 eggs

Preheat oven to 400 degrees. Lightly grease and flour 12 standard muffin cups (or line them with paper liners).

Sauté bacon in a heavy skillet over medium-high heat until golden brown and just crisp. Do not overcook. Use a slotted spoon to remove bacon to paper towels. Reserve fat and set bacon aside to cool. Sauté onion in the bacon fat over medium-high heat until light brown, 8 to 10 minutes. Place onion in a strainer set over a bowl and allow the fat to drain out.

In a small bowl, combine buttermilk with ½ cup of cornmeal and stir well. Set aside. In a separate bowl, whisk together remaining cornmeal with flour, baking soda, and baking powder. Set aside.

Cream butter and shortening with an electric mixer in a large bowl until light. Add eggs one at a time, mixing well after each addition. On low speed, stir in buttermilk mixture and mix until just combined. Slowly add flour mixture and stir on low speed until the mixture is just combined. Do not overmix. Scrape down the sides and bottom of the bowl with a rubber scraper and stir in onion and bacon until just combined.

Fill the muffin cups two-thirds full. Place in the oven and reduce heat to 350 degrees. Bake for 20 to 25 minutes, until golden brown and a toothpick inserted into the center of one of the muffins comes out clean. Cool on a rack.

MAKES 12 MUFFINS

VARIATIONS

HAM CORN MUFFINS
Replace the bacon and onion with 1 cup finely diced ham.

HAM AND CHEESE CORN MUFFINS
Replace the bacon and onion with ¾ cup finely diced ham and 1¼ cups grated sharp cheddar.

SWEET CORN CAKES

½ cup all-purpose flour
½ cup yellow cornmeal
1 teaspoon baking powder
1 tablespoon sugar
1 egg, lightly beaten
1 cup Creamed Corn (page 114), or canned
2 tablespoons vegetable oil
About ½ cup milk

Combine dry ingredients into a bowl. Mix egg, corn, and oil in another bowl. Combine the two mixtures and then add enough milk to make a thin batter.

Heat a griddle, grease it, and ladle out about ¼ cup of batter for each cake. Cook until the bubbles on top burst, taking a peek from time to time to make sure the bottom isn't getting too dark. Turn and cook until golden on the other side.

MAKES 10 TO 12 CAKES

SKILLET CORNBREAD

The important thing for this recipe is to have the skillet as hot as you can get it.

1 cup yellow cornmeal
1 cup all-purpose flour
½ teaspoon sugar (optional)
4 teaspoons baking powder
½ teaspoon salt
¼ cup safflower oil or bacon drippings
1 egg
1½ cups milk, approximately.

Place a large cast-iron skillet in the oven and turn temperature to 400 degrees.

While the oven and the pan are preheating, mix dry ingredients in a bowl. Mix oil, egg, and milk, then stir into dry ingredients. Add a bit more milk if batter is stiff.

Remove skillet from the oven. Grease quickly with vegetable oil or bacon fat and pour the batter in, smoothing with a spatula if necessary. Bake about 20 minutes, until golden brown.

Serve hot from the skillet.

SERVES 6 TO 8

BUTTERMILK–SOUR CREAM CORNBREAD

This corn bread does occasionally stick to the bottom of the pan, even when the pan has been sprayed. You might want to line the bottom of the pan with wax paper to be on the safe side.

2 cups white cornmeal
3½ teaspoons baking powder
½ teaspoon baking soda
1½ teaspoons salt
1½ cups low-fat sour cream
2 large eggs, lightly beaten
2 tablespoons corn oil
⅔ cup buttermilk

Preheat oven to 425 degrees. Coat well an 8 × 11-inch pan with vegetable-oil spray or spray and line bottom with wax paper. Set aside.

Sift together the dry ingredients. Set aside. Lightly beat together sour cream, eggs, and oil. Mix quickly with the dry ingredients (do not overmix) and pour into the pan. Pour buttermilk over the top of the batter.

Bake for 30 to 35 minutes or until lightly browned. Cut into 12 pieces.

SERVES 12

CORNSTICKS

To make these successfully, there are two very important things to remember. You must have a pair of seasoned black iron stick-pans, and these pans, with oil in each slot, must be smoking hot when you put the batter in.

2½ tablespoons cooking oil
2 cups white cornmeal
4 teaspoons baking powder
1½ teaspoons salt
1 egg
1½ cups milk

Preheat oven to 450 degrees 30 minutes before you plan to bake the sticks. Prepare the pans by putting ½ oil in each slot. put the pans in to heat up.

When the pans are hot, put the cornmeal, baking powder, and salt in a bowl and mix. Beat the eggs lightly and add it to the milk. Mix the dry and liquid ingredients together very quickly. Do not overmix.

Remove the first pan. Be sure to have a heatproof pad or board ready to set it down on, as the pan can scorch the top of a counter. Fill each slot, using a tablespoon. It will puff up to fill. Do not overfill. Put the filled pan in the oven and repeat with the second pan. Bake for 20 minutes.

Take pans from oven and remove the sticks carefully with a fork. Loosen any batter that has overflowed and hardened around the edges. They should then pop right out. If one doesn't come out immediately, move on quickly to the next one and come back to the reluctant one when you have finished and the pan has cooled slightly.

MAKES 16 CORNSTICKS

CORN MUFFINS

1 tablespoon vegetable oil
³⁄₄ cup all-purpose flour
1¹⁄₄ cups yellow cornmeal
2 tablespoons sugar
2 teaspoons baking powder
1 teaspoon salt
1 cup milk
4 tablespoons (¹⁄₂ stick) unsalted butter,
    melted
1 egg, beaten

Preheat oven to 375 degrees. Liberally spray a 12-cup muffin tin with vegetable-oil spray, then put ¹⁄₄ teaspoon of the vegetable oil in each tin. Place in the oven while you mix the batter quickly.

Combine all liquid ingredients and mix well. Pour the wet into the dry mixture and stir lightly—do not overmix. Spoon the batter into the prepared heated tin to about three-quarters full.

Bake until just turning golden, about 20 to 25 minutes.

MAKES 12 MUFFINS

FRESH CORN MUFFINS

Try adding caraway seeds to this for a change. You'll like the result.

2 cups white cornmeal
¹⁄₂ cup all-purpose flour
3¹⁄₂ teaspoons baking powder
¹⁄₂ teaspoon baking soda
1¹⁄₂ teaspoons salt
1¹⁄₂ cups buttermilk
2 eggs, lightly beaten
2 tablespoons unsalted butter, melted
3 cups fresh corn kernels, cut and scraped
    from the cob (about 4 large ears)

Preheat oven to 450 degrees. Grease two 12-cup muffin tins. Set aside.

Sift together cornmeal, flour, baking powder, baking soda, and salt. Stir in buttermilk and then the eggs. Do not overmix. Add butter and corn, then stir just enough to blend. Fill prepared cups and bake for about 25 minutes, until lightly browned.

MAKES 18 TO 24 MUFFINS, DEPENDING ON THE SIZE OF CUPS

309

COLD-WATER CORN CAKES

These corn cakes resemble pancakes. The consistency of the batter is the key here. It should be thin enough to run quickly out toward the edge of the skillet, leaving a few holes around the edge as it does. This will give the cake a crunchy texture. Since cornmeals vary widely, so will the quantity of water.

3/4 cups yellow cornmeal
1/2 cup all-purpose flour
1/2 teaspoon baking soda
1/2 teaspoon salt
1/2 to 1 cup peanut oil for frying
2 1/2 cups cold water

Preheat oven to 225 degrees.

In a medium bowl, combine cornmeal, flour, baking soda, and salt. Cover a baking sheet with paper towels.

Pour 1/2 cup of the oil into a heavy 9-inch skillet, preferably cast iron, and set over high heat. Meanwhile, stir 2 1/2 cups of cold water into the cornmeal mixture until blended. Add up to 1 cup more water, as necessary, to make a very thin batter.

When the oil begins to smoke, pour about 1/4 cup of the batter into the center of the pan; it will form a thin layer over the bottom. Cook for 3 to 4 minutes, until browned, turn over and cook until browned on the other side, about 30 seconds to 1 minute. (Since each round almost fills the pan, turning can be a bit awkward. Use a turner and a small spatula to slide it over.) Drain on the paper towels and keep warm in the oven. Continue making rounds, replenishing the oil as necessary, until all of the batter is used; you may have to add 1 or 2 tablespoons more water if the batter becomes too thick.

MAKES 4 TO 6 CAKES

JALAPEÑO CORN MUFFINS

If hot peppers are not to your taste, substitute the canned, mild variety.

1 1/2 cups yellow cornmeal
1 cup all-purpose flour
1 tablespoon baking powder
1 teaspoon chili powder
1 teaspoon ground cumin
1/2 teaspoon paprika
1 can (17 ounces) creamed corn
1/4 cup chopped pickled jalapeño, without seeds
1/4 cup safflower oil or bacon fat
1/4 cup milk
2 eggs, lightly beaten
4 ounces monterey jack, grated, or muenster

Preheat oven to 400 degrees. Generously grease 12 standard muffin cups.

In a large bowl, sift together cornmeal, flour, baking powder, chili powder, cumin, and paprika. In another bowl, mix thoroughly the creamed corn, jalapeños, oil, milk, and eggs. Combine with the dry ingredients; do not overmix. Fold in cheese and fill cups three-fourths full.

Bake until golden on top, about 20 minutes.

MAKES 12 MUFFINS

ZUCCHINI CORN CAKES

These tasty cakes may be made as they are here or, if you want to give them a little extra zip, add 2 teaspoons minced or pressed garlic and 1/2 cup crumbled feta or asiago cheese to the batter.

For breakfast, serve them with butter, maple syrup, and sausage (and eggs). For a savory lunch or appetizer, serve them with Corn and Avocado Salsa (page 356) and crème fraîche. For dinner, serve them with Mexican Pork Stew (page 245).

*1 1/3 cups yellow or blue cornmeal (preferably
    medium stone-ground)*
1/2 teaspoon salt
1/2 teaspoon baking soda
1/4 cup all-purpose flour
2 eggs
1/3 cup corn oil
1 1/2 cups buttermilk
*1 1/2 cups grated zucchini or any other
    summer squash*
*1 cup corn kernels, drained (fresh, frozen,
    or canned)*

Stir together cornmeal, salt, baking soda, and
flour. In a separate bowl, mix eggs, corn oil,
and buttermilk until smooth. Add grated zucchini and corn, then stir in the sifted ingredients. Blend until smooth.

Cook 3-inch cakes until golden brown on a
hot, lightly oiled griddle or heavy skillet.
SERVES 4 TO 6

SPOON BREAD

TOMATO SPOON BREAD

If you have a favorite spoon bread recipe, use
it. Simply add to it the amount of tomatoes
called for here.

2 cups milk
2 eggs
2 tablespoons unsalted butter
2/3 cup white cornmeal
1 teaspoon salt
2 teaspoons sugar (optional)
2 teaspoons baking powder
*4 to 6 tablespoons coarsely chopped Oven-
    Dried Tomatoes (page 142)*

Preheat oven to 450 degrees and generously
butter a 1 1/2-quart soufflé dish.

Combine 2/3 cup of milk with eggs and beat
well. Set aside. Combine remaining milk and
the butter in a saucepan over low heat. Bring
just to a simmer. Over slightly increased heat,
add cornmeal in a steady stream, stirring constantly. Stir in salt and sugar. Off the heat, add
milk mixture, whisking until smooth. Sprinkle
baking powder over all, and whisk to combine.
Stir in the tomatoes. Pour into the soufflé dish,
and bake until puffy and golden, about 30
minutes. Serve immediately.
SERVES 6

VARIATION

For Green Chili Spoonbread, substitute 1 4-
ounce can mild green chilies, drained and
minced, for the "sun-dried" tomatoes.

CORN KERNEL SPOON
BREAD

Spoon bread suits me anytime.

1 1/4 cups milk
3/4 cup white cornmeal
3/4 teaspoon salt
2 tablespoons unsalted butter
1 can (17 -ounces) yellow creamed corn
3/4 teaspoon baking powder
3 large eggs, separated

Preheat oven to 375 degrees. Grease a 2-quart
baking dish.

Heat milk in a saucepan over low heat until
bubbles form around the edge. Stir in cornmeal and salt in a steady stream, and continue
to cook over low heat, stirring constantly, until
the mixture thickens, about 10 minutes. Stir in
the butter and corn, then the baking powder.
Stir in egg yolks and set aside.

Beat egg whites in a medium bowl until stiff
peaks form. Fold whites into the batter. Pour
into the prepared dish and bake until puffy
and golden, about 35 minutes.
SERVES 6

QUICK BREAD

BISHOP'S BREAD

Pam Lockard has triplets and another daughter, so she is pretty busy around the house. However, she says she has time to make this easy and tasty old-fashioned bread.

2½ cups sifted all-purpose flour
2 cups (firmly packed) light brown sugar
1 teaspoon salt
½ cup solid vegetable shortening
1 teaspoon baking powder
1 teaspoon baking soda
1 teaspoon ground cinnamon
¾ cup milk
1 tablespoon distilled white vinegar
1 large egg

Preheat oven to 375 degrees. Grease a 9 × 13-inch baking pan. Set aside.

Combine flour, brown sugar, and salt in a large bowl. Cut in the shortening with a pastry blender or 2 knives until it resembles the texture of coarse meal. Set aside ¾ cup of this mixture in a small bowl to use later as the topping.

Add baking powder, baking soda, and cinnamon to the large bowl and mix. Stir in milk, vinegar, and egg and mix at high speed until mixture is smooth.

Pour batter into the prepared pan and sprinkle the reserved crumb topping evenly over the top.

Bake for 25 minutes, or until golden. Let cool in the pan before cutting into 3 × 2-inch pieces. Serve warm or at room temperature.
SERVES 18

CINNAMON–OATMEAL RAISIN BREAD

Not too sweet, yet comforting, tasty, and spicy. Who could ask for anything more?

1 cup rolled oats
¾ cup milk, scalded
1 cup golden raisins
1½ cups sifted whole wheat flour
1¼ cups sifted all-purpose flour
1 tablespoon baking powder
1 teaspoon baking soda
1 teaspoon salt
1 tablespoon ground cinnamon
½ teaspoon freshly grated nutmeg
12 tablespoons (1½ sticks) unsalted butter, softened
1 cup (firmly packed) light brown sugar
3 large eggs
½ cup sour cream
2 teaspoons vanilla extract

Combine oats, milk, and raisins in a bowl. Stir to moisten thoroughly, then set aside for 45 minutes to 1 hour.

Preheat oven to 350 degrees. Butter and flour two 9 × 5 × 3-inch loaf pans.

Combine flours, baking powder, baking soda, salt, and spices in a bowl. Set aside.

Cream butter and brown sugar until smooth, about 3 minutes. Add eggs, one at a time, beating well after each addition. Beat in sour cream and vanilla, then add oatmeal–raisin mixture (all the milk will have been absorbed).

Lightly mix in the flour mixture, one third at a time. The dough should be thick, lumpy, and sticky. Divide batter between the 2 pans.

Bake loaves on the center rack of the oven for 35 to 40 minutes, or until a cake tester comes out *almost* clean. Do not overbake. Allow bread to cool in the pans for about 15 minutes, then unmold onto racks. When completely cooled, wrap in foil and keep at room temperature for a few days or freeze. The flavor improves with age.
MAKES 2 LOAVES

GOLDEN RAISIN GINGERBREAD

This gingerbread is marvelous with tea or coffee. But it can also be served warm with ice cream or Bourbon Whipped Cream (page 365) as a dessert.

Most gingerbread recipes are pretty much the same, but this one calls for light raisins, which I like best, instead of the usual dark ones. If you don't like raisins, leave them out altogether.

2¼ cups sifted all-purpose flour
1 teaspoon baking soda
1 teaspoon baking powder
½ teaspoon salt
1 tablespoon ground ginger
½ teaspoon ground cinnamon
8 tablespoons (1 stick) unsalted butter, softened
½ cup (firmly packed) dark brown sugar
½ cup (firmly packed) light brown sugar
2 large eggs
⅓ cup sour cream
⅔ cup buttermilk
1 cup golden raisins

Preheat oven to 350 degrees. Grease and flour a 9-inch square baking pan. If you want to turn cake out of the pan, line bottom with wax paper. Set aside.

Remove ¼ cup of the flour and set aside. Combine remaining flour with baking soda, baking powder, salt, and spices. Set aside.

Cream butter and brown sugars until smooth, about 3 minutes. Add eggs, one at a time, mixing well after each addition. Beat in sour cream and buttermilk, then add the dry mixture and beat until smooth.

Dredge raisins in reserved ¼ cup of flour and fold into batter (including any remaining flour). Pour batter into the prepared pan and bake for 35 to 45 minutes, or until a cake tester comes out clean. Let cool on cake rack.

SERVES 8

HAM CAKE

1 cup all-purpose flour
3 large eggs, lightly beaten
½ cup milk
½ cup peanut oil
Pinch of salt and freshly ground black pepper
2 cups pea-size cubes cooked ham
2 cups grated gruyère
1 package active dry yeast

Preheat oven to 350 degrees. Butter a 4 × 10-inch or 9 × 5-inch loaf pan.

Mix thoroughly the flour, eggs, milk, oil, salt, and pepper. Fold in the ham and cheese. Sprinkle yeast over the top and mix well. Pour into prepared pan. Bake until golden, about 1 hour. If any oil oozes out, pour it off. Serve lukewarm or toasted.

MAKES 1 LOAF

313

STICKY BUNS, MUFFINS, AND POPOVERS

STICKY BUNS

These work fine as regular-size buns, but you might want to go wild and make them giant size—twice as big. I might add that sticky buns get their name honestly.

> 1 package active dry yeast
> ¼ cup lukewarm water (105° to 115° F.)
> 1 cup milk, scalded
> 4 tablespoons (½ stick) unsalted butter
> ¼ cup granulated sugar
> 1 teaspoon salt
> 1 large egg, lightly beaten
> 4 cups sifted all-purpose flour

CARAMEL NUT TOPPING
> 4 tablespoons (½ stick) unsalted butter, melted
> ⅔ cup light corn syrup
> 1½ cups (firmly packed) light brown sugar
> 1 tablespoon ground cinnamon
> 1½ cups small pecan halves

FILLING
> 3 tablespoons unsalted butter, melted
> ½ cup (firmly packed) light brown sugar

Start by making the dough. Put yeast in a small bowl and stir in lukewarm water. Set aside for 10 minutes.

Pour scalded milk over butter, sugar, and salt in a large bowl. Mix well to dissolve sugar and set aside to cool to lukewarm (105 to 115 degrees).

When milk has cooled, stir in yeast mixture and beaten egg. Add flour, ½ cup at a time, and stir to form a soft dough. Beat vigorously for a few minutes. Cover bowl with a damp kitchen towel and set aside in a warm, draft-free spot until dough rises to double its bulk, about 1½ to 2 hours.

Make the topping. When dough has risen, combine melted butter, syrup, brown sugar, and cinnamon in a small saucepan, preferably nonstick. Stir over low heat until smooth and sugar has dissolved.

Meanwhile, grease 16 standard muffin cups or 8 giant 4-inch cups. Divide nuts evenly among the cups and then pour melted syrup over them. Set aside.

Divide dough in half, and roll one portion at a time out on a lightly floured board into a rectangle roughly 12 × 8 inches and about ¼ inch thick. Brush dough with half the melted butter for the filling and then sprinkle on half the brown sugar. Starting on one of the short sides, roll up dough jelly roll fashion into a cylinder. Cut the cylinder into 8 equal slices. Place 1 slice, spiral side up, in each of 8 muffin cups. Repeat with the remaining portion of dough so all cups are filled.

Cover muffin tins with a damp cloth and let dough rise a second time until doubled, another 1½ to 2 hours.

When dough has almost finished rising the second time, preheat oven to 375 degrees. Line a couple of jelly roll pans or baking sheets with foil and place the muffin tins on the pans before placing them in the oven. The sugar sometimes boils over the edges, and the pans make cleanup easier. Bake for 25 minutes, or until brown. Invert muffin tins onto a sheet of foil immediately and let cool.

MAKES 16 STANDARD OR 8 GIANT BUNS

314

DRIED STRAWBERRY AND CHERRY MUFFINS

1 cup dried strawberries
1 cup dried cherries
1/2 cup boiling water
2 cups all-purpose flour
1/2 teaspoon ground cinnamon
2 teaspoons baking powder
1 teaspoon baking soda
1/2 teaspoon salt
2/3 cup sugar
2 eggs, lightly beaten
1/3 cup unsalted butter, melted and cooled

Put strawberries and cherries in a heatproof bowl and pour in the boiling water. Set aside until cool.

Preheat oven to 400 degrees. Grease and lightly flour 12 standard muffin cups (or line them with paper liners).

Stir together flour, cinnamon, baking powder, baking soda, salt, and sugar in a large bowl.

Stir eggs and butter into the strawberries and cherries. Using a large rubber spatula, stir the egg–fruit mixture into the flour mixture and stir until just blended. Do not overmix.

Fill the muffin cups two-thirds full. Place in the oven and reduce heat to 350 degrees. Bake for 25 minutes, or until a cake tester comes out clean.
MAKES 12 MUFFINS

VARIATION
DRIED BLUEBERRY AND CHERRY MUFFINS
Substitute 1 cup dried blueberries for the dried strawberries. The blueberries don't need to be soaked; simply fold them in after you add the cherries.

HAM AND CHEESE MUFFINS

2 cups all-purpose flour
1 tablespoon baking powder
1/2 teaspoon salt
1 egg, at room temperature
1 cup buttermilk, at room temperature
1/4 cup canola oil
8 ounces boneless ham steak, cut into small dice
1 1/4 cups grated sharp cheddar

Preheat oven to 450 degrees. Lightly grease and flour 12 muffin cups (or line them with paper liners).

In a large bowl, stir together flour, baking powder, and salt. Set aside.

Whisk together egg, buttermilk, and oil in a small bowl. Stir in ham and cheese. Using a rubber spatula, stir egg mixture into dry ingredients just until combined. Do not overmix. Use a ladle to fill each of the prepared muffin cups about two-thirds full. Place in the oven and lower the temperature to 400 degrees. Bake until golden brown, about 20 minutes.
MAKES 12 MUFFINS

VARIATIONS
BACON AND CHEESE MUFFINS
Substitute 6 slices thick-cut bacon for the ham. Dice bacon and sauté it in a heavy skillet over medium-high heat until it is just crisp. Do not overcook it. Drain on paper towels and let cool. Combine bacon and cheese with the egg mixture and continue as above.
SAUSAGE AND CHEESE MUFFINS
Substitute 8 ounces Italian sausage (hot or sweet) for the ham. Remove sausage from the casing and sauté it in a heavy skillet over medium-high heat until completely cooked. Drain on paper towels and let cool. If necessary, roughly chop the cooked sausage. Mix sausage and cheese with the egg mixture and continue as above.

APPLE–CINNAMON MUFFINS

These are perfect to serve in the afternoon or for breakfast.

> 2 cups sifted all-purpose flour
> 1 tablespoon baking powder
> 1½ teaspoons ground cinnamon
> 1 teaspoon salt
> 3 large eggs
> ⅔ cup milk
> 6 tablespoons (¾ stick) unsalted butter, melted and cooled
> ½ teaspoon vanilla extract
> ½ cup (firmly packed) light brown sugar
> 1 cup peeled, seeded, and chopped apple

Preheat oven to 400 degrees. Grease or line 12 muffin cups. Set aside.

Sift together flour, baking powder, cinnamon, and salt. Set aside. Combine eggs, milk, butter, and vanilla in a bowl and mix well. Beat in brown sugar, then add flour mixture. Stir in apple, but do not overmix; batter should be lumpy. Divide batter among the cups.

Bake for 20 to 25 minutes, or just until a cake tester comes out clean.

MAKES 12 MUFFINS

RAISIN BRAN MUFFINS

> 3 cups raisin bran cereal
> ½ cup raisins
> 1 cup hot black coffee
> 2½ cups all-purpose flour
> 1 cup sugar
> 2½ teaspoons baking soda
> 2 eggs, lightly beaten
> ½ cup unsalted butter, melted and cooled
> 2 cups buttermilk

Preheat oven to 400 degrees. Grease and lightly flour 24 standard muffin cups (or line them with paper liners).

Place cereal and raisins in a large bowl. Pour in coffee and stir to combine. Set aside.

Whisk together flour, sugar, and baking soda in a large mixing bowl. Set aside.

Stir eggs, butter, and buttermilk into the cereal mixture. Add this to the flour mixture and stir with a rubber spatula until just combined. Do not overmix. Fill the prepared muffin tins two-thirds full. Bake for 18 to 20 minutes, until a cake tester comes out clean.

MAKES 24 MUFFINS

BANANA WALNUT MUFFINS

> 2 cups sifted all-purpose flour
> 1 tablespoon baking powder
> 1 teaspoon salt
> 3 large eggs
> ⅔ cup milk
> 6 tablespoons (¾ stick) unsalted butter, melted and cooled
> ½ cup (firmly packed) dark brown sugar
> ½ teaspoon vanilla extract
> 1½ cups mashed banana (2 to 3 ripe bananas)
> ⅓ cup chopped walnuts.

Preheat oven to 400 degrees. Grease or line 12 muffin cups. Set aside.

Sift together flour, baking powder, and salt. Set aside. Combine eggs, milk, and melted butter in a bowl. Mix well, then beat in brown sugar and vanilla. Add the dry ingredients and mix slightly. Stir in bananas and nuts. Combine but do not overmix; the batter should be lumpy. Divide among the cups. Bake for 20 to 25 minutes, or until a cake tester come out clean.

MAKES 12 MUFFINS

JAM MUFFINS
Use your favorite jam to fill these.

2¹/₂ cups all-purpose flour
1 teaspoon baking soda
2 teaspoons baking powder
1¹/₄ cups (firmly packed) brown sugar
²/₃ cup canola oil
2 eggs, lightly beaten
1 cup buttermilk
6 tablespoons jam
¹/₂ cup sliced almonds

Preheat oven to 400 degrees. Grease and lightly flour 18 muffin cups (or line them with paper liners).

In a medium bowl, whisk together flour, baking soda, and baking powder. Set aside.

Combine sugar, oil, and eggs in a large mixing bowl. Stir well with a large rubber spatula. Add buttermilk and stir to combine. Stir the dry ingredients into the wet until just combined. Do not overmix.

Fill the muffin cups two-thirds full. Place 1 teaspoon of jam in the center of each muffin. Surround the jam with sliced almonds. Place in the oven and reduce heat to 350 degrees. Bake until golden brown, about 20 minutes.

MAKES 18 MUFFINS

BLUEBERRY MUFFINS
If you use strawberries here, select medium ones and cut them in half. They'll give off a good bit of liquid as they cook, so the muffins will not rise as high as blueberry muffins, but they still taste mightly good.

2 cups plus 3 tablespoons all-purpose flour
¹/₂ teaspoon salt
4 teaspoons baking powder
¹/₂ teaspoon ground cinnamon
¹/₂ cup plus 2 tablespoons sugar
2 large eggs, well beaten
6 tablespoons (³/₄ stick) unsalted butter,
    melted and cooled
²/₃ cup milk
2¹/₂ cups blueberries or blackberries,
    raspberries, or strawberries

Preheat oven to 425 degrees. Using 16 regular muffin cups, either grease the tins or place paper cups in the tins. Set aside.

Sift together 2 cups of the flour, the salt, baking powder, and cinnamon. Set aside.

Beat together sugar and eggs, then add butter and milk. Briefly stir into the dry ingredients; do not overmix. Sprinkle remaining flour over berries and toss to coat. Fold these into the batter. Fill the muffin cups two-thirds full. Bake 20 to 25 minutes, or until a tester come our clean.

MAKES 16 MUFFINS

RICE MUFFINS

The rice in these muffins gives them a nice chewy texture.

1½ cups medium rye flour
½ cup all-purpose flour
1½ teaspoons baking powder
¼ teaspoon baking soda
Pinch of cayenne
⅔ cup coarsely chopped green onions, with some of the green
⅔ cup coarsely chopped celery
6 tablespoons (¾ stick) unsalted butter
2 cups cooked white rice, drained well
5 eggs, lightly beaten
½ cup water

Preheat oven to 400 degrees. Generously grease 12 muffin cups.

Sift together flours, baking powder, baking soda, and cayenne in a large bowl.

Sauté green onions and celery in butter until wilted, about 5 minutes. Toss in rice.

Mix eggs and water. Stir into dry mixture; do not overmix. Fold in vegetables and rice. Spoon into cups until three-fourths full. Bake for 20 minutes or until golden.

MAKES 12 MUFFINS

NUT MUFFINS

Notice that I specify toasted nuts in this recipe.

¾ cup whole wheat flour
½ cup bran flakes
1¼ teaspoons baking powder
½ teaspoon salt
½ cup milk
1 egg
1 tablespoon dark molasses
2 tablespoons unsalted butter, melted and cooled
1 cup toasted nut meats

Preheat oven to 425 degrees. Grease a 12-cup muffin pan or coat cups with vegetable cooking spray.

In a large bowl, mix flour, bran flakes, baking powder, and salt. In a separate bowl, combine milk, egg, and molasses. Mix until molasses is dissolved. Pour into the dry mixture all at once and add the melted butter. Quickly stir just to combine; do not overmix. Batter should be lumpy. Stir in nuts. Divide among the muffin cups. Bake until browned on top, about 15 to 17 minutes. Let cool about a minute in the pan, then loosen edges and turn out.

MAKES 12 MUFFINS

PECAN POPOVERS

Make sure the pecans are finely chopped, otherwise they will not mix throughout.

6 tablespoons all-purpose flour
1 cup plus 2 tablespoons finely chopped pecans
¼ teaspoon salt
1½ cups milk
3 eggs, lightly beaten
1 tablespoon plus 1½ teaspoons butter, melted and cooled

Preheat oven to 450 degrees. Generously butter twelve ½-cup custard cups.

Mix flour and pecans in a large bowl. Add salt. Mix in milk, eggs, and cooled butter. Stir, but do not overmix. Pour into prepared custard cups, filling each about three-fourths full. Place on a baking sheet and bake for 15 minutes.

Turn heat to 350 degrees and bake another 20 minutes. Do not open oven while cooking, but check temperature before you start to make sure it's correct.

As soon as you remove the popovers from the oven, puncture sides with a knife to let any steam out. This will prevent them from collapsing. Serve immediately.

MAKES 12 POPOVERS

POPOVERS

Use four-ounce custard cups to bake your popovers.

1 cup milk
1 tablespoon unsalted butter, melted
1 cup all-purpose flour
1/4 teaspoon salt
2 eggs, lightly beaten

Preheat oven to 475 degrees. Grease 6 to 8 custard cups and set aside.

Beat milk, butter, flour, and salt together until smooth; it will be the consistency of heavy cream. Add eggs, one at a time, mixing after each, but do not overbeat. Fill the cups three-fourths full place on a baking sheet. and bake for 15 minutes. Lower the heat to 350 degrees and bake another 20 minutes. Do not peek. They should be nicely browned and pulling away from the sides.

MAKES 9 POPOVERS

PANCAKES

PANCAKES

Of all the berries, I like raspberries the best for pancakes.

1 cup self-rising cake flour
2 teaspoons sugar
1/4 teaspoon baking soda
1/4 teaspoon salt
1 large egg, lightly beaten
1 cup buttermilk
1 to 2 tablespoons unsalted butter, melted and cooled
1 cup raspberries

Have a griddle well oiled with vegetable oil and hot.

Sift together the dry ingredients in a large bowl. Combine egg, buttermilk, and butter in a small bowl, mixing well. Quickly stir into dry ingredients; do not overmix. Sprinkle berries on top and fold in gently.

Place on the griddle by large spoonfuls. Cook until golden on the underside, about 2 to 3 minutes, then turn. Cook another minute or so until done.

SERVES 4 TO 6

CRÈME FRAÎCHE PANCAKES

This recipe makes a very thin and very light pancake. Serve them with Sautéed Bananas (page 457), Hazelnut Honey Butter (page 352), and syrups and jams.

4 large eggs
1/2 teaspoon salt
1 teaspoon baking soda
1/2 cup unbleached all-purpose flour
2 tablespoons sugar
2 cups crème fraîche
2 tablespoons unsalted butter, melted and cooled
Vegetable oil to grease griddle

Place all ingredients except the butter and oil into a blender. Blend until smooth, pouring in butter. This takes only 15 to 20 seconds. Stir once to make sure it is all mixed.

Grease a well-heated griddle with vegetable oil. Pour out a scant 1/4 cup of batter. When the bubbles on top burst, turn the pancake. Continue, greasing the griddle as necessary.

SERVES 6

319

WILD SOURDOUGH PANCAKES

This recipe came to me from Cassandra Mitchell, who owns the popular The Diner in Yountville, California. Cassandra got it from her grandmother Jane Grosfield, of Big Timber Mountain.

The pancakes have a distinctive flavor and lightness. Start the sourdough process when you have time to play with it.

2 cups all-purpose flour
2 cups warm water (105° to 115° F.)
½ cup Wild Sourdough Starter (recipe
   follows)
3 large eggs
4 tablespoons butter, melted
2 tablespoons sugar
1 teaspoon sugar
1 teaspoon salt
1½ teaspoons baking soda

The night before you make the pancakes, combine flour, warm water, and starter until blended and smooth (do *not* use a metal spoon or bowl). Cover with a clean kitchen towel and set aside in a warm place.

Make a batter by stirring in all the other ingredients, mixing well but not hard. Cook on a hot, lightly greased griddle. Let bubbles from on top before turning. If batter seems too thick, thin with a little milk.

SERVES 4 TO 6

WILD SOURDOUGH STARTER

In a glass jar or crockery bowl, mix 1 cup bleached all-purpose flour with enough water to make a thick paste that is still on the runny side. Set the jar out uncovered on the counter or the porch to let it start fermenting. It will bubble and start to smell beerlike after a couple of days. Once it does, you're ready to go with the pancakes.

MAKES 1 CUP

CARROT CAKE WAFFLES

1 cup all-purpose flour
1 tablespoon sugar
1 teaspoon baking powder
½ teaspoon baking soda
⅛ teaspoon salt
1 cup buttermilk
1 whole egg
1 tablespoon vegetable oil
1 cup finely grated carrot (about 2 large
   carrots)
½ cup sweetened coconut flakes
½ cup canned crushed pineapple, drained
   of extra liquid
½ teaspoon ground ginger
2 egg whites

Prepare hot waffle iron with a thin coating of nonstick spray.

Put dry ingredients in a large mixing bowl, making a well in the center. Mix buttermilk, egg, and oil in a medium bowl; add to dry ingredients and stir to combine.

Mix carrot, coconut, pineapple, and ginger in a medium bowl. Add to buttermilk mixture, combining with just a few quick strokes. Beat egg whites until stiff peaks form and fold into the batter with several over-and-under motions. The batter may still be streaky, but do not overmix.

Measure into prepared waffle machine and cook according to manufacturer's instructions.

SERVES 4 TO 6

320

STUFFED CREPES WITH RED BELL PEPPER SAUCE

I always thought it was too much trouble to make crepes until a friend, who is a professional, showed me how simple they are to prepare. They may be made in advance and stowed in the refrigerator all day, or if you really get a head of steam up, you can make a big batch and freeze them separated by wax paper.

Any other strong-flavored green could be substituted for the escarole.

6 tablespoons unsalted butter
1 cup finely chopped onion
4 cups lightly packed stemmed escarole, broccoli rabe, spinach, chicory, or swiss chard
½ cup Chicken Stock (page 41)
1 teaspoon salt
¼ teaspoon freshly ground black pepper
¼ teaspoon freshly grated nutmeg
1 cup ricotta cheese
1¼ cups freshly grated parmesan
1 large egg
12 crepes (recipe follows)
Red Bell Pepper Sauce (page 93)

Melt 2 tablespoons of the butter over medium-high heat and sauté onion and escarole until wilted, about 5 minutes. Add stock and cook until it is almost entirely evaporated, about 6 to 8 minutes. Place in a strainer and gently press out any remaining liquid. Chop coarsely and set aside. Combine salt, pepper, and nutmeg with the ricotta, ½ cup parmesan, and egg. Mix well and fold in the chopped escarole.

Preheat oven to 350 degrees.

Spread 1 generous tablespoon of the filling over the bottom half of a crepe, leaving a ¼-inch border around the lower edge. Fold top half over filling and press down lightly. Fold over one more time, making a triangle with a rounded side. Repeat.

Place crepes in 1 or 2 buttered baking dishes and sprinkle each crepe with 1 tablespoon of remaining parmesan and dot it with ½ teaspoon of remaining butter. Cover tightly with foil and bake for 30 minutes. Uncover and bake until just beginning to turn golden, about 10 more minutes.

Allow 2 crepes per serving, placing them on heated plates with some of the red bell pepper sauce.

SERVES 6

CREPES

2 large eggs
1 cup milk
½ cup water
2 teaspoons unsalted butter, melted and cooled
1 teaspoon salt
⅔ cup all-purpose flour

Place eggs, milk, water, butter, and salt in a bowl and whip it with a fork until smooth. Sprinkle flour over all while continuing to beat with a fork; when smooth, set aside.

Using additional butter, lightly rub the inside of a 7-inch crepe or omelet pan. Heat over high heat. Pour ¼ cup of the batter into the pan and cook until top is no longer shiny, loosening it around the egges with your spatula as it cooks, about 1½ minutes. Turn and lightly brown other side, another 1½ minutes. Set crepe aside. Repeat until all batter is used, wiping out the pan with a paper towel and rebuttering it after each crepe. Place a paper towel between finished crepes. If you are not using these right away, separate crepes with wax paper.

PIZZAS, FRITTERS, CRISPBREADS, AND SANDWICHES

TO ME, THE BIGGEST PART OF even the smallest sandwich is the balance between the bread and what it encloses. I hate those things with monster fillings called "over-stuffed." I dislike equally sandwiches that consist of a thin layer of something between two slices of bread so thick that you can hardly get them into your mouth. ✦ Pizza and focaccia are really variations on the open-faced sandwich theme and focaccia can make a good base for a heartier sandwich. In the summer I like to keep dough in the refrigerator (some pizza places sell it ready made) to make pizzas on the grill. ✦ In this section you'll find the crackers and crispbreads that can accompany a meal or stand on their own as a special snack. And finally, let's not forget sandwich spreads—very useful for producing a quick bite.

PIZZA AND FOCACCIA

TOMATO-TARRAGON PIZZA

The recipe for this dough comes from Donna Scala, formerly of Ristorante Piatti in Yountville, California. I make it with a mixer, but it can be done by hand. This dough recipe makes enough for three 8-inch pizzas. (You can freeze the extra pizzas or dough.) The topping is enough for one pizza.

If you like pizza, a pizza stone is worth the investment (they're available at most cooking stores). A flat pizza paddle is also a help, although you can use a thin baking sheet in its place.

PIZZA DOUGH
1³/₄ cups unbleached all-purpose flour
1¹/₂ teaspoons salt
1 package active dry yeast
²/₃ cup warm water (105° to 115° F.)
2 tablespoons olive oil

Cornmeal

TOMATO-TARRAGON TOPPING
¹/₂ cup chopped white onions
1 tablespoon unsalted butter
2 cups peeled, seeded, and chopped tomatoes
3 tablespoons minced fresh tarragon
¹/₄ teaspoon salt
¹/₄ teaspoon freshly ground black pepper
3 tablespoons olive oil
¹/₄ cup freshly grated parmesan
2 ounces romano, shaved

To make dough: Put flour and salt in the bowl of a heavy-duty electric mixer fitted with a dough hook. In a small bowl, dissolve yeast in the water and let sit for a few minutes, until foamy. With the mixer at low speed, combine yeast mixture with flour. Add olive oil and continue mixing. When the ingredients are well blended, increase the speed to medium and continue for 3 minutes. Switch back to low for another 3 minutes. Turn the dough out on a floured surface and cover with a damp towel. Let it rise for 1 hour.

Divide the dough into 3 equal balls. The dough should have a smooth and somewhat "tense" surface. Place each ball in a separate large plastic bag and seal. Let rise again at room temperature, or refrigerate to let rise a second time overnight.

Put a pizza stone in the oven and preheat the oven to 500 to 550 degrees. Remove dough from the refrigerator and set aside at room temperature for about 15 minutes before rolling.

To make topping: Sauté onions in butter over medium heat, stirring, until browned, 6 to 8 minutes. Set aside.

Toss tomatoes with tarragon, salt, and pepper. Put in a colander and set aside in the sink to drain.

Meanwhile, roll out a ball of pizza dough into an 8- to 9-inch round. Sprinkle the pizza paddle or baking sheet lightly with cornmeal and transfer the dough to it. Turn up the edge, making a shallow rim all around. Sprinkle half the olive oil on the dough, brushing to cover evenly. Scatter onions over this, and top with parmesan. Spoon on the tomatoes and spread evenly. Drizzle with the remaining oil.

Sprinkle the preheated pizza stone with cornmeal. Slide the pizza off the paddle onto the stone and bake until browned, 7 to 9 minutes. Remove and sprinkle with the shaved romano. Cut into wedges and serve.
SERVES 2

INDIVIDUAL GRILLED PIZZA

Top these individual pizzas with Fresh Tomato Sauce (page 92) or one of the toppings that follow.

> 1 package active dry yeast
> 1 teaspoon sugar
> 1 cup warm water (105° to 115° F.)
> 3 cups unbleached all-purpose flour
> 1 teaspoon salt
> 1/4 cup olive oil
> Toppings (recipes follow)

In a small bowl, combine yeast, sugar, and water. Stir to dissolve. Set aside until foamy, 5 to 10 minutes.

Combine flour and salt in a large bowl. Stir olive oil into the yeast mixture. Add the yeast mixture to the flour and mix well. Add a bit more flour if the dough is too moist. Turn out the dough onto a lightly floured surface and knead gently until soft and elastic, 8 to 10 minutes.

Oil a large bowl and place the dough in it. Oil the top of the dough. Cover with plastic wrap or a clean kitchen towel and set aside in a warm, draft-free spot until doubled in size, about 1 hour.

While the dough is rising, prepare the grill.

Punch down the dough and turn out onto a lightly floured surface. Cut the dough into 6 equal pieces.

Using a metal sheet pan and rolling pin (with additional flour as needed), roll out pizza dough one piece at a time. The dough should be as thin as possible, even if the shape becomes less than perfect in the process. Transfer the rolled dough to the grill for about 1 to 2 minutes but do not attempt to turn the dough. Grill on one side only, being careful not to burn the crust, and remove from heat.

Continue with the remaining dough until the 6 pizza bases are completed.

Assemble the pizza toppings on the grilled side of each pizza base and return to the grill. Cover until completely warmed, being careful not to burn the crust.

SERVES 6

TOMATO AND BASIL TOPPING

Some people add a little minced garlic to this, but I like it better without. If anything, I'd add shallots.

> 4 medium tomatoes, peeled, seeded, and coarsely chopped
> 1 small onion, minced
> 12 large fresh basil leaves, minced
> Salt and freshly ground black pepper, to taste

Toss all ingredients together and let stand at room temperature.

Spread sauce on prebaked pizza crust. Return to the grill to warm through.

MAKES ENOUGH FOR 2 INDIVIDUAL PIZZAS

MARGARITA TOPPING

> 1 large tomato, thinly sliced
> 1/2 cup shredded mozzarella
> 10 basil leaves, sliced in thin strips (chiffonade)

Arrange sliced tomato on top of the prebaked crust. Top with shredded cheese and sprinkle with basil. Finish on the grill until the cheese melts and the pizza is heated through.

MAKES ENOUGH FOR 1 INDIVIDUAL PIZZA

SAUSAGE AND MUSHROOM TOPPING

> 8 ounces sweet Italian sausage
> 2 tablespoons olive oil
> 1/4 pound cremini mushrooms, sliced (about 1 cup)
> 1/4 cup tomato sauce
> 1/2 cup shredded mozzarella

324

Preheat oven to 350 degrees.

Remove sausage from casing, crumble in a pie pan, and cook until meat is no longer pink, about 8 to 10 minutes. Drain and set sausage aside to cool.

In a large sauté pan over medium-high heat, heat oil until almost smoking. Add mushrooms and sauté until golden, about 6 to 8 minutes.

Assemble pizza by spreading tomato sauce on baked crust. Sprinkle with shredded cheese, mushrooms, and sausage. Finish on grill until cheese is melted and pizza is heated through.

MAKES ENOUGH FOR 4 INDIVIDUAL PIZZAS

ZUCCHINI, YELLOW SQUASH, AND GREEN PEPPER TOPPING

1 small zucchini
1 small yellow squash
½ large green bell pepper, cored and seeded
1 tablespoon olive oil
¼ cup tomato sauce
½ cup shredded mozzarella

Slice the zucchini and yellow squash in half lengthwise, quarter, and cut into ¼-inch pieces. Roughly chop the green pepper. Combine with zucchini and yellow squash and sauté in olive oil over high heat until golden brown, about 5 minutes. Set aside.

Spread tomato sauce on prebaked crust. Top with shredded cheese and vegetables. Finish on the grill until cheese is melted and pizza is heated through.

MAKES ENOUGH FOR 4 INDIVIDUAL PIZZAS

ROASTED GARLIC, SHALLOT, SPINACH, AND GOAT CHEESE TOPPING

1 head of garlic
2 teaspoons olive oil
6 large shallots
1 pound spinach, stemmed and cleaned
¼ cup tomato sauce
¼ cup shredded mozzarella
2 ounces goat cheese, crumbled

Preheat oven to 400 degrees.

Cut the top off the head of garlic, so the individual cloves are exposed. Drizzle with 1 teaspoon of the olive oil. Wrap in foil and set aside.

Peel shallots and toss them in the remaining teaspoon of olive oil. Wrap all of them together in one sheet of foil. Seal tightly and roast along with the garlic until soft and tender, about 45 minutes.

While garlic and shallots are roasting, place spinach, still wet from washing, in a large hot sauté pan. Cook just until wilted, about 1 to 2 minutes, turning frequently. Set aside.

To assemble pizza, spread tomato sauce and shredded mozzarella on the prebaked crust. Add spinach and goat cheese. Squeeze roasted garlic from the skins directly onto the pizza, distributing as evenly as possible, and top with the shallots. Finish on the grill until cheese is melted and pizza is heated through.

MAKES ENOUGH FOR 4 INDIVIDUAL PIZZAS

GARLIC PIZZA SQUARES

If you like garlic, here's the recipe for you.

3 envelopes active dry yeast
2 tablespoons sugar
1 cup warm water (105° to 115° F.)
4 cups unbleached all-purpose flour
1 tablespoon plus ¹/₂ teaspoon salt
3 tablespoons olive oil
2 tablespoons unsalted butter
2 tablespoons minced garlic
¹/₈ teaspoon freshly ground black pepper

Mix yeast and sugar in a small bowl and pour warm water over. Stir and let stand until dissolved, about 10 to 15 minutes.

Mix flour and 1 tablespoon of the salt. Make a well in the center. Add 1 tablespoon of the olive oil to the yeast mixture and stir. Pour into the well and mix into a stiff dough. Knead until elastic and shinny, about 7 minutes. Place dough in an oiled crockery bowl, cover loosely with a clean kitchen towel, and let rise in a warm, draft-free spot until doubled in bulk, about 1 hour.

Meanwhile, mix remaining olive oil and salt, butter, garlic, and pepper in a small pan. Cook over very low heat until garlic is just softened, being careful not to brown garlic. Set aside.

When dough is ready, preheat oven to 425 degrees. Grease 2 baking sheets.

Roll out dough until very thin, ¹/₄ inch thick. Cut into 5-inch squares and place on baking sheets. Paint the top of each with the garlic–oil mixture. Bake until golden, about 10 to 15 minutes.

MAKES ABOUT 12 SQUARES

ONION AND BLACK OLIVE PIZZA BREAD

You can use any topping on this you fancy— just like a regular pizza. This makes enough dough for two breads, so freeze half.

1 package active dry yeast
Pinch of sugar
1 cup warm water (105° to 115° F.)
3 cups unbleached all-purpose flour
1 teaspoon salt
¹/₄ cup plus 2 tablespoons olive oil
1 small onion, halved and sliced
12 to 18 black oil-cured olives, pitted and
   coarsely chopped, tossed in a bowl with
   about 1 tablespoon of their own oil
Salt and freshly ground black pepper, to
   taste

In a small bowl, combine yeast, sugar, and water. Let sit for about 15 minutes, until foamy. Combine flour and salt in a large bowl. Stir ¹/₄ cup of the olive oil into the yeast mixture, then add to the flour, mixing well. Add a bit more flour if the dough is too damp. Turn dough out onto a floured surface and knead it lightly for a few minutes. Dough should be soft and elastic.

Oil a large bowl and place dough in it, oil the top of the dough, cover it with plastic wrap, and let it rise in a warm, draft-free spot until doubled in size, about 45 minutes.

When ready to assemble bread, preheat oven to 400 degrees and divide dough into 2 balls. Wrap one tightly in plastic wrap and refrigerate (for up to 2 days) or freeze.

Oil a small pizza pan, about 12 inches, and roll out the dough to fit it. Pat the dough in place, leaving a thick border all around. Brush dough with 1 tablespoon of the olive oil. Toss onion with remaining oil. Sprinkle oiled onion over dough and then sprinkle on the olives. Salt and pepper and bake until golden, about 20 minutes.

SERVES 3 TO 4

326

FOCACCIA

Focaccia toppings can be as simple or as complicated as you like. Do a little experimenting.

1 package active dry yeast
1 tablespoon sugar
1 cup warm water (105° to 115° F.)
1 teaspoon salt
1/4 cup plus 1 tablespoon olive oil
3 cups unbleached all-purpose flour
Kosher salt
1/2 cup thinly sliced red onion
1 teaspoon finely chopped fresh rosemary
Olive oil for dipping (optional)

In a large mixing bowl, dissolve yeast and sugar in the water. Set aside. When foamy, add salt and 1/4 cup of the olive oil. Stir. Mix in 2 cups of the flour with a wooden spoon to make a very sticky dough. Work in the balance of the flour a little at a time with your hands, until all is used and a smooth dough is formed. Knead in a mixer or on a floured board until smooth and elastic. Turn into a lightly oiled bowl, oil the top of the dough, and cover with plastic wrap or a clean kitchen towel. Let double in bulk in a warm, draft-free spot, about 1 hour.

Oil a 9-inch square pan. Punch down the dough and pat it evenly into the oiled pan. Cover and let rise for another 30 minutes.

Preheat oven to 450 degrees.

After the dough has risen the second time, poke it with your finger in about 12 different places. Brush with 1 tablespoon olive oil, allowing some to collect in the holes. Sprinkle with kosher salt, red onion, and rosemary.

Bake until golden brown, about 40 minutes. Cut into 4 strips and cut each of these in half. Serve hot with extra olive oil for dipping, if desired.

SERVES 8

VARIATION

Increase the amount of sliced onions to 2 cups. Omit the rosemary.

CRISPBREADS AND CRACKERS

MELBA TOAST

Preheat oven to about 250 degrees, or as low as it can be set. Cut slices of very thin white or whole wheat bread in half. Place on baking sheets and toast until golden. This may take 1 hour or less, depending on how how your oven will go and how dark you like the toast. Store in an airtight container.

TOASTED PITA BREAD TRIANGLES

Preheat oven to 325 degrees. Pull pita breads in half and then cut each half into triangles. Place these on a baking sheet and toast in oven until crisp and golden. Turn once. Store in an airtight container.

PUFFED TORTILLA TRIANGLES

These are so popular that you might want to double or even triple this recipe.

Safflower or canola oil
8 to 10 flour tortillas, each cut into 4
*   triangles*
Kosher salt, to taste

Put omelet pan over medium-high heat. Pour about 1/4 inch of oil in the pan. When hot (the oil should be shimmering), add 4 tortilla triangles and fry, turning once, until puffy and golden on each side, about 30 seconds per side. Drain and sprinkle with salt. Repeat until all are done.

SERVES 8

GRILLED PITA CHIPS

Brush both sides of pita bread with olive oil and sprinkle with salt. Grill until crisp and covered with grill marks on both sides, about 1 minute per side. Remove and immediately cut into triangles to serve.

TOASTED ICE-WATER CRACKERS

These crackers have a marvelous flavor and keep especially well in a container with a tight-fitting lid. The flavor even seems to improve in a day or so. They make an ideal accompaniment to soups and lunches and shouldn't require much additional butter.

> *24 saltine crackers*
> *Ice water*
> *4 tablespoons (1/2 stick) melted butter, or*
>   *more to taste*

Preheat oven to 400 degrees. Grease a baking sheet or two.

Have ready a bowl of ice water and the melted butter as well as a small soft brush. Drop the crackers in the water about six at a time. After 28 or 30 seconds, carefully but quickly lift them out, allow water to drip off, and place on a baking sheet. Do not try to do too many at one time, because by the time you get to the last ones they will have become too soggy. I've found six to be the ideal number. When you have a full baking sheet, brush each cracker generously with the melted butter. Don't use too much pressure, because you don't want to flatten the crackers.

Toast in the oven for 10 minutes, then turn heat down to 300 degrees. Continue to toast for an additional 10 to 15 minutes. Cool and store in a container with a tight lid.

MAKES 24 CRACKERS

FRIED CROUTONS

These croutons are not the small cubes of toast that you find in salads or floating on top of soup. Instead, they are slices of French or Italian bread that have been fried until golden and crisp.

To make them, simply cut a loaf of French or Italian bread on a diagonal with a serrated knife into 3/4-inch slices. Butter both sides lightly with softened unsalted butter. Set aside.

Put 1/2 cup of olive oil in a large skillet and mash about 6 cloves of garlic into it as the oil heats. When the garlic begins to brown, discard. Pour oil out and reserve, leaving a thin coating on the bottom of the pan. Turn heat to medium and fry the bread slices, turning as necessary. Add more oil and continue frying the bread until all have been done. Serve warm or at room temperature.

MAKES ABOUT 20 CROUTONS

SUN-DRIED TOMATO TOASTS

These are also good with soup.

> *1 baguette, 12 to 15 inches long, cut into*
>   *1/2-inch rounds*
> *1 ounce sun-dried tomatoes, sliced thin*
> *6 tablespoons olive oil*
> *Freshly ground black pepper, to taste*
> *1 tablespoon freshly grated romano*

Preheat oven to 250 degrees.

Place bread rounds on a baking sheet. Combine tomatoes and oil in a small saucepan and heat over low heat until just hot. Spoon over bread rounds, dividing evenly. Sprinkle with pepper and then cheese. Bake for about 8 minutes until dried out slightly.

MAKE SEVERAL DOZEN

WHOLE WHEAT BENNE WAFERS

For those of you who don't know, benne seeds are sesame seeds. The African name for these seeds is used in the South.

2/3 cup sifted whole wheat flour
Pinch of salt
1/4 teaspoon baking powder
8 tablespoons (1 stick) unsalted butter, softened
1 cup (firmly packed) light brown sugar
1 large egg
1 teaspoon vanilla extract
1 1/4 cups benne (sesame) seeds, toasted (see Note)

Preheat oven to 350 degrees. Lightly grease several sheets of cooking parchment. Put them on baking sheets and set aside.

Combine whole wheat flour, salt, and baking powder and set aside.

Cream butter and brown sugar until fluffy, about 3 minutes. Add egg and vanilla and combine well. Add the dry mixture, beating enough to combine. Then stir in benne seeds.

Drop by small teaspoonfuls onto the lined sheets, leaving 2 inches in between. These spread and become very thin. If you bake 2 baking sheets at once, reverse them halfway through the cooking time.

Bake for 6 to 8 minutes, or until lightly browned. Allow waters to cool on the sheet for about 30 seconds, then gently remove them to a cooling rack. To preserve their crispness, store in an airtight jar.

Note: To toast benne or sesame seeds, place in a single layer on a jelly-roll pan. Roast in a 350-degree oven until golden, about 15 minutes.

MAKES ABOUT 6 DOZEN

CHEESE TOASTS

1 cup freshly grated parmesan
1/2 cup commercial mayonnaise
1 baguette, sliced 1/4-inch thick

Combine cheese and mayonnaise and spread on bread slices. Broil until brown and bubbly, about 1 to 2 minutes. Serve immediately.

MAKES 18 OR MORE

SALT WAFERS

These crisp little squares were inspired by Nathalie Dupree's Brittlebread.

1 3/4 cups all-purpose flour
1 cup whole wheat flour
2 tablespoons sugar
3/4 teaspoon salt
1/4 teaspoon freshly ground black pepper
1/2 teaspoon baking soda
8 tablespoons (1 stick) unsalted butter
1 cup low-fat sour cream
Kosher salt for topping

Preheat oven to 400 degrees.

Sift together flours, sugar, salt, pepper, and baking soda. Cut in the butter with a pastry blender or 2 knives. Beat in the sour cream.

Roll out dough until paper-thin on a floured surface. Cut into 2-inch squares and place on 2 ungreased baking sheets. Sprinkle each with salt.

Bake for about 7 minutes and then turn off heat. Let crisp as the oven cools.

MAKES ABOUT 60 WAFERS

329

HOT-WATER SODA WAFERS WITH CHIVES

These tend to toughen up if allowed to sit around too long, so they are best eaten shortly after baking.

1½ cups water
1 teaspoon salt
4 tablespoons (½ stick) unsalted butter
½ teaspoon baking soda
2 cups all-purpose flour
3 or more tablespoons snipped fresh chives

Preheat oven to 425 degrees.

Place water, salt, and butter in a medium saucepan and bring to a boil. Meanwhile, toss baking soda and flour together. When water is boiling, add flour all at once, stirring constantly with a wooden spoon. Continue to stir over low heat for another minute, until the mixture is well combined and has formed a ball.

Pull off walnut-size pieces of dough and quickly roll each into a ball. Flatten slightly and sprinkle with chives. Place on an ungreased baking sheet and press with heel of the hand until very thin. Prick with a fork in several places. Continue until all dough is used.

Bake for 15 minutes or until browned and crisp. Let cool slightly on a rack.

MAKES ABOUT 48 WAFERS

CORN WAFERS

These wonderful, crisp little wafers are so easy to prepare you will want to make them every time you serve soup.

¾ cup white cornmeal
½ teaspoon salt
1 cup boiling water
2 tablespoons margarine, melted
Unsalted butter

Preheat oven to 425 degrees. Grease 2 baking sheets or coat with vegetable cooking spray.

Mix cornmeal and salt in a bowl and pour in boiling water, stirring all the while to keep lumps from forming. Stir in margarine.

Drop 1 tablespoon at a time onto the baking sheets. This batter should be liquid enough to spread out into a 3-inch circle. If it doesn't spread, add a bit more water. Bake until golden brown around the edges and crispy, about 20 minutes. Serve with butter.

MAKES ABOUT 36 WAFERS

CRACKER BREAD

1 think you'll be pleasantly surprised at how easy this is to make.

3 tablespoons shelled sunflower seeds
1¼ cups all-purpose flour
¾ teaspoon sugar
¾ teaspoon baking powder
¼ teaspoon baking soda
½ teaspoon salt
6 tablespoons grated parmesan
2 tablespoons cold unsalted butter, cut into
    small pieces
½ cup buttermilk
Kosher salt

Preheat oven to 425 degrees. Lightly oil the backs of three baking sheets.

In a bowl, mix seeds, flour, sugar, baking power, baking soda, salt, and 3 tablespoons of the parmesan. Add butter and mix with your fingers until the mixture is mealy. Stir in buttermilk quickly. The dough should be moist but not sticky. (If it is sticky, knead in a little more flour briefly.)

Divide the dough into 3 balls. Place one in the center of one of the greased baking sheets. Roll out paper-thin, literally. Sprinkle with a tablespoon of the reserved parmesan and press the cheese into the surface of the dough. Cut into large cracker shapes or strips with a pizza cutter or a knife. Be careful; if you drag the tip of a knife over the dough to cut it, the dough will snag and wrinkle in spots. Slightly separate the crackers on the sheet. Prick with the tines of a fork and sprinkle with kosher salt. Repeat with the other two thirds of the dough.

Bake until golden, about 8 minutes. Cool on a rack.

MAKES ABOUT 48 CRACKERS

CHEESE PECAN TWISTS

These are made with frozen puff pastry and couldn't be simpler. Incidentally, if at any point while you are preparing these the pastry should become sticky and difficult to work with, return it to the freezer for 3 or 4 minutes.

1 10 × 15-inch sheet of commercial puff pastry
¼ cup milk
1 large egg white
1¼ cups freshly grated parmesan
¾ cup finely ground pecans

Preheat oven to 400 degrees.

Lay pastry on a flat surface. Beat milk and egg white together and brush pastry liberally with it. Mix cheese and pecans and sprinkle half on top of the pastry. Press down lightly. Turn pastry over and brush with the milk–egg wash and sprinkle with the balance of the cheese mixture. Press down lightly. Using a pizza wheel or a sharp knife, cut pastry crosswise into 1 × 10-inch strips. Pick up each strip by one end and, holding it vertically, twist it a few times and place on a parchment-lined baking sheet. Bake for 15 to 20 minutes. Do not let pecans burn. Cool on a rack.

MAKES 15 TWISTS

VARIATION

To make Paprika Twists, substitute 1 cup freshly grated romano, ¼ cup paprika, and 1 tablespoon cayenne for the parmesan and pecans.

TORTILLAS

HAM FAJITAS WITH FRESH SALSA RANCHERA AND SCRAMBLED EGGS

FRESH SALSA RANCHERA
1 cup diced ripe red tomato
2 teaspoons chopped and drained canned mild green chilies
2 teaspoons canned tomato with jalapeño
1 teaspoon fresh cilantro leaves, torn (not chopped)

FILLING
1 tablespoon olive oil
1 large red onion, thinly sliced (about 2 cups)
1 pound ham, thickly sliced and cut into 1-inch strips
6 (8-inch) flour tortillas

SCRAMBLED EGGS
12 large eggs
3 tablespoons heavy cream (optional)
3 tablespoons unsalted butter
Salt and freshly ground black pepper, to taste

1 cup grated white sharp cheddar

To make salsa ranchera: Combine ingredients and set aside at room temperature until ready to serve.

To make filling: In a heavy skillet over medium-high heat, heat olive oil until almost smoking. Sauté onion, stirring occasionally, until just beginning to brown, 10 to 12 minutes. Add ham and combine.

Preheat oven to 200 degrees.

To make tortillas easier to fold, stack, wrap in foil, and place in the warm oven for 10 to 15 minutes.

To make scrambled eggs: While onion is cooking, place a heatproof plate in the pre-heated oven.

Lightly beat four of the eggs and add a tablespoon of the cream, if using.

In a large skillet over low heat, melt 1 tablespoon of the butter. Add eggs and cook slowly, stirring with a fork as the eggs begin to set. When scrambled, remove to warm plate and return to oven. Repeat, four eggs at a time, until finished. Season with salt and pepper.

Remove warm tortillas from the oven. Working with one at a time, and keeping the rest wrapped, fill the tortilla with the ham mixture, sprinkle with cheese, and fold into quarters. Place in a heavy skillet, folded side down. Put a heatproof "weight" plate on top of the folded tortillas to hold them while they heat. Cook over medium-high heat until cheese starts to melt, about 2 to 3 minutes.

Place each fajita on an individual plate and accompany with scrambled eggs.

SERVES 6

BLUE CORN ENCHILADAS

RED CHILI SAUCE
   15 to 18 dried hot red chili peppers
   ¼ cup olive oil
   1 large head of garlic, cut in half
   1 pound ground beef shoulder
   1 cup pure chili powder
   1 teaspoon salt
   1 tablespoon unbleached all-purpose flour
   4 cups Chicken Stock (page 41)
   ½ teaspoon dried oregano
   ½ teaspoon ground cumin

ASSEMBLY
   12 blue corn tortillas
   Vegetable oil
   ¼ cup Caramelized Onions (page 130)
   1 cup shredded cheddar
   1 cup shredded monterey jack
   Mild goat or farmer cheese

To make sauce: Under running water, split dried peppers and wash out seeds. Cover with hot water and soak for 10 to 15 minutes.

Meanwhile, heat oil in a large, heavy skillet over medium-high heat and sauté the garlic for a minute. Add the meat and chili powder and fry until very brown, stirring all the while, about 8 to 10 minutes. Stir in the salt and flour.

Drain the peppers and purée them in a food processor to make a smooth paste.

Add stock to the meat and bring to a simmer. Add pepper purée and seasonings. Bring to a boil, then turn back to a simmer, reducing until thickened (like tomato sauce), about 20 minutes.

To assemble: Preheat oven to 350 degrees. Lightly oil a 14-inch oval casserole.

Warm the tortillas in a very lightly oiled heavy pan over high heat, turning once, until soft, about 30 seconds per side.

Fill each tortilla with ¼ cup of the chili sauce and a teaspoon of the caramelized onion. Mix the cheddar and jack and divide 1½ cups evenly among the tortillas. Roll the enchiladas and place seam side down in the casserole. Pour the remaining cup of sauce over the enchiladas and sprinkle with the remaining ½ cup of cheese. Bake uncovered for 30 minutes or until bubbly. Sprinkle with crumbled goat cheese before serving.

SERVES 6

CHICKEN FAJITAS WITH AVOCADO DRESSING

AVOCADO DRESSING
4 tablespoons fresh cilantro leaves
1 jalapeño, seeded and minced
1/2 cup coarsely chopped red onion
2 avocados
1 teaspoon fresh lemon juice

CHICKEN FILLING
2 tablespoons olive oil
2 cups thinly sliced red onion
1 red bell pepper, cored, seeded, and
*   julienned*
1 green bell pepper, cored, seeded, and
*   julienned*
2 garlic cloves, minced
1/4 pound cooked chorizo sausage, cut
*   lengthwise and then into 1/4-inch pieces*
2 whole chicken breasts, skinless and
*   boneless, split in half (4 pieces)*

ASSEMBLY
6 (8-inch) flour tortillas
1 cup chopped tomato
1 cup shredded romaine lettuce

To make avocado dressing: Using a food processor, purée cilantro, jalapeño, and onion.

Scoop out avocados into a medium-size bowl and mash. Add the puréed ingredients, stirring well to combine. Sprinkle lemon juice over dressing, cover with plastic wrap, and set aside.

To make filling: Heat 1 tablespoon of the olive oil in a heavy skillet over high heat until almost smoking. Sauté onion and bell peppers in a single layer (this may take two batches), turning only once, to brown both sides. This will take about 8 to 10 minutes. Add garlic and sausage and stir over heat to combine. Remove and keep warm.

Using the same pan, sauté chicken in remaining oil until cooked through, about 4 minutes on each side. Remove and let cool slightly before cutting into thin strips.

To assemble: Spread a small amount of avocado dressing on a flour tortilla, top with chicken-vegetable mixture, and add tomato and lettuce. Roll to serve.

SERVES 6

FRITTERS

PLAIN FRITTERS

The trick with fritters is to have the batter just thick enough so you have to use a second spoon to urge it off the spoon into the hot oil. Make fritters comparatively small. If they are too large, they will not cook all the way through before burning on the outside.

1 cup white cornmeal
1/3 cup all-purpose flour
2 teaspoons baking powder
3/4 teaspoon salt
2 eggs, lightly beaten
1 cup Creamed Corn (page 114), or canned
4 to 6 tablespoons milk
2 tablespoons minced onion
Oil for frying

Sift dry ingredients into a mixing bowl. Combine eggs and corn in another bowl, and mix lightly with the dry ingredients. Add milk a few tablespoons at a time, until the correct consistency is achieved. Stir in onion.

Heat oil in a deep-fryer to about 365 degrees. Drop batter by the tablespoonfuls into hot oil and cook until golden, several minutes. Drain on paper towels.

MAKES ABOUT 24 FRITTERS

ONION FRITTERS

Modern version of an old favorite.

1½ cups roughly chopped yellow onion
½ cup roughly chopped shallots
2 tablespoons olive oil
3 green onions, finely chopped (use all of the
    green)
⅔ cup all-purpose flour
½ teaspoon salt
⅛ teaspoon freshly ground black pepper
1 large egg, separated
1 tablespoon unsalted butter, melted and
    cooled
¾ cup flat beer
Vegetable oil for frying

In a large skillet set over medium-high heat, fry onion and shallots in olive oil until golden brown, 12 to 15 minutes. Stir in green onions and sauté, stirring constantly, for 1 minute. Remove the pan form the heat and set aside to cool.

Meanwhile, combine flour, salt, and pepper in a bowl; make a well in the center. In another bowl, whisk together egg yolk, melted butter, and beer. Pour the liquids into the dry ingredients and blend until the batter is smooth and thick. Stir in the cooled onion mixture. Cover and let batter rest for several hours, or cover and refrigerate overnight.

Just before frying, beat the egg white until soft peaks form. Gently fold the white into the prepared batter; do not overmix.

In a deep-fryer, heat oil to about 365 degrees. Working in batches, drop generous tablespoonfuls of the batter into the hot oil. Do not crowd the pan. Cook, turning gently, until dark golden brown all over and cooked through. Test the first fritter for doneness before going on; they can be deceptive, looking done on the outside while still raw in the middle. Drain the fritters on paper towels while you finish frying the rest. Serve hot.

MAKES ABOUT 24 FRITTERS

CORN AND PROSCIUTTO FRITTERS

I grew up on fritters, but for some reason they don't seem to be served much these days. Whatever, I think they are worth the trouble. These are nice served with Tomato Coulis (page 353).

1½ cups all-purpose flour
2 teaspoons baking powder
1 teaspoon salt
2 tablespoons unsalted butter, melted
2 eggs, lightly beaten
Milk
⅓ cup sliced and shredded prosciutto or
    chopped cooked ham
1 cup fresh corn kernels, cut and scraped
    from the cob (about 2 medium ears)
Safflower oil for frying

Mix dry ingredients in a bowl. Make a well in the center and pour in butter and eggs. Blend well, then add a few tablespoons of milk. Mix well; the dough should be smooth but not runny, and you should only just be able to shake the batter from the spoon. Keep adding milk and mixing until you reach this consistency. Stir in prosciutto and corn.

In a deep-fryer, heat oil to about 365 degrees. Drop the batter by generous tablespoonfuls into hot, but not smoking, oil and cook, turning gently, until dark golden; do not let burn. Test one fritter first before going on with the others to make sure you are cooking it the right length of time. Drain fritters on paper towels, then place in a warm oven until you have finished the lot.

MAKES ABOUT 24 FRITTERS

TOMATO FRITTERS

The traditional Shaker version of these fritters calls, I think, for combining cracker crumbs instead of flour with the tomato. Perhaps that is more authentic, but I prefer it this way.

2 tablespoons tomato paste
3 tomatoes, peeled, seeded, and puréed
    (about ³/₄ cup)
¹/₂ cup plus 2 tablespoons all-purpose flour
¹/₂ teaspoon sugar
¹/₂ teaspoon baking powder
¹/₄ teaspoon salt
¹/₂ cup grated gruyère
1 egg, lightly beaten
¹/₄ teaspoon Worcestershire Sauce
Vegetable oil for frying

Combine tomato paste and tomato purée in a bowl and set aside.

Sift together flour, sugar, baking powder, and salt in a mixing bowl. Stir in tomato mixture, cheese, egg, and Worcestershire; mix well.

Heat about ¼ inch of oil over moderately high heat and drop in batter in heaping tablespoonfuls. Fry for about 20 seconds on each side, until golden. Do not let the oil get too hot, or the fritters will brown on the outside without completely cooking on the inside. Try one first, to make sure of what you are doing, and adjust heat if necessary. Drain on paper towels.
MAKES ABOUT 12 FRITTERS

RASPBERRY FRITTERS

If you use blackberries to make the fritters, just follow the instructions. If you use blueberries, stir them into the batter all at once. Strawberries don't work very well here.

1¹/₂ cups all-purpose flour
2 rounded teaspoons baking powder
¹/₂ teaspoon salt
1 tablespoon granulated sugar
2 tablespoons unsalted butter, melted
2 large eggs, lightly beaten
Milk
1 cup lightly sugared raspberries
Oil for frying
Confectioners' sugar and/or Berry Syrup
    (page 370)

Mix dry ingredients in a bowl. Make a well in the center and pour in the butter and eggs. Blend well. Add milk a tablespoon at a time, stirring after each addition until you have a batter that's smooth but not runny. You should only just be able to shake the batter off the spoon. Don't mix the berries in.

Heat oil in a deep pot (you should have at least 2 inches of oil) until very hot, about 365 degrees. Stir some batter into a quarter of the berries. Drop by tablespoonfuls into the hot oil and fry until golden. Be careful not to burn them. Fritters can deceive you, looking done on the outside while remaining uncooked inside, so try one or two until you get it right. Fry the fritters in batches, until all batter and berries are used.

Sprinkle with confectioners' sugar or drizzle with a bit of Berry Syrup.
MAKES ABOUT 12 FRITTERS

335

ENGLISH APPLE FRITTERS

These are tasty and sturdy. The batter is the simplest kind and tastes almost like a dough-nut. The sprinkling of sugar should be liberal.

> 4 medium firm-textured pie apples, such as
>   Granny Smith
> Lemon juice (optional)
> 2 eggs, lightly beaten
> 1 cup milk
> 1¾ cups all-purpose flour
> Pinch of salt
> Oil for frying
> Granulated sugar mixed with cinnamon
>   and a pinch of nutmeg

Core the apples (do not peel) and cut them into ¼-inch slices. If you like, rub them with lemon juice.

Mix the eggs and milk and combine with flour. Add salt. Do not overmix.

Heat 1 inch of oil to 350 degrees. Coat apples with batter and fry on each side until golden. Drain and sprinkle generously with the spiced sugar.

SERVES 6 TO 8

HUSH PUPPIES

Hush puppies are close relatives of fritters.

> 1 cup white cornmeal
> ¾ teaspoon salt
> 1 teaspoon baking powder
> ¼ cup finely chopped green onions, with
>   some of the green
> ½ cup boiling water
> 1 egg, well beaten
> Vegetable oil for deep-frying

Thoroughly mix cornmeal, salt, and baking powder in a large bowl. Mix in green onions. Pour in boiling water, stirring well. Stir in egg.

Heat oil in a deep-fryer to about 365 degrees. Drop batter by generous teaspoonfuls into hot oil and fry until golden brown. Drain on paper towels.

MAKES ABOUT 18 HUSH PUPPIES

VARIATION

Another version of this recipe can be made by simply mixing cornmeal, salt, and green onions, pouring hot water over all, and leaving out the egg.

Put about 1 inch of oil in a skillet, heat to very hot, and drop batter in by teaspoonfuls. Turn once and fry until brown. Drain on paper towels.

VEGETABLE CROQUETTES

You may use leftover vegetables here in place of the leek, carrot, and celery combination. If you do, you will need about one generous cup of cooked vegetables, coarsely chopped.

> ¾ cup cooked rice
> ¾ cup shredded Swiss cheese, loosely packed
> ¼ teaspoon dry mustard
> ¾ teaspoon salt
> ½ teaspoon freshly ground black pepper
> Dash of cayenne
> 3 tablespoons unsalted butter
> 1 medium leek, washed carefully, cut into
>   ½-inch rings, using some of the green
> 1 medium carrot, peeled and shredded
> 1 small celery rib, finely chopped
> 2 tablespoons all-purpose flour
> ½ cup evaporated low-fat milk or whole
>   milk
> Several cups toasted bread crumbs
> Oil for frying (or a combination of oil and
>   butter)

Mix rice, cheese, mustard, salt, pepper, and cayenne and set aside.

Melt 1 tablespoon butter in a medium skillet and add the vegetables. Wilt over low heat for 5 minutes and set aside.

Melt the remaining 2 tablespoons butter in a saucepan and mix in the flour carefully. Meanwhile, have the milk warming. When butter and flour are thoroughly mixed, add the warmed milk, stirring constantly. Continue to cook, stirring, until you have a thick smooth sauce.

Add the vegetables to the rice mixture and combine. Add the sauce and mix thoroughly.

Set out a large plate or sheet of wax paper and spread the bread crumbs on it. Drop the vegetable mixture by generous tablespoonfuls onto the crumbs and roll around to coat and form a cigar shape. Place them on a plate as you finish coating.

Add about ⅛ inch of oil to a skillet. Bring to medium heat and carefully add the croquettes. Do not crowd them—you may want fry them in batches. When they are brown on one side, turn them over with two forks. When done on that side, remove with a slotted pancake turner and drain on paper towels. Let cool.

MAKES ABOUT 12 CROQUETTES

DUMPLINGS

BERRY DUMPLINGS

Some people love dumplings while others can take 'em or leave 'em. I think the problem for those who don't like them is that they have had dumplings that weren't cooked properly or were handled too much in the preparation, which makes them tough. To ensure they are cooked property, I poach my berry dumplings separately from what they are served with—in a poaching liquid that's a combination of apple juice and chicken stock.

I like berry dumplings with spicy mixtures of stewed meats, such as pork and sausages, or in chili-flavored vegetable stews. They lend a light touch to such rich dishes.

Although I've tried using other types of berries, I think blueberries are the best.

2 cups Chicken Stock (page 41)
2 cups unsweetened apple juice
1 cup all-purpose flour
1½ teaspoons baking powder
½ teaspoon salt
¼ teaspoon baking soda
Pinch of freshly grated nutmeg
1 large egg, lightly beaten
2 tablespoons butter or margarine, melted and cooled
⅔ cup buttermilk
½ cup blueberries, roughly puréed

Combine stock and apple juice in a wide pot and put on to heat. Meanwhile, sift dry ingredients together into a bowl. Mix egg, butter and buttermilk. Pour this into the dry ingredients all at once and mix quickly. Add the blueberry purée and mix it in with a few strokes.

With the stock at a rolling boil, drop dumpling dough by the scant tablespoon into the liquid; do not crowd. Carefully turn the dumplings over with a fork after about 10 minutes. Cook until puffed and cooked through, about 15 minutes. Remove with a slotted spoon.

SERVES 6

337

EMPANADAS

BEEF-FILLED EMPANADAS

This is George and Sherry Zabriskie's recipe.

FILLING

3 tablespoons unsalted butter or margarine
1/3 cup chopped yellow onion
1/2 pound ground beef
1/3 cup currants
2 tablespoons slivered almonds
1 teaspoon ground cinnamon
2 teaspoons chili powder
3 tablespoons brown sugar
1 egg, lightly beaten
Salt and freshly ground black pepper, to
*   taste*

DOUGH

8 tablespoons (1 stick) unsalted butter or
*   margarine, at room temperature*
4 ounces cream cheese, at room temperature
1 1/2 cups all-purpose flour
1/2 teaspoon baking powder
1/4 teaspoon cider vinegar
2 tablespoons very cold water or milk
1 tablespoon vegetable oil
1 egg, beaten with 2 tablespoons water

To make filling: Heat enough butter to sauté onion until golden. With a slotted spoon or spatula, remove onion to a medium-size mixing bowl.

Sauté beef in remaining butter over moderate heat until cooked through, about 3 minutes. Put in bowl with onion. Add remaining filling ingredients and mix well. Season and set aside.

Preheat oven to 400 degrees.

To make dough: Combine butter and cream cheese, using a fork. Sift flour over mixture. Add baking powder, vinegar, and water and combine.

With generously floured hands, work the dough until you have a smooth resilient ball, 3 or 4 minutes. At first, the dough will stick to your fingers, but keep working in the flour until the dough finally holds together.

Flour both a work surface and a rolling pin, and roll out the dough about 1/8 inch thick. Cut out as many 6-inch circles as possible and set aside. Gather up scraps and roll out again and cut more circles. There should be 10 circles.

Oil a large baking sheet. Spoon 2 tablespoons filling in the middle of each circle. Dampen edges and fold over to make a half-moon shape. Seal with tines of a fork. Brush with egg glaze and bake until golden, 15 to 20 minutes. Let cool on a rack.

SERVES 4 TO 6

SANDWICHES

GRILLED CHEESE SANDWICHES

Butter
Very thin slices of whole wheat bread
Honey mustard
Emmentaler
Cornichons

Spread butter on one side of the bread and honey mustard on the other side. Top with cheese and a final slice of buttered bread. Start in a cold skillet and grill on both sides over medium heat. Serve with cornichons.

VARIATIONS

Omit the mustard and substitute mild goat cheese and slices of prosciutto for the emmentaler.

Omit the mustard and substitute mozzarella slices and strips of peeled and seeded roasted bell pepper (see Note, page 74) for the emmentaler.

Substitute very thin slices of wheat bread for the wheat bread and omit the mustard. Use Swiss cheese slices, wilted cucumbers, and strips of crisp bacon instead of the emmentaler.

Substitute very thin slices of soft rye bread for the wheat bread, green peppercorn mustard for the honey mustard, and sharp cheddar slices for the emmentaler, and add wilted green onions.

Substitute very thin slices of soft rye bread for the wheat bread and omit the mustard. Instead of the emmentaler, try mashed blue cheese and chopped walnuts.

ROASTED RED PEPPER AND BUTTER SANDWICHES

I prefer Pepperidge Farm bread for these sandwiches.

*1 large red bell pepper, roasted, peeled, and
  seeded (see Note, page 74), chopped
8 tablespoons (1 stick) unsalted butter,
  softened
1 teaspoon salt
1/2 teaspoon freshly ground black pepper
12 slices very thin white bread
12 slices very thin whole wheat bread*

Place roasted red pepper (and any roasting liquid) in the bowl of a food processor fitted with a metal blade. Process until smooth. Add butter, salt, and pepper and process until well combined.

Using a spatula, smooth butter mixture on one side of white bread. Top each slice of buttered bread with a slice of whole wheat bread. Stack several sandwiches together and, using a sharp serrated knife, remove the crusts. Slice each stack into four sandwich triangles.

MAKES 12 SANDWICHES

GRILLED PORTOBELLO BURGER

*6 portobello mushrooms, wiped clean and
  stems removed
1/4 cup olive oil
1 teaspoon salt
1/2 teaspoon freshly ground black pepper
6 1/4-inch slices red onion
6 1/4-inch slices tomato
6 slices melting cheese (monterey jack,
  havarti)
6 round rolls (kaiser rolls, onion rolls,
  hamburger buns)*

Prepare a grill or broiler.

Coat mushrooms with olive oil, but do not saturate. Season with salt and pepper.

Grill mushrooms crown side down until grill marks start to appear. This will take between 3 and 5 minutes. Invert mushrooms, now crown side down, and place onion, tomato, and cheese in the natural pocket that the crown forms. Cover grill and cook, checking occasionally, until the cheese starts to melt, about 2 minutes.

Toast buns on grill.

Fill each bun with a portobello burger and serve.

MAKES 6 BURGERS

THE TUSCAN SANDWICH

You can put any number of grilled elements in my Tuscan sandwich—mushrooms, onions, and seeded tomato slices. Make it with or without cheese. However, after experimenting with others, I've decided I like the version here the best.

8 thick lengthwise slices from several large
  zucchini
8 thick lengthwise slices from 2 medium
  eggplants
Olive oil
Balsamic vinegar
2 large red bell peppers, roasted, peeled,
  and seeded (see Note, page 74)
4 slices Italian bread, about 1/4 inch thick,
  generously rubbed on one side with garlic
  and brushed well with olive oil
8 medium slices mozzarella
Salt and freshly ground black pepper, to
  taste
Fried Thin Onion Rings (page 132)

Prepare a grill or broiler.

Rub zucchini and eggplant slices with olive oil and then sprinkle with vinegar. Set aside. Cut peppers into wide strips and set aside.

Grill zucchini and eggplant about 6 inches from the coals until tender and turning golden, about 4 or more minutes on each side. (This timing is only approximate, since it will ultimately depend on how close the vegetables are to the heat and how hot the coals are.) Set aside. Grill the bread, bare side down first, until lightly toasted. Turn and grill the oiled side.

Assemble the sandwiches by layering the eggplant, pepper, and zucchini on each slice of the grilled bread, oiled side up. Salt and pepper the layers. Top with mozzarella and run the sandwiches under the broiler just long enough to melt the cheese slightly. Place on individual plates and sprinkle with the fried onions and serve immediately.

SERVES 4

GRILLED SHRIMP WITH COLESLAW ON PEPPER BREAD

1 1/2 cups hot picante sauce
3 tablespoons olive oil
1 1/2 pounds small shrimp, cleaned and
  deveined
1/4 recipe Coleslaw (page 56)
6 Pepper Breads (recipe follows)

Combine picante sauce with olive oil. Add shrimp and marinate at room temperature for 1 hour.

Prepare a grill or sauté pan.

Remove shrimp from marinade and drain on paper towels. Grill or sauté shrimp until bright pink, about 2 to 3 minutes, turning frequently, over high heat. Do not overcook.

Top each bread with coleslaw and shrimp.

MAKES 6 SANDWICHES

PEPPER BREAD

3 cups all-purpose flour
2 teaspoons baking powder
1 teaspoon salt
1/2 cup boiling water
1/2 cup plus 2 tablespoons cold water
3 teaspoons peanut oil
1 1/2 teaspoons coarsely ground black pepper

Put the flour, baking powder, and salt in the bowl of a food processor fitted with a metal blade and pulse to combine. Withe motor running, pour boiling water in a thin stream through the feed tube. Add the cold water and process until mixture forms a ball. Process for 1 minute longer.

Turn out dough onto a lightly floured surface. Knead briefly. Cover with plastic wrap and let sit for 15 minutes.

Divide the dough into 6 pieces. Working with one piece at a time, and keeping the others covered, turn out dough onto a floured surface and roll into a circle 8 inches in diameter. Spoon ½ teaspoon of the oil over the top of the bread, and sprinkle with ¼ teaspoon of pepper.

Roll the bread as tightly as possible, jelly roll fashion. Anchoring one end of the resulting tube on the work surface with a finger, coil the bread as tightly as possible and pinch the other end against the coil to make a smooth round. Flatten gently with the palm of your hand. Roll the bread out again gently until it is about ¼ inch thick and 6 inches across.

Repeat with remaining dough. Cover any dough that is not being cooked with dampened paper towel.

Heat a heavy cast-iron skillet over medium heat. Once the skillet is hot, rub it lightly with an oiled paper towel. Lower the heat to medium-low and place the bread in the skillet. Cook for 3 minutes or until the bottom is golden brown. Turn and repeat on the other side. Transfer to a rack to cool. Wrap in plastic wrap to keep soft.

MAKES 6 INDIVIDUAL BREADS

HOT TURKEY PATTY SANDWICH

Grace Monroe, who has worked for me for years now, makes wonderful flavorful patties from ground turkey meat for a quick lunch or dinner. They are good hot or at room temperature. And, of course, they may also be made with ground chicken. Ballpark mustard really does make a difference here.

2 slices country white bread
Mayonnaise and yellow mustard, to taste
1 Grace's Turkey Patty (recipe follows)
Lettuce
Dill pickle, sliced

Spread the bread lightly with mayonnaise and mustard. Add the patty, some lettuce, and slices of dill pickle.

MAKES 1 SANDWICH

GRACE'S TURKEY PATTIES

1¼ pounds ground turkey
½ cup finely chopped onion
½ cup finely chopped green bell pepper
½ teaspoon freshly ground black pepper
2 cups Chicken Stock (page 41) reduced to ⅓ cup
1½ tablespoons vegetable oil

Combine turkey, onion, green bell pepper, black pepper, and stock. Mix well and form into 6 patties.

Heat oil in a medium skillet and brown patties quickly on both sides over medium heat. Reduce heat and continue cooking until done through, about 15 minutes.

MAKES 6 PATTIES

SHALLOT BUTTER SANDWICHES

1 recipe Shallot Butter (page 351), softened
16 slices very thin whole wheat bread, crusts trimmed

Spread 8 slices of bread generously with the butter, top each with another slice, and cut in half. Wrap them tightly, 4 to a packet, in plastic wrap and refrigerate until ready to use.

MAKES 8 SANDWICHES

CHEESE STEAK SANDWICHES

2 baguettes, cut into 6 sandwich rolls, split
lengthwise and opened
1 can (13 ounces) low-sodium beef broth
1½ pounds precooked roast beef, thinly
sliced
½ pound muenster or American cheese,
thinly sliced

Preheat oven to 350 degrees. Place open bread on a baking sheet, crust side down.

In a heavy saucepan over medium heat, bring beef broth to a boil and reduce to a simmer. Using tongs, drop sliced roast beef into simmering stock until meat is heated, about 2 minutes.

Remove meat and place on prepared bread. Top with sliced cheese. Heat in oven until cheese is melted and edges of bread are crisp, about 3 to 5 minutes.

Remove baking sheet from oven. Fold bread over to cover the melted meat and cheese.

SERVES 6

SPREADS AND CANAPES

WHITE BEAN SPREAD

To make sandwiches, spread the purée on thickly sliced bread and top with watercress and green onions. You can make soup of this by adding reserved bean liquid and chicken stock to the desired consistency.

1 pound small dried white beans, soaked
overnight or by the quick-soak method
(see Note, page 25)
½ pound salt pork
2 bay leaves
2 garlic cloves
2 whole cloves
½ teaspoon dried thyme
2 tablespoons olive oil
1 tablespoon finely chopped fresh Italian
flat-leaf parsley
2 teaspoons fresh lemon juice
½ teaspoon freshly ground black pepper
½ teaspoon salt
8 drops Tabasco Sauce

Drain the beans. Pour on fresh water to come about 2 inches over them. Add pork, bay leaves, garlic, cloves, and thyme. Simmer, skimming as needed, for 1½ hours, or until tender.

Drain, reserving the liquid. Remove bay leaves and pork. Discard the bay leaves. Cut any lean meat from the pork, discarding the fat and rind. Put the pork in a food processor and chop coarse. Then add beans, along with olive oil, parsley, lemon juice, pepper, salt, and Tabasco. Purée. Correct the seasoning.

Store in the refrigerator with a light film of olive oil on top to keep it from drying out.

MAKES ABOUT 4 CUPS

CUCUMBER SPREAD

As you might imagine, the cucumbers give this a very refreshing flavor. However, you must work on it to ensure that it isn't too bland. Make as much or as little as you like.

Cucumbers
Salt
Pot cheese or cottage cheese
Mayonnaise or light cream
Tabasco Sauce
Grated onion
Worcestershire Sauce
Paprika
Freshly ground black pepper
Crumbled crisp bacon

Peel and seed the cucumbers, then cut into medium chunks. Sprinkle generously with salt and place in the refrigerator for several hours, covered. Remove and drain. Discard liquid and dry the chunks between paper towels. Mince the cucumbers. Meanwhile, mix the pot cheese with just enough mayonnaise or cream to make it spreadable. Season with Tabasco, grated onion, Worcestershire, paprika, and pepper (no salt needed). Stir in the cucumbers and bacon just before using.

FRESH SALMON SPREAD

1/4 cup Salmon Salad (page 282)
4 ounces cream cheese, softened
1 small onion, roughly chopped
6 dashes Tabasco Sauce
1/2 teaspoon Worcestershire Sauce

Place all ingredients in the bowl of a food processor. Process for several minutes until smooth.
MAKES ABOUT 1 CUP

SMOKED SALMON SPREAD

3 ounces smoked salmon, roughly chopped
3 ounces cream cheese, softened
1 small onion, roughly chopped
1 tablespoon capers, rinsed and drained

Place all ingredients in the bowl of a food processor. Process for several minutes until smooth.
MAKES ABOUT 1 CUP

VARIATIONS

Substitute 1 tablespoon chopped fresh dill for the capers. Add fresh lemon juice to taste.
   Omit the onion.

RADISH CANAPÉS

I had forgotten just how tasty this simple canapé could be and was glad to rediscover it.

1 loaf homemade-style white bread, sliced
   medium thin
8 tablespoons (1 stick) unsalted butter,
   softened
2 to 3 bunches red radishes
Finely snipped fresh chives

Cut the bread into 2½-inch rounds with a cookie cutter, making 24 in all. Spread each round generously with softened butter. Slice the radishes thin and arrange on bread in concentric circles. Sprinkle with chopped chives. Lightly cover with a damp cloth and keep chilled until serving time.
   Any scraps and leftover pieces of bread can be made into bread crumbs.
MAKES 24 CANAPÉS

OLIVE AND SUN-DRIED TOMATO SPREAD

*1/4 cup pitted and roughly chopped oil-cured
    black olives*
*1/2 cup roughly chopped pimiento-stuffed
    green olives*
1/2 cup roughly chopped sun-dried tomatoes
1/2 cup roughly chopped canned pimientos
*3 tablespoons finely chopped fresh Italian
    flat-leaf parsley*
2 anchovy fillets, mashed
2 teaspoons minced garlic
1/2 teaspoon dried oregano
1 teaspoon fresh lemon juice
1/2 teaspoon freshly ground black pepper
4 ounces cream cheese, softened

Stir together all of the ingredients except the
cream cheese until well combined. Stir in the
cream cheese and mix until thoroughly
blended.
MAKES 1½ CUPS

LIMA BEAN SPREAD

This is good use for leftover beans. Amounts
depend on how much you have.

Cooked lima beans, well drained
Chopped watercress
Mayonnaise
Fresh lemon juice
Tabasco Sauce
Minced green onions

The best way to do this is to purée the cooked
beans and chopped watercress first. Taste the
mixture at this point before adding the mayonnaise and lemon juice, because you may not
need much of either. Ditto with the Tabasco,
which should be mixed with the mayonnaise if
you are using it. Stir in the green onions just
before you use the spread.

GRILLED TUNA SPREAD WITH ROASTED PEPPERS

This is a good use for leftover grilled tuna steak
(or swordfish). Make as much as you want, but
keep the ratio of mayonnaise to sour cream to
about three to one.

*Grilled tuna steak or canned tuna packed in
    oil, drained*
Mayonnaise
Sour cream
*Roasted red bell pepper, peeled and seeded
    (see Note, page 74)*
Fresh lemon juice
*Salt and freshly ground black pepper, to
    taste*

Purée tuna, mayonnaise, sour cream, and bell
pepper in a food processor until smooth. Add
lemon juice, salt, and pepper. Store this in the
refrigerator with a sheet of wax paper pressed
onto the top until ready to use.

SAUCES, SALSAS, CHUTNEY, AND MORE

THIS SECTION IS DEVOTED TO LITTLE indulgences that can put distinctive snap into a dish or a meal. All are easy to make and open-to-suggestion when it comes to uses. For instance, the flavored vinegars are not just for vinaigrette, but also lend an intriguing accent to sauces and gravies. The herbed butters can be used as sandwich spreads as well as for topping meats, fish, and vegetables. And some of these salsas can serve as salads on their own. ✦ Though I don't spend much time putting up preserves, when fruit is at its peak of natural flavor I do make small batches of ones that keep well for several weeks in the refrigerator. I particularly like mixing two different fruits together for preserves— and I'm never shy about using two sauces on one dessert. Where I come from, pickles and relishes appear on the table at most meals. The pickle and relish recipes you'll find here are Southern-traditional. Try them—I'll bet you'll be whistling *Dixie*.

SOME CLASSIC SAUCES

HORSERADISH SAUCE

The important thing in this recipe is to be sure the onion is lightly browned. This adds considerably to the sauce's flavor. I also usually use more than the quarter cup of horseradish called for here, but let your taste be your guide.

4 tablespoons (½ stick) unsalted butter (or half butter and half margarine)
½ cup minced onion
3 tablespoons unbleached all-purpose flour
2 cups Chicken Stock (page 41), hot
1 tablespoon fresh lemon juice
¼ teaspoon freshly ground black pepper
¼ cup prepared horseradish, or more to taste
Salt (optional)

Melt butter in a large skillet. Add onion and cook over medium-high heat until lightly golden, about 15 minutes. Sprinkle in flour and cook, stirring, for a minute or so. Stir in stock, mixing as you go to eliminate any lumps. Stir in lemon juice and pepper. Reduce the heat to low and simmer, stirring occasionally, until the sauce thickens, about 10 minutes. Stir in the horseradish. Add a little salt if necessary.

You can let this cool and reheat it.

MAKES ABOUT 2 CUPS

VARIATION
HORSERADISH AND GREEN PEPPERCORN SAUCE

Prepare the recipe as above. When you stir in the horseradish, add 1 tablespoon Dijon mustard and 2 tablespoons drained, brine-packed green peppercorns.

CREOLE SAUCE

Make this sauce as hot or as mild as you like by increasing or decreasing the quantity of hot chili.

1 4-inch hot red chili, roasted, peeled, and seeded (see Note, page 74)
6 ounces shallots, peeled
2 large garlic cloves
⅓ cup snipped fresh chives
2 tablespoons vegetable oil
½ teaspoon salt
3 tablespoons fresh lime juice
⅔ cup boiling water

Cut the chili into strips. Put it, along with shallots, garlic, and chives, in a food processor. Chop fine. Transfer to a bowl and add the oil, salt, lime juice, and boiling water. Stir and let cool, then cover. You do not have to refrigerate this.

MAKES 2 CUPS

CAPER SAUCE

This sauce is great with fish.

1 teaspoon vegetable oil
2 tablespoons minced red onion
1 garlic clove, minced
¼ cup white wine vinegar
2 cups heavy cream
1 tablespoon chopped fresh Italian flat-leaf parsley
1 tablespoon capers, rinsed and drained
Salt and white pepper, to taste

Heat oil in a medium saucepan over medium-high heat. Add onion and garlic and sauté until translucent. Add vinegar and reduce to about 1 tablespoon. Then add cream and reduce to about one cup.

Remove from the heat, stir in parsley and capers, and season with salt and pepper.

MAKES ABOUT 1 CUP

PARSLEY-PECAN SAUCE

Another great sauce for fish.

*2 cups tightly packed fresh Italian flat-leaf
    parsley, leaves and tender stems only*
1/2 cup olive oil
1/2 cup broken pecan meats
1 large garlic clove, cut into several pieces
1/2 cup freshly grated parmesan
1/2 cup fresh grated romano
2 tablespoons unsalted butter, cut into pieces
Salt

Place parsley in a food processor and process
until coarsely chopped, turning machine off
and on and scraping down sides. Add all other
ingredients except salt, and process until mixture makes a smooth paste. Correct seasoning
with salt. Store, tightly covered, in the refrigerator.

    This sauce freezes successfully. Thaw in the
refrigerator.

MAKES ABOUT 2 CUPS

VARIATION

Substitute pine nuts for the pecans.

HERB SAUCE

Vary the herbs to suit the dish you're saucing.

1 tablespoon unsalted butter
1 tablespoon plus 2 teaspoons minced shallot
1 teaspoon minced garlic
1 teaspoon minced fresh rosemary
1 tablespoon all-purpose flour
1 1/4 cups milk, warmed
1/2 teaspoon salt, or to taste
Pinch of white pepper
*Pinch of cayenne or several dashes of
    Tabasco Sauce*
1 teaspoon Worcestershire Sauce
2 tablespoons minced fresh chives
*1 tablespoon minced fresh Italian flat-leaf
    parsley*

Melt butter in a small saucepan. Sauté shallot,
garlic, and rosemary over medium heat until
wilted, about 5 minutes. Stir in flour and cook
for a minute or two. Whisk in milk slowly.
Cook over medium-low heat, stirring all the
while, until slightly thickened, about 5 minutes more. Off the heat, stir in remaining
ingredients. Serve warm.

MAKES ABOUT 1 1/2 CUPS

YOGURT AND
CUCUMBER SAUCE

This traditional Greek sauce, called tzatziki, is
often served as a dip with triangles of toasted
(or plain) pita bread. It is an excellent sauce for
vegetable croquettes or for crudités.

2 cups plain yogurt
*1 cup peeled, seeded, and shredded
    cucumber*
1 teaspoon fresh lemon juice
1 teaspoon minced garlic
Salt and freshly ground black pepper, to taste

Cut a double piece of cheesecloth into a square
that will cover the inside of a medium-size fine
sieve. Rinse and wring it dry and line the sieve.
Add yogurt and let drain over a bowl for 2
hours. Discard the drained liquid and combine the remaining ingredients with the
yogurt. Refrigerate for at least 1 hour.

SERVES 4 TO 6

VARIATION

Sprinkle with chopped fresh dill for the color
and flavor of it.

TARRAGON CUCUMBER SAUCE

1 large English cucumber, peeled, seeded, and coarsely chopped
2 tablespoons tarragon vinegar
1 tablespoon canola oil
1/2 cup Chicken Stock (page 41)
2 tablespoons minced red onion
1 tablespoon chopped fresh Italian flat-leaf parsley
1 teaspoon salt
1/4 teaspoon white pepper

Purée cucumber, vinegar, oil, and stock in a food processor. Transfer to a bowl and whisk in the other ingredients.
MAKES ABOUT 1 1/2 CUPS

MAYONNAISE

HOMEMADE MAYONNAISE

If you are concerned about the safety of eggs in your area, do not make raw egg mayonnaise.

1 teaspoon dry mustard
1 teaspoon salt
Pinch of freshly ground black pepper
3 tablespoons fresh lemon juice
1 large egg
1 1/4 cups vegetable oil
3/4 cup olive oil
Dash of Tabasco Sauce (optional)

Place mustard, salt, pepper, lemon juice, and egg in a food processor. Combine the oils. With the motor running, pour oil in a slow, steady stream through the feed tube until all has been emulsified. Stir in Tabasco if using.
MAKES ABOUT 2 CUPS

VARIATIONS

Substitute 1 to 2 teaspoons Dijon mustard or green peppercorn mustard for the dry mustard. Substitute lime juice for the lemon juice.

GARLIC MAYONNAISE

2 whole medium heads of garlic, top 1/4 inch sliced off
2 teaspoons olive oil
Pinch of salt
Pinch of freshly ground black pepper
2 cups mayonnaise, preferably homemade (recipe above)
3 tablespoons fresh lemon juice (1 lemon)
1/4 teaspoon salt
1/4 teaspoon white pepper

Preheat oven to 275 degrees.
Place garlic heads in a small pan lined with foil. Drizzle oil over each and sprinkle with salt and pepper. Bake until tender, 45 minutes or more.
Peel and purée the roasted garlic. Combine the purée with the other ingredients. Chill.
MAKES ABOUT 2 CUPS

MUSTARD-DILL MAYONNAISE

1/2 cup mayonnaise, preferably homemade (recipe above)
1/3 cup Dijon mustard
1 tablespoon tarragon vinegar
1/4 teaspoon white pepper
2 tablespoons chopped fresh dill

Whisk mayonnaise, mustard, vinegar, and white pepper until blended. Fold in dill. Refrigerate until ready to use.
MAKES ABOUT 1 CUP

348

JALAPEÑO–LIME MAYONNAISE

6 saffron threads
½ cup dry white wine
2 cups mayonnaise, preferably homemade
(recipe above)
1 teaspoon seeded and minced jalapeño
Salt and freshly ground black pepper, to
taste

Combine saffron and wine in a very small saucepan and simmer over medium-low heat until reduced to about 1 tablespoon, 8 to 10 minutes. Strain, reserving the wine, and set aside to cool.

Make the mayonnaise using lime juice. Whisk in the jalapeño. Stir in the reduced wine and adjust seasoning.
MAKES 2½ CUPS

WATERCRESS MAYONNAISE

½ large bunch watercress, leaves only
1 shallot, coarsely chopped
2 tablespoons tarragon vinegar
½ teaspoon salt
Pinch of freshly ground black pepper
Pinch of cayenne
1 cup mayonnaise, preferably homemade
(recipe above)

Place all ingredients except mayonnaise in a food processor. Purée, scraping down sides often. Add mayonnaise and mix until just blended.
MAKES ABOUT 1 CUP

MUSTARD SAUCE

1 cup mayonnaise, preferably homemade
(recipe above)
½ cup heavy cream, whipped into peaks
1 tablespoon Dijon mustard
1 teaspoon dry mustard

Mix mayonnaise, whipped cream, and mustards and refrigerate until ready to use.
MAKES 1½ CUPS

TARTAR SAUCE

There are many ingredients in this sauce because I like it that way, but it can also be made with just mayonnaise, pickles, and chives.

1 cup mayonnaise, preferably homemade
(recipe above)
1 tablespoon finely chopped fresh Italian
flat-leaf parsley
1 tablespoon chives, snipped fine
1 tablespoon small capers, rinsed and
drained
2 tablespoons sweet pickles, chopped fine
1 large green onion, with some of the green,
chopped fine
¼ teaspoon Dijon mustard
3 or 4 grinds of fresh black pepper
Salt, to taste
Chopped fresh dill

Mix all the ingredients except dill and refrigerate until ready to use. Sprinkle dill generously over the sauce before serving.
MAKES ABOUT 1 CUP

VARIATIONS
Use ⅔ cup mayonnaise and ⅓ cup yogurt. Add Tabasco Sauce to taste.

Substitute 4 tablespoons snipped fresh dill for the parsley. Add 1 canned jalapeño, seeded and rinsed.

349

TOMATO TARTAR SAUCE

1 cup puréed peeled and seeded fresh tomato
  or canned tomatoes
1 cup dry white wine
1/2 cup tomato juice
1 teaspoon minced garlic
2 cups mayonnaise, preferably homemade
  (page 348)
1/4 cup minced white onion
1/4 cup drained sweet pickle relish
1 tablespoon minced fresh tarragon
1/2 teaspoon Louisiana Hot Sauce
1/2 teaspoon salt
Whites of 2 hard-cooked eggs, minced

Combine tomato purée, wine, tomato juice, and garlic in a small saucepan and bring quickly to a boil, stirring, over high heat. Turn the heat down to a simmer and reduce the mixture to 1 cup without stirring, about 20 to 25 minutes. Let cool.

Add the cooled tomato reduction to the mayonnaise, onion, and relish in a food processor. Purée and scrape out into a bowl. Mix in all other ingredients, correct seasoning if necessary, and chill.

MAKES ABOUT 3 CUPS

FLAVORED BUTTER

PARSLEY–PINE NUT BUTTER

This tangy butter would be very good on simple broiled fish with just a bit of lemon and black pepper.

1 1/2 cups (loosely packed) fresh Italian flat-
  leaf parsley
1/4 cup pine nuts
1 large garlic clove, cut into several pieces
1/4 teaspoon salt
3 tablespoons olive oil
8 tablespoons (1 stick) unsalted butter,
  softened

Place parsley, pine nuts, garlic, and salt in a small food processor. Pulse until mixture is coarsely chopped, then continue to process, adding olive oil, until smooth. Beat into softened butter.

MAKES ABOUT 3/4 CUP

PARSLEY BUTTER

Herbed butters should only be made with the freshest of herbs because it is this freshness that gives them their distinctiveness. In place of parsley you could use chives or dill.

1/2 pound (2 sticks) unsalted butter, softened
1/2 cup finely chopped fresh Italian flat-leaf
  parsley, no stems

Put butter in a small bowl and sprinkle parsley over all. Whip with a fork until combined. Scrape into a crock. Use softened.

MAKES ABOUT 1 1/4 CUPS

350

SHALLOT BUTTER

I love the flavor of this butter, which in French is called *beurre marchand de vins*. It is essentially the same as *beurre Bercy* except that it is made with red wine instead of white.

1 tablespoon minced shallots
1/4 cup dry red wine
1/2 cup Beef Stock (page 42) or canned beef
    broth
Freshly ground black pepper
8 tablespoons (1 stick) unsalted butter,
    softened
1 1/2 tablespoons finely chopped fresh Italian
    flat-leaf parsley

Simmer shallots, wine, stock, and pepper until reduced to about 1 1/2 tablespoons. Set aside to cool. Beat the cooled shallot mixture into softened butter and add parsley a little at a time. Scrape into a container and refrigerate. Soften before using.

MAKES ABOUT 3/4 CUP

CUCUMBER BUTTER

The trick to this very uncomplicated but tasty butter is to get the cucumbers dry enough.

1/2 large cucumber, peeled, seeded, chopped,
    and lightly salted
8 tablespoons (1 stick) unsalted butter,
    softened
1/4 teaspoon lemon juice
Salt (optional)

Let the salted chopped cucumber stand in a colander for about 30 minutes, then squeeze as much liquid from it as possible. One way of doing this is to dump the drained cucumber onto a tea towel, fold the towel over, and twist it as if you were wringing it out.

Whip the cucumber pulp into the butter along with the lemon juice. Add salt if desired.

MAKES ABOUT 3/4 CUP

SAVORY TOMATO BUTTER

1/4 cup minced onion
8 tablespoons (1 stick) unsalted butter, plus
    2 teaspoons
3 cups peeled and seeded tomatoes, puréed

Sauté onion over medium heat in the 2 teaspoons of butter until it just begins to color, 3 to 4 minutes. Add tomato purée and bring to a boil. Turn the heat down to a simmer and cook for about 5 minutes. Strain the mixture through a fine strainer, pressing to get out most of the liquid. Put the liquid in a clean saucepan. Bring to a boil over medium-low heat and cook, stirring occasionally, until reduced to 2 or 3 tablespoons, about 30 minutes. During the last 10 minutes or so, take care to keep it from scorching. Let it cool.

Beat the reduction into the remaining butter. Refrigerate until ready to use.

MAKES ABOUT 3/4 CUP

APRICOT BUTTER

Apricot butter has a very subtle aftertaste of fruit and is slightly sweet. Because you are adding so much to the butter, it does not get as hard as regular butter would, which makes it easy to spread.

1/2 pound (2 sticks) unsalted butter, softened
2 medium apricots or 1 large peach, peeled,
    pitted, and cut into quarters
2 to 3 tablespoons apricot jam

Put all the ingredients in a food processor and process until smooth. Scrape into a container and store, covered, in the refrigerator.

MAKES ABOUT 2 CUPS

TABASCO BUTTER

1/2 pound (2 sticks) unsalted butter, softened
1/2 teaspoon Tabasco Sauce

Whip butter with a wire whisk or hand mixer until fluffy, adding Tabasco as you go along. Scrape into a small crock. Refrigerate until ready to use.
MAKES 1 CUP

BERRY BUTTER

Use the same type of fresh berry as in the syrup. This butter is perfect on toast in the morning or on scones or little oatmeal biscuits with afternoon tea. It would make a wonderful dessert served with cheese and thin rounds of crusty French bread.

12 tablespoons unsalted butter, softened
1/2 cup Berry Syrup (page 370)
1/2 cup berries, crushed

Put all ingredients in a bowl and blend thoroughly with a hand mixer at high speed. Smooth mixture into a bowl and cover. Keep refrigerated.
MAKES ABOUT 1 CUP

HAZELNUT–HONEY BUTTER

Naturally, you may make this with other kinds of nuts.

8 tablespoons (1 stick) unsalted butter, softened
1/2 cup finely chopped toasted hazelnuts
1/4 cup honey

Combine all ingredients in a small bowl. Mix well. Refrigerate if not using immediately.
MAKES ABOUT 1 CUP

TOMATO SAUCE

BASIC TOMATO SAUCE
This sauce is cooked very briefly so it retains its fresh flavor.

1/4 cup olive oil
2 tablespoons minced garlic
8 medium to large tomatoes (about 4 pounds), peeled, seeded, and coarsely chopped
Pinch of sugar
Salt and freshly ground black pepper, to taste
3 tablespoons sliced fresh basil, in thin julienne

Place oil in a large skillet and heat over high heat. Add garlic and cook about 1 minute, stirring. Add tomatoes and continue cooking over high heat, stirring, until heated through and some liquid has evaporated, about 5 minutes. Add sugar and season to taste. Stir in the basil off the heat, then serve.
MAKES ABOUT 8 CUPS

SPICY TOMATO SAUCE
Add 1/4 teaspoon crushed red pepper or more to taste.

ALL-PURPOSE TOMATO SAUCE
You can use canned tomatoes here—if you must.

1/4 cup olive oil
3 cups chopped onions
1 3/4 to 2 cups shredded carrots
1 tablespoon minced garlic
12 cups peeled, seeded, and coarsely chopped tomatoes (with any juice)
2 1/2 teaspoons salt, or to taste

1 teaspoon freshly ground black pepper
1 tablespoon minced fresh basil

Heat oil in a deep pot and sauté onions and carrots over medium-high heat until wilted, 4 to 5 minutes. Stir in garlic. Add tomatoes and bring to a simmer. Stir in salt, pepper, and basil. Simmer to reduce and thicken, about 10 to 15 minutes. Do not overcook.

Transfer to a food processor and process just enough to make a coarse texture.

MAKES ABOUT 12 CUPS

TOMATO COULIS

This would make a delightful summer pasta sauce, with or without the addition of fresh basil or tarragon. It's also perfect for fish.

1/4 cup olive oil
1 tablespoon minced garlic
5 cups peeled, seeded, and puréed ripe
*   tomatoes*
1 teaspoon salt
1/2 teaspoon freshly ground black pepper
2 medium ripe tomatoes, peeled, seeded,
*   and chopped*
2 tablespoons finely minced fresh Italian
*   flat-leaf parsley*
1 teaspoon white wine vinegar

Heat oil in a saucepan over medium heat. Add garlic and cook for 1 minute, or until softened but not browned. Add tomato purée, salt, and pepper. Bring to a boil, stirring occasionally, and turn heat to low. Continue to cook, stirring occasionally, for another 10 to 12 minutes. Add chopped tomatoes and cook an additional 5 minutes, stirring occasionally, until sauce is thickened. Stir in parsley and vinegar.

MAKES ABOUT 4 CUPS

SWEET AND TART TOMATO BUTTER

This spread comes from painter Neil Welliver's mother, Mamie, who grew up in rural Pennsylvania. Use it for fruit sandwiches or breakfast toast.

8 large tomatoes, peeled
1 cup sugar
1/2 teaspoon salt
1 teaspoon cinnamon
2 whole cloves
1 tablespoon fresh lemon juice

Remove the seeds from half the tomatoes and coarsely chop the tomatoes. Measure out 4 cups of chopped tomatoes and put in a nonreactive saucepan. Mix in all the other ingredients. Simmer over very low heat, stirring occasionally to prevent scorching, until thickened and reduced to 2 cups, about 2 hours. When cool, remove and discard the cloves, cover tightly and refrigerate.

MAKES 2 CUPS

SUN-DRIED TOMATO DIP

1/4 cup oil-packed sun-dried tomatoes
1/2 pound goat cheese
1/4 teaspoon freshly ground black pepper

Purée sun-dried tomatoes in a food processor until almost smooth. Add cheese and pepper and pulse until well combined. Transfer to a serving bowl.

MAKES 3/4 CUP

TOMATO OIL

You can gild the tomato by using this oil to dress tomato salad, with a good squeeze of lemon and a grind of black pepper.

>   3 pounds tomatoes, unpeeled but coarsely chopped
>   1/4 cup olive oil
>   1 teaspoon minced fresh basil
>   1 teaspoon minced fresh tarragon

Put tomatoes in a food processor and pulse a few times. Transfer to a strainer and press out all pulp and liquid. Discard seeds and skins. Put tomato pulp in a small saucepan over medium-high heat and reduce to 1 cup, about 30 minutes. Do not allow to scorch. Put it through the strainer again and return to the heat. Reduce to 1/2 cup, about 10 minutes. Mix in the olive oil and herbs. When cool, cover and refrigerate.

MAKES ABOUT 3/4 CUP

VINAIGRETTE

ALL-PURPOSE VINAIGRETTE

Use this simple vinaigrette to dress any salad.

>   2 tablespoons balsamic vinegar
>   1 teaspoon Dijon mustard
>   3/4 teaspoon salt
>   1/2 teaspoon freshly ground black pepper
>   5 tablespoons olive oil
>   3 tablespoons canola oil

Whisk together vinegar, mustard, salt, and pepper. Whisk in the oils. Use immediately, or store in a tightly covered jar in the refrigerator. Bring to room temperature and shake well before using.

MAKES ABOUT 3/4 CUP

WARM TOMATO VINAIGRETTE

This warm vinaigrette goes with everything from fish to okra.

>   1/4 cup olive oil
>   1/4 cup minced shallots
>   1 cup peeled, seeded, and finely chopped tomatoes
>   1/4 cup red wine vinegar
>   1 medium garlic clove, minced
>   2/3 cup dry white wine
>   1/4 teaspoon salt
>   Freshly ground black pepper, to taste
>   2 tablespoons minced gherkins
>   3 tablespoons small capers, rinsed and drained

Heat oil and add shallots. Cook over low heat until wilted, about 5 minutes. Do not brown. Add tomatoes and simmer for 5 minutes. Add vinegar, garlic, wine, salt, and pepper. Simmer for another 15 to 20 minutes, until reduced to a thick sauce. Correct the seasoning, and stir in the gherkins and capers.

MAKES ABOUT 1 1/2 CUPS

HOT WALNUT OIL VINAIGRETTE

This is particularly good with grated carrots. Allow about half a cup of carrots per person.

>   3 tablespoons walnut oil
>   2 tablespoons safflower oil
>   2 tablespoons red wine vinegar
>   1 teaspoon Dijon mustard
>   1 teaspoon salt, or to taste
>   Dash of freshly ground black pepper

Whisk together all of the ingredients and put into a small saucepan. Heat when ready to serve. Toss with hot cooked vegetables or drizzle over greens.

MAKES ABOUT 1/2 CUP

354

SHALLOT VINAIGRETTE

Here's a good sauce for fish or artichokes. It keeps well in the refrigerator.

3/4 cup white wine vinegar
1 3/4 cups olive oil
1 teaspoon salt
1 teaspoon white pepper
1 tablespoon minced basil or thyme
1 teaspoon minced shallots
1 teaspoon minced garlic

Whisk together vinegar, oil, salt, and pepper. Stir in the herb, shallots, and garlic. Refrigerate.
MAKES 2 1/2 CUPS

BERRY VINEGAR

You can make berry vinegar using raspberries, blackberries, or blueberries. Strawberries don't work too well; their flavor doesn't seem quite potent enough.

I find these sweet-tart vinegars have lots of uses—for instance, in vinaigrette to dress salads containing strong, peppery, or slightly bitter combinations of greens. Or for piquing sauces and gravies. They can do wonders added to chicken gravy (simmer it down a bit after adding) or sprinkled over grilled vegetables.

To make the vinegar, boil any small glass container in water for a few minutes, dry it, and fill with one kind of berries. Pour enough apple cider vinegar over the berries to cover them. Cap the container, and place it in a spot where the sun will heat it every day. Let the vinegar mature for 8 days, then strain the liquid by pouring it through a sieve into another sterilized bottle with a cap. Discard the berries.

ROASTED CORN SALSA

Roasting corn can give it a good nutty flavor, but if you don't have the time or inclination, make this with steamed corn.

2 medium ears of corn, kernels cut from cob
3/4 cup chopped yellow or red onion
2 tablespoon minced jalapeño
3 tablespoons minced fresh cilantro
1 3/4 cups chopped tomatoes
3/4 cup chopped red bell pepper
1 tablespoon fresh lemon juice
1 tablespoon fresh orange juice
1 tablespoon fresh lime juice
1/4 teaspoon salt
Pinch of freshly ground black pepper
1/2 teaspoon soy sauce

Place a heavy skillet over high heat. When it's very hot, add the corn. Toss constantly until roasted, about 8 minutes. Toss the corn with all the other ingredients. Serve at room temperature, adding more soy sauce if necessary.
MAKES ABOUT 4 CUPS

FRESH BERRY SALSA

This is especially good made with sliced strawberries.

2 cups diced ripe tomatoes
1/2 cup diced yellow bell pepper
1 cup berries
3 tablespoons seeded and minced jalapeño pepper
1/2 cup diced white onion
3 tablespoons minced fresh cilantro
1 teaspoon salt
3 tablespoons balsamic vinegar

Mix all the ingredients in a bowl and refrigerate, covered, for 1 hour. Let salsa come back to room temperature before serving.
MAKES ABOUT 4 CUPS

BASIC TOMATO SALSA

This recipe came to me from John Schmitt of those cookin' California Schmitts. He holds forth at the Boonville Hotel, which he owns and runs with his wife in Boonville, California. John says you can add either fresh oregano or mint to this.

2 cups diced ripe tomatoes
1/2 to 3/4 cup diced red onion
3 to 4 large basil leaves, cut into thin strips
Juice of 1 small orange
1 1/2 teaspoons balsamic vinegar
1/2 jalapeño, or to taste, seeded and minced
Salt and freshly ground black pepper, to taste

Mix all ingredients together about 30 minutes before serving so the flavors will blend but still remain distinct.

MAKES ABOUT 2 1/2 CUPS

PEACH–TOMATO SALSA

You may certainly add more green onion and jalapeño to this.

2 large ripe peaches, about 1 pound, peeled and pitted
1 tablespoon fresh lemon or lime juice
2 medium tomatoes, peeled and seeded
6 large green onions, chopped
1 tablespoon chopped bottled hot peppers
1 tablespoon minced fresh cilantro (optional)
3/4 cup olive oil
1/4 cup sherry vinegar
2 teaspoons honey

Cut peaches into medium dice and toss with lemon juice. Cut tomatoes into medium julienne strips.

Combine peaches and tomatoes. Add green onions, jalapeños, and cilantro if using. Mix.

Whisk together oil, vinegar, and honey and pour over the other ingredients.

You may leave this unrefrigerated if you are using it within several hours; otherwise, cover it and refrigerate.

Serve with a slotted spoon, allowing most of the juice to drain off.

MAKES ABOUT 3 CUPS

PEACH–BELL PEPPER SALSA

2 cups diced ripe tomatoes
1/2 cup diced yellow bell pepper
1 cup diced peeled ripe peaches
3 tablespoons seeded and minced jalapeño
1/2 cup diced white onions
3 tablespoons minced fresh cilantro
1 teaspoon salt
3 tablespoons balsamic vinegar

Mix all ingredients together and refrigerate, covered, for 1 hour. Allow to come back to room temperature before serving.

MAKES ABOUT 3 CUPS

CORN AND AVOCADO SALSA

1 medium white onion, finely diced
1 tablespoon minced garlic
1/4 cup rice wine vinegar
Juice and grated zest of 1 medium lime
2 tablespoons coarsely chopped fresh cilantro
2 tablespoons finely diced red bell pepper
1 medium jalapeño, stemmed, seeded, and finely minced
1 cup fresh corn kernels, cut from the cob
1 medium to large ripe avocado, peeled, pitted, and cut into 1/2-inch cubes

Place all ingredients except avocado in a glass bowl and toss well. Add avocado and toss, being careful not to mash avocado pieces.

MAKES ABOUT 2 CUPS

PAPAYA SALSA

1 medium papaya, peeled, seeded, and
  finely diced
1 medium red bell pepper, finely diced
6 green onions, with some of the green,
  finely diced
½ cup chopped fresh cilantro
1 to 2 small jalapeños, seeded and minced
Juice of 2 medium limes
½ teaspoon kosher salt

Combine ingredients in a bowl and toss to mix.
MAKES 2½ CUPS

CHUTNEY

FRESH BERRY CHUTNEY

⅔ cup golden raisins
½ cup fresh orange juice
2 cups berries
5 green onions, minced, with some of the
  green
1 garlic clove, minced
1 small red chili (about 4 inches), seeded
  and minced
1½ tablespoons minced fresh ginger
3 tablespoons minced fresh cilantro
1 to 1½ tablespoons fresh lime juice
Salt

Put raisins in a small nonreactive bowl and
cover with orange juice. Let sit for about 30
minutes. Drain, reserving raisins and discarding juice.

Toss raisins with remaining ingredients,
mixing well. Let marinate for about an hour
before serving.
MAKES ABOUT 2½ CUPS

APPLE AND GREEN PEAR CHUTNEY

2 cups apple cider vinegar
3 cups dark brown sugar, tightly packed
10 large tart apples (3¾ to 4 pounds),
  peeled, cored, and coarsely chopped
5 firm green pears (about 2¼ pounds),
  peeled, cored, and coarsely chopped
2 large red bell peppers (about ¾ pound),
  cleaned and coarsely chopped
1 cup dried currants
1 cup coarsely chopped onion
½ cup peeled and finely chopped fresh
  ginger
2 large lemons, seeded and finely chopped
  (including rind)
2 teaspoons whole mustard seeds
1 tablespoon coarsely chopped fresh mint
  leaves
1 tablespoon salt

In a large, nonreactive pot, bring vinegar and
brown sugar to a boil over high heat. Add all
other ingredients and turn heat to a simmer.
Cook, stirring occasionally, until thickened,
about 45 minutes. Pour into sterilized jars and
seal.
MAKES 7 TO 8 PINTS

FRESH MANGO CHUTNEY

You may substitute other fruits in this basic recipe. If the fruit has very firm flesh, blanch it first.

1 cup sugar
³/₄ cup sherry vinegar
1 medium white onion, cut into thin
*   julienne strips*
2 tablespoons unsalted butter
1 cup sun-dried cherries
1 cup diced mango

In a nonreactive saucepan over medium heat, simmer sugar and sherry vinegar until it starts to darken and becomes syrupy, about 15 minutes.

Meanwhile, sauté onion in the butter over medium-high heat until golden and caramelized, about 10 to 12 minutes. Remove from the heat and combine with the syrup. Stir in cherries and mango. Serve warm.

MAKES ABOUT 2½ CUPS

FRESH TOMATO CHUTNEY

This is a very good addition to lamb or any other grilled meat. You can make it as hot or as mild as you like.

²/₃ cup golden raisins
¹/₂ cup fresh orange juice
2 cups peeled, seeded, and chopped tomatoes
5 green onions, minced, with some of the
*   green*
1 medium garlic clove, minced
1 small red chili (about 4 inches), seeded
*   and minced*
1¹/₂ tablespoons minced fresh ginger
3 tablespoons minced fresh cilantro
1 to 1¹/₂ tablespoons fresh lime juice
Salt, to taste

Put raisins in a small nonreactive bowl and cover with orange juice. Let sit for about 30 minutes. Drain, reserving raisins and discarding juice.

Toss raisins with remaining ingredients, and let marinate for about 1 hour before using.

MAKES ABOUT 2½ CUPS

FRESH PINEAPPLE CHUTNEY

As you might imagine, this is marvelous with curry. But it's also a great foil for simply roasted meats.

1 cup (firmly packed) dark brown sugar
²/₃ cup white wine vinegar
¹/₃ cup fresh lime juice
¹/₂ cup coarsely chopped onion
2 large shallots, peeled and thinly sliced
¹/₃ cup peeled and coarsely chopped fresh
*   ginger*
1 cinnamon stick, 2 or 3 inches long
1 tablespoon mustard seeds
1 teaspoon crushed red pepper
2 cups fresh pineapple, cut into ³/₄-inch
*   chunks*

Combine all the ingredients except the pineapple in a nonreactive saucepan. Bring quickly to a boil over high heat, cover, and turn the heat to low. Simmer for 15 minutes. Uncover the pan and turn the heat up. Boil gently to thicken and reduce the liquid slightly, 5 to 10 minutes.

Remove the pan from the heat and stir in the pineapple. Return to the heat and simmer for another 4 minutes, until thick. Cool to room temperature, then refrigerate, covered, until chilled.

MAKES ABOUT 2 CUPS

RELISH AND ONION TOPPING

ONION AND RAISIN RELISH

This relish is great with ham, pork loin, and other roasted meats.

½ cup golden raisins
⅓ cup dried currants
1¼ pounds red or yellow onions, thickly sliced
2 tablespoons unsalted butter
¾ cup Chicken Stock (page 41) or canned chicken broth
1 teaspoon honey
½ teaspoon finely chopped fresh or pickled jalapeño

Put raisins and currants in a small bowl and cover them with hot water. Set aside.

In a heavy saucepan set over medium-high heat, sauté onions in butter, stirring occasionally, until just tender, about 7 minutes.

Reduce the heat to medium, add stock and honey, cover, and simmer until most of the liquid has been absorbed and the mixture has thickened slightly, about 10 minutes.

Drain the raisins and currants, and stir them into the mixture with the jalapeño. Cover and simmer for 5 minutes. Serve this cool or at room temperature.

MAKES ABOUT 2 CUPS

TOMATO AND JALAPEÑO RELISH

3 cups peeled, seeded, and chopped tomatoes (6 medium tomatoes)
1½ teaspoons minced jalapeño
1½ teaspoons minced serrano
1½ cups chopped jicama
¾ cup roughly chopped onion
½ cup olive oil
¼ cup balsamic vinegar
½ cup fresh orange juice
1 teaspoon salt
½ teaspoon freshly ground black pepper

In a medium mixing bowl, combine tomatoes, jalapeño, serrano, jicama, and onion. Stir.

Combine oil, vinegar, orange juice, salt, and pepper in a jar with a tight-fitting lid. Shake well. Pour over the tomato mixture and stir. Taste and adjust the salt and pepper if necessary.

MAKES ABOUT 4 CUPS

FRESH CORN RELISH

2 cups fresh corn kernels, cut and scraped from the cob (about 3 medium ears)
2 tablespoons minced jalapeño
½ cup finely chopped serrano
½ cup diced red bell pepper
½ cup diced green bell pepper
2 tablespoons minced fresh cilantro
1 tablespoon plus 1 teaspoon fresh lime juice
2 teaspoons olive oil
½ teaspoon salt
½ teaspoon freshly ground black pepper

Combine corn, jalapeño, serrano, bell peppers, and cilantro in a bowl. Stir. Drizzle the lime juice and olive oil over the mixture and sprinkle on the salt and pepper. Mix very well.

MAKES 3½ CUPS

PEPPERED ONION RELISH

Shallots could be added to this mixture.

2 tablespoons unsalted butter
4 cups diced onions
1 teaspoon salt
1 tablespoon sugar
½ teaspoon freshly ground black pepper
2 tablespoons white pepper

Heat butter over high heat until it begins to brown; add onions. Continue to cook over fairly high heat, tossing, until onions are browned but not burned, about 3 to 4 minutes. Add other ingredients and cook for another minute. Check seasoning.

MAKES ABOUT 3 CUPS

SWEET VIDALIA ONION SAUCE

This sauce is great on pork.

2 tablespoons unsalted butter
3 cups thin strips Vidalia onions (about 1½ pounds)
½ cup Sauternes (or other sweet wine)
3 cups beef, veal, or lamb stock (or a combination)
1 large bay leaf
½ teaspoon freshly ground black pepper
Salt, to taste

Heat 1 tablespoon of the butter in a large sauté pan. Add onions and cook over medium-high heat, stirring occasionally, until they are caramelized, about 12 to 15 minutes. Add Sauternes, stock, bay leaf, and pepper. Continue to cook on medium heat for another 15 minutes to reduce. Whisk in the remaining tablespoon of butter off the heat. Check for salt and serve.

MAKES 2 CUPS

ONION–HOT PEPPER TOPPING

I use the long red, semihot Mexican peppers here. If you have the strength for them, you may use hotter ones. But if you do, warn your guests.

5 tablespoons olive oil
3 large red onions, very thinly sliced
3 long red, medium-hot peppers, cut in half lengthwise, seeded, and cut into ½-inch pieces
½ to ¾ teaspoon salt
¾ teaspoon sugar
5 teaspoons red wine vinegar

In a large skillet over medium heat, warm half the olive oil. Toss in onions and peppers to coat. Turn heat to low and wilt the onions, being careful not to burn them. After about 6 minutes, add the balance of the olive oil and the salt and sugar. Cook several more minutes, stirring occasionally to keep from burning. When onions have started turning dark, about 10 minutes, sprinkle with the vinegar and cook 2 minutes more.

MAKES ABOUT 2 CUPS

RADISH RELISH

¾ cup finely chopped radishes
1 teaspoon minced shallots
1 teaspoon minced garlic
1 tablespoon whole capers, rinsed and drained
2 tablespoons olive oil
½ teaspoon salt
¼ teaspoon white pepper

Mix all ingredients together. Cover and marinate overnight in the refrigerator.

MAKES ABOUT 1 CUP

ANCHOVIES, CAPERS, BASIL, AND PINE NUTS

You may also add a few black olives to this condiment if you like.

16 flat anchovy fillets, drained
1/4 cup rinsed and drained capers
1/4 cup minced fresh basil
1/4 cup pine nuts
2 teaspoons lemon juice
2 tablespoons olive oil

Mince anchovies, capers, basil, and nuts together by hand, then stir in the lemon juice and oil. Or put all the ingredients in a small food processor and chop it together; care should be taken not to overprocess the mixture. The finished paste should be coarse.

MAKES ABOUT 1 CUP

FRUIT SAUCE

WARM APPLESAUCE WITH CREAM

4 cups peeled, cored, and coarsely chopped
    tart apples
2 cups water
1/2 cup honey
1 1/2 teaspoons vanilla extract or bourbon
1 cup heavy cream (or more)

Cook the apples in the water in a large saucepan over low heat for about 15 to 20 minutes, or until they are soft. Purée in a food processor and return to the pan. Add honey and vanilla. Simmer for another 30 minutes until liquid is reduced.

Serve this warm with cold heavy cream.

MAKES ABOUT 3 1/2 CUPS

RASPBERRY SAUCE FOR MEAT

This is especially good with crisp duck. You can also make this with blackberries.

1 cup raspberries
1 cup port
3 1/2 cups Chicken Stock (page 41), reduced
    to 2 1/2 cups
1 teaspoon salt, or to taste
1/2 teaspoon white pepper (optional)

Bring berries and wine to a boil in a nonreactive saucepan over high heat. Continue at a rolling boil until reduced by half, 10 to 12 minutes. Add stock and bring to a boil again. Strain, season, and serve.

MAKES ABOUT 3 CUPS

ORANGE-ANAHEIM PEPPER SAUCE

1/3 cup fresh orange juice
Zest of 2 medium oranges
1/4 cup dry white wine
3 tablespoons white wine vinegar
3 tablespoons minced Anaheim pepper,
    including a few seeds
2 tablespoons heavy cream
1/2 pound (2 sticks) cold unsalted butter, cut
    into 1-inch pieces
1/4 teaspoon salt
Pinch of white pepper

Place juice in a small nonreactive pot with the zest, wine, and vinegar. Reduce over high heat until syrupy, about 10 minutes. Off the heat, add pepper and cream and whisk to combine. Return to medium heat and whisk in butter a piece at a time until all is incorporated. Sprinkle in salt and pepper, adding more if desired.

MAKES ABOUT 1 1/2 CUPS

CRANBERRY, ORANGE, AND RAISIN SAUCE

This is a slight variation on an old favorite.

1 package (12 ounces) fresh cranberries
1 large seedless orange, scrubbed
1 cup sugar
1¹/₂ cups golden raisins
³/₄ cup fresh orange juice

The day before serving, wash and pick over cranberries. Cut the orange into eighths. Place in a food processor with the cranberries and chop coarse. Stir in sugar and refrigerate overnight. Place raisins in a small bowl and cover with orange juice. Macerate overnight.

Combine cranberry–orange mixture with macerated raisins and orange juice. Stir to mix.
SERVES 8

CRANBERRY–HOT PEPPER SAUCE

I like the surprising kick hot pepper jelly gives cranberry sauce. You can make it as fiery as you please.

1 package (12 ounces) fresh cranberries,
washed and picked over
1 cup water
1 cup sugar
1 jar (4 or 5 ounces) jalapeño jelly

Combine berries, water, and sugar. Cook until the berries begin to burst open. Remove from the heat and stir in the jar of jelly. Let cool and refrigerate.
SERVES 8

FRESH APPLESAUCE WITH SAUTÉED APPLES

The combination of sautéed apples with the sauce gives this old standby a marvelous texture. Incidentally, the sauce freezes quite well. The method is rather inexact, but it is easy and you can make it to your own taste.

22 to 26 large apples, peeled, quartered,
and seeded
Juice of lemon
Honey, to taste
Freshly grated nutmeg, to taste
Ground cinnamon, to taste
3 to 4 tablespoons unsalted butter, or to taste

Drop a third of the apples into a bowl of cold water with the lemon juice. Place the remaining apples in a 6-quart pot. Add 1 cup water and cover. Place over low heat. In about 20 to 30 minutes, give the apples a stir and repeat at intervals until applesauce reaches the desired consistency, which may take 1 hour or more. If a smooth sauce is desired, put through a potato ricer or food mill. Sweeten with honey and sprinkle with nutmeg and cinnamon.

To serve, cut remaining apples into eighths and sauté in butter until translucent. Dust with cinnamon and arrange on top of the bowl of sauce.
MAKES ABOUT 3 QUARTS

FRUIT SAUCE FOR DESSERTS

QUICK RASPBERRY SAUCE

2 cups washed raspberries
Sugar
Fresh lemon juice
Kirsch (optional)

Place berries in a blender or food processor with several tablespoons of sugar. Purée and taste for sweetness. Add more if necessary. Add a teaspoon of lemon juice and taste again, adding more juice if you like. Do the same with kirsch if you are using it.

Strain out the seeds and refrigerate until ready to use.
MAKES ABOUT 1 CUP

VARIATIONS
Substitute strawberries.
Substitute blueberries. Do not strain.
Add crème de cassis to taste.

COOKED BERRY SAUCE

Simmer a box of fresh or frozen berries (blackberries, blueberries, raspberries, or strawberries) with ¼ to ½ cup of sugar (depending on how sweet you like it) for about 5 minutes, or until it starts to thicken very slightly. You want to be able to pour the sauce easily when it is cool. Strain out the seeds with a fine sieve (not necessary with blueberries) and refrigerate.

COOKED FRUIT SAUCE

A sauce that's perfect for custards and ice cream can be made from almost any fruit or combination of fruits. Something else to recommend this sauce is that it can be prepared from frozen fruit.

Peel and pit the fruit (such as peaches, nectarines, pears, plums, or mangoes), then add sugar to taste and a squeeze of lemon juice. Simmer for 5 or more minutes. Purée in a food processor and let cool before refrigerating.

You may also add a bit of grated lemon zest to the finished purée as well as a dash of liqueur.

RASPBERRY-CARAMEL SAUCE

1 pint golden or red raspberries
½ cup water
1½ cups sugar
½ cup Sauternes
1 tablespoon fresh lemon juice
Kirsch, to taste (optional)

Purée berries and strain to remove seeds. Measure 1 cup purée. Set aside.

Place 4 tablespoons of water and sugar in a heavy saucepan. Let stand until sugar is moist. Cook over medium-high heat until sugar is light golden in color, stirring constantly. Sugar will begin to smell caramelized. Remove from the heat and set pan in sink. Carefully stir in remaining water. Return pan to stove over medium heat and add wine. Cook, stirring constantly, until caramel has completely dissolved. Remove from heat and add purée, a tablespoon at a time. Add lemon juice and a few drops of Kirsch if desired.
MAKES ABOUT 1½ CUPS

VARIATION
Substitute strawberries, blueberries, or blackberries for the raspberries.

PEAR SAUCE

Pear sauce keeps quite well in the refrigerator, so you could actually make it several days ahead if you like.

> 3 large pears, cored, peeled, and cut into
>   quarters
> ³/₄ cup port
> ¹/₄ cup water
> 6 tablespoons honey
> Grated zest of ¹/₂ large lemon
> 3 tablespoons fresh lemon juice

Put pears in a small saucepan. Mix remaining ingredients and pour over pears. Simmer until fork-tender. Remove pears with a slotted spoon and put in the bowl of a food processor. Reduce the liquid to a little over ¹/₂ cup. Add a tablespoon or two to the pears (reserve the rest) and purée. Refrigerate.

MAKES ABOUT 1¹/₂ CUPS

BLACKBERRY SAUCE

> 1 cup fresh or frozen blackberries, puréed,
>   with seeds strained out
> 1 tablespoon unsalted butter
> 1 tablespoon fresh lime or lemon juice
> ¹/₃ cup sugar
> ³/₄ cup dry white wine
> ¹/₄ cup crème de cassis (black currant
>   liqueur)
> 1 tablespoon cornstarch

In a saucepan, blend blackberry purée, butter, lime juice, sugar, and wine. Mix cassis and cornstarch and stir in. Cook over medium heat, stirring, until the sauce thickens, 3 to 5 minutes or less. Chill completely.

This sauce may be made in advance and frozen. Let it thaw in the refrigerator before using.

MAKES ABOUT 1¹/₂ CUPS

APRICOT PURÉE

Fresh fruit purées are wonderful over ice cream or sorbet. Dried fruits work well, too, and are a nice change when it's hard to find good fruit. Leftover syrup should be cooled and refrigerated in an airtight container.

> Boiling water
> 18 dried apricot halves
> 3 cups sugar
> 1¹/₂ cups water
> White wine

Pour boiling water over apricots and let stand for 30 minutes. Put the sugar and 1¹/₂ cups water in a saucepan and bring to a boil. Then turn heat down and simmer for 5 minutes. Drain apricots and add to the syrup. Simmer for 15 minutes. Remove apricots with a slotted spoon and purée them in a food processor. Add enough white wine (and more syrup if you want it sweeter) to make a thick pouring consistency.

SERVES 6

BERRY AND BLACK CHERRY SAUCE

> 1 can (17 ounces) pitted black cherries,
>   drained, reserving the syrup
> 2-inch strip of lemon zest
> 1 tablespoon fresh lemon juice
> 1¹/₂ tablespoons cornstarch
> 2 tablespoons water
> 1 cup berries (halved, if strawberries)

Place cherry syrup in a medium saucepan and add zest and lemon juice. Set aside.

Mix cornstarch with water until smooth. Stir into the syrup and cook over medium heat, stirring all the while, until mixture is clear and thickened, about 10 minutes. Add the cherries off the heat and let cool. Just before serving, mix in the berries.

MAKES ABOUT 2 CUPS

BOYSENBERRY SAUCE

½ cup sugar
½ cup water
1 package frozen boysenberries, thawed

Combine sugar and water in a small saucepan and bring quickly to a boil. Remove from heat and cool. Purée berries in a blender or food processor and add syrup to them. Strain out seeds.

MAKES ABOUT 2 CUPS

FLAVORED WHIPPED CREAM

CHOCOLATE WHIPPED CREAM

This is great with plain angel food cake.

1 ounce unsweetened chocolate
¼ cup sugar
1 cup plus 2 tablespoons heavy cream

Combine the chocolate, sugar, and 2 tablespoons of the cream in a small, heavy-bottomed saucepan. Place over low heat and stir until the chocolate is melted. Place the saucepan in a bowl of ice water and stir several times. Let the chocolate mixture cool.

In a medium bowl, whip the remaining cream until soft peaks form. Add the cooled chocolate mixture and whip to combine well.

Refrigerate, covered, until you're ready to serve it. Stir several times just before serving.

MAKES ABOUT 1½ CUPS

BANANA WHIPPED CREAM

This whipped cream has many users—try it on everything from fresh fruit to custards and cakes.

1 cup heavy cream
1 tablespoon sugar
½ teaspoon vanilla extract
1 ripe medium banana, mashed

In a chilled bowl, whip the cream and sugar until it almost stands in soft peaks. Add the vanilla and banana. Beat to blend.

MAKES ABOUT 1½ CUPS

BOURBON WHIPPED CREAM

Bourbon whipped cream is marvelous on most cobblers and fruit desserts, as well as on simple cakes. Of course, whipped cream may be flavored with other liquors, such as rum, as well as liqueurs and fruit brandies.

Add 1 teaspoon of sugar to 1 cup of heavy cream as it is being whipped, and then stir in about 2 tablespoons of bourbon when the whipping is finished.

MAKES ABOUT 1 CUP

SPICED WHIPPED CREAM

1 cup heavy cream
½ teaspoon ground cinnamon
½ teaspoon ground allspice
½ teaspoon freshly grated nutmeg
½ teaspoon ground cloves
½ teaspoon ground ginger
½ teaspoon vanilla extract
1 tablespoon sugar

Make whipped cream by combining ingredients and whipping to soft peaks.

MAKES ABOUT 1 CUP

365

COCONUT WHIPPED CREAM

2 cups cold heavy cream
2 tablespoons confectioners' sugar
4 tablespoons sweetened coconut flakes

Refrigerate bowl and whisk or beaters until ready to use.

Pour cold heavy cream into the cold bowl and whisk or beat until cream begins to solidify but is still short of forming peaks. Add the sugar with the coconut and fold in just to combine.

MAKES ABOUT 2 CUPS

VANILLA SAUCE

VANILLA SAUCE

This vanilla sauce is a very basic kind of sweet sauce. Although I like the flavor of liquor in it, you could add orange juice and more lemon zest in place of the rum.

1/3 cup sugar
1 tablespoon cornstarch
3/4 cup water
2 tablespoons unsalted butter
1 1/2 teaspoons grated lemon zest
2 teaspoons vanilla extract
2 tablespoons rum

Combine sugar and cornstarch in the top of a double boiler. Add the water and mix. Cook over hot water until the mixture begins to thicken, then add the rest of the ingredients. Cook for several minutes more, until the mixture thickens again.

MAKES ABOUT 1 CUP

VANILLA CUSTARD SAUCE

Serve this on simple sliced cake or warm fruit.

2 cups half-and-half
1 vanilla bean
3 large eggs
1/4 cup sugar
1/4 teaspoon salt

Put half-and-half and vanilla bean in the top of a double boiler. Heat to the boiling point, then take from the heat and remove vanilla bean. Slit the bean open and scrape the seeds out into the half-and-half. (Dry off the bean and use it to flavor granulated sugar.)

Beat eggs with a fork, then add sugar and salt. Mix well, and add a few tablespoons of hot half-and-half to warm the eggs. Put half-and-half back over barely simmering water and stir in the warmed egg mixture. Continue to cook, stirring constantly, until the custard coats the back of a spoon.

Remove pan from the heat and press a sheet of wax paper or plastic wrap onto the surface of the custard to keep a film from forming. Let cool completely before refrigerating.

MAKES ABOUT 2 1/2 CUPS

CRÈME ANGLAISE

5 egg yolks
1/2 cup sugar
2 cups half-and-half
1 teaspoon vanilla extract

Place yolks and sugar in a bowl and whip until the mixture becomes thick and light-colored.

Bring half-and-half to a boil over medium heat and slowly add it to the yolk mixture, stirring all the while. Pour the sauce into a double boiler and cook over gently boiling water, stirring constantly, making sure you get into the edges of the pan. Cook until slightly thickened, about 5 minutes or more. Remove from heat, stir in vanilla, and place pan into cold water, stirring occasionally until mixture is lukewarm.

MAKES ABOUT 2½ CUPS

BUTTERSCOTCH, CHOCOLATE, AND PRALINE SAUCE

BUTTERSCOTCH SAUCE

This is perfect over ice cream, sprinkled with nuts.

1 cup (firmly packed) light brown sugar
¼ cup half-and-half
2 tablespoons light corn syrup
2 tablespoons unsalted butter
½ teaspoon vanilla extract

Combine brown sugar, half-and-half, corn syrup, and butter in a small saucepan over low heat. Bring to a boil slowly, stirring until thickened, about 4 to 5 minutes. Remove from heat and stir in vanilla. Let cool before refrigerating.

MAKES ABOUT 1½ CUPS

CHOCOLATE SAUCE

I don't have to explain chocolate sauce. We all grew up on it.

6 ounces semisweet chocolate, or 4 ounces
*   semisweet and 2 ounces unsweetened*
½ cup light corn syrup
¼ cup half-and-half or cream
1 tablespoon unsalted butter
½ teaspoon vanilla extract

Coarsely chop the chocolate, then melt it over hot water in the top of a double boiler along with the syrup. Mix well, and add half-and-half. Blend well, and stir in the butter. Remove pan from heat and add vanilla and mix.

Serve warm or let cool and refrigerate.

MAKES ABOUT 1½ CUPS

PRALINE SAUCE

2 cups cane syrup
⅓ cup boiling water
⅓ cup (firmly packed) dark brown sugar
1 cup coarsely chopped pecans
½ teaspoon vanilla extract

Combine all ingredients except vanilla in a saucepan. Bring to a boil over medium heat, stirring, and let boil for about 30 seconds. Remove from heat, and stir in vanilla. Cool, then refrigerate.

MAKES ABOUT 3 CUPS

WHISKEY AND RUM SAUCE

BOURBON CREAM SAUCE

2 large eggs, separated, at room
*   temperature*
1 cup sifted confectioners' sugar
½ cup heavy cream, whipped
1 tablespoon bourbon

Beat egg yolks with confectioners' sugar until smooth. Fold in whipped cream and set aside. Beat egg whites until they make soft peaks, then fold into the cream mixture. Stir in bourbon.

MAKES ABOUT 2 CUPS

BOURBON SAUCE

In the part of the South where I grew up, there was a distinct preference for dessert sauces containing spirits.

1/2 cup (1 stick) unsalted butter
1 egg
1 cup superfine sugar
1/2 cup bourbon, more or less, depending on
*   taste*

Cut butter into small pieces and put in to the top of a double boiler over hot but not boiling water. While this is melting, beat egg lightly and combine it with the superfine sugar. Pour this mixture into the melted butter and cook for several minutes until the sugar granules disappear and egg is cooked, being careful not to let the water boil. Remove pan from the hot water and add bourbon to the sauce after it has cooked. Serve at room temperature.

MAKES 2 CUPS

IRISH COFFEE SAUCE

Irish coffee sauce is marvelous on Chocolate Angel Food Cake (page 424) or any chocolate dessert. It's also good with plain custards.

1 cup sugar
7 tablespoons water
1 cup freshly made strong coffee
2 tablespoons Irish whiskey or bourbon

Put sugar and water in a medium to large saucepan and bring to a boil over medium heat. Simmer, stirring, until the mixture begins to turn a caramel color, about 10 minutes. Toward the end of the cooking, the mixture will become very foamy as it starts to darken. Stir constantly at this point and, just as it becomes medium caramel color, turn off the heat but continue to stir—it will become darker off the heat.

Add coffee, being careful since the mixture tends to spatter when the coffee first makes contact (the reason for the large pan). Mix well and let cool. Stir in whiskey and refrigerate.

MAKES ABOUT 2 CUPS

RUM BUTTER SAUCE

3/4 cup sifted confectioners' sugar
8 tablespoons (1 stick) unsalted butter,
*   softened*
2 tablespoons dark rum
1 tablespoon grated orange zest
1 teaspoon freshly grated nutmeg

Beat sugar into butter, a little at a time. Gradually beat in remaining ingredients. Put in a small container and smooth the top. Decorate it with an additional sprinkling of nutmeg.

MAKES ABOUT 1 CUP

WHISKEY SAUCE

1 1/2 teaspoons cornstarch
1 tablespoon water
1/2 cup heavy cream
2 tablespoons sugar
2 tablespoons whiskey

Whisk together cornstarch and water. Bring cream to a boil in a small saucepan over medium heat. Add cornstarch mixture, whisking vigorously. Let mixture boil. Then remove from heat and stir in sugar and whiskey. Let cool, then refrigerate.

MAKES ABOUT 3/4 CUP

368

CONSERVES AND PRESERVES

FIG CONSERVE

This recipe comes from my aunt who lives in Natchez, where there are a lot of figs. It can be used like any other jam. I'm told it will keep for months in the refrigerator, but it has never stayed around long enough for me to find out.

1 lemon
1 pint small ripe figs, trimmed
1 cup sugar
1/4 cup chopped pecans

Cut the lemon into sections and remove seeds. Chop coarse in a food processor or chopper. Put figs and lemon in a saucepan, add sugar, and boil until thick. Stir in pecans and cool. This can be poured into sterilized jars and sealed. It may also be kept in the refrigerator, unsealed.

MAKES ABOUT 1½ PINTS

BLACKBERRY-WALNUT CONSERVE

How perfectly the flavor of blackberries combines with walnuts to make this tart and crunchy conserve.

12 to 16 ounces fresh or frozen blackberries
1/2 cup sugar
1 tablespoon fresh lemon juice
2 tablespoons vodka
1 1/2 cups coarsely chopped walnuts
1/4 teaspoon ground cinnamon (optional)

Combine berries, sugar, lemon juice, and vodka in the top of a double boiler. Stir and cook over low heat for 20 minutes or until thickened. Mix in walnuts and cinnamon if using. Let cool and store, tightly covered, in the refrigerator.

MAKES ABOUT 2 CUPS

VARIATION

Substitute other berries for the blackberries.

REFRIGERATOR BERRY PRESERVES

This jam is not too sweet. Simply add more sugar to the next batch if you like your jam sweeter. You may also add a little commercial pectin if you like; follow package directions.

1 quart berries
1 to 1 1/2 cups sugar
1 teaspoon fresh lemon juice

Wash and hull the berries. If using strawberries, quarter them. In a small enamel pot, alternate layers of berries and sugar. Bring to a boil, stirring from time to time, and then turn heat down. Add lemon juice and simmer for 8 to 10 minutes, stirring often.

With a slotted spoon, remove fruit to a small jar. Continue simmering juice until it is reduced by half and syrupy. Pour over berries. Let cool. Cover and keep refrigerated.

MAKES ALMOST 1 PINT

369

RED ONION MARMALADE

This is one of those crossover foods that can be served with meats—as it often is in the South—or with toast for breakfast.

4 tablespoons unsalted butter
1/2 cup sugar
1 1/2 pounds red onions, thinly sliced
2/3 cup dry red wine
1/3 cup plus 1 tablespoon white wine vinegar
3 tablespoons crème de cassis

Melt butter with sugar in a large nonreactive saucepan set over low heat until sugar completely dissolves. Add onions, cover, and cook until very soft, about 30 minutes.

Stir in wine, vinegar, and crème de cassis. Increase the heat to medium and bring to a boil. Lower the heat and simmer, uncovered, for 30 minutes. Increase the heat to high and boil, stirring constantly, until thick, about 5 minutes. Remove from the heat and set aside to cool to room temperature. Refrigerate in a covered container for up to 2 weeks.

MAKES ABOUT 1 CUP

BLACKBERRY KETCHUP

This is extremely easy to make and is so much better than commercial tomato ketchup that once you try it, you will be hooked. I must admit that I don't bottle it the proper way. I just sterilize the container and keep it in the refrigerator. It may stay like that for a few months. To keep it longer, you should do a proper bottling job.

2 cups blackberries
1/2 cup cider vinegar
1/2 cup water
3/4 cup (firmly packed) dark brown sugar
1/2 teaspoon ground cloves
1/2 teaspoon ground ginger
1 teaspoon ground cinnamon

1/4 teaspoon cayenne
1/2 teaspoon salt
2 tablespoons unsalted butter

Mix berries with vinegar and water in a saucepan. Bring to a boil, lower the heat to a simmer, cook for 5 minutes, and then sieve out the seeds. Return to the saucepan and add the remaining ingredients. Simmer for about 10 minutes, until thickened. Let cool and pour into a sterilized bottle with a tight cap.

MAKES ABOUT 2 CUPS

SYRUP

BERRY SYRUP

This syrup has many uses. For instance, it is wonderful on pancakes or as a topping for custards and ice creams. And it takes only a few minutes to make—perfect for the times when you have gathered too many berries and don't quite know what to do with them. Any berry will do, but raspberries are particularly good.

1 pint berries
1 1/2 cups sugar
2 teaspoons fresh lemon juice

Put berries in a small enameled pan and top with sugar. Place over low heat, stirring occasionally. When bubbly, cook for about 10 minutes. Add lemon juice. Let cool slightly and put through a sieve. Discard the seeds. Pour into a container, cover tightly, and store in the refrigerator.

MAKES ABOUT 2 CUPS

BERRY HONEY

It's really better to use frozen berries for this because they are usually cheaper and the flavor is all that counts.

1 cup frozen berries
1 1/2 cups honey
1/4 cup water
1 teaspoon or more grated lemon zest
   (optional)

Combine berries, 1/2 cup of the honey, and water in a small saucepan. Simmer slowly over low heat for about 15 minutes. Stir in the balance of the honey, then let cool. Stir in lemon zest if using. Refrigerate.
MAKES ABOUT 2 1/2 CUPS

BLUEBERRY CINNAMON SYRUP

Here's another case where frozen berries work just fine. If you use frozen blueberries, don't cook them instead, remove hot syrup from the heat and just dump them in.

1 cup sugar
1 cup water
1 long stick of cinnamon, broken in half
2 long strips of lemon zest
10 black peppercorns
1 pint blueberries, picked over

Combined sugar, water, cinnamon, lemon zest, and peppercorns in a saucepan. Bring to a boil, stirring. Add blueberries and cook for a minute or two. Cool, then refrigerate until well chilled.
MAKES ABOUT 3 CUPS

SIMPLE SYRUP

To make simple syrup, combine 1 part water with 2 parts sugar. Slowly boil for 5 minutes. Cool before using. Refrigerate in a tightly sealed jar. The syrup keeps almost indefinitely.

BEVERAGES

CHAMPAGNE AND APPLEJACK

Applejack, or apple brandy, is an American cousin to French calvados. Combined with champagne, it makes an awfully good (and potent) drink.

Simple Syrup (recipe above)
Applejack
Champagne
Lemon twists (optional)

Have all of the ingredients chilled, as well as the glasses. Put 1/2 teaspoon of simple syrup in each champagne flute (or more according to taste) along with half a jigger of applejack. Fill the glass with champagne. Stir once to mix, no more, as too much stirring will dissipate the bubbles in the wine. If you like, run a lemon twist around the rim of each glass and then twist it over the drink. Let the twist float on the top.

CAFÉ AU LAIT

This café au lait is simply strong coffee combined with caramelized sugar and warm milk. The caramelized sugar is a little twist our cook added when she made it for me as a child. I don't know if it is something she thought of or it if is usual in some parts of the country. Here's how to do it.

After you have made a pot of good strong coffee, scald several cups of milk and set aside. Put 2 tablespoons sugar in a pot and melt it over medium heat. When it turns golden, add the hot milk and stir until mixed. Pour in the coffee to taste. Guests may add more sugar, coffee, or warm milk if they like.

FLAVORED VODKA

Berry vodkas make refreshing summer drinks on ice with club soda or tonic water. Add a twist or slice of lemon or lime. You can also put them in the freezer to be drunk neat.

Fill a glass bottle about two-thirds full with raspberries, blueberries, blackberries, or sliced strawberries. Pour vodka over them, filling the bottle all the way. Cap it and refrigerate for several days before using.

ICED COFFEE WITH BRANDY

Spiced and spiked iced coffee served in this manner was a favorite of a friend of mine, Margaret Williams, from New Orleans. When accompanied by tea cakes, it becomes dessert, coffee, and after-dinner liqueur all in one—perfect for a party.

6 cups very strong black coffee
Zest of 1 small orange, cut into ¹/₂-inch-wide
   strips
3 cinnamon sticks
18 whole cloves
3 teaspoons sugar, or more to taste
1¹/₂ cups brandy, or more to taste
Crushed ice

Pour hot coffee into a large heatproof pitcher. Add orange zest, cinnamon sticks, cloves, and sugar. Taste and add more sugar if you like. Stir in the brandy. Cool and refrigerate, covered, until ready to use. Serve in Pilsner glasses over crushed ice.

MAKES 12 DRINKS

PIES, TARTS, COBBLERS, AND CRISPS

IF YOU ARE ONE OF THOSE PEOPLE WHO HAS NEVER MADE A PIE you are going to be delighted to find out how easy it is. All you have to do is learn to handle pie dough—and with a food processor and two pieces of wax paper, this part is a cinch. ✦ Don't forget that dessert pie crusts can be made from other things like nuts, cookies, and even crumbs from other cakes. Savory pies make good first courses or light suppers. ✦ That said, I'll add that perfectly decent pie crusts are usually available in the dairy and freezer sections of most large supermarkets. ✦ Cobblers and crisps—composed of little more than fruit with crust or crumble topping—are among the

best foolproof sweets. This is one category that many cooks try to fancy up, but remember, cobblers and crisps are desserts with no secrets other than their simplicity.

FRUIT PIES

APPLE PIE

The true American classic—and I don't believe in messing around with the classics.

> *1 recipe Hot-Water Pastry (page 406)*
> *4 cups peeled, cored, and thinly sliced tart*
>   *apples (about 4 large apples)*
> *1 cup sugar*
> *1/4 teaspoon salt*
> *1/2 teaspoon ground cinnamon*
> *Finely grated zest of 1/2 lemon*
> *1 tablespoon fresh lemon juice*
> *4 tablespoons (1/2 stick) unsalted butter, cut*
>   *into bits*
> *Ice cream or whipped cream flavored with*
>   *vanilla*

Preheat oven to 450 degrees.

Divide pastry dough into 2 parts, one slightly larger than the other. Roll out the larger part on a floured surface. Line a 9-inch pie pan with it and trim, leaving 1/2 inch around the edge. Set aside.

Place apple slices in a large bowl. Combine sugar, salt, and cinnamon, then mix with the apples, coating slices well. Sprinkle lemon zest and juice over all and toss. Pile into the pie pan, mounding it in the middle. Dot with the butter.

Roll out the top crust and trim to just fit. Fold the half-inch excess left on the bottom crust over the top and seal by crimping edges together. Make several steam slits in the top.

Bake pie for 10 minutes, then turn oven down to 350 degrees and continue baking for an additional 30 minutes, or until the top is golden.

Serve with ice cream or slightly whipped, vanilla-flavored sweetened cream.

SERVES 6 TO 8

APPLE AND GREEN TOMATO PIE

Green tomatoes give this American classic a new twist. This recipe makes a thin and runny pie. The pie will have to be served from the pan in which it is baked. The first piece will be a mess, but keep going. It gets neater.

> *1 recipe Flaky Pastry (page 405)*
> *1 cup sugar*
> *1/4 teaspoon salt*
> *1/2 teaspoon cinnamon*
> *1 tablespoon grated lemon zest*
> *2 cups peeled, cored, and thinly sliced tart*
>   *apples*
> *2 cups thinly sliced green tomatoes, with any*
>   *large seeds removed*
> *1 tablespoon fresh lemon juice*
> *8 tablespoons (1 stick) unsalted butter, cut*
>   *into thin strips*
> *Fresh cream, whipped cream, or ice cream*

Preheat oven to 450 degrees.

Roll out one of the disks of dough on a floured surface. Line an 8-inch pie pan with it and trim, leaving 1/2 inch around the edge. Set aside.

Put sugar, salt, cinnamon, and lemon zest in a bowl. Mix. Add apples and tomatoes and toss. Add lemon juice and toss lightly. Pile mixture into the prepared pastry, mounding the middle. Put slices of butter on top.

Roll out remaining pastry dough and trim to fit the top of the pie. Cover the apple mixture. Seal with tines of a fork and cut holes for steam. Brush with cream to make crust brown more if you like. (You may also sprinkle the top with more sugar.) Put in oven and bake for 10 minutes. Turn oven down to 350 degrees and continue to bake for another 35 minutes. Remove to a rack to cool. Serve with fresh cream, whipped cream, or ice cream.

SERVES 6

STRAWBERRY PIE

You can use this basic recipe to make black-berry, blueberry, or raspberry pies; just adjust the amount of sugar. And you can use any crust. The one here is sweetened and has a touch of lemon.

¹/₂ recipe Sweet Pastry (page 406)
About 1¹/₂ quarts fresh berries
1 cup sugar
3 tablespoons cornstarch
¹/₂ cup water
1 tablespoon unsalted butter
1 cup heavy cream, whipped and flavored
*   with 1 teaspoon vanilla extract*

Preheat oven to 425 degrees.

Roll out the dough on a lightly floured sur-face. Place in a 9-inch pie pan, and trim, leav-ing ¹/₂ inch all around. Fold edge under and then crimp. Place a sheet of foil on top of the pastry and weight it down with dried beans. Bake for 5 to 7 minutes, or until edges begin to firm. Remove foil and beans, and continue baking for another 10 minutes, or until golden brown. Carefully loosen edges. When almost cool, slide off onto a serving plate. Set aside.

Mash enough berries to fill 1 cup. Cut bal-ance in half, saving a few perfect ones for a garnish.

Combine the crushed berries, sugar, corn-starch, and water in a small saucepan and cook over medium heat, stirring constantly, until mixture comes to a boil. Continue cooking for about 2 minutes over low heat until mixture is thickened and clear. Stir in butter and cook until melted, then let cool slightly.

Place the halved berries in the baked crust and pour the cooked ones over them. Shake the serving plate gently so the glaze seeps down around the uncooked berries.

Chill for a few hours, then serve topped with the flavored whipped cream.

SERVES 6 TO 8

KEY LIME PIE

I have tried many versions of this old favorite, and I think I have found the best. This is a small pie, but its richness means you will only serve small portions. When strawberries are in season, this pie is good served with a few sliced over the top of each piece.

1 pint fresh strawberries, sliced and
*   sprinkled with 1 tablespoon sugar*
*   (optional)*
¹/₂ recipe Flaky Pastry (page 405)
¹/₂ cup fresh lime juice
1 can (14 ounces) sweetened condensed milk
2 egg whites, stiffly beaten

Let the strawberries sit uncovered in the refrig-erator for an hour so that they will chill and give up some juice.

Preheat oven to 425 degrees. Roll out dough to ¹/₄-inch thickness and place in an 8-inch pie pan. Trim and crimp the edges and prick the bottom of the pan with the tines of a fork. Bake for 10 to 12 minutes, or until golden brown. Look in on the crust several times dur-ing this brief baking period and prick any bub-bles that may have formed in the dough. It is important to do this to keep the bottom of the crust flat. This crust shrinks considerably in the pan so don't be alarmed; however, this makes it quite easy to remove. Let cool in the pan and then carefully slide out onto a serving plate.

Mix the lime juice with the condensed milk and stir until well incorporated. Beat egg whites until stiff and fold into the condensed milk mixture. Pour and scrape into the cooled crust and refrigerate the pie until ready to serve.

SERVES 6

PUMPKIN CHIFFON PIE

There is one secret to this marvelous spicy pie with its gingersnap crust: Avoid refrigerating it because if you do, the crust will get cold and harden. So make and bake the crust and set it aside. If you must refrigerate it, let it come back to room temperature before going on with the recipe. Prepare the filling and refrigerate it. Then assemble the whole thing, which takes only minutes, just before you want to serve the pie.

GINGERSNAP CRUST
2 cups finely crushed gingersnap cookies
2 to 3 tablespoons sugar (depending on the
*   sweetness of the cookies)*
Pinch of salt
8 tablespoons (1 stick) unsalted butter,
*   melted*

FILLING
1 envelope unflavored gelatin
1 cup evaporated milk
2 cups solid-pack canned pumpkin
³/4 cup (firmly packed) light brown sugar
Pinch of salt
2 large eggs, separated, at room
*   temperature*
1 teaspoon ground cinnamon
¹/2 teaspoon freshly grated nutmeg
¹/2 teaspoon ground allspice
¹/2 teaspoon ground ginger
¹/4 teaspoon ground cloves
3 tablespoons granulated sugar

1 cup heavy cream, whipped

Preheat oven to 325 degrees. Very heavily butter a 9-inch pie pan. Set aside.

To make crust: Combine crushed cookies, sugar, and salt in a bowl. Pour in melted butter, and toss with a fork until crumbs are moistened. Press mixture evenly into the buttered pie pan. Place pan on a baking sheet and bake for 10 minutes. Cool completely on a rack before filling.

To make filling: Whisk gelatin into evaporated milk and set aside to soften.

In a large saucepan (nonstick if possible), combine pumpkin, brown sugar, and salt. Place over moderate heat and cook until warmed through. Add the milk mixture and cook, stirring constantly, until the mixture comes to a boil. Remove from the heat and set aside.

Beat egg yolks in a small bowl. Add about ¹/3 cup of the pumpkin mixture and stir to warm the yolks. Then add the yolks to the saucepan and stir over moderately low heat until well blended. Add spices and cook, stirring, until very thick, about 2 to 3 minutes.

Place a round of wax paper directly on the surface and let cool to room temperature.

Beat egg whites to soft peaks. Add granulated sugar and continue to beat until stiff. Fold the whites into the pumpkin mixture only just until no white streaks show. Top with a round of wax paper and refrigerate until well chilled.

To serve, mound the filling into the crust and smooth the top. Pile the whipped cream on top and serve at once.
SERVES 6 TO 8

BLUEBERRY PIE

I prefer fruit pies made without flour. The only problem with this is that the slices don't look too great. This recipe calls for flour, so try it that way; some other recipes (like my apple pie) don't use flour. Make up your own mind which you prefer.

Whole Wheat Short Pastry (page 407)
¹/4 cup all-purpose flour
²/3 cup sugar
2 teaspoons finely grated lemon zest
6 cups fresh blueberries
2 tablespoons fresh lemon juice
4 tablespoons (¹/2 stick) unsalted butter, cut
*   into bits*

376

Preheat oven to 400 degrees.

Combine flour, sugar, and zest for the filling. Add the berries and toss to coat. Toss in lemon juice. Set aside.

Roll out the larger piece of dough into a 13-inch circle. Fit dough into a 10-inch pie pan, without stretching. Trim edges, leaving a ½-inch overhand.

Pour the filling in and dot with butter.

Roll out the remaining dough into a 12-inch circle. Place over filling and trim the edges. Fold over and crimp the edges. Cut 3 to 4 steam slits in the top.

Place on a foil-covered baking sheet in the center of the oven. Bake for 20 minutes, then reduce heat to 350 and bake for an additional 25 minutes, or until browned. Let cool to room temperature on a rack.

SERVES 6 TO 8

SUMMER FRUIT PIE

This is a marvelous combination for a pie.

1 recipe Flaky Pastry (page 405)
2 ripe peaches, peeled, pitted, and cut into
  ½-inch slices
2 nectarines, peeled, pitted, and cut into
  ½-inch slices
2 large red plums, peeled, pitted, and cut
  into ½-inch slices
12 large strawberries, halved
12 bing cherries, pitted
½ cup plus 1 tablespoon sugar
1 tablespoon quick-cooking tapioca
Milk

Preheat oven to 450 degrees.

Roll out one of the disks of dough ¼ inch thick on a floured surface and line a 9-inch pie pan.

Place all the fruit in a bowl and toss with the ½ cup sugar and tapioca. Heap into pie pan.

Roll out remaining pastry to ¼ inch thick and place on top of fruit. Trim, seal, and crimp. Brush top crust with a small amount of milk, vent it, and sprinkle with the remaining tablespoon of sugar. Bake 15 minutes. Reduce heat to 350 degrees and bake for another 30 minutes, until top is golden. Cool before serving.

SERVES 8

DEEP-DISH BLACKBERRY PIE

1 recipe Flaky Pastry (page 405)
5 cups blackberries, washed
1 cup plus 1 tablespoon sugar
2 tablespoons all-purpose flour
4 tablespoons unsalted butter, cut into bits
1 tablespoon fresh lemon juice
½ teaspoon ground cinnamon

Preheat oven to 425 degrees.

Roll out half the dough on a lightly floured surface. Line an 8-inch deep-dish pie pan, leaving a ½-inch overhang all around.

Place the berries in a bowl. Mix 1 cup of sugar with the flour and sprinkle over the berries. Sprinkle the chilled butter pieces and lemon juice over all and toss together. Mound into the lined pie pan.

Roll out the other portion of dough and place it over the top. Cut it to fit and bring the extra half inch around the outside of the bottom crust up over the top crust and seal. Crimp; cut steam slits in the top. Mix the remaining tablespoon of sugar with the cinnamon and sprinkle it over the top. Bake until crust is dark golden, about 35 to 40 minutes.

SERVES 6 TO 8

MERINGUE PIES

LEMON MERINGUE PIE

This version of the old favorite has a very strong lemon flavor.

½ recipe Sweet Pastry (page 406)
4 eggs, separated
1 cup sugar
1 tablespoon all-purpose flour
Juice and grated zest of 1 large lemon

Preheat oven to 425 degrees.

Roll out pastry to ¼ inch thick and place in an 8-inch pie pan. Prick crust all over with a fork. Bake for 5 minutes, until just lightly browned. Puncture any bubbles that form in the bottom and sides. Set aside.

Beat egg yolks until very light. Add ½ cup sugar and the flour and blend well. Add lemon juice and zest. Cook in a double boiler over low heat until this mixture thickens. Stir constantly. Let cool.

Preheat oven to 350 degrees.

Beat egg whites and slowly add the remaining sugar, beating all the while. Reserve half the whites for meringue and gently fold the balance into the yolk mixture.

Fill the piecrust with the lemon mixture and top with the meringue, taking care to seal all the filling inside. Bake for 20 minutes, or until it turns golden.

SERVES 6 TO 8

BUTTERSCOTCH MERINGUE PIE

Jim Fobel's Aunt Myra makes this pie, which is unlike any other I know and tastes better than it looks. Aunt Myra deserves a medal.

1 recipe All-Shortening Pie Pastry
(page 405)

FILLING
1 cup (firmly packed) light brown sugar
½ cup all-purpose flour
¼ teaspoon salt
1 can (13 ounces) evaporated milk
4 large egg yolks, at room temperature
4 tablespoons (½ stick) unsalted butter, cut
* into bits*
1 teaspoon vanilla extract

MERINGUE
4 large egg whites, at room temperature
¼ teaspoon salt
¼ teaspoon cream of tartar
½ cup granulated sugar

Preheat oven to 425 degrees. Roll out dough on a lightly floured surface to fit into a 9-inch pie pan and fold edges under all around the rim and crimp. Prick bottom all over with tines of a fork.

Bake crust for 12 minutes, puncturing any bubbles in the bottom of the dough that may form. The crust should be crisp and golden. Cool on a rack.

To make filling: Combine brown sugar, flour, and salt in a bowl. Add enough water to the evaporated milk to measure 2 cups.

In another small bowl, lightly beat egg yolks and then whisk in ½ cup of the diluted milk. Whisk the yolk mixture into the dry ingredients until thoroughly blended. Whisk in remaining diluted milk.

Transfer mixture to the top of a double boiler and cook over simmering water, whisking constantly, for 10 to 15 minutes, or until very thick. Remove from heat and stir in butter and vanilla. Cover with a round of wax paper placed directly on the surface and let cool for 15 minutes.

Pour filling into pie shell and cover again with wax paper. Let cool to room temperature and then refrigerate until well chilled, about 3 hours.

To prepare meringue: Preheat oven to 350 degrees.

Beat egg whites with salt and cream of tartar until soft peaks form. Gradually add sugar and continue beating until whites are stiff and glossy; do not overbeat or meringue will be dry.

Remove wax paper from filling and pile meringue on top, mounding in the center and spreading out to overlap the crust slightly all around.

Bake in the center of the oven for 12 to 15 minutes, or until meringue turns slightly golden. Chill for 3 hours before serving.

To slice, dip a sharp knife into very hot water before making each cut.

SERVES 8 TO 10

CHOCOLATE CREAM PIE WITH CHOCOLATE MERINGUE

This is pretty sweet for a chocolate pie, but also pretty darn good. You could forego the meringue, but that is part of the fun.

1 recipe All-Shortening Pie Pastry
(page 405)

FILLING
3 large egg yolks, at room temperature
3/4 cup sugar
1/4 cup cornstarch
1/2 teaspoon salt
2 cups buttermilk
3 ounces semisweet or bittersweet chocolate, melted
2 tablespoons unsalted butter
1 teaspoon vanilla extract

MERINGUE
4 large egg whites, at room temperature
1/2 teaspoon cream of tartar
Pinch of salt
6 tablespoons sugar
1 ounce semisweet or bittersweet chocolate, melted and cooled to room temperature

Preheat oven to 350 degrees.

Roll the dough out onto a lightly floured surface into a 12-inch circle. Line a 9-inch pie pan with it and trim the edges, leaving ½ inch of the crust to fold under and crimp. Line crust with a sheet of foil and fill with dried beans or aluminum pie weights. Place on a baking sheet and bake for 10 minutes. Remove foil and beans. Continue to bake for an additional 5 to 8 minutes, or until golden. Cool on a wire rack.

To make filling: Beat egg yolks and place them in a large nonstick saucepan. Stir in sugar, cornstarch, salt, and buttermilk. Cook over moderate heat, stirring constantly, until very thick and mixture stirs into fairly stiff mounds.

Off the heat, stir in melted chocolate. Add butter and vanilla, stirring until butter melts completely. Place a round of wax paper directly on the surface of the chocolate cream and chill.

Preheat oven to 350 degrees. Mound the filling in the crust and smooth the top.

To make meringue: Beat egg whites, cream of tartar, and salt until foamy, then add sugar, one tablespoon at a time. At the lowest speed, fold in melted chocolate. Work quickly and gently so meringue does not deflate too much.

Mound meringue on top of filling and smooth out to sides, sealing it to the edges of the crust (this is important). Bake for 5 to 10 minutes—just until meringue is lightly browned. Let cool on a rack to room temperature. Chill thoroughly before serving cold.

SERVES 6 TO 8

INDIVIDUAL CRUSTLESS LEMON MERINGUE PIES

1½ cups superfine sugar
¼ cup plus 1 tablespoon cornstarch
½ teaspoon salt
*4 large eggs, at room temperature,
    separated, plus 1 large egg white, at
    room temperature*
½ cup fresh lemon juice
2 cups cold water
1½ teaspoons finely grated lemon zest
*5 tablespoons unsalted butter, cut into 5
    equal pieces*

Preheat oven to 350 degrees. Butter 6 ½-cup ramekins.

Combine 1 cup of the sugar, the cornstarch, ¼ teaspoon of the salt, the egg yolks, and lemon juice in a large, heavy saucepan. Add the cold water and whisk until blended.

Cook over moderate heat, whisking constantly, until mixture comes to a boil. Boil, stirring constantly with a wooden spoon, for 1 minute. Remove from heat and stir in lemon zest and butter. Keep stirring until butter is completely melted.

Pour into prepared ramekins and cover with rounds of wax paper cut to fit directly onto the surface. Cool to room temperature, then place ramekins on a baking sheet for transfer to the oven.

Combine 5 egg whites and remaining ¼ teaspoon salt in a large bowl, beating until soft peaks form. Gradually add the remaining ½ cup sugar and beat until stiff.

Remove wax paper from ramekins and pile meringue onto filling. Spread meringue, slightly overlapping the edges of the ramekin, to seal the filling. This is an important step.

Bake in center of oven until top is pale golden, about 10 minutes. Cool on a wire rack to room temperature. Refrigerate until chilled and custard is set.

SERVES 6

MERINGUES WITH BERRIES AND WHIPPED CREAM

You can buy meringue shells ready to use in most first-rate bakeries and patisseries, but should you want to make them, they are fairly simple if you are content with mound shapes instead of cups. My meringues include chopped nuts, which I like, but they can be made without them.

The meringues can be made in advance. Be sure to store them in an airtight container or they will disintegrate quickly. If it is a very humid day, it might be impossible to make meringues—the warm oven cannot dry them properly.

2 egg whites, at room temperature
¼ teaspoon salt
½ teaspoon cream of tartar
½ cup sugar
½ teaspoon vanilla extract
*½ cup finely chopped nuts (walnuts,
    pecans, almonds, or any combination)*
*Berries, hulled and sliced (or left whole),
    lightly sweetened*
Whipped cream

Preheat the oven to 225 degrees. Use an oven thermometer to make sure the temperature is accurate. Generously oil a large cookie sheet.

Beat egg whites until frothy, then add salt and cream of tartar. Continue beating until they form soft peaks and then add sugar, a tablespoon at the time, beating about 20 or 30 seconds between additions. Halfway through this, add the vanilla.

After all the sugar and the vanilla have been added, beat at high speed for another 2 minutes, as this should be very stiff. Gently fold in the nuts with a rubber spatula, using an over-and-under motion.

With a large spoon, make individual mounds of the mixture on the cookie sheet. You can put them quite close together because they do not expand. Bake for 1 hour and let stay in the turned-off oven for another 30 minutes.

When cool, cut in half and top with berries and a dollop of whipped cream.

SERVES 6

COCONUT CREAM PIE WITH COCONUT MERINGUE

If you can't find a fresh coconut or don't want to bother, use store-bought unsweetened coconut. This recipe calls for a coconut crust, but you could, of course, use a pastry one.

COCONUT CRUST
2 cups shredded or grated coconut
4 tablespoons (½ stick) unsalted butter, melted

FILLING
¼ cup cornstarch
½ cup sugar
¼ teaspoon salt
2 cups milk
⅔ cup cream of coconut
3 large egg yolks, at room temperature
1 teaspoon vanilla extract
1 tablespoon unsalted butter
1 cup shredded coconut

MERINGUE
3 large egg whites, at room temperature
¼ teaspoon cream of tartar
Pinch of salt
½ teaspoon vanilla extract
5 tablespoon sugar

¼ cup shredded coconut

To make crust: Preheat oven to 325 degrees.

Combine coconut with melted butter. Toss with a fork until moistened, then use your hands to pat the mixture evenly into a 9-inch pie pan. Press into place so it adheres to the pan.

Bake the crust for about 20 minutes, or until golden brown and set. Let cool completely.

To make filling: Combine cornstarch, sugar, and salt in a large saucepan. Slowly add milk and cream of coconut, stirring constantly, over moderate heat until thickened.

In a separate bowl, whisk together yolks and about ⅓ cup of the hot milk mixture. Stir to warm yolks, then add warmed yolks to the milk mixture and continue to cook over low heat, stirring constantly and taking care not to let custard boil, until it is thick and smooth.

Off the heat, stir in vanilla and butter, then fold in coconut. Cover with a round of wax paper pressed directly on surface of custard (to keep film from forming on top), and let cool completely.

Preheat oven to 325 degrees.

To make meringue: Combine egg whites with cream of tartar, salt, and vanilla. Beat at low speed just until foamy. Increase speed and beat until whites form soft peaks. Add sugar, one tablespoon at a time, and beat faster until fluffy and stiff, but not hard. Do not overbeat.

Pour filling into the pie shell and smooth the top. Mound the meringue in the center and spread out to the edges, making sure meringue seals the filling completely, going all the way out to the crust.

Sprinkle the coconut over the top and bake for 10 to 12 minutes, until set and browned. Let cool on a rack to room temperature. Chill for at least 2 hours before serving.

SERVES 6 TO 8

PISTACHIO AND PECAN MERINGUE CAKES WITH STRAWBERRY FILLING

This recipe is enough for two meringue cakes, but you can halve it easily. This unconventional cooking method makes a moist and tender meringue.

MERINGUES
12 egg whites, at room temperature
1 teaspoon cream of tartar
3 1/3 cups sugar
1/2 cup chopped pecans
1/2 cup chopped pistachios

RASPBERRY SAUCE
1 pound fresh or frozen raspberries
1 cup fresh orange juice
Sweetener (optional)

ASSEMBLY
1 pint heavy cream
2 pints fresh strawberries, hulled and sliced
Mint leaves (optional)

To make meringues: Preheat oven to 375 degrees. Line four 9-inch cake pans with foil and butter generously or spray with vegetable spray. Set aside.

In the bowl of a large mixer, beat egg whites until foamy. Add cream of tartar. Continue beating until soft peaks form. Add sugar gradually while beating at high speed until all the sugar is incorporated and stiff peaks form, 8 to 10 minutes. Divide among the 4 pans, smooth the tops, and sprinkle the chopped nuts evenly over each.

Bake for about 25 minutes, until brown and rather firm to the touch. Let cool in the pans.

To assemble: Whip the cream until soft peaks form.

Carefully remove meringue layers form the foil—they are very fragile—and divide whipped cream between 2 of the layers, smoothing the top of each. Place a layer of sliced strawberries over cream and top each with the remaining layers.

Slice with a serrated knife and serve individual slices on a slick of raspberry sauce. Garnish with mint if you like.

SERVES 12

NUT PIES

PECAN CRUST BUTTERSCOTCH PIE

I think nut crusts are too often overlooked. They're easy to make and you may use any kind of nut, or a combination of several. And nut crusts are marvelous with almost any cream pie. Experiment!

1 cup (firmly packed) light brown sugar
1/2 cup all-purpose flour
1/4 teaspoon salt
2 cups milk
3 large egg yolks
3 tablespoons unsalted butter
1 1/2 teaspoons vanilla extract
1/2 cup coarsely chopped toasted pecans
1 baked and cooled Nut Crust (page 408),
    made with pecans
1 cup heavy cream
1 tablespoon rum

Put brown sugar, flour, and salt in a bowl and combine well. In another bowl, whisk together 1/2 cup of the milk and the egg yolks. Whisk this into the sugar–flour mixture, then add the balance of the milk and combine well.

Place in the top of a double boiler and cook over barely boiling water, whisking, until very thick, 12 to 15 minutes. Off the heat, stir in butter and vanilla, then the pecans.

Cover with a round of wax paper, placed directly on the surface. Let filling cool about 15 minutes, then pour it into the crust. Cover as before with wax paper; when it cools to room temperature, chill it for at least 3 hours.

Whip the cream lightly and stir in the rum. Place a big spoonful on top of each piece before serving.

SERVES 8

MACADAMIA CREAM PIE

Most nut pies have syrup-based fillings in a regular crust. This one is different—and the macadamia crust combined with the nutty cream mixture is delightful. Toast the nuts for crust and filling all at once.

> 2 1/2 cups milk
> 1 vanilla bean, cut in pieces
> 1/4 cup cornstarch
> 3/4 cup sugar
> 1/4 teaspoon salt
> 3 large egg yolks, at room temperature, lightly beaten
> 1 tablespoon unsalted butter
> 3/4 cup finely chopped toasted macadamia nuts (see Note, page 408)
> 1 baked and cooled Nut Crust (page 408), made with macadamia nuts
> 3/4 cup coarsely chopped toasted macadamia nuts
> Whipped cream flavored with vanilla extract

Scald 2 cups of the milk with the vanilla bean. Set aside to steep for at least 45 minutes.

Stir together the remaining 1/2 cup milk and the cornstarch in a large saucepan. Add the sugar and salt. Strain the scalded milk to remove the vanilla bean, then add gradually to the milk in the saucepan, stirring over moderate heat. Stir and cook until thick, then reduce the heat to low and cook for 1 minute.

Add 1/3 cup of the mixture to the egg yolks and stir to warm them. Add the warmed yolks to the saucepan and cook for 1 to 2 minutes,

just until thick and creamy. Do not allow to boil. Off the heat, stir in the butter until melted. Place the pan in a bowl of ice and beat until cooled slightly. Top with a round of wax paper and let cool to room temperature.

Stir the finely chopped nuts into the cooled custard and pour into the crust. Sprinkle coarsely chopped nuts on top and serve with flavored whipped cream.

SERVES 6 TO 8

PECAN PIE

The marvelous old classic revisited.

PASTRY
> 1 3/4 cups all-purpose flour
> 1/2 cup sugar
> 1/4 teaspoon salt
> 1/2 teaspoon baking powder
> 1/2 teaspoon nutmeg
> 1 teaspoon cinnamon
> 8 tablespoons (1 stick) cold unsalted butter, cut into pieces
> 1 egg, lightly beaten

FILLING
> 1 cup light corn syrup
> 1 cup sugar
> 8 tablespoons (1 stick) unsalted butter, melted
> 4 eggs
> 1/2 teaspoon vanilla extract
> 1 cup coarsely chopped pecans

To make pastry: Place all ingredients, except the egg, in a food processor and pulse until mixture is the texture of coarse meal. Add egg and pulse until dough just begins to cling together. Gather into a ball, wrap, flattening slightly, and refrigerate for about 1 hour.

Roll out dough between 2 sheets of wax paper into about a 10-inch circle, 1/8 inch thick. Line an 8-inch pie pan with it and crimp the edges.

383

To complete pie: Preheat oven to 350 degrees. Mix syrup and sugar at low speed in a large bowl for about 2 minutes to dissolve sugar. Beat in butter, eggs, and vanilla briefly. Mix in pecans and pour into prepared crust.

Bake until set, about 45 to 55 minutes.

Cool and serve plain or topped with some whipped cream or ice cream.

SERVES 8

CHOCOLATE PIES

CHOCOLATE CUSTARD PIE

This produces a very liquidy pie because of its pudding filling. If this bothers you, make individual pastry tarts in a muffin pan instead of one pie. Refrigerating it for several hours before serving will also make it set more.

> *2 ounces semisweet or bittersweet chocolate*
> *2 tablespoons unsalted butter*
> *3 cups milk*
> *³/₄ cup sugar*
> *¹/₂ cup flour*
> *¹/₄ teaspoon salt*
> *3 egg yolks, lightly beaten*
> *1 teaspoon vanilla extract*
> *¹/₂ recipe Flaky Pastry (page 405)*
> *¹/₂ pint heavy cream, whipped*

Melt chocolate and butter together in a small saucepan. Add milk. Combine sugar, flour, and salt in another saucepan. Add chocolate mixture to sugar mixture, stirring over low heat until thick. Add egg yolks and continue cooking for 3 minutes. Remove from heat and stir in vanilla. Let cool slightly and pour into baked 9-inch piecrust or individual crusts. Top with whipped cream at the table.

Note: There will be some custard left over, which keeps for a few days. I like it served ice-cold on top of a slice of slightly stale pound cake, which has been sprinkled with rum or brandy first and topped with whipped cream.

SERVES 6 TO 8

CHOCOLATE BROWNIE PIE

Like most healthy American, I like a chocolate fix now and again. However, I don't think I qualify as a "chocolate freak," as some of my friends call themselves. This pie is for chocolate freaks. Enjoy

CHOCOLATE PASTRY

> *³/₄ cup unbleached all-purpose flour*
> *3 tablespoons (firmly packed) light brown sugar*
> *12 tablespoons (1¹/₂ sticks) frozen unsalted butter, cut into small pieces*
> *1 ounce bittersweet chocolate, grated*
> *³/₄ teaspoon vanilla extract*
> *4¹/₂ teaspoons evaporated skimmed milk*

FILLING

> *3 ounces bittersweet chocolate*
> *2 ounces semisweet chocolate*
> *12 tablespoons (1¹/₂ sticks) unsalted butter, softened*
> *1 cup plus 2 tablespoons sugar*
> *2 eggs, lightly beaten*
> *1¹/₂ teaspoons vanilla extract*
> *¹/₂ cup coarsely chopped pecans*
> *¹/₂ cup plus 1 tablespoon all-purpose flour*

TOPPING

> *1 cup (firmly pakced) light brown sugar*
> *3 tablespoons heavy cream*
> *2 tablespoon unsalted butter*
> *1 teaspoon instant dark coffee granules*
> *¹/₂ cup confectioners' sugar, sifted*

384

Preheat oven to 350 degrees.

To make pastry: Put flour, brown sugar, butter, and chocolate in a food processor and process to the texture of coarse meal. Mix vanilla with milk and add to the other mixture. Process just to combine. Press into the bottom and sides of a 9-inch pie pan. This is likely to be rather sticky, so flour your fingers if necessary. Set aside.

To make filling: Melt chocolates in the top of a double boiler. Add butter by the tablespoon, mixing after each addition. Off the heat, add sugar. Mix thoroughly. Add eggs, half at a time. Stir in vanilla and nuts. Add flour in small quantities, mixing after each addition. Pour into the pastry shell and bake for 30 minutes, or until a cake tester inserted in the center comes out clean. Let cool.

To make topping: Put brown sugar, cream, and butter in a saucepan. Bring to a boil and turn off the heat. Add the coffee granules and confectioners' sugar. Beat with a whisk or hand mixer until smooth. Pour over the top of the pie. It will begin to set very quickly.

SERVES 6 TO 8

OTHER PIES

AUNT LADY CARTER'S ANGEL PIE

3 egg whites
1/2 cup granulated sugar
1/3 cup confectioners' sugar
1 1/2 cups heavy cream
1 ounce or more semisweet or sweet chocolate

Preheat oven to 300 degrees.

Beat egg whites until stiff but not dry. Beat in granulated sugar, then fold in confectioners' sugar. Pour batter into an ungreased 9-inch pie pan and bake for 1 hour. This will puff up and be lightly golden, like ordinary meringue.

Let cool.

About 2 hours before serving, whip the cream. Crush the top of the meringue if it has not already settled, and fill crust with the cream. Grate the chocolate over the top. Refrigerate until ready to serve.

SERVES 6 TO 8

VARIATION

Fold 1 cup chopped toasted pecans or walnuts and 1 teaspoon vanilla into the whipped cream.

CHESS PIE

My Aunt Cora remembers how her grandmother Rose Cheney Pearce made this wonderful simple pie when she, Cora, was a child. Families were larger then, and she always made two at one time. She used a pastry crust, but here we have substituted a vanilla-wafer one. Mrs. Pearce would then make something called "angel food pie" from the egg whites, which she would whip in a large china platter with a wire whisk, counting 100 times for each white before adding the sugar. Her recipe for "angel food pie" has not survived, but, fortunately, Aunt Lady Carter's Angel Pie has.

VANILLA-WAFER CRUST
2 cups finely ground vanilla wafers
2 tablespoons sugar
Pinch of salt
8 tablespoons (1 stick) unsalted butter,
melted

FILLING
6 large egg yolks
³⁄₄ cup sugar
6 tablespoons (³⁄₄ stick) unsalted butter,
softened
¹⁄₄ cup heavy cream

Preheat oven to 325 degrees. Heavily butter a 9-inch pie pan. Set aside.

To make crust: Toss wafer crumbs with sugar and salt. Add melted butter and toss again with a fork to moisten. Press mixture into the pie pan, lining the bottom and sides and making it as smooth as possible. Place pan on a baking sheet in the center of the oven and bake for 10 minutes, or until set. Let cool on a rack.

Turn oven up to 350 degrees.

To make filling: Beat yolks, sugar, and butter together until smooth, then beat in the cream. Pour mixture into the pie crust and bake for about 30 minutes, or until golden brown and set. Watch carefully to make sure it doesn't overcook.

SERVES 6 TO 8

OSGOOD PIE

Osgood pie is a relative of mince pie but better. This one goes over big.

¹⁄₂ recipe Sweet Pastry (page 406)
3 tablespoons all-purpose flour
1 cup golden raisins
1 cup coarsely chopped pecans or pecan
pieces
6 tablespoons (³⁄₄ stick) unsalted butter,
softened
³⁄₄ cup (firmly packed) light brown sugar
3 large eggs, separated, at room
temperature
2 tablespoons sour-mash whiskey, such as
Jack Daniel's
1 teaspoon distilled white vinegar
1 teaspoon ground cinnamon
¹⁄₂ teaspoon freshly grated nutmeg
¹⁄₂ teaspoon ground allspice
Pinch of salt
1 cup heavy cream, whipped with 2
teaspoons sour-mash whiskey and 2
tablespoons sugar

Preheat oven to 350 degrees.

Roll out the crust and fit into a 9-inch pie pan. Place pan on a baking sheet and set aside.

Toss flour, raisins, and pecans in bowl to coat well. Set aside.

Cream butter and brown sugar until smooth, about 3 minutes. Add egg yolks, one at a time, beating after each addition. Add whiskey, vinegar, cinnamon, nutmeg, and allspice. Mix well, then add the floured nut and raisin mixture.

Beat egg whites with salt until stiff. Gently fold whites into the nut mixture.

Mound filling into the pie crust and smooth the top. Bake in the center of the oven for 25 to 30 minutes, or until puffed and set.

Serve warm or at room temperature, topped with a dollop of spiked whipped cream.

SERVES 6 TO 8

BOYSENBERRY PYRAMIDS

This gorgeous dessert is remarkably easy to make and can even be partly made a day before.

MASCARPONE CREAM
  1/2 cup crème fraîche
  2 1/2 tablespoons mascarpone cheese
  1 tablespoon sugar

PRYAMIDS
  7 cups large fresh boysenberries
  1/2 cup sugar
  2 tablespoons Sauternes
  3 sheets phyllo dough
  2 tablespoons unsalted butter, melted
  1 tablespoon ground almonds
  1 tablespoon confectioners' sugar

To make cream: Whip crème fraîche into soft peaks and beat in mascarpone and sugar. Refrigerate until ready to use. This can be done the day before. Stir again before using.

To make pyramids: Put 3 cups of the berries in a saucepan and sprinkle with sugar and Sauternes. Mix, stirring lightly over medium heat, until the mixture boils and thickens, about 20 minutes. Be careful not to let this scorch. Cool and refrigerate. (This keeps well.)

Preheat oven to 350 degrees.

Brush 1 sheet of phyllo with melted butter. Sprinkle with sugar and ground almonds. Put a second sheet on top, butter it, and sprinkle with sugar and almonds. Put on the third sheet and sprinkle with confectioners' sugar.

Cut rounds out of stacked phyllo to fit six 4 1/2-inch pie tins. Lay rounds inside and bake for 5 to 7 minutes or until just golden.

When cool, remove rounds to individual plates and spread with mascarpone cream. Dip remaining berries in the thick boysenberry syrup, individually, and mound on top of the cream to form a pyramid.

SERVES 6

IMPOSSIBLE PIE

I suppose this recipe gets its name from the fact that all the ingredients are dropped into a food processor (or blender) and whirled around, then poured into a pie pan and baked—making it seem unlikely that anything good could come from such a mess. But the mixture magically makes its own crustlike bottom and is very tasty. It couldn't be easier.

  1 cup sugar
  4 large eggs
  2 cups milk
  8 tablespoons (1 stick) unsalted butter or margarine, melted
  1/2 cup sifted all-purpose flour
  1 teaspoon vanilla extract
  1 cup fresh flaked coconut
  1/2 cup honey-roasted peanuts
  Bourbon Whipped Cream (page 365)

Preheat oven to 350 degrees.

Combine all the ingredients except the whipped cream in the bowl of food processor and process for 1 minute. Pour mixture into a 10-inch pie pan.

Bake for 1 hour or until set. Serve with spiked whipped cream.

SERVES 8

TARTS

DATE TART

The recipe for this very easy tart was given to me by my Aunt Freddie. It is a rich and dense dessert that needs cream to balance it. You can make it as a pie, or in a proper tart pan. If it is made in a pie pan, you may have a little difficulty getting the first piece out, but after that it will be all right.

3 eggs, separated
³/₄ cup sugar
2 tablespoons all-purpose flour
One 10-ounce package pitted dates, coarsely chopped
1 cup coarsely chopped pecans
Whipped cream or heavy cream

Preheat oven to 325 degrees.

Beat egg yolks well and gradually add sugar. Continue beating until lemon yellow. Combine flour with chopped dates and pecans and add to the egg yolk mixture. Mix well.

In a separate bowl, whisk egg whites until they stand in stiff peaks. Dump them on top of the other mixture and fold in with an over-and-under motion.

Pour into a well-greased floured pan. Bake for 45 minutes.

Let cool before serving topped with cream, whipped or not.

SERVES 6 TO 8

VARIATION

Make the filling with ½ cup chopped dates, ½ cup chopped figs, and ¼ cup golden raisins.

BLACKBERRY JAM TART

Obviously, you could use any jam you like. I've even made it with Mayhew jam.

PASTRY
1 cup all-purpose flour
¹/₄ cup sugar
¹/₂ teaspoon baking powder
Pinch of salt
4 tablespoons (¹/₂ stick) cold unsalted butter
1 large egg, lightly beaten

FILLING
3 large eggs, separated
5 tablespoons sugar
Pinch of salt
6 tablespoons unsalted butter, melted and cooled
6 tablespoons soft white bread crumbs
6 tablespoons ground walnuts
6 tablespoons blackberry jam

To make pastry: Put flour, sugar, baking powder, and a pinch of salt in a bowl and mix. Cut in butter with a pastry blender or 2 knives. Stir in egg with a fork to moisten evenly, then gather pastry together and knead it for a minute or so on a floured surface. Form into a flattened circle and refrigerate, tightly wrapped, for at least 1 hour.

Preheat oven to 375 degrees.

Roll out pastry and line bottom and about halfway up the sides of a 9-inch cake pan with a removable bottom.

To make filling: Beat together egg yolks, sugar, a pinch of salt, and butter. When thoroughly mixed, stir in bread crumbs and walnuts. Whip egg whites until they form stiff peaks and fold into the egg–nut mixture.

Spread jam evenly over bottom of tart. Spread egg–nut mixture evenly over the jam and bake for 30 to 35 minutes, or until it has risen and turned slightly golden. Loosen edges and when cooled slide off onto serving plate.

SERVES 6 TO 8

BITTER LEMON TART

This is one of the desserts my pal Lee Klein passed on to me.

2 large lemons
½ cup plus 2 tablespoons sugar
2 large eggs
Grated zest of ½ lemon
1 baked and cooled Lee Klein's Pie Crust
  (page 406)

The night before, drop lemons in boiling water, turn off heat, and let stand 5 minutes. Drain and carefully peel, scraping away all the white pith.

Using a very sharp knife, slice the lemons as thin as you can, discarding any seeds as you go. Layer these slices with the sugar in a small bowl, scraping any juice over them that may have been squeezed out during slicing. Cover with plastic wrap and let stand, unrefrigerated, until the next day.

When ready to assemble pie, preheat oven to 375 degrees.

Using a slotted spoon, remove lemon slices from the liquid and spread over the crust (which is still in its pan). Beat the eggs and mix with the lemon liquid and lemon zest. Pour over lemon slices. Bake for 25 to 30 minutes, until puffy.

Serve this with a little sweetened cream if you like.

SERVES 6 TO 8

GRAPE TART WITH RED CURRANT GLAZE

The best kind of grapes to use for this are the medium-size seedless red ones or the tiny champagne grapes one sees in the markets these days.

1 cup all-purpose flour
⅓ cup confectioners' sugar
8 tablespoons (1 stick) unsalted butter,
  softened
2 tablespoons granulated sugar
1 egg
¾ cup sour cream
1 large bunch seedless grapes
Juice of ½ small lemon
½ cup red currant jelly, heated
Cream, flavored with sugar, rum, bourbon,
  or vanilla

Preheat oven to 350 degrees.

Put flour, confectioners' sugar, and butter in a mixing bowl and, using your fingers, work it to form a stiff dough. Press and pat it into the bottom of a 14 × 4½-inch tart pan. It is not necessary to line the sides.

Mix granulated sugar, egg, and sour cream and spread over the dough. Arrange grapes in an even layer over the sour cream mixture. Sprinkle with lemon juice.

Bake until the dough is done and turning golden around the edges, about 50 minutes.

Let tart cool for about 10 minutes, then loosen around the edges and slide off onto a tart plate. Spread heated jelly over all and smooth evenly (with your fingers if necessary). Serve with flavored cream.

SERVES 6 TO 8

VARIATION

Substitute 1 pint large blueberries for the grapes.

PLUM TART

Other kinds of fruit, such as peaches, can also be used.

SWEET PASTRY CRUST

1¹/₂ cups all-purpose flour
3 tablespoons sugar
¹/₄ teaspoon salt
9 tablespoons (1 stick plus 1 tablespoon) frozen unsalted butter, cut into bits
1 egg yolk
1¹/₂ tablespoons cold water

FILLING

10 ripe red plums
¹/₄ cup fresh lemon juice
2 tablespoons sugar
3 tablespoons honey
1 cup whipped cream

To make crust: Mix dry ingredients using a food processor. Add butter and process just until mixture resembles coarse cornmeal. Mix the egg yolk and water, then add to the bowl of the food processor with motor running and process just until the dough almost forms a ball. Refrigerate until ready to use.

Preheat oven to 400 degrees.

Drop plums in boiling water for about a minute to make peeling easier and then use a paring knife. Cut each in half and remove pit. Place plums in a bowl with the lemon juice, coating well.

Remove dough from refrigerator. On a floured surface, roll out to fit into an 11-inch rectangular tart pan with a removable bottom. Arrange plums neatly in rows on the pastry, then sprinkle with the sugar. Bake for 25 to 30 minutes, until pastry has turned golden and plums are tender. Let cool thoroughly. Remove tart from pan. Warm the honey and glaze each plum. Fill between the rows with whipped cream.

SERVES 8 TO 10

ALMOND TART WITH APRICOT ICE CREAM

This tart would be fine with simple whipped cream, but the ice cream sends it over the top.

PASTRY

2¹/₂ cups all-purpose flour
¹/₂ cup sugar
Pinch of salt
14 tablespoons (1³/₄ sticks) frozen unsalted butter, cut into small pieces
1 whole egg plus 1 egg yolk
1 teaspoon vanilla extract
¹/₂ teaspoon grated lemon zest

ALMOND FILLING

²/₃ cup unpeeled almonds
¹/₂ cup plus 2 tablespoons sugar
¹/₂ pound (2 sticks) plus 1 tablespoon unsalted butter
1 whole egg plus 1 egg yolk
1 teaspoon vanilla extract
¹/₄ teaspoon almond extract
1 cup sliced toasted almonds
Apricot ice cream

To make pastry: Mix flour, sugar, and salt in a food processor fitted with a metal blade. Add butter and process until mixture is the texture of meal.

In a small bowl, beat together egg, egg yolk, vanilla, and zest. With the motor running, pour this mixture through the feed tube. Process just until dough begins to cling together. Remove dough and knead lightly on a sparsely floured board until dough is no longer sticky and forms a ball. Divide in half; flatten, wrap in plastic, and refrigerate for at least 1 hour.

Remove one half of the dough and let it stand for 30 minutes at room temperature, then knead again lightly. Roll it out on a floured surface to a thickness of ¹/₄ to ³/₈ inch. Roll it onto the pin, then unroll over a 10-inch tart pan and line, building up the edges with the excess. If the dough should come apart, piece it and press together in the pan.

To make filling: Place unpeeled almonds and sugar in a food processor with a metal blade. Grind to a coarse powder, then transfer to a mixer with a heavy-duty paddle. Add butter and beat until light and fluffy, about 5 minutes. (You can use a hand mixer.) Exchange paddle for a whisk attachment and add egg and yolk, whisking until well mixed. Add vanilla and almond extracts and continue whisking for another 5 minutes.

Spread the mixture in the tart shell and sprinkle top with the almonds. Bake until shell is golden and filling is set, about 40 minutes. Cool on a rack.

Serve with apricot ice cream.
SERVES 8

NAPA VALLEY APPLE TART
Neatness counts here.

> *1 recipe Sweet Pastry (page 406)*
> *6 to 8 Golden Delicious apples, peeled,*
>   *halved, cored, and sliced ¼ inch thick*
> *½ cup sugar*
> *4 tablespoons (½ stick) unsalted butter*
> *½ cup sieved apricot preserves*
> *1 to 2 tablespoons calvados (apple brandy)*

Preheat oven to 400 degrees.

Roll out the pastry into a large round or rectangle approximately ⅛ inch thick. Roll dough onto rolling pin and transfer to a 16 × 12-inch baking sheet. Place apple slices on top, slightly overlapping, leaving a 2-inch border all around. Fold border back onto the apples. Sprinkle with sugar and dot with pieces of butter. Bake for 1 hour, until golden.

When cool, mix apricot preserves and brandy in a small bowl and brush carefully over the apples.
SERVES 12

PEAR TART
I have used raspberry jelly to glaze this tart because I like the combination of the flavors of pear and raspberry. You might experiment with other jams if you like.

> *1 recipe Hot-Water Pastry (page 406)*
> *6 small pears, peeled, cored, and sliced thin*
> *Fresh lemon juice*
> *3 tablespoons sugar*
> *1 tablespoon cornstarch*
> *¼ teaspoon freshly grated nutmeg*
> *⅛ teaspoon finely ground black pepper*
> *½ cup raspberry jelly, heated, or raspberry*
>   *preserves, heated and sieved*
> *Whipped cream flavored with pear brandy*

Preheat oven to 350 degrees.

Roll out dough on a floured surface. Line a long rectangular tart pan, about 14 × 4½ inches. Slightly separate the pear slices and lay each pear on the dough crosswise (or in an even pattern) in the pan. Sprinkle lemon juice over. Combine sugar, cornstarch, nutmeg, and pepper, and sift over the pears.

Bake for 50 minutes, or until pears are tender. While still hot, loosen the edges and slide the tart onto a serving platter. Pour melted jelly or preserves over the top and smooth out, with fingers if necessary.

Serve with flavored whipped cream.
SERVES 6

WALNUT TART

This tart can be made in a pie pan or a rectangular 14 × 4½ × 1-inch tart pan. If you use the tart pan, put a sheet of lightly oiled foil between the outer tart frame and the bottom sheet to make it easier to remove the tart from the frame.

> 1 baked and cooled Lee Klein's Pie Crust (page 406)
> 1½ cups coarsely chopped walnuts
> 3 eggs
> 1 cup light corn syrup
> 1 tablespoon unsalted butter, melted and cooled
> ½ teaspoon vanilla
> 1 tablespoon all-purpose flour
> 1 cup sugar
> Walnut halves
> ½ pint whipping cream, flavored with 1 teaspoon vanilla

Preheat oven to 375 degrees.

Spread chopped nuts in prepared pastry shell. Beat eggs and blend with corn syrup, butter, and vanilla. Set aside. Combine flour and sugar and blend with the egg mixture. Pour mixture over nuts in pastry shell and let stand until nuts float to the top, so that they will glaze during baking. Trim with walnut halves if desired. Bake 40 to 50 minutes, until filling is set and top browned. Serve with flavored whipped cream.

SERVES 8

LITTLE PIES

PRUNE AND PORT TARTLET FILLING

> 1 cup fresh orange juice
> ½ cup plus 1 tablespoon port
> ½ cup finely diced pitted prunes
> 4 teaspoons sugar
> 2 teaspoons cornstarch
> ¼ cup roughly chopped toasted pecans

Put orange juice, ½ cup port, prunes, and sugar into a medium saucepan over medium-high heat. Bring to a boil, reduce the heat, and simmer for 8 minutes. Let cool slightly. Combine cornstarch with the remaining tablespoon port. Stir into the fruit mixture and return to the heat. Cook over medium-high heat, stirring constantly, until thickened, about 2 minutes. Stir in nuts. Set aside to cool completely.

Preheat oven to 450 degrees.

MAKES ABOUT 1 CUP

VARIATION

Substitute dried peaches for the prunes and walnuts for the pecans.

PUFF PASTRY TARTLETS

I like sweet tarts best when made with puff pastry, but you can also use Hot-Water Pastry (page 406) or Flaky Pastry (page 405). A tart mold makes preparing these a breeze.

*1 sheet store-bought puff pastry, cold but not
    frozen (see Note)*
*Prune and Port Filling at room
    temperature*
1 egg, beaten

Roll out the pastry to about ⅛ inch thick on a lightly floured board. Cut out 12 rounds of pastry, each about 3½ inches in diameter.

Spoon about 3 tablespoons of the filling into the center of 6 of the rounds, mounding it up. Brush the edge of the rounds lightly with beaten egg.

Place the remaining rounds over the filling and press the edges to seal. Crimp the edges with a fork, and trim them with a sharp knife. Alternatively, you can use a tart mold to seal and crimp the tarts. Brush the tarts with the beaten egg, and use a skewer to poke a steam vent in the top of each tart.

Transfer the tarts to baking sheets with a flat spatula and place them in the refrigerator for 30 minutes. Preheat the oven to 450 degrees. Bake for 15 to 18 minutes, or until golden brown. Cool on a wire rack.

Note: A 17½-ounce box of puff pastry contains 2 sheets. For best results, puff pastry should remain cold. If the pastry starts to get soft and sticky, return it to the refrigerator for a few minutes to firm it up again.

MAKES 6 LITTLE PIES

JAM AND BERRY TARTLETS

The buttered soft bread crumbs in the filling keep it from being runny when you bite into it. Almost any kind of jam can be combined with any kind of berries. Fig Conserve (page 369) and fresh raspberries would be a luscious combination.

*1 recipe Lee Klein's Pie Crust (page 406),
    unbaked*
1 cup tangerine marmalade
*½ cup soft bread crumbs, mixed with melted
    butter*
1 teaspoon grated lemon zest (optional)
12 strawberries, sliced if large
Sugar for sprinkling

Preheat oven to 350 degrees. Lightly grease a baking sheet.

Roll out half the dough into a thin sheet. Have ready the marmalade mixed with the soft buttered bread crumbs and the lemon zest if using. If you have a tart maker, heap a tablespoon of the jam–crumb mixture onto the center of a 5-inch square of rolled-out dough. Top with a berry or two. Place another square of pastry on top of this. Cut and seal with the tart maker. Remove to the baking sheet and sprinkle the top generously with sugar. When the first sheet of dough is used, repeat with the second.

If you don't have a tart maker, use the same square, but put the filling in one side and fold the dough over on itself. Seal the three open sides by pressing them together with the tines of a fork. You will then have a tart shaped vaguely like a hotdog bun. Bake until golden, about 20 to 25 minutes. Remove to a rack to cool.

MAKES 6 LITTLE PIES

SAVORY TARTS

CHEESE AND ONION PIE

Don't be fooled by the simplicity of this dish. It's a winner.

2 pounds onions, thinly sliced
¼ cup olive oil
½ teaspoon dried thyme
½ teaspoon dried oregano
¼ teaspoon freshly ground black pepper
½ cup Chicken Stock (page 41) or canned chicken broth
1 baked and cooled Lee Klein's Pie Crust (page 406)
6 ounces sharp cheddar, grated (about 1½ cups)

Sauté onions in olive oil in a large skillet set over medium-high heat, stirring occasionally, until golden brown, 10 to 12 minutes.

Stir in thyme, oregano, pepper, and stock. Cook, stirring, until most of the stock evaporates. Remove from the heat and set aside.

Preheat oven to 400 degrees.

Spread the onions into the prebaked pie shell and sprinkle with the grated cheese. Bake until the cheese is bubbling and browned, about 15 to 20 minutes.

SERVES 6 TO 8

YELLOW ONION TART

4 tablespoons unsalted butter
1 pound yellow onions, very thinly sliced
1 bay leaf
½ teaspoon salt
¼ teaspoon freshly ground black pepper
1 recipe Flaky Tart Crust (page 408)
1 egg white, lightly beaten
3 eggs or egg substitute
½ cup milk
½ cup evaporated skimmed milk
Dash of freshly grated nutmeg

Melt butter over medium heat in a large skillet. Add onions, bay leaf, salt, and pepper; cover and cook, stirring occasionally, until very dark brown, about 30 minutes. Remove from heat and set aside.

Preheat oven to 400 degrees.

Roll out the dough into a large round. Fit dough into a 10-inch round fluted tart pan with a removable bottom; crimp the edges. Line dough with foil and weight down with pie weights, dried beans, or rice. Bake tart shell for 10 minutes, until set.

Remove the weights and foil, and bake the shell for 10 minutes longer, until golden. Remove from the oven and immediately brush with the lightly beaten egg white. Return to the oven and bake for 1 minute. Remove and place on a wire rack. Reduce the oven temperature to 350 degrees.

In a bowl, whisk together eggs, milk, evaporated skimmed milk, and nutmeg. Spread the onions into the tart shell. Remove the bay leaf. Pour the milk mixture over the onions.

Bake the tart until the filling is set, about 30 minutes.

SERVES 6 TO 8

394

ONION–BACON PIE

1 recipe Flaky Tart Crust (page 408)
1/4 pound thick-sliced smoked bacon, cut into
    squares
3 tablespoons butter
2 pounds sweet onions (Vidalia, if possible),
    coarsely chopped
1 teaspoon minced garlic
1 tablespoon minced fresh rosemary
4 large eggs
1 1/2 cups heavy cream
1 1/2 teaspoons salt
1/4 teaspoon freshly ground black pepper

Preheat oven to 425 degrees.

Roll out dough on a floured surface and line a 10-inch pie pan. Cut off excess, leaving about 1/2 inch all around, which will be tucked under before you crimp edges. Prick bottom in 4 or 5 places with the tines of a fork. Very carefully line the pan with foil and weight it down with a layer of dried beans or pie weights.

Bake for 10 minutes. Remove foil and beans and bake another 10 minutes, until golden. Set aside to cool.

Reduce oven temperature to 350 degrees.

Cook bacon in a large skillet until most of the fat has been rendered but bacon is not brown or crisp. Remove bacon with a slotted spoon and drain on paper towels. Discard fat and wipe out skillet.

Melt butter in skillet and sauté onions until well wilted but not browned, about 5 minutes. Add garlic and rosemary after onions have cooked for about 2 minutes. Mix.

To assemble pie, sprinkle bacon over cooled bottom crust and top with the onion mixture. Beat eggs until foamy, then whisk in cream, salt, and pepper. Pour over all and bake until puffy and set, about 45 minutes.

SERVES 6 TO 8

RUSTIC ZUCCHINI TART

To me, rustic means you don't have to fuss too much. This suits me just fine.

PASTRY
3/4 cup all-purpose flour
1 teaspoon dried thyme
1/4 teaspoon freshly ground black pepper
1/2 teaspoon salt
3 tablespoons cold unsalted butter, cut into
    bits
1 tablespoon cold solid vegetable shortening
1 tablespoon ice water

FILLING
3 tablespoons unsalted butter
1 teaspoon dried basil
2 cups sliced onions
1 tablespoon minced garlic
2 1/2 cups shredded zucchini
1 cup grated mozzarella

To make pastry: Mix flour, thyme, pepper, and salt in a bowl. Cut in butter and shortening with 2 knives or a pastry blender. Stir in water to make a ball. Flatten dough between 2 sheets of wax paper and refrigerate at least 30 minutes.

Preheat oven to 400 degrees.

Roll out the dough into a rough circle about 12 inches in diameter. Place circle on a baking sheet and crimp the edges. Prick with the tines of a fork and bake until golden brown, about 15 minutes. Remove from oven and cool on a wire rack. Reduce oven temperature to 350 degrees.

To make filling: Heat butter over medium heat, stir in basil, and then add onions and garlic. Sauté until wilted, about 5 minutes. Add zucchini and sauté until some of the liquid evaporates, another 5 minutes.

Spread cheese evenly over pastry and top with the zucchini mixture. Smooth over.

Bake until well heated and cheese has melted, about 15 minutes.

SERVES 6

PIPERADE PIE

If you don't have a large deep-dish pie pan, make two smaller pies. You could also cheat a bit and use two frozen crusts. They won't have cheese in them, so sprinkle a heaping tablespoon of grated parmesan on top of each pie to make up for it.

> 1/2 recipe Cheese Pastry (page 407)
> 1 1/4 cups coarsely chopped red bell peppers
> 3/4 cup coarsely chopped onion
> 6 tablespoons coarsely chopped green
>   onions, with some of the green
> 4 1/2 tablespoons olive oil
> 1 tablespoon minced garlic
> 3 cups peeled, seeded, and chopped tomatoes
> 2 tablespoons coarsely chopped fresh basil
> 2 teaspoons salt, or to taste
> 1 1/2 teaspoons freshly ground black pepper
> 6 dashes Tabasco Sauce
> 3 tablespoons unsalted butter, melted
> 6 large eggs, lightly beaten

Roll out pastry on a lightly floured surface and line a deep 10- or 11-inch pie pan, crimping the edges and pricking with the tines of a fork. Then line the pan with foil. Cover the bottom with a layer of dried beans or pie weights. Bake for 15 minutes, until the pastry is set. Remove the weights and foil. Bake another 10 minutes, or until golden. Set aside to cool.

Sauté peppers, onion, and green onions in the olive oil in a large skillet over medium heat until vegetables are wilted, about 10 minutes. Stir in garlic. Add tomatoes, basil, salt, pepper, and Tabasco. Bring to a slow simmer and continue cooking to reduce the liquid, about another 10 minutes. Remove from the heat and stir in melted butter, then mix in eggs.

Pour into the baked pie shell and bake for about 15 to 20 minutes, or until the filling is set but not dry.

Let rest for a few minutes to set before slicing.

SERVES 8

LEEK AND GOAT CHEESE PIE

Chez Panisse's version of this classic pie was the inspiration for this variation.

> 6 medium leeks
> 6 tablespoons (3/4 stick) unsalted butter
> Salt and freshly ground black pepper, to taste
> 1/4 pound pancetta or bacon, diced
> 1 egg
> 1/2 cup heavy cream
> 1 teaspoon Dijon mustard
> 1/4 teaspoon curry powder
> 1/3 pound mild goat cheese
> 1 sheet of store-bought puff pastry, rolled
>   into a 10-inch round about 1/8 inch thick
> 1/2 cup fresh bread crumbs

Preheat oven to 400 degrees.

Trim leeks, leaving just a small amount of the green. Julienne them and wash very carefully in several changes of water. Drain and pat dry.

Heat 4 tablespoons of the butter in a medium skillet over low heat. Add leeks and cook for about 15 minutes, until wilted. Sprinkle with salt and pepper and cover. Continue cooking, shaking pan occasionally, for another 10 minutes. Set aside to cool slightly.

Meanwhile, cut pancetta into medium dice and fry in a separate pan over medium heat until crispy, about 3 minutes. Drain off fat.

Beat egg and cream together, then add mustard and curry powder. Crumble half of the cheese into the egg–cream mixture. Add the cooled leeks and pancetta. Mix well and set aside.

Melt the remaining 2 tablespoons of butter in a small saucepan and set aside.

Place pastry on a baking sheet. Roll up around the edges to make a 1/2-inch-deep shell. Use a double thickness of folded foil around this edge to keep it in place. Fill shell with the leek mixture. Crumble remaining cheese over the top, sprinkle with bread crumbs, and drizzle with the melted butter.

Bake for 15 minutes to set pie. Remove foil and reduce heat to 350 degrees. Continue baking until nicely browned, about 30 minutes more.

SERVES 8

SAVORY LITTLE PIES

LITTLE PIES

Some of the recipes for little pies call for a specific pastry and have directions for folding and sealing. If not, follow these directions.

1 recipe pastry (see pages 405 to 407)
1 recipe filling, at room temperature
1 egg, beaten

Divide the dough in half and roll out 1 piece to about ⅛ inch thick on a lightly floured board. Cut out 6 to 8 circles about 3½ inches in diameter.

Spoon about 3 tablespoons of the filling into the center of each circle, mounding it up. Brush the edge of the circle lightly with beaten egg.

Roll out the remaining piece of pastry and cut out 6 to 8 more circles. Place these over the filling and press the edges to seal. Crimp the edges with a fork, and trim them with a sharp knife. Brush the pies with the beaten egg, and use a skewer to poke a steam vent in the top of each pie. Alternatively, you can use a tart mold to seal and crimp the pies.

Transfer the pies to a baking sheet with a flat spatula and bake as directed. Cool them on a wire rack.

MAKES 8 TO 10 LITTLE PIES

CHICKEN, WALNUT, AND RED PEPPER LITTLE PIES

I don't think I would tamper too much with this one, except maybe for the nuts, which might be changed to pecans or hazelnuts. I like it pretty well as it is.

1 tablespoon unsalted butter
8 ounces coarsely ground chicken breast (uncooked)
1 tablespoon margarine
2 tablespoons chopped onion
3 tablespoons very finely chopped red bell pepper
2 tablespoons coarsely chopped walnuts
1 recipe Butter–Margarine Tart Crust (page 407)

Preheat oven to 350 degrees. Grease a baking sheet.

Melt butter in a skillet and sauté chicken just until it turns white. Remove from the pan and set aside. Add margarine to the pan and sauté onion and red pepper until soft. Add chicken and walnuts. Cook for just a minute.

Prepare the pies as directed recipe on page 397. Bake on baking sheet for 25 minutes, or until golden. Cool on rack.

MAKES 8 LITTLE PIES

HAM AND FIG
LITTLE PIES WITH
CHEDDAR CRUST

I especially like figs and so I use them in many recipes. If they are not one of your favorites, you could probably use any dried fruit. The cheddar crust could be used for a number of other combinations. I've never tried it, but I bet it would make a wonderful apple tart.

CHEDDAR CRUST

1½ cups unbleached all-purpose flour
½ teaspoon salt
5 tablespoons grated sharp cheddar
4 tablespoons frozen unsalted butter
4 tablespoons frozen margarine
4 to 5 tablespoons ice water

FILLING

2 tablespoons finely diced onion
3 ounces mushrooms, cleaned and diced
1 tablespoon unsalted butter
1 tablespoon margarine
3 ounces ham, diced
4 medium dried figs, chopped
1 tablespoon pine nuts
Dash of freshly ground black pepper
1 egg, beaten

To make crust: Put all ingredients except the ice water in a food processor. Process until the mixture has the texture of small peas. Add water and process until the mass begins to make a ball. Remove and form into a ball and place between two sheets of wax paper. Flatten slightly and refrigerate for at least 30 minutes.

Preheat oven to 350 degrees. Grease a baking sheet.

To make filling: Sauté onion and mushrooms in butter. Remove from the heat and add remaining ingredients. Mix well.

Roll out the dough and cut into 4-inch squares. Place abut 1½ tablespoons of the filling in the center of half the squares. Brush the edges with beaten egg. Cover each with another square of dough. Using a round tart cutter, cut and seal each square. Or crimp the edges with a fork. Puncture with a skewer to vent. Continue, rerolling the dough as necessary, until it is all used.

Bake on a greased baking sheet for 25 minutes, or until golden.

MAKES 8 LITTLE PIES

ORIENTAL BEEF FILLING
FOR LITTLE PIES

1 tablespoon all-purpose flour
1 tablespoon olive oil
1 boneless ribeye steak (6 ounces), all fat removed, finely chopped
3 large garlic cloves, minced
1 cup finely chopped green onions
1 tablespoon minced fresh ginger
½ cup Chicken Stock (page 41)
1 tablespoon soy sauce

Heat a small cast-iron skillet over medium-high heat. Add flour and cook, stirring occasionally with the edge of a metal spatula, until it begins to brown, 6 to 8 minutes. Do not let the pan get too hot. Remove from the heat and let cool.

Heat a large cast-iron skillet over medium-high heat. Add olive oil and heat until hot. Add beef and cook, stirring, until browned, 2 to 3 minutes. Add garlic and cook for an additional minute. Add green onions and ginger, and cook for 1 more minute. Sprinkle with the browned flour and stir. Add stock and soy sauce, and cook, stirring, until thickened. Cool to room temperature.

Preheat oven to 425 degrees.

Prepare the pies according to the master recipe on page 397. Bake for 30 minutes, or until golden. Cool on a rack.

MAKES ENOUGH FOR 6 LITTLE PIES

PORK FILLING FOR LITTLE PIES

Make sure the potato is cut into very fine dice—no more than ¼ inch

1 tablespoon all-purpose flour
4 tablespoons olive oil
1 large onion, finely chopped
1 pork tender loin (12 ounces), all fat removed, finely chopped
½ teaspoon salt
¼ teaspoon freshly ground black pepper
⅔ finely chopped green onions
1 cup Chicken Stock (page 41)
1 large russet potato, peeled and finely diced

Heat a small cast-iron skillet over medium-high heat. Add flour and cook, stirring occasionally with the edge of a metal spatula, until it begins to brown, 6 to 8 minutes. Do not let the pan get too hot. Remove from the heat and let cool.

Place olive oil into a large, heavy skillet and heat over high heat. Add onion and cook, stirring occasionally, until lightly browned, 4 to 5 minutes. Sprinkle pork with salt and pepper and add it to the onion. Cook until well browned, 3 to 4 minutes. Add green onions and browned flour and cook, stirring, for 1 minute. Add stock and cook, stirring from the bottom, until slightly thickened. Remove the pan from the heat and add potato. Cool to room temperature.

Preheat oven to 325 degrees.

Prepare the pies as directed on page 397. Bake for 60 minutes, or until golden. Cool on a rack.

MAKES ENOUGH FOR 8 LITTLE PIES

HAM AND CHICKEN FILLING FOR LITTLE PIES

1 tablespoon olive oil
1 boneless, skinless chicken breast
Salt and freshly ground black pepper, to taste
1 tablespoon all-purpose flour
1 small boneless ham steak (6 ounces), finely chopped
1 cup toasted pecans, finely chopped
½ cup Chicken Stock (page 41)
2 tablespoons Dijon mustard

Heat oil in a small, heavy skillet. Sprinkle chicken with salt and pepper and cook until nicely browned, 2 to 3 minutes per side. Set aside to cool, then chop fine.

Heat a small cast-iron skillet over medium-high heat. Add flour and cook, stirring occasionally with the edge of a metal spatula, until it begins to brown, 6 to 8 minutes. Do not let the pan get too hot. Remove from the heat and let cool.

Place ham, chicken, and pecans in a large, heavy skillet and heat over medium-high heat until just heated through, about 2 minutes. Sprinkle with the browned flour and stir. Add stock and mustard and cook, stirring, until thickened, 3 or 4 minutes. Cool to room temperature.

Preheat oven to 425 degrees.

Prepare the pies as directed on page 397. Bake for 30 minutes, or until golden. Cool on a rack.

MAKES ENOUGH FOR 8 LITTLE PIES

BLACK OLIVE LITTLE PIES

I am very partial to capers, but I find people to be about evenly divided between those who share my enthusiasm and those who don't. Their strong, distinctive flavor appeals to me, but they could be omitted here if you like.

1/2 cup pitted Greek black olives in oil
1/2 cup pitted Italian black olives in oil
1 teaspoon capers, rinsed and drained
5 tablespoon olive oil
3 tablespoons fresh lemon juice
6 tablespoons finely chopped onion
3 medium garlic cloves, chopped
1 small tomato, peeled, seeded, and chopped
1 recipe Butter–Margarine Tart Crust
  (page 407)

Preheat oven to 350 degrees. Grease a baking sheet.

Chop olives and add capers, olive oil, and lemon juice. Put a few tablespoons of the oil from the olive mixture in a skillet and sauté onion and garlic. Add tomato and continue to cook for just a minute or two, to give any tomato liquid a chance to evaporate. Mix the tomato mixture in with the olive mixture.

Roll out the pastry and cut into 4- to 5-inch squares. Put 2 tablespoons of the filling in the center of each and dampen the edges of the square with a bit of the olive oil. Fold over to make a triangle. Seal the edges with the tines of a fork. Puncture with a skewer to vent. Put the tarts on a baking sheet and bake for 25 to 30 minutes. Let cool on a rack.

MAKES 6 TO 8 LITTLE PIES

VEGETABLE FILLING FOR LITTLE PIES

It's important to chop the vegetables fine for these little pies.

1/4 cup olive oil
1/2 pound eggplant, peeled and cut into
  small dice
1/2 cup finely chopped onion
1/4 cup finely chopped red bell pepper
1/2 cup finely chopped zucchini
1 garlic clove, minced
1 tablespoon finely chopped fresh basil
1/4 teaspoon dried oregano
1/2 teaspoon salt
1/2 pound tomatoes (about 2 small), peeled,
  seeded, and finely chopped
2 tablespoons minced fresh Italian flat-leaf
  parsley
2 tablespoons capers, rinsed and drained
1 tablespoon fresh lemon juice
1/4 cup grated parmesan

Heat olive oil in a large cast-iron skillet over moderately high heat. Add eggplant, onion, red pepper, zucchini, garlic, basil, oregano, and salt. Toss to coat the vegetables with the oil. Cover and simmer over low heat for about 20 minutes, stirring occasionally, until vegetables have softened. Add tomatoes, increase the heat to medium-high, and cook uncovered, stirring occasionally, until the mixture has thickened. Remove from the heat and stir in parsley, capers, lemon juice, and cheese. Let cool.

Preheat oven to 425 degrees.

Prepare the pies as directed on page 397. Bake for 30 minutes, or until golden. Cool on a rack.

MAKES ENOUGH FOR 10 LITTLE PIES

CHICKEN FILLING FOR LITTLE PIES

1 tablespoon all-purpose flour
1 large onion, finely diced
1 tablespoon olive oil
1 cup finely diced cooked chicken breast
3/4 cup Chicken Stock (page 41)
1 tablespoon minced capers
1/2 cup finely chopped toasted pecans
1/4 teaspoon freshly ground black pepper

Heat a small cast-iron skillet over medium-high heat. Add flour and cook, stirring occasionally with the edge of a metal spatula, until it begins to brown, 6 to 8 minutes. Do not let the pan get too hot. Remove from the heat and let cool.

Sauté onion in olive oil in a heavy skillet over medium-high heat until golden brown, 8 to 10 minutes, stirring occasionally. Add chicken and stir to combine. Sprinkle in browned flour and stir. Add stock and cook, stirring, until thickened, about 2 minutes. Stir in capers, pecans, and pepper. Cool to room temperature.

Preheat oven to 425 degrees.

Prepare the pies as directed on page 397. Bake for 30 minutes, or until golden. Cool on a rack.

MAKES ENOUGH FOR 8 LITTLE PIES

COBBLERS

APPLE COBBLER

1/2 pound (2 sticks) plus 2 tablespoons cold unsalted butter
2 egg yolks
1 teaspoon salt
3 cups all-purpose flour
2 to 3 tablespoons ice water
6 cups thin-sliced peeled and cored tart apples
1 tablespoon fresh lemon juice
1 teaspoon grated lemon zest
1 cup sugar
1 teaspoon ground cinnamon
Whipped cream

Preheat oven to 400 degrees.

Cut the 2 sticks of butter into small pieces and place in the bowl of a food processor with egg yolks. Process until smooth. Sprinkle salt over all and add flour; pulse to mix coarsely. Sprinkle water over all and pulse until mixture just begins to cling together. Form into a ball, wrap in plastic wrap, and refrigerate.

Toss apples with lemon juice, zest, sugar, and cinnamon. Set aside.

Unwrap dough and roll out into a 15-inch circle between 2 sheets of wax paper. Line an 8-cup soufflé dish with the dough, allowing the excess to drape over the edges. If dough breaks, patch it. Spoon in apple mixture and dot with the remaining 2 tablespoons of butter. Flop dough on top of the apples, using any pieces that may have broken off.

Bake until apples are soft, about 1 hour.

Serve with whipped cream.

SERVES 8

PEAR–RASPBERRY COBBLER

Pears and raspberries complement each other perfectly. And this dish looks as good as it tastes. You may use frozen raspberries when they are not in season.

1 recipe Cobbler Pastry (page 408)
6 cups peeled, cored, and sliced firm pears
1¼ cups fresh raspberries
¾ cup sugar
4 tablespoons (½ stick) unsalted butter, cut into bits
Cream or ice cream

Preheat oven to 425 degrees. Grease a deep 9 × 7-inch ovenproof dish. Set aside.

Roll out dough into a rough rectangle and line the prepared dish, letting excess crust drape over the edge. Heap pears into dish, mounding slightly in the middle. Sprinkle berries evenly over dish and then pour sugar evenly over all. Dot with butter. Bring dough up and let it flop over fruit, using any that falls off to patch in the middle.

Bake for 45 minutes, or until golden brown. Let cool and serve with cream or ice cream.
SERVES 6 TO 8

BLACKBERRY COBBLER

Blackberries grow wild in most areas of the country where there are damp spots or streams. They are delectable when cooked in a cobbler and fun to find and pick growing wild.

1 recipe Cobbler Pastry (page 408)
6 to 7 cups blackberries, washed and picked over
¾ cup sugar
4 tablespoons (½ stick) unsalted butter, cut into 12 pieces
Additional sugar or crushed sugar cubes

Preheat oven to 425 degrees. Lightly grease a 9-inch round ovenproof dish (2 or more inches deep).

Roll out the dough on a floured surface to a ragged circle about 15 inches in diameter. Roll onto the rolling pin window-shade fashion, then unroll over the prepared dish. Allow excess to drape over the sides.

Mound berries in the dish, sprinkle with sugar, and dot with butter. Flop the edges on top of the berries, using any pieces that may have broken off to patch. Sprinkle with a little additional sugar or crushed sugar cubes. Bake until golden and bubbly, about 45 minutes.
SERVES 6

VARIATION

Substitute boysenberries for the blackberries. Add 2 tablespoons quick-cooking tapioca for a less runny filling if you like.

PLUM COBBLER

The quantity of plums here is fairly flexible. I have called for a dozen large ones; obviously, if they are not big, you would want more. You can't really go too wrong with this easy recipe.

12 large unpeeled plums, washed, pitted, and cut into 8 pieces
¾ cup (firmly packed) light brown sugar (or less)
7 tablespoons unsalted butter
Juice of ¼ lemon

BUTTERMILK BISCUIT TOPPING
1 cup sifted all-purpose flour
1 teaspoon baking powder
¼ teaspoon baking soda
½ teaspoon salt
¾ cup buttermilk

Whipped cream or ice cream

Preheat oven to 425 degrees. Butter a deep 9 × 7-inch ovenproof dish. Set aside.

Mix plums and sugar and spread evenly in the dish. Dot with 4 tablespoons of the butter and squeeze the lemon juice over all. Bake, uncovered, for 25 minutes.

Meanwhile, sift together flour, baking powder, baking soda, and salt. Cut in the remaining 3 tablespoons butter with a pastry blender or 2 knives. When plums are baked, stir buttermilk into dry ingredients and drop by large table-spoonfuls onto the plums. Bake an additional 25 minutes, or until biscuits have browned.

Serve warm or at room temperature with whipped cream or ice cream.

SERVES 6

PEACH COBBLER

This cobbler is about as simple as a dessert can be.

1 recipe Cobbler Pastry (page 408)
7 very large ripe peaches, peeled and pitted
1 cup sugar
4 tablespoons (1/2 stick) unsalted butter
1 cup heavy cream, whipped, or light cream

Preheat oven to 450 degrees. Lightly grease a 1½- to 2-quart dish.

Roll out the pastry into a large ragged circle. Dust it with flour and roll up on your rolling pin window-shade fashion. Unroll over the prepared dish. Carefully slip it down into the dish so that you have lined the bottom and sides, allowing the excess to hang over if necessary.

Cut the peaches into 8 or 9 slices each and heap into the dish. Cover with sugar and dot with butter. Flop the loose ends of the pastry over the top. Any extra loose pieces of dough can be used to fill in. Put in preheated oven and turn down to 425 degrees. Bake for 45 minutes. Let cool and serve with whipped or plain cream.

SERVES 6

CRISPS, CRUMBLES, AND BROWN BETTY

APPLE-CHERRY CRISP

Apples are about the best year-round staple for making baked fruit desserts. Here they are joined by wonderful dried tart cherries soaked in calvados (apple brandy)—a nice twist on an old standby.

6 ounces dried tart cherries
1/3 cup calvados
About 6 cups sliced, peeled, and cored apples, such as Granny Smith or McIntosh

CINNAMON TOPPING
1 cup sifted all-purpose flour
3/4 cup sugar
1/2 teaspoon ground cinnamon
1/4 teaspoon salt
8 tablespoons (1 stick) unsalted butter, softened, cut into bits

Whipped cream flavored with vanilla extract

Preheat oven to 350 degrees. Combine dried cherries with calvados and set aside for at least 10 minutes.

Mix marinated cherries (and remaining calvados) with apples and place evenly in a deep 9 × 7-inch greased baking dish.

Combine ingredients for cinnamon topping in a medium bowl and mix with your hands until mixture is the texture of rough meal. Spread evenly over the apples, smoothing with your hand.

Bake for about 35 minutes, or until the top begins to turn color and the mixture is bubbling. Serve with flavored whipped cream or ice cream.

SERVES 6

PEACH CRISP WITH BOURBON SAUCE

This peach dish is best if it is not too sweet because it is served with Bourbon Sauce, which is sweet. Should the sauce not appeal to you, serve sweetened whipped cream or ice cream in its place.

7 large peaches
Juice of 1 lemon
Grated zest of 1/2 lemon
1/4 teaspoon freshly grated nutmeg (optional)

OAT TOPPING
5 1/3 tablespoons cold unsalted butter
1 cup sifted all-purpose flour
3/4 cup rolled oats
1 cup (firmly packed) brown sugar
1/2 cup pecans or walnuts, coarsely chopped (optional)

Bourbon Sauce (page 368)

Preheat oven to 325 degrees. Butter a 9 × 9-inch ovenproof dish.

Dip peaches in boiling water for 30 seconds. Peel and pit them. Slice thin and place in the prepared baking dish. Sprinkle with lemon juice and grated zest. Add the nutmeg if you like.

Cut butter into 8 to 10 pieces and combine with flour, oats, and sugar in a medium bowl. Mix together using a pastry blender or 2 knives. When it is crumbly, work in the nuts if you are using them. Sprinkle the topping over the peaches and press down to cover evenly. Bake for 30 minutes, or until peaches are tender. Serve at room temperature with the sauce.
SERVES 8

AMBROSIA CRUMBLE

This makes a refreshing finish to any meal—with or without the whipped cream.

1/2 large pineapple, peeled, cored, and cut into 1/2-inch cubes
4 large seedless oranges, peeled (with white pith cut off) and sectioned
3 tablespoons fresh lemon juice
1 cup shredded unsweetened coconut
3/4 cup granulated sugar
1 cup all-purpose flour
1/2 cup (firmly packed) light brown sugar
8 tablespoons (1 stick) unsalted butter, softened
Banana Whipped Cream (page 365) or vanilla ice cream

Preheat oven to 350 degrees.

Generously butter an 8-inch square or oval pan or baking dish.

Toss pineapple and oranges with lemon juice and half of the coconut. Heap into the buttered dish. Sprinkle 1/4 cup of the granulated sugar over all.

Mix together remaining coconut with remaining 1/2 cup granulated sugar. Add flour and brown sugar and use your fingers to rub in the butter until the mixture is crumbly. Pat onto the fruit.

Bake until the top begins to turn golden, about 45 minutes.

Serve with flavored whipped cream or vanilla ice cream.
SERVES 6

VARIATION
Add 3 ripe bananas, cut into 1-inch pieces, to the fruit mixture.

BLUEBERRY BROWN BETTY

Some recipes for brown betty call for finely ground toasted bread crumbs, but I much prefer large, soft bread crumbs.

6 cups blueberries, washed and picked over
1/2 cup (firmly packed) light brown sugar
1/2 teaspoon ground cinnamon
Grated zest and juice of 1/2 large lemon
2 cups large, very coarse fresh bread crumbs (see Note)
5 1/3 tablespoons unsalted butter, melted

Preheat oven to 350 degrees. Butter a deep 9 × 7-inch ovenproof dish.

Toss together berries, brown sugar, cinnamon, and lemon zest and juice. Place half the berries in the prepared dish. Toss half the bread crumbs with half the melted butter. Spread the crumbs over the berries. Top with the remaining berries and then the last of the crumbs and butter as above.

Bake for 30 minutes, then cover lightly with foil and bake another 15 minutes, or until berries are bubbling.

Note: Cut crusts off slices of dense white bread and tear into large pieces. Place in a processor and pulse just enough to make large, soft bread crumbs. Or just pinch off small pieces of bread by hand.

SERVES 6 TO 8

PASTRY FOR PIES, TARTS, AND COBBLERS

FLAKY PASTRY

You may add one teaspoon of sugar to the dough if you wish.

2 1/4 cups all-purpose flour
1/2 teaspoon salt
12 tablespoons (1 1/2 sticks) cold unsalted butter, roughly chopped
1/4 cup ice water

Put flour and salt into the bowl of a food processor and pulse once or twice to mix. Add butter and process only until it resembles coarse meal. Add water and process just until the dough is formed into a ball. Remove and dust with flour if dough is sticky. Form the dough into 2 disks, wrap in plastic, and refrigerate for 1 hour.

MAKES ENOUGH FOR ONE 2-CRUST PIE OR 10 TARTLETS

ALL-SHORTENING PIE PASTRY

1 1/2 cups sifted all-purpose flour
1/4 teaspoon salt
1/2 cup cold solid vegetable shortening
2 to 3 tablespoons ice water

Combine flour and salt in a large bowl. Cut in shortening until the mixture resembles coarse meal. Sprinkle with ice water and combine with a fork. Gather dough into a ball. Place between 2 sheets of wax paper and flatten. Refrigerate for 1 hour.

MAKES ENOUGH FOR ONE 1-CRUST PIE

SWEET PASTRY

2 cups all-purpose flour
1/2 teaspoon salt
1/2 teaspoon sugar
1/2 teaspoon grated lemon zest (optional)
14 tablespoons cold unsalted butter, cut into walnut-size pieces
1/4 cup ice water

Sift the dry ingredients together; stir in lemon zest. Quickly cut in butter with 2 knives or a pastry blender until it is the size of small peas. Sprinkle with ice water and mix with as few strokes as possible. Form into a long, flat disk, wrap in plastic wrap, and refrigerate for at least an hour, more if possible. (This may also be done in a food processor.)
MAKES ENOUGH FOR ONE 2-CRUST PIE

HOT-WATER PASTRY

This recipe comes from Mrs. Cashdollar's famous recipe in *Country Desserts*.

3/4 cup solid vegetable shortening
1/4 cup boiling water
1 tablespoon milk
1 teaspoon salt
2 cups all-purpose flour, or more as needed

Put shortening in a bowl and pour boiling water over it. Stir until smooth, then add milk.

Combine salt and flour in the bowl of a food processor, and pour the shortening mixture over the flour. Process until the dough forms a mass. Form into a ball, flatten slightly between 2 sheets of wax paper or plastic wrap, and refrigerate for at least 1 hour.
MAKES ENOUGH FOR ONE 2-CRUST PIE
OR 8 TARTLETS

SHORT CRUST

2 cups unbleached all-purpose flour
2 tablespoons sugar (optional)
1/4 teaspoon salt
8 tablespoons (1 stick) cold unsalted butter, cut into bits
1 large egg yolk
2 to 3 tablespoons ice water

Combine flour, sugar if using, and salt in a food processor. Add butter and egg yolk. Pulse until mixture resembles coarse meal.

With the motor on, add 2 tablespoons of the ice water and process just until dough masses into a ball (add another tablespoon of water if needed). Remove dough from processor and knead in any remaining flour. Chill, wrapped in plastic, for 30 minutes or so.
MAKES ENOUGH FOR ONE 2-CRUST PIE

LEE KLEIN'S PIE CRUST

This recipe gives instructions for "blind" baking an empty pie or tart shell.

1 1/4 cups all-purpose flour
1 tablespoon sugar (optional)
1/2 teaspoon salt
6 tablespoons frozen unsalted butter
4 tablespoons frozen vegetable shortening
3 tablespoons ice water

Preheat oven to 425 degrees.

Mix flour, sugar, and salt in a food processor. Pulse just a couple of times. Add butter and vegetable shortening. Add water and pulse a few more times. Gather into a ball. There should be bits of butter showing in the dough. Form into a ball, flatten it, and wrap in wax paper. Refrigerate for at least 30 minutes before using.

Roll pastry out on a floured surface and line pie pan. Prick bottom with tines of a fork. Cover with a piece of foil and weight with dried beans. Bake until set, about 5 minutes. Remove foil and beans and continue baking until the pastry is beginning to turn golden, pricking any blisters that may form on the bottom the crust, about 10 or more minutes. This should not completely bake, since it will have to be cooked again when the filling is added.

MAKES ENOUGH FOR ONE 1-CRUST PIE

WHOLE WHEAT SHORT PASTRY

2^1/$_4$ cups sifted whole wheat pastry flour
^{1}/$_4$ cup sugar
^{1}/$_2$ teaspoon salt
^{1}/$_2$ cup cold solid vegetable shortening, cut into bits
1 teaspoon distilled white vinegar
About 6 tablespoons ice water

Combine whole wheat flour, sugar, and salt in the bowl of a food processor. Sprinkle the shortening on top and pulse several times until the mixture resembles coarse meal.

With the motor running, add vinegar and 2 tablespoons of the ice water. Process briefly, add 1 tablespoon more water, and pulse. Keep adding water, 1 tablespoon at the time, until the dough forms a mass.

Divide dough in half, one part slightly larger than the other. Wrap separately in plastic or wax paper and chill for at least 1 hour.

MAKES ENOUGH FOR ONE 2-CRUST PIE

CHEESE PASTRY

2 cups all-purpose flour
Pinch of salt
8 tablespoons (1 stick) cold unsalted butter, cut into bits
4 tablespoons cold solid vegetable shortening
2 cups grated cheddar
^{1}/$_4$ cup ice water

Toss flour and salt together in a large bowl. Cut in butter, shortening, and cheese with 2 knives or a pastry blender until the mixture resembles coarse meal. Stir in the water, mixing well but quickly. Form into 2 disks and wrap in plastic. Refrigerate for 30 minutes.

MAKES ENOUGH FOR 8 LITTLE PIES

BUTTER–MARGARINE TART CRUST

1^1/$_2$ cups unbleached all-purpose flour
^{1}/$_2$ teaspoon salt
4 tablespoons (^{1}/$_2$ stick) frozen unsalted butter
6 tablespoons (^{3}/$_4$ stick) frozen margarine
5 to 6 tablespoons ice water

Put all of the ingredients except the ice water in a food processor. Process until the mixture has the texture of small peas. Add the water and process until the mass begins to form a ball. Remove, shape into a ball, and place between two pieces of wax paper. Flatten slightly and refrigerate.

MAKES ENOUGH FOR 6 TO 8 LITTLE PIES

NUT CRUST

I think nut crusts are too often overlooked. They're easy to make and you may use any kind of nut, or a combination of several. And nut crusts are marvelous with almost any cream pie. Experiment!

If you are using toasted nuts in the filling as well as the crust, do the whole batch at once. Also, when you use an egg white in the crust, save the yolk to go into the filling.

1 1/2 cups finely chopped toasted nuts (see Note)
1/4 cup sugar
White of 1 large egg

Combine nuts and sugar, then stir in the egg white, mixing well. Mound in the center of the pie pan. Pat gently to cover bottom and sides evenly. Rinse hands in cold water if they become sticky, leaving them damp, and continue patting crust in place.

Bake until set, about 20 minutes. Place on a rack until completely cool. When you first remove crust from the oven, if it has puffed up in spots, gently pat it back down while it is still hot.

Note: To toast nuts, spread in a single layer on a rimmed baking sheet. Bake in a 350° degree oven for about 8 to 10 minutes, until starting to turn color, stirring if necessary to keep from burning. Let cool before using.

MAKES ONE 9-INCH CRUST

FLAKY TART CRUST

1 1/2 cups all-purpose flour
6 tablespoons (3/4 stick) cold unsalted butter
2 tablespoons cold solid vegetable shortening
1/4 teaspoon salt
3 tablespoons ice water

In a food processor, combine flour, butter, shortening, and salt. Pulse until the mixture resembles coarse meal. Add the water and process until the mixture starts to come together. Pat the dough into a disk and wrap in plastic. Chill for at least 1 hour.

MAKES ENOUGH FOR ONE 10-INCH TART

COBBLER PASTRY

1 1/2 cups all-purpose flour
1/4 teaspoon salt
5 tablespoons frozen unsalted butter
4 tablespoons frozen solid vegetable shortening
4 to 5 tablespoons ice water

Combine flour and salt in a food processor. Add butter and shortening and process until shortening is the size of small peas. Add 4 tablespoons water and process until dough begins to cling together (this shouldn't take too long—10 seconds or so). If more water is required, add it. Gather dough into a ball. Wrap in plastic wrap or wax paper. Refrigerate until ready to use.

MAKES ENOUGH FOR 1 COBBLER

CAKES AND COOKIES

THE SAD TRUTH IS THAT PEOPLE DON'T BOTHER TO MAKE CAKES from scratch the way they used to. I say sad because, in my view, cake-making is as rewarding—and crowd-pleasing—as cooking can be. I guess it was the advent of the cake mix that did it in. Whatever, I would like to see this trend, if not stopped, at least slowed down. Take it from me, cakes are among the most basic

desserts you can put together—right up there with cobblers. Follow any one of these recipes and be the first on your block fight back this anti-cake-making movement. You won't be sorry. ✦ As for cookies, they always make me think of ice cream, lemonade, warm weather, and my grandmothers. In any order you choose. Actually, I seem to remember Grandmother Bailey smelled like a cookie. And that in those days almost all cookies were crisp with modest but intense flavors and were served in the afternoon as a little treat—with something wet like iced tea.

LAYER CAKES

BANANA LAYER CAKE

My Aunt Cora first made this cake and then, as her recipe was passed around, most other family members followed suit.

Lighter than banana bread, it uses fresh bananas between the layers. These are fairly perishable, but in our case the cake never lasted long enough for that to make much difference.

> 2¹/₂ cups sifted cake flour
> 2¹/₂ teaspoons baking powder
> ¹/₂ teaspoon baking soda
> Pinch of ground cloves
> 1¹/₄ teaspoons ground cinnamon
> ¹/₂ teaspoon freshly grated nutmeg
> ¹/₂ teaspoon salt
> 1¹/₄ cups sugar
> 8 tablespoons (1 stick) unsalted butter, softened
> 2 large eggs
> 1 teaspoon vanilla extract
> 1¹/₂ cups mashed ripe bananas
> Several bananas for filling, sliced lengthwise

BOILED FROSTING
> 1¹/₂ cups sugar
> ¹/₂ cup water
> 3 large egg whites, at room temperature
> Pinch of salt
> 1 teaspoon vanilla extract
>
> Additional sugar for filling

Preheat oven to 375 degrees. Grease and lightly flour two 9-inch round cake pans. Set aside.

Sift together flour, baking powder, baking soda, cloves, cinnamon, nutmeg, and salt. Set aside. Cream sugar and butter until fluffy, about 3 minutes. Beat in eggs, one at a time, beating well after each addition. Stir in vanilla. Mix in the flour mixture, alternating with the mashed bananas.

Pour the batter into the prepared cake pans and bake for 25 minutes, or until a cake tester comes out clean. Let cool.

To make frosting: Combine sugar and water in a heavy saucepan over high heat and boil until the syrup reaches the soft-ball stage (238 degrees). Beat egg whites with salt until they form soft peaks. Pour hot syrup, very slowly, into the beaten egg whites, then beat constantly with an electric mixer until frosting stands in stiff peaks and is of spreading consistency. Stir in vanilla.

To assemble the cake, place 1 layer on a flat cake plate, and cover the top with thin slices of ripe bananas. Sprinkle generously with sugar. Put the other layer on top and hold in place with toothpicks. Cover the top and sides with frosting.
SERVES 12

INTERMONT WHITE CAKE

My Aunt Cora used to make this cake for celebrations. It has a marvelous light texture and looks beautiful piled generously with white mountain icing. This is scrumptious with homemade Peach Pit Ice Cream or Vanilla-Bean Custard Ice Cream (pages 494 and 491).

> 3 cups sifted cake flour (not self-rising)
> 1 tablespoon baking powder
> ¹/₂ teaspoon salt
> 12 tablespoons (1¹/₂ sticks) unsalted butter, softened
> 2 cups sugar
> 1 teaspoon vanilla extract
> 1 teaspoon almond extract
> 1 cup milk
> 6 large egg whites, at room temperature

WHITE MOUNTAIN ICING

1 cup boiling water
2¼ cups sugar
1 tablespoon light corn syrup
3 large egg whites, at room temperature

Preheat oven to 375 degrees. Grease and lightly flour two 9-inch round cake pans. Set aside.

Sift together flour, baking powder, and salt. Set aside. Cream butter and 1½ cups of the sugar until fluffy, about 3 minutes. Mix in vanilla and almond extracts. Add the dry mixture in 4 parts, alternating with the milk.

Whisk egg whites until foamy, then start adding the remaining ½ cup sugar, continuing to beat until whites stand in stiff peaks. Fold whites into the batter with an over-and-under motion. Pour batter into the prepared pans and bake for 35 minutes, or until a cake tester comes out clean. Let cool slightly, then loosen edges and remove from the pans to cake racks to cool completely.

To make icing: Combine the boiling water with 2 cups of the sugar and the corn syrup in a large saucepan set over medium heat. Cook at a rolling boil until mixture reaches soft-ball stage (238 degrees on a candy thermometer).

Meanwhile, whisk egg whites until foamy, then start adding the remaining ¼ cup sugar. Continue whisking until whites stand in stiff peaks.

When syrup is at the correct temperature, pour into the beaten whites in a thin, steady stream, beating all the while. Ice between the cake layers, then ice the top and sides of the cake.

SERVES 12

COCONUT CAKE

This simple cake can be made in two parts. Make the cake the day before, and ice it the day of the party. Serve with Chocolate Whipped Cream (page 365)

1¾ cups sifted all-purpose flour
¼ teaspoon salt
2½ teaspoons baking powder
8 tablespoons (1 stick) unsalted butter, softened
1 cup sugar
2 eggs
⅔ cup milk
1 teaspoon vanilla extract

COCONUT ICING

1 tablespoon light corn syrup
1 cup sugar
⅓ cup water
1 egg white
1 teaspoon vanilla extract
1 cup grated fresh coconut, or more to taste

Preheat oven to 350 degrees. Lightly grease and flour two 8-inch cake pans. Set aside.

Sift flour again with salt and baking powder. Set aside. Using a hand mixer, cream together butter and sugar until it is light yellow. Add eggs, one at a time, beating after each. Add milk and flour alternately, ending with flour, and mixing thoroughly after each addition. Stir in vanilla and pour into the prepared pans. Bake for 35 to 40 minutes, or until a cake tester comes out clean. Let cool in the pan, then invert onto racks.

To make icing: Put syrup, sugar, and water in a small saucepan and bring to a brisk boil. Turn the heat down to a normal boil and cook until a candy thermometer registers between 238 and 240 degrees. This will take about 7 to 10 minutes, so you can get the egg white ready in the meantime—put it in a bowl and beat until stiff. At 238 degrees, the sugar syrup will spin a very fine thread; if it goes up past 240 degrees, it will harden too quickly. So at 238 degrees, pour the syrup in a steady stream into the beaten egg white, beating all the while with a hand mixer. Add vanilla and mix it in.

Cover the top of the bottom cake layer by putting a big blob of icing in the center and coaxing it out to the edges. Sprinkle this generously with coconut. Put the top layer on very gently, securing with toothpicks. Ice the top in the same way you did the bottom layer. Using a spatula (dipped in water if necessary), ice the sides. Sprinkle the top and sides with coconut.
SERVES 12

NATCHEZ LEMON CAKE

An old cake recipe, wonderfully moist and tart—and like most old Southern dessert recipes, very sweet.

CAKE

2/3 cup unsalted butter, or half butter and
   half margarine, softened
1 1/2 cups sugar
2 tablespoons freshly grated lemon zest
2 1/2 teaspoons fresh lemon juice
4 eggs
2 cups plus 3 tablespoons all-purpose flour
2 1/2 teaspoons baking powder
1/4 teaspoon salt
3/4 cup milk

LEMON FILLING

1 1/2 cups sugar
1/4 cup cornstarch
Pinch of salt
1 cup water
6 tablespoons fresh lemon juice
4 teaspoons freshly grated lemon zest
2 tablespoons unsalted butter
6 egg yolks, lightly beaten

Whipped cream (optional)
Berry purée (optional)

Preheat oven to 375 degrees. Grease and flour three 9-inch round cake pans. Set aside.

To make cake: Cream butter and sugar until light and fluffy. Add lemon zest and juice, then add eggs, one at a time, mixing well after each.

Sift flour with baking powder and salt. Add to batter, alternating with milk and beginning and ending with flour.

Pour batter into prepared pans. Bake, being careful not to let pans touch one another, for 20 minutes, or until a cake tester comes out clean. Let cool slightly in the pan, then loosen edges and invert cakes onto cooling racks. When completely cooled, dust crumbs off layers.

To make filling: Sift sugar, cornstarch, and salt into the top of a double boiler. Stir in water, lemon juice, and zest. Add butter and cook, stirring, for 6 minutes. Cover and cook another 10 minutes without stirring. Remove from the heat and stir in egg yolks. Return to heat and cook about 3 minutes, until mixture begins to coat spoon. If any globs of egg yolk have solidified in the mixture, pick them out. Cool for 45 minutes, stirring occasionally.

To assemble, place 1 layer on a cake plate with the bottom side up and spoon on some of the filling a little at a time so it will be absorbed, continuing until it starts to run off. Hold the second layer in one hand, bottom side up, and spoon filling over it, allowing it to soak in as with the first layer. Carefully turn it over and position on top of the first layer, wet side down. Spoon more filling on top. (Filling will not be absorbed as readily as it was on the undersides.) Prepare the top layer as you did the second, bottom side up, then turn it over and place on top of second layer. Spoon remaining filling over top layer and let it run down sides.

This filling is very liquid and takes a while to set. Serve cake with whipped cream or a berry purée.
SERVES 12

FRESH PEACH CAKE

I'm told this is an old Pennsylvania Dutch recipe, but I wouldn't swear to it. Wherever it came from, it's hard to resist.

CREAM FILLING
    2 cups heavy cream
    1/2 cup sugar
    1 1/2 teaspoons vanilla extract

CAKE
    2 cups sifted unbleached all-purpose flour
    5 tablespoons plus 1 teaspoon cornstarch
    2 teaspoons baking powder
    3/4 teaspoon salt
    6 tablespoons (3/4 stick) margarine, softened
    6 tablespoons (3/4 stick) unsalted butter, softened
    1 1/4 cups plus 2 tablespoons sugar
    3/4 cup milk
    1 1/2 teaspoons vanilla extract
    9 large egg whites, stiffly beaten

PEACH FILLING
    5 to 6 large peaches
    Juice of 1/2 lemon
    2 tablespoons sugar

To make cream filling: Mix cream, sugar, and vanilla. Cover and refrigerate for at least 2 hours.

Preheat oven to 350 degrees. Generously grease three 8-inch round cake pans, then line the bottoms with wax paper. Grease the paper and lightly flour. Set aside.

To make cake: Sift flour with cornstarch, baking powder, and salt. Set aside.

Cream margarine, butter, and sugar until fluffy, about 3 minutes. Add dry mixture in 4 parts, alternating with milk and ending with flour. Mix in vanilla.

Place the beaten egg whites on top of the mixture and fold in with an over-and-under motion. Do not beat, but be sure it is well mixed. Pour batter into cake pans and bake on the middle rack of the oven for 20 to 25 minutes, or until a cake tester comes out clean. Let cakes cool in pans for 10 minutes, then invert onto cooling racks. Let cool completely.

To make peach filling: Dip peaches in hot water for about 10 seconds, then run cold water over them. Slip the skins off and cut each into about a dozen slices; discard pits. Toss peach slices with lemon juice and sugar.

Whip the chilled cream filling until it is stiff, then mix in the vanilla.

The peaches will have given up a bit of juice by now, so pour some of it over the bottom cake layer, a little at a time, to give it a chance to soak in. Put a third of the peach slices on the bottom layer and cover with some whipped cream. Repeat with the remaining layers, holding them in place with toothpicks if necessary.

Keep cake refrigerated, very loosely covered with foil or wax paper, until ready to serve.

SERVES 12 TO 18

PLUM JAM CAKE

You can use any flavor of jam you like, but because the cake is rather sweet, a tart jam is best. Serve it with a flavored whipped cream.

1/2 pound (2 sticks) unsalted butter, softened
2 cups granulated sugar
3 1/4 cups unbleached all-purpose flour
2 teaspoons baking powder
2/3 cup milk
8 egg whites
1 teaspoon almond extract
Plum jam
1/4 cup confectioners' sugar

Preheat oven to 350 degrees. Grease and lightly flour three 8-inch round cake pans.

Cream butter until light and add 1 cup of the sugar. Cream again until very light in color.

Sift together flour and baking powder. Add to creamed mixture, alternating with milk and mixing thoroughly. The batter will be very stiff.

Beat egg whites until they start making soft peaks. Add the remaining sugar 1/4 cup at a time, beating after each addition. Fold half the egg whites into the batter, then fold in the remaining whites and the almond extract. Pour into the prepared pans and bake for 25 to 30 minutes, or until cake tester comes out clean.

To assemble, melt jam over low heat and spread on the bottom layer, allowing it to run over the sides. Repeat with the next 2 layers (holding them in place with toothpicks). Sprinkle with confectioners' sugar.

SERVES 12

ALMOND–BLACKBERRY JAM CAKE

Almonds are my favorite in this cake, but obviously any other nut can be substituted. Use the best jam you can find.

1 3/4 cups sifted all-purpose flour
1/4 teaspoon baking soda
8 tablespoons (1 stick) unsalted butter, softened
1 1/2 cups sugar
3 large eggs, separated
2/3 cup sour cream
1 teaspoon vanilla extract
1 cup slivered almonds, toasted and coarsely chopped
1 to 1 1/2 cups blackberry jam
Lightly whipped cream flavored with a few tablespoons of blackberry brandy (optional)

Preheat oven to 325 degrees. Grease and lightly flour two 8-inch round cake pans.

Sift flour with baking soda in a large bowl. Set aside a few tablespoons of the flour mixture on a plate. Cream butter and sugar in a medium bowl with an electric mixer until light and fluffy, about 3 minutes. Add egg yolks, one at a time, beating well after each addition.

Stir dry ingredients into egg and butter mixture alternately with sour cream, beginning and ending with flour. Stir in vanilla and mix well.

Lightly dredge almonds in reserved flour on the plate, shaking off any excess. Stir into the batter.

In a very clean medium bowl (copper if you have one), beat egg whites until stiff peaks form. Gently stir one third of the whites into the batter to soften it; fold in the remaining whites.

Pour into the prepared pans, shaking to spread out the thick batter evenly. Bake until golden and a cake tester comes out clean, 40 to 50 minutes. Let the layers cool in the pans on wire racks for 30 minutes before turning out.

Heat the jam in a small saucepan over low heat until it's runny.

Brush the crumbs off both layers and place one layer on a cake plate. Pour and spread about half the jam over the bottom layer. Top with the second layer and secure it in place with toothpicks. Spread the top with the remaining jam and let it run down the sides of the cake.

Serve with flavored whipped cream if you care to.

SERVES 12

VARIATION

Substitute 1 cup blanched hazelnuts for the almonds. Toast and chop the nuts.

GOLDEN PECAN CAKE WITH PECAN DIVINITY ICING

This is one of everyone's favorites. It should be served with ice cream, whipped cream, or vanilla sauce.

3 cups sifted all-purpose flour
1¹/₂ teaspoons baking powder
¹/₄ teaspoon salt
1 cup coarsely chopped toasted pecans
¹/₂ pound (2 sticks) unsalted butter, softened
2 cups sugar
5 large eggs
1 cup milk
1 teaspoon vanilla extract

PECAN DIVINITY ICING
3 cups sugar
¹/₂ cup light corn syrup
²/₃ cup water
2 large egg whites, at room temperature
Pinch of salt
1 teaspoon vanilla extract

1 cup chopped toasted pecans (see Note)

Preheat oven to 350 degrees. Oil and lightly flour three 9-inch round cake pans. Set aside.

Sift together flour, baking powder, and salt. Remove ¹/₄ cup of the mixture and toss with the pecans. Set both aside.

Cream butter and sugar until light and fluffy, about 3 minutes. Add eggs, one at a time, mixing well after each addition. Add dry ingredients in 3 batches, alternating with milk and mixing well after each addition. Add vanilla and mix, then fold in the floured pecans. (Do not overmix.)

Pour batter into prepared pans and bake for 30 minutes, or until tops are golden and sides have left the pan. Remove and let cool slightly before inverting onto cooling racks. Let cool completely.

To make icing: Combine sugar, syrup, and water in a large saucepan. Bring to a boil over medium heat and continue to boil until mixture reaches soft-ball stage (238 degrees on a candy thermometer).

Meanwhile, beat egg whites with salt until stiff. When syrup is ready, pour into the beaten egg whites in a thin, steady stream, beating all the while. When creamy, stir in vanilla.

Ice the cake by filling between layers first and sprinkling with pecans, then ice the top and sides and sprinkle top with remaining nuts.

Note: Chopped candied cherries and freshly grated coconut can also be sprinkled between the layers and on top along with the pecans.

SERVES 12

PLANTATION PECAN CAKE

Margaret Williams used to serve this cake, which is popular wherever pecans are grown. Sometimes the cake was cooked in a tube pan and at other times in layers, as it is here. Whichever way, it has always been one of my favorites.

1½ cups sifted all-purpose flour
1 teaspoon baking powder
½ teaspoon salt
1½ cups finely chopped or grated pecans
8 tablespoons (1 stick) unsalted butter, softened
1½ cups sugar
¼ cup bourbon mixed with ½ cup water
½ cup egg whites, stiffly beaten (about 5 large eggs)
1 cup heavy cream, whipped
Confectioners' sugar

Preheat oven to 375 degrees. Grease two 8-inch round cake pans and cut wax paper to fit the bottom of each. Grease the paper and then lightly flour the inside of each pan. Set aside.

Sift together flour, baking powder, and salt. Combine with pecans and set aside.

Cream butter and sugar until fluffy, about 3 minutes. Add the dry mixture in 4 parts, alternating with the bourbon water and mixing well after each addition. Pile the beaten egg whites on top of the batter and carefully fold in with an over-and-under motion.

Pour batter into pans and bake for about 25 minutes, or until a cake tester comes out clean. Let layers cool for about 10 minutes, then run a knife around the edges of the pans and invert onto cooling racks.

To serve cake, spread whipped cream between the 2 layers, holding them in place with a couple of toothpicks if necessary. Sift confectioners' sugar over the top.

SERVES 12

TUBE CAKES

APPLESAUCE SPICE CAKE

This cake remains moist and fresh for a long time, especially if stored in an airtight container. As a matter of fact, its flavor seems to improve the second day.

It can be served for dessert with the addition of a flavored cream or a sauce. But it really shines with coffee or tea.

½ pound (2 sticks) unsalted butter, softened
2 cups superfine sugar
2 cups unsweetened applesauce
3 cups sifted all-purpose flour
1 cup coarsely chopped pecans
1 cup raisins
1 teaspoon ground cinnamon
1 teaspoon freshly grated nutmeg
½ teaspoon ground mace
1¾ teaspoons baking soda
1 teaspoon vanilla extract

BROWN SUGAR FROSTING
2 cups (firmly packed) light brown sugar
6 tablespoons heavy cream
4 tablespoons (½ stick) unsalted butter
1 teaspoon vanilla extract
1 cup sifted confectioners' sugar

Preheat oven to 325 degrees. Grease a 9-inch tube pan. Cut a piece of wax paper to fit the bottom and grease it lightly. Dust the pan with flour, shaking out excess.

Cream butter and sugar until fluffy, about 3 minutes. Then fold in applesauce. This will not mix completely.

Remove ¼ cup of the flour and use it to dredge the nuts and raisins. Sift together remaining flour, spices, and baking soda. Fold the dry mixture into the creamed mixture, then add vanilla and the nuts and raisins.

Pour batter into the prepared pan and bake

for 1½ hours, or until a cake tester comes out clean. Let cool in the pan, then invert to remove.

To make frosting: Put the brown sugar, cream, and butter in a large saucepan and slowly bring to a rolling bowl over medium heat, stirring all the while. Remove pan from heat and stir in vanilla and confectioners' sugar. Pour frosting onto the top of the cake and let run down the sides. This frosting tends to set rather quickly, so don't try to spread it with a spatula; it will look best if allowed to flow naturally.

SERVES 12

OLD-FASHIONED COCONUT CAKE

Mrs. Curtis McCaskill of Laurel, Mississippi, who is noted thereabouts for her wonderful desserts, told me how to make this cake. It is a very large cake with a marvelous flavor that is delicious served with fruit. It also keeps quite well.

3 cups sifted all-purpose flour
¼ teaspoon baking soda
½ pound (2 sticks) unsalted butter, softened
3 cups sugar
6 large eggs
1 cup sour cream
1 tablespoon coconut flavoring
½ teaspoon vanilla extract
Boiled Frosting (page 410) or White
    Mountain Icing (page 410)
Grated fresh coconut

Preheat oven to 350 degrees. Grease and lightly flour a 10-inch tube pan.

Sift flour and baking soda, then set aside.

Cream butter and sugar until fluffy, about 3 minutes. Then add eggs, one at a time, beating well after each addition. Add dry mixture, alternating with sour cream. Stir in the flavorings and pour into the prepared pan. Bake for about 70 minutes (or slightly more), or until a cake tester comes out clean. Let cake cool completely before removing from the pan.

Ice the cake, then sprinkle it generously with coconut.

SERVES 12

CREAM CHEESE BUNDT CAKE

Don't let the simplicity of this recipe deceive you, it has a distinctive flavor and texture. And thanks to Mickey Ellis for giving me the recipe for the cake.

¾ cup margarine, softened
6 tablespoons unsalted butter, softened
2 cups granulated sugar
6 ounces cream cheese, softened
1½ teaspoons vanilla extract
4 large eggs
2 cups all-purpose flour
Pinch of salt
Confectioners' sugar (optional)

Grease and flour a Bundt pan. Cream together margarine, butter, and sugar until light. Beat in cream cheese until smooth. Beat in vanilla. Beat in eggs, one at a time, then stir in flour and salt. Spoon into pan and put in a cold oven. Turn oven on to 275 degrees and bake until tester comes out clean, about 1 hour and 10 minutes (check for doneness after 1 hour).

Let cool and remove from pan. Serve with the syrup or dust with confectioners' sugar.

SERVES 8

417

SUNSHINE CREAM CAKE

This version of the classic is served at Watts Tea Room in Milwaukee, Wisconsin.

9 large eggs, separated, at room
    temperature
1/4 cup water
1 1/2 teaspoon vanilla extract
1 1/2 teaspoons ground cinnamon
1 cup sugar
1 cup cake flour, sifted 3 times
1 teaspoon cream of tartar

FRENCH CUSTARD FILLING
4 large egg yolks, lightly beaten
3/4 cup sifted confectioners' sugar
3/4 cup milk
1 teaspoon vanilla extract
1/2 pound (2 sticks) unsalted butter, softened

Boiled Frosting (page 410)
Grated orange zest

Preheat oven to 350 degrees.

Combine egg yolks, water, vanilla, cinnamon, and 1/2 cup of the sugar in a large bowl. Beat together until light and fluffy. Add flour, 1/4 cup at a time, until well blended.

Whip egg whites with cream of tartar until they form soft peaks. Add remaining 1/2 cup sugar and beat until stiff peaks begin to form. Fold whites into batter. Pour into an ungreased 9-inch tube pan and bake for 35 minutes. Let cool in pan for about 15 minutes, then remove from pan to rack to finish cooling.

To make filling: Combine egg yolks, confectioners' sugar, and milk in the top of a double boiler and cook, stirring constantly, until custard coats a stirring spoon and begins to thicken. Let cool.

Combine vanilla and butter in a bowl and cream until fluffy, about 2 minutes. Add custard slowly and continue beating until smooth.

To assemble, cut cake carefully into 3 layers. Spread custard filling between the layers, then ice top and sides with frosting. Garnish with grated orange zest.

SERVES 12

BROWN SUGAR GLAZED CAKE

This marvelous-tasting cake is from the fabulous Edna Lewis, who created it from her memory of such delicious simple cakes served when she was a child.

2 cups minus 2 tablespoons sifted all-
    purpose flour
1 tablespoon baking powder
1/4 teaspoon salt
8 tablespoons (1 stick) unsalted butter,
    softened
1 1/2 cups superfine sugar
3 large eggs
2/3 cup milk
1 tablespoon vanilla extract

BROWN SUGAR GLAZE
1 cup (firmly packed) light brown sugar
3 tablespoons cold water

Preheat oven to 375 degrees. Butter and flour a Bundt pan. Set aside.

Sift flour, baking powder, and salt together. Set aside.

Cream butter and sugar until fluffy, about 3 minutes. Add eggs, one at a time, beating after each addition. Add the dry mixture in 3 parts, alternating with the milk. Stir in vanilla and pour batter into the prepared pan.

Bake on the center rack of the oven for 35 minutes, or until a cake tester comes out clean.

Loosen the sides of the cake with a knife and let cool in the pan about 15 minutes before removing to a rack to cool completely.

To make glaze: Place brown sugar and water in a medium saucepan set over medium heat and let boil until it reaches the soft-ball stage (238 degrees on a candy thermometer). Do not stir at any time during the cooking, but skim foam off top if necessary.

Remove to a bowl of ice water, and when glaze becomes thick enough to spread, place cake on a rack set atop a layer of wax paper. Smooth or pour the glaze over the cake, letting it drop down the sides. If the glaze thickens too much, reheat to pouring consistency.

SERVES 8

Bake for about 2 hours, or until a cake tester comes out clean. Let cake cool in the pan, then loosen edges and invert onto a serving plate.

SERVES 18 TO 24

PAN AND LOAF CAKES

WHITE FRUITCAKE
This is the fabled Windsor fruitcake

3 cups sifted all-purpose flour
1 teaspoon baking powder
¼ teaspoon salt
1½ teaspoons ground cinnamon
1 teaspoon ground allspice
1 teaspoon ground cloves
1 teaspoon freshly grated nutmeg
½ pound (2 sticks) unsalted butter, softened
2 cups sugar
6 large eggs, well beaten
½ cup dry sherry
2 cups blanched almond halves
1½ cups coarsely chopped pecans
½ cup coarsely chopped walnuts
1 box (15 ounces) golden raisins
1½ cups diced candied citron
1½ cups diced candied pineapple
½ cup diced candied orange peel

Preheat oven to 300 degrees. Grease a 10-inch tube pan and line the bottom with wax paper. Grease the paper and flour the inside of the entire pan. Set aside.

Sift together flour, baking powder, salt, cinnamon, allspice, cloves, and nutmeg. Set aside.

Cream butter and sugar until fluffy, about 3 minutes. Beat in eggs thoroughly, then add sherry and mix well. Mix in nuts and fruits. Add the dry mixture in 4 parts, mixing thoroughly after each addition. Pour batter into the prepared pan.

WARM GINGERBREAD
Gingerbread is extremely easy to make. The one thing to remember is that if you want to turn it out of the pan to serve it, you must line the bottom of the oiled and floured pan with oiled wax paper.

2½ cups all-purpose flour
½ teaspoon baking powder
3 teaspoons baking soda
2 teaspoons ground ginger
1½ teaspoons ground cinnamon
½ teaspoon ground cloves
½ teaspoon freshly grated nutmeg
¾ cup (firmly packed) dark brown sugar
2 eggs
¾ cup molasses
¾ cup shortening or unsalted butter, melted
1 cup boiling water
Ice cream or whipped cream

Preheat oven to 350 degrees. Oil and lightly flour a 10 × 8-inch baking pan. Line with wax paper.

Sift together all the dry ingredients except the brown sugar and set aside. Beat together eggs, molasses, and sugar. When smooth, add melted shortening and mix well. Add the sifted mixture to the egg mixture a third at a time. Mix well. Add the boiling water and mix well. Pour into the prepared pan and bake for 30 to 40 minutes, until a toothpick comes out clean. Serve with ice cream or whipped cream.

SERVES 8

CARROT CAKE WITH CREAM CHEESE ICING

What more can be said about carrot cake, which the "back to the earth" hippies of the 1960s made famous. This version is moist and spicy—and terrific.

> 2 cups sifted whole wheat pastry flour
> 1½ teaspoons baking soda
> 1½ teaspoons ground cinnamon
> 1½ teaspoons ground allspice
> 1½ cups vegetable oil
> 1 cup sugar
> 4 large eggs
> ½ cup buttermilk
> 4 cups finely grated carrots (about 1¾ pounds)
> ½ cup chopped walnuts

CREAM CHEESE ICING
> 1 package (8 ounces) cream cheese, at room temperature
> ⅓ cup sour cream
> 2 tablespoons unsalted butter, softened
> 1 cup sifted confectioners' sugar

Preheat oven to 325 degrees. Grease a 13 × 9-inch glass baking pan. Set aside.

Sift together flour, baking soda, cinnamon, and allspice. Set aside.

Beat together oil and sugar until sugar is dissolved and mixture is smooth, about 3 minutes. Add eggs, one at a time, mixing well after each addition. Gradually add the dry mixture, alternating with buttermilk. Beat well.

Fold in carrots and walnuts, combining well, then pour batter into prepared pan and smooth the top with a spatula.

Bake for 40 to 45 minutes, or until a cake tester comes out clean. Let cool on cake rack.

To make icing: Cream the cream cheese, sour cream, and butter until fluffy. Add confectioners' sugar and beat until thickened. Spread over room-temperature cake and refrigerate until served.

SERVES 12

SHERRY SPICE CAKE WITH CREAMY BROWN SUGAR GLAZE

> 2⅓ cups sifted cake flour
> 1½ teaspoons baking powder
> ½ teaspoon baking soda
> 1 teaspoon freshly grated nutmeg
> 1 teaspoon ground cinnamon
> ½ teaspoon ground cloves
> ½ teaspoon salt
> 1½ cups sugar
> 12 tablespoons (1½ sticks) unsalted butter
> 3 eggs, separated
> ½ cup plus 1 tablespoon buttermilk
> ¼ cup dry sherry

CREAMY BROWN SUGAR GLAZE
> 2 cups (firmly packed) light brown sugar
> ¾ cup heavy cream
> 4 tablespoons (½ stick) unsalted butter
> 1 teaspoon vanilla extract
> 1 cup confectioners' sugar

Preheat oven to 350 degrees. Lightly grease and flour a 9 × 5-inch loaf pan or 9-inch tube pan. Set aside.

Sift together flour, baking powder, baking soda, nutmeg, cinnamon, cloves, and salt onto a sheet of wax paper. Set aside.

Sift sugar into a bowl with butter. Cream together until very light and fluffy, about 3 minutes. Beat in egg yolks, one at a time. Combine buttermilk and sherry, then add to creamed mixture, alternating with flour mixture. Beat egg whites until stiff and fold into batter. Pour into prepared pan and bake about 1 hour, or until a cake tester comes out clean. Let cool on a wire rack, then invert pan and remove cake.

To make glaze: Put brown sugar, cream, and butter in a saucepan and bring slowly to a rolling boil, stirring all the while. Remove from heat and stir in vanilla and then confectioners' sugar. Pour over top of cake and let

420

run down the sides naturally. Do not try to spread.

SERVES 12

PEACH CRUMBLE CAKE

Crumble cake is easy to make and may be varied by changing the fruit and the spices, so let your imagination be your guide.

8 tablespoons (1 stick) unsalted butter, softened
1/2 cup (firmly packed) light brown sugar
1/2 cup plus 3 tablespoons granulated sugar, or more to taste
1 cup sifted all-purpose flour
1 teaspoon baking powder
2 large eggs
10 large peaches, peeled, pitted, and cut in half
1 tablespoon fresh lemon juice, or more to taste
1/2 teaspoon ground cinnamon, or more to taste
Vanilla-flavored whipped cream or ice cream

Preheat oven to 350 degrees. Lightly butter an 8-inch square baking dish. Set aside.

Cream butter, brown sugar, and 1/2 cup of granulated sugar until light and fluffy, about 3 minutes. Sift together flour and baking powder, then beat into the butter mixture. Beat in eggs.

Scrape the mixture into the prepared baking dish and place peach halves on top of the batter, flat side down. Sprinkle with lemon juice. Mix remaining sugar with cinnamon and sprinkle it over the peaches.

Bake for 1 hour, or until golden. Serve with flavored whipped cream or ice cream.

SERVES 6

PINEAPPLE UPSIDE-DOWN CAKE

What could be more of a family favorite—especially for the kids—than this?

1 can (8 ounces) pineapple rings
2 tablespoons unsalted butter
1/2 cup (firmly packed) dark brown sugar
Maraschino cherries, cut into halves
1/3 cup vegetable shortening
3/4 cup granulated sugar
1 egg
1 3/4 cups all-purpose flour
2 1/2 teaspoons baking powder
1/4 teaspoon salt
1 1/2 teaspoons vanilla extract
Ice cream or whipped cream

Preheat oven to 350 degrees.

Drain pineapple, reserving the liquid. Melt butter in a deep 9-inch ovenproof skillet. Stir in brown sugar and 1 tablespoon of the reserved pineapple juice. Arrange pineapple rings in the pan, filling all centers with cherry halves. Set aside.

Beat shortening, granulated sugar, and egg together until well blended, about 3 to 4 minutes. Combine flour, baking powder, and salt. Measure remaining pineapple juice and add water if necessary to make 2/3 cup. Add the dry mixture and pineapple juice to the shortening mixture alternately and beat. Pour over pineapple rings and place in oven. Bake for 45 minutes, or until done in the middle (see Note). Cool for 5 minutes before running a knife around the edge and inverting cake onto a plate.

Serve with ice cream or whipped cream.

Note: This cake can be a bit deceptive, looking done on top while being uncooked in the middle, so test center with a wooden pick before removing cake from the oven.

SERVES 8

BLACKBERRY ROLL

When blackberries are plentiful, I freeze them in measured batches just large enough to make specific dishes.

2¼ cups unbleached all-purpose flour
¾ cup plus 2 tablespoons sugar
1½ teaspoons salt
½ pound (2 sticks) unsalted butter, cut into small bits
4½ tablespoons ice water
4 cups blackberries
2 tablespoons unsalted butter, melted
½ cup hot water

Preheat oven to 450 degrees.

Put flour, 2 tablespoons sugar, salt, and three fourths of the butter in a food processor. Process to a coarse texture. Add the ice water and continue to process until mixture is just beginning to form a ball. Remove it, make it into a ball, and place between two sheets of wax paper, pressing the ball flat before refrigerating it.

Combine 3 cups of the berries and the remaining ¾ cup sugar and set aside.

Roll out the dough on a floured surface to the thickness of a piecrust. Cut out a rectangle about 15 × 9 inches. Discard any leftover dough. Brush dough with melted butter and spoon on berries. Dot with the remaining bits of butter and roll up as you would a jelly roll. Place this, seam side down, in a greased baking dish. Cut several diagonal slits in the top of the roll. Sprinkle the top with additional sugar and then arrange the remaining cup of berries around the roll. Bake at 450 degrees for 10 minutes and then pour the hot water around the roll. Turn the heat down to 350 degrees and bake for another 40 to 45 minutes.

Serve slices with juice spooned on top.

SERVES 6

BLACKBERRY BUCKLE WITH BLACKBERRY SAUCE

This is a Southern variation on a New England favorite.

2 cups plus 2 tablespoons all-purpose flour
2 teaspoons baking powder
½ teaspoon salt
4 tablespoons (½ stick) unsalted butter, softened
¾ cup sugar
1 large egg
½ cup milk
1 pint fresh blackberries

TOPPING
4 tablespoons (½ stick) unsalted butter, softened
½ cup sugar
⅓ cup all-purpose flour
½ teaspoon ground cinnamon

BLACKBERRY SAUCE
1 cup fresh blackberries
6 tablespoons superfine sugar
1 tablespoon lemon juice
1 tablespoon crème de cassis or blackberry liqueur

Whipped cream flavored with blackberry brandy, crème de cassis, or rum

Preheat oven to 375 degrees. Grease an 8-inch round springform pan. Set aside.

Sift together 2 cups of the flour, baking powder, and salt. Set aside. Cream butter and sugar until fluffy, about 3 minutes. Beat in egg, then add the flour mixture in 3 parts, alternating with milk. Toss berries with the remaining 2 tablespoons of flour (to separate and scatter them evenly through the dough) and fold in. Pour batter into the prepared pan.

To make topping: Combine ingredients for the topping with a fork to make a crumbly mixture. Sprinkle this over the batter.

422

Bake for 1 hour. If a cake tester does not come out clean, bake for another 5 to 10 minutes. Let cake cool.

To make sauce: While cake is baking, sprinkle berries with sugar and refrigerate for about 1 hour. Purée in a food processor with lemon juice and crème de cassis.

Run a knife around edges of the cake and release sides of the pan. Serve with blackberry sauce and whipped cream.

SERVES 8

VARIATION

Substitute blueberries for blackberries in the cake and in the sauce.

TORTES

CALIFORNIA NUT TORTE

I've got to say this is about one of the best nut cakes I've ever had, and I'm a nut cake nut.

CRUST
  ½ cup medium-ground hazelnuts
  ½ cup medium-ground roasted almonds
  3½ tablespoons pastry flour
  2½ tablespoons sugar
  ⅓ cup unsalted butter, cut into bits

FILLING
  1 cup plus 2½ tablespoons (firmly packed) light brown sugar
  2 whole eggs plus 1 egg yolk
  ½ teaspoon baking powder
  1¾ cups coarsely chopped walnuts
  1 cup shredded, sweetened coconut
  ½ cup unbleached all-purpose flour
  Confectioners' sugar for dusting (optional)
  Crème Anglaise (page 366) or whipped cream

Preheat oven to 350 degrees.

To make crust: Mix hazelnuts, almonds, flour, sugar, and butter with a paddle in a mixer until just combined but slightly crumbly. Press into a 2-inch-deep 8-inch-round cake pan, going about one third up the side of the pan.

To make filling: Place brown sugar, egg and egg yolk, and baking powder in a mixer with a paddle and blend. Mix in walnuts, coconut, and flour and pour into prepared crust. Bake 50 minutes, until golden but soft and caramelly in the middle. Let cool and set in the pan for about 15 minutes before inverting onto the serving plate.

Dust with confectioners' sugar if desired and serve with Crème Anglaise or whipped cream.

SERVES 8 TO 10

ALMOND-PEAR TORTE

You can actually use any kind of nuts. Almonds and pears are a classic combination.

  2 to 3 pears, peeled, cored, and cut into ⅛-inch slices
  1 cup water mixed with 2 tablespoons fresh lemon juice
  1 cup sugar
  6 eggs, separated
  1 cup finely ground blanched almonds
  ½ cup lightly toasted fine white bread crumbs
  ½ teaspoon vanilla extract
  ½ cup apple jelly, melted
  Ice cream or whipped cream

Soak pear slices in the lemon water to keep them from turning brown.

Preheat oven to 350 degrees. Lightly grease the bottom of an 8-inch springform cake pan.

Sift sugar into a large bowl and cream with egg yolks until light in color, about 3 or 4 minutes. Stir in almonds, bread crumbs, and vanilla. Mix well. Beat egg whites until stiff, then fold lightly into the batter.

Pour batter into pan and bake for 40 minutes, or until cake tester comes out clean. Cool in pan before removing. Drain the pear slices thoroughly, then arrange on top of the torte. Glaze with melted jelly.

Serve with ice cream or whipped cream.

SERVES 10

ANGEL FOOD CAKES

ANGEL FOOD CAKE WITH LEMON SAUCE AND RASPBERRIES

Both the sauce and the cake may be made the day before.

1¹/₃ cups sugar, sifted 3 times
1 cup cake flour, sifted 5 times
11 egg whites, at room temperature
1 teaspoon salt
1¹/₂ teaspoons cream of tartar
1 teaspoon vanilla extract

LEMON SAUCE
1¹/₂ teaspoons cornstarch
³/₄ cup fresh lemon juice
6 tablespoons sugar, or more to taste

1 pint fresh raspberries, or more to taste

Preheat oven to 400 degrees. Line bottom of pan with a circle of parchment. Set aside.

Mix ¹/₃ cup of the sugar with the flour. Beat egg whites with a hand mixer at medium speed until foamy. Add salt and after about a minute turn mixer to high and add cream of tartar. Beat another few minutes and turn back to medium. Gradually add the remaining sugar, mixing all the while, until mixture makes stiff

glossy peaks. Stir in vanilla. Fold in flour–sugar mixture a fourth at a time. Stop when everything is well incorporated. Do not overmix.

Pour and scrape into pan and bake for 8 minutes. Turn heat down to 325 degrees and bake an additional 25 to 35 minutes, until a cake tester comes out clean and the top is light golden. Let cool slightly before removing from pan.

To make sauce: Mix cornstarch with lemon juice in a small saucepan and cook over low heat, stirring, until mixture thickens slightly, about 1 or 2 minutes. Stir in sugar and continue to cook, stirring, for another 2 to 3 minutes.

Serve topped with the warm lemon sauce and raspberries.

SERVES 12

CHOCOLATE ANGEL FOOD CAKE

The most important things about making this particular cake are being sure that the cocoa is well mixed in with the flour and letting the cake cool after baking. Otherwise, it is simplicity itself and will keep very well.

³/₄ cup sifted cake flour
4 tablespoons unsweetened cocoa powder
1¹/₄ cups egg whites, at room temperature
¹/₄ teaspoon salt
1 teaspoon cream of tartar
1¹/₄ cups sifted sugar
1 teaspoon vanilla extract or lemon juice
Irish Coffee Sauce (page 368)
1 cup heavy cream, whipped
Powdered espresso

Put a rack in the center of the oven and preheat oven to 375 degrees.

Tear off two squares of wax paper. Put flour and cocoa in a sifter and sift onto one of the squares. Repeat this process, going back and forth between squares, until flour and cocoa are well mixed—four or five times. Set aside.

Beat egg whites and salt together for a few seconds and then sprinkle on the cream of tartar. Continue beating until stiff. Fold in sugar, a little at a time, with an over-and-under motion, always in the same direction. Fold in vanilla. Fold in the flour–cocoa mixture, also a little at a time, but don't take too long to finish. Pour the batter into an ungreased 10-inch angel food cake pan or tube pan and bake for 30 minutes, until a cake tester inserted in the center comes out clean. Let cool completely before removing from pan.

To serve, put a slick of Irish Coffee Sauce on each dessert plate and on top of that a slice of cake (cut the cake with a bread knife). Finish it off by spooning whipped cream over the top and dusting on some of the powdered espresso.

SERVES 12

CHOCOLATE CAKES

FLOURLESS CHOCOLATE CAKE

Serve this in small wedges—it's intense! And complement it with a dab of whipped cream.

CAKE

5 ounces bittersweet or semisweet chocolate
3 ounces unsweetened chocolate
8 tablespoons (1 stick) unsalted butter,
*   softened*
5 large eggs, separated, at room
*   temperature*
²/₃ cup sugar
1¹/₂ teaspoons vanilla extract
Pinch of salt

CHOCOLATE GLAZE

3 ounces semisweet chocolate
3 tablespoons unsalted butter, softened
1 tablespoon brandy or bourbon (optional)

Preheat oven to 350 degrees. Butter and flour a 10-inch springform pan. Line the bottom with a round of parchment or wax paper, then butter the paper. Set aside.

To make cake: Melt chocolates and butter together in a saucepan set over low heat, stirring to blend well. Set aside to cool.

Beat egg yolks with sugar until thick and lemon yellow in color, about 5 minutes. Stir in vanilla.

Whisk the egg whites with salt until stiff. Set aside.

Gently fold the chocolate mixture into the yolks, then fold in one third of the egg whites. Fold in remaining whites until no streaks of white remain.

Pour batter into the prepared pan and bake in the center of the oven for 35 to 45 minutes, or until a cake tester inserted in the center comes out clean. The cake will rise a great deal during baking.

Cool cake in pan for 10 minutes, then remove sides of the pan. Invert the cake onto a rack and remove the bottom, but do not remove the parchment. Let cake cool completely; it will fall considerably. Remove parchment before glazing.

To make glaze: Melt chocolate and butter together in a saucepan over low heat, stirring until smooth. Stir in the brandy.

Place the cake on a rack set over a sheet of wax paper. Pour glaze over cake and spread lightly with a spatula if necessary to coat cake evenly, allowing extra glaze to run down sides.

SERVES 12

DEVIL'S FOOD CAKE WITH CHOCOLATE BUTTERCREAM ICING

Although a chocolate frosting is the classic for devil's food, some people prefer other frostings, such as vanilla or coffee, for a contrast in color and flavor. I generally like classics the way they are, especially this one.

1²/₃ cups sifted cake flour
¼ cup unsweetened cocoa powder
1 teaspoon baking soda
½ teaspoon salt
8 tablespoons (1 stick) unsalted butter, softened
1½ cups (firmly packed) dark brown sugar
1½ teaspoons vanilla extract
2 large eggs
2 ounces semisweet or bittersweet chocolate, melted and cooled
¾ cup strong hot coffee (not instant)

CHOCOLATE BUTTERCREAM ICING
½ pound (2 sticks) unsalted butter, softened
1 large egg yolk, at room temperature
6 ounces semisweet chocolate, melted and cooled
1 tablespoon powdered instant espresso
1 teaspoon vanilla extract
1¼ cups sifted confectioners' sugar

Preheat oven to 350 degrees. Grease and flour two 9-inch round cake pans.

Sift together flour, cocoa, baking soda, and salt. Set aside.

Cream butter and brown sugar until smooth, about 3 minutes, then stir in vanilla. Add eggs, one at a time, beating 2 minutes after each addition. Beat in the melted chocolate and gradually stir in hot coffee.

Add flour mixture, one third at a time, beating well after each addition. Pour batter into the prepared pans and bake for 25 minutes, or until a cake tester comes out clean.

Let the layers cool in the pan for 10 min-utes. Unmold onto cake racks and let cool completely.

To make icing: Cream butter until fluffy, about 3 minutes. Beat in egg yolk, then add melted chocolate and beat well. Add espresso and vanilla and beat for 3 minutes. Gradually add confectioners' sugar and beat, scraping bowl as necessary, until smooth and creamy.

When cake has cooled, ice between the layers, then ice top and sides of cake.

SERVES 12

CHOCOLATE LAYER CAKE

You can't have too many chocolate cake recipes.

2¼ cups cake flour
¾ teaspoon baking powder
¾ teaspoon baking soda
1½ cups milk
7 ounces semisweet chocolate, chopped fine
6 ounces unsalted butter, softened
2 cups sugar
4 eggs
1 teaspoon vanilla extract

CHOCOLATE FROSTING
3 cups heavy cream
2 tablespoons unsalted butter
1 pound semisweet chocolate, chopped fine

Preheat oven to 350 degrees.

Butter two 8-inch cake pans. Line bottoms with parchment and butter the parchment. Flour insides of both pans baking and shake out any excess.

Sift together flour, baking powder, and soda. Set aside. Bring milk to a slow boil over medium heat in a medium saucepan. Add chocolate and stir until melted. Set aside.

Cream butter and sugar together until light and fluffy. Beat in eggs, one at a time, then vanilla. Add flour mixture and chocolate mix-ture alternately, mixing well after each addition. Pour into prepared pans and bake until tester comes out clean, about 35 minutes. Cool in pans and turn out.

To make frosting: Combine cream and butter in a saucepan and bring to a boil over medium heat, stirring, until butter is melted and mixture is smooth. Remove from heat and stir in chocolate until chocolate is melted. Refrigerate to cool. Chill a mixing bowl and pour mixture in. Whip with a hand mixer until frosting forms soft peaks. Do not overmix.

Slice off rounded top of each cake layer. Slice each layer in two to make 4 thin layers. Put layers together with the frosting, holding them in place with toothpicks as you assemble the cake. Frost outsides and refrigerate until ready to serve. Cut with a warm knife.

SERVES 12

FLOURLESS CHOCOLATE AND WALNUT CAKE

1 pound semisweet chocolate, broken into squares
8 tablespoons (1 stick) unsalted butter, cut into pieces, at room temperature
2 tablespoons sugar
4 tablespoons finely ground walnuts
4 large eggs, separated, at room temperature
1/8 teaspoon salt

Preheat oven to 425 degrees. Line the bottom of an 8-inch springform pan with wax or parchment paper cut to fit. Coat lightly with nonstick cooking spray but do not flour.

Melt chocolate in a double boiler over hot (but not simmering) water, stirring occasionally. When chocolate appear to be almost liquid, remove pan from double boiler, add butter, and mix well.

Using a wooden spoon, blend in sugar, walnuts, and lightly beaten egg yolks.

Beat egg whites with salt in another bowl until stiff peaks form. Fold about one third of

egg whites into chocolate mixture until blended. Add remaining egg whites but do not overmix.

Pour into prepared pan and bake in center of oven for exactly 15 minutes. Transfer to a cooling rack. When cake is room temperature, remove springform mold and invert cake onto a serving plate. Peel off paper liner. Refrigerate for at least 4 hours.

This very dense, rich cake can be served thinly sliced alone or with whipped cream or ice cream.

SERVES 8

POUND CAKES

SOUR CREAM POUND CAKE

If moist and flavorful is what you want, this pound cake is the ticket—and it is simple to make. Also remember that pound cakes freeze extremely well and actually improve with age.

1 3/4 cups sifted unbleached all-purpose flour
1/4 teaspoon baking soda
8 tablespoons (1 stick) unsalted butter, softened
1 1/2 cups sugar
3 large eggs, separated, at room temperature
2/3 cup sour cream
1 teaspoon vanilla extract

Preheat oven to 325 degrees. Butter and flour a 9 × 5-inch loaf pan. Set aside.

Sift together flour and baking soda. Set aside.

Cream butter and sugar until fluffy, about 3 minutes. Add egg yolks and beat well.

Add one third of the flour mixture and beat to incorporate, then add sour cream and beat again. Repeat until flour mixture and sour cream are mixed in. Stir in vanilla.

Beat egg whites until very stiff, then fold into the batter with an over-and-under motion. Pour into the prepared pan.

Bake on the center rack of the oven for about 1 hour 20 minutes, or until golden on top and a cake tester comes out clean.

Let cake cool in the pan on a rack. It can be stored in an airtight container or frozen indefinitely.

SERVES 12

SOUR CREAM POUND CAKE WITH POACHED FRUIT

3 cups water
1½ cups sugar
3 peaches, cut in half and pitted
6 apricots, cut in half and pitted
4 plums, cut in half and pitted
2 pears, cut in half, peeled, and cored
14 kumquats, cut in half, or chopped zest of two oranges
1 recipe Sour Cream Pound Cake (page 427)

In a small stockpot, combine water and sugar. Bring to a boil, stirring until sugar is dissolved. Add prepared fruit and return to boil. Reduce heat and simmer until fruit is tender, about 6 to 10 minutes, depending on ripeness.

Remove from heat and transfer fruit with the poaching liquid to a deep container. Let cool to room temperature. Cover and refrigerate. (This may be done a day ahead.)

Slice pound cake and serve topped with poached fruits and their syrup.

SERVES 12

LAYERED BOURBON ICEBOX CAKE

Here is a Southern trifle.

6 egg yolks
⅔ cup sugar
¾ cup bourbon
½ teaspoon freshly grated nutmeg
½ teaspoon ground cinnamon
⅛ teaspoon ground allspice
1 plain loaf pound cake, in ½-inch slices

Whip together yolks and sugar in the top of a double boiler. Stir in bourbon and spices. Cook over lightly boiling water, stirring constantly, for 5 minutes until thick and custard-like. Press a sheet of wax paper onto the top and let cool.

When custard is cool, assemble cake by layering cake slices and custard in a glass bowl, ending with the custard. Cover and refrigerate for half a day before serving.

This will keep very well for several days.

SERVES 12

CAYENNE POUND CAKE

Here is an interesting twist on an old *Joy of Cooking* recipe.

½ pound (2 sticks) unsalted butter, softened
1 cup sugar
5 eggs, at room temperature
1 teaspoon vanilla extract
2 cups all-purpose flour
Pinch of cayenne
½ teaspoon cream of tartar
½ teaspoon salt

Preheat oven to 325 degrees and grease a 9 × 5-inch loaf pan. Set aside.

Cream butter and sugar until light and fluffy. Add eggs, one at a time, mixing well after each. Stir in vanilla. Sift flour and measure, then sift again with the other dry ingredients. Gradually add to the butter–sugar mixture, stirring. When well mixed, pour into the pan and bake for 1 hour, or until a cake tester comes out clean.

SERVES 12

PUDDING CAKES

FIG PUDDING CAKE

Many Texans make fig preserves. The delicious little morsels are used in this cake. If you are not lucky enough to have homemade, use store-bought preserves. Since the cake should be stale when you assemble this dessert, make it the day before and leave it out, uncovered, to dry overnight.

CAKE
2 large eggs, separated
2 tablespoons warm coffee
1 teaspoon vanilla extract
1 teaspoon fresh lemon juice
1/2 cup sugar
Pinch of salt
1/2 cup sifted self-rising cake flour

ASSEMBLY
3 large eggs
3 cups milk
1/2 cup plus 1 tablespoon sugar
1 teaspoon vanilla extract
Freshly ground nutmeg, to taste
1 cup fig preserves including syrup,
    chopped and mashed lightly together
2 tablespoons unsalted butter, softened

To make cake: Cut a piece of wax paper to fit the bottom of a deep 8-inch soufflé dish and place it in the bottom of the dish. Do not grease the dish. Preheat oven to 325 degrees.

Combine egg yolks, coffee, vanilla, and lemon juice. Beat with an electric hand mixer at high speed until thickened, about 2 minutes. Add sugar and beat another 30 seconds or so to combine well. Set aside. Beat egg whites until foamy, add salt, and beat until whites form stiff peaks. Fold the whites into the yolk mixture. Sift flour, a little at a time, over the egg mixture, folding in after each addition. Pour into the prepared pan and bake until a tester comes out clean, about 25 minutes.

Let rest in the pan for about 30 minutes before loosening the edges and removing from the dish. Let cool completely. Peel off the wax paper and slice the layer in half, crosswise. Leave it uncovered to dry out overnight.

To assemble dessert: Put a kettle of water on to boil and preheat oven to 300 degrees.

Put eggs in a small pitcher and whisk lightly. Whisk in milk, 1/2 cup of the sugar, vanilla, and nutmeg. Set aside.

Butter an 8-inch soufflé dish and place the bottom layer of the cake in it. Spread this with the fig preserves. Add the top layer of the cake and spread it with the softened butter. Put the dish in a larger ovenproof pan. Pour the custard through a strainer over the top of the cake, lightly beating it as you pour. Sprinkle with the remaining tablespoon of sugar. Surround the dish with boiling water and bake until set, about 1 hour and 15 minutes. Remove from water bath and let cool. Refrigerate, covered. You may serve this from the soufflé dish or turn it out onto a serving plate by loosening the edges and inverting it over the plate and holding the plate in place while giving it a firm downward shake.

SERVES 8

BANANA PUDDING CAKE

2 tablespoons unsalted butter, softened
1/2 cup plus 2 tablespoons sugar
1/8 teaspoon salt
3 large eggs, separated, plus 1 large egg
  white, at room temperature
3 tablespoons unbleached all-purpose flour
1 ripe banana, mashed
1/4 cup fresh lemon juice
1 cup milk

Preheat oven to 325 degrees. Butter a 2-quart soufflé dish. Fold a dish towel and place it in the bottom of a large, deep baking pan and set prepared soufflé dish on top. Bring several quarts of water to a boil, reserving for water bath.

Crumble butter, sugar, and salt together in a medium mixing bowl, using the back of a wooden spoon. Beat in egg yolks, then flour, mixing until smooth. Slowly add mashed banana and lemon juice to combine. Stir in milk.

Beat egg whites to stiff, moist peaks. Gently fold whites into batter until smooth. Do not overmix. It may still look a little streaky.

Immediately ladle (don't pour) batter into soufflé dish. Set baking pan on oven rack and pour enough boiling water into baking pan to come halfway up side of the soufflé dish. Bake until center of pudding cake is set and springs back when gently touched, about 25 minutes.

Remove baking pan from oven and let soufflé dish continue to stand in water bath for 10 minutes. Pudding cakes can be served warm, at room temperature, or chilled.
SERVES 6

LEMON PUDDING CAKE

You can serve this dessert either warm or chilled, and I can't really say which I like best. There is, however, an advantage to serving the cake chilled: You can make it a day in advance. Be sure to allow the cake to cool completely on a rack before you refrigerate it.

4 tablespoons (1/2 stick) unsalted butter,
  softened
1 1/2 cups sugar
4 eggs, separated
3 tablespoons all-purpose flour
1 3/4 cups milk
1/2 cup fresh lemon juice
1 1/2 tablespoons grated lemon zest

Preheat oven to 350 degrees. Generously butter a 2-quart soufflé dish.

Cream together butter and sugar until light and fluffy. Add egg yolks, one at a time, beating well after each addition. Stir in flour, combining well. Pour in one third of the milk and stir until smooth, then stir in the remaining milk. Stir in lemon juice and zest.

In a very clean, deep bowl, beat egg whites until stiff peaks form. Fold the beaten whites into the batter. Pour into the prepared soufflé dish. Place the soufflé dish in a larger baking pan and pour boiling water into the large pan to reach about 1 inch up the side of the soufflé dish. Bake until golden and puffy, about 1 hour. Cool on a rack.

If you are going to chill the cake, keep it on the rack, covered with a tea towel, for at least 1 hour, or until at room temperature. Cover tightly with plastic wrap and refrigerate for several hours or overnight. Serve from the dish.

VARIATION
Substitute lime juice and zest for the lemon.
SERVES 6

PEAR PUDDING CAKE

So easy!

1 cup sugar
6 tablespoons all-purpose flour
1½ teaspoons baking powder
Pinch of salt
2 eggs, lightly beaten
1 tablespoon bourbon
1 tablespoon grated lemon zest
1 cup coarsely chopped walnuts
1 cup peeled and coarsely diced firm pear
Vanilla Sauce (page 366) or vanilla
  ice cream
Pear slices
Lemon juice
Lemon zest, grated or cut in strips

Preheat oven to 350 degrees. Generously butter an 8-inch square baking dish.

Sift together sugar, flour, baking powder, and salt. Add eggs and beat for several minutes, until thoroughly mixed. Stir in bourbon and lemon zest, mixing well again. Fold in nuts and pear. Pour into baking dish and bake until puffy and brown, about 30 to 35 minutes.

Serve with Vanilla Sauce or vanilla ice cream, garnished with a few slices of fresh pear bathed in fresh lemon juice and topped with a bit of lemon zest if you like.

SERVES 6

CHOCOLATE TOFFEE NUT PUDDING CAKE

This version of the old classic pudding cake came from my friend Laurie Wolf. You can serve this cake with Chocolate Whipped Cream (page 365), with vanilla ice cream, or plain. And it's equally good hot and at room temperature.

1 cup all-purpose flour
¾ cup granulated sugar
7 tablespoons unsweetened cocoa powder
2 teaspoons baking powder
¼ teaspoon salt
½ teaspoon instant espresso powder
1 teaspoon vanilla extract
½ cup milk
2 tablespoons canola oil
1 cup crushed Heath bars
1 cup chopped walnuts, plus additional for
  garnish
1 cup (firmly packed) light brown sugar
1¾ cups boiling water

Preheat oven to 350 degrees and place a rack in the center of the oven. Generously butter a 1½-quart soufflé dish or a 9 × 9-inch pan.

Combine flour, granulated sugar, 3 tablespoons of the cocoa, baking powder, salt, and espresso powder in a large bowl. Stir to mix well. Stir vanilla into milk. Add milk and oil to the dry ingredients and mix well. Stir in Heath bars and nuts. The batter will be very stiff. Scrape it into the prepared dish with a rubber spatula.

Combine brown sugar and remaining 4 tablespoons cocoa in a small bowl. Sprinkle this mixture over the top of the batter. Gently pour the boiling water over the batter—do not stir—and place in the preheated oven.

Bake 35 minutes, until the top looks crispy and cracked and a tester comes out clean when inserted into the "cake" part. Let rest a few minutes before serving with chocolate or plain whipped cream and chopped walnuts.

SERVES 12

CHEESECAKES

CHOCOLATE MOUSSE CHEESECAKE

Lynn Grossman, who gave me this recipe, is my kind of cook: She never leaves a recipe alone. For instance, sometimes her chocolate cheesecake has chocolate chips in it, and once she even put in broken pieces of chocolate Oreo cookies. Then sometimes the crust is made with chocolate cookie crumbs instead of graham cracker crumbs, or a mixture of chocolate and graham cracker.

> *³/₄ cup graham cracker crumbs*
> *4 tablespoons (¹/₂ stick) unsalted butter, softened*
> *2 tablespoons sugar*

FILLING
> *24 ounces cream cheese, softened*
> *2 large eggs*
> *1 cup sugar*
> *8 ounces semisweet chocolate, melted*
> *2 tablespoons heavy cream*
> *7 tablespoons very strong coffee or espresso*
> *³/₄ cup sour cream*
> *1 teaspoon dark rum*

Preheat oven to 350 degrees.

Put cracker crumbs, butter, and sugar in a food processor and give it a few whirls to mix. Press into the bottom of an 8-inch springform mold. Set aside.

To make filling: Put cream cheese, eggs, and sugar into the processor bowl and mix until smooth. Add remaining ingredients and blend thoroughly. Pour batter on top of the crust.

Bake for 45 minutes without opening the oven door (make sure your oven temperature is accurate). Cake will be slightly soft in the middle, but will firm up as it cools. At the end of the baking time, turn off heat and prop oven door open slightly with a pot holder or knife. Let cake cool in the oven for 1 hour before removing. Refrigerate.

Remove cake from the refrigerator at least 15 minutes before serving.
SERVES 10

SAVORY CHEESECAKE

This would make a perfect first course, with or without salad.

> *³/₄ cup toasted bread crumbs*
> *³/₄ cup finely chopped toasted walnuts*
> *3 tablespoons unsalted butter, melted*
> *³/₄ pound aged asiago or aged tomme, grated*
> *1¹/₄ pounds cream cheese, at room temperature*
> *4 eggs*
> *1 medium garlic clove, crushed or minced*
> *¹/₄ teaspoon dried tarragon, or 1 tablespoon minced fresh tarragon*
> *Salt and freshly ground black pepper, to taste*

Preheat oven to 350 degrees.

Place bread crumbs, walnuts, and butter in a food processor and process until thoroughly combined. Press into the bottom and slightly up the sides of an 8-inch springform pan. Set aside.

Beat asiago and cream cheese with a hand mixer until smooth. Add eggs, one at a time, beating well after each addition. Add garlic and tarragon and combine well. Add salt and pepper. Pour into the prepared pan and bake for 40 minutes to 1 hour, checking after 45 minutes. Cake should be golden and puffed, not loose in the center. Remove from oven and let stand for 30 minutes before cutting.
SERVES 8

432

SHORTCAKES

STRAWBERRY SHORTCAKE

This recipe calls for a warm, buttered, slightly sweet biscuit instead of the usual sponge cake. The fact that it must be served warm—as well as its generous size—disqualifies it as a dessert to serve at the end of a meal. Instead, have it as a treat.

  4 cups hulled and sliced strawberries
  1 tablespoon sugar, or to taste
  2 cups whipping cream
  1/2 teaspoon vanilla extract
  2 cups all-purpose flour
  2 1/2 teaspoons baking powder
  1 teaspoon salt
  6 tablespoons (3/4 stick) cold unsalted butter,
      cut into 12 pieces
  1 cup milk
  Whole strawberries
  Additional unsalted butter for biscuits

Place hulled and sliced berries in a bowl and mash about a quarter of them. Add sugar. Refrigerate.

Whip cream and add vanilla (also sugar if you like; I don't). Refrigerate.

When ready to serve, preheat oven to 450 degrees. Mix dry ingredients and then cut in butter with a pastry blender or 2 knives. When the mixture resembles coarse cornmeal, add 3/4 cup milk all at once and mix well, and quickly. Turn out onto a floured board and knead briefly.

Roll out dough to 1/2 inch thickness, cut into about eight 3-inch rounds, place on an ungreased baking sheet, and brush the tops with milk. You may also sprinkle them with sugar. Bake 12 to 15 minutes, or until golden.

Assemble dessert by splitting the still-hot biscuits and putting them on individual plates.

Spread both halves lightly with butter. When this has melted, add berries and a topping of whipped cream to the bottom half. Cover with the other half. Add more whipped cream and berries. Garnish with a whole berry or two.
SERVES 8

MIXED BERRY SHORTCAKE

Use any combination of berries you like for this.

  2 cups all-purpose flour
  2 tablespoons sugar, plus additional for
      berries
  1/4 teaspoon salt
  4 teaspoons baking powder
  2 eggs, lightly beaten
  4 tablespoons (1/2 stick) cold unsalted butter,
      cut into small pieces
  2 cups heavy cream
  2 pints mixed berries

Preheat oven to 400 degrees.

Mix dry ingredients together in a large bowl. Mix in eggs. Cut butter in with a pastry blender or 2 knives. Mix in enough cream to make a dry dough. Roll out 1/2 inch thick on a floured surface and cut into 8 biscuits. Place on an ungreased baking sheet and bake until golden, about 12 minutes.

Whip the remaining cream and refrigerate; sweeten the berries to taste and refrigerate.

To serve, split the biscuits. Place the bottom half on a dessert plate and cover with berries and some of their juice. Replace top and add more berries and a dollop of whipped cream.
SERVES 8

433

PEACH AND BERRY SHORTCAKE WITH WARM CREAM SAUCE

1 cup all-purpose flour
1½ teaspoons baking powder
¼ teaspoon salt
¼ cup sugar
⅛ teaspoon freshly grated nutmeg
4 tablespoons (½ stick) unsalted butter, softened
¼ cup milk
1 small egg

WARM CREAM SAUCE
4 tablespoons (½ stick) unsalted butter
¼ cup sugar
2 cups heavy cream

3 large peaches, peeled, pitted, and sliced
2 baskets of mixed berries

Preheat oven to 400 degrees.

Measure flour, baking powder, salt, sugar, and nutmeg into a mixing bowl. Cut in butter with a pastry blender or 2 knives until very fine, like cornmeal. Measure milk in a large measuring cup, then drop in egg and mix with a fork. Make a well in the dry ingredients and pour in milk–egg mixture all at once. Mix with a fork just long enough for all ingredients to gather together. Drop in 6 portions by large forkfuls onto a greased baking sheet. Bake for 15 minutes or until nicely browned.

To make cream sauce: Combine ingredients in a heavy-bottomed saucepan large enough to have room for the cream to boil up. Simmer over low heat until cream boils. Whisk down and let boil up at least once more, then let simmer very gently for a few minutes. This can be done several hours ahead. It takes about 15 to 20 minutes to cook. For thicker cream, simmer it longer. Should it get too thick, thin out with a little extra cream.

Reheat the shortcakes, uncovered, until warm and crisp on top. Split the biscuits and place bottoms on individual serving plates. Top with sliced peaches. Replace tops, then spoon berries over each and spoon warm cream sauce over all.

SERVES 6

BLUEBERRY SHORTCAKE

I love the old-fashioned shortcake biscuits called for here—so will you.

2 cups sifted all-purpose flour
2½ teaspoons baking powder
¼ teaspoon salt
1 tablespoon sugar
8 tablespoons (1 stick) cold butter, cut into bits
½ cup light cream or half-and-half
1½ pints fresh blueberries
Sugar, to taste
Additional unsalted butter for biscuits
Vanilla-flavored whipped cream

Preheat oven to 450 degrees.

Sift flour, baking powder, salt, and sugar into a large bowl. Cut butter in with a pastry blender or 2 knives. Pour cream in all at once, and stir quickly until dough leaves sides of bowl.

Turn out onto a floured surface and dust top lightly with additional flour. Roll out the dough with a floured pin to a 1-inch thickness. Cut into 8 large biscuits and bake on an ungreased baking sheet until golden, about 8 to 10 minutes.

While the biscuits are baking, mash a few berries in a bowl and add sugar. Toss with other whole berries.

When biscuits are done, split and butter each half. Arrange biscuit bottoms on individual plates. Pile berries on each and place a dab of whipped cream on the berries. Add the biscuit tops and more berries and cream if you like.

SERVES 8

DROP COOKIES

CITRUS LACE COOKIES

The juice in these cookies gives them an unusual flavor, which is especially good when you serve the cookies with sorbets and ice creams.

1½ cups sugar
1 cup slivered almonds
¾ cup all-purpose flour
½ cup citrus juice (grapefruit, orange, or lemon)
8 tablespoons (1 stick) unsalted butter, melted

Preheat oven to 400 degrees.

Combine sugar, almonds, and flour in a bowl. Add juice and melted butter and stir well. If you have time, leave this in the refrigerator for several hours before using; it makes the dough easier to handle.

Drop the mixture by rounded teaspoonfuls onto nonstick baking sheets, spreading the mounds into flat 2-inch circles with the back of a spoon that has been dipped into hot water. These cookies double in width, so leave enough space between them on the pan. Bake for about 5 minutes, or until golden brown. Watch them carefully since they burn easily.

Remove sheets from oven and let cookies rest for about a minute to firm slightly. Remove the cookies with a spatula and drape them over a rolling pin or wine bottles to shape them. Cool and store in a cool dry spot or sealed in a cookie tin.

MAKES ABOUT 3 DOZEN COOKIES

VERMONT GINGER AND SPICE COOKIES

These are semisoft cookies. The recipe comes from someone who wrote to me from Vermont years ago. Sad to say, I no longer know who it was. These cookies could be made larger. Just give them room to spread.

4 cups sifted all-purpose flour
¾ teaspoon baking soda
¾ teaspoon ground ginger
1½ teaspoons ground cinnamon
1½ teaspoons ground cloves
½ teaspoon salt
½ pound (2 sticks) unsalted butter, softened
2¼ cups sugar
½ cup unsulfured molasses
2 medium eggs
1 teaspoon vanilla extract

Preheat oven to 350 degrees.

Sift together flour, baking soda, ginger, cinnamon, cloves, and salt. Set aside.

Cream butter with the sugar until fluffy, about 3 minutes. Stir in molasses and mix in eggs, one at a time, stirring thoroughly after each addition. Stir in vanilla.

Add the dry mixture in 3 parts, mixing thoroughly after each addition.

Pour out the remaining sugar on a piece of wax paper. Using 2 tablespoons, drop walnut-size lumps of dough onto the sugar and roll around to coat. Place on an ungreased baking sheet 2 inches apart. Bake for about 14 minutes or until light golden. Remove to a cooling rack. Continue until dough is used up.

MAKES ABOUT 5 DOZEN COOKIES

435

LEMON CRISPS

1 cup blanched almonds
Zest of 1 lemon, cut into strips
*8 tablespoons (1 stick) unsalted butter, at
    room temperature*
¹/₂ cup sugar
1 egg
1 tablespoon fresh lemon juice
1 teaspoon vanilla extract
¹/₂ cup sifted all-purpose flour

Preheat oven to 325 degrees. Lightly grease 2 baking sheets.

Put almonds on a baking sheet and bake them, stirring occasionally, until golden brown, about 10 minutes. Let cool.

Raise oven heat to 375 degrees.

Put almonds and lemon zest in the bowl of a food processor. Pulse until finely chopped.

Put butter and sugar in a large bowl and beat with an electric mixer on medium speed until light and fluffy, about 3 minutes. Beat in egg, lemon juice, and vanilla. Add the almond–zest mixture and mix well. Add flour and stir just to combine.

Drop the dough by scant teaspoonfuls onto the baking sheets and bake for about 12 minutes, until the edges brown. Let cool slightly before transferring the cookies to a wire rack.

MAKES ABOUT 4 DOZEN COOKIES

ROCKS

This recipe came from a Texas woman named Susie Jastro and was part of a booklet put together by her family to celebrate the eighty-first birthday of their cook, Anna Glover. I've cut the original recipe in half; otherwise, these are just as she made them.

2³/₄ cups sifted all-purpose flour
1 teaspoon baking soda
¹/₂ teaspoon ground cinnamon
¹/₂ teaspoon freshly ground nutmeg
¹/₂ teaspoon grated orange zest
*8 tablespoons (1 stick) unsalted butter,
    softened*
1¹/₂ cups (firmly packed) dark brown sugar
2 tablespoons milk
2 large eggs, lightly beaten
1 cup raisins
1 cup currants
4 ounces pitted dates, coarsely chopped
³/₄ cup coarsely chopped walnuts

Preheat oven to 300 degrees.

Set aside ¼ cup of the flour. Sift the balance with baking soda, cinnamon, and nutmeg. Sprinkle zest over the top and set aside.

Cream butter and sugar until smooth, about 2 minutes. Add milk and eggs, mixing well. Stir in the flour mixture in 4 parts, mixing thoroughly after each addition. Set aside.

Mix raisins, currants, dates, and nuts and toss well with the reserved flour. Fold these (along with any extra flour) into the batter. Drop in rounded tablespoonfuls onto ungreased baking sheets.

Bake for 23 to 25 minutes, or until very slightly browned. Remove with a spatula to a cooling rack.

MAKES ABOUT 4 DOZEN COOKIES

CHOCOLATE CHUNK COOKIES

Chunk is the operative word here, because this recipe calls for coarsely chopped extra-bittersweet chocolate bars. The cookies are similar to the usual chocolate-chip ones, but the larger pieces of chocolate make all the difference.

2 cups sifted all-purpose flour
1 teaspoon baking soda
1/2 teaspoon salt
10 tablespoons (1 1/4 sticks) unsalted butter, softened
1/2 cup (firmly packed) light brown sugar
1/2 cup (firmly packed) dark brown sugar
1/4 cup granulated sugar
1 large egg
1 1/2 teaspoon vanilla extract
3/4 cup coarsely chopped walnuts
9 ounces extra-bittersweet chocolate (such as 3 Lindt "Traditional" bars), coarsely chopped

Preheat oven to 375 degrees.

Combine flour, baking soda, and salt. Set aside.

Cream butter and sugars until smooth, about 4 minutes. Add egg and mix well. Add flour mixture and beat thoroughly. Stir in vanilla, then fold in nuts and then chocolate.

Drop in 2-tablespoon clumps onto an ungreased baking sheet, leaving several inches between for expansion.

Bake for 10 to 12 minutes, or until the bottoms are lightly browned. Repeat with remaining batter until used up.

MAKES ABOUT 30 COOKIES

COFFEE-CHOCOLATE-MACADAMIA SPREADS

I'm really partial to the taste of macadamia nuts. Here they are part of a big, soft, and chewy cookie.

1 1/2 cups sifted whole wheat pastry flour
1/2 teaspoon baking soda
1/4 teaspoon salt
10 tablespoons (1 1/4 sticks) unsalted butter, softened
1 1/3 cups (firmly packed) dark brown sugar
2 large eggs
1 teaspoon vanilla extract
1 tablespoon powdered instant espresso
3 ounces semisweet or bittersweet chocolate, melted and cooled to room temperature
3/4 cup macadamia nuts, halved

Preheat oven to 350 degrees. Lightly grease 2 baking sheets. Set aside.

Combine whole wheat flour, baking soda, and salt. Set aside.

Cream butter and brown sugar until smooth, about 4 minutes. Add eggs, one at a time, beating well after each addition. Beat in vanilla and powdered espresso.

Add the flour mixture, a third at a time, beating well after each addition until thoroughly mixed. Blend in chocolate and fold in nuts.

Drop in 2-tablespoon clumps onto the prepared sheets, leaving plenty of room for them to spread out. (That's why they are called "spreads.")

Bake for about 12 minutes, or just until soft and lightly crisped around the edges. Remove to a cooling rack. They will harden a bit as they cool.

MAKES ABOUT 2 DOZEN COOKIES

MILK CHOCOLATE MACAROONS

Everyone knows macaroons, but when made with milk chocolate they become something else altogether. If milk chocolate is not your taste, change it to bittersweet.

> *3 large egg whites, at room temperature*
> *Pinch of salt*
> *²⁄₃ cup superfine sugar*
> *1 teaspoon vanilla extract*
> *6 ounces milk chocolate, melted and cooled to room temperature*
> *2 cans (3¹⁄₂ ounces each) sweetened grated coconut (about 2¹⁄₃ cups)*

Preheat oven to 325 degrees. Line 2 baking sheets with foil, then lightly grease the foil and set aside.

Whisk egg whites with salt until they form soft peaks. Gradually add sugar, a little at a time, whisking at high speed all the while, until very stiff but not dry. Quickly fold in vanilla and chocolate, then fold in coconut.

Drop in 1¹⁄₂-inch clumps on the prepared sheets, leaving an inch or so between for spreading.

Bake for 20 to 22 minutes, or until set, but with peaks only lightly browned. Remove from foil and let cool on a rack. Store in an airtight jar.

MAKES ABOUT 30 COOKIES

HAZELNUT MERINGUE COOKIES

Jean Thackery gave me the recipe for these cookies. They literally melt in your mouth. This is a great way of using up extra egg whites.

> *3 egg whites*
> *¹⁄₂ teaspoon cream of tartar*
> *¹⁄₈ teaspoon salt*
> *³⁄₄ cup sugar*
> *2 cups coarsely ground hazelnuts*

Preheat oven to 200 degrees. Lightly butter and flour (barely) a sheet of baking parchment. Place on a baking sheet.

Beat egg whites until foamy, add cream of tartar and salt, and beat until stiff peaks form. Gradually stir in sugar. Fold in nuts.

Drop batter by tablespoonfuls onto the prepared paper. These do not rise or spread, so they may be placed fairly close together but not touching.

Bake for 1 hour and 15 minutes. Turn off oven and let meringues cool in the oven. Peel off paper and store in an airtight container.

MAKES ABOUT 3 DOZEN COOKIES

VARIATION

Substitute pecans or walnuts for the hazelnuts

OATMEAL-RAISIN COOKIES

Pamela Krausmann, who has got to be one of the most knowledgeable food people around, created this recipe, which makes the best oatmeal-raisin cookies I've had.

> *1¹⁄₂ cups sifted all-purpose flour*
> *1 teaspoon baking soda*
> *1 teaspoon ground cinnamon*
> *¹⁄₂ pound (2 sticks) unsalted butter, softened*
> *¹⁄₂ cup (firmly packed) dark brown sugar*
> *1 cup granulated sugar*
> *1 large egg, well beaten*
> *1 teaspoon vanilla extract*
> *1¹⁄₂ cups old-fashioned rolled oats*
> *1 cup raisins*

Sift together flour, baking soda, and cinnamon. Set aside.

Cream butter and sugars until fluffy, about 3 minutes. Mix beaten egg in thoroughly, then stir in vanilla. Add the dry mixture. Mix in oatmeal and then raisins. Give it a final mixing. Refrigerate, covered, for 1 hour.

438

Preheat oven to 350 degrees. Grease a baking sheet.

Place walnut-size pieces of dough on the prepared sheet, allowing space for cookies to spread.

Bake for 10 minutes, or until set. Repeat for remaining dough until used up.

MAKES ABOUT 5 DOZEN COOKIES

DROPPED BROWNIE COOKIES

The little bit of pepper here adds zip. I'm sure you can imagine how good these would be with a glass of cold milk or ice cream.

4 ounces semisweet chocolate
1 ounce unsweetened chocolate
8 tablespoons (1 stick) unsalted butter
1 cup sugar
1 teaspoon vanilla extract
1/2 teaspoon salt
1/2 teaspoon freshly ground black pepper
2 eggs, lightly beaten
1 1/2 cups all-purpose flour
1 teaspoon baking powder
1 3/4 cups chopped toasted walnuts

Preheat oven to 350 degrees.

Combine semisweet and unsweetened chocolates with butter in a small saucepan and melt over medium-low heat. Remove from the heat and transfer to a mixing bowl. Add sugar, vanilla, salt, and pepper. Mix well and let cool slightly. Stir in eggs. Combine flour and baking powder and stir into the mixture. Then stir in nuts.

Drop by rounded teaspoonfuls onto an ungreased baking sheet.

Bake for 12 minutes. Let cool for a few minutes before removing to a rack to cool completely.

MAKES ABOUT 30 COOKIES

COCONUT–WALNUT JUMBLES

Coconut jumbles are a longtime favorite and for good reason—they're simple to make and always a hit with the kids.

10 tablespoons (1 1/4 sticks) unsalted butter, softened
3/4 cup sugar
1 large egg
1 can (3 1/2 ounces) sweetened grated coconut
1 cup sifted all-purpose flour
1/2 teaspoon vanilla extract
1 cup coarsely chopped walnuts

Preheat oven to 425 degrees. Lightly grease a baking sheet.

Cream butter and sugar until fluffy, about 3 minutes. Then beat in egg. Mix coconut and flour in together. This will make a fairly thick batter, but it is easy to mix. Stir in vanilla and then fold in nuts. Drop by rounded teaspoonfuls onto the baking sheet, leaving enough space between cookies for them to expand.

Bake for about 10 minutes, or until cookies turn golden on top. Be careful not to burn bottoms. Remove to a cooling rack. Repeat with remaining batter until used up.

MAKES ABOUT 3 DOZEN COOKIES

VARIATION

Omit the walnuts if you prefer plain jumbles.

439

BLOWOUTS

I guess these are called "blowouts" because they will blow your taste buds away. They certainly have enough good things in them.

2 cups sifted all-purpose flour
1 teaspoon baking soda
¼ teaspoon salt
½ cup chunky-style peanut butter, at room temperature
8 tablespoons (1 stick) unsalted butter, at room temperature
½ cup (firmly packed) light brown sugar
¼ cup granulated sugar
1 large egg
1 teaspoon vanilla extract
¼ cup milk
¾ cup semisweet chocolate chips
¾ cup honey-roasted peanuts
¾ cup coarsely chopped frozen miniature peanut butter cups (about 12)

Preheat oven to 350 degrees.

Combine flour, baking soda, and salt. Set aside.

Beat peanut butter and butter together until fluffy. Add sugars and beat until light and smooth. Then add egg and beat about 3 minutes. Add vanilla and mix well. Stir in flour mixture and beat thoroughly. Sprinkle milk over the mixture and beat to soften the dough. Fold in chocolate chips and peanuts, then carefully add chopped peanut butter cups.

Drop in 2-tablespoon clumps onto an ungreased baking sheet. Leave enough space between them so they can expand slightly (about 1 inch).

Bake for 10 to 12 minutes, or until just browned. Do not overbake or the cookies will be too dry. Remove with a spatula to a cooling rack. Repeat with remaining batter until it is all used.

MAKES ABOUT 30 COOKIES

PECAN LACE COOKIES

Pecan lace cookies should be a bit brittle, so they can't be underbaked. Test one or two before you bake the whole batch. If you have any crumbs or crumbled cookies left over, they make a wonderful topping for rich ice cream—something you should remember anytime you have cookie crumbs. If they are soft, lightly toast them.

1 cup sifted whole wheat pastry flour
1 cup combined chopped pecans and quick-cooking oats (equal portions is good, but more pecans to the mix is okay too)
½ cup light corn syrup
½ cup (firmly packed) dark brown sugar
8 tablespoons (1 stick) unsalted butter, softened
1 teaspoon vanilla extract

Preheat oven to 375 degrees. Line 2 baking sheets with foil (just fold over one end so it stays in place; it is easy to slide off).

On a sheet of wax paper, mix whole wheat flour, nuts, and oats. Set aside.

In a medium saucepan (nonstick if you have it), combine corn syrup, brown sugar, and butter over moderate heat. Bring to a boil, stirring, then remove from heat.

Stir in vanilla and add the dry ingredients. Stir very thoroughly. The mixture will bubble up and turn opaque.

Drop by tablespoonfuls onto the lined baking sheet, leaving several inches between for cookies to spread out to make 3- to 4-inch circles.

Bake for 9 minutes, or until set and golden. Remove the baking sheets from oven and slide the foil onto a cooling rack. Re-line the sheets and continue until you use all the batter.

When completely cooled, peel off foil or store cookies on the foil. When cool, they peel off very easily.

MAKES ABOUT 30 COOKIES

PRALINE COOKIES

A friend of my Aunt Freddie's in Natchez, Mississippi, gave me this recipe. It makes delicious crunchy treats and is simple to do. I make these and all other cookies on parchment, which makes it easy to remove the cookies.

1 cup (firmly packed) light brown sugar
1 large egg white, stiffly beaten
2 cups coarsely chopped pecans
1 teaspoon vanilla extract

Preheat oven to 275 degrees. Grease (or spray with vegetable cooking spray) 2 sheets of parchment paper and place them on baking sheets.

Sift brown sugar, then add to beaten egg white and mix well. Stir in nuts and vanilla. Drop by teaspoonfuls onto the lined baking sheets and bake for about 30 minutes, or until set and golden. Carefully remove cookies from parchment, using a spatula, while they are still hot. Cool on racks. (If you allow them to cool on the sheet, they will break apart as you try to remove them.)

MAKES ABOUT 3 DOZEN COOKIES

PECAN COOKIES

Almost any nuts or combination of nuts can be substituted for the pecans in this recipe.

8 tablespoons (1 stick) unsalted butter
3/4 cup (firmly packed) light brown sugar
1 egg, beaten
1 1/4 cups all-purpose flour
1/2 teaspoon baking soda
1/2 teaspoon salt
1 teaspoon vanilla extract
1/2 cup pecans, coarsely chopped

Preheat oven to 375 degrees. Grease 2 baking sheets.

Cream butter and sugar together. Add egg and mix well. Sift together flour, soda, and salt. Add to butter mixture. Add vanilla and 1 teaspoon hot water. Mix. Add pecans and mix.

Drop by rounded teaspoonfuls onto baking sheets. Bake for 12 minutes, or until golden brown. Remove to a rack and cool.

MAKES ABOUT 3 DOZEN COOKIES

WALNUT COOKIES

This is a wafer cookie. As with most thin cookies, the important thing here is the consistency of the dough. It should not fall from the spoon but should be so thick that you must force it out with another spoon. If too thin, add another tablespoon or more or flour.

1 1/2 cups (firmly packed) brown sugar
1/2 cup water
1/2 teaspoon vanilla extract
8 tablespoons (1 stick) unsalted butter
1 1/4 cups all-purpose flour
1 cup finely chopped walnuts

Preheat oven to 350 degrees. Line baking sheets with parchment paper and butter generously.

Put 1/2 cup of the sugar and the water in a pan and boil for 3 minutes. Remove from heat and add vanilla and butter. Let stand until butter melts. Add the remaining sugar, the flour, and nuts, mixing well after each addition.

Drop by tablespoonfuls on the baking sheet, leaving 2 inches in between. Bake for 8 to 9 minutes. Let cool a few minutes before removing with a spatula.

MAKES ABOUT 2 DOZEN COOKIES

ROLLED COOKIES

TEA CAKES

Tea cakes were once very popular. By themselves, they are unassuming, but when served with, for instance, strong vanilla ice cream or fruit, they come into their own.

> *8 tablespoons (1 stick) unsalted butter,*
>   *softened*
> *³/₄ cup sugar*
> *1 egg*
> *¹/₂ teaspoon baking soda*
> *1¹/₂ teaspoons white vinegar*
> *2¹/₃ cups all-purpose flour*
> *¹/₂ teaspoon salt*

Preheat oven to 350 degrees. Very lightly grease 2 medium baking sheets.

Cream butter and sugar together. Add egg and beat well. Dissolve soda in vinegar and mix in. Combine flour and salt and gradually add. Mix thoroughly to make a stiff batter that can be rolled thin.

Roll dough out on floured surface to ¹/₄-inch thickness. Cut with fancy biscuit cutter and place on baking sheets. Bake for 12 minutes, or until light gold. Remove to cooling rack.

Note: If you like, sugar can be sprinkled on top of cakes before baking. Their flavor improves if they are made a day or so ahead of time. They keep extremely well in a jar with a tight lid.

MAKES ABOUT 2 DOZEN COOKIES

FILLED COOKIES

Carolyn Hart supplied me with this recipe, which she said was her maternal grandmother's and a family tradition. Try it and you'll see why. Each cookie has a little surprise in the middle. After you get the hang of making them, you can devise your own fillings, using the one here as a guide.

> *3 cups sifted all-purpose flour*
> *2 teaspoons baking powder*
> *¹/₄ teaspoon salt*
> *8 tablespoons (1 stick) unsalted butter,*
>   *softened*
> *1 cup less 2 tablespoons sugar*
> *1 large egg*
> *¹/₂ cup milk*
> *1 teaspoon vanilla extract*

FILLING
> *¹/₂ cup chopped raisins*
> *¹/₄ cup chopped walnuts*
> *3 tablespoons sugar*
> *¹/₄ cup water*
> *¹/₂ teaspoon vanilla extract*

Sift flour, baking powder, and salt together. Set aside.

Beat butter and sugar together until fluffy, about 3 minutes. Beat egg lightly and combine with milk and vanilla. Add to the butter, alternating with the flour mixture and ending with the flour. Beat well after each addition. This will be a fairly sticky dough. Form into a ball, wrap in plastic wrap, and put into the freezer for about 1 hour.

To make filling: Combine all the ingredients except the vanilla and heat until thickened. Off the heat, stir in vanilla and set aside to cool.

Preheat oven to 375 degrees.

Divide dough in half and return the first half to the refrigerator while you work with the other. Place the dough on a well-floured surface and dust with flour. Turn the dough over and make sure there is flour underneath. Roll out thin and cut into 3-inch circles with a floured cutter. As you place a circle on an ungreased baking sheet, put a generous tablespoon of filling in the center and cover with another circle of dough, pressing the edges together slightly with the tines of a fork. Continue until all the dough and filling are used. Combine the scraps of dough and roll out to make the last cookies.

Bake for about 15 minutes, or until dough begins to brown slightly.

MAKES ABOUT 18 LARGE COOKIES

LEMON SAND TARTS

These are perfect to serve with ice cream or iced tea.

1¼ cups sugar
12 tablespoons (1½ sticks) unsalted butter, softened
1 egg plus 1 egg yolk
½ teaspoon vanilla extract
2 teaspoons fresh lemon juice
1 teaspoon grated lemon zest
3 cups all-purpose flour
¼ teaspoon salt
Sugar for sprinkling

Cream sugar and butter until light and fluffy. Beat in egg and egg yolk, then stir in vanilla, lemon juice, and zest. Beat in flour and salt to form a stiff dough. Gather into a ball and flatten between sheets of wax paper. Refrigerate for 1 hour.

Preheat oven to 400 degrees. Grease 2 baking sheets.

Roll dough until thin, cut into 2-inch rounds, and sprinkle rounds with additional sugar. Place on baking sheets and bake for 9 minutes, or until just beginning to turn golden.

MAKES ABOUT 4 DOZEN COOKIES

NEW WORLD SPICE COOKIES

½ pound (2 sticks) unsalted butter, at room temperature
1 cup sugar
1 egg, at room temperature
½ cup molasses
3¾ cups all-purpose flour
¼ cup unsweetened cocoa powder
2 tablespoons pumpkin pie spice
1½ teaspoons ground cloves
¾ teaspoon baking soda
Pinch of salt

Preheat oven to 350 degrees. Lightly grease 2 baking sheets or line with parchment.

Cream butter and sugar until light and fluffy, using an electric mixer. Add egg and beat thoroughly. Beat in molasses.

Combine the remaining ingredients in a medium bowl.

Continue to beat butter–sugar mixture at low speed and gradually add flour mixture. You may need to mix this by hand to make sure the ingredients are well combined.

Shape the dough into 2 balls and pat into disks. Wrap in wax paper or plastic wrap and refrigerate for 1 to 2 hours.

On a lightly floured surface, roll out the dough about ⅜ to ½ inch thick. (These cookies are better a little on the "cakey" side.)

Using a 3-inch biscuit cutter, cut the dough. Transfer to prepared baking sheets with a spatula.

Bake for 10 to 12 minutes, rotating the baking sheets once. Because these cookies are thick, let them rest for several minutes on the hot baking sheets before transferring them to wire cooling racks.

MAKES ABOUT 3 DOZEN COOKIES

SHAPED COOKIES

VANILLA CRESCENTS

I suspect everyone's had a version of this cookie, as it crops up in some form or another in all cuisines.

This particular recipe was given by Grandmother Haidin to Mardee Regan's mother when she married. Mardee has simplified it even more by chopping the vanilla bean and nuts in the processor at the same time, then adding the rest of the ingredients for a quick whirl. A breeze to make.

2¼ cups sugar
1 vanilla bean, crushed and broken into
  chunks
½ cup shelled walnuts
½ pound (2 sticks) unsalted butter, softened
2⅓ cups sifted all-purpose flour

Preheat oven to 350 degrees.

Place ¼ cup of the sugar and the vanilla bean in the bowl of a food processor fitted with a metal blade. Pulse off and on a few times to chop the bean, then add walnuts. Process until finely chopped. Add butter and flour and process, scraping down sides of the bowl, until dough is pliable. Remove and gather into a ball.

Pinch off walnut-size pieces of dough and shape into balls. Then shape balls into small crescents about the size of your thumb. Place crescents ½ inch apart on an ungreased baking sheet (these do not expand).

Bake for 10 minutes, then reduce the oven temperature to 300 degrees and bake for an additional 10 to 15 minutes, or until cookies are tan and dry.

Pour out remaining sugar on a piece of wax paper. Roll the hot cookies in sugar and let cool on wire racks.

MAKES ABOUT 3 DOZEN COOKIES

SUGAR COOKIES

These have a flavor that complements ice cream very nicely. And they keep well.

2½ cups all-purpose flour
1½ teaspoons baking powder
½ teaspoon salt
¼ teaspoon ground cinnamon
¼ teaspoon freshly grated nutmeg
3 cups sugar
¾ cup safflower oil
2 eggs
1 teaspoon vanilla extract

Preheat oven to 375 degrees.

Sift together flour, baking powder, salt, cinnamon, and nutmeg. Combine 1 cup of the sugar and oil, then beat in eggs, one at a time. Stir in vanilla. Add to flour mixture all at once and mix well.

Spread out remaining sugar on a piece of wax paper. Squeeze off walnut-size balls and roll in sugar. Flour your hands and flatten each cookie as thin as you can. Place on an ungreased baking sheet about 2 inches apart. Sprinkle tops with more sugar if necessary.

Bake for 12 minutes or until light golden. Cool on racks.

MAKES 5 DOZEN COOKIES

CRACKED SUGAR COOKIES

Cracked sugar cookies get that name from the way their tops look after baking. They have a real old-fashioned flavor. My Louisiana cousin, Mackie Kyle, gave me this recipe, which she says has been around for a long time.

1¼ cups sugar
½ pound (2 sticks) unsalted butter, softened
3 large egg yolks, lightly beaten
1 teaspoon vanilla extract
2½ cups sifted all-purpose flour
1 teaspoon baking soda
½ teaspoon cream of tartar

Preheat oven to 350 degrees. Lightly grease a baking sheet.

Cream sugar and butter until fluffy, about 3 minutes. Beat in yolks and vanilla. Sift the dry ingredients together, then add to the batter in 4 parts, mixing well after each addition.

Form dough into balls the size of a walnut and place balls on baking sheet about 2 inches apart. Do not flatten. Bake for about 11 minutes. Cool on a wire rack. Repeat with remaining dough until used up.

MAKES ABOUT 4 DOZEN COOKIES

PEPPER SUGAR COOKIES

This cookie is similar to one of my favorites, so I was bound to like it.

1/2 pound (2 sticks) unsalted butter, softened
1 1/4 cups sugar
2 eggs
1 teaspoon vanilla extract
1/2 teaspoon salt
1 teaspoon cream of tartar
2 1/4 cups all-purpose flour
1 tablespoon ground allspice
1/2 teaspoon freshly ground black pepper

Cream butter and 1 cup of sugar until light and fluffy. Add eggs, one at a time, beating well. Add vanilla and mix. Sift together salt, cream of tartar, and flour, then add to the batter, beating until you have a semistiff dough. Refrigerate for 20 minutes.

Preheat oven to 350 degrees.

Mix remaining 1/4 cup of sugar, allspice, and pepper in a bowl and spread on a sheet of wax paper. Roll dough into balls by the spoonful, then roll in the spiced sugar to coat. Place on a baking sheet, allowing space for them to expand. Bake until lightly golden, about 10 to 12 minutes.

MAKES 4 TO 5 DOZEN COOKIES

SNICKERDOODLES

A true American classic. Heaven only knows how these cookies really got their name—although I'm sure many people will swear they know. If you like, you can lightly press a small pecan half on top of each ball of dough just before baking (in addition to the pecans already in the dough) to make these a little more decorative.

2 3/4 cups sifted all-purpose flour
2 teaspoons cream of tartar
1 teaspoon baking soda
1/4 teaspoon salt
1/2 pound (2 sticks) unsalted butter, softened
1 1/2 cups sugar
2 large eggs
1/4 cup sugar mixed with 1 tablespoon ground cinnamon

Combine flour, cream of tartar, baking soda, and salt and sift again. Set aside.

Cream butter and sugar until fluffy, about 3 minutes. Add eggs, one at a time, beating well after each addition. Add the flour mixture in 4 parts and beat thoroughly after adding each part.

Wrap dough in plastic and refrigerate for at least 1 hour.

Preheat oven to 400 degrees.

Roll dough into balls about the size of a walnut, then roll each in the sugar–cinnamon mixture. Place about 2 inches apart on an ungreased baking sheet.

Bake for 8 to 10 minutes, or until just lightly browned but still soft. Repeat until remaining dough is used up.

MAKES ABOUT 3 DOZEN COOKIES

VENETIAN COOKIES

I found this cookie recipe in a box of papers that had belonged to my mother. They are very good with ice cream or iced tea. They are not very sweet, so if you like, increase the amount of sugar by half. Taste one after they are done, and if you want still more sweetness, roll them in confectioners' sugar while they are still hot.

¹/₂ pound (2 sticks) unsalted butter, softened
¹/₂ cup confectioners' sugar
2 cups all-purpose flour
1¹/₂ teaspoons vanilla extract
2 cups finely chopped walnuts

Preheat oven to 300 degrees.

Cream together butter and sugar. Add flour, a little at a time, then mix in vanilla. Stir in nuts. Make into balls and flatten slightly. Bake for 15 minutes. These do not brown.

MAKES ABOUT 30 COOKIES

THREE-NUT COOKIES

1¹/₂ cups all-purpose flour
1 teaspoon cream of tartar
¹/₂ teaspoon baking soda
Pinch of salt
8 tablespoons (1 stick) unsalted butter, softened
³/₄ cup sugar
1 egg
1¹/₂ cups very coarsely chopped macadamia nuts
1 cup slivered almonds
1 cup finely grated pecans
¹/₂ cup (firmly packed) light brown sugar
1 tablespoon ground cinnamon

Preheat oven to 400 degrees. Grease 2 baking sheets.

Sift together flour, cream of tartar, baking soda, and salt. Set aside.

In a large bowl, cream butter and sugar until fluffy. Beat in egg. Add the dry ingredients to the wet mixture in 2 parts. Mix well. Stir in macadamia nuts and almonds.

Thoroughly mix pecans, brown sugar, and cinnamon.

Pinch off walnut-size pieces of dough and form into balls. Roll each ball in the pecan–sugar mixture and place on a baking sheet about 2 inches apart. Do not flatten. Bake until browned, about 10 minutes.

MAKES ABOUT 2 DOZEN COOKIES

SHASTA MOUNTAIN PEANUT BUTTER COOKIES

8 tablespoons (1 stick) unsalted butter, at room temperature
¹/₄ cup granulated sugar, plus additional for rolling
1 cup (firmly packed) dark brown sugar
1 cup chunky peanut butter
¹/₂ teaspoon vanilla extract
1 egg
2 ounces (¹/₃ cup) salted peanuts, chopped
1¹/₃ cups unbleached all-purpose flour
¹/₄ teaspoon salt
¹/₂ teaspoon baking soda

In a mixing bowl, combine butter, granulated sugar, brown sugar, and peanut butter. Beat with an electric mixer on medium speed until light and smooth, 3 to 4 minutes. Add vanilla, egg, and peanuts and stir until just combined.

Whisk together flour, salt, and baking soda. Add all at once to the butter mixture. Stir until just combined. The dough will be stiff. Cover and refrigerate for at least 4 hours or overnight.

Preheat oven to 350 degrees.

With your hands, shape 1¹/₂-tablespoon measures of the cookie dough (just smaller than golf balls) and roll in granulated sugar to coat. Place about 3 inches apart on a greased baking sheet and flatten with the bottom of a glass, then score crisscross with the tines of a fork.

Bake for 12 to 15 minutes, or until set and slightly golden. Let cool slightly on the baking sheet before removing. Cool on a rack.

MAKES ABOUT 12 LARGE COOKIES

ICEBOX AND OTHER COOKIES

PEANUT BUTTER COOKIES

This is my Aunt Freddie's recipe, and one that I use all the time. These are the simplest cookies imaginable, and have a taste that most of us associate with our childhoods. They also freeze quite well.

1/2 pound (2 sticks) unsalted butter, softened
1 cup sugar
1 cup (firmly packed) brown sugar
1 cup chunky peanut butter
2 eggs, well beaten
2 1/2 cups all-purpose flour
3/4 teaspoon baking soda
Pinch of salt
1 teaspoon vanilla extract

Put butter, sugars, and peanut butter in a bowl. Cream thoroughly. Add eggs and mix well. Sift flour, baking soda, and salt into the mixture. Blend well. Add vanilla and mix. Roll into a long log. Wrap the log up in wax paper or plastic wrap and refrigerate for 24 hours. (You can make two rolls and freeze one.)

To bake, preheat oven to 350 degrees.

Cut cookies from roll and bake on a lightly greased baking sheet for 12 to 15 minutes.

MAKES ABOUT 4 DOZEN COOKIES

ICEBOX COOKIES

Icebox cookies take no effort to mix, but they must be refrigerated to make handling the dough easier. They may be baked as you need them. They can stay in the refrigerator for up to a week.

1/2 pound (2 sticks) unsalted butter, softened
1/2 cup less 1 tablespoon superfine sugar
1 large egg yolk
1/2 teaspoon vanilla extract
1/2 teaspoon almond extract
1 3/4 cups sifted unbleached all-purpose flour

Beat butter and sugar until fluffy, about 3 minutes. Then beat in egg yolk, vanilla, and almond extract. Stir in flour in 2 parts, blending well after each addition. Divide the dough in half and roll each half into a 3-inch-wide log. Wrap in plastic wrap and refrigerate for several hours.

Preheat oven to 375 degrees.

Using a knife with a very sharp, thin blade, make 1/8-inch dough slices and place them on an ungreased baking sheet with space between for them to expand. Bake for about 11 minutes, or until they just start to turn color but not brown. Remove to a rack to cook. Repeat with remaining dough until used up.

These cookies are already rather sweet, but you could sprinkle them with flavored granulated sugar after they have cooled slightly if you like.

MAKES ABOUT 3 DOZEN COOKIES

447

BUTTERSCOTCH PECAN COOKIES

Several years ago, I received a very nice letter from a lady who remarked on how much she liked cookies for dessert and how glad she was to see that I shared her enthusiasm. With the letter, she enclosed a favorite cookie recipe of hers. And here it is. Unfortunately, her letter lost its last page with her name. So if you read this, many thanks. I'm glad others may now enjoy this cookie as much as we both have.

These cookies are wonderful served with butter pecan ice cream.

8 tablespoons (1 stick) unsalted butter
1 cup (firmly packed) dark brown sugar
1 large egg
$1/2$ cup finely chopped pecans
$1/2$ teaspoon vanilla extract
$1^1/2$ cups unbleached all-purpose flour
$1/2$ teaspoon salt
$1/2$ teaspoon baking powder
$1/4$ teaspoon baking soda

Cream butter and sugar until smooth. Add egg and pecans. Mix thoroughly, then stir in vanilla. Set aside while you sift the remaining ingredients together. Combine well with the butter–sugar mixture.

On a floured surface, divide the dough in half (this will be very sticky). Shape a log from each half that is about 2 inches in diameter and wrap securely with plastic. Refrigerate for at least 1 hour, more if you have time.

Preheat oven to 350 degrees.

Cut chilled dough into $1/8$-inch slices. Place 1 inch apart on an ungreased baking sheet and bake until cookies are golden but not browned, about 15 to 16 minutes. Remove with a spatula while warm. Place on a rack to cool.

MAKES ABOUT 3 DOZEN COOKIES

FRUITCAKE COOKIES

These cookies, which are wonderful for the holidays, were the idea of my friend and food maven Carole Bannett. The recipe was devised by David Coltin, the moving force behind Society Bakery of Boston, Massachusetts.

This recipe makes about 150 small cookies, but before they are cooked, the dough must be frozen. We have divided the dough in 6 parts. That way you can take out one part and bake the cookies as you need them.

$1/2$ pound dried figs, chopped
$1/4$ pound raisins
$1/4$ pound glacéed cherries, chopped coarsely
1 tablespoon honey
2 tablespoons dry sherry
1 tablespoon fresh lemon juice
Pinch of salt
6 ounces small walnut pieces
$1/2$ pound (2 sticks) unsalted butter, softened
$1/2$ teaspoon ground cloves
$1/2$ cup superfine sugar
$1/3$ cup (firmly packed) light brown sugar
1 large egg
$2^2/3$ cups sifted all-purpose flour mixed with
$1/4$ teaspoon salt

Combine fruits, honey, sherry, lemon juice, salt, and walnuts. Let marinate, covered, overnight.

Cream butter, cloves, and sugars until smooth, about 3 minutes. Add egg and incorporate. Add the flour and salt mixture in 3 parts, mixing after each addition but being careful not to overmix. Mix in fruit and nuts, and any liquid. Chill dough briefly, then divide into 6 equal portions and roll into logs with lightly floured hands. Put in freezer for about 1 hour.

Preheat oven to 350 degrees.

Cut the chilled logs into very thin rounds with a sharp knife and place on an ungreased baking sheet with about $1/2$ inch between. Bake for 10 to 13 minutes, or until light golden.

MAKES ABOUT 150 SMALL COOKIES

SPICE SABLES

These meltingly good rolled cookies are the brainchild of talented pastry chef André Fecteau.

2 cups sifted all-purpose flour
1 1/2 teaspoons ground cinnamon
1/2 teaspoon freshly grated nutmeg
1/2 teaspoon ground allspice
12 tablespoons (1 1/2 sticks) unsalted butter, softened
1/2 teaspoon salt
1/2 cup (firmly packed) light brown sugar
2 tablespoons Grand Marnier
1/2 cup finely ground blanched almonds

Sift together flour, cinnamon, nutmeg, and allspice. Set aside.

Cream butter, salt, and brown sugar until smooth. Stir in Grand Marnier and then almonds. Beat in the dry mixture and pat into a ball. Wrap in plastic wrap and refrigerate for 1 hour.

Preheat oven to 325 degrees. Grease and flour several baking sheets. Roll out and pat the dough (it will not stretch like pie or biscuits dough but is more grainy) on a floured surface until 1/4 inch thick. Cut into cookies with a 3-inch floured cookie cutter in the shape of your choice. Place on prepared baking sheet.

Bake for 15 to 20 minutes, or until lightly browned. Remove to a cooling rack.

MAKES ABOUT 2 DOZEN COOKIES

PECAN-COCONUT BISCOTTI

1 egg plus 1 egg white
1/2 cup vegetable oil
3/4 cup sugar
1 teaspoon vanilla extract
1/2 teaspoon salt
3/4 cup coarsely chopped pecans
1/2 cup sweetened flaked coconut
1 1/2 cups all-purpose flour
1 1/2 teaspoons baking powder

Combine egg, egg white, and oil in a large bowl. Beat with an electric mixer on low speed until well combined. Add sugar, vanilla, salt, pecans, and coconut and mix on low speed until completely blended, 1 or 2 minutes.

Stir together flour and baking powder in a small bowl. Add all at once to the egg mixture and mix on low speed until just combined. Cover with plastic wrap and refrigerate overnight.

Preheat oven to 325 degrees. Lightly coat 2 baking sheets with vegetable spray.

Divide the dough into 2 balls. Place one ball of dough on each baking sheet. Flatten each ball into a long loaf the length of the baking sheet and about 4 inches wide.

Bake for 30 minutes, or until crisp and lightly browned. Remove from the oven and let cool for several minutes. Using 2 large spatulas, carefully remove the baked loaf from the sheets and place on a large cutting board. Cut each loaf on the diagonal into about 18 strips. Return the cookies to the baking sheets, laying the strips on their sides, and bake for 15 to 20 minutes, or until rich golden brown.

MAKES ABOUT 3 DOZEN BISCOTTI

VARIATION

Substitute macadamia nuts for the pecans. Add 2 tablespoons anise seeds.

PECAN TILES

2 egg whites
Pinch of salt
½ teaspoon vanilla extract
½ cup superfine sugar
6 tablespoons all-purpose flour
¾ cup finely chopped pecans
3 tablespoons unsalted butter, melted

Preheat oven to 375 degrees. Grease 2 baking sheets.

Whip egg whites in a large bowl with salt until foamy but not forming peaks. Fold in vanilla and sugar.

Combine flour with pecans, mixing well. Sprinkle this over egg whites and incorporate. Stir in butter. The batter should be liquid enough to spread out into a thin 3-inch circle when dropped onto the baking sheet. If it is not, spread rounds with a small spatula.

Bake until golden brown around the edges, about 6 minutes. Drape each cookie over a rolling pin or the side of a wine bottle while it is still hot and pliable. Allow to remain there long enough to hold its "tile" shape. (If cookies get too hard before you can mold them all, place them back in the oven for another few seconds.)

MAKES ABOUT 20 COOKIES

CINNAMON WALNUT TWISTS

½ cup sugar
½ cup walnuts
1 teaspoon ground cinnamon
1 teaspoon grated lemon zest
1 sheet frozen puff pastry, thawed
1 egg white, lightly beaten

Preheat oven to 400 degrees.

Combine sugar, walnuts, cinnamon, and lemon zest in the bowl of a food processor fitted with a metal blade, pulsing until finely ground.

Roll out the puff pastry sheet on a lightly floured surface. Brush one side with egg white. Sprinkle nut mixture over the egg white and very lightly pat nuts to stick.

Cut the dough in half lengthwise and then into 1-inch strips. Fold each strip of dough in half and pinch to close. Twist once and place on a lightly greased baking sheet.

Bake until golden brown, about 10 to 12 minutes. Remove and cool on a rack.

MAKES ABOUT 2 DOZEN COOKIES

BAR COOKIES

CHOCOLATE SQUARES

½ pound (2 sticks) plus 2 tablespoons
  unsalted butter or margarine, slightly
  softened
½ cup (firmly packed) light brown sugar
½ cup granulated sugar
2 egg yolks
1 cup all-purpose flour
1 cup quick oatmeal
12 ounces milk chocolate
¾ cup finely chopped walnuts

Preheat oven to 350 degrees.

Cream ½ pound of the butter and the sugars. Beat in egg yolks, then add flour and oatmeal. Press into a lightly greased 17 × 11-inch low-sided pan. Bake 20 minutes, until set. Meanwhile, melt the chocolate and remaining 2 tablespoons butter together.

Remove pan from the oven, spread top with the chocolate mixture, and sprinkle with nuts. Cut into squares.

MAKES ABOUT 40 SQUARES

OUTRAGEOUS BROWNIES

If ever a cookie was aptly named, this one is. They are certainly outrageous—outrageously good. There must be a million versions of brownies, but this one by Ina Garten certainly ranks with the very best.

1 pound (4 sticks) unsalted butter
1 pound plus 3 cups semisweet chocolate chips
6 ounces unsweetened chocolate
6 large eggs
2 tablespoons plus 1 1/2 teaspoons powdered instant espresso
2 tablespoons vanilla extract
2 1/4 cups sugar
1 cup shifted unbleached all-purpose flour
1 tablespoon baking powder
1 teaspoon salt
3 cups chopped walnut pieces

Preheat oven to 350 degrees. Grease and flour an 15 × 10-inch jelly roll pan. Set aside.

Melt together butter, 1 pound of the chocolate chips, and unsweetened chocolate until smooth in the top of a double broiler. Cool to room temperature.

Combine, but do not whisk, eggs, powdered espresso, vanilla, and sugar. Stir in the cooled chocolate mixture. Set aside.

Sift together flour, baking powder, and salt. Mix into the batter. Finally, fold in remaining chocolate chips and the walnuts. Pour into the greased pan.

Bake about 30 minutes, or until a tester just comes out clean. Do not overbake. Cool thoroughly and cut into 3 × 2-inch bars.

Note: Halfway through baking, open the oven, lift the pan, and smack it on the rack. Turn the pan around and smack the other side. This stops the rising process and gives the brownies their sinfully dense texture.

MAKES 25 BROWNIES

SHASTA MOUNTAIN BROWNIES

6 ounces bittersweet chocolate
1/2 pound (2 sticks) unsalted butter
1/2 pound chocolate chip cookies (homemade if possible)
4 eggs
2 1/4 cups sugar
1 teaspoon vanilla extract
1 cup all-purpose flour
4 ounces pecans, chopped

Preheat oven to 350 degrees. Lightly grease and flour two 9-inch square pans.

Melt chocolate and butter together in a small bowl. (You can do this in a microwave or on the stove over a pot of simmering water.) Stir and set aside to cool slightly.

Place cookies in the bowl of a food processor. Pulse to chop the cookies coarse.

Combine eggs, sugar, and vanilla in a large bowl. Beat with an electric mixer on medium speed until thick and lemon colored, about 3 minutes. Add melted chocolate and butter, and stir to combine. Mix in flour gradually, just to incorporate. Fold in chopped cookies and three quarters of the nuts.

Spread the batter in the 2 prepared pans and sprinkle with the remaining nuts. Bake about 40 minutes, or until set. The brownies will, be soft in the center. Cool on a rack. Cut each pan of brownies into 9 squares.

MAKES 18 LARGE BROWNIES

BLONDIES

As far as I know, true blondies don't have chocolate in them, but I couldn't resist adding just a little. So these have a chocolate bottom.

8 tablespoons (1 stick) unsalted butter, softened
1 cup (firmly packed) light brown sugar
2 large eggs
1¹/₂ teaspoons vanilla extract
1 cup sifted cake flour (not self-rising)
¹/₄ teaspoon salt
¹/₃ cup coarsely chopped walnuts
¹/₂ cup coarsely chopped bittersweet chocolate (3-ounce bar)

Preheat oven to 350 degrees. Butter an 8-inch square baking pan. Set aside.

Cream butter and brown sugar until fluffy, about 3 minutes. Add eggs, one at a time, beating well after each addition. Stir in vanilla. Add flour and salt and beat until well mixed. Fold in walnuts and then chocolate pieces. Pour batter into the pan and smooth the top.

Bake in the center of the oven for 30 to 35 minutes, or until a cake tester comes out clean. Cool in the pan before cutting into 2-inch squares.

MAKES 16 BLONDIES

ROCKY ROAD SQUARES WITH CARAMEL SAUCE

Not only does this adult version of a kid's dessert tickle your palate, it may be made in advance and stored in the freezer for months.

10 ounces semisweet chocolate, chopped
3 tablespoons unsalted butter
3 egg yolks
¹/₄ cup sugar
4 egg whites
2¹/₂ cups chopped pecans, toasted
4 ounces mini marshmallows
Caramel sauce

Melt chocolate and set it aside. Whip butter until light and fluffy. Beat in the melted chocolate. Whip egg yolks with half the sugar until light yellow. Set aside. Whip egg whites with the other half of the sugar until soft peaks form. Fold yolk mixture into the chocolate–butter mixture, then fold in the egg whites. Fold in pecans and marshmallows.

Open the top end of a 1-quart paper milk carton completely. Rinse it out and dry it. Spoon mixture into carton, shaking it down lightly, until carton is filled. Cover and place in the freezer.

To serve, rip the carton off and cut slices with a knife dipped into hot water and dried. Serve with caramel sauce or puréed strawberries.

Note: You may also make this in a buttered 1-quart terrine. The milk carton doesn't need buttering.

SERVES 6 TO 8

CAPPUCCINO BROWNIES

8 ounces milk chocolate, coarsely chopped
1 tablespoon instant coffee powder
4 tablespoons unsalted butter, softened
1/2 cup sugar
2 eggs, at room temperature
2 teaspoons vanilla extract
1/8 teaspoon ground cinnamon
Pinch of salt
1/2 cup unbleached all-purpose flour
1 cup pecans, toasted and coarsely chopped

Preheat oven to 350 degrees. Grease and lightly flour an 8-inch square pan. Set aside.

Melt chocolate and instant coffee in a double boiler over hot, not simmering, water. Stir until smooth and set aside.

Using an electric mixer, beat butter until fluffy, gradually adding sugar. Beat in eggs, one at a time, until mixture is light in color. Add vanilla, cinnamon, and salt and beat just until blended.

Stir in chocolate and coffee mixture and mix well. Add flour and stir to combine. Pour the batter into the prepared pan, scraping the bowl with a spatula. Top with chopped nuts.

Bake for about 25 to 30 minutes, until edges are firm but the center is still soft. Cool to room temperature on a wire rack. Cut into squares. To loosen brownies, slide a knife around the sides of the pan and shake pan gently.

MAKES 16 BROWNIES

LEMON SQUARES

Here's a recipe from Carolyn Hart, this one from her Auntie Pearl, to be exact.

1/2 pound (2 sticks) unsalted butter, softened
2 cups plus 1 tablespoon sifted all-purpose flour
1/2 cup sifted confectioners' sugar
4 large eggs, at room temperature
2 cups granulated sugar
Grated zest of 1 large lemon
6 tablespoons fresh lemon juice
1/2 teaspoon baking powder
1 1/2 cups chopped walnuts

Preheat oven to 325 degrees. Grease a 13 × 9-inch baking pan. Set aside.

Beat together butter, 2 cups of flour, and the confectioners' sugar until fluffy. Scrape mixture into the prepared pan and smooth into a thin layer covering the bottom. Bake for 15 minutes.

Meanwhile, beat eggs and sugar until light. Add lemon zest and juice, and mix. Sprinkle the tablespoon of flour and the 1/2 teaspoon of baking powder over all, then pour in the nuts. Combine well.

Pour lemon mixture into crust and return to oven to bake for another 35 minutes, or until filling is set.

Let cool slightly, then cut into 2-inch squares. Loosen crust around the edges before removing squares from the pan.

MAKES 2 DOZEN SQUARES

LEMON WALNUT BARS

Lemon bars are just about everyone's favorite.

BASE
1 cup all-purpose flour
1/3 cup confectioners' sugar, sifted
1/2 cup finely ground walnuts
1/2 teaspoon grated lemon zest
2/3 cup unsalted butter, cut in small chunks

FILLING
2 eggs
1 cup granulated sugar
7 tablespoons fresh lemon juice
2 tablespoons all-purpose flour
1/2 teaspoon baking powder
Confectioners's sugar, to taste

Preheat oven to 375 degrees.

To make base: Combine flour, confectioners' sugar, walnuts, and zest in a bowl and blend well. Add butter chunks. Using your fingers, combine until mixture resembles coarse meal. Press mixture into an ungreased 8-inch square pan. Bake until set, about 20 minutes.

To make filling: Beat eggs and granulated sugar in a bowl until light in color. Add lemon juice and continue beating another 5 minutes. In a separate bowl, combine flour and baking powder. Add the flour mixture to the egg mixture slowly, stirring all the while until smooth.

Pour the filling over the partially baked base and return to the oven and continue baking until set, about 25 minutes. Remove from the oven and cool. Sift confectioners' sugar over the top and cut into squares or bars.

MAKES 12 TO 16 BARS

SHORTBREAD

This is a very old recipe. Like many such, it is wonderfully simple. The end product improves with age. You will note that the recipe calls for granulated sugar rather than confectioners' sugar; this contributes to its crunchy texture.

8 tablespoons (1 stick) unsalted butter
1/2 cup sugar
2 cups all-purpose flour

Preheat oven to 300 degrees.

Mix all the ingredients together with your hands until dough resembles coarse meal. The theory is that the warmth of your hands softens the butter and makes the shortbread crispy.

Pat the mixture into an ungreased 9-inch square pan. Pierce the dough every 2 inches with a fork. Bake for 40 minutes, or until slightly brown. Cut into squares while still warm.

MAKES 16 SHORTBREADS

BROWN SUGAR SHORTBREAD

This recipe is a variation on the time-tested classic.

1/2 pound (2 sticks) unsalted butter, softened
1 cup (firmly packed) light brown sugar
1 teaspoon vanilla extract
2 1/4 cups sifted all-purpose flour

Preheat oven to 325 degrees. Butter a 9-inch cake pan and set aside.

Beat butter, brown sugar, and vanilla together until fluffy, about 3 minutes. Add flour in 4 batches and combine well after each addition. (You may do this with your hands.) Scrape the dough into the prepared pan and pat into an even layer. Prick the surface with the tines of a fork.

Since shortbread becomes solid when it cools, score the top (do not cut all the way through the dough) before baking so it will be easy to break apart into wedges.

Bake in the upper third of the oven for about 30 minutes, or until the top is puffy and lightly browned.

MAKES 12 SHORTBREADS

VARIATION
Replace 1 cup of the flour with 1 cup finely chopped pecans.

HAZELNUT SHORTBREAD
I always make shortbread of some kind because it keeps so well and is so good with ice cream, tea, and any kind of fruit.

1 cup sugar
1¼ cups all-purpose flour
Pinch of salt
1 cup coarsely chopped, lightly toasted hazelnuts
½ pound (2 sticks) unsalted butter, softened
1 teaspoon vanilla extract

Preheat oven to 350 degrees. Butter two 8-inch square baking pans.

Combine sugar, flour, salt, and hazelnuts. Mix with a fork. Add butter and start to mix with your hands. When combined, sprinkle vanilla over all and mix thoroughly. Pat into the prepared pans and score the tops to make it easier to cut after baking.

Bake until set and turning slightly golden, about 25 to 30 minutes. Let cool for a few minutes before cutting. If shortbread is allowed to cool completely before cutting, you will need to break it apart into serving pieces.

MAKES 18 SHORTBREADS

TEXAS COOKIES
Don't ask me why my mother called these Texas cookies. Another one of those mysteries.

1 cup all-purpose flour
½ teaspoon baking powder
½ teaspoon salt
8 tablespoons (1 stick) unsalted butter, softened
2 cups (firmly packed) brown sugar
2 eggs
1 teaspoon vanilla extract
2 cups coarsely chopped pecans

Preheat oven to 350 degrees.

Sift together flour, baking powder, and salt. Set aside. Cream together butter and sugar and beat in eggs, one at a time. Mix in vanilla. Add flour mixture, a little at a time. When well mixed, spread on a very well oiled jelly-roll pan. Sprinkle pecans over it and bake for about 25 minutes. Cut into squares when almost cool and remove the cookies with a spatula.

MAKES 24 COOKIES

455

OTHER DESSERTS

DESSERT SEEMS TO BE THE PART OF THE MEAL MOST PEOPLE associate with childhood favorites, even when these are gussied up to suit restaurant menus. My method of selecting the desserts here was rather random and subjective, so don't be disappointed if your treasured treat from childhood has been overlooked. There are plenty of other possibilities. ✦ Although I have never been much of a candy maker, I have fond memories as a small boy of pulling taffy, of fudge and divinity and that hometown specialty, the praline. Candy thermometers make the results of these candy recipes less iffy— and personally, I wouldn't try making candy without one. ✦ Puddings and custards must surely be the most soothing of all desserts. They are also among the easiest to make, composed simply and primarily of sweetened milk or cream with eggs. ✦ Finally, fresh fruit can't be beat as a light and refreshing way to end a meal.

FRUIT AND FRUIT SALAD

SAUTÉED BANANAS

This is done rather quickly, so wait until the last minute.

4 tablespoons (½ stick) unsalted butter
1 tablespoon (firmly packed) dark brown
* sugar*
Pinch of salt
Pinch of white pepper
8 medium bananas, peeled and sliced
* diagonally into 1-inch pieces*

Put butter, brown sugar, salt, and pepper in a large skillet and heat over high heat. When bubbly, add bananas and cook, tossing lightly, just long enough to coat and heat through, 1 to 2 minutes. Serve hot.
SERVES 8

SWEET SIMPLICITY

Most of us know from eating them sun-warmed right off the vine or bush that berries don't really need to be enhanced to taste sublime. But human nature being what it is, most of us can't seem to resist a little embellishing. If berries are perfect when just picked at their ripest, just add a sprinkle of sugar and a little heavy cream, or whipped cream flavored with vanilla, or—better still—flavor them with eau-de-vie made from the fruit.

Another good match is crème fraîche with a sprinkle of dark raw sugar on top.

BANANAS IN BROWN SUGAR AND RUM

Most places in New Orleans call this Bananas Foster. It is a delightful dessert. If the bananas are very small, allow 1½ per person.

8 tablespoons (1 stick) unsalted butter
½ cup (firmly packed) dark brown sugar
6 small bananas, peeled and split in half
* lengthwise*
6 ounces light or dark rum
Whipped cream or vanilla ice cream

Put butter and sugar in a shallow pan. Melt them very slowly and add bananas. Cook for 2 minutes on each side, until just tender. Turn only once. (Start bananas on their round side—I find them easier to turn that way.) Place on individual plates. Add rum to the pan, swirl around, and bring to a boil. Do not overcook. Pour over the bananas.

Serve with whipped cream or vanilla ice cream.
SERVES 6

STRAWBERRIES WITH BROWN SUGAR AND SOUR CREAM

This combination also works well with freshly sliced, peeled peaches. But it's best to toss them with a bit of lemon juice to prevent discoloration.

2 pints large strawberries, washed
1 cup (firmly packed) dark brown sugar
1 pint sour cream

Place berries, brown sugar, and sour cream in separate bowls and allow guests to help themselves, first to the strawberries, then the toppings of sour cream and brown sugar.
SERVES 8

MARINATED
STRAWBERRIES

Strawberries are served this way all over Italy.
The lemon juice combines wonderfully with
the strawberries.

*2 pints strawberries, washed, hulled, and
    sliced in half*
3 tablespoons sugar
3 tablespoons fresh lemon juice

Combine all of the ingredients and refrigerate
until ready to serve.
SERVES 6

FRESH FIGS WITH
CREAM

What a treat these are!

20 small fresh figs, stemmed and peeled
1½ to 2 cups heavy cream
Grated lemon zest (optional)

Cut each fig in half and divide the lot evenly
among 6 to 8 individual serving dishes. Pour 4
tablespoons of cream over each. Sprinkle with
a little finely grated lemon zest if you like.
SERVES 6 TO 8

CANDIED GRAPEFRUIT
RIND

Gael Greene gave me the recipe for these delicious little strips of rind.

1 large grapefruit
Equal amounts of water and sugar
Sugar for coating

With a knife, remove peel from grapefruit in
thick slices, leaving some of the fruit on the
rind. Cover with cold water in a pot, bring to a
boil, and boil 10 minutes. Drain. Cover again
with cold water and repeat 2 more times.

Drain. Cover with a mixture of equal amounts
of cold water and sugar. The quantity will vary
according to the amount of grapefruit peel you
have. Bring to a boil. Boil 10 minutes. Drain.
Let dry slightly until cool. Cut into long strips
and press into sugar to coat the rind.

MANGO WITH
BLACKBERRIES

6 mangoes, peeled and roughly chopped
2 tablespoons unsalted butter, melted
¼ cup (firmly packed) light brown sugar
1 pint blackberries

Preheat oven to 300 degrees. Butter six ½-cup
ramekins and set aside.
    Toss together mangoes, butter, and brown
sugar. Spoon into ramekins. Heat in oven until
warm, about 15 minutes. Top warm mango
mixture with blackberries. Cool on a wire rack.
SERVES 6

FRESH FIGS MARINATED
IN LEMON

It is important to prepare these well enough in
advance to allow the flavors and texture to
develop.

4 cups water
1 cup sugar
½ cup fresh lemon juice
*2 lemons, cut into thick slices and seeds
    removed*
12 large green figs, stems left on
*Devonshire cream or Vanilla Sauce
    (page 366)*

Bring water, sugar, and lemon juice to a boil.
Add lemon slices and simmer for 3 minutes.
    Meanwhile, wash figs and place in a glass
bowl. Pour hot liquid and lemons over all.
Cover with a plate that fits inside the bowl to

keep the figs submerged. Let cool, then cover with plastic wrap and refrigerate for several days.

Serve with Devonshire (clotted) cream or vanilla sauce.

SERVES 6

MELON BALLS WITH MINT

Two small melons are more than enough for four people. When buying them, get different varieties. Make as many melon balls as you think you'll need. Garnish with slivers of mint leaf if available and pique their flavor with lemon or lime juice (or both) and a grating of lemon zest. If the melon balls must sit in the refrigerator (always covered) for any length of time, pour out any liquid that may accumulate in the bottom of the bowl and dry it out. Do not add the garnishes and citrus juice until you are ready to serve.

MELON BALLS WITH CHERRIES

When cherries are in season, I serve them mixed with melon. I have a cherry pitter that makes fast work of them, but this is not really necessary. As a matter of fact, cherries look much more appealing with their stems on.

Either way, select a nice, ripe melon such as a Santa Claus or a honeydew, and cut it into cubes or make balls with a baller. I like the taste of cherries with these melons better than I do with cantaloupe. Give the whole thing a squeeze of lemon or lime juice and you are done. You might top it off with a bit of freshly grated lemon zest.

MELON SLICES WITH RASPBERRY PURÉE

Quick Raspberry Sauce (page 363)

Cut rind from melon wedges. Slice each wedge into ¼-inch pieces and fan out on individual plates.

Pour raspberry sauce over melon.

SERVES 6

BRANDIED PEACHES

When peaches are in season, I make a batch of these to serve with meats and meat pies. They can be canned, but I don't go through all of that.

3 cups sugar
3 cups water
4 whole cloves
4 whole allspice berries
One 4-inch cinnamon stick
3 pounds unblemished peaches, dipped in hot water and peeled
4 tablespoons brandy

Put sugar and water in a large kettle and bring to a boil. Add cloves, allspice, and cinnamon. Simmer for 5 minutes. Carefully add peaches. Simmer for 5 minutes, until tender. Remove peaches to a large sterile jar with a snap lid. Pour in the cooking syrup and top with brandy. When cool, snap shut and store in the refrigerator.

Let this mature for a few days before serving.

MAKES 2 QUARTS

GRILLED PINEAPPLE WITH RUM CREAM SAUCE

This delicious rum sauce can also be used on baked or grilled bananas.

1 large ripe pineapple, peeled, cored, and
*   cut into 12 lengthwise strips*
Vegetable oil
4 tablespoons (1/2 stick) unsalted butter
1/2 cup (firmly packed) dark brown sugar
1/2 cup heavy cream
1/4 cup light rum
1/4 cup fresh lime juice
Thin slices of lime (optional)

Prepare an outdoor grill or a grill pan.

Dip pineapple spears in vegetable oil and grill or broil 5 minutes on both sides.

Meanwhile, combine the 4 tablespoons butter, brown sugar, and cream in a small saucepan. Bring to a boil over medium heat. When all the sugar is melted (almost at the same time it comes to a boil), remove from heat and stir in rum and lime juice. Place 2 slices of pineapple on each serving plate and spoon sauce over. Garnish with thin slices of lime if desired.

SERVES 6

BAKED STUFFED PEARS WITH VANILLA SAUCE

The ubiquitous pear is always dependable for making cold-weather desserts.

3 large pears, peeled, cut in half, and cored
Fresh lemon juice
1/3 cup raisins or dried currants
3 tablespoons sugar
2 tablespoons unsalted butter
1 tablespoon cognac (optional)
2 teaspoons ground cinnamon
1/2 teaspoon freshly grated nutmeg
Vanilla Sauce (page 366), warm

Preheat oven to 400 degrees. Generously grease a baking dish into which pear halves will fit snugly.

Rub pear halves generously with lemon juice (to keep from discoloring) and set aside.

Grind or chop raisins very fine and mix with the other ingredients (except the Vanilla Sauce) to make a paste. Fill each pear cavity with the mixture. Place pears, filled side down, in baking dish. Bake until tender, about 30 minutes. Let cool slightly, then carefully remove with a spatula.

Serve warm on a pool of the warm Vanilla Sauce. Pass additional sauce if desired
SERVES 6

BAKED WINTER FRUIT

This comes out with the figs all plumped up and the apples still having a little crunch.

1/2 pound dried figs
1 large lemon, cut in half, with one half
*   juiced and the other cut into thin rings*
*   and seeded*
1 pound firm pears, peeled, cored, and
*   quartered*
1/3 cup sugar
1 pound apples, peeled, cored, and cut in
*   eighths*

Preheat oven to 350 degrees. Butter a deep 8-cup casserole.

Place figs on the bottom of the casserole, sprinkle with half the lemon juice, and scatter half the lemon slices over. Put the pears on top of this and sprinkle with half the sugar, remaining lemon juice, and the balance of the lemon slices. Top with the apples and sprinkle with the balance of the sugar.

Bake, uncovered, for about 30 minutes. Cover loosely with foil and turn off oven. Leave in oven for another hour. The apples should retain some of their texture, and the pears will be soft.
SERVES 6

WARM CURRIED FRUIT

You might also want to add a cup or so of freshly grated coconut.

> 2 cups thickly sliced peeled and cored pears
> 2 cups thickly sliced peeled and cored apples
> 2 cups thickly sliced peeled and pitted peaches
> 2 cups coarsely chopped fresh pineapple
> 2 cups seedless grapes
> 2 tablespoons fresh curry powder
> 5⅓ tablespoons (⅔ stick) unsalted butter, slightly softened
> ¾ cup (firmly packed) light brown sugar

Preheat oven to 325 degrees. Mix fruit in a large bowl and set aside. Mix curry powder, butter, and brown sugar, then toss with the fruit. Scoop out fruit into a shallow, buttered baking dish.

Bake, covered, for 45 minutes. Uncover and continue baking for another 15 minutes, until fruit is soft.

Serve warm.

SERVES 12

TROPICAL FRUIT COMPOTE

Use any mélange of fruit you see in the market, but always toss it with the orange juice (unless you are using peeled orange sections in the mixture). I generally make a big batch of this so people can dip into it all day long. Leftovers, if there are any, are fine for breakfast.

> 3 medium bananas, cut into medium slices
> ½ medium pineapple, peeled, cored, and cut into small triangles
> 2 medium papayas, peeled, seeded, and cut into medium chunks
> 2 large mangoes, peeled and cut into chunks
> 4 kiwi fruits, peeled and cut into thick rings
> Juice of 1 medium orange

Toss all the fruit together with the orange juice. Chill, covered, for just 30 minutes before serving.

If this must wait longer, reserve the bananas until just before serving.

SERVES 8 TO 10

FRESH FRUIT WITH YOGURT AND WARM SUN HONEY

Some suggested combination of fruits are: all berries (raspberries, blueberries, strawberries), sliced peaches and blueberries, or sliced mango, papaya, and oranges.

> 1 cup honey
> 3 cups plain yogurt (high-quality cow's, sheep's, or goat's whole-milk yogurt)
> 6 cups fresh fruit

Pour honey in to a serving pitcher. Cover top loosely with plastic wrap and place in the sun to warm. This will take at least 1 hour, maybe more.

Divide yogurt among 6 bowls. Place a platter of assorted fresh fruit and the pitcher of honey on the table for guests to help themselves.

SERVES 6

461

FRESH FRUIT SALAD

2 medium navel oranges
1 cup seedless grapes, cut into halves
1 cup blueberries
2 cups cantaloupe or honeydew melon
    chunks
1/2 cup fresh orange juice
Sugar, to taste

Peel the oranges. Plunge into boiling water for 30 to 45 seconds, remove from the water, and, using a sharp paring knife, scrape off any white pith. Slice along the membranes to remove the orange sections, then cut the sections in half.

Combine oranges with the remaining ingredients and toss well.

SERVES 6

LAYERED FRESH FRUIT WITH RASPBERRY SAUCE

Use any fruits that might be handy, following this recipe simply as a guide.

2 oranges, juiced
1/2 fresh pineapple, peeled and cut into
    medium cubes
1 medium banana, sliced
2 or 3 purple plums, pitted and sliced
1 pint strawberries, hulled and thickly sliced
1 large nectarine, thickly sliced
1 large peach, peeled, pitted, and thickly
    sliced
1 small bunch red or green seedless grapes
    (about 1/3 pound)
Quick Raspberry Sauce (page 363)

Place orange juice in a medium bowl. Select a large glass jar with a wide mouth in which to layer fruit. Alternating various fruits according to color, dip the fruit into the orange juice and place in the jar. After using all the fruit, pour any leftover orange juice over all. Cover and refrigerate.

Serve a portion of each fruit and pass the raspberry sauce on the side.

SERVES 6 TO 8

ORANGE, COCONUT, AND DATE AMBROSIA

Banana or fresh pineapple or both could be added to this.

5 navel oranges, peeled
1 cup freshly grated coconut
5 large medjhool dates, cut into quarters
2 tablespoons sugar
1 cup fresh orange juice

Dip peeled oranges into boiling water for 20 seconds. This will make it easier to scrape off the remaining pith after oranges are peeled. Cut each slice into quarters. Place in a glass bowl. Add coconut, dates, and sugar. Pour orange juice over all and toss. Refrigerate until ready to serve.

SERVES 6

PAPAYA, BANANA, AND COCONUT AMBROSIA

I'm especially fond of papaya and banana together—and with a sprinkling of coconut, it's even better. Now, if you are making this far ahead, chill just the papaya and orange juice mix. Add the bananas at the last minute.

2 papayas, peeled, seeded, and cut into
    chunks
2 bananas, peeled and cut into thick slices
6 tablespoons fresh orange juice
6 tablespoons or more grated fresh coconut

Combine papayas, bananas, and orange juice. Chill for 30 minutes or more. Divide among 6 chilled dishes and sprinkle with coconut.

SERVES 6

POACHED FRUIT

POACHED ORANGES

6 oranges
1/2 cup (firmly packed) brown sugar
1/4 cup cider vinegar
2 cup water
1/2 stick cinnamon
6 whole cloves

To peel oranges, dip in boiling water for 1 minute. Remove and, using a sharp paring knife, scrape off the white pith. Slice each orange into 4 slices and place in heatproof bowl.

In a small saucepan over medium heat, combine the sugar, vinegar, water, cinnamon, and cloves. Bring to a boil, lower heat, and simmer for 3 to 5 minutes. Pour syrup over sliced oranges. Allow to sit until cool. Serve at room temperature or refrigerate.

SERVES 6

POACHED APRICOTS, PINK PEPPERCORNS, AND MINT WITH CRÈME FRAÎCHE

I never serve fresh apricots unless they are at the very height of their season. Like peaches, they are often mealy when they have not been allowed to ripen naturally—and I think there is nothing worse.

2 cups water
2 tablespoons pink peppercorns
1 1/2 cups sugar
18 to 24 ripe apricots, depending on size
4 fresh mint sprigs, tied (optional)
Crème fraîche or Devonshire cream

Bring water to a boil and add peppercorns. Simmer for a few minutes, then add sugar. When sugar is well dissolved, add apricots. Cook until just tender; the time will vary according to the size and age of the fruit, but use the point of a sharp knife to test for doneness.

Remove the apricots with a slotted spoon, place in a bowl, and bury the mint in the fruit. Pour the syrup and peppercorns over, then let cool. Discard mint and refrigerate fruit.

Serve the apricots with crème fraîche or Devonshire (clotted) cream.

SERVES 6

GINGERED PEACHES

You can substitute figs for the peaches here if they are in season. They are just as good, but probably are more expensive unless you live in South or West. Serve the peaches with Pecan Tiles (page 450).

2 1/2 cups water
2 cups sugar
3 tablespoons finely chopped peeled fresh
  ginger
6 tree-ripened unblemished peaches

Mix water and sugar in a saucepan over medium heat. When simmering, add ginger. Simmer very slowly for 10 minutes.

Meanwhile, plunge peaches into boiling water for about 10 seconds and then slip off skins. Slide peaches into the boiling syrup and simmer slowly, carefully turning occasionally so peaches poach evenly. When tender—in about 10 minutes—let cool in the syrup. Transfer to a glass container with a slotted spoon and pour syrup over all. Refrigerate until ready to use.

SERVES 6

463

POACHED PEARS WITH RASPBERRY-CARAMEL SAUCE

3 cups water
1 bottle fumé blanc or other dry white wine
Rinds of 4 lemons
2 teaspoons vanilla extract
2 cups sugar
¼ to ⅓ cup honey may be substituted
*6 medium pears, carefully peeled with stems
     on and bottoms cut off so they will sit flat
     on the plate, then rubbed with lemon
     juice*
Raspberry-Caramel Sauce (page 363)
Fresh berries (optional)
Mint leaves (optional)
Whipped cream (optional)

Put water, wine, lemon rind, vanilla, sugar, and honey in a deep saucepan and bring quickly to a boil. Turn back to a simmer and lower pears in carefully. Poach, uncovered, until pears are tender, about 15 minutes. Cool in the poaching liquid, then drain.

Serve individually on plates slicked with sauce. Garnish with fresh berries, mint leaves, and a dab of whipped cream if desired.
SERVES 6

PEPPERMINT PEARS

Serve these pears with Brown Sugar Shortbread (page 454).

¾ cup sugar
¾ cup water
½ lemon, cut into several pieces
*6 medium pears (preferably, Anjou), cored,
     peeled, and halved*
4 or 5 large sprigs of fresh peppermint, tied
Sprigs of fresh mint
*Crème fraîche or yogurt sprinkled with
     cinnamon*

Combine sugar and water in a saucepan and bring to a boil. Drop in lemon pieces and simmer for about 5 minutes. Add pears and simmer until tender but not mushy.

Remove pears with a slotted spoon, place in a bowl, and bury the mint bundle among them. Pour syrup over all and let cool. Refrigerate.

To serve, discard mint and garnish pears with a sprig of fresh mint and a dollop of crème fraîche or yogurt sprinkled with cinnamon if desired or serve plain in the syrup.
SERVES 6

POACHED CHERRIES AND PLUMS

This basic poaching liquid may be used to cook any combination of fruit. Serve the fruit with Shortbread (page 454).

2 cups cold water
2 cups sugar
12 peppercorns
2 cinnamon sticks (optional)
8 whole cloves (optional)
2 cups dry white wine
12 assorted plums
1 cup fresh cherries, with stems if possible

Combine water and sugar in a pot large enough to hold the fruit. Simmer over medium heat until the sugar is dissolved, then add peppercorns, cinnamon sticks, and cloves. Simmer over lowest heat for another 5 minutes. Add wine, increase heat, and bring to a light boil. Add fruit, and simmer until it is just tender, about 3 to 5 minutes, depending on the age and kind of fruit. Do not overcook.

Remove fruit to a glass bowl with a slotted spoon. When cool, remove loosened plum skins if desired. Do not try to skin cherries. Meanwhile, reduce the poaching liquid over high heat until thickened slightly, about 15 minutes. Cool and pour over fruit.
SERVES 6

PERFECT POACHED PEARS

This poaching liquid may be reused over and over. Just strain it after each use and keep it refrigerated. It is good for poaching peaches, apples, and apricots as well as pears. Incidentally, at the end of its usefulness (when enough has been cooked away so you can't poach anymore), this liquid can be reduced and used as an ice-cream topping.

POACHING LIQUID
3 bottles muscat blanc, or 1 1/2 bottles plus
    4 3/4 cups water
1 whole nutmeg
1 whole cinnamon stick
1 large bay leaf
1 vanilla bean, split lengthwise
1 1/2 teaspoons whole cloves
1 1/2 teaspoons whole cardamom seeds
1 1/2 teaspoons whole allspice
1 tablespoon chopped fresh ginger
1 medium lemon, quartered

5 medium pears, peeled and cored with
    stems attached (see Note)

1 recipe Spiced Whipped Cream (page 365)
Mint leaves (optional)

Combine the poaching ingredients in a nonreactive saucepan and simmer for 30 minutes. Strain out solids and set liquid aside.

Place poaching liquid and pears in a deep nonreactive saucepan and weight down with a saucer that can withstand high heat. (This is to keep pears submerged.) Bring to a simmer and poach until pears are tender but not falling apart, 10 to 20 minutes. Place entire pot in the refrigerator until pears are chilled.

To serve, make a bed of the whipped cream on individual plates and add drained pears. Garnish near the stems with a mint leaf (held in place with a dab of cream) if you wish.

Note: The extra pear is insurance in case you have an accident with one.
SERVES 4

POACHED APRICOTS WITH PEAR PURÉE

This makes a very pretty dessert and can be arranged on individual plates in the kitchen.

14 small fresh apricots
Simple Syrup (page 371)
1 cinnamon stick (optional)
1 whole clove (optional)
3 ripe pears
1 tablespoon fresh lemon juice
Grated zest of 1/2 lemon
Grind of nutmeg
Lemon zest strips (optional)
Mint sprigs (optional)

Dip apricots into hot water for a few minutes and skin them. Put in a saucepan with enough simple syrup to just cover. Add cinnamon and clove if using. Simmer gently until just tender and then let cool in the syrup. Refrigerate in the syrup.

Peel and core the pears. (If you are not going to make the purée immediately, rub the outside of the pears with lemon juice.) Cut each pear into 4 pieces and put them in a food processor. Remove the pits from 2 of the poached apricots, and put apricots in with the pears. Add lemon juice, zest, and nutmeg and processor to a coarse purée.

To serve, put a spoonful of purée on each plate and top with 2 apricots and more purée. Decorate with lemon strips and mint sprigs if desired.
SERVES 6

POACHED DRIED FRUIT

If you can't find the dried strips of orange, substitute the julienne zest of one orange.

3 cups dried fruit (pears, apricots, peaches,
    pitted prunes, and papaya), quartered or
    halved (uniform in size)
1/4 cup soft, dried strips of orange
1 1/2 cups sugar
3 cups water
4 whole peppercorns
Zest of 1 orange, cut into julienne

Arrange the dried fruit mixture and the dried orange in a heatproof glass bowl large enough to hold both the fruit and the liquid.

Combine sugar and water in a medium saucepan. Stir over low heat to dissolve sugar. Raise heat and bring to a boil. Pour this syrup over dried fruit and let cool.

When fruit has cooled, drain syrup into saucepan and add peppercorns and orange zest julienne. Bring to a boil and reduce by half. Arrange fruit in individual bowls, spoon syrup over each portion, and serve.

SERVES 6

APPLE DUMPLINGS WITH ALMOND SAUCE

This recipe came to me from Mrs. Yvonne LeBoeuf of Houma, Louisiana, who said it has been in her family for over a hundred years. The dumpling dough is very stiff and dense; it probably must be that way to keep it from dissolving during the cooking time.

DUMPLINGS

3 cups coarsely chopped, peeled tart apples
Grated zest of 1 lemon
3 3/4 cups sifted unbleached all-purpose flour
1 1/2 tablespoons baking powder
3/4 cup cold milk
2 large eggs, lightly beaten
Whipped cream flavored with vanilla
    (optional)

ALMOND SAUCE

4 cups water
8 tablespoons (1 stick) unsalted butter
8 tablespoons (1 stick) margarine
3/4 cup sugar
Pinch of salt
3/4 teaspoon vanilla extract
3/4 cup slivered almonds

Preheat oven to 350 degrees.

Combine chopped apples and lemon zest in a bowl. Set aside.

Sift flour and baking powder into the bowl of a food processor fitted with a metal blade. Combine milk and eggs and add to flour all at once. Process until the mixture clings together and forms a ball. This makes a very stiff dough. Roll out dough on a floured surface until very thin. Cut dough into twelve 4-inch squares and place a tablespoon of the apple mixture in the middle of each. Bring the 4 corners of each square together, slightly twisting and squeezing to seal. Make 12 dumplings, discarding any scraps of dough (see Note). Place dumplings in a deep 9- to 10-inch baking dish or ovenproof casserole, squeezing together if necessary. Sprinkle leftover chopped apple over all and set aside.

To make sauce: Bring the water to a boil in a medium saucepan and add butter, margarine, sugar, salt, and vanilla. Cook until dissolved. Sprinkle almonds over the dumplings and then pour liquid over dumplings.

Bake, uncovered, about 1 hour, or until the dumplings are golden and the sauce is reduced. Serve dumplings with sauce spooned over each portion. They may also be topped with flavored whipped cream.

Note: Since this dough is so stiff and dry, it is hard to utilize the scraps for rerolling. I have purposely made the quantity of dough generous to account for this.

SERVES 6 TO 12

SOUFFLÉS AND MOUSSES

TRIPLE CHOCOLATE TERRINE WITH CRÈME ANGLAISE AND RASPBERRY SAUCE

Chocolate lovers, here it is!

10 ounces bittersweet chocolate
4 ounces milk chocolate
3 ounces white chocolate
³/₄ teaspoon unflavored gelatin
¹/₄ cup water
¹/₂ cup plus 2 tablespoons warm
  Crème Anglaise (page 366)
2 egg whites
3 tablespoons sugar
¹/₂ cup plus 2 tablespoons heavy cream
¹/₂ cup finely ground walnuts
Crème Anglaise
Raspberry Sauce

Place chocolates in a bowl over hot water and melt, stirring occasionally. Dissolve gelatin in the water and add to the crème anglaise. Stir this mixture into the chocolates and set aside.

Whip egg whites and sugar until they become stiff. Set aside.

In a large bowl, whip the cream until stiff. Fold in the chocolate mixture until incorporated completely. Fold in egg whites, then fold in walnuts. Pour into a 9 × 5-inch loaf pan 2³/₄ inches deep. Cover with plastic wrap and refrigerate overnight.

When ready to serve the terrine, dip the pan in hot water for about 15 seconds and turn out onto a serving dish. The terrine may not come out the first try; tap the pan over the platter until it does, or if it is really reluctant, dip it in hot water again. Once unmolded, smooth top of terrine with a spatula and refrigerate to set again, about 30 minutes. Slice with a knife dipped into hot water and serve with crème anglaise and raspberry sauce.
SERVES 8

COLD BERRY SOUFFLÉ

6 large eggs, separated, at room
  temperature
¹/₂ cup granulated sugar
1 tablespoon unflavored gelatin
1 cup puréed berries
1 tablespoon kirsch
1 cup heavy cream
¹/₄ cup confectioners' sugar
¹/₄ cup cream of tartar
¹/₄ teaspoon salt
Whole berries for serving
Quick Raspberry Sauce (page 363)
  (optional)

Put an oiled wax paper collar around a 6-cup soufflé dish. (If you don't want to bother with a collar, use a slightly larger dish.)

Place egg yolks, granulated sugar, and gelatin in a bowl and beat until light and thick. Put mixture in the top of a double boiler and stir in berry purée. Cook over barely boiling water just long enough to dissolve the sugar and gelatin, several minutes, then set aside to cool.

Stir kirsch into the egg–berry mixture. Whip the cream, adding confectioners' sugar, one tablespoon at a time, until stiff. Fold cream into the berry mixture.

Beat egg whites until foamy. Add cream of tartar and salt and continue to beat until soft peaks form. Fold the whites into the berry mixture and pour into the prepared soufflé dish. Refrigerate for several hours, or until set.

Serve the soufflé topped with additional berries and Quick Raspberry Sauce if desired.
SERVES 6 TO 8

FROZEN LIME SOUFFLÉ

I prefer a boysenberry sauce for this soufflé, but blackberries or raspberries could be substituted.

1 cup sugar
¼ cup water
6 egg yolks
Juice of 3 medium lemons
Juice of 4 medium limes
2 cups heavy cream
Boysenberry Sauce (page 365)
Fresh mint leaves (optional)
Candied lime peel (optional)

Tie baking paper collars around six ½-cup ramekins to extend 1 inch above the rim.

Combine sugar and water in a small saucepan. Stir to dissolve and place over high heat until mixture boils. Do not stir. (It might crystallize.) Continue to boil until mixture reaches 240 degrees or the soft-ball stage. Remove from heat.

Meanwhile, with a heavy-duty mixer, beat egg yolks until pale and thick. With mixer running, add the hot sugar syrup in a steady steam. Continue to beat until bowl reaches room temperature, about 15 minutes. Beat in lemon and lime juices. Separately, beat cream to soft peaks and gently fold into the yolk mixture. Divide among the ramekins and freeze for at least 4 hours. Serve with sauce and garnish with mint and candied lime peel if you wish.

SERVES 6

CAROL'S CHOCOLATE SOUFFLÉ

Many people consider chocolate soufflé the ultimate dessert. Classically, the soufflé must be put together at the last minute, which can be a forbidding chore for most home chefs. In Carol Cutler's recipe (from her book called *Cuisine Rapide*), this grand finale can be presented with ease, since it can wait in the mold several hours before going into the oven.

1 tablespoon unsalted butter, softened
¾ cup sugar
½ cup water
1 tablespoon instant coffee
6 ounces semisweet chocolate
6 eggs (see Note)
½ cup heavy cream
1 tablespoon Grand Marnier or other orange liqueur
12 ounces cream cheese, softened

Preheat oven to 375 degrees.

Liberally grease with butter a 6-cup soufflé dish or other mold. Sprinkle in ¼ cup of the sugar and rotate the mold to coat it evenly. If any spot is left uncoated, butter it and sprinkle on a little more sugar. Shake out the excess.

Put the remaining ½ cup sugar, water, coffee, and chocolate in a small saucepan and melt together over low heat. Remove from heat and let cool slightly.

Break eggs into a blender jar and add cream and Grand Marnier. Blend for about 30 seconds, or until eggs and cream are thoroughly mixed. With the blender running, scrape in melted chocolate and then the cream cheese, breaking the cheese into chunks to add it. When the batter is completely mixed, blend at high speed for a few seconds.

Pour the batter into the prepared dish (it will be about three-quarters full) and put in the hot oven. Bake for 50 to 60 minutes for a soufflé that is still moist in the center. Test by gently

468

shaking the dish. If the center is still soft, it will jiggle. An absolutely flat or slightly convex surface indicates that the soufflé has been cooked firm throughout. This means you will not have the soft center to use as a sauce over the baked portions.

Notes: For a lighter soufflé, use 2 additional egg whites.

This soufflé can be prepared several hours in advance, poured into the mold, and kept in a cool spot. If the kitchen is very hot, put the soufflé in the refrigerator; but allow an extra 5 minutes for the baking.

SERVES 6 TO 8

BLACKBERRY MOUSSE

You could use other berries for this or even a combination of several kinds. And you can always try it with fresh berries.

1 pound frozen blackberries
1 cup sugar
2 tablespoons fresh lemon juice
2 tablespoons water
1 envelope unflavored gelatin
1 cup heavy cream, whipped
4 large egg whites, beaten until stiff but not dry
Sprigs of fresh mint

Combine berries, sugar, and lemon juice in a nonreactive saucepan. Bring to a boil over medium heat. Remove from heat and let cool. Purée and set aside.

Put the water in a small saucer and sprinkle the gelatin over it. Set aside for a few minutes.

Stir the softened gelatin into the berry purée. Fold in whipped cream. Fold in beaten egg whites. Place in individual goblets or in a soufflé dish and refrigerate for at least 1 hour before serving.

Serve garnished with fresh mint.

SERVES 8

LEMON MOUSSE WITH BERRY PURÉE

I think this looks best in two separate bowls rather than one large one. If you don't use one of them, you can freeze it. (You should eat a frozen mousse before it thaws completely.)

2 envelopes unflavored gelatin
Juice and grated zest of 4 large lemons (you should have ½ cup juice)
10 eggs, separated
1½ cups superfine sugar
1½ cups heavy cream
Pinch of salt

BERRY PURÉE
Raspberries, strawberries, or blueberries, or a combination
Sugar, to taste
Crème de cassis (optional)

In a small saucepan, sprinkle gelatin over lemon juice and let soften for 5 minutes.

Meanwhile, beat egg yolks until they are light yellow and gradually add 1 cup of the superfine sugar, beating all the while. Stir in lemon zest.

Melt the gelatin mixture over low heat until the gelatin dissolves; do not let it boil. Let cool for a few minutes. Drizzle gelatin mixture over egg yolks and mix well. Set aside to cool thoroughly.

Beat cream until stiff and fold it gently into the cooled egg yolk mixture.

Beat egg whites with salt until stiff. Gradually add remaining ½ cup superfine sugar, beating constantly. Fold egg whites into the cream mixture. Divide the mousse between two bowls and refrigerate for at least 3 hours.

To make berry purée: Purée berries in a food processor or blender and add sugar along with a dash of cassis if desired.

SERVES 8

TANGERINE MOUSSE

I am very partial to the flavor of tangerines; it is not as sharp as that of regular oranges. And now that tangerine juice can be bought frozen, this dessert almost makes itself.

6 eggs, separated
1/2 cup sugar
1 tablespoon gelatin
1 cup frozen tangerine juice concentrate, thawed
Grated zest of 1 orange
2 tablespoons Grand Marnier
1 cup heavy cream
4 tablespoons confectioners' sugar
1/4 teaspoon cream of tartar
1/4 teaspoon salt
Cooked Berry Sauce (page 363)
Fresh berries

Put egg yolks in a bowl with sugar and gelatin. Beat until light in color and thickened. Pour this into the top of a double boiler and add juice and orange zest. Heat just enough to dissolve the gelatin and sugar. Do not allow to boil or the egg might curdle. Set aside to cool. When cool, stir in the Grand Marnier.

Start whipping the cream and then add confectioners' sugar. Continue whipping until cream forms stiff peaks. Pour it over the egg–juice mixture. Fold in carefully.

Whip egg whites until foamy, then add cream of tartar and salt. Continue whipping until it forms soft peaks. Fold this into the other mixture. Pour into a 6-cup soufflé dish and refrigerate, covered with plastic wrap, until set— or better still, overnight. Serve with berry sauce and garnish with a few fresh berries.

Note: For a more impressive presentation, use a soufflé dish with shorter sides and tie a lightly oiled parchment paper collar around it (or use plain wax paper). When you remove the collar, the soufflé will have set and will be sticking up slightly above the dish.

SERVES 6 TO 8

FLANS AND CUSTARDS

COCONUT CARAMEL FLAN

Flans are always a welcome treat after a spicy meal. This one is very rich but especially nice.

2 cups sugar
2 tablespoons water
1/2 teaspoon fresh lemon juice
4 1/3 cups milk
1 vanilla bean, split lengthwise
4 whole eggs plus 8 egg yolks
7 ounces shredded unsweetened coconut, toasted

Preheat oven to 325 degrees.

In a small saucepan, combine 1 cup of the sugar with the water and lemon juice. Over low heat, bring to a boil, then raise heat to medium and cook without stirring for 8 to 10 minutes, until golden. Quickly pour into an ungreased 8-cup mold. Using a pot holder, swirl caramel around until it cools, coating the bottom and sides of the mold.

Bring milk and vanilla bean to a boil. Remove bean and set pan off the heat. In a large mixing bowl, beat eggs, yolks, and remaining cup of sugar until well blended. Stirring constantly, add the hot milk and coconut. Pour into the prepared mold and place in larger ovenproof pan. Surround with hot water. Bake about 1 hour, until a knife inserted in the center comes out clean. Remove from the hot water bath and let cool.

To serve, run a sharp knife around the mold and turn out onto a dish with a lip, being careful not to spill melted caramel as you do. Cool slightly before serving.

SERVES 8

COCONUT FLAN

The secret ingredient in this dessert is the coconut milk, which lends a very subtle taste. It is often available in health food stores. Do not use sweetened coconut cream. This dessert is best eaten the day it is cooked.

3/4 cup sugar
2 tablespoons water
4 large eggs, plus 1 egg yolk, at room temperature
2 cups canned unsweetened coconut milk or milk
1 cup heavy cream
1/2 cup shredded fresh coconut (or more)

Preheat oven to 300 degrees.

Mix 1/2 cup of the sugar with the water in a saucepan and bring to boil over medium heat. Continue cooking until the mixture begins to caramelize, stirring all the while with a wooden spoon. When it is dark golden, pour into a 4 1/2- to 6-cup ring mold. Using a pot holder (or metal tongs) to hold it, tilt the mold to coat the inside. Continue tilting and turning until the liquid sets. Set aside.

Lightly beat together eggs and egg yolk. Set aside.

Scald coconut milk and cream together in a large saucepan. Lightly beat the remaining 1/4 cup sugar into the eggs. Put a few tablespoons of the milk mixture into the egg mixture to heat it, then add warmed eggs to the milk. Mix well.

Sprinkle coconut into the prepared mold and strain the cream mixture through a sieve into it. Place mold in a roasting pan, surround with hot water, and bake for about 50 minutes, or until set. Let cool, then cover and refrigerate. Flan should be served cold.
SERVES 6 TO 8

VARIATION

To make espresso flan, omit coconut and add a tablespoon of powdered instant espresso to the mixture before pouring it into the mold. Serve in a pool of Irish Coffee Sauce (page 368).

CHOCOLATE MACADAMIA FLAN

3/4 cup sugar
3 tablespoons water
1 cup coarsely chopped macadamia nuts, toasted
3 large eggs, plus 3 egg yolks
3 cups half-and-half
6 ounces semisweet chocolate, coarsely chopped
1 1/2 teaspoons instant espresso powder
1 1/2 teaspoons vanilla extract
Whipped cream, sweetened and flavored with vanilla, Grand Marnier, or framboise

Preheat oven to 300 degrees.

Combine 1/2 cup of the sugar with the water in a small saucepan and bring to a boil. Cook over medium-low heat, stirring occasionally, until syrup begins to caramelize, about 6 minutes. When dark golden, pour into a 6-cup metal ring mold. Working quickly and using a pot holder, tilt the mold around to coat the bottom and sides as the syrup cools. When completely cooled, sprinkle with nuts and set aside.

Lightly beat together eggs and yolks and set aside.

Scald the half-and-half in the top of a double boiler. Stir in chocolate, remaining sugar, espresso powder, and vanilla. Continue stirring until the chocolate is melted. Slowly pour milk mixture into the eggs, stirring. Pour through a strainer, then into the mold. Place mold in a larger ovenproof pan and surround with boiling water. Bake until set, about 40 to 50 minutes. Let cool and refrigerate, covered.

To serve, loosen edges of flan with a knife. Invert onto a serving plate, and if flan doesn't come out with a gentle shake, very sharply shake down to unmold.

Serve with a dollop of the flavored whipped cream.
SERVES 8

HONEY CUSTARD

I bet you'll be surprised at how tasty this very easy little custard is. You'll probably make it often once you give it a try.

> 2 cups milk
> 1/4 cup honey
> 1 teaspoon vanilla extract
> 3 large eggs
> Pinch of salt
> Grinding of nutmeg or sprinkling of cinnamon
> Cooked Berry Sauce (page 363) or flavored whipped cream (see pages 365 to 366)

Preheat oven to 375 degrees. Generously butter 6 individual 1/2-cup custard cups. Set aside.

Scald milk, being careful not to scorch it. Off the heat, stir in honey and then vanilla. Beat eggs and salt together, then stir in several tablespoons of the milk mixture to warm the eggs. While continuing to stir, pour the warmed eggs into the milk. Add nutmeg or cinnamon and strain through a sieve into the prepared cups. Place cups in a shallow baking pan and surround with boiling water.

Bake custards for 40 minutes, or until a knife inserted into the center comes out clean. Let cool out of the water. Refrigerate covered.

Serve in the cups, or unmold the custards by running a knife around the edge of each, inverting them over individual plates, and, holding them in place firmly, giving them a sharp downward shake. Top with a berry sauce or flavored whipped cream.

SERVES 6

APPLE–ALMOND CUSTARD

You might substitute some other nut for the almonds and pears for apples as a variation on this easy dessert.

> 1 1/2 Golden Delicious apples, peeled, cored, and coarsely chopped
> 2 tablespoons sugar
> 2 tablespoons unsalted butter
> 6 tablespoons coarsely ground almonds
> 1 cup milk
> 2 tablespoons honey
> 2 large eggs
> 1/4 teaspoon salt
> 1 teaspoon calvados or vanilla extract
> Sweetened puréed fruit (optional)
> Flavored whipped cream (see pages 365 to 366)

Preheat oven to 350 degrees. Generously butter six 1/2-cup ovenproof custard cups. Place cups in an ovenproof pan large enough to hold them comfortably.

Divide chopped apple among the cups. Sprinkle each with a teaspoon of sugar and place a teaspoon of butter on each. Surround the cups with warm tap water and bake for 25 minutes, until apples are tender and just beginning to brown very slightly. Sprinkle each with a generous tablespoon of ground almonds. Return to oven for another 5 minutes.

Meanwhile, scald milk and stir in honey. Lightly beat eggs and pour into the milk, stirring. Add salt and calvados, mixing well. Strain mixture into the 6 cups, filling each.

Bake for 30 minutes, or until a knife comes out clean when inserted into the middle of the custard. Let cool and refrigerate until ready to serve.

To serve, run a knife around the edges of the cups and invert onto individual dessert plates. Holding the cup in place, give it a little shake to get custard to come out.

You may top these with a little sweetened puréed fruit or a dab of flavored whipped cream (or both) if you like.

SERVES 6

FRESH FIG BAKED CUSTARD

I know figs are expensive during the colder months, but it really doesn't take too many to make a cup, and that's all you need here.

1 cup sugar
6 tablespoons all-purpose flour
2¹/₂ teaspoons baking powder
Pinch of salt
2 eggs, lightly beaten
1 teaspoon vanilla extract
1 teaspoon bourbon
1 cup chopped pecans
1 cup steamed and mashed fresh figs
1 teaspoon grated lemon zest
Heavy cream (optional)

Preheat oven to 350 degrees. Generously butter an 8-inch square baking pan. Set aside.

Mix sugar, flour, baking powder, and salt in a large bowl. Combine beaten eggs, vanilla, and bourbon. Pour into dry ingredients, stirring. Add pecans, figs, and lemon zest. Continue to mix (with a hand mixer) until very well blended, several minutes.

Pour and scrape mixture into prepared pan and bake for 30 to 35 minutes, or until a knife inserted in middle comes out clean.

Serve as is, or with a topping of heavy cream, either whipped or not.

SERVES 6

JUBILEE CUSTARD

Sherrye Henry told me this is one of the family recipes she took with her from Tennessee when she got married. It makes a beautiful dessert.

1 envelope unflavored gelatin
3 tablespoons cold water
1¹/₄ cups milk
Dash of salt
2 large eggs, separated, at room temperature
1 teaspoon vanilla extract
¹/₄ cup sugar
1 cup heavy cream
Berry and Black Cherry Sauce (page 364)

Stir gelatin into the cold water and set aside. While gelatin is dissolving, combine milk and salt in a double boiler and heat slowly.

Meanwhile, lightly beat egg yolks and stir in a few tablespoons of the heated milk to warm them. Stirring all the while, slowly pour the warmed yolks into the milk and continue to cook, stirring, over barely boiling water until slightly thickened. Add the softened gelatin and stir until completely dissolved. Remove from the heat and add vanilla. Mix and let cool until just beginning to thicken.

Beat egg whites until stiff, adding sugar one tablespoon at a time. Set aside for a minute while you whip the cream. Fold the beaten egg whites and whipped cream into the custard mixture. Coat the inside of 6-cup mold with vegetable cooking spray and pour custard in. Refrigerate until set.

To serve, unmold (this may take a firm shake) and accompany with cherry sauce.

SERVES 8

BRANDY CUSTARD WITH FRESH BERRIES

This recipe came to me from a friend who had gotten it from her grandmother. I've tried many old recipes and have discovered that many of the desserts are sweeter than similar ones popular today. For that reason, I have reduced the amount of sugar called for in the original.

2 cups whole milk
2 eggs, separated
1/2 to 3/4 cup sugar
2 tablespoons all-purpose flour
1 tablespoon brandy, or more to taste
Freshly grated nutmeg
Fresh raspberries or other berries

Bring milk to boil in a double boiler. Beat egg yolks well and mix with half the sugar and the flour. Stir into the hot milk. Continue to stir until thickened. Strain immediately.

Beat egg whites until very stiff and add the remaining sugar. Beat long enough to incorporate. Stir into the custard mixture. Add brandy and pour into six 1/2-cup custard pots. Top with nutmeg. Fresh berries can be sprinkled on top or served on the side. This custard may be chilled slightly but should not be refrigerated for long.
SERVES 6 TO 8

COEUR DE CRÈME

Mardee Regan, who worked with me on my *Country Desserts* book, gave me this recipe, her own variation of classic *coeur de crème*. You'll love it. Serve it with sweetened fresh fruit.

8 ounces cream cheese, softened
3/4 cup sifted confectioners' sugar
1 teaspoon fresh lime juice
1 teaspoon grated lemon zest
1 teaspoon vanilla extract
1 tablespoon framboise
1 1/4 cups heavy cream, whipped

Beat cream cheese with a hand mixer until fluffy, then beat in confectioners' sugar, lime juice, and lemon zest. Mix vanilla and framboise into the whipped cream and then add to cream cheese mixture.

Line a *coeur de crème* mold or a closely woven basket with a double layer of dampened fine cheesecloth. Pour in mixture and smooth top. Cover with a layer of dampened cheesecloth and place the mold or basket on a plate and allow the *coeur de crème* to "weep" in the refrigerator overnight. Discard any liquid.
SERVES 6

CHOCOLATE POTS DE CRÈME

This is fairly rich, so plan on serving small portions—as good as it is.

1/4 cup sugar
2 cups light cream or half-and-half
Dash of salt
8 ounces semisweet or bittersweet chocolate, grated
4 egg yolks
1 teaspoon vanilla extract
Flavored whipped cream (see pages 365 to 366)

Place sugar, cream, salt, and chocolate in the top of a double boiler and melt over very low heat for 30 minutes, stirring often. Meanwhile, beat yolks until thick and cream colored. Spoon a little of the chocolate mixture into the yolks and mix. While beating, pour the balance of the chocolate mixture slowly into the yolks. Return mixture to the double boiler and cook another 30 minutes, stirring, or until thick. Stir in vanilla.

Pour 1/4 cup of chocolate mixture into each of 8 small *pot de crème* cups. When slightly cool, cover and refrigerate for 4 to 6 hours until firm.

Top each serving with a dab of flavored whipped cream.

SERVES 8

AMARETTI-MASCARPONE CUSTARD

Mascarpone cheese is soft and creamy and makes an excellent base for this simple Italian dessert.

3 egg yolks
1/2 pound mascarpone cheese, at room temperature
1 tablespoon fresh lemon juice
1/4 cup sugar
1/3 cup brandy
8 whole amaretti cookies
4 egg whites, at room temperature

Combine egg yolks and cheese in a bowl and mix thoroughly. Add lemon juice and sugar and mix. Set aside.

In a bowl, sprinkle brandy over 8 lightly crushed amaretti halves (the other halves are used later) and set aside.

Beat egg whites until stiff. Add the crushed cookies to the cheese mixture in 4 batches and mix. Gently fold in egg whites.

Pour into individual custard cups and top each with a cookie half. Refrigerate for at least 1 hour.

SERVES 8

PUDDINGS

BUTTERSCOTCH PUDDING

This is real butterscotch pudding because it has Scotch whiskey in it.

6 tablespoons (3/4 stick) unsalted butter
1 1/4 cups (firmly packed) dark brown sugar
3 cups milk
1/4 cup plus 2 tablespoons cornstarch
1/2 teaspoon salt
3 large egg yolk s, lightly beaten
1 teaspoon vanilla extract
3 tablespoons mild Scotch whiskey
1/2 cup chopped walnuts (optional)
Whipped cream flavored with vanilla extract (optional)

Combine butter and brown sugar in a large saucepan and cook over moderate heat until smooth. Add 2 1/2 cups of the milk and continue to cook until steam rises from the surface.

Meanwhile, mix remaining 1/2 cup milk with the cornstarch and salt. Stir until smooth, then add to the butter mixture. Cook, stirring, until very thick, about 10 minutes.

Stir about 1/2 cup of the warm mixture into the egg yolks to warm them, then stir warmed yolks into the pudding. Cook for 3 minutes, stirring.

Remove from the heat and add vanilla and whiskey (and walnuts if using). Pour into 6 dessert glasses and chill. Puddings may be topped with a dab of flavored whipped cream.

SERVES 4 TO 6

SUMMER PUDDING

I had never made a summer pudding until several years ago, but now I am a convert. I think you will be, too, if you aren't already. Use almost any combination of berries you have on hand; here, I use a combination of blueberries and strawberries.

*1½ pounds combined blueberries and
   strawberries
Grated zest of 1 lemon
¼ cup plus 2 tablespoons sugar
5 or more slices white bread, crusts trimmed
Whipped cream flavored with vanilla
   extract*

Remove stems and pick over berries, cutting the strawberries in half. Combine fruit with the lemon zest and sugar in a small nonaluminum saucepan. Cover and simmer for 10 minutes. Take care, lest the whole thing boil over when it starts to cook.

Cut each slice of bread into 3 strips and line the bottom and sides of a 4-cup soufflé dish (patching with pieces of bread if necessary). Strain the fruit pulp, reserving the juice. Pour several tablespoons of the juice over the bottom slices of bread and let it set for a few minutes.

Fill the soufflé dish almost to the top with fruit pulp, then pour in enough juice to moisten. Cover top with a layer of bread and dampen this with a little juice, too. Put a small plate, which just fits inside the dish, on top and wrap the whole thing in plastic wrap. Set on a plate in the refrigerator with a weight on top. (A large can may be used as a weight.) Leave for 24 hours.

To serve, run a knife around the edges and invert the dish onto a serving platter, being careful not to spill the accumulated juice. If juice has not stained all the bread through, you may do so with the reserved juice.

Serve with whipped cream and reserved juice.

SERVES 4

BANANA CLAFOUTI

Clafouti is traditionally made with fresh black cherries, but I thought it might be fun to give this old-timer a new twist.

*5 tablespoons sugar
3 large firm but ripe bananas
2 cups half-and-half
3 eggs, beaten
¼ cup all-purpose flour
1 tablespoon finely grated orange zest
1 teaspoon vanilla extract
¼ teaspoon salt
Confectioners' sugar*

Preheat oven to 375 degrees.

Butter an 8 × 8-inch or 10 × 7-inch shallow baking dish. Sprinkle 2 tablespoons of the sugar in the bottom. Cut each banana into 3 long strips and line the bottom of the dish with them.

In a bowl, beat together all the remaining ingredients, except the confectioners' sugar, and pour carefully over the bananas. Bake for 40 to 50 minutes, or until puffed and golden. Let cool on a rack for 15 minutes. Sift confectioners' sugar over the top for garnish.

SERVES 6

PUMPKIN PUDDING

1 cup sugar
2 cups whole milk
1½ tablespoons all-purpose flour
6 tablespoons solid-packed canned pumpkin
¼ teaspoon ground cinnamon
¼ teaspoon freshly grated nutmeg
⅛ teaspoon ground cloves
⅛ teaspoon ground allspice
2 egg yolks, lightly beaten
2 tablespoons unsalted butter, at room temperature
2 teaspoon vanilla extract

Whisk together sugar, milk, flour, pumpkin, and spices in a heavy saucepan, making sure everything is well dissolved into the milk. Place over medium heat and, using a wooden spoon, stir the mixture slowly until it begins to boil. This will take about 15 minutes. Continue to boil for another 2 to 3 minutes, being careful not boil over.

Remove the pan from the heat. Pour about ½ cup of the hot mixture into the egg yolks, whisking well to temper the yolks. When the mixture is smooth, add it to the main pudding mixture and return the pot to the heat. Stir until thickened slightly, about 1 or 2 minutes.

Take the pan off the heat, add butter and vanilla, and stir to incorporate.

Pour the hot pudding into 6 small ramekins or dessert bowls. Cool on a rack until room temperature. Refrigerate until ready to serve.
SERVES 6

CHOCOLATE STEAMED PUDDING

Mrs. John Thomas of Austin, Texas, had this recipe with her when she was still Mary Fulton Berry. That was at the turn of the century, when she was brought from Scotland to America by her family.

1 cup sifted all-purpose flour
2 teaspoons baking powder
1 tablespoon unsalted butter, melted
½ cup sugar
1 large egg, lightly beaten
1½ ounces semisweet chocolate, melted and slightly cooled
½ cup milk
Bourbon Cream Sauce (page 367)

Generously butter a 4-cup mold with a lid and set aside.

Sift together flour and baking powder. Set aside. Combine melted butter and sugar, beating well, then add egg and continue to beat until mixed. Stir in melted chocolate and add the flour in 3 parts, alternating with milk. Mix well, then pour into the prepared mold.

Place lid securely on the mold and put mold into a larger pot. Surround mold halfway up with hot water. Cover the pot and steam the pudding over low heat for 1 hour. Let pudding rest for about 15 minutes before serving with the Bourbon Cream Sauce.
SERVES 4 TO 6

BREAD PUDDING

BREAD PUDDING SOUFFLÉ

For this, you need three elements: bread pudding, meringue, and sauce. The first and last may be made in advance. You can freeze leftover bread pudding for another batch of soufflés or you can serve it as is, with the Whiskey Sauce.

BREAD PUDDING
1 cup sugar
³/₄ teaspoon ground cinnamon
Pinch of freshly grated nutmeg
1 whole egg plus 1 egg white, lightly beaten
1 cup half-and-half
1 teaspoon vanilla extract
4 to 5 cups cubed New Orleans French Bread (page 245)
¹/₄ cup raisins

MERINGUE
8 egg whites
¹/₂ cup sugar

Whiskey Sauce (page 368)

To make bread pudding: Preheat oven to 350 degrees. Grease an 8 × 8-inch pan.

Mix sugar, cinnamon, and nutmeg in a large bowl. Beat in egg and egg white, then stir in half-and-half and vanilla. Add bread and raisins and stir. Pour into prepared pan and bake until lightly browned and a toothpick comes out clean, about 45 minutes. Cool.

To make meringue: Preheat oven to 350 degrees. Butter six ¹/₂-cup custard cups.

In a large bowl, whip egg whites until foamy. Continue to whip, adding sugar gradually, until shiny and thick.

In a large bowl, break half the bread pudding—reserve the rest for another use—into

small bits (use your hands or a large spoon) and gently stir in half the meringue. Then fold in half of the remaining meringue, reserving the rest. Spoon the mixture into the prepared cups and top each with a swirl of the reserved meringue. Bake in a water bath until tops are golden, about 20 minutes.

To serve, warm the Whiskey Sauce in a double boiler. Poke down the tops of the soufflés and spoon in a bit of the sauce.
SERVES 6

BREAD PUDDING WITH WHISKEY SAUCE

This is a more down-home version of bread pudding, with enough difference to make it distinctive. This recipe came to me courtesy of Joel English, who supervises the cooking at Mandich Restaurant, which she and her husband run together. Mandich's is in New Orleans, a city where they know all about bread pudding.

4 large eggs
1 cup sugar
4 tablespoons (¹/₂ stick) unsalted butter, melted
4 cups milk
1 tablespoon vanilla extract
1 24-inch loaf stale French bread
¹/₂ cup raisins
¹/₂ cup canned fruit cocktail, drained
Whiskey Sauce (page 368)

Preheat oven to 350 degrees. Generously butter a 6-cup soufflé dish or oval baking dish. Set aside.

Mix eggs, sugar, and melted butter in a large bowl. Add milk and vanilla and mix well. Break the bread into small chunks and put into the mixture. When bread has softened, break into smaller bits with your hands and let it continue to soak until all the milk is absorbed. Fold in raisins and fruit cocktail. Pour mixture into the prepared dish and place dish in a larger ovenproof pan. Surround with boiling water, and bake about 1 hour and 15 minutes, or until firm and brown on top.

Serve with whiskey sauce.

SERVES 8

BREAD PUDDING

One of my all-time favorite desserts. And a "crowd pleaser," I might add.

10 or more 1-inch-thick slices day-old
   French bread, with crusts trimmed
8 tablespoons (1 stick) unsalted butter,
   softened
4 large eggs
3/4 cup plus 2 tablespoons sugar
4 cups milk
2 tablespoons vanilla extract
Freshly grated nutmeg
Whipped cream flavored with bourbon or
   liqueur (see pages 365 to 366)

Preheat oven to 350 degrees. Generously butter a 6-cup soufflé dish or low oval baking dish. Set aside.

Spread bread slices generously with softened butter and place, buttered side up, in the baking dish. There should be enough pieces to cover the bottom.

Beat eggs and 3/4 cup of sugar until smooth. Pour milk in while stirring, then add vanilla and nutmeg. Mix very well.

Carefully pour the mixture through a strainer into the baking dish. Sprinkle the tops of the bread slices with the remaining 2 tablespoons of sugar.

Place dish in a larger ovenproof pan and surround with hot water.

Reduce the oven heat to 325 degrees and bake for 45 minutes, or until set. (Pudding will be a little jiggly when you remove it from the oven but will set when refrigerated.)

Serve with flavored whipped cream.

SERVES 8

TRIFLE AND TIRAMISU

CHERRY AND CHOCOLATE TRIFLE

1 tablespoon sugar
1 tablespoon cornstarch
1/4 cup liquid egg substitute or 1 egg, lightly
   beaten
1 cup skim milk
1 teaspoon vanilla extract
3 tablespoons dry sherry
1/4 pound angel food cake, cut into
   1-inch cubes
3/4 cup dried cherries, reconstituted with
   cabernet and heated until soft and
   plump, drained and chopped
4 ounces bittersweet chocolate
1/2 bottle dry red wine

Mix sugar and cornstarch in a small saucepan. Add egg substitute or egg and milk. Mix well. Heat to a simmer, stirring constantly, and continue to cook until thickened, several minutes. Remove from heat and add vanilla. Press a round of wax paper onto surface and let cool.

To assemble, sprinkle sherry over cake cubes and divide one third of them among individual dessert bowls or wine glasses. Spoon one third of the custard onto each serving, followed by one third of the cherries. Repeat the layers—cake, custard, and cherries—twice more. Cover and refrigerate.

To serve, heat chocolate and wine together, stirring until chocolate melts. Drizzle this over the trifles.

SERVES 4

PECAN–ALMOND CUSTARD

This is an old recipe that originated in Virginia, or so I am told. It is related to trifle and is probably an American version of this English standard. You could substitute stale pound cake sprinkled with sherry or a mixture of stale cake and macaroons for ladyfingers, which seem difficult to find nowadays.

8 ladyfingers
2 tablespoons coarsely chopped pecans
2 tablespoons coarsely chopped toasted
*   almonds*
1 1-ounce square bittersweet chocolate,
*   grated*
2 cups half-and-half
1 cup milk
6 eggs, beaten
1/2 cup sugar
1/8 teaspoon salt
1 cup tart jelly (optional)

Preheat oven to 325 degrees and put a kettle of water over low heat.

Butter a 1½-quart casserole and arrange ladyfingers on the bottom (and a few up the sides if you have any left over). Sprinkle with pecans and almonds and then the chocolate. Set aside.

In the top of a double boiler, start the half-and-half and milk heating. Meanwhile, beat eggs with sugar and salt. Set aside. When milk is almost boiling, add the egg–sugar mixture, stirring all the while. Cook until slightly thickened and pour over ladyfingers. Place casserole in a pan of hot water and bake for 45 minutes, or until firm. Let cool (out of the water bath). You may melt the jelly and pour it over the top of the custard before serving if you like. Do not refrigerate if you can avoid it.

SERVES 6

TRIFLE

Trifle, a favorite Victorian dish, is the perfect party dessert. Make it well ahead of time, so that the sherry and brandy have enough time to seep into the cake. Serve in a glass bowl.

About 3/4 pound leftover pound cake, sponge
*   cake, or Madeira cake*
1 cup berry or currant jam
1/4 cup slivered almonds
1/4 cup brandy
3/4 cup dry sherry
1 1/2 cups milk
1 cup heavy cream
1 vanilla bean
1 teaspoon cornstarch
3 tablespoons sugar
5 eggs
2 cups whipped heavy cream
1/2 cup candied citron
6 crystallized violets or fresh strawberries

Cut cake into very thick slices and spread each with a generous amount of jam. Arrange the slices on the bottom of a large glass bowl. If you prefer to use individual glass dishes, divide the cake equally among the dishes. Sprinkle almonds over the cake slices, pour on brandy and sherry, and let soak for about 45 minutes (but not longer or the cake will become too soggy).

Bring milk, cream, and vanilla bean to a boil in the top of a double boiler. Remove from the heat and discard the vanilla bean.

Mix cornstarch with sugar and eggs and gradually add vanilla cream mixture to it. Return the mixture to the double boiler and stir until the custard becomes thick and creamy. Do not allow to boil.

Let the custard cool a little and then pour it over the cake. Let the trifle set, and when it is fully cooled, spread any remaining jam on top, then cover with whipped cream.

Decorate the trifle with citron slices and crystallized violets or fresh strawberries and refrigerate until ready to serve.

SERVES 8

RASPBERRY TIRAMISU

This would be equally good made with other kinds of berries. If you should substitute blackberries, remember they can be rather tart. Sprinkle them with a bit of sugar and let them rest before using.

SPONGE CAKE

    2 large eggs, separated
    2 tablespoons warm coffee
    1 teaspoon vanilla extract
    1 teaspoon fresh lemon juice
    1/2 cup sugar
    Pinch of salt
    1/2 cup sifted self-rising cake flour

ASSEMBLY

    1 cup cold espresso
    2 1/2 cups fresh raspberries
    2 tablespoons water
    1 cup sugar
    1 pound mascarpone cheese
    2 cups heavy cream
    2 tablespoons dark rum
    1 ounce bittersweet chocolate, grated
    Cooked Berry Sauce (page 363), made with
        raspberries

To make cake: Cut a piece of wax paper and fit it into the bottom of a 2-quart soufflé dish. Do not grease the dish. Preheat oven to 325 degrees.

Combine egg yolks, coffee, vanilla, and lemon juice. Beat with an electric hand mixer at high speed until thickened, about 2 minutes. Add sugar and beat another 30 seconds or so to combine well. Set aside. Beat egg whites until foamy, add salt, and beat until whites form stiff peaks. Fold whites into the yolk mixture. Sift flour, a little at a time, over the batter, folding in after each addition. Pour into dish and bake until a tester comes out clean, about 20 to 25 minutes.

Let cake rest in the dish for about 30 minutes. Loosen edges and remove from the dish. Let cool completely. Peel off wax paper and leave uncovered to dry out overnight.

To assemble: Cut cake in half crosswise. Lightly toast the 2 cut sides of the cake under the broiler. Put the bottom slice, toasted side up, back into the dish it was cooked in. Sprinkle with 1/2 cup of the espresso.

Combine raspberries, water, and 1/2 cup of the sugar in a saucepan. Cook over low heat, stirring, until sugar dissolves, about 4 minutes. Set aside. Place cheese, cream, remaining 1/2 cup sugar, and rum in a bowl and beat with a hand mixer. Spread half of the mixture over the bottom layer of cake in the dish. Cover this with the berries, spreading them evenly. Place the top layer of cake, toasted side up, over the berries and sprinkle with the balance of the espresso. Spread the balance of the cheese mixture over this and sprinkle with the grated chocolate. Cover with plastic wrap and refrigerate for at least 1 hour before serving. Remove from the refrigerator about 30 minutes or so before serving. Cut out serving portions and top each with Cooked Berry Sauce.

SERVES 12

CHEESE DESSERTS

OLIVE, CHEESE, AND PLUMS

Buy loose unpitted black olives in brine, drain and wash, then drain once more. Put them in a bowl. Add enough good olive oil to just cover. Since this oil will be tasted undiluted, be sure that it is of high quality. Sprinkle with fines herbs or a favorite combination of dried herbs and mix. Let sit.

Place a thick round of mild goat cheese on a plate and pour over it a liberal amount of good olive oil. Add 6 to 8 juniper berries and roll them around in the oil so that they are well coated. Snip fresh rosemary and chives over the cheese and give a generous grind of black pepper to finish.

If you like plums and they are large, buy 1½ plums per guest. If they are small, buy 2 for each. Serve gratte paille cheese at room temperature with the plums.

CHAMPAGNE GRAPES WITH CHEESE

Champagne grapes are a particular favorite of mine, and I look forward to their brief season at the end of the summer. They are very small, sweet, and seedless—and worth the wait.

A very simple and quick dessert is to put out a bowl of these little beauties atop a bed of cracked ice and serve along with several good cheeses. Try a goat cheese and maybe something soft with a bloomy white rind. Camembert, the old standby, is one .

Incidentally, one of the best investments I ever made was a pair of grape scissors. They really do their work—grape stems being too difficult to break comfortably without a little help.

CAMBAZOLA CHEESE AND ASIAN PEARS

¾ pound cambazola cheese, thinly sliced and at room temperature
1 Asian pear (see Note), thinly sliced and rubbed with fresh lemon juice
¼ pound assorted small lettuce leaves (optional)
Lemon–Oil Dressing (page 48)
French bread, thinly sliced and toasted

Place a slice of cheese on individual plates along with 2 slices of Asian pear. Add a few lettuce leaves for garnish and drizzle with dressing.

Serve this with thin slices of toasted French bread.

Note: Asian pear tastes like a smooth-textured cross between a pear and an apple. If not available, use firm Bosc pears or jicama.
SERVES 8

PEACHES AND FRESH PECORINO WITH HONEY AND BLACK PEPPER

I had something similar to this in a restaurant once. Now I like to serve it after a pasta that has no cheese on it.

You must use only *fresh* pecorino for this, not aged. If fresh is not available, substitute gruyère.

6 medium-thick slices fresh pecorino cheese
3 medium peaches, peeled, halved, and rubbed with fresh lemon juice
Freshly ground black pepper, to taste
About 4 tablespoons honey

Arrange slices of cheese on individual plates with a half peach each. Grind black pepper over all and spoon honey over each.
SERVES 6

482

CHILDREN'S FAVORITES

CHOCOLATE–PECAN– RAISIN CLUSTERS

You might just as easily make butterscotch–walnut–raisin clusters as these chocolate pecan ones. To do so, substitute butterscotch morsels for the chocolate and walnuts for the pecans.

8 ounces semisweet or milk chocolate
3/4 cup golden or dark raisins
3/4 cup broken pecans or walnuts

Melt chocolate in the top of double boiler over simmering water. Stir in raisins and nuts. Drop in clusters on a sheet of wax paper. Let cool slightly, then chill to set chocolate.
MAKES ABOUT 2 DOZEN CLUSTERS

POPCORN BALLS

I think this is my favorite. I've always been hooked on popcorn, so popcorn balls are a natural for me. I also like Cracker Jacks. You can add nuts to this, too.

3 quarts unsalted popcorn
2 cups cane syrup, dark corn syrup, or maple syrup
1 tablespoon cider vinegar
1/2 teaspoon salt
2 teaspoons vanilla extract

Place popcorn in a large bowl and set aside. Grease 2 large forks. Set aside.

 Combine syrup, vinegar, and salt in a deep pot. (Pot must be deep because the syrup boils up and will overflow if not large enough.) Bring to a boil over medium heat until it reaches the firm-ball stage (250 degrees on a candy thermometer). Add the vanilla and mix well.

Pour over the popcorn and toss to coat with the greased forks. Butter your hands liberally and form popcorn into balls, pressing lightly to make them stick together. Continue forming balls, rebuttering your hands after each, until all the corn is used.
MAKES ABOUT 1 DOZEN BALLS

MOLASSES POPCORN BALLS

Another family recipe. If you don't want to go to the trouble of making these into balls, just stir the corn with the syrup until set and serve in a bowl.

1 cup sugar
1 tablespoon distilled white vinegar
1/2 cup water
2 tablespoons molasses
1 tablespoon unsalted butter
1/2 teaspoon salt
6 to 8 cups popped corn

Put sugar, vinegar, and water in a large saucepan and bring to a boil over moderate heat. Boil for 5 minutes.

 Add molasses, butter, and salt and cook until a few drops drizzled into a cup of cold water become hard brittle. Remove from heat and stir in the popcorn.

 Butter your hands and slip them into baggies. Working quickly, shape mixture into balls, squeezing tight. When cool, wrap the balls in wax paper. Store in an airtight container.
MAKES 6 TO 8 LARGE OR 15 SMALL BALLS

MARSHMALLOW–BUTTERSCOTCH–PEANUT SQUARES

This is a variation on that old favorite made from breakfast cereal. They could probably be made with chocolate morsels instead of butterscotch, or you could make them as is and sprinkle chocolate morsels on top.

> 6 tablespoons (³/₄ stick) unsalted butter or
>   margarine
> 10 ounces miniature marshmallows
> 6 cups crisped rice cereal
> 2 cups butterscotch morsels
> ¹/₄ cup milk
> 1 cup honey-roasted peanuts

Butter a 13 × 9 × 2-inch baking pan and set aside.

Melt 4 tablespoons of the butter in a large saucepan. Add marshmallows and cook over low heat until melted and smooth.

Off the heat, add cereal, and stir to coat. Pat mixture into prepared pan. Set aside.

In another saucepan, melt the remaining butter and add butterscotch morsels. Stir until soft, then add milk, stirring until smooth. Mix in peanuts and coat well. Pour evenly over the cereal and smooth top lightly.

Let set before cutting into squares.

MAKES 2 DOZEN SQUARES

CHOCOLATE COOKIE LOG

This dessert, made with chocolate wafers, is a variation on the one Nabisco printed on the back of their chocolate wafer package. It's a marvelous, easy-to-make dessert. I know a lot of adults who like it, too. You might dress it up for the grown-ups sometime.

> 2 cups heavy cream
> 1¹/₂ teaspoons vanilla extract
> 2 tablespoons superfine sugar
> 1 package (8¹/₂ ounces) chocolate wafers

Whip the cream until soft peaks form, then stir in vanilla and sugar. Continue whipping until stiff.

Spread cream generously on the chocolate wafers, then put wafers in stacks of 4 or 5. Arrange stacks lengthwise on a serving plate to make 1 long row.

Frost the outside of the log with the remaining cream. Refrigerate for at least 3 hours (or overnight), or freeze until firm (covered with plastic wrap; let thaw in refrigerator 1 hour before serving).

To serve, slice log on the diagonal.

SERVES 8

VARIATION

Mix 3 tablespoons unsweetened cocoa powder into the cream along with the vanilla and sugar.

GROWN-UP VARIATION

Omit the sugar and add 2 tablespoons framboise or other liqueur, or 2 tablespoons bourbon, to the vanilla and cream.

FREDDIE'S GRAHAM CRACKER PICKUPS

This is a treat my remarkable Aunt Freddie came up with. I don't have any idea where she got the idea, but it is a surprisingly tasty combination of flavors.

24 whole graham crackers (48 squares)
8 tablespoons (1 stick) unsalted butter, softened
1/2 cup sugar
1 cup coarsely chopped pecans

Preheat oven to 350 degrees.

Arrange crackers on a jelly-roll pan. Cream butter and sugar until mixed, then stir in pecans. Divide the mixture among the crackers and spread over each.

Bake for 12 to 14 minutes, or until melted and the color of maple syrup.

Let cool on a wire rack. Store in an airtight container.

MAKES 4 DOZEN SQUARES

CANDY

CHOCOLATE FUDGE

This is Liz Smith's (of the famous candy-making Smiths) own fudge. Years ago, we used to make it in the country to finish off the Saturday evening festivities.

2 cups sugar
2 heaping tablespoons unsweetened cocoa powder
1 cup milk
Dash of salt
4 tablespoons (1/2 stick) unsalted butter, cut into bits
2 teaspoons vanilla extract

Generously grease a 12-inch plate.

Mix sugar, cocoa, milk, and salt in a small saucepan and bring to a boil over medium heat, stirring occasionally. Boil until it reaches the soft-ball stage, 240 degrees on a candy thermometer.

Stir in butter and vanilla and continue to beat until candy begins to set. Quickly turn into prepared plate. When set, cut into squares.

MAKES ABOUT 18 PIECES

MAMIE EISENHOWER FUDGE

I don't know if this really was Mamie's recipe, but I've always heard it referred to that way.

4 1/2 cups sugar
Pinch of salt
2 tablespoons unsalted butter
1 can (12 ounces) evaporated milk
2 cups semisweet chocolate chips
2 cups milk chocolate chips
1 jar (7 1/2 ounces) marshmallow cream
2 cups coarsely chopped walnuts

Combine sugar, salt, butter, and milk in a large saucepan and bring to a boil over medium heat. Simmer to soft-ball stage, or until a candy thermometer reaches 240 degrees.

Meanwhile, combine chocolate chips and marshmallow cream in a large bowl. Butter a 13 × 9-inch pan.

When the sugar mixture is ready, add the chocolate mixture and mix until chocolates are melted and mixture is smooth. Stir in walnuts quickly, and pour into prepared pan. Let cool and cut into squares.

MAKES A WHOPPING 5 POUNDS

PEANUT BUTTER FUDGE

Who doesn't remember the taste of this old standby? Often the peanut butter was combined with chocolate, but here it stands alone. A winner both ways.

2 cups sugar
³/₄ cup milk
¹/₂ teaspoon salt
1 teaspoon vanilla extract
2 tablespoons unsalted butter
6 tablespoons chunky-style peanut butter

Generously butter a 12-inch plate.

Combine sugar, milk, and salt in a small saucepan. Over medium heat, boil slowly to the soft-ball stage, 240 degrees on a candy thermometer. Off the heat, stir in vanilla, butter, and peanut butter. Mix well and pour onto a buttered plate. Let cool, then cut into squares.

MAKES ABOUT 2 DOZEN PIECES

PRALINES

This is my Aunt Freddie's recipe. There are many others to choose from, but all are very similar.

2 cups granulated sugar
1 cup (firmly packed) dark brown sugar
8 tablespoons (1 stick) unsalted butter
1 cup milk
2 tablespoons light corn syrup
4 cups pecan halves and pieces

In a large saucepan, combine sugars, butter, milk, and corn syrup. Bring to a boil over medium heat, and continue, stirring occasionally, until mixture reaches soft-ball stage, 240 degrees on a candy thermometer; this will take about 20 minutes. After the mixture has been boiling for about 10 minutes, stir in pecans and continue to cook to required temperature.

Drop by tablespoons onto wax paper and let cool.

MAKES ABOUT 18 PRALINES

CHOCOLATE-NUT TOFFEE

Chocolate-nut toffee is the invention of John Prescott's mother. Together they own a confection company called Katherine's Own. This particular candy was made exclusively for me to sell at Saks Fifth Avenue—and what a hit it was.

Actually, the doing of this candy is rather tedious, but now when you buy toffee, you will know how much loving care goes into it.

1 pound (4 sticks) lightly salted butter
2 cups sugar
1 cup slivered almonds
4 ounces semisweet chocolate
4 ounces bittersweet chocolate
1 cup chopped pecans

Combine butter and sugar in a large saucepan and bring to a boil over medium heat. Stirring with an over-and-under motion (like folding egg whites into a batter), cook until sugar is dissolved. Add almonds and continue to cook, stirring with the same motion all the while, until mixture reaches the hard-crack stage, 295 to 300 degrees on a candy thermometer; it will be smoking and dark brown. This can take from 45 minutes to 1 hour.

Pour out onto a marble slab or into a jelly roll pan and let harden for about 6 hours.

Melt chocolates together and spread evenly over the top of the toffee. Sprinkle with chopped pecans and let rest for several hours. Break into pieces and store in an airtight container.

MAKES ABOUT 3 POUNDS

BLACK WALNUT DIVINITY

Mrs. Sloan Smith (none other than columnist Liz Smith's mother) made this divinity every Christmas, to everyone's immense delight.

2½ cups sugar
½ cup water
½ cup light corn syrup
2 large egg whites, at room temperature
Pinch of salt
1 cup black or English walnuts or pecans,
    coarsely chopped
1 teaspoon vanilla extract

Generously grease a 12-inch plate.

Combine sugar, water, and corn syrup in a small pan and bring to a boil. Continue boiling until syrup makes a firm ball, 249 degrees on a candy thermometer. While syrup is cooking, beat egg whites with salt until they form soft peaks.

When the syrup is the right temperature, pour about half of it into the whites, beating all the while. Return the balance of the syrup to the heat and cook until it reaches the hard-ball stage, 260 degrees. Pour, in a steady stream, into the egg white mixture, beating all the while. Continue to beat for a few minutes, then fold in nuts and vanilla. Pour into prepared plate and let cool. Cut into squares while lukewarm.

When completely cool, wrap individual pieces in plastic wrap, since divinity will harden if left exposed to the air.

MAKES ABOUT 18 PIECES

NUT BRITTLE

I'll go out on a limb and say that this is my favorite simple candy. If you have never made it, try it.

2 cups pecan or walnut pieces or whole
    peanuts
1 cup sugar
1 cup light corn syrup
1 tablespoon baking soda

Butter a baking sheet (or coat with nonstick spray) and set aside.

Combine nuts, sugar, and corn syrup in a medium saucepan set over medium heat. Bring to a boil, stirring constantly, then let boil, without stirring, until the mixture reaches the hard-crack stage, 295 degrees on a candy thermometer.

Remove saucepan from the heat and stir in the baking soda. This will foam up; mix quickly and then pour onto prepared baking sheet.

When cool enough to handle, stretch the brittle to get it as thin as possible. Let cool completely and break into pieces. Store in an airtight container.

MAKES ABOUT 1¼ POUNDS

ICE CREAMS AND SORBETS

THE VERY TASTE OF RICH HOMEMADE CUSTARD ICE CREAM— which, as far as I am concerned, is the quintessential country summer dessert—never fails to evoke the sweetness of the small-town family Sundays I knew as a boy. When I was growing up in Louisiana—as even now—people sat down to the main meal as soon as church was over. And during the deepest days of summer the ice cream churn really got a workout. From these comforting memories came a lot of the ice cream recipes, along with variations and relatives, for this section. ✦ If you  don't own an electric ice cream maker, such a machine is a good investment and can be interesting to experiment with. Should you have had little experience in making ice creams you will find all kinds of possibilities to pique your interest here—custard-based ice creams,, sherbets and sorbets, granités, ices and even some yogurt-based favorites. You can't go wrong with any of them.

ICE CREAM

WHITE CHOCOLATE ICE CREAM

Here is yet another recipe devised by the multitalented food writer and consultant Lee Klein.

2 cups half-and-half
⅓ cup superfine sugar
Pinch of salt
4 large egg yolks
1½ teaspoons vanilla extract
4 ounces white chocolate
1 tablespoon milk or cream
6 tablespoons buttermilk
2 teaspoons fresh lemon juice
Fresh berries (optional)

Put half-and-half in a small saucepan and bring to a boil. Transfer to the top of a double boiler and stir in sugar and a pinch of salt. Beat egg yolks. With half-and-half mixture set over boiling water, add a little of the half-and-half to the yolks to warm them, then pour the yolks into the half-and-half in a thin stream, stirring, until mixture coats a spoon, several minutes. Strain and stir in vanilla. Set aside off the heat.

Break the white chocolate into small pieces and place in a small pan with milk. Melt the white chocolate over low heat and immediately stir into the half-and-half mixture. Set aside to cool.

When cool, stir in buttermilk and lemon juice. Refrigerate, covered, until cold. Pour into a commercial ice-cream maker and freeze according to manufacturer's directions.

Serve with berries if desired.

MAKES ABOUT 1½ PINTS

CHOCOLATE NOUGAT ICE CREAM

Here's an incredibly rich chocolate ice cream you'll love.

2 bars (3½ ounces each) Tobler bittersweet
*   chocolate, finely chopped*
2 cups half-and-half
½ cup milk
3 large egg yolks, at room temperature
Pinch of salt
⅔ cup sugar
1 teaspoon vanilla extract

Combine chocolate, half-and-half, and milk in a medium saucepan. Cook, stirring, over low heat until chocolate melts and mixture is smooth, being careful not to scorch. Set aside.

Beat egg yolks with salt and sugar until sugar is dissolved. Add ½ cup of the chocolate mixture to the yolks to warm them, mix thoroughly, then add yolk mixture to the balance of the chocolate mixture. Return to heat and cook slowly, stirring all the while, until thick enough to coat a spoon, about 2 minutes.

Stir in vanilla off the heat and let cool.

Pour mixture into an ice-cream maker and freeze according to manufacturer's directions.

MAKES ABOUT 1 QUART

489

CHOCOLATE–CHOCOLATE CHIP ICE CREAM

½ cup sugar
8 ounces semisweet chocolate, coarsely chopped
2½ cups half-and-half
Pinch of salt
1½ teaspoons vanilla extract
1 cup semisweet chocolate chips

Put sugar in a food processor and process until finely ground, about 20 seconds. Add chopped chocolate and process until chocolate and sugar form small pellets.

Meanwhile, bring half-and-half just to a boil in a small saucepan over medium heat. When hot, pour into the processor and process until sugar and chocolate are melted.

Pour mixture into a bowl and add salt and vanilla. Let cool slightly, then stir in chocolate chips. Chill thoroughly, then freeze in an ice-cream maker according to manufacturer's directions.

MAKES ABOUT 1 QUART

BLOWOUT ICE CREAM

This is one of those ice-cream concoctions that you might want to experiment with. Use this recipe as a guide for making your own madness. Anything goes!

1 recipe Vanilla-Bean Custard Ice Cream (page 491)
4 to 8 Outrageous Brownies (page 451), cut into chunks or crumbled
½ cup coarsely chopped honey-roasted peanuts
2 teaspoons powdered instant espresso (optional)
½ cup semisweet chocolate chips (optional)
2 tablespoons bourbon or coffee-flavored liqueur (optional)

Follow the directions for making the ice cream. When the mixture is frozen almost solid, remove the freezing canister and fold in any or all of the remaining ingredients. Spoon into a container and freeze until solid, at least 3 hours.

MAKES 1 TO 1½ QUARTS, DEPENDING ON WHAT YOU ADD

ESPRESSO ICE CREAM

This is a variation on coffee ice cream but with a stronger flavor.

2 cups heavy cream
1 cup milk
5 large egg yolks, at room temperature
⅔ cup superfine sugar
1 teaspoon vanilla extract
1 tablespoon powdered instant espresso, plus extra for sprinkling on top

Combine cream and milk in a large saucepan and bring just to a boil over high heat, stirring all the while. Set aside.

Whisk together egg yolks and sugar until frothy. Gradually add the hot mixture, whisking, until well mixed. Pour back into the saucepan and cook over moderate heat until mixture coats a spoon and is thickened, about 2 minutes. Do not overcook.

Stir in vanilla and powdered espresso. Place plastic wrap directly onto the surface of the cream. Let cool to room temperature. Chill mixture.

Pour mixture into ice-cream maker and freeze according to manufacturer's directions.

Serve with additional powdered espresso sprinkled on top.

MAKES ABOUT 1½ PINTS

VANILLA-BEAN CUSTARD ICE CREAM

This is the real thing, rich as all get out with cream and eggs and the custard flecked with vanilla seeds. If you like vanilla, here is the granddaddy of them all.

1 cup milk
⅔ cup sugar
2 vanilla beans, cut in half lengthwise
9 large egg yolks, at room temperature
2 cups heavy cream

Combine milk, sugar, and vanilla beans in the top of a double boiler and heat over barely simmering water. Lightly beat yolks. When milk mixture is almost to the point of boiling, pour a little into the yolks to warm them. Stir and add a bit more hot milk.

Pour warmed yolks into the milk in a slow, steady stream, stirring all the while. Continue to cook, stirring constantly, over hot, not boiling, water until mixture coats the spoon.

Press a sheet of wax paper or plastic wrap directly onto the surface of the custard and let cool to room temperature.

Add cream to the custard and refrigerate for several hours.

Just before freezing, remove vanilla beans and scrape their seeds into the mixture. Stir and pour into an ice-cream maker and freeze according to manufacturer's directions.

MAKES 1 QUART

STRAWBERRY ICE CREAM WITH STRAWBERRY PURÉE

When berries are first in season, I love to make homemade strawberry ice cream. I serve it with sweetened strawberry purée, garnished with one or two nice big ripe berries rolled in confectioners' sugar.

1 cup strawberries, washed, hulled, and sliced, plus 6 whole extra perfect ones for garnish
Few drops of fresh lemon juice
Sugar, to taste
Confectioners' sugar
1 recipe Berry Ice Cream (page 492), made with strawberries

Purée sliced berries and add a few drops of lemon juice along with sugar. Refrigerate until serving.

Roll whole berries in confectioners' sugar on a plate and serve with the ice cream and purée.

SERVES 6

CINNAMON CUSTARD ICE CREAM

This is perfect with apple pie or cobbler.

2 cups heavy cream
2 cups half-and-half
¾ cup sugar
3 whole eggs
3 egg yolks
¼ cup honey
2 tablespoons ground cinnamon
2 tablespoons hot water

Combine cream, half-and-half, and ½ cup of the sugar in a saucepan and scald over medium heat, stirring.

Slightly beat egg, yolks, and remaining sugar in a stainless steel bowl. Add a cup of the scalded cream mixture to the eggs, whisking lightly. Add egg mixture to the remainder of the scalded mixture. Whisk. Combine honey, cinnamon, and hot water and whisk this in. Strain, press a piece of plastic wrap onto the surface, and let cool. Chill in the refrigerator. Pour into an ice-cream maker and freeze according to manufacturer's directions.

MAKES ABOUT 1 QUART

BERRY ICE CREAM

Ice cream may be made with just about any ripe berry, either with the seeds and pulp or just pulp alone.

6 tablespoons sugar
1½ teaspoons unbleached all-purpose flour
Pinch of salt
1 cup half-and-half
1 large egg, lightly beaten
1 cup milk
1 teaspoon vanilla extract
1 pint fresh berries, crushed

Mix sugar, flour, and salt in the top of a double boiler. Stir in half-and-half, then cook over boiling water for about 5 minutes, stirring all the while. Cover and continue cooking over boiling water for 10 minutes longer. Remove from heat and spoon a little of the hot mixture into the beaten egg to heat it. Add the warmed egg to the milk and return double boiler to the heat.

Place mixture over hot, not boiling, water and stir constantly until mixture coats a spoon, about 5 minutes. Strain and chill.

When cold, stir in milk, vanilla, and berries.

Pour mixture into an ice-cream maker and freeze according to manufacturer's directions.
MAKES ABOUT 1½ PINTS

RUM CHERRY ICE CREAM

Soak the cherries in kirsch for an even more intense flavor.

¾ cup dried cherries
Light rum
2½ cups half-and-half
½ cup sugar
4 large egg yolks
¼ teaspoon vanilla extract

Place cherries in a bowl and cover with rum. Let soak for several hours.

Heat half-and-half and sugar together until sugar is dissolved and bubbles begin to form around edge of the pot. Whisk yolks until creamy and then whisk in ½ cup of the heated half-and-half mixture. Pour the warmed yolks back into the half-and-half and continue to cook, stirring, until the custard mixture coats the back of a spoon. Do not overcook or the custard will curdle. Stir in vanilla, let cool completely, then chill.

Pour into an ice-cream maker and freeze according to manufacturer's directions. Drain the cherries. When the mixture begins to thicken as it freezes, add the cherries and freeze until ice cream is the proper consistency.
MAKES ABOUT 1¾ PINTS

TOASTED COCONUT ICE CREAM

Toasting improves the taste of coconut immeasurably. This mixture is uncooked, unless you call toasting the coconut cooking, so it is very simple to prepare.

1¼ cups canned cream of coconut
1 cup milk
½ cup heavy cream
Pinch of salt
1 cup shredded fresh coconut, toasted, plus additional for serving

Combine cream of coconut, milk, and cream in a large bowl. Sprinkle salt over mixture and whisk until well mixed. Sprinkle toasted coconut over all and gently fold in.

Pour the mixture into an ice-cream maker and freeze until firm according to manufacturer's directions. Serve with additional toasted coconut on top if desired.
MAKES ABOUT 1½ PINTS

FREDDIE'S FIG PRESERVES

This is my Aunt Freddie's recipe.

5 pounds small fresh figs, stemmed
5 cups sugar
1½ lemons, seeded and thinly sliced

Wash figs in cold water. Put in a heavy pot with the sugar and just enough water to cover the sugar and keep figs from sticking. Stir. Add lemon slices and cook over moderate heat about 10 minutes or until syrup is thick and fruit is tender. Skim off foam that comes to the top.

When the juice has become a syrup, divide among sterilized jars and seal. Turn jars upside down to ensure perfect seal. Process in boiling water for 5 minutes.

MAKES EIGHT ½-PINT JARS

FIG PRESERVES ICE CREAM

You can use store-bought fig jam or make you own fig preserves, which are very easy.

2 cups milk
2 eggs
1 cup sugar
1 tablespoon vanilla extract
1 cup heavy cream
1 cup Freddie's Fig Preserves
  (recipe above)

Scald milk. Meanwhile, beat eggs and sugar together until lemon colored. Add a little of the milk to the mixture to heat it, then pour into hot milk, stirring all the while. Continue to cook over very low heat (or in a double boiler) about 10 minutes, or until thickened. Whip the cream and fold in. Mix in preserves.

Pour into an ice-cream freezer and freeze according to manufacturer's directions.

MAKES ABOUT 1 QUART

FIG ICE CREAM

This recipe is an old one from Louisiana, where there is an endless supply of fresh figs in early summer. The ice cream has a delightful and subtle flavor.

1 cup sugar
¼ cup water
1 tablespoon distilled white vinegar
Pinch of salt
2 large egg whites, stiffly beaten
4 cups crushed fresh figs
1½ cups milk

Combine sugar, water, vinegar, and salt in a saucepan. Over moderate heat, boil rapidly to the thread stage, 230 degrees on a candy thermometer.

Pour mixture in a thin stream into the beaten egg whites and then combine with figs. Stir in milk.

Pour mixture into an ice-cream maker and freeze according to manufacturer's directions.

MAKES 1 TO 1½ QUARTS

MAPLE-BLACK WALNUT ICE CREAM

This recipe couldn't be simpler, and it is a good way to use up some of that maple syrup that we all seem to get as gifts.

2 cups half-and-half
¾ cup good-quality maple syrup
1 cup coarsely chopped black walnuts

Combine half-and-half and maple syrup in a medium bowl and mix well. Add walnuts.

Pour into an ice-cream maker and freeze according to manufacturer's directions.

MAKES ABOUT 1½ PINTS

LEMON CUSTARD ICE CREAM

Almost everyone knows about lemon sherbet and lemon ice, but what about lemon ice cream? It has a flavor and texture all its own and, although richer than ice or sherbet, is equally refreshing.

²/₃ cup sugar
2¹/₂ cups half-and-half
5 large egg yolks, at room temperature
Grated zest of 1 large lemon
¹/₂ cup fresh lemon juice

Combine sugar and half-and-half in a large saucepan and cook over low heat until sugar dissolves, stirring all the while. Set aside.

Beat egg yolks until creamy, then add ¹/₂ cup of the cream to warm them. Return cream mixture to medium-low heat and stir in the warmed yolks. Cook until the mixture coats the back of a spoon, about 5 minutes.

Off the heat, stir in zest and lemon juice. Mix well and let cool. Chill.

Pour mixture into an ice-cream maker and freeze according to manufacturer's directions.
MAKES ABOUT 1¹/₂ PINTS

VARIATION

Substitute lime juice for the lemon juice. Use lemon zest, not lime zest.

PEACH PIT ICE CREAM

This unusual recipe makes a delicious ice cream with a strong peachy flavor.

1¹/₄ pounds ripe unblemished peaches
   (about 8 large)
¹/₄ cup fresh lemon juice
1¹/₂ cups heavy cream
1¹/₂ cups milk
³/₄ cup sugar
3 large egg yolks, at room temperature

Peel and pit peaches, reserving peach skins and pits. In a food processor or blender, purée peach flesh with lemon juice. You should have about 2¹/₄ cups of purée. Cover and refrigerate.

Place skins and pits in a large saucepan along with cream and milk. Simmer, covered, over low heat for 20 minutes, being careful not to let mixture boil. It may look slightly separated because of the acid in the fruit, but don't worry. Stir in sugar to dissolve and remove from the heat. Whisk yolks and add about ¹/₂ cup of the hot liquid to warm them. Mix well and pour warmed yolks into the hot mixture, stirring constantly. Return saucepan to the heat and cook until custard coats the back of a spoon, about 8 minutes. Again, be careful not to let mixture boil; boiling may cause custard to curdle.

Press a sheet of wax paper or plastic wrap directly onto the surface of the mixture and let cool. When cool, strain and combine with the fruit pulp. Mix and chill.

Pour mixture into an ice-cream maker and freeze according to manufacturer's directions.
MAKES ABOUT 1 QUART

RUM–RAISIN ICE CREAM

Another time, you can vary this recipe by using dried figs instead of dark raisins.

1 cup dark raisins
1/3 cup dark rum
2 1/2 cups half-and-half
2/3 cup (firmly packed) light brown sugar
1/2 teaspoon ground cinnamon

Many hours ahead, or even the night before, mix the raisins and rum and let raisins soak until the liquid is absorbed.

Combine half-and-half and brown sugar in a large saucepan and simmer over low heat, stirring, until sugar is dissolved. Let cool, then stir in cinnamon. Chill.

Just before freezing, stir in raisins, reserving any rum that was not absorbed.

Pour mixture into an ice-cream maker and freeze until almost firm. If you have any leftover rum, add it now. Otherwise, continue freezing until firm according to manufacturer's directions.

MAKES ABOUT 1 1/2 PINTS

PEPPERMINT ICE CREAM

6 tablespoons sugar
1 1/2 teaspoons unbleached all-purpose flour
Pinch of salt
1 cup half-and-half
1 egg, beaten
1 teaspoon vanilla extract
1 cup whole milk
6 peppermint canes or round candies,
   crushed

Mix sugar, flour, and salt in the top of a double boiler. Stir in half-and-half. Cook over boiling water for 5 minutes, stirring all the while. Cover and cook for 10 minutes more. Turn off heat. Spoon a little of the hot milk mixture into the beaten egg and then return all to the dou-ble boiler. This time, cook over hot, not boiling, water, stirring constantly, for about 5 minutes, or until mixture begins to coat spoon. Strain and chill. Add vanilla, whole milk, and peppermint candy. Put into an ice-cream maker and freeze according to manufacturer's directions.

MAKES 1 1/2 PINTS

VARIATION

For a low-fat version, substitute 1 cup evaporated skimmed milk for the half-and-half and for the whole milk.

PEANUT BRITTLE ICE CREAM

2 cups half-and-half
2/3 cup (firmly packed) light brown sugar
3 tablespoons light corn syrup
3 large egg yolks, at room temperature
2 teaspoons vanilla extract
1 cup coarsely chopped or broken peanut
   brittle

Combine half-and-half, brown sugar, and corn syrup in a medium saucepan and cook over medium heat, stirring all the while, until the sugar dissolves completely. Remove from heat.

Beat egg yolk until creamy, then add 1/2 cup of the hot cream mixture, stirring to heat them. Put saucepan back on heat and add the warmed yolks, stirring. Continue to cook over medium-low heat until mixture coats the spoon.

Remove from heat, let cool, and stir in vanilla. Chill and pour into an ice-cream maker and freeze until partially set, about 20 minutes. Stir in peanut brittle and continue freezing until firm following manufacturer's directions.

MAKES ABOUT 1 QUART

HONEY AND HONEY-ROASTED PEANUT ICE CREAM

The person who thought up honey-roasted peanuts must have had me in mind. I love them. Here I've added them to honey ice cream.

1 cup heavy cream
1 cup milk
2/3 cup honey
3 large egg yolks, at room temperature
Pinch of salt
1 cup coarsely chopped honey-roasted
  peanuts

Combine cream and milk in a medium saucepan. Cook slowly over moderate heat until heated through, about 2 minutes. Off the heat, add honey and mix until completely dissolved. Set aside.

Beat egg yolks with salt until frothy, then add 1/2 cup of the honey–cream mixture to heat the yolks. Return saucepan to low heat and add warmed yolks. Stirring all the while, cook until the mixture coats the back of a spoon.

Remove from heat and let cool before stirring in peanuts. Chill mixture.

Pour mixture into an ice-cream maker and freeze according to manufacturer's directions.
MAKES ABOUT 1½ PINTS

BOURBON–PECAN ICE CREAM

This is a nice Southern variation on an old favorite combination. The pecans and bourbon could also be added to a simple custard ice cream.

2½ cups half-and-half
1/3 cup (firmly packed) light brown sugar
1/3 cup granulated sugar
1 cup coarsely chopped pecans
2 to 3 tablespoons bourbon

Combine half-and-half with sugars in a small saucepan. Slowly heat until sugars dissolve, then set aside to cool. Stir in pecans and bourbon, then pour into an ice-cream maker and freeze until firm according to manufacturer's directions.
MAKES ABOUT 1½ PINTS

BOURBON–MINT ICE CREAM

2 cups milk
1/4 cup bourbon
2 tablespoons chopped fresh mint
3 eggs
1 cup sugar
1/2 teaspoon salt
1½ cups heavy cream
1½ teaspoons vanilla extract

Place milk, bourbon, and mint in a saucepan and bring just to a boil over low heat. Meanwhile, beat eggs and sugar until lemon yellow. Pour in a little hot milk to heat it, then pour egg mixture into warm milk, stirring all the while. Return to low heat (or transfer to a double boiler), and cook, stirring constantly, for 10 minutes, or until mixture coats a spoon. Strain and cool, then refrigerate.

Stir in cream and vanilla and pour mixture into an ice-cream maker. Freeze according to manufacturer's directions.
MAKES 1 QUART

CREOLE CREAM CHEESE ICE CREAM

This makes an ultra-creamy ice cream.

1 cup sugar
3¼ cups half-and-half
4 egg yolks, lightly beaten
¾ cup sour cream
½ cup cream cheese or sour cream

Place sugar, half-and-half, and egg yolks into a heavy saucepan and mix well. Cook over moderate heat, stirring constantly, until mixture coats the back of a spoon, 8 to 10 minutes; do not boil. Remove from heat and strain into a bowl set into another bowl of cracked ice. Stir to cool. Whisk in sour cream and cream cheese. Freeze in an ice-cream maker according to manufacturer's directions.

MAKES ABOUT 1 QUART

YOGURT ICE CREAM

You can vary the flavor of this recipe by using a different kind of frozen juice concentrate—or you can make a combination of juices.

4 cups vanilla yogurt
⅔ cup frozen tangerine juice concentrate, thawed

Combine yogurt and concentrate in a large bowl and mix thoroughly. Pour into an ice-cream maker and freeze until firm according to manufacturer's directions.

MAKES ABOUT 1 QUART

SORBETS

PLUM SORBET

I had never thought of making sorbet from plums until a friend brought me a big basket of them. So many, in fact, I had to think of some way to use them all. This is the happy result.

2 cups water
⅓ cup sugar
1 tablespoon fresh lemon juice
2 pounds dark plums, pitted

Combine water, sugar, and lemon juice in a saucepan and heat. Add plums and bring to a simmer over medium heat. Simmer, skimming if necessary, for 8 to 10 minutes. Pour the whole mixture into a food processor and purée. Let cool, then freeze in an ice-cream maker according to the manufacturer's directions.

MAKES ABOUT 1½ PINTS

CASSIS SORBET

2½ cups water
1½ cups sugar
¾ cup crème de cassis (black currant liqueur)
3 tablespoons fresh lemon juice
2 tablespoons grated lemon zest

Stir water and sugar together in a saucepan over medium heat until sugar dissolves. Set aside to cool. Add cassis, lemon juice, and lemon zest. Mix and chill. Pour into an ice-cream maker and freeze according to manufacturer's directions.

Serve in chilled bowls.

MAKES ABOUT 1½ PINTS

CRANBERRY–PEAR SORBET

This is rather tart, so if you have a sweet tooth, add more sugar, tasting as you go along.

2/3 cup sugar
2/3 cup water
3 cups fresh or frozen cranberries, puréed
2 ripe pears, peeled, cored, and puréed
Grated zest of 2 oranges
2 tablespoons kirsch
1 egg white

Combine sugar and water in a small saucepan and bring to a boil, stirring. When sugar is dissolved, let cool, then chill.

Mix chilled syrup, cranberries, pears, orange zest, and kirsch. Blend well. Freeze until mushy in an ice-cream machine or in metal ice trays.

Place slush in a food processor with egg white. Process until smooth and fluffy. Refreeze in the ice-cream machine and refrigerate at least 1 hour before serving.

MAKES 1 QUART

PINEAPPLE–BANANA SORBET

The flavors of these two tropical fruits are delicious together.

2 cups sugar
2 cups water
1 large pineapple, peeled and cored
2 large ripe bananas, peeled
1/4 cup fresh lemon juice
1/4 cup fresh orange juice

Dissolve sugar in the water over medium heat. Set aside to cool.

Cut pineapple and bananas into chunks and process until almost smooth. Add juices and process to mix. It is not necessary, but it makes a smoother consistency if this mixture is then passed through a strainer.

Add the reserved syrup to the fruit and mix. Pour into an ice-cream maker and freeze according to manufacturer's directions.

MAKES 1 QUART

APPLE SORBET

Our market got in a shipment of rather sad-looking apples. But since everyone was getting a little tired of peaches, as marvelous as they had been, we decided to buy some and make sorbet.

4 small tart apples, peeled, cored, and
    quartered
2/3 cup sugar
2 teaspoons lemon juice
1 cup water
Calvados or other apple brandy (optional)

Put apples, sugar, lemon juice, and water in a medium saucepan and simmer until apples are tender, about 10 minutes. Purée and let cool.

Freeze in an ice-cream freezer according to the manufacturer's directions. When serving, you may make an indentation in the top of each portion with the back of a spoon and fill with brandy, preferably calvados.

MAKES ABOUT 1 QUART

BELLINI SORBET

This sorbet was inspired by the Bellini cocktail made famous at Harry's Bar in Venice. It melts pretty fast, so serve it in chilled bowls.

3/4 cup sugar
1/2 cup water
2 pounds ripe peaches, peeled and pitted
1 tablespoon fresh lemon juice
1 tablespoon crème de cassis
1 1/2 cups dry champagne

Mix sugar and water in a saucepan. Bring to a slow simmer, stirring. When sugar melts in a few minutes, remove from heat and let cool.

Meanwhile, purée peaches with lemon juice in a food processor. Mix with the cooled syrup. Stir in cassis and champagne.

Place mixture in an electric ice-cream freezer and process according to manufacturer's directions. Or place mixture in a shallow metal pan in the freezer, stirring occasionally as the mixture freezes.

MAKES ABOUT 1 QUART

BLACK WALNUT SORBET

As most of you know, black walnuts have a distinctive taste. If you like them, you'll love this. There is really no substitute for the black walnut extract or the liqueur, so if you can't find it, don't make this.

> 3 cups water
> 1 cup sugar
> 1 cup shelled black walnuts, toasted and
>   finely chopped
> 1 tablespoon black walnut extract, or 1/2 cup
>   black walnut liqueur (see Note)
> 2 tablespoons fresh lemon juice

Bring water and sugar to a boil. Remove from heat and add black walnuts, and let macerate overnight.

Add extract or liqueur and lemon juice. Strain and freeze mixture in an ice-cream freezer according to manufacturer's directions. Or you may freeze this without straining.

Note: Grutzmacher's black walnut liqueur is available at some liquor stores and Wagner's black walnut extract is available at good specialty food stores.

MAKES ABOUT 1 QUART

SHERBET

GRAPEFRUIT SHERBET WITH CANDIED GRAPEFRUIT RIND

The light, fresh taste of the grapefruit, with the surprise of its crystallized rind, makes a refreshing finish to a meal.

> 1/2 to 1 grapefruit, unpeeled, cut into
>   1/2-inch pieces (1 1/2 cups)
> 1/2 cup superfine sugar
> 1 1/2 cups water
> 2 tablespoons fresh grapefruit juice
> 2 teaspoons fresh lemon juice
> 1 egg white, beaten into soft peaks
> 2 jiggers vodka
> Candied Grapefruit Rind (page 458)

Put grapefruit in a small saucepan with only enough water to cover and boil slowly until tender (5 to 10 minutes). Drain, discarding the water. Combine grapefruit with 3 tablespoons of the sugar. Put in food processor fitted with a metal blade and mix until grapefruit is puréed.

In a small saucepan, combine remaining sugar and the water. Heat over slow heat until sugar dissolves. Remove and let cool. Put this syrup in freezer for 10 to 15 minutes.

Put grapefruit purée in another saucepan and simmer slowly until thick, 15 to 20 minutes. Keep an eye on it and don't let it scorch. Remove from heat and stir in grapefruit juice. Combine chilled syrup, grapefruit purée, and lemon juice. Just before freezing, add beaten egg white and stir in vodka. Put in automatic ice-cream freezer. Serve with pieces of candied rind.

MAKES 1 QUART

COCONUT NUTMEG MILK SHERBET

You can also make this with low-fat milk.

2½ cups sweetened grated coconut
3 cups milk
¼ cup (firmly packed) dark brown sugar
¾ to 1 teaspoon freshly grated nutmeg
Pinch of salt

Cook coconut in a heavy saucepan over medium heat, stirring constantly, until it begins to caramelize. Set aside 2 tablespoons to use as topping. Pour in milk and bring to a simmer. Add brown sugar. Stir and simmer until sugar is dissolved. Pour into a food processor and process until smooth. Let cool, then chill. Stir in nutmeg and salt. Freeze in an ice-cream maker, following manufacturer's directions.

MAKES ABOUT 1 QUART

BLOOD ORANGE SHERBET

When sliced, blood oranges are one of the most beautiful fruits because of the color variations in any particular batch. They are marvelous simply peeled, sliced, and sprinkled with sugar. Try a scoop of blood orange sherbet with them for a real treat.

⅓ cup sugar
1 cup water
2 cups strained blood orange juice
2 teaspoons fresh lemon juice
2 tablespoons finely grated blood orange zest
2 tablespoons orange-flavored liqueur or
    vodka (optional)
3 large egg whites, beaten until stiff

Combine sugar and water in a small saucepan and heat until sugar is melted and mixture is clear. Remove and chill.

In a glass bowl, combine chilled sugar syrup, orange juice, lemon juice, zest, and liqueur. Mix thoroughly, then fold in the egg whites using an over-and-under motion. Continue folding until no egg whites streaks remain in the mixture.

Pour mixture into an ice-cream maker and freeze until firm according to manufacturer's directions.

MAKES ABOUT 1½ PINTS

BERRY SHERBET

The good thing about this sherbet is that you can use any kind of frozen or fresh berries—raspberries, blackberries, blueberries, or a mixture.

4 cups berries
¾ cup sugar
1 cup water
1 tablespoon vodka
2 egg whites, lightly beaten
Fresh berries

Place berries in a small saucepan and heat, stirring occasionally, for 10 minutes, or until the juice is rendered out. Push berries through a sieve to remove seeds (if using raspberries or blackberries; this is not necessary with blueberries). Discard seeds and set juice aside.

Put sugar and water in a saucepan and bring to a simmer. Simmer slowly for 10 minutes. Combine juice and vodka with syrup, then let cool. Stir in egg whites and freeze in an ice-cream freezer according to manufacturer's directions.

Serve garnished with extra berries if they are fresh.

MAKES 1 QUART

PINEAPPLE SHERBET

Undoubtedly you've had pineapple sherbet many times, but if you have never had it made with shredded fresh pineapple, you have a treat in store.

1 large pineapple, trimmed and cored, the
*   flesh shredded with a fork (about 2 cups*
*   pineapple flesh)*
1 cup unsweetened pineapple juice
2/3 to 1 1/3 cups superfine sugar (depending
*   on the sweetness of pineapple)*
3 tablespoons fresh lemon juice
Rum

Taste pineapple to judge its sweetness, so you will know about how much sugar you will want to use.

Combine pineapple juice with desired amount of sugar in a medium saucepan. Heat, stirring, until all the sugar is dissolved. Let cool slightly, then add lemon juice and fresh pineapple. Add more sugar if mixture is too tart. (And remember, once frozen, mixture will taste less sweet.) Let cool, then chill.

Pour mixture into an ice-cream maker and freeze until firm according to manufacturer's directions.

Top with a bit of rum, if desired, when serving.

MAKES ABOUT 1 1/2 PINTS

ICES

APPLEJACK ICE

Eating applejack ice is like having a crisp, icy-cold apple with just a little kick of brandy. Delicious after a rich meal.

1 1/2 cups unsweetened applesauce
1 1/2 cups unsweetened apple juice
3 1/3 cups superfine sugar
1/4 cup fresh lemon juice
1/4 cup applejack (apple brandy)
Cinnamon sticks or ground cinnamon

Stir together applesauce, apple juice, sugar, and lemon juice in a large bowl. Strain, if desired, through a fine sieve. Pour the mixture into an ice-cream maker and freeze until somewhat firm, about 20 minutes. Pour in applejack and freeze until firm according to the manufacturer's directions.

Serve garnished with a cinnamon stick or with a light sprinkling of cinnamon over the top.

MAKES ABOUT 1 1/2 PINTS

BERRY ICE

If you have Berry Syrup (page 370), you can easily make berry ice, or granita.

Measure out a quantity of syrup and then add one third the amount of water. Mix well and freeze it in an ice-cream freezer or in metal ice-cube trays (without the dividers) in your refrigerator freezer. Stir every 20 to 30 minutes until it sets. Break up any large pieces before serving. If it should freeze solid, break it all up and put in a food processor and give it a few quick whirls. Refrigerate to let it set again for a few minutes.

SUGARLESS BERRY ICE

2 packages (10 ounces each) frozen berries,
*   almost thawed*
²/₃ cup chilled unsweetened apple juice or ice
*   water*
2 tablespoons eau-de-vie or fruit brandy of
*   the berry you are using (optional)*

Purée the almost-thawed berries in a food
processor or blender, strain, then stir in apple
juice.

   Pour the mixture into an ice-cream maker
and freeze according to the manufacturer's
directions until almost firm. If you are using
eau-de-vie, add it now; if not, continue freezing until firm.

MAKES ABOUT 1½ PINTS

GRAPE ICE

Don't use seedless grapes for this; grapes with
seeds have much better flavor.

2 cups white grape juice
½ cup sugar
1½ pounds wine or concord grapes,
*   stemmed*
3 tablespoons fresh lemon juice, or to taste

Combine grape juice and sugar in a medium
saucepan and simmer over low heat until
sugar dissolves and mixture is clear, about 5
minutes.

   Meanwhile, purée grapes in a food processor. Push mixture through a sieve to remove
skins and seeds, then stir grape purée and
lemon juice into grape juice mixture and chill.

   Pour mixture into an ice-cream maker and
freeze according to manufacturer's directions.

MAKES ABOUT 1½ PINTS

BLACKBERRY ICE

During their season, I try to get enough blackberries so that I can make syrup to keep in the
freezer. Should you do this, it is best to freeze
the juice in quantities just large enough to
make a batch of berry ice. That way, you won't
have to defrost the whole thing each time you
want to make it.

2 cups blackberries
¾ cup sugar
1 teaspoon fresh lemon juice
¾ cup water

Put blackberries and sugar in a small enameled pan and bring to a boil. Simmer for about
5 minutes and then add lemon juice. Using a
very fine sieve, strain out the seeds. You may
put this aside at this point or freeze it for later
use.

   To make the ice, add the water to the syrup
and pour into several metal ice-cube trays
(without the dividers). Stir every 20 or 30 minutes as it begins to freeze. If it gets too solid,
break it up and put in a food processor for a
few whirls.

   You may, of course, make the ice in an electric ice-cream maker.

MAKES ABOUT 1 PINT

RASPBERRY ICE

Almost any variety of berry can be used here,
with or without the seeds and pulp, sweetened
to taste. Remember, though, that freezing
diminishes the sweetness of the mixture, so it
should taste a little sweeter before freezing
than you might like.

3½ cups fresh raspberries
2 tablespoons fresh lemon juice
1 cup ice water
½ to ¾ cup superfine sugar, depending on
*   sweetness of berries*
2 large egg whites, beaten to soft peaks

In a food processor or blender, purée berries with lemon juice, then set aside. Mix water and sugar in a small saucepan and set over low heat, stirring until sugar is dissolved. Let cool.

Combine purée and sugar mixture and mix well. Fold in egg whites. Pour the mixture into an ice-cream maker and freeze until firm according to manufacturer's directions.

MAKES ABOUT 1½ PINTS

GRAPEFRUIT ICE

½ to 1 medium grapefruit, unpeeled
½ cup superfine sugar
1½ cups water
2 teaspoons fresh lemon juice
1 large egg white, beaten to soft peaks
Vodka (optional)

Squeeze out 2 tablespoons juice from grapefruit and set aside. Cut grapefruit into ½-inch pieces (for about 1½ cups) and put into a saucepan with just enough water to cover. Over low heat, boil slowly until tender, about 10 minutes. Drain, discarding the water. Combine grapefruit with 3 tablespoons of the sugar and purée in a food processor.

In a medium saucepan, combine remaining sugar and the water. Stir over low heat until sugar dissolves. Remove and let cool, then freeze for 10 to 15 minutes. Meanwhile, simmer grapefruit purée until thick, about 15 to 20 minutes. Make sure it doesn't scorch. Stir in grapefruit and lemon juices and the sugar syrup and chill. Just before freezing, fold in egg white.

Pour the mixture into an ice-cream maker and freeze according to manufacturer's directions.

If desired, make an indentation on the top of each scoop with a tablespoon and fill with vodka.

MAKES ABOUT 1 QUART

LEMON ICE WITH RUM

1½ cups fresh lemon juice
1 tablespoon grated lemon zest
3 cups Simple Syrup (page 371)
Rum

Put lemon juice, zest, and syrup in a metal bowl and mix. Put the bowl in the freezer with a plate over it. Give the mixture a stir now and again as it begins to freeze. It is ready to eat when it gets granular. If it should freeze too solid, give it a few whirls in a blender (in batches) or food processor.

Splash rum over each serving.

MAKES ABOUT 1½ PINTS

LIME ICE

This makes a very tart ice, so if you have a sweet tooth, add more sugar.

1½ cups fresh lime juice
½ cup water
2¼ cups confectioners' sugar

Combine all the ingredients and mix well. Refrigerate for several hours, then freeze in an ice-cream freezer.

If you would like to do this in the freezer compartment of your refrigerator, put the mixture in metal ice-cube trays (without the dividers) and freeze, stirring every 20 to 30 minutes to keep it from freezing solid. Garnish with lime slices.

MAKES A LITTLE LESS THAN 1 QUART

LEMONY LIME ICE

Another easy recipe, with a little bite.

*1 to 1½ cups fresh lime juice (or a
  combination of lime and lemon)
3 cups Simple Syrup (page 371) (see Note)
Grated zest of 1 lemon*

Combine 1 cup of the juice with the simple
syrup. Since lime juice is very tart, add juice
carefully until you get a balance you like.
(Remember that when the mixture is frozen, it
will not taste as sweet as it does at this stage.)
Stir in grated zest, pour mixture into an ice-
cream maker, and freezer according to manufacturer's directions.

*Note: Make the syrup from 3 cups each sugar
and water.*

MAKES 2½ PINTS

MIXED TROPICAL FRUIT
ICE

Buy whatever looks good in the market—
watermelon and other melons, pineapple,
starfruit, mangoes, or papaya, in any combination. Cut up the fruit as for fruit salad and force
the fruit pulp through a sieve. Add sugar and
fresh lemon juice to taste. Then pour the mixture into metal ice-cube trays (without the
dividers), or some other kind of metal container, and freeze, stirring occasionally to keep
it from becoming solid.

PEAR ICE

What a marvelously refreshing flavor this has.

*1½ cups pear purée (made from 3 ripe
  medium pears, peeled and cored)
1½ cups Simple Syrup (page 371)
  (see Note)
1 tablespoon fresh lemon juice
Pear brandy (optional)*

In a large bowl, mix pear purée, simple syrup,
and lemon juice. Pour into an ice-cream
maker and freeze according to manufacturer's directions.

If desired, to serve, make an indentation in
the top of each scoop of ice with the back of a
tablespoon and fill with a tablespoon of pear
brandy.

*Note: Make the syrup from 1½ cups each
sugar and water.*

MAKES 1½ TO 2 PINTS

504

INDEX

Acorn Squash
  Baked, 139
  Buttered, 141
  Casserole, Sweet, 140
  and Green Beans, Puréed, 155
  and Turnip Soup, 19
All-Purpose Vinaigrette, 354
All-Shortening Pie Pastry, 405
Almond
  -Apple Custard, 472
  -Blackberry Jam Cake, 414
  -Pear Torte, 423
  -Pecan Custard, 480
  Sauce, Apple Dumplings with, 466
  Tart with Apricot Ice Cream, 390
Amaretti-Mascarpone Custard, 475
Ambrosia
  Crumble, 404
  Orange, Coconut, and Date, 462
  Papaya, Banana, and Coconut, 462
Ancho Chili Cream, 39
Anchovies, Capers, Basil, and Pine Nuts (relish), 360
Anchovy Vinaigrette, 50, 104
Angel Biscuits, 305
Angel Food Cake
  Chocolate, 424
  with Lemon Sauce and Raspberries, 424
Angel Hair. See also Pasta
  with Spinach, Tomatoes, and Three Cheeses, 83
Angel Pie, Aunt Lady Carter's, 385
Apple(s)
  -Almond Custard, 472
  Applesauce
    with Sautéed Apples, Fresh, 362
    Spice Cake, 416
    Warm, with Cream, 361
  Braised, and Red Onions, 164

-Cherry Crisp, 403
-Cinnamon Muffins, 316
Cobbler, 401
Dumplings with Almond Sauce, 466
Fritters, English, 336
and Green Pear Chutney, 357
and Green Tomato Pie, 374
Pear, and Celery Salad, Chopped, 63
Pie, 374
Sautéed, 164
Sorbet, 498
Tart, Napa Valley, 391
Applejack and Champagne, 371
Applejack Ice, 501
Applesauce
  with Sautéed Apples, Fresh, 362
  Spice Cake, 416
  Warm, with Cream, 361
Apricot(s)
  Butter, 351
  Pink Peppercorns, and Mint, Poached, with Crème Fraîche, 463
  Poached, with Pear Purée, 465
  Purée, 364
  Steamed Carrots with, 112
Artichoke(s)
  with Black Olive Butter, 100
  Bottoms, Stuffed, 100
  Mushroom, and Fennel Ragout, 124
  Salad, Warm, 57
  Steamed, 100
Arugula, 47–48. See also Salad
  Boston Lettuce, and Julienne Red Pepper Salad, 47
  and Lettuce Salad with Rice Wine Vinaigrette, 48
  and Swiss Cheese Salad, 48
Asian Pears, Cambazola Cheese and, 482
Asparagus
  Glazed, 101
  and Onion Sauce, Fettuccine with, 80
  Pockets, Grilled, 101

Raw, and Lettuce Salad with Mustard Vinaigrette, 57
with Shallots, 101
Simple Sautéed, 101
Soup, 9
Tiny Fresh, 102
Vinaigrette, 58
with Warm Tomato Vinaigrette, 102
Aspic
  Red Bell Pepper, 137
  Tomato
    with Crabmeat Salad, 257
    Fresh, 145
    Fresh, and Feta Cheese, 72
    with Mayonnaise, 72
Avocado(s)
  and Corn Salsa, 356
  Dressing, Chicken Fajitas with, 333
  with Lime Vinaigrette, 59
  Mayonnaise, Creole Tomatoes with, 71
  Onion, Tomato, and Hot Pepper Salad, Chopped, 59
  Salad with Cilantro Vinaigrette, 58
  Sliced, Salad with Lemon Vinaigrette, 58

Baby Lettuces, Mixed, with Honey-Lemon Dressing, 46
Bacon
  and Baked Tomato Sauce, Spaghetti with, 88
  Bean, Potato, and Red Pepper Soup, 25
  Butter Beans with, 105
  Fresh Porcini Mushrooms Baked with, 128
  -Molasses Dressing, 215
  and Onion Corn Muffins, 307; variations, 307
  -Onion Pie, 395

Sauce, Fettuccine with Spicy
Tomato and, 85
Smoked, and Wild
Mushrooms in Puff
Pastry, 125
Balsamic Vinaigrette, 44
Ballpark Mustard Dressing, 76
Banana(s)
in Brown Sugar and Rum, 457
Clafouti, 476
Layer Cake, 410
Papaya, and Coconut
Ambrosia, 462
-Pineapple Sorbet, 498
Pudding Cake, 430
Sautéed, 457
Walnut Muffins, 316
Whipped Cream, 365
Bar Cookies, 450–55
Blondies, 452
Brownies, Outrageous, 451
Brownies, Shasta Mountain,
451
Cappuccino Brownies, 453
Chocolate Squares, 451
Lemon Squares, 453
Lemon Walnut Bars, 454
Marshmallow-Butterscotch -
Peanut Squares, 484
Rocky Road Squares with
Caramel Sauce, 452
Shortbread, 454; Brown
Sugar, 454; Hazelnut, 455
Texas, 455
Barbecued
Brisket, Slow Oven-, 227
Corn on the Cob, 114
Onions, 130
Shrimp and Capellini with
Shrimp Sauce, 267
Sirloin, Oven-, 228
Basmati Rice. See also Rice
Loaf, 177
and Wild Rice Salad, 179
and Wild Rice with Swiss
Chard, 174
Bean(s). 191–95. See also Green
Bean; Lentils; Lima Bean;
White Bean
about quick-soaking, 25
Bacon, Potato, and Red
Pepper Soup, 25
Black Bean
Cuban, 192
and Jicama Salad, 195

and Macaroni Soup, 24
Butter Beans with Bacon, 105
and Pasta Soup, 27
Pinto Beans, 191
Red Bean
Mustard Green, Sweet
Potato, and Ham Soup,
31
and Rice Salad, 178
Succotash, 192
Salad, Two-, 61
Soup, Five-, 24
Walnuts, Pumpkin, and
Prunes, Lamb and Pork
with, 238
Beaten Biscuits, 303
Béchamel Sauce, Light, 187
Beef, 226–31
Beefsteak Florentine, 231
Brisket of, Boiled, 227
Brisket, Slow Oven -
Barbecued, 227
-Filled Empanadas, 338
Filling, Oriental, for Little
Pies, 398
Garlic Smoked Tenderloin of,
226
Lemon Stroganoff, 229
Mediterranean Patties, 249
Roast, Tenderloin of, with
Shallot Butter, 226
Roast, Tenderloin Steak, 226
Salad, 230
Sirloin, Oven-Barbecued, 228
Stew, Best, 228
Stew with Rum and Olives,
230
Stock, 42
Beet(s)
Baby, and Greens, 106
Buttered, 105
Carrot, and Sweet Potato
Soup, 9
and Carrots, Purée of, 151
Cold (Salad), 59
Endive, and Red Onion Salad,
Chopped, 60
Grated Baked, 105
and Lamb Soup, 32
Pickled, and Wilted Red
Onions Salad, 60
Salad, Fresh, 59
Salad with Onion, 60
and Turnips, 147
Bell Pepper(s). See also Green,
Red, Yellow Peppers

and Onion, 136
Bellini Sorbet, 498
Benne. See also Sesame
seeds, about toasting, 329
Wafers, Whole Wheat, 329
Berry(ies). See also Name of
Berry
and Black Cherry Sauce, 364
Butter, 352
Chutney, Fresh, 357
Dumplings, 337
Honey, 371
Ice, 501; Sugarless, 502
Ice Cream, 492
and Jam Tartlets, 393
Meringues with, and
Whipped Cream, 380
and Peach Shortcake with
Warm Cream Sauce, 434
Preserves, Refrigerator, 369
Salsa, Fresh, 355
Sauce, Cooked, 363
Sherbet, 500
Shortcake, Mixed, 433
Soufflé, Cold, 467
Summer Pudding, 476
Sweet Simplicity, 457
Syrup, 370
Vinaigrette, 52
Vinegar, 355
Beverage
Café au Lait, 372
Champagne and Applejack,
371
Iced Coffee with Brandy, 372
Vodka, Flavored, 372
Bibb Lettuce. See also Salad
and Boston Lettuce Salad with
Fruit Vinaigrette, 50
and Cheese Salad, 48
Salad with Peppercorn
Vinaigrette, 49
Biscotti, Pecan-Coconut, 449
Biscuits, 303–6. See also Bread;
Muffins; Popovers; Rolls
Angel, 305
Biscuits, 303; Beaten, 303
Buttermilk, 304; Drop, 304
Cottage Cheese, 305
Flaky, with Parsley Butter, 306
Mozzarella, 306
Sausage and Cheese Drop,
306
Shortcake, I, 304; II, 304
Bishop's Bread, 312

Bitter Lemon Tart, 389
Black Bean(s). *See also* Beans
    Cuban, 192
    and Jicama Salad, 195
    and Macaroni Soup, 24
Black Cherry and Berry Sauce,
    364
Black Olive Little Pies, 400
Black Walnut
    Divinity, 487
    -Maple Ice Cream, 493
    Sorbet, 498
Blackberry(ies)
    -Almond Jam Cake, 414
    Buckle with Blackberry Sauce,
        422; blueberry variation,
        422
    Cobbler, 402; boysenberry
        variation, 402
    Ice, 502
    Jam Tart, 388
    Ketchup, 370
    Mango with, 458
    Mousse, 469
    Pie, Deep-Dish, 377
    Roll, 422
    Sauce, 364
    Vinaigrette, 53
    -Walnut Conserve, 369
Blondies (cookies), 452
Blood Orange Sherbet, 500
Blowout Ice Cream, 490
Blowouts (cookies), 440
Blue Corn Enchiladas, 332
Blueberry(ies)
    Brown Betty, 405
    Cinnamon Syrup, 371
    Muffins, 317
    Pie, 376
    Shortcake, 434
    Summer Pudding, 476
Boar, Mock, Roasted with a
    Mustard Coating, 240
Boar, Wild, Sausage and Grilled
    Venison, 253
Boiled Crab, Crawfish, Shrimp,
    Corn, and Potatoes, 272
Boston Lettuce Salad. *See also*
    Salad
    Arugula, and Julienne Red
        Pepper, 47
    and Bibb Lettuce with Fruit
        Vinaigrette, 50
    and Fennel, 65

    with Peas and Anchovy
        Vinaigrette, 50
    and Raw Asparagus, with
        Mustard Vinaigrette, 57
    with Sherry Vinaigrette, 49
    with Toasted Goat Cheese, 49
    with Walnut Vinaigrette and
        Cambazola, 50
Bourbon
    Icebox Cake, Layered, 428
    -Mint Ice Cream, 496
    -Pecan Ice Cream, 496
    Sauce, 368; Bourbon Cream,
        367
    Whipped Cream, 365
Boysenberry Pyramids, 387
Boysenberry Sauce, 365
Bran Raisin Muffins, 316
Brandied Peaches, 459
Brandy Custard with Fresh
    Berries, 474
Bread, 294–300. *See also*
    Biscuits; Crispbread;
    Muffins; Popovers; Rolls;
    Spoon Bread; Sticky Buns
    Bishop's, 312
    Cajun Three-Pepper, 297;
        Oreganato, 297
    Cinnamon-Oatmeal Raisin,
        312
    Corn, Buttermilk-Sour
        Cream, 309
    Corn, Skillet, 308
    Cornsticks, 309
    Cracker, 330
    Crumb Cups, Chili-Tomato
        Eggs in, 2
    English Muffin Loaf, 296
    Focaccia, 327
    French, New Orleans, 295
    Garlic, 295
    Gingerbread, Golden Raisin,
        313
    Ham Cake, 313
    Monkey, 294
    Parmesan Onion Puffs, 300
    Pepper, 340
    Pepper, Skillet, 300
    Pizza, Onion and Black Olive,
        326
    Scallion, Deep-Fried, 299
    Scotch Unkneaded, 298
    Sesame Breadsticks, 298
    Sourdough, 294
    Sunflower, 296
    Tomato Gougère, 299

    and Tomato Salad, 70
Bread Pudding, 479
    Soufflé, 478
    with Whiskey Sauce, 478
Breadsticks, Sesame, 298
breakfast. *See* Eggs
Broccoli
    Basic, 106
    and Carrot Purée, 152
    Pasta with, 79
    Refrigerator Pickled, 160
    Sautéed, 106
    Steamed, and Cauliflower,
        107
Broccoli Rabe
    and Sausage, Two-Bean Soup
        with, 26
    Soup, 10; Puréed, 10
Brown Betty, Blueberry, 405
Brown Butter, Eggs in, 3
Brown Sauce for Pasta, 94
Brown Sugar Glazed Cake, 418
Brown Sugar Shortbread, 454
Browned Butter Eggs, Baked, 3
Brownie(s)
    Cappuccino, 453
    Chocolate Pie, 384
    Cookies, Dropped, 439
    Outrageous, 451
    Shasta Mountain, 451
    Brownie(s)
Brussels Sprouts with Mustard,
    107
Brussels Sprouts, Roasted
    Shallots, and Roasted
    Yellow Bell Peppers, 107
Bucatini. *See also* Pasta
    with Black Pepper, Bread
        Crumbs, and Pecorino, 89
Bulgur
    Buttered with Black Olives,
        167
    Pasta and Grain Pilaf, 167
    Salad, 167
    Tabbouleh, 168
Bundt Cake, Cream Cheese, 417
Buns, Sticky, 314
Butter
    Beans with Bacon, 105
    Flavored, 350–52. *See also*
        Flavored Butter
    -Margarine Tart Crust, 407
    Rum Sauce, 368
Buttermilk
    Biscuits, 304; Drop, 304

Chicken with Deep Gravy, 199
Dressing (for Pasta), 82
Rolls, Quick, 300
-Sour Cream Corn Bread, 309
Vegetable Soup, Chilled,
    23
Butternut Squash
    Duck, and Turnip Soup, 30
    and Leek Purée, 155
    Purée, 140
    and Zucchini Soup, 23
Butterscotch
    -Marshmallow-Peanut
        Squares, 484
    Meringue Pie, 378
    Pecan Cookies, 448
    Pie, Pecan Crust, 382
    Pudding, 475
    Sauce, 367

Cabbage. See also Coleslaw
    and Carrots with Ginger,
        Sautéed, 109
    Green, Steamed, 108
    and Lamb, Penne with, 87
    Potato, Bell Pepper, and
        Onion Mélange, 110
    and Potato Gratin, 187
    Slaw, Warm, 110
    Steamed, 108
    Stuffed with Grains, Nuts, and
        Vegetables, 108
    Stuffed with Pork and Apple,
        244
Cabernet Sauce, Roast
        Tenderloin of Venison
        with, 253
Cabernet Wine Sauce, Roasted
        Lamb Loin with, 235
Caesar Salad, Southwestern, 51;
        Cornbread Croutons for,
        51
Café au Lait, 372
Cajun Three-Pepper Bread, 297
Cake, 410–34. See also Angel
        Food; Cheesecake; Layer
        Cake; Pan and Loaf Cake;
        Pound Cake; Pudding
        Cake; Shortcake; Torte;
        Tube Cake
    Almond-Blackberry Jam, 414
    Almond-Pear Torte, 423

Angel Food, with Lemon
        Sauce and Raspberries,
        424
Applesauce Spice, 416
Banana Layer, 410
Banana Pudding, 430
Berry Shortcake, Mixed, 433
Blackberry Buckle with
        Blackberry Sauce, 422;
        blueberry variation, 422
Blackberry Roll, 422
Blueberry Shortcake, 434
Bourbon Icebox, Layered,
        428
Brown Sugar Glazed, 418
Carrot, with Cream Cheese
        Icing, 420
Chocolate
    Angel Food, 424
    Layer, 426
    Mousse Cheesecake, 432
    Toffee Nut Pudding, 431
Coconut, 411; Old -Fashioned,
        417
Cream Cheese Bundt, 417
Devil's Food, with Chocolate
        Buttercream Icing, 426
Fig Pudding, 429
Flourless Chocolate, 425; and
        Walnut, 427
Fruitcake, White, 419
Gingerbread, Warm, 419
Intermont White, 410
Lemon Pudding, 430
Natchez Lemon, 412
Nut Torte, California, 423
Peach
    and Berry Shortcake with
        Warm Cream Sauce,
        434
    Crumble, 421
    Fresh, 413
Pear Pudding, 431
Pecan, Golden, with Pecan
        Divinity Icing, 415
Pecan, Plantation, 416
Pineapple-Upside Down, 421
Pistachio and Pecan
        Meringue, with
        Strawberry Filling, 382
Plum Jam, 414
Pound, Cayenne, 428
Savory Cheesecake, 432
Sherry Spice, with Creamy
        Brown Sugar Glaze, 420

Sour Cream Pound, 427; with
        Poached Fruit, 428
Strawberry Shortcake, 433
Sunshine Cream, 418
Calf Liver and Onions, Classic,
        235
Cambazola Cheese and Asian
        Pears, 482
Canapés, Radish, 343
Candied Grapefruit Rind, 458
Candy, 485–87. See also
        Children's Favorites
    Black Walnut Divinity, 487
    Chocolate Fudge, 485
    Chocolate-Nut Toffee, 486
    Mamie Eisenhower Fudge,
        485
    Nut Brittle, 487
    Peanut Butter Fudge, 486
    Pralines, 486
Capellini. See also Pasta
    and Barbecued Shrimp with
        Shrimp Sauce, 267
Caper Sauce, 346
Cappuccino Brownies, 453
Caramel Coconut Flan, 470
Caramel-Raspberry Sauce, 363
Carrot(s), 110–12
    with Apricots, Steamed, 112
    and Baked Onions, Purée of,
        152
    Beet, and Sweet Potato Soup,
        9
    and Beets, Purée of, 151
    and Broccoli Purée, 152
    Cake with Cream Cheese
        Icing, 420
    Cake Waffles, 320
    and Cauliflower, Puréed, 151
    and Cucumber Salad, Sweet,
        63
    and Cucumber, Thai Salad
        with, 63
    Custard, 112
    and Dill Soup, 11
    and Endive Salad with Berry
        Vinaigrette, 52
    Honey, 112
    Lemon, 111
    and Red Bell Pepper Soup, 12
    Slaw, 62
    and Tomato Soup, 11
    and Turnips, Candied, 110

508

Turnips, and Onions, Glazed, 111
and Yellow Bell Peppers, Buttered, with Parsley, 111
White Pepper, 111
Cassis Sorbet, 497
Cauliflower
 and Carrots, Puréed, 151
 and Cress Soup, 12
 and Mashed Potatoes, 185
 Roasted Onion, and Leek Purée, 152
 Roasted Onion, and Pear, Purée of, 153
 Steamed Broccoli and, 107
Cayenne Pound Cake, 428
Celery
 Apple, and Pear Salad, Chopped, 63
 Fennel, and Parsley Salad with Shaved Parmesan, 65
 Root Rémoulade, 113
Champagne
 and Applejack, 371
 Grapes with Cheese, 482
 Rabbit with Apple and Green Pear Chutney, 251
 Vinaigrette, 46
Charcoaled Bourbon-Marinated Lamb Steaks, 236
Cheese
 and Ham Muffins, 315; bacon, sausage variations, 315
 -and-Herb-Stuffed Pasilla Chiles, 135
 and Onion Pie, 394
 Pastry, 407
 Pecan Twists, 331; paprika variation, 331
 Sandwiches, Grilled, 338
 and Sausage Drop Biscuits, 306
 Steak Sandwiches, 342
 Toasts, 329
 and Turkey Enchilada Casserole, 216
Cheese Dessert, 482
 Cambazola Cheese and Asian Pears, 482
 Champagne Grapes with Cheese, 482
 Olive, Cheese and Plums, 482

Peaches and Fresh Pecorino with Honey and Black Pepper, 482
Cheesecake, Chocolate Mousse, 432
Cheesecake, Savory, 432
Cherry(ies)
 -Apple Crisp, 403
 Black, and Berry Sauce, 364
 and Chocolate Trifle, 479
 Dried, and Dried Strawberry Muffins, 315
 Melon Balls with, 459
 and Plums, Poached, 464
 Rum, Ice Cream, 492
Chess Pie, 386
Chèvre Vinaigrette, 47
Chicken, 197–216
 -Apple Sausage, 222
 Breasts
  Grilled, Conchiglie with, and Goat Cheese, 91
  Grilled Marinated, 199
  Grilled, with Tabasco-Honey Glaze, 201
  Roasted, with Pan Gravy, 206
  Sesame, 200
 Buttermilk, with Deep Gravy, 199
 Champagne, with Apple and Green Pear Chutney, 251
 Cutlets, Italian, 200
 and Dill Soup, 29
 and Dumpling Pie, Double-Crust, 212
 Enchiladas with Andouille Sausage, 205
 Enchiladas, and Walnut, with Roasted Green Chili Sauce, 204
 Fajitas with Avocado Dressing, 333
 Filling for Little Pies, 401
 Garlic, 197
 Greek Lemon, 197
 Gumbo variation, 269
 Gumbo Ya Ya, 206
 and Ham Filling for Little Pies, 399
 Lemon, with Sour Cream Sauce, 202
 Loaf, 210
 and Okra Gumbo, 207
 Pancakes with Peach Salsa, 210

Pot Pie with Biscuit Topping, 211
Pot Pie with Cornbread Crust, 213
 with Prunes and Hot Peppers, 203
 with Raspberry Vinegar, 202
Rigodon, 208
Salad
 Chipotle, 216
 Traditional, 214
 Warm, with Hazelnut Vinaigrette, 215
 Warm Spicy, with Bacon-Molasses Dressing, 215
Sauce Piquant, 201
Sausage Patties, 222
Soup, Lemon, 28
Southern Fried Pecan, 198
Spicy, Milk-Fried, with Pan Gravy, 198
and Spicy Sausage, Macaroni Casserole with, 214
Stock, 41
with Tuna Sauce, 208
Walnut, and Red Pepper Little Pies, 397
and White Bean Chili, 209
Children's Favorites, 483–84. See also Candy
 Chocolate Cookie Log, 484
 Chocolate-Pecan-Raisin Clusters, 483
 Graham Cracker Pickups, Freddie's, 485
 Marshmallow-Butterscotch-Peanut Squares, 484
 Molasses Popcorn Balls, 483
 Popcorn Balls, 483
Chiles, Pasilla, Cheese-and-Herb-Stuffed, 135
Chiles Rellenos, Baked, 136
Chili
 Ancho, Cream, 39
 Chicken and White Bean, 209
 Green, and Corn Chowder, 14
 Green, Polenta, 170
 Sauce, Roasted Green, Chicken and Walnut Enchiladas with, 204
 Sauce with Sausage (for pasta), 95
 Sausage, 250

Spoon Bread, 311
-Tomato Eggs in Bread
    Crumb Cups, 2
-Tomato Sauce, Eggs Poached
    in, 2
Chipotle Chicken Salad, 216
Chocolate
    Angel Food Cake, 424
    Brownie(s)
        Cappuccino, 453
        Cookies, Dropped, 439
        Outrageous, 451
        Pie, 384
        Shasta Mountain, 451
    Cake, 425–27
        Devil's Food, with
            Chocolate Buttercream
            Icing, 426
        Flourless, 425
        Flourless and Walnut, 427
    Layer, 426
    and Cherry Trifle, 479
    -Chocolate Chip Ice Cream,
        490
    Chunk Cookies, 437
    -Coffee-Macadamia Spreads,
        437
    Cookie Log, 484; variations,
        484
    Cream Pie with Chocolate
        Meringue, 379
    Custard Pie, 384
    Fudge, 485
    Fudge, Mamie Eisenhower,
        485
    Macadamia Flan, 471
    Milk, Macaroons, 438
    Mousse Cheesecake, 432
    Nougat Ice Cream, 489
    -Nut Toffee, 486
    -Pecan-Raisin Clusters, 483
    Pots de Crème, 474
    Sauce, 367
    Soufflé, Carol's, 468
    Squares, 451
    Steamed Pudding, 477
    Terrine, Triple, with Crème
        Anglaise and Raspberry
        Sauce, 467
    Toffee Nut Pudding Cake,
        431
    Whipped Cream, 365
    White, Ice Cream, 489
Chowder. See also Soup

Corn, 13
    and Green Chili, 14
    and Oyster, 38
    White, and Oyster, with
        Ancho Chili Cream, 39
    Okra, 16
    Smoked Salmon and Corn, 37
Chutney, 357–58. See also Relish
    Apple and Green Pear, 357
    Berry, 357
    Mango, Fresh, 358
    Pineapple, Fresh, 358
    Tomato, Fresh, 358
Cilantro Vinaigrette, 58
Cinnamon
    Custard Ice Cream, 491
    -Oatmeal Raisin Bread, 312
    Walnut Twists, 450
Citrus Dressing, 70
Citrus Lace Cookies, 435
Clafouti, Banana, 476
Clams. See also Seafood
    Baked, 272
Cloverleaf Rolls, 302
Cobbler, 401–3
    Apple, 401
    Blackberry, 402; boysen-
        berry variation, 402
    Pastry, 408
    Peach, 403
    Pear-Raspberry, 402
    Plum, 402
Coconut
    Cake, 411
    Cake, Old-Fashioned, 417
    Cream Pie with Coconut
        Meringue, 381
    Flan, 471; Coconut Caramel,
        470
    Nutmeg Milk Sherbet, 500
    Orange, and Date Ambrosia,
        462
    Papaya, and Banana
        Ambrosia, 462
    -Pecan Biscotti, 449
    Toasted, Ice Cream, 492
    -Walnut Jumbles, 439
    Whipped Cream, 366
Coeur de Crème, 474
Coffee
    Café au Lait, 372
    -Chocolate-Macadamia
        Spreads, 437
    Iced, with Brandy, 372
    Sauce, Irish, 368
Cold Soup. See also Soup

Asparagus, 9
Buttermilk Vegetable,
    Chilled, 23
Carrot and Red Bell Pepper,
    12
Corn, Creamed, and Red Bell
    Pepper, 13
Corn and Green Chili
    Chowder, 14
Crab Gazpacho, 34
Green, 14
Greens, Turnip, and Corn, 15
Pimiento, Cold, 17
Radish, Cold, 18
Sweet Pea, 17
Sweet Potato Vichyssoise, 18
Tomato
    Cold Roasted, and Red Bell
        Pepper, 21
    Cold Roasted, with Chervil,
        20
    Uncooked, 22
Cold-Water Corn Cakes, 310
Coleslaw, I, II, 56. See also Slaw
    Grilled Shrimp with, on
        Pepper Bread, 340
    New Orleans, 56
Composed Salad, 73
Compote, Tropical Fruit, 461
Conchiglie with Grilled Chicken
    Breasts and Goat Cheese,
    91
Confit of Garden Vegetables, 156
Conserve and Preserves, 369–70.
    See also Relish
    Berry, Refrigerator, 369
    Blackberry Ketchup, 370
    Blackberry-Walnut, 369
    Fig (conserve), 369
    Fig, Freddie's (preserves), 493
    Red Onion Marmalade, 370
Consommé, Mushroom, 15
Cookies, 435–55. See also Bar;
    Drop; Icebox; Rolled;
    Shaped Cookies
    Blondies, 452
    Blowouts, 440
    Brownie(s)
        Dropped, 439
        Cappuccino, 453
        Outrageous, 451
        Shasta Mountain, 451
    Butterscotch Pecan, 448
    Chocolate
        Chunk, 437

510

Cookie Log, 484; variations, 484
Squares, 451
Cinnamon Walnut Twists, 450
Citrus Lace, 435
Coconut-Walnut Jumbles, 439
Coffee-Chocolate -Macadamia Spreads, 437
Cracked Sugar, 444
Filled, 442
Fruitcake, 448
Ginger and Spice, Vermont, 435
Hazelnut Meringue, 438; variations, 438
Icebox, 447
Lemon
  Crisps, 436
  Sand Tarts, 443
  Squares, 453
  Walnut Bars, 454
Macaroons, Milk Chocolate, 438
Oatmeal-Raisin, 438
Peanut Butter, 447; Shasta Mountain, 446
Pecan, 441
  -Coconut Biscotti, 449
  Lace, 440
  Tiles, 450
Pepper Sugar, 445
Praline, 441
Rocks, 436
Rocky Road Squares with Caramel Sauce, 452
Shortbread, 454; Brown Sugar, 454; Hazelnut, 455
Snickerdoodles, 445
Spice, New World, 443
Spice Sables, 449
Sugar, 444
Tea Cakes, 442
Texas, 455
Three-Nut, 446
Vanilla Crescents, 444
Venetian, 446
Walnut, 441
Corn, 113–16
  and Avocado Salsa, 356
  Barbecued, on the Cob, 114
  Blue, Enchiladas, 332
  Bread, Buttermilk-Sour Cream, 309
  Bread, Skillet, 308

Cakes
  Cold-Water, 310
  Sweet, 307
  Zucchini, 310
Chowder, 13
off the Cob, 113
on the Cob, Steamed, 113
Cornbread Croutons, 51
Cornbread Stuffing, 219
Cornsticks, 309
Crab Bisque, 34
Creamed, 114
Creamed, and Red Bell Pepper Soup, 13
Fried, 114
and Green Chili Chowder, 14
Greens, and Turnip Soup, 15
Kernel Spoon Bread, 311
Maque Choux, 116
Muffins, 308
  Bacon and Onion, 307; ham variations, 307
  Fresh, 308
  Jalapeño, 310
New Potato, and Red Bell Pepper Salad, 191
Okra, and Tomatoes, Sautéed, 129
Omelet, 4
and Oyster Chowder, 38
Peppers Stuffed with, 137
Potatoes, Crab, Crawfish, and Shrimp, Boiled, 272
and Prosciutto Fritters, 334
Pudding, Creamed, 116
Relish, Fresh, 359
and Rice, 116
Roasted, Salsa, 355
Salad, 64
and Salmon Croquettes, 282
Skillet Baked, 115
Skillet Creamed, 115
and Smoked Salmon Chowder, 37
Smoked Salmon, and Goat Cheese, Rotini with, 90
Timbales, 115
Wafers, 330
White, and Oyster Chowder with Ancho Chili Cream, 39
White, Sauce, Fettuccine with Gorgonzola and, 80
Yellow Tomatoes, and Peppers, Rigatoni with, 84

Cornbread Croutons, 51
Cornbread Stuffing, 219
Cornmeal. See also Spoon Bread
  Fried Oysters, 274
  Pan-Fried Green Tomatoes, 146
Cornsticks, 309
Cottage Cheese Biscuits, 305
Coulis, Tomato, 353
Court-Bouillon, 266
Couscous-Stuffed Tomatoes, Warm, 143
Crab(s), Crabmeat, 256–60. See also Seafood
  Cakes, Baked, 257
  Cakes, Maryland, 258
  Claws, Stone, with Hot Ketchup Mayonnaise, 260
  Corn Bisque, 34
  Crawfish, Shrimp, Corn, and Potatoes, Boiled, 272
  Dungeness, Cakes with Jalapeño-Lime Mayonnaise, 258
  Gazpacho, 34
  Gulf Shrimp, and Oyster Stew, 268
  with Ravigote Sauce, 259
  Salad, Tomato Aspic with, 257
  Soft-Shell, Fried, 256
  Soft-Shell, with Lemon Butter Sauce, 256
Cracked Sugar Cookies, 444
Cracker Bread, 330
Crackers, Ice-Water, Toasted, 328
Cranberry
  -Hot Pepper Sauce, 362
  Orange, and Raisin Sauce, 362
  -Pear Sorbet, 498
Crawfish, 260–62. See also Seafood
  Bisque, 35
  Crab, Shrimp, Corn, and Potatoes, Boiled, 272
  Fettuccine, 261
  Sauce, Pasta with, 89
  and Shrimp Creole, New Orleans, 265
  Smothered, with Ham Stuffing, 260
  with Spicy Tomato Sauce, 261
  -Stuffed Eggplant "Tortillas" with Tomatillo Sauce, 262

511

Cream Cheese Bundt Cake, 417
Cream Cheese Ice Cream, Creole, 497
Crème Anglaise, 366
Crème Fraîche Pancakes, 319
Creole
    Cream Cheese Ice Cream, 497
    Sauce, 346
    Tomatoes with Avocado Mayonnaise, 71
Crepes, 321
Crepes, Stuffed with Red Bell Pepper Sauce, 321
Cress. *See also* Watercress and Cauliflower Soup, 12
    Lentil, and Fennel Soup, 27
Crisp(s)
    Apple-Cherry, 403
    Lemon, 436
    Peach, with Bourbon Sauce, 404
Crispbread and Crackers, 327–31
    Cracker Bread, 330
    Crackers, Ice-Water, Toasted, 328
    Croutons, Fried, 328
    Melba Toast, 327
    Pita Bread Triangles, Toasted, 327
    Pita Chips, Grilled, 328
    Toasts, Cheese, 329
    Toasts, Sun-Dried Tomato, 328
    Tortilla Triangles, Puffed, 327
    Twists, Cheese Pecan, 331; paprika variation, 331
    Wafers
        Corn, 330
        Hot-Water Soda, with Chives, 330
        Salt, 329
        Whole Wheat Benne, 329
Croquettes, Vegetable, 336
Croutons, Fried, 328
Crudités, Vegetable, 158–59. *See also* Vegetables
Crumble, Ambrosia, 404
Crust. *See* Pastry
Cuban Black Beans, 192
Cucumber(s)
    and Carrot Salad, Sweet, 63
    and Carrot, Thai Salad with, 63
    and Green Pepper Salad, 68

and Mint Salad, 64
Pickles in a Hurry, Terrell's, 161
Salad with Sesame Dressing, 64
Sauce, Fresh, 278
Sauce, Gorgonzola Soufflé with, 6
Spread, 343
Steamed Caraway, 117
Tarragon Sauce, 348
Walnut, and Endive Salad with Walnut Vinaigrette, 64
and Yellow Peppers, Marinated, with Dill and Mint, 117
and Yogurt Sauce, 347
Curried Fruit, Warm, 461
Curried Shrimp and Potato Soup, 38
Custard, 472–75. *See also* Flan; Pudding
    Amaretti-Mascarpone, 475
    Apple-Almond, 472
    Brandy, with Fresh Berries, 474
    Chocolate Pots de Crème, 474
    Cinnamon, Ice Cream, 491
    Coeur de Crème, 474
    Fig, Fresh Baked, 473
    Honey, 472
    Ice Cream, Vanilla Bean, 491
    Jubilee, 473
    Lemon, Ice Cream, 494
    Pecan-Almond, 480
    Rigodon (chicken), 208

Date, Orange, and Coconut Ambrosia, 462
Date Tart, 388
Dessert, 457–504. *See also* Individual Listing; Fruit, Name of Fruit
    Cake, 410–34
    Candy, 485–87
    Cheese, 482
    Children's Favorites, 483–84
    Cookies, 435–55
    Custard and Flan, 470–75
    Frozen (Ice, Ice Cream, Sherbet, Sorbet), 489–504
    Mousse and Soufflé, 467–70
    Pie, Tart, Cobbler, and Crisp, 374–408

Pudding, 475–79
Trifle and Tiramisù, 479–81
Dessert Sauce, 363–68
    Apricot Purée, 364
    Berry and Black Cherry, 364
    Blackberry, 365
    Bourbon, 368; Bourbon Cream, 367
    Boysenberry, 365
    Butterscotch, 367
    Chocolate, 367
    Crème Anglaise, 366
    Irish Coffee, 368
    Pear, 364
    Praline, 367
    Raspberry, Quick, 363; variations, 363
    Rum Butter, 368
    Vanilla, 366; Vanilla Custard, 366
    Whiskey, 368
Dessert Toppings, 365–66. *See also* Whipped Cream
Devil's Food Cake with Chocolate Buttercream Icing, 426
Dip, Sun-Dried Tomato, 353. *See also* Spread
Dirty Rice, 176
Divinity, Black Walnut, 487
Dressing. *See also* Vinaigrette
    Bacon-Molasses, 215
    Ballpark Mustard, 76
    Buttermilk (for pasta), 82
    Caesar, 51
    Citrus, 70
    Egg, 54
    Honey-Lemon, 46
    Honey-Mustard, 74
    Lemon-Oil, 48
    Mayonnaise, 56. *See also* Mayonnaise
    Oil and Lemon, 53
    Port, 47
    Sesame, 64
Dried Fruit, Poached, 466
Dried Strawberry and Cherry Muffins; 315; blueberry and cherry variation, 315
Drop Buttermilk Biscuits, 304
Drop Cookies, 435–41
    Blowouts, 440
    Brownie, 439

Chocolate Chunk, 437
Citrus Lace, 435
Coconut-Walnut Jumbles, 439
Coffee-Chocolate -Macadamia
    Spreads, 437
Ginger and Spice, Vermont,
    435
Hazelnut Meringue, 438;
    pecan or walnut varia-
    tions, 438
Lemon Crisps, 436
Macaroons, Milk Chocolate,
    438
Oatmeal-Raisin, 438
Pecan, 441
Pecan Lace, 440
Praline, 441
Rocks, 436
Walnut, 441
Duck(ling)
    and Orange Sausage, 223
    and Pork Rillettes, 223
    Roast, with Blackberry Sauce,
        220
    Sausage and New Potatoes,
        224
    Turnip, and Squash Soup, 30
Dumpling(s)
    Apple, with Almond Sauce,
        466
    Berry, 337
    and Chicken Pie, Double -
        Crust, 212
    Spaetzle, 170
Dungeness Crab Cakes with
    Jalapeño-Lime
    Mayonnaise, 258

Egg(s), 2–7
    Baked Browned Butter, 3
    in Brown Butter, 3
    Chili-Tomato, in Bread
        Crumb Cups, 2
    Corn Omelet, 4
    Dressing, 54
    Gorgonzola Soufflé with
        Cucumber Sauce, 6
    Hard-Cooked, and Garden
        Green Salad, 54
    Mexican, 5
    in Piquant Mayonnaise, 5
    Poached in Chili-Tomato
        Sauce, 2

Salad, Chopped Lettuce and,
    55
Salad, Special, on Water
    Biscuits, 7
Scrambled
    Ham Fajitas with Fresh
        Salsa Ranchera and,
        331
    and Onions, 5
    Salad, 6
    and Skillet Potatoes with Chili
        and Ham, 182
    Tomato Soufflé, 4
    and Vegetables, Rice with, 176
Eggplant, 117–19
    Grilled, with Ricotta and Two
        Tomatoes, 118
    Pan-Grilled, on Sun-Dried
        Tomato Toasts, 118
    Ratatouille and Italian
        Sausage, 249
    Sticks, Fried, 117
    "Tortillas," Crawfish -Stuffed,
        with Tomatillo Sauce, 262
    Whole Baby, in Oil, 119
    Zucchini, and Parmesan
        Tortino, 150
Empanadas, Beef-Filled, 338
Enchilada(s)
    Blue Corn, 332
    Casserole, Turkey and
        Cheese, 216
    Chicken, with Andouille
        Sausage, 205
    Chicken and Walnut, with
        Roasted Green Chili
        Sauce, 204
Endive Salad, 52–53. See also
    Salad
    with Blackberry Vinaigrette,
        53
    and Carrot, with Berry
        Vinaigrette, 52
    Chopped Beet, and Red
        Onion, 60
    Cucumber, and Walnut, with
        Walnut Vinaigrette, 64
    with Oil and Lemon Dressing,
        53
    Radicchio, Apple, and Pepper
        with Roquefort Dressing,
        52
    and Radicchio, with Red Wine
        Vinaigrette, 52
English Apple Fritters, 336
English Muffin Loaf, 296

Espresso Ice Cream, 490

Fajitas, Chicken, with Avocado
    Dressing, 333
Fajitas, Ham, with Fresh Salsa
    Ranchera and Scrambled
    Eggs, 331
Fennel
    and Boston Lettuce Salad, 65
    Broiled, with Pancetta, 119
    Celery, and Parsley Salad with
        Shaved Parmesan, 65
    and Green Pea Purée with
        Mint, 154
    Lentil, and Cress Soup, 27
    Mushroom, and Artichoke
        Ragout, 124
    Niçoise, 120
    and Onions, Penne with, 79
    and Orange Salad with
        Shaved Parmesan and
        Black Olives, 65
Feta
    Cheese and Fresh Tomato
        Aspic, 72
    and Chopped Herbs, Tomato
        Slices with, 144
    and Tomato Salad, 71
Fettuccine. See also Pasta
    with Asparagus and Onion
        Sauce, 80
    Crawfish, 261
    with Four Cheeses, 88
    with Gorgonzola and White
        Corn Sauce, 80
    with Red Bell Pepper Sauce,
        82
    with Spicy Tomato and Bacon
        Sauce, 85
Fig(s)
    Conserve, 369
    Fresh
        Baked Custard, 473
        with Cream, 458
        Marinated in Lemon, 458
    and Ham Little Pies with
        Cheddar Crust, 398
    Ice Cream, 493
    Preserves, Freddie's, 493
    Preserves Ice Cream, 493
    Pudding Cake, 429
Filled Cookies, 442
Fish, 278–92. See also Seafood

513

Cold Poached Gulf, with
        Fresh Cucumber Sauce,
        278
Court-Bouillon for poaching,
        266
Fillets, 289–91
    Baked, 291
    Broiled, with Onion-Hot
        Pepper Topping, 290
    Oven-Fried, 290
    Pistachio-Coated, 289
    Steamed and Seared,
        White, 289
Monkfish, Baked, 278
Pompano, Grilled, with
        Thyme and Garlic Butter,
        279
Salmon. *See also* Smoked
        Salmon
    Baked, Thin-Sliced, 279
    and Corn Croquettes, 282
    Fillet, Baked, with Wasabi
        Crust and Orange -
        Anaheim Chili Sauce,
        280
    King, with Aspic and Herb
        Butter, 280
    Spread, Fresh, 343
    Smoked, Cakes with Caper
        Sauce, 291
    Smoked, with Roasted
        Peppers and Zucchini,
        292
Snapper, Grilled Teriyaki,
        283
Snapper, Whole Red, 283
Soup, 40
Stock, 42
Swordfish Steak Salad, 284
Trout in a Shoestring Potato
        Crust, 285
Trout, Steelhead, Wrapped in
        Vine Leaves, 284
Tuna
    Salad, Fresh, 287
    Salad, Warm Yellowfin,
        287
    Salmon, and Sturgeon,
        Grilled, 286
    Sauce, Chicken with, 208
    and Shrimp Salad, 288
    Spaghetti with, and Olives,
        Capers, and Cayenne,
        90

Spread, Grilled, with
        Roasted Peppers, 344
Steaks, Grilled, 288
Uncooked, and Tomato
        Sauce, Pasta Shells
        with, 91
White Bean Salad with, 194
Five Bean Soup, 24
Flaky
    Biscuits with Parsley Butter,
        306
    Pastry, 405
    Tart Crust, 408
Flan, 470–71. *See also* Custard;
        Pudding
    Chocolate Macadamia, 471
    Coconut, 471; Coconut
        Caramel, 470
Flavored
    Butter, 350–52
        Apricot, 351
        Berry, 352
        Hazelnut-Honey, 352
        Parsley, 350
        Parsley-Pine Nut, 350
        Shallot, 351
        Tabasco, 352
        Tomato, Sweet and Tart,
            353
    Vinaigrette, 54
    Vodka, 372
    Whipped Cream, 365–66
        Banana, 365
        Bourbon, 365
        Chocolate, 365
        Coconut, 366
        Spiced, 365
Flourless Chocolate Cake, 425
Flourless Chocolate and Walnut
        Cake, 427
Focaccia, 327
French Bread, New Orleans, 295
French Rolls, 301
Fritters, 333–36. *See also*
        Dumplings; Empanadas
    Apple, English, 336
    Corn and Prosciutto, 334
    Hush Puppies, 336
    Onion, 334
    Plain, 333
    Raspberry, 335
    Tomato, 335
    Vegetable Croquettes, 336
Frozen Dessert, 489–504. *See
        also* Ice; Ice Cream;
        Sherbet; Sorbet

Frozen Lime Soufflé, 468
Fruit. *See also* Name of Fruit
    Ambrosia Crumble, 404
    Compote, Tropical, 461
    Cooked, Sauce, 363
    Curried, Warm, 461
    Dried, Poached, 466
    Fresh, with Yogurt and Warm
        Sun Honey, 461
    Fruitcake Cookies, 448
    Fruitcake, White, 419
    Ice, Tropical, Mixed, 504
    Layered Fresh, with
        Raspberry Sauce, 462
    Pies, 374–77
    Poached, 463–66
    Salad, Fresh, 462
    Sauce, 361–65. *See also*
        Dessert Sauce
    Side Dishes, 164. *See also*
        Apples; Peaches
    Summer, Pie, 377
    Syrup, 370–71. *See also* Syrup
    Vinaigrette, 50
    Winter, Baked, 460
Fruitcake Cookies, 448
Fruitcake, White, 419
Fudge
    Chocolate, 485
    Mamie Eisenhower, 485
    Peanut Butter, 486
Fusilli. *See also* Pasta
    with Red Onion, Tomato,
        Basil, and Goat Cheese,
        83

Game, 251–54. *See also* Rabbit;
        Venison
Garden Salad
    with Balsamic Vinaigrette and
        Fontina, 44
    Green, and Hard-Cooked
        Egg, 54
    Summer, 74
Garlic
    Bread, 295
    Chicken, 197
    Mayonnaise, 348
    Pizza Squares, 326
    Roasted
        with Herbs, 120
        Mashed Potatoes, 185

514

and Shallot, Spinach, and
Goat Cheese Topping
for Pizza, 325
Smoked Tenderloin of Beef,
226
Gazpacho, Crab, 34
Ginger Sesame Rice, 171
Ginger and Spice Cookies,
Vermont, 435
Gingerbread, Golden Raisin, 313
Gingerbread, Warm, 419
Gingered Peaches, 463
Gnocchi, Adriana's, 168
Goat Cheese
Boston Lettuce Salad with, 49
Conchiglie with Grilled
Chicken Breasts and, 91
Fusilli with Red Onion,
Tomato, Basil, and, 83
Lentils with, 195
Mashed Potatoes, 187
Orecchiette with Tomatoes,
Cilantro, and, 85
Rotini with Smoked Salmon,
Corn, and, 90
Gorgonzola Soufflé with
Cucumber Sauce, 6
Gougère, Tomato, 299
Graham Cracker Pickups,
Freddie's, 485
Grain and Pasta Pilaf, 167
Grains, Nuts, and Vegetables,
Cabbage Stuffed with, 108
Grape(s)
Champagne, with Cheese, 482
Ice, 502
and Melon Salad, 76
Tart with Red Currant Glaze,
389; blueberry variation,
389
Grapefruit
Ice, 503
Rind, Candied, 458
Sherbet with Candied
Grapefruit Rind, 499
Greek Lemon Chicken, 197
Green(s), 120–22
Baby Beets and, 106
Garden, Salad and Hard-
Cooked Egg, 54
and Mushroom Salad, 67
Linguine with, and Pine Nuts,
81
Mustard, 121. *See also*
Mustard Green

with New Potato Salad and
Lemon-Dill Chardonnay
Vinaigrette, 69
Salad, 44–55. *See also* Salad
Turnip, and Corn Soup, 15
Turnip, Old-Fashioned, 120
Wilted Mixed Summer, 121
Wilted Mustard, with Olive
Oil and Lemon, 122
Winter, Braised, 122
Green Bean(s). *See also* Wax
Beans
and Acorn Squash, Puréed,
155
Baby, Onion, and Toasted
Pine Nut Salad, 61
Baby, Salad, 62
and Cheese Salad, 62
Haricots Verts with Anchovy
Vinaigrette, 104
with Jicama, 103
and Mushrooms, 103
in Mustard Marinade, 102
and New Potatoes, 181
Pockets, Grilled, 104
and Potato Purée, 153
Purée, Wagon Wheels with,
79
Salad, Warm, 62
Two-Bean Salad, 61
Warm, and New Potato Salad,
69
White Beans and Pine Nuts,
Rigatoni with, 78
Green Bell Pepper. *See also*
Peppers
and Cucumber Salad, 68
Green Chili. *See* Chili
Green Pea(s). *See* Peas
Green Peppercorn Mustard
Rolls, 301
Green Sauce, Uncooked, 93
Green Soup, 14
Green Tomato(es)
and Apple Pie, 374
Cornmeal Pan-Fried, 146
Ratatouille, 146
Grilled Cheese Sandwiches, 338
Grits
Baked Bouillon, 166
Baked Creamy, 166
with Butter, 166
Grouper, Cold Poached Gulf
Fish with Fresh
Cucumber Sauce, 278
Gumbo, 269

Chicken and Okra, 207
Ya Ya (chicken), 206

Ham. *See also* Pork
Baked, 247
Cake, 313
and Cheese Muffins, 315;
bacon, sausage variations,
315
and Chicken Filling for Little
Pies, 399
Fajitas with Fresh Salsa
Ranchera and Scrambled
Eggs, 331
and Fig Little Pies with
Cheddar Crust, 398
Fresh, with Pan Gravy, 242
Green Pea Soup with, 16
Mustard Green, Red Bean,
and Sweet Potato Soup, 31
Salad, 247
Steaks, Baked Marinated, 247
Stuffing, Smothered Crawfish
with, 260
Haricots Verts. *See also* Green
Beans
with Anchovy Vinaigrette, 104
Hazelnut
-Honey Butter, 352
Meringue Cookies, 438; varia-
tions, 438
Shortbread, 455
Vinaigrette, 215
Herb Sauce, 347
Honey
Berry, 371
Carrots, 112
Custard, 472
and Honey-Roasted Peanut
Ice Cream, 496
-Lemon Dressing, 46
-Mustard Dressing, 74
Horseradish Sauce, 346; green
peppercorn variation,
346
Hot-Water Pastry, 406
Hot-Water Soda Wafers with
Chives, 330
Hush Puppies, 336

Ice, 501–4. *See also* Sherbet;
Sorbet
Applejack, 501

Berry, 501
Blackberry, 502
Grape, 502
Grapefruit, 503
Lemon, with Rum, 503
Lemony Lime, 504
Lime, 503
Pear, 504
Raspberry, 502
Sugarless Berry, 502
Tropical Fruit, Mixed, 504
Ice Cream, 489–97. *See also* Ice;
    Sherbet; Sorbet
Berry, 492
Blowout, 490
Bourbon-Mint, 496
Bourbon-Pecan, 496
Chocolate-Chocolate Chip,
    490
Chocolate Nougat, 489
Cinnamon Custard, 491
Coconut, Toasted, 492
Creole Cream Cheese, 497
Espresso, 490
Fig, 493
Fig Preserves, 493
Honey and Honey-Roasted
    Peanut, 496
Lemon Custard, 494
Maple-Black Walnut, 493
Peach Pit, 494
Peanut Brittle, 495
Peppermint, 495; low-fat vari-
    ation, 495
Rum Cherry, 492
Rum-Raisin, 495
Strawberry, with Strawberry
    Purée, 491
Vanilla-Bean Custard, 491
White Chocolate, 489
Yogurt, 497
Ice-Water Crackers, Toasted, 328
Iceberg Lettuce, Chopped, and
    Tomato Salad with
    Pepper Mayonnaise, 71
Icebox Cake, Layered Bourbon,
    428
Icebox Cookies, 447–49
Butterscotch Pecan, 448
Fruitcake, 448
Icebox, 447
Peanut Butter, 447
Pecan-Coconut Biscotti, 449
Spice Sables, 449
Icebox Rolls, 302
Iced Coffee with Brandy, 372

Impossible Pie (coconut-peanut),
    387
Irish Coffee Sauce, 368
Italian
Chicken Cutlets, 200
Rice, Baked, 172
Sausage and Ratatouille, 249

Jalapeño Corn Muffins, 310
Jalapeño-Lime Mayonnaise, 349
Jam and Berry Tartlets, 393
Jam Muffins, 317
Jicama
and Black Bean Salad, 195
Green Beans with, 103
Slaw, 56
Jubilee Custard, 473

Ketchup, Blackberry, 370
Key Lime Pie, 375
Kidney Beans, Two-Bean Salad,
    61
Kohlrabi and Pear Purée, 154
Kohlrabi, Sautéed, 122

Lace Cookies, Citrus, 435
Lace Cookies, Pecan, 440
Lamb, 235–39
and Beet Soup, 32
and Cabbage, Penne with, 87
Loin, Roasted, with Cabernet
    Wine Sauce, 235
Medallions, Broiled, 238
Mediterranean Patties, 249
Ouzo Lemon, with Yogurt,
    237
and Pork with Walnuts,
    Pumpkin, Prunes, and
    Beans, 238
Pumpkin, and Lima Bean
    Soup, 33
Shanks with Black Olives and
    Orange Zest, 236
Steaks, Charcoaled Bourbon-
    Marinated, 236
and Zucchini Pies, 239
Lasagna, Vegetable, 158
Layer Cake, 410–16
Almond-Blackberry Jam, 414
Banana, 410
Chocolate, 426
Coconut, 411
Intermont White, 410

Lemon, Natchez, 412
Peach, Fresh, 413
Pecan, Golden, with Pecan
    Divinity Icing, 415
Pecan, Plantation, 416
Plum Jam, 414
Layered Bourbon Icebox Cake,
    428
Layered Fresh Fruit with
    Raspberry Sauce, 462
Leek(s)
and Butternut Squash Purée,
    155
and Herb Custard, Braised,
    124
Niçoise, 123
Roasted Onion, and
    Cauliflower Purée, 152
Steamed, with Red Onion,
    123
and Vidalia Onions with
    Tarragon Vinaigrette, 66
and Wax Beans, Purée of, 152
Lemon
Bitter, Tart, 389
Cake, Natchez, 412
Carrots, 111
Chicken
    Greek, 197
    Soup, 28
    with Sour Cream Sauce,
        202
Crisps, 436
Custard Ice Cream, 494
Ice with Rum, 503
Lemony Lime Ice, 504
Meringue Pies, 378;
    Individual Crustless, 380
Mousse with Berry Purée, 469
-Oil Dressing, 48
Pudding Cake, 430
Rice, 171
Sand Tarts, 443
Squares, 453
Stroganoff, 229
Vinaigrette, 58; -Dill
    Chardonnay, 69
Walnut Bars, 454
Lemony Lime Ice, 504
Lentil(s)
Fennel, and Cress Soup, 27
with Goat Cheese, 195
Salad, 195
Lettuce-Prosciutto Risotto, 173

516

Lettuce Salad (Bibb, Boston,
Mesclun, etc.), 46–50, 55.
See also Name of Lettuce;
Salad
Light Béchamel Sauce, 187
Lima Bean(s)
and Cheese Salad, 61
Lamb, and Pumpkin Soup, 33
and Pears, Baked, 104
Spread, 344
Steamed, with Brown Butter,
105
Lime
Ice, 503
Lemony Ice, 504
Pie, Key, 375
Soufflé, Frozen, 468
Vinaigrette, 59
Linguine. *See also* Pasta
with Greens and Pine Nuts, 81
Little Pies, 392–93; Savory,
397–401. *See also* Pies;
Savory Pies and Tarts
Liver and Onions, Classic, 235
Lobster. *See also* Seafood
Soup, 36
with Tarragon Mayonnaise,
264

Macadamia
Chocolate Flan, 471
-Coffee-Chocolate Spreads,
437
Cream Pie, 383
Macaroni. *See also* Pasta
and Black Bean Soup, 24
Casserole with Chicken and
Spicy Sausage, 214
and Cheese Salad, 98
Macaroons, Milk Chocolate, 438
Mâche Salad, 54. *See also* Salad
and Radicchio, with Sparkling
Wine Vinaigrette, 53
Mamie Eisenhower Fudge, 485
Mandarin Grilled Quail, 220
Mango with Blackberries, 458
Mango, Chutney, Fresh, 358
Maple-Black Walnut Ice Cream,
493
Maque Choux, 116
Margarita Topping for Pizza,
324
Marinade, Mustard, 102
Marinated
Chicken Breasts, Grilled, 199

Cucumbers and Yellow
Peppers with Dill and
Mint, 117
Fresh Figs, in Lemon, 458
Ham Steaks, Baked, 247
Lamb Steaks, Charcoaled
Bourbon-, 236
and Pickled Vegetables,
160–63. *See also* Name of
Vegetable; Vegetables
Shrimp with Green Chili
Polenta and Corn Salsa,
265
Strawberries, 458
Summer Mélange, 75
Veal, Roast Loin of, in Port
Wine and Orange, 233
Marmalade, Red Onion, 370
Marshmallow-Butterscotch-
Peanut Squares, 484
Maryland Crab Cakes, 258
Mascarpone-Amaretti Custard,
475
Mayonnaise, 348–50
Avocado, 71
Dressing, 56
Garlic, 348
Homemade, 348
Jalapeño-Lime, 349
Ketchup, 194
Mustard-Dill, 348
Mustard Sauce, 349
Pepper, 71
Tartar Sauce, 349;
Tomato Tartar Sauce, 350
Watercress, 349
Meat, Raspberry Sauce for, 361
Meatloaf, Best Yankee, with
Oven-Cured Tomatoes,
248
Mediterranean Patties, 249
Melba Toast, 327
Melon
Balls with Cherries, 459
Balls with Mint, 459
and Grape Salad, 76
Slices with Raspberry Purée,
459
menus, summer, xvi–xxi; winter,
xxii–xxvii
Meringue(s)
with Berries and Whipped
Cream, 380
Hazelnut Cookies, 438; pecan
or walnut variations, 438
Pies, 378–82. *See also* Pies

Mesclun Salad. *See also* Salad
with Chèvre Vinaigrette, 47
with Pears, Blue Cheese, and
Port Dressing, 47
Mexican Eggs, 5
Mexican Pork Stew, 245
Molasses Popcorn Balls, 483
Monkey Bread, 294
Monkfish, Baked, 278
Mousse. *See also* Soufflé
Blackberry, 469
Chocolate Terrine, 467
Lemon, with Berry Purée, 469
Tangerine, 470
Mozzarella Biscuits, 306
Muffins, 307–10, 314–18. *See also*
Bread; Biscuits; Popovers;
Rolls; Sticky Buns
Apple-Cinnamon, 316
Banana Walnut, 316
Blueberry, 317
Corn, 308
Bacon and Onion, 307;
variations, 307
Fresh, 308
Jalapeño, 310
Dried Strawberry and Cherry,
315; blueberry variation,
315
Ham and Cheese, 315; bacon,
sausage variations, 315
Jam, 317
Nut, 318
Raisin Bran, 316
Rice, 318
Mushroom(s), 124–28
Broth, Julienned Pork in, with
Pasta Shells, 246
Consommé, 15
Fennel, and Artichoke
Ragout, 124
and Green Beans, 103
and Greens Salad, 67
Grilled Portobello, with Black
Olives and Tomatoes, 126
Marinated
with Carrots and Green
Onions, 161
with Oregano, 160
with Rosemary and Chives,
161
Spiced, 162
Oyster, Fried, 125
Porcini, Baked Wild Rice and,
177

Porcini, Fresh, Baked with
Bacon, 128
Portobello, Stuffed, 127
and Rice, Buttered, 171
Salad, Savoy, 128
Salad, Warm Grilled, 127
Sautéed, 126
and Walnut Salad, 67
Mustard
-Dill Mayonnaise, 348
Marinade, Green Beans in,
102
Rolls, Green Peppercorn, 301
Sauce, 349
Vinaigrette, 57; Balsamic, 98
Mustard Green(s), 121
Red Bean, Sweet Potato, and
Ham Soup, 31
Wilted, with Olive Oil and
Lemon, 122

Napa Valley Apple Tart, 391
Natchez Seafood Salad, 270
New Orleans French Bread, 295
New Orleans Shrimp and
Crawfish Creole, 265
New World Spice Cookies,
443
Noodles. *See also* Pasta
Cold Sesame, with Carrots,
and Cucumbers, 78
Nut. *See also* Name of Nut
Brittle, 487
-Chocolate Toffee, 486
Chocolate Toffee Pudding
Cake, 431
Cookies, Three-, 446
Crust, 408
Muffins, 318
Pies, 382–83. *See also*
Macadamia; Pecan
Torte, California, 423

Oatmeal-Cinnamon Raisin
Bread, 312
Oatmeal-Raisin Cookies, 438
Oil Dressings. *See* Dressing
Okra. *See also* Gumbo
and Chicken Gumbo, 207
Chowder, 16
Pickled, 162
Pilaf, 176
Steamed, with Warm Tomato
Vinaigrette, 129

Tomatoes, and Corn, Sautéed,
129
Olive(s)
Beef Stew with, and Rum, 230
Black
Lamb Shanks with, and
Little Pies, 400
and Onion Pizza Bread, 326
Orange Zest, 236
Orzo with Onions and, 82
and Shaved Parmesan,
Fennel and Orange
Salad with, 65
Cheese, and Plums (dessert),
482
Green, Walnut and Parsley
Sauce, 95
Rice, and Green Pea Salad
with Orange-Cilantro
Vinaigrette, 67
Salad, 163
and Sun-Dried Tomato
Spread, 344
Tuna, Capers, and Cayenne,
Spaghetti with, 90
Omelet, Corn, 4
Onion(s), 130–34
about slipping skins of, 111
and Asparagus Sauce,
Fettuccine with, 80
and Bacon Corn Muffins, 307
-Bacon Pie, 395
Baked, and Carrots, Purée of,
152
Barbecued, 130
and Bell Peppers, 136
and Black Olive Pizza Bread,
326
Caramelized, 130
Carrots, and Turnips, Glazed,
111
and Cheese Pie, 394
and Fennel, Pasta with, 79
Fritters, 334
Green, Spring Peas and, 134
-Hot Pepper Topping, 360
Liver and, Classic, 235
and Mashed Potatoes, 186
Orzo with, and Black Olives,
82
Parmesan Puffs, 300
Peppered, Relish, 360
Pickled, 160
and Potato Salad, Roasted,
133
Potatoes Anna, 131

and Raisin Relish, 359
Red
and Apples, Braised, 164
Marmalade, 370
Tomato, Basil, and Goat
Cheese, Fusilli with, 83
Wilted, and Pickled Beet
Salad, 60
Refrigerator Wilted, 134
Rings, 133
Rings, Fried Thin, 132
Roasted
with Balsamic Vinegar, 130
Cauliflower, and Leek
Purée, 152
Pear, and Cauliflower,
Purée of, 153
Sautéed, 130
Sautéed, Spring Sausage with,
250
in Seasoned Olive Oil, 131
Stuffed, Cuban Style, 132
Vidalia
and Leeks with Tarragon
Vinaigrette, 66
Salad, Roasted, 133
Sauce, Sweet, 360
Sautéed, 131
and Yellow Squash, 149
Yellow, Tart, 394
Orange(s)
-Anaheim Pepper Sauce, 361
Blood, Sherbet, 500
-Cilantro Vinaigrette, 67
Coconut, and Date Ambrosia,
462
Cranberry, and Raisin Sauce,
362
and Fennel Salad with Shaved
Parmesan and Black
Olives, 65
Poached, 463
Orecchiette. *See also* Pasta
with Tomatoes, Cilantro, and
Goat Cheese, 85
Oreganato Bread, 297
Oriental Beef Filling for Little
Pies, 398
Orzo
with Butter and Parsley, 86
with Mustard Balsamic
Vinaigrette, 98
with Onions and Black Olives,
82
and Rice Pilaf, 174
and Vegetable Salad, 97

Osgood Pie (pecan-raisin), 386
Osso Buco Soup, 31
Ouzo Lemon Lamb with Yogurt, 237
Oyster(s), 273–75. *See also* Seafood
  Baked Jalapeño, 275
  and Corn Chowder, 38
  Cornmeal Fried, 274
  Gulf Shrimp, and Crab Stew, 268
  Mandich, 273
  Salad with Radish Relish, 274
  Tartare with Sparkling Wine Sauce, 273
  and White Corn Chowder, with Ancho Chili Cream, 39
Oyster Mushrooms. *See also* Wild Mushrooms
  Fried, 125

Pan and Loaf Cake, 419–22
  Blackberry Buckle with Blackberry Sauce, 422; blueberry variation, 422
  Blackberry Roll, 422
  Carrot, with Cream Cheese Icing, 420
  Gingerbread, Warm, 419
  Peach Crumble, 421
  Pineapple Upside-Down, 421
  Sherry Spice, with Creamy Brown Sugar Glaze, 420
Pancakes, 319. *See also* Corn Cakes; Crepes; Waffles
  Chicken, with Peach Salsa, 210
  Crème Fraîche, 319
  Sweet Potato, 189
  Wild Sourdough, 320
Papaya, Banana, and Coconut Ambrosia, 462
Papaya Salsa, 357
Parmesan Onion Puffs, 300
Parsley
  Butter, 350
  -Pecan Sauce, 347
  -Pine Nut Butter, 350
Pasta, 78–98
  Angel Hair with Spinach, Tomatoes, and Three Cheeses, 83
  and Bean Soup, 27

  with Broccoli, 79
  Bucatini with Black Pepper, Bread Crumbs, and Pecorino, 89
  Capellini and Barbecued Shrimp with Shrimp Sauce, 267
  Conchiglie with Grilled Chicken Breasts and Goat Cheese, 91
  with Crawfish Sauce, 89
  Fettuccine
    with Asparagus and Onion Sauce, 80
    Crawfish, 261
    with Four Cheeses, 88
    with Gorgonzola and White Corn Sauce, 80
    with Red Bell Pepper Sauce, 82
    with Spicy Tomato and Bacon Sauce, 85
  Fusilli with Red Onion, Tomato, Basil, and Goat Cheese, 83
  and Grain Pilaf, 167
  Linguine with Greens and Pine Nuts, 81
  Macaroni
    and Black Bean Soup, 24
  Casserole with Chicken and Spicy Sausage, 214
  and Cheese, 98
  Noodles, Cold Sesame, with Carrots and Cucumbers, 78
  Orecchiette with Tomatoes, Cilantro, and Goat Cheese, 85
  Orzo
    with Butter and Parsley, 86
    with Mustard Balsamic Vinaigrette, 98
    with Onions and Black Olives, 82
  and Rice Pilaf, 174
  and Vegetable Salad, 97
  Penne
    with Cabbage and Lamb, 87
    with Fennel and Onions, 79
    with Mixed Grilled Vegetables, 84
  and Rice, 173
  Rigatoni with White Beans, Green Beans, and Pine Nuts, 78

  Rigatoni with Yellow Tomatoes, Peppers, and Corn, 84
  Rotini with Smoked Salmon, Goat Cheese, and Corn, 90
  Salads, 97–98. *See also* Salad
  Sauces, 92–96. *See also* Pasta Sauce
  Sausage, 86
  Sausage Cake, 96
  and Seafood Salad, 287
  Shells, Julienned Pork in Mushroom Broth with, 246
  Shells with Uncooked Tuna and Tomato Sauce, 91
  and Shrimp Salad, 271
  Spaghetti
    with Bacon and Baked Tomato Sauce, 88
    with Garlic and Rosemary Oil, 81
    with Tuna, Olives, Capers, and Cayenne, 90
  Summer Salad, 97
  Tortellini and Wild Mushrooms with Buttermilk Dressing, 82
  Wagon Wheels with Green Bean Purée, 79
  and White Bean Salad, 194
Pasta Sauce, 92–96
  Buttermilk Dressing for, 82
  Chili, with Sausage, 95
  Crawfish, 89
  Green Olive, Walnut, and Parsley, 95
  Ricotta, Basil, and Prosciutto, 96
  Tomato
    Fresh, 92
    and Red Bell Pepper, 93
    Smoked, 92
  Two Sauces for (Brown; Tomato), 94
  Uncooked Green, 93
  Uncooked Tomato, 92
Pastry (for Cobblers, Pies, Tarts), 405–8
  Butter-Margarine Tart Crust, 407
  Cheese, 407
  Cobbler, 408
  Flaky, 405
  Flaky Tart Crust, 408

519

Hot-Water, 406
Nut Crust, 408
Pie, All-Shortening, 405
Pie Crust, Lee Klein's, 406
Short Crust, 406
Short, Whole Wheat, 407
Sweet, 406
Pea(s), Green
and Fennel Purée with Mint,
154
Rice, and Olive Salad with
Orange-Cilantro
Vinaigrette, 67
Salad, 66
in Shallot Butter, Garden, 134
Soup with Ham, 16
Spring, and Green Onions,
134
Steamed, 135
Sweet, Soup, 17
Tiny, with Dill Butter, 134
and Watercress Purée, 153
Peach(es)
Bellini Sorbet, 498
and Berry Shortcake with
Warm Cream Sauce, 434
Brandied, 459
Cake, Fresh, 413
Cobbler, 403
Crisp with Bourbon Sauce,
404
Crumble Cake, 421
and Fresh Pecorino with
Honey and Black Pepper,
482
Gingered, 463
Peppered, 164
Pit Ice Cream, 494
-Tomato Salsa, 365
Peanut
Brittle Ice Cream, 495
Honey-Roasted, and Honey
Ice Cream, 496
-Marshmallow-Butterscotch
Squares, 484
and Rice Pilaf, 174
Peanut Butter Cookies, 447;
Shasta Mountain, 446
Peanut Butter Fudge, 486
Pear(s). See also Asian Pears
-Almond Torte, 423
Apple, and Celery Salad,
Chopped, 63
Baked Stuffed, with Vanilla
Sauce, 460
-Cranberry Sorbet, 498

Green, and Apple Chutney,
357
Ice, 504
and Kohlrabi Purée, 154
and Lima Beans, Baked, 104
Peppermint, 464
Perfect Poached, 465
Poached, with Raspberry -
Caramel Sauce, 464
Pudding Cake, 431
-Raspberry Cobbler, 402
Roasted Onion, and
Cauliflower, Purée of, 153
Sauce, 364
Tart, 391
and Turnips, Puréed, 154
Pecan
-Almond Custard, 480
-Bourbon Ice Cream, 496
Butterscotch Cookies, 448
Cake, Golden, with Pecan
Divinity Icing, 415
Chicken, Southern Fried, 198
-Chocolate-Raisin Clusters,
483
-Coconut Biscotti, 449
Cookies, 441
Crust Butterscotch Pie, 382
Lace Cookies, 440
-Parsley Sauce, 347
Pie, 383
and Pistachio Meringue Cakes
with Strawberry Filling,
382
Plantation Cake, 416
Popovers, 318
Rice, 173
Tiles (cookies), 450
Pecorino, Fresh, and Peaches
with Honey and Black
Pepper, 482
Penne. See also Pasta
with Cabbage and Lamb, 87
with Fennel and Onions, 79
with Mixed Grilled
Vegetables, 84
Pepper(s). See also Red Bell
Peppers; Yellow Bell
Peppers
about roasting, 74
Bell, and Onion, 136
Chiles, Pasilla, Cheese -and-
Herb-Stuffed, 135
Chiles Rellenos, Baked, 136
Green, and Cucumber Salad,
68

Hot, and Prunes, Chicken
with, 203
Mixed in Oil and Vinegar, 136
Onion Topping, Hot-, 360
Salad, Roasted (various col-
ors), 68
Stuffed with Corn, 137
and Summer Squash with
Balsamic Vinegar Butter,
149
Wild Rice with, 175
Pepper Bread, 340
Cajun Three-, 297
Grilled Shrimp with Coleslaw
on, 340
Skillet, 300
Pepper Sugar Cookies, 445
Peppercorn Vinaigrette, 49
Peppered
Loin of Venison with Red
Wine Sauce, 252
Onion Relish, 360
Peaches, 164
Peppermint Ice Cream, 495; low-
fat variation, 495
Peppermint Pears, 464
Pickled and Marinated
Vegetables, 160–63. See
also Name of Vegetable;
Vegetables
Pickles in a Hurry, Terrell's, 161
Pickles, Watermelon Rind, 162
Pie(s), 374–401. See also Savory
Pies and Tarts; Tart(let)s
Angel, Aunt Lady Carter's,
385
Apple, 374
Apple and Green Tomato, 374
Black Olive Little, 400
Blackberry, Deep-Dish, 377
Blueberry, 376
Boysenberry Pyramids, 387
Butterscotch Meringue, 378
Cheese and Onion, 394
Chess, 386
Chicken Filling for Little, 401
Chicken, Walnut, and Red
Pepper Little, 397
Chocolate
Brownie, 384
Cream, with Chocolate
Meringue, 379
Custard, 384
Coconut Cream, with Coconut
Meringue, 381
Crust, Lee Klein's, 406

Ham and Chicken Filling for Little, 399
Ham and Fig with Cheddar Crust, Little, 398
Impossible (coconut -peanut), 387
Key Lime, 375
Leek and Goat Cheese, 396
Lemon Meringue, 378; Individual Crustless, 380
Little, 397
Macadamia Cream, 383
Meringues with Berries and Whipped Cream, 380
Onion-Bacon, 395
Oriental Beef Filling for Little, 398
Osgood (pecan-raisin), 386
Pastry, All-Shortening, 405. See also Pastry
Pecan, 383
Pecan Crust Butterscotch, 382
Piperade, 396
Pork Filling for Little, 399
Pumpkin Chiffon, 376
Strawberry, 375
Summer Fruit, 377
Vegetable Filling for Little, 400
Pilaf
Okra, 176
Orzo and Rice, 174
Pasta and Grain, 167
Rice and Peanut, 174
Pimiento Soup, Cold, 17
Pineapple
-Banana Sorbet, 498
Chutney, Fresh, 358
Grilled with Rum Cream Sauce, 460
Sherbet, 501
Upside-Down Cake, 421
Pinto Beans, 191
Piperade Pie, 396
Pistachio-Coated Fish, 289
Pistachio and Pecan Meringue Cakes with Strawberry Filling, 382
Pita Bread Triangles, Toasted, 327
Pita Chips, Grilled, 328
Pizza, 323–27
Bread, Onion and Black Olive, 326
Focaccia, 327

Garlic Squares, 326
Individual Grilled, 324; various toppings, 324–25
Tomato-Tarragon, 323
Plum(s)
and Cherries, Poached, 464
Cobbler, 402
Jam Cake, 414
Olive, and Cheese (dessert), 482
Sorbet, 497
Tart, 390
Poached Fruit, 463–66
Apple Dumplings with Almond Sauce, 466
Apricots, with Pear Purée, 465
Apricots, Pink Peppercorns, and Mint with Crème Fraîche, 463
Cherries and Plums, 464
Dried Fruit, 466
Gingered Peaches, 463
Oranges, 463
Pears, Perfect, 465
Pears with Raspberry -Caramel Sauce, 464
Peppermint Pears, 464
Polenta
Green Chili, 170
Green Chili, Marinated Shrimp with, and Corn Salsa, 265
Oven, Tomato Fondue, and Sonoma Jack Cheese, 169
Pompano, Grilled, with Thyme and Garlic Butter, 279
Popcorn Balls, 483; Molasses, 483
Popovers, 319; Pecan, 318
Porcini Mushrooms. See also Wild Mushrooms
Baked Wild Rice and, 177
Fresh, Baked with Bacon, 128
Pork, 239–48. See also Ham; Sausage
Butt, Boiled Smoked, with Vegetables, 248
Cabbage Stuffed with, and Apple, 244
Chops with Raspberry Sauce, 242
Chops and Rice, 243
and Duck Rillettes, 223
Filling for Little Pies, 399
Fresh Ham with Pan Gravy, 242

Julienned in Mushroom Broth with Pasta Shells, 246
and Lamb with Walnuts, Pumpkin, Prunes, and Beans, 238
Medallions with Prunes and Port, 243
Mock Boar Roasted with a Mustard Coating, 240
Ribs, Baked Country -Style, 242
Rillettes, 245
Roast(ed)
Loin of, with Natural Gravy, 240
Loin with Pan Juices, 241
in Milk, 241
Tenderloin, with Mustard Wine Sauce, 239
Stew, Mexican, 245
Port Dressing, 47
Portobello Mushrooms. See also Wild Mushrooms
Burger, Grilled, 339
Grilled, with Black Olives and Tomatoes, 126
Stuffed, 127
Pot Pie, Chicken, with Biscuit Topping, 211
Pot Pie, Chicken, with Cornbread Crust, 213
Potato(es), 180–87. See also Sweet Potatoes
Bean, Bacon, and Red Pepper Soup, 25
Buttered, 180
Cabbage, Bell Pepper, and Onion Mélange, 110
and Cabbage Gratin, 187
Chips, Oven-Baked, 181
Corn, Crab, Crawfish, and Shrimp, Boiled, 272
and Curried Shrimp Soup, 38
and Green Bean Purée, 153
Grilled, Pockets, 184
Mashed
and Cauliflower, 185
Goat Cheese, 187
and Onions, 186
Roasted Garlic, 185
New
Baked in Chicken Stock, 184
Boiled, 180

and Duck Sausage, 224
and Green Beans, 181
Red Bell Pepper, and Corn
  Salad, 191
Salad, with Greens and
  Lemon-Dill
  Chardonnay
  Vinaigrette, 69
Skillet, 180
Spicy Boiled, 181
and Warm Green Bean
  Salad, 69
Onion Anna, 131
and Onion Salad, Roasted,
  133
Oven-Roasted Cottage Fries,
  182
Oven Slices, 182
and Red Bell Pepper Soup, 18
Roasted, 184
Roasted Red, 184
Rosemary, with Parmesan,
  Crispy, 183
Salad, 191
  Red, 190
  Warm, with Sherry
    Vinaigrette, 190
  Warm Vinegar, 190
Scalloped, 186
Scottish Skillet, 182
Skillet, and Eggs with Chili
  and Ham, 182
Stuffed Baked, 183
Pots de Crème, Chocolate, 474
Poultry. See Chicken; Duck;
  Quail; Squabs; Turkey
Poultry Sausages, 222–24. See
  also Chicken; Duck;
  Sausage
Pound Cake, 427–28
  Bourbon Icebox, Layered,
    428
  Cayenne, 428
  Sour Cream, 427; with
    Poached Fruit, 428
Praline(s), 486
  Cookies, 441
  Sauce, 367
Prawns, Grilled, with Papaya
  Salsa, 268
Preserves. See also Conserve and
  Preserves
  Fig, Freddie's, 493
Prosciutto-Lettuce Risotto, 173
Prosciutto Ricotta, and Basil
  Sauce, 96

Prune(s)
  and Hot Peppers, Chicken
    with, 203
  and Port, Pork Medallions
    with, 243
  and Port Tartlet Filling, 392;
    peach and walnut varia-
    tion, 392
  Walnuts, Pumpkin, and
    Beans, Lamb and Pork
    with, 238
Pudding, 475–79. See also
  Custard; Mousse;
  Pudding Cake
  Banana Clafouti, 476
  Bread, 479
    Soufflé, 478
    with Whiskey Sauce, 478
  Butterscotch, 475
  Chocolate Steamed, 477
  Pumpkin, 477
  Summer, 476
Pudding Cake, 429–31
  Banana, 430
  Chocolate Toffee Nut, 431
  Fig, 429
  Lemon, 430
  Pear, 431
Puff Pastry Tartlets, 393. See also
  Pastry
Pumpkin
  Chiffon Pie, 376
  Lamb, and Lima Bean Soup,
    33
  seeds, about roasting, 204
  Pudding, 477
  Walnuts, Prunes, and Beans,
    Lamb and Pork with, 238

Quail
  Baked, 221
  Mandarin Grilled, 220
  Skillet-Cooked, 221
Quick Bread, 312–13
  Bishop's, 312
  Cinnamon-Oatmeal Raisin,
    312
  Ham Cake, 313
  Raisin Gingerbread, Golden,
    313

Rabbit, Champagne, with Apple
  and Green Pear Chutney,
  251

Radicchio, 52–53. See also Salad
  Endive, Apple, and Pepper
    with Roquefort
    Vinaigrette, 52
  and Endive Salad, with Red
    Wine Vinaigrette, 52
  Grilled, 138
  and Mâche Salad with
    Sparkling Wine
    Vinaigrette, 53
Radish
  Canapés, 343
  Relish, 360
  Soup, Cold, 18
Raisin
  Bran Muffins, 316
  -Chocolate-Pecan Clusters,
    483
  Cinnamon-Oatmeal Bread,
    312
  Cranberry, and Orange Sauce,
    362
  Gingerbread, Golden, 313
  -Oatmeal Cookies, 438
  and Onion Relish, 359
  -Rum Ice Cream, 495
Raspberry(ies)
  -Caramel Sauce, 363
  Fritters, 335
  Green Salad with, and
    Raspberry Vinaigrette, 45
  Ice, 502
  -Pear Cobbler, 402
  Sauce for Meat, 361
  Sauce, Quick, 363; variations,
    363
  Tiramisù, 481
  Vinaigrette, 45
Ratatouille, Green Tomato, 146
Ratatouille and Italian Sausage,
  249
Red Bean. See also Beans
  Mustard Green, Sweet Potato,
    and Ham Soup, 31
  and Rice Salad, 178
  Succotash, 192
Red Bell Pepper(s). See also
  Peppers
  Aspic, 137
  and Carrot Soup, 12
  and Creamed Corn Soup, 13
  and Onion, 136
  Piperade Pie, 396
  and Potato Soup, 18
  Roasted

and Butter Sandwiches, 339
Grilled Tuna Spread with, 344
Shrimp, White Beans, and, 267
and Tomato Soup, Cold, 21
and Zucchini, Smoked Fish with, 292
Salad, New Potato, and Corn, 191
Sauce, Fettuccine with, 82
Sauce, Stuffed Crepes with 321
and Tomato Sauce, 93
and Yellow Pepper Salad, Sautéed, 68
Red Onions. *See* Onions
Red Wine Vinaigrette, 44
Refrigerator Berry Preserves, 369
Refrigerator Pickled Broccoli, 160
Relish, 359–60. *See also* Chutney
Anchovies, Capers, Basil, and Pine Nuts, 360
Blackberry Ketchup, 370
Corn, Fresh, 359
Onion-Hot Pepper Topping, 360
Onion and Raisin, 359
Peppered Onion, 360
Radish, 360
Tomato and Jalapeño, 359
Vidalia Onion, Sweet, 360
Rémoulade, Shrimp, 264
Rice, 170–80. *See also* Basmati Rice; Wild Rice
and Andouille Sausage, Baked Tomatoes Stuffed with, 144
Baked Green, 180
Baked Italian, 172
and Corn, 116
Dirty, 176
with Eggs and Vegetables, 176
with Fresh Dill, 171
Ginger Sesame, 171
Green Pea, and Olive Salad with Orange-Cilantro Vinaigrette, 67
Lemon, 171
Lettuce-Prosciutto Risotto, 173

Loaf, 177
Long-Grain and Wild, Mixed, 175
Muffins, 318
and Mushrooms, Buttered, 171
and Orzo Pilaf, 174
and Pasta, 173
Pasta and Grain Pilaf, 167
and Peanut Pilaf, 174
Pecan, 173
and Pork Chops, 243
and Red Bean Salad, 178
Salad, 178
Seafood Risotto, 263
Smoked Salmon and Spinach Risotto, 172
White and Wild, Salad with Vegetables, 179
Wine Vinaigrette, 48
Yellow, Steamed, 171
Ricotta, Basil, and Prosciutto Sauce, 96
Rigatoni. *See also* Pasta
with White Beans, Green Beans, and Pine Nuts, 78
with Yellow Tomatoes, Peppers, and Corn, 84
Rigodon (chicken), 208
Rillettes (pork), 245
Risotto
Baked Italian Rice, 172
Lettuce-Prosciutto, 173
Seafood, 263
Smoked Salmon and Spinach, 172
Rocks (cookies), 436
Rocky Road Squares with Caramel Sauce, 452
Rolled Cookies, 442–43
Filled, 442
Lemon Sand Tarts, 443
Spice, New World, 443
Tea Cakes, 442
Rolls, 300–2. *See also* Biscuits; Bread; Muffins; Popovers; Sticky Buns
Buttermilk, Quick, 300
Cloverleaf, 302
French, 301
Green Peppercorn Mustard, 301
Icebox, 302
Roquefort Vinaigrette, 52
Rotini. *See also* Pasta

with Smoked Salmon, Goat Cheese, and Corn, 90
Rum
Butter Sauce, 368
Cherry Ice Cream, 492
-Raisin Ice Cream, 495
Rustic Salad, 55

Salad, 44–76
Artichoke, Warm, 57
Arugula
Boston Lettuce, and Julienne Red Pepper, 47
and Lettuce, with Rice Wine Vinaigrette, 48
and Swiss Cheese, 48
Asparagus, Raw, and Lettuce, with Mustard Vinaigrette, 57
Asparagus Vinaigrette, 58
Avocado(s)
Chopped, Onion, Tomato, and Hot Pepper, 59
with Cilantro Vinaigrette, 58
with Lime Vinaigrette, 59
Sliced, with Lemon Vinaigrette, 58
Beef, 230
Beet(s)
Chopped, Endive, and Red Onion Salad, 60
Cold, 59
Fresh, 59
with Onion, 60
Bibb Lettuce and Cheese, 48
Bibb Lettuce with Peppercorn Vinaigrette, 49
Black Bean and Jicama, 195
Boston Lettuce
and Bibb Lettuce, with Fruit Vinaigrette, 50
with Peas and Anchovy Vinaigrette, 50
with Sherry Vinaigrette, 49
with Toasted Goat Cheese, 49
with Walnut Vinaigrette and Cambazola, 50
Bulgur, 167

Caesar, Southwestern, 51;
    Cornbread Croutons for,
    51
Carrot and Cucumber, Sweet,
    63
Carrot Slaw, 62
Celery, Apple, and Pear,
    Chopped, 63
Chicken
    Chipotle, 216
    Traditional, 214
    Warm, with Hazelnut
        Vinaigrette, 215
    Warm Spicy, with Bacon -
        Molasses Dressing, 215
Coleslaw, New Orleans, 56
Coleslaw I, II, 56
Composed, 73
Corn, 64
Crabmeat, Tomato Aspic
    with, 257
Cucumber
    and Mint, 64
    with Sesame Dressing, 64
    Walnut, and Endive, with
        Walnut Vinaigrette, 64
Egg(s)
    Hard-Cooked, and Garden
        Green, 54
    in Piquant Mayonnaise, 5
    Scrambled, 6
    Special, on Water Biscuits,
        7
Endive
    with Blackberry
        Vinaigrette, 53
    and Carrot, with Berry
        Vinaigrette, 52
    with Oil and Lemon
        Dressing, 53
    Radicchio, Apple, and
        Pepper with Roquefort
        Vinaigrette, 52
    and Radicchio, with Red
        Wine Vinaigrette, 52
Fennel
    and Boston Lettuce, 65
    Celery, and Parsley, with
        Shaved Parmesan, 65
    and Orange, with Shaved
        Parmesan and Black
        Olives, 65
Feta and Tomato, 71
Fruit, Fresh, 462

Garden, with Balsamic
    Vinaigrette and Fontina,
    44
Green(s)
    and Mushroom, 67
    with Raspberries and
        Raspberry Vinaigrette,
        45
    with Sherry-Red Wine
        Vinaigrette, 45
Green Bean
    Baby, 62
    Baby, Onion, and Toasted
        Pine Nut, 61
    and Cheese, 62
    Warm, 62
    Warm, and New Potato, 69
Green Pea, 66
Green Pepper and Cucumber,
    68
Ham, 247
Jicama Slaw, 56
Lentils, 195
Lettuce(s)
    Baby, Mixed, with Honey -
        Lemon Dressing, 46
    Chopped, and Egg Salad,
        55
    Chopped, and Tomato,
        with Pepper
        Mayonnaise, 71
Lima Bean and Cheese, 61
Mâche, 54
Mâche and Radicchio, with
    Sparkling Wine
    Vinaigrette, 53
Melon and Grape, 76
Mesclun, with Chèvre
    Vinaigrette, 47
Mesclun, with Pears, Blue
    Cheese, and Port
    Dressing, 47
Mixed Green(s)
    with Champagne
        Vinaigrette, 46
    with Red Wine Vinaigrette,
        44
    with Sherry-Rice Wine
        Vinaigrette, 46
    with White Wine
        Vinaigrette, 44
Mushroom
    Savoy, 128
    and Walnut, 67
Warm, Grilled, 127
Olive, 163

Onion(s)
    and Potato, Roasted, 133
    Roasted Vidalia, 133
    Vidalia, and Leeks with
        Tarragon Vinaigrette,
        66
Oyster, with Radish Relish,
    274
Pasta
    Macaroni and Cheese, 98
    Orzo with Mustard
        Balsamic Vinaigrette,
        98
    Orzo and Vegetable, 97
    and Seafood, 287
    Summer, 97
Pepper, Roasted, 68
Potato, 191
    New, with Greens and
        Lemon-Dill
        Chardonnay
        Vinaigrette, 69
    New, Red Bell Pepper, and
        Corn, 191
    Red, 190
    Warm, with Sherry
        Vinaigrette, 190
    Warm Vinegar, 190
Red Bean and Rice, 178
Red and Yellow Pepper,
    Sautéed, 68
Rice, 178
Rice, Green Pea, and Olive,
    with Orange -Cilantro
    Vinaigrette, 67
Rustic, 55
Salmon, 282
Seafood, Natchez, 270
Shrimp and Pasta, 271
Simple, 45
Smoked Salmon, 292
Spring, Chopped, 75
Summer Garden, 74
Summer Mélange, Marinated,
    75
Swordfish Steak, 284
Thai with Carrot and
    Cucumber, 63
Tomato(es)
    Aspic with Mayonnaise, 72
    and Bread, 70
    with Citrus Dressing, 70
    Creole, with Avocado
        Mayonnaise, 71

Fresh, and Feta Cheese
    Aspic, 72
  with Lemon Slices, 70
  and Red Onion with Olives
    and Romano, 70
  Shrimp, White Bean and,
    Warm, 270
  Sliced, with Lemon Juice,
    73
Tuna
  Fresh, 287
  and Shrimp, 288
  Warm Yellowfin, 286
Two-Bean, 61
Vegetable, 74; Cooked, 74. *See
    also* Vegetable Salad
Watercress, with Egg
    Dressing, 54
Watermelon and Red Onion,
    76
White Bean
  and Pasta, 194
  with Tuna, 194
  and Walnut, 193
White and Wild Rice, with
    Vegetables, 179
Wilted, with Pancetta, 55
Wilted Red Onions and
    Pickled Beet, 60
Winter, Chopped, 76
Winter Vegetable Mélange, 75
Salad Dressing. *See* Dressing;
    Vinaigrette
Salmon. *See also* Smoked
    Salmon
  about baking, 281
  Baked, Thin-Sliced, 279
  and Corn Croquettes, 282
  Fillet, Baked, with Wasabi
    Crust and Orange-
    Anaheim Chili Sauce, 280
  King, with Aspic and Herb
    Butter, Cold, 280
  Salad, 282
  Spread, Fresh, 343
  Tuna, and Sturgeon, Grilled,
    286
Salsa, 355–57
  Berry, Fresh, 355
  Corn and Avocado, 356
  Corn, Roasted, 355
  Papaya, 357
  Ranchera, 331
  Tomato, Basic, 356
Salt Wafers, 329
Sand Tarts, Lemon, 443

Sandwiches, 339–42
  Cheese Steak, 342
  Grilled Cheese, 338; varia-
    tions, 338
  Portobello Burger, Grilled,
    339
  Roasted Red Pepper and
    Butter, 339
  Shallot Butter, 341
  Shrimp, Grilled, with
    Coleslaw on Pepper
    Bread, 340
  Turkey Patty, Hot, 341
  The Tuscan, 340
Sauce, 346–53. *See also* Dressing;
    Vinaigrette
  Béchamel, Light, 187
  Cabernet, 253
  Cabernet Wine, 235
  Caper, 346
  Chocolate, 367
  Cranberry, Orange, and
    Raisin, 362
  Cranberry-Hot Pepper, 362
  Crawfish, 89
  Crème Anglaise, 366
  Creole, 346
  Cucumber, Fresh, 278
  Flavored Butter, 350–52. *See
    also* Flavored Butter
  Fruit, 361–65. *See also* Name
    of Fruit
  Grainy Mustard, 252
  Herb, 347
  Horseradish, 346; variation,
    346
  Irish Coffee, 368
  Mayonnaise, 348–50. *See also*
    Mayonnaise
  Mustard, 349
  Orange-Anaheim Pepper, 361
  Parsley-Pecan, 347
  Pasta, 92–96. *See also* Pasta
    Sauce
  Praline, 367
  Raspberry, for Meat, 361
  Raspberry, Quick, 363; -
    Caramel, 363;
  Red Chili, 332
  Rum Butter, 368
  Salsa, 355–57. *See also* Salsa
  Tartar, 349; Tomato, 350
  Tomatillo, 262
  Tomato, 352–53
    about making fresh, 83
    All-Purpose, 352

  Baked, Spaghetti with
    Bacon and, 88
  Basic, 352
  Coulis, 353
  Pasta, 94
  and Red Bell Pepper, 93
  Smoked, 234
  Tomato Butter, Sweet and
    Tart, 353
  Vanilla, 366; Vanilla Custard,
    366
  Vidalia Onion, Sweet, 360
  Whiskey, 368
  Yogurt and Cucumber, 347
Sausage(s)
  Andouille, Chicken
    Enchiladas with, 205
  Andouille, and Rice, Baked
    Tomatoes Stuffed with,
    144
  Balls, Hot Tomato and Rice
    Soup with, 21
  and Cheese Drop Biscuits, 306
  Chicken-Apple, 222
  Chicken Patties, 222
  Chili, 250
  Chili Sauce with, 95
  Duck
    and New Potatoes, 224
    and Orange, 223
    and Pork Rillettes, 223
    Italian, and Ratatouille, 249
    and Mushroom Topping
      for Pizza, 324
  Pasta, 86
  Pasta Cake, 96
  Roasted, Mixed, 250
  smoking method for, 224
  Spicy, and Chicken, Macaroni
    Casserole with, 214
  Spring, with Sautéed Onions,
    250
  Two-Bean Soup with Broccoli
    Rabe and, 26
  Venison, and Veal Casserole,
    254
  and White Bean Soup, 26
  Wild Boar, and Grilled
    Venison, 254
Savory Cheesecake, 432
Savory Pies and Tarts, 394–401
  Black Olive Little Pies, 400
  Cheese and Onion Pie, 394
  Chicken Filling for, 401
  Chicken, Walnut, and Red
    Pepper Pies, 397

525

Ham and Chicken Filling for, 399
Ham and Fig Little Pies, with Cheddar Crust, 398
Leek and Goat Cheese Pie, 396
Little Pies, 397
Onion-Bacon Pie, 395
Onion, Yellow, Tart, 394
Oriental Beef Filling for, 398
Piperade Pie, 396
Pork Filling for, 399
Vegetable Filling for, 400
Zucchini, Rustic, Tart, 395
Scallion Bread, Deep-Fried, 299
Scallop(s). *See also* Seafood
Roasted Tomato, and Rice Soup, 37
Seviche, 275
Scalloped Potatoes, 186
Scotch Unkneaded Bread, 298
Scottish Skillet Potatoes, 182
Scrambled Egg Salad, 6
Scrambled Eggs and Onions, 5
Seafood, 256–75. *See also* Fish; Name of Shellfish
Cakes, Mixed, with Jalapeño Tartar Sauce and Thin Fried Onions, 259
Crawfish Sauce, Pasta with, 89
Gumbo, 269
and Pasta Salad, 287
Risotto, 263
Salad, Natchez, 270
Stuffed Artichokes, 266
Semolina, Gnocchi, Adriana's, 168
Sesame. *See also* Benne
Breadsticks, 298
Chicken Breasts, 200
Ginger Rice, 171
Noodles, Cold, with Carrots and Cucumbers, 78
Dressing, 64
Seviche, Scallop, 275
Shallot(s)
Asparagus with, 101
Butter, 351
Garden Peas in, 134
Sandwiches, 341
Pan-Roasted, 138
Roasted, Brussels Sprouts, and Roasted Yellow Bell Peppers, 107
Vinaigrette, 355
Shaped Cookies, 444–46

Cracked Sugar, 444
Peanut Butter, Shasta Mountain, 446
Pepper Sugar, 445
Snickerdoodles, 445
Sugar, 444
Three-Nut, 446
Vanilla Crescents, 444
Venetian, 446
Shasta Mountain Brownies, 451
Shasta Mountain Peanut Butter Cookies, 446
Shellfish. *See* Name of Shellfish (Clams, Crawfish Oysters, etc.); Seafood
Sherbet, 499–501. *See also* Ice; Sorbet
Berry, 500
Blood Orange, 500
Coconut Nutmeg Milk, 500
Grapefruit Sherbet with Candied Grapefruit Rind, 499
Pineapple, 501
Sherry Spice Cake with Creamy Brown Sugar Glaze, 420
Sherry Vinaigrette, 49
-Red Wine, 45
-Rice Wine, 46
Short Crust, 406
Short Pastry. *See also* Pastry
Whole Wheat, 407
Shortbread, 454; Brown Sugar, 454; Hazelnut, 455
Shortcake, 433–34
Berry, Mixed, 433
Biscuits I, 304; II, 304
Blueberry, 434
Peach and Berry, with Warm Cream Sauce, 434
Strawberry, 433
Shrimp. *See also* Seafood
Barbecued, and Capellini with Shrimp Sauce, 267
Crab, Crawfish, Corn, and Potatoes, Boiled, 272
and Crawfish Creole, New Orleans, 265
Curried, and Potato Soup, 38
Grilled, with Coleslaw on Pepper Bread, 340
Gulf, Crab, and Oyster Stew, 268
Marinated, with Green Chili Polenta and Corn Salsa, 265

and Pasta Salad, 271
Pasta and Seafood Salad, 287
Prawns, Grilled, with Papaya Salsa, 268
Rémoulade, 264
and Tuna Salad, 288
Warm, White Bean, and Tomato Salad, 270
White Beans, and Roasted Red Peppers, 267
Simple Syrup, 371
Simple Vinaigrette, 45
Skillet Corn Bread, 308
Skillet Pepper Bread, 300
Slaw. *See also* Coleslaw
Carrot, 62
Jicama, 56
Warm, 110
Smoked Fish Cakes with Caper Sauce, 291
Smoked Fish with Roasted Peppers and Zucchini, 292
Smoked Salmon
and Corn Chowder, 37
Goat Cheese, and Corn, Rotini with, 90
Salad, 292
and Spinach Risotto, 172
Spread, 343
Snapper, Grilled Teriyaki, 283
Snapper, Whole Red, 283
Snickerdoodles, 445
Sorbet, 497–504. *See also* Ice; Ice Cream; Sherbet
Apple, 498
Bellini (peach), 498
Black Walnut, 498
Cassis, 497
Cranberry-Pear, 498
Pineapple-Banana, 498
Plum, 497
Sorrel Soup, 19
Soufflé. *See also* Mousse
Berry, Cold, 467
Bread Pudding, 478
Chocolate, Carol's, 468
Frozen Lime, 468
Gorgonzola with Cucumber Sauce, 6
Tomato, 145; Light, 4
Soup and Chowder, 9–42. *See also* Cold Soup
Acorn Squash and Turnip, 19
Asparagus, 9

Bean, Bacon, Potato, and Red
    Pepper, 25
Bean, Five, 24
Beef Stock, 42
Beet, Carrot, and Sweet
    Potato, 9
Black Bean and Macaroni, 24
Broccoli Rabe, 10; Puréed, 10
Buttermilk Vegetable,
    Chilled, 23
Carrot
    and Dill, 11
    and Red Bell Pepper, 12
    and Tomato, 11
Cauliflower and Cress, 12
Chicken
    and Dill, 29
    Lemon, 28
    Stock, 41
Corn
    Chowder, 13
    Creamed, and Red Bell
        Pepper, 13
    and Green Chili Chowder,
        14
    and Oyster Chowder, 38
    White, and Oyster
        Chowder with Ancho
        Chili Cream, 39
Crab Corn Bisque, 34
Crab Gazpacho, 34
Crawfish Bisque, 35
Curried Shrimp and Potato,
    38
Duck, Turnip, and Squash, 30
Fish, 40
Fish Stock, 42
Green, 14
Green Pea, with Ham, 16
Greens, Turnip, and Corn, 15
Gumbo (seafood), 269
Ham, Mustard Green, Red
    Bean, and Sweet Potato,
    31
Lamb and Beet, 32
Lamb, Pumpkin, and Lima
    Bean, 33
Lentil, Fennel, and Cress, 27
Lobster, 36
Mushroom Consommé, 15
Okra Chowder, 16
Osso Buco, 31
Pasta and Bean, 27
Pimiento, Cold, 17
Potato and Red Bell Pepper,
    18

Radish, Cold, 18
Smoked Salmon and Corn
    Chowder, 37
Sorrel, 19
Spinach, 19
Spring, 22
Sweet Pea, 17
Sweet Potato Vichyssoise, 18
Tomato
    Cold Roasted, with Chervil,
        20
    Cold Roasted, and Red Bell
        Pepper, 21
    and Rice, with Sausage
        Balls, Hot, 21
    Roasted, Rice, and Scallop,
        37
    Summer, 22
    Uncooked, 22
Turkey Stock, 41
Turkey Vegetable, 29
Two-Bean, with Broccoli Rabe
    and Sausage, 26
Vegetable Stock, 40
White Bean and Sausage, 26
Zucchini and Butternut
    Squash, 23
Sour Cream Pound Cake, 427;
    with Poached Fruit, 428
Sourdough Bread, 294
Sourdough Pancakes, Wild, 320
Southwestern Caesar Salad, 51;
    Cornbread Croutons for,
    51
Spaetzle, 170
Spaghetti. See also Pasta
    with Bacon and Baked
        Tomato Sauce, 88
    with Garlic and Rosemary Oil,
        81
    with Tuna, Olives, Capers,
        and Cayenne, 90
Spaghetti Squash with Roasted
    Vegetables, 140
Spare Ribs, Baked Country-
    Style, 242
Sparkling Wine Vinaigrette, 53
Spice
    Applesauce Cake, 416
    Cookies, New World, 443
    and Ginger Cookies,
        Vermont, 435
    Sables (cookies), 449
    Sherry Cake with Creamy
        Brown Sugar Glaze, 420
Spiced Whipped Cream, 365

Spinach
    Creamy, 139
    Risotto, Smoked Salmon and,
        172
    Sautéed, 139
    Soup, 19
    Tomatoes, and Three
        Cheeses, Angel Hair with,
        83
Spoon Bread, Corn Kernel, 311
Spoon Bread, Tomato, 311;
    green chili variation, 311
Spread
    Cucumber, 343
    Lima Bean, 344
    Olive and Sun-Dried Tomato,
        344
    Radish Canapés, 343
    Salmon, Fresh, 343
    Smoked Salmon, 343
    Sun-Dried Tomato Dip, 353
    Tuna, Grilled, with Roasted
        Peppers, 344
    White Bean, 342
Spring
    Peas and Green Onions, 134
    Salad, Chopped, 75
    Sausage with Sautéed Onions,
        250
    Soup, 22
Squabs, Grilled Herbed, 221
Squares. See Bar Cookies
Squash. See Name of Squash
    (Acorn, Butternut,
        Spaghetti, Summer,
        Yellow, Zucchini)
Steamed Pudding, Chocolate,
    477
Steelhead Trout Wrapped in
    Vine Leaves, Oak-
    Grilled, 284
Stew
    Beef, Best, 228
    Beef, with Rum and Olives,
        230
    Gulf Shrimp, Crab, and
        Oyster, 268
    Pork, Mexican, 245
Sticky Buns, 314
Stock
    Beef, 42
    Chicken, 41
    Fish, 42
    Turkey, 41
    Vegetable, 40

527

Stone Crab Claws with Hot
    Ketchup Mayonnaise,
    260
Strawberry(ies)
    with Brown Sugar and Sour
        Cream, 457
    and Cherry, Dried, Muffins,
        315
    Ice Cream with Strawberry
        Puree, 491
    Marinated, 458
    Pie, 375
    Shortcake, 433
    Summer Pudding, 476
Strong Vinaigrette, 144
Sturgeon, Tuna, and Salmon,
    Grilled, 286
Succotash, Red Bean, 192
Sugar Cookies, 444; Cracked
    Sugar, 444; Pepper Sugar,
    445
Sugarless Berry Ice, 502
Summer
    Fruit Pie, 377
    Garden Salad, 74
    Greens, Wilted Mixed,
        121
    Mélange, Marinated (salad),
        75
    menus, xvi-xxi
    Pasta Salad, 97
    Pudding, 476
    Squash and Peppers with
        Balsamic Vinegar Butter,
        149
    Tomato Soup, 22
Sun-Dried Tomato(es)
    Dip, 353
    Grilled Eggplant with Ricotta
        and Two Tomatoes, 118
    and Olive Spread, 344
    Toasts, 328
    Toasts, Pan-Grilled Eggplant
        on, 118
Sunflower Bread, 296
Sunshine Cream Cake, 418
Sweet Corn Cakes, 307
Sweet Pastry, 406
Sweet Peas. See Peas
Sweet Potato(es)
    Beet, and Carrot Soup, 9
    Cakes, 189
    Chips, 188
    Ham, Mustard Green, and
        Red Bean Soup, 31
    Pan-Roasted, 188

Pancakes, 189
    Spiced, 188
    Vichyssoise, 18
    Whipped, 189
Sweet Simplicity (berries), 457
Swiss Chard, Basmati and Wild
    Rice with, 174
Swordfish Steak Salad, 284
Syrup, 370-71
    Berry, 370; Berry Honey, 371
    Blueberry Cinnamon, 371
    Simple, 371

Tabasco Butter, 352
Tabbouleh, 168
Tangerine Mousse, 470
Tarragon Cucumber Sauce, 348
Tarragon Vinaigrette, 66
Tart(let)s, 388-95. See also Pies
    Almond, with Apricot Ice
        Cream, 390
    Apple, Napa Valley, 391
    Bitter Lemon, 389
    Blackberry Jam, 388
    Crust, Butter-Margarine, 407
    Crust, Flaky, 408
    Date, 388
    Filling, Prune and Port, 392;
        peach and walnut varia-
        tion, 392
    Grape, with Red Currant
        Glaze, 389; blueberry
        variation, 389
    Jam and Berry, 393
    Lemon Sand (cookies), 443
    Pear, 391
    Plum, 390
    Puff Pastry, 393
    Savory, 394-96. See also
        Savory Pies and Tarts
    Walnut, 392
    Yellow Onion, 394
    Zucchini, Rustic, 395
Tartar Sauce, 349; Tomato, 350
Tea Cakes, 442
Terrine, Triple Chocolate, with
    Crème Anglaise and
    Raspberry Sauce, 467
Texas Cookies, 455
Thai Salad with Carrot and
    Cucumber, 63
Three-Nut Cookies, 446
Three-Pepper Cajun Bread, 297
Tiles, Pecan (cookies), 450
Tiramisù, Raspberry, 481

Toasts, Cheese, 329
Toasts, Sun-Dried Tomato, 328
Tomato(es), 141-46 See also Sun-
    Dried Tomatoes
    Aspic
        Fresh, 145
        with Crabmeat Salad, 257
        with Mayonnaise, 72
    and Bacon Sauce, Spicy,
        Fettuccine with, 85
    Baked Honey, 142
    Baked, Stuffed with
        Andouille Sausage and
        Rice, 144
    and Basil Topping for Pizza,
        324
    and Bread Salad, 70
    and Carrot Soup, 11
    Cherry, Sautéed, 141
    Chopped Avocado, Onion,
        and Hot Pepper Salad, 59
    and Chopped Lettuce Salad
        with Pepper Mayonnaise,
        71
    Chutney, Fresh, 358
    Cilantro, and Goat Cheese,
        Orecchiette with, 85
    with Citrus Dressing, 70
    Couscous-Stuffed, Warm, 143
    and Feta Salad, 71
    Fondue, Oven Polenta, and
        Sonoma Jack Cheese, 169
    Fresh, and Feta Cheese Aspic,
        72
    Fritters, 335
    Gougère, 299
    Green
        and Apple Pie, 374
            Cornmeal Pan-Fried,
            146
        Ratatouille, 146
    with Honey and Black Pepper,
        146
    and Jalapeño Relish, 359
    with Lemon Slices, 70
    and Lemons, 146
    Oil, 354
    Okra, and Corn, Sautéed, 129
    Oven-Cured, 142; Best Yankee
        Meatloaf with, 248
    Oven-Dried, 142
    -Peach Salsa, 356
    and Red Bell Pepper Sauce,
        93
    Red Onion, Basil, and Goat
        Cheese, Fusilli with, 83

and Red Onion with Olives
and Romano, 70
and Rice Soup with Sausage
Balls, Hot, 21
Roasted, Rice, and Scallop
Soup, 37
roasting, 20
Salad
Aspic with Mayonnaise, 72
and Bread, 70
with Citrus Dressing, 70
Creole, with Avocado
Mayonnaise, 71
Fresh, and Feta Cheese
Aspic, 72
with Lemon Slices, 70
and Red Onion with Olives
and Romano, 70
Shrimp, White Bean and,
Warm, 270
Sliced, with Lemon Juice,
73
Salsa, Basic, 356
Sauce, 352–54
about making fresh, 83
All-Purpose, 352
Baked, Spaghetti with
Bacon and, 88
Basic, 352
Coulis, 353
Pasta, 94
and Red Bell Pepper, 93
Smoked, 234
Sweet and Tart Butter, 353
Shrimp, and White Bean,
Warm Salad, 270
Sliced, with Lemon Juice, 73
Slices with Feta and Chopped
Herbs, 144
Slow-Baked, 142
Smoked, 143
Soufflé, 145
Soufflé, Light, 4
Soup
Cold Roasted, with Chervil,
20
Cold Roasted, and Red Bell
Pepper, 21
Summer, 22
Uncooked, 22
Spinach, and Three Cheeses,
Angel Hair with, 83
Spoon Bread, 311; green chili
variation, 311
Stewed, 141
-Tarragon Pizza, 323

Two, Grilled Eggplant with
Ricotta and, 118
Vinaigrette, 284; Warm, 354
Yellow, Peppers, and Corn,
Rigatoni with, 84
and Yellow Squash, Grilled,
148
Torte, Almond-Pear, 423
Torte, California Nut, 423
Tortellini and Wild Mushrooms
with Buttermilk Dressing,
82
Tortilla(s), 331–33
Blue Corn Enchiladas, 332
Chicken Fajitas with Avocado
Dressing, 333
Ham Fajitas with Fresh Salsa
Ranchera and Scrambled
Eggs, 331
Triangles, Puffed, 327
Trifle, 480
Cherry and Chocolate, 479
Pecan-Almond Custard, 480
Raspberry Tiramisù, 481
Triple Chocolate Terrine with
Crème Anglaise and
Raspberry Sauce, 467
Tropical Fruit Compote, 461
Tropical Fruit Ice, Mixed, 504
Trout
in a Shoestring Potato Crust,
285
Smoked Fish with Roasted
Peppers and Zucchini,
292
Steelhead, Wrapped in Vine
Leaves, 284
Tube Cake, 416–19
Applesauce Spice, 416
Brown Sugar Glazed, 418
Coconut, 417
Cream Cheese Bundt, 417
Fruitcake, White, 419
Sunshine Cream, 418
Tuna, 286–88
Olives, Capers and Cayenne,
Spaghetti with, 90
Pasta and Seafood Salad, 287
Salad, Fresh, 287
Salad, Warm Yellowfin, 286
Salmon, and Sturgeon,
Grilled, 286
Sauce, Chicken with, 208
and Shrimp Salad, 288
Spread, Grilled, with Roasted
Peppers, 344

Steaks, Grilled, 288
Uncooked, and Tomato
Sauce, Pasta Shells with,
91
White Bean Salad with, 194
Turkey
Breast, Boned, with Peanut
Sauce, 217
Breast, Roasted Herb, 217
and Cheese Enchilada
Casserole, 216
Patty, Hot, Sandwich, 341
Roast, with Pan Gravy, 218
Stock, 41
Vegetable Soup, 29
Turnip(s)
and Acorn Squash Soup, 19
and Beets, 147
and Carrots, Candied, 110
Carrots, and Onions, Glazed,
111
Custard, 147
Grated, 148
Greens, and Corn Soup, 15
Greens, Old-Fashioned, 120
and Pears, Puréed, 154
The Tuscan Sandwich, 340
Twists, Cinnamon Walnut (cook-
ies), 450
Two-Bean Salad, 61
Two-Bean Soup with Broccoli
Rabe and Sausage, 26

Uncooked
Green Sauce, 93
Tomato Sauce, 92
Tomato Soup, 22
Unkneaded Bread, Scotch, 298

Vanilla
-Bean Custard Ice Cream, 491
Crescents, 444
Sauce, 366
Veal, 231–35
Chops
with Blackberries, 234
Grilled, 232
Grilled, with Smoked
Tomato Sauce, 234
Liver and Onions, Classic, 235
Marinated Roast Loin of, in
Port Wine and Orange,
233
Osso Buco Soup, 31

Roast, 231
Roast Tenderloin of, with
  Natural Sauce, 233
Shanks, Country, 232
and Venison Sausage
  Casserole, 254
Vegetable(s), 100–63. *See also*
  Name of Vegetable
Assorted (crudités), 158
Buttermilk Soup, Chilled, 23
Cold, with Mustard Sauce
  (crudités), 159
Croquettes, 336
Crudités with Herb
  Mayonnaise, 159
Filling for Little Pies, 400
Garden, Confit of, 156
Grains, and Nuts, Cabbage
  Stuffed with, 108
Grilled Mixed, Penne with, 84
Lasagna, 158
Marinated Mixed, 163
and Orzo Salad, 97
Raw, on Ice, 159
Rice with Eggs and, 176
Roasted, Spaghetti Squash
  with, 140
Salad, 74
  Cooked, 74
  Spring, Chopped, 75
  Summer Garden, 74
  Summer Mélange,
    Marinated, 75
  Winter, Chopped, 76
  Winter Vegetable Mélange,
    75
Spring Soup, 22
Stock, 40
Terrine with Watercress
  Mayonnaise, 157
Turkey Soup, 29
White and Wild Rice Salad
  with, 179
Vegetable Purées, 151–55. *See
  also* Name of Vegetable
Vegetable Salads, 57–76. *See also*
  Name of Vegetable
Vegetable Soups, 9–23. *See also*
  Name of Vegetable
Venetian Cookies, 446
Venison
  with Grainy Mustard Sauce,
    252
  Grilled, and Wild Boar
    Sausage, 253
  Peppered Loin of, with Red

Wine Sauce, 252
Roast Tenderloin of, with
  Cabernet Sauce, 253
Sausage and Veal Casserole,
  254
Vermont Ginger and Spice
  Cookies, 435
Vichyssoise, Sweet Potato, 18
Vidalia Onion(s). *See also* Onions
  and Leeks with Tarragon
    Vinaigrette, 66
  Salad, Roasted, 133
  Sauce, Sweet, 360
  Sautéed, 131
Vinaigrette. *See also* Dressing
  All-Purpose, 354
  Anchovy, 50, 104
  Balsamic, 44
  Berry, 52
  Blackberry, 53
  Champagne, 46
  Chèvre, 47
  Cilantro, 58
  Flavored, 54
  Fruit, 50
  Hazelnut, 215
  Lemon, 58
  Lemon-Dill Chardonnay, 69
  Lime, 59
  Mustard, 57
  Mustard Balsamic, 98
  Orange-Cilantro, 67
  Peppercorn, 49
  Raspberry, 45
  Red Wine, 44
  Rice Wine, 48
  Roquefort, 52
  Shallot, 355
  Sherry, 49
  Sherry-Red Wine, 45
  Sherry-Rice Wine, 46
  Simple, 45
  Sparkling Wine, 53
  Strong, 144
  Tarragon, 66
  Tomato, 284
  Tomato, Warm, 354
  Walnut, 50
  Walnut Oil, Hot, 354
  White Wine, 44
Vinegar, Berry, 355
Vodka, Flavored, 372

Wafers
  Corn, 330

Hot-Water Soda, with Chives,
  330
Salt, 329
Whole Wheat Benne, 329
Waffles. *See also* Pancakes
Carrot Cake, 320
Wagon Wheels. *See also* Pasta
  with Green Bean Purée, 79
Walnut(s). *See also* Black Walnut
  and Chicken Enchiladas with
    Roasted Green Chili
    Sauce, 204
  and Chocolate Flourless Cake,
    427
  Cinnamon Twists, 450
  -Coconut Jumbles, 439
  Cookies, 441
  Lemon Bars, 454
  and Mushroom Salad, 67
  Oil Vinaigrette, Hot, 354
  Pumpkin, Prunes, and Beans,
    Lamb and Pork with, 238
  Tart, 392
  Vinaigrette, 50
  and White Bean Salad, 193
Watercress. *See also* Cress
  and Green Pea Purée, 153
  Mayonnaise, 349
  Salad with Egg Dressing, 54
  Stir-Fried, 148
Watermelon and Red Onion
  Salad, 76
Watermelon Rind Pickles, 162
Wax Beans and Leeks, Purée of,
  152
Whipped Cream, Flavored,
  365–66. *See also* Flavored
  Whipped Cream
Whiskey Sauce, 368
White Bean(s), 192. *See also*
  Beans
  and Chicken Chili, 209
  Green Beans, and Pine Nuts,
    Rigatoni with, 78
  and Pasta Salad, 194
  Salad with Tuna, 194
  and Sausage Soup, 26
  Shrimp, and Roasted Red
    Peppers, 267
  Shrimp, Warm, and Tomato
    Salad, 270
  Spread, 342
  Vinaigrette, 193
  and Walnut Salad, 193
  Warm, with Red Onions, 192
White Cake, Intermont, 410

530

INDEX

White Chocolate Ice Cream, 489
White Fish
  Fillets
    Baked, 291
    Broiled with Onion-Hot
      Pepper Topping, 290
    Oven-Fried, 290
    Pistachio-Coated, 289
    Steamed and Seared, 289
    Smoked Fish Cakes with
      Caper Sauce, 291
  Smoked, with Roasted
    Peppers and Zucchini,
    292
White Wine Vinaigrette, 44
Whole Wheat Benne Wafers,
  329
Whole Wheat Short Pastry, 407
Wild Boar Sausage and Grilled
  Venison, 253
Wild Mushroom(s)
  Oyster Mushrooms, Fried,
    125
  Porcini, Baked Wild Rice and,
    177
  Porcini, Fresh, Baked with
    Bacon, 128
  Portobello
  Burger, Grilled, 339
  Grilled, with Black Olives and
    Tomatoes, 126
  Stuffed, 127
  and Smoked Bacon in Puff
    Pastry, 125
  and Tortellini with Buttermilk
    Dressing, 82

Wild Rice
  and Basmati Salad, 179
  and Basmati with Swiss
    Chard, 174
  and Long-Grain Rice, Mixed,
    175
  with Peppers, 175
  and Porcini Mushrooms,
    Baked, 177
  and White, Salad with
    Vegetables, 179
Wild Sourdough Pancakes, 320
Wilted
  Mixed Summer Greens,
    121
  Mustard Greens with Olive
    Oil and Lemon, 122
  Onions, Refrigerator, 134
  Red Onions and Pickled Beet
    Salad, 60
  Salad with Pancetta, 55
Winter
  Fruit, Baked, 460
  Greens, Braised, 122
  menus, xxii-xxvii
  Salad, Chopped, 76
  Vegetable Mélange, 75

Yellow Bell Pepper(s). *See also*
    Peppers
  and Carrots, Buttered, with
    Parsley, 111
  and Cucumbers, Marinated,
    with Dill and Mint, 117
  and Onion, 136
  and Red, Sautéed, Salad, 68

Roasted, Brussels Sprouts,
    and Roasted Shallots, 107
  Tomatoes, and Corn, Rigatoni
    with, 84
Yellow Squash, 148–50
  Green Summer Squash, and
    Roasted Onions, Purée of,
    155
  and Onions, 149
  Soufflé with Tomato and Red
    Bell Pepper Sauce, 150
  and Tomato, Grilled, 148
Yogurt
  and Cucumber Sauce, 347
  Fresh Fruit with, and W
    Warm Sun Honey, 461
  Ice Cream, 497

Zucchini
  Broiled, 149
  and Butternut Squash Soup,
    23
  Corn Cakes, 310
  Eggplant, and Parmesan
    Tortino, 150
  Green Summer Squash,
    Yellow Squash, and
    Roasted Onions, Purée of,
    155
  and Lamb Pies, 239
  Shredded, 149
  Tart, Rustic, 395
  Yellow Squash, and Green
    Pepper Topping for Pizza,
    325

CONVERSION CHART
Equivalent Imperial and Metric Measurements

American cooks use standard containers, the 8-ounce cup and a tablespoon that takes exactly 16 level fillings to fill that cup level. Measuring by cup makes it very difficult to give weight equivalents, as a cup of densely packed butter will weigh considerably more than a cup of flour. The easiest way therefore to deal with cup measurements in recipes is to take the amount by volume rather than by weight. Thus the equation reads:

1 cup = 240 ml = 8 fl. oz. $^{1}/_{2}$ cup = 120 ml = 4 fl. oz.

It is possible to buy a set of American cup measures in major stores around the world.

In the States, butter is often measured in sticks. One stick is the equivalent of 8 tablespoons. One tablespoon of butter is therefore the equivalent to ½ ounce/15 grams.

LIQUID MEASURES

Fluid ounces	U.S.	Imperial	Milliliters
	1 teaspoon	1 teaspoon	5
¼	2 teaspoons	1 dessertspoon	10
½	1 tablespoon	1 tablespoon	14
1	2 tablespoons	2 tablespoons	28
2	¼ cup	4 tablespoons	56
4	½ cup		110
5		¼ pint or 1 gill	140
6	¾ cup		170
8	1 cup		225
9			250, ¼ liter
10	1¼ cups	½ pint	280
12	1½ cups		340
15		¾ pint	420
16	2 cups		450
18	2¼ cups		500, ½ liter
20	2½ cups	1 pint	560
24	3 cups		675
25		1¼ pints	700
27	3½ cups		750
30	3¾ cups	1½ pints	840
32	4 cups or 1 quart		900
35		1¾ pints	980
36	4½ cups		1000, 1 liter
40	5 cups	2 pints or 1 quart	1120
48	6 cups		1350
50		2½ pints	1400
60	7½ cups	3 pints	1680
64	8 cups or 2 quarts		1800
72	9 cups		2000, 2 liters

SOLID MEASURES

U.S. and Imperial Measures		Metric Measures	
ounces	pounds	grams	kilos
1		28	
2		56	
3½		100	
4	¼	112	
5		140	
6		168	
8	½	225	
9		250	¼
12	¾	340	
16	1	450	
18		500	½
20	1¼	560	
24	1½	675	
27		750	¾
28	1¾	780	
32	2	900	
36	2¼	1000	1
40	2½	1100	
48	3	1350	
54		1500	1½
64	4	1800	
72	4½	2000	2
80	5	2250	2¼
90		2500	2½
100	6	2800	2¾

OVEN TEMPERATURE EQUIVALENTS

Fahrenheit	Celsius	Gas Mark	Description
225	110	¼	Cool
250	130	½	
275	140	1	Very Slow
300	150	2	
325	170	3	Slow
350	180	4	Moderate
375	190	5	
400	200	6	Moderately Hot
425	220	7	Fairly Hot
450	230	8	Hot
475	240	9	Very Hot
500	250	10	Extremely Hot

EQUIVALENTS FOR INGREDIENTS

all-purpose flour—plain flour
arugula—rocket
confectioners' sugar—icing sugar
cornstarch—cornflour
eggplant—aubergine

granulated sugar—castor sugar
half and half—12% fat milk
lima beans—broad beans
scallion—spring onion
shortening—white fat

unbleached flour—strong, white flour
vanilla bean—vanilla pod
zest—rind
zucchini—courgettes or marrow